The Relatio
Literature and Science

An Annotated Bibliography
of Scholarship, 1880–1980

Edited by

WALTER SCHATZBERG
RONALD A. WAITE
JONATHAN K. JOHNSON

The Modern Language Association of America
New York   1987

Library of Congress Cataloging-in-Publication Data

The Relations of literature and science: an annotated bibliography of
scholarship, 1880–1980 / edited by Walter Schatzberg, Ronald A.
Waite, Jonathan K. Johnson.

Incorporates the work of the annual bibliographies of the Division
on Literature and Science of the Modern Language Association of
America from 1939 to 1980 with some additions and deletions and new
entries for the period back to 1880.
Includes indexes.
ISBN 0-87352-172-2.   ISBN 0-87352-173-0 (pbk.).
1. Literature—History and criticism—Bibliography.   2. Literature
and science—Bibliography.   I. Schatzberg, Walter.   II. Waite,
Ronald A., 1956– .   III. Johnson, Jonathan K., 1958–
IV. Modern Language Association of America. Division on Literature
and Science.
Z6511.R44   1987
[PN55]
016.809'93356—dc19   87-26241

Cover illustration of the paperback edition: *Der Astronomus* (1568), woodcut,
by Jost Amman, in *The Book of Trades (Ständebuch)*, by Jost Amman and
Hans Sachs (New York: Dover, 1973).

Published by The Modern Language Association of America
10 Astor Place, New York, NY 10003-6981

Contents

Introduction

This annotated bibliography on the relations of literature and science is offered as a resource tool for literary scholars, historians of science, and historians of ideas who are working in this field, which has had a distinct identity in literary scholarship for over fifty years. In 1939 at the Modern Language Association convention, in New Orleans, the discussion group General Topics 7: Relations of Literature and Science was founded. In 1976 the group was reorganized as the Division on Literature and Science. Thus, annually since 1939 a program on literature and science has been presented at the MLA convention and a bibliography of scholarship on the relations of literature and science has been compiled by the division's bibliography committee.[1] In 1949 Fred A. Dudley edited a compilation of the bibliographies since 1939, adding some titles back to 1930; in 1968 he edited a selected bibliography covering the years 1930 to 1967.

The present bibliography incorporates the work of the annual bibliographies from 1939 to 1980 with some significant additions and deletions. We have extended the bibliography back to 1880 to cover a complete century of scholarship on literature and science. We have not included background studies that focus on broad or general issues of cultural history and history of science but have instead concentrated on scholarly studies that deal specifically with some aspect of the relation of literature and science.

To supplement the annual bibliographies we paid careful attention to book production between 1880 and 1980 and systematically gleaned items from several hundred journals published in that period. We consulted the major bibliographies of literary scholarship, most notably the *MLA International Bibliography*, specialized bibliographies such as the *Bibliographie der deutschen Sprach- und Literaturwissenschaft* (Eppelsheimer, Köttlewesch, et al.) and *A Critical Bibliography of French Literature* (Cabeen, Brooks, et al.), and numerous bibliographies on individual authors.

This volume is organized to move from the general to the particular; that is, from studies of the general relations between literature and science to studies of their relations during the various historical periods from classical antiquity to the present. Each period is divided into general studies and surveys and studies of individual authors. A thematically organized subject index complements this structure and facilitates use of the bibliography as explained below.

The most difficult task in compiling this bibliography was establishing clear principles for inclusion. Since there are no simple guidelines concerning the nature of literature and science, the relation between the two domains is by no means self-evident. One relation is signaled by the phrase "literature *in* science." By this, we refer to studies that highlight the literary qualities of a scientist's work, such as imaginativeness, poetic language, or prose style. Consequently, among individual authors we have included scientists like Johannes Kepler, Galileo Galilei, Francis Bacon, and Charles Darwin, who are represented by studies that focus on their scientific works as writing per se or that in some way call attention to their work as writers.

A second relation is indicated by the phrase "literature *and* science." With this designation we refer to those works—found primarily in the first section, Interactions of Literature and Science—that compare the two domains to explore their similarities and differences. The controversy between the two discourses is popularly associated with the conflict between Matthew Arnold and T. H. Huxley in the 1880s and even more with the "two cultures" debate between C. P. Snow and F. R. Leavis in the 1950s and 1960s. Other studies that explore literature and science seek a harmony or common ground between the two, along the lines of shared creativity, use of language, or historicity. In "Literature and Science: The State of the Field," George S. Rousseau expresses one of the most provocative and challenging views on this subject, calling for greater theoretical clarity in the scholarship. We hope this bibliography will serve as a point of departure for scholars who wish to respond to Rousseau's charge that they incorporate contemporary developments in literary theory into their work on literature and science.

In "Literature and Science" George Slusser and George Guffey make a useful distinction between "science and literature" and "science *in* literature," the heading that identifies the third and largest classification in our bibliography. To this category belong all studies that examine some aspect of a writer's imaginative use of science in the language, the thematic content, or the structure of, say, a poem, a play, or a novel. There is no better way to describe this, the primary thrust of our bibliography, than to refer the reader to the subject index, which lists all topics pertinent to the relations of literature and science as well as all literary figures, scientists, or other persons mentioned in either the annotations or the titles. The headings for major themes such as astronomy, biology, evolution, or physics, as well as those for frequently mentioned literary figures, include comprehensive subheadings that enable the reader to see at a glance the range of literary figures influenced by a particular science or the range of sciences discussed in relation to a particular writer. For example, listed under "Evolution" are such authors as Robert Browning, Ralph Waldo Emerson, Thomas Hardy, and Alfred, Lord Tennyson, while astronomy, cosmology, evolution, and geology are among the sciences given under the Tennyson heading. With this arrangement a scholar interested in, for example, Tennyson's relation to evolution can locate all relevant items quickly, simply by researching the items cited for evolution under Tennyson and for Tennyson under evolution.

For a comprehensive study of evolution in literature one would examine all the relevant items under evolution, Charles Darwin, and Darwinism—a total of 223 items referring to 63 literary figures. A further example along these lines is the topic of modern physics in literature. A survey of the subject index suggests headings such as Einstein, entropy, physics, quantum mechanics, theory of relativity, and thermodynamics, which encompass 125 items referring to 46 literary figures. Yet another example would be the literary use of astronomy from antiquity to the present: the subject index under astronomy offers a wealth of material for every major period and every major literary figure.

By using the subject index and the system of classification indicated in the Contents, the reader can explore the impact of science, individual sciences or scientists, scientific theories, or scientific themes on individual authors, specific literary periods, or Western literary history altogether. Although working straight through all the entries, selecting a specific period, or choosing a specific author are all feasible ways of using the bibliography, we advise readers to familiarize themselves thoroughly with the subject index, which offers a problem-oriented approach to literature-and-science scholarship.

Let us now turn to the important issue of the guidelines directing our choice of entries. We have carefully selected approximately 2,500 items for inclusion, checking each for bibliographic accuracy and for relevance to the theme of the bibliography. One consideration was the designation "science." We accepted George Sarton's general understanding of science as systematized knowledge that is cumulative and progressive. With some significant differences we followed the practice of the *Isis Cumulative Bibliography* (Whitrow; Neu), which includes among the sciences physics, chemistry, astronomy, meteorology, geology, mineralogy, geography, biology, botany, zoology, anatomy, and natural history. We also followed the *Isis Cumulative Bibliography* in including those pseudosciences that practiced empirical, experimental methods and achieved prominence as sciences in their own time, such as alchemy, astrology, Elizabethan humoral psychology, mesmerism, phrenology, and physiognomy.

Our designation "literature" includes only Western imaginative literature, predominantly American, English, French, and German. Separate sections of the bibliography pertain to individual literary figures, and while some scientists appear in this list, they are included, as already mentioned, solely for studies that treat their works from a literary perspective. For Goethe, who was both a scientist and a poet, we include only those studies that stress the presence of science in his literary works. Evaluative and historical studies of Goethe's scientific works appear in great quantity and fall outside the scope of this project.

We have included studies on literature and medicine that consider the scientific aspect of medicine, but we have excluded studies that merely describe physicians or patients as literary characters or that examine images of medical practitioners in literature. A useful survey of medical themes in literature from antiquity to the present is the annotated bibliography *Literature and Medicine*, compiled by Joanne Trautmann and Carol Pollard. For an excellent analysis of the scholarship on the interrelation of literature and medicine we recommend George S. Rousseau's "Literature and Medicine: The State of the Field."

From the burgeoning scholarship on science fiction we have included primarily items that highlight the imaginative use of science and that focus centrally on some aspect of science in science fiction. We have excluded, however, studies whose sole purpose is the literary analysis of science fiction works or the examination of social, political, or religious themes in science fiction. Of the currently available bibliographies of science fiction scholarship we recommend for their broad scope the bibliographies that Marshall B. Tymn and Roger C. Schlobin have been compiling annually since 1970 (see also Tymn and Tymn, Schlobin, and Currey).

We have included some items on the relation of literature and technology, such as Wylie Sypher's *Literature and Technology: The Alien Vision*, but have excluded studies on machine imagery and on the impact of industrialization on literature. Nor have we covered the social sciences such as psychology, anthropology, and economics. Inclusion of scholarship on the relations of literature and these social sciences would require separate volumes. For the same reason we have not covered philosophy and linguistics.

It is important to point out that this is an annotated and not a critical bibliography. Faced with the variety of approaches to the subject of literature and science, we chose to speak with the voice of a dispassionate scholarly narrator. Consequently, instead of evaluating the quality of a scholarly study we primarily highlight the literature-and-science relation in each entry. The annotations are intended to provide a concise general guide to the topics, authors, scientists, and texts considered in the studies cited, with an emphasis on the elements that are relevant to the bibliography's theme.

In the 1980s many significant articles and books on the relations of literature and science have appeared, and we anticipate a supplementary annotated bibliography on literature and science scholarship of the 1980s. This supplement will, moreover, include items from the 1880–1980 period that we have overlooked and that our readers will kindly call to our attention.

Walter Schatzberg
Ronald A. Waite
Jonathan K. Johnson

NOTE

[1]The annual bibliographies for the years 1950 to 1965 appeared in *Symposium*: 5 (1951): 382–86; 6 (1952): 241–45; 7 (1953): 207–11; 8 (1954): 208–13; 9 (1955): 196–201; 10 (1956): 182–87; 11 (1957): 178–84; 12 (1958): 256–62; 13 (1959): 361–66; 15 (1961): 311–19; 17 (1963): 307–17; 18 (1964): 374–81; 19 (1965): 277–84; 21 (1967): 366–81. The annual bibliographies for the years 1972–73 to 1978–79 appeared in *CLIO*: 4 (1974): 73–93; 5 (1975): 97–121; 6 (1976): 71–88; 7 (1977): 135–55; 8 (1978): 97–116; 9 (1979): 111–32; 10 (1980): 57–84. Subsequent bibliographies were published in booklet form by Clark University Press under the title *Relations of Literature and Science: A Bibliography of Scholarship*: 1980–81 (1982), 31 pp.; 1981–82 (1983), 33 pp.; 1982–83 (1984), 32 pp. Thereafter the annual bibliographies appear in *Publications of the Society for Literature and Science*.

WORKS CITED

Cabeen, David C., Richard A. Brooks, et al., eds. *A Critical Bibliography of French Literature*. Enl. ed. Syracuse: Syracuse UP, 1952.

Dudley, Fred A., ed. *The Relations of Literature and Science: A Selected Bibliography 1930–49*. Pullman: Dept. of English, State C of Washington, 1949.

———, ed. *The Relations of Literature and Science: A Selected Bibliography 1930–67*. Ann Arbor: UMI, 1968.

Eppelsheimer, Hanns W., Clemens Köttlewesch, et al., eds. *Bibliographie der deutschen Sprach- und Literaturwissenschaft*. Vol. 1. Frankfurt: Kolstermann, 1945. 20 vols. 1945–80.

Neu, John, ed. *Isis Cumulative Bibliography, 1966–1975: A Bibliography of the History of Science from Isis Critical Bibliographies 91–100*. 2 vols. London: Mansell in conj. with the History of Science Society, 1980–85.

Rousseau, George S. "Literature and Medicine: The State of the Field." *Isis* 72 (1981): 406–24.

———. "Literature and Science: The State of the Field." *Isis* 69 (1978): 583–91.

Slusser, George, and George Guffey. "Literature and Science." *Interrelations of Literature*. Ed. Jean-Pierre Barricelli and Joseph Gibaldi. New York: MLA, 1982. 176–204.

Sypher, Wylie. *Literature and Technology: The Alien Vision*. New York: Random, 1968.

Trautmann, Joan, and Carol Pollard. *Literature and Medicine: An Annotated Bibliography*. Rev. ed. Pittsburgh: U of Pittsburgh P, 1982.

Tymn, Marshall B., ed. *The Year's Scholarship in Science Fiction, Fantasy, and Horror Literature: 1980*. Kent: Kent State UP, 1983.

Tymn, Marshall B., and Roger C. Schlobin, eds. *The Year's Scholarship in Science Fiction and Fantasy: 1972–1975*. Kent: Kent State UP, 1979.

———, eds. *The Year's Scholarship in Science Fiction and Fantasy: 1976–1979*. Kent: Kent State UP, 1982.

Tymn, Marshall B., Roger C. Schlobin, and L. W. Currey, eds. *A Research Guide to Science Fiction Studies: An Annotated Checklist of Primary and Secondary Sources for Fantasy and Science Fiction*. New York: Garland, 1977.

Whitrow, Magda, ed. *Isis Cumulative Bibliography: A Bibliography of the History of Science Formed from Isis Critical Bibliographies 1–90, 1913–65*. 6 vols. London: Mansell in conj. with the History of Science Society, 1971–84.

Acknowledgments

We wish to express our appreciation to the following colleagues, who contributed annotations for articles and books in their fields of specialization: Maria Baker (Clark Univ.), Raymond E. Barbera (Clark Univ.), Charles Blinderman (Clark Univ.), Dennis R. Dean (Univ. of Wisconsin, Parkside), Carol C. Donley (Hiram Coll.), Wolfgang Bernard Fleischmann (Montclair State Coll.), Anne Godlewska (Queen's Univ.), Ludmilla J. Jordanova (Univ. of Essex), J. Fannin King (Clark Univ.), Jutta Kolkenbrock-Netz (Univ. Bochum), Donald D. Kummings (Univ. of Wisconsin, Parkside), Kent P. Ljungquist (Worcester Polytechnic Inst.), Wendy Owanisian-Wagner (Clark Univ.), Stuart Peterfreund (Northeastern Univ.), Roy Porter (Wellcome Inst. for the History of Medicine), Knud Rasmussen (Clark Univ.), Lance Schachterle (Worcester Polytechnic Inst.), Elinor S. Shaffer (Univ. of East Anglia), Sharon R. Trachte (Clark Univ.), Brigitte Voykowitsch (Clark Univ.), Robert L. Walters (Univ. of Western Ontario), John A. Woodcock (Indiana Univ., Bloomington).

We are especially grateful to Lu Ann Renzoni-Pacenka for her expertise with word-processor technology and to the staff of the Goddard Library of Clark University for fulfilling our many requests.

Abbreviations

AGald	Anales galdosianos
AHR	American Historical Review
AJP	American Journal of Philology
AJPhys	American Journal of Physics
Akzente	Akzente: Zeitschrift für Literatur
AL	American Literature
ALR	American Literary Realism, 1870–1910
AmerS	American Studies
AmerSci	American Scientist
AMH	Annals of Medical History
AN&Q	American Notes and Queries
Anglia	Anglia: Zeitschrift für englische Philologie
AnM	Annuale Mediaevale
AnS	Annals of Science
AQ	American Quarterly
AR	Antioch Review
Arcadia	Arcadia: Zeitschrift für vergleichende Literaturwissenschaft
Archiv	Archiv für das Studium der neueren Sprachen und Literaturen
ArielE	Ariel: A Review of International English Literature
ArQ	Arizona Quarterly
ASch	American Scholar
ASILO	Adalbert Stifter Institut des Landes Oberösterreich: Vierteljahrsschrift
Atlantic	Atlantic Monthly
ATQ	American Transcendental Quarterly
AUMLA	Journal of the Australasian Universities Language and Literature Association
AUR	Aberdeen University Review
BA	Books Abroad
BHM	Bulletin of the History of Medicine
BHR	Bibliothèque d'humanisme et renaissance
BJRL	Bulletin of the John Rylands Library
BlakeN	Blake: An Illustrated Quarterly
BlakeS	Blake Studies
BLM	Bonniers litterära magasin
BNYPL	Bulletin of the New York Public Library
BrechtJ	Brecht-Jahrbuch
BRMMLA	Bulletin of the Rocky Mountain Modern Language Association
BSAM	Bulletin de la Société des Amis de Montaigne

BST	*Brontë Society Transactions*
BSTCF	*Ball State Teachers College Forum*
BSUF	*Ball State University Forum*
BuR	*Bucknell Review*
BYUS	*Brigham Young University Studies*
C&L	*Christianity and Literature*
C&M	*Classica et mediaevalia*
Cassinia	*Cassinia: Proceedings of the Delaware Valley Ornithological Club*
CCrit	*Comparative Criticism: A Yearbook*
CE	*College English*
Centerpoint	*Centerpoint: A Journal of Interdisciplinary Studies*
CentR	*Centennial Review*
ChauR	*Chaucer Review*
CJ	*Classical Journal*
CL	*Comparative Literature*
CLAJ	*College Language Association Journal*
ClasPhil	*Classical Philology*
ClassQ	*Classical Quarterly*
CLC	*Columbia Library Columns*
ClioI	*CLIO: An Interdisciplinary Journal of Literature, History, and the Philosophy of History*
CLS	*Comparative Literature Studies*
ColF	*Columbia Forum*
CollG	*Colloquia germanica: Internationale Zeitschrift für germanische Sprach- und Literaturwissenschaft*
CollL	*College Literature*
CompD	*Comparative Drama*
ConL	*Contemporary Literature*
Conradiana	*Conradiana: A Journal of Joseph Conrad*
Crit	*Critique: Studies in Modern Fiction*
Criticism	*Criticism: A Quarterly for Literature and the Arts*
Critique	*Critique: Revue générale des publications françaises et étrangères*
CritQ	*Critical Quarterly*
CS	*Cahiers du sud*
CVE	*Cahiers victoriens et edouardiens*
DA	*Dissertation Abstracts*
DAI	*Dissertation Abstracts International*
Daphnis	*Daphnis: Zeitschrift für mittlere deutsche Literatur*
DB	*Doitsu Bungaku*
DDJ	*Deutsches Dante Jahrbuch*
DHLR	*D. H. Lawrence Review*
DilR	*Diliman Review*
DiS	*Dickens Studies*
DR	*Dalhousie Review*
DSARDS	*Dante Studies with the Annual Report of the Dante Society*
DSN	*Dickens Studies Newsletter*
DU	*Deutschunterricht*
DubR	*Dublin Review*

DUJ	*Durham University Journal*
DVLG	*Deutsche Vierteljahrsschrift für Literaturwissenschaft und Geistesgeschichte*
EA	*Etudes anglaises*
EAL	*Early American Literature*
E&S	*Essays and Studies by Members of the English Association*
ECLife	*Eighteenth-Century Life*
ECr	*Esprit créateur*
ECS	*Eighteenth-Century Studies*
EDH	*Essays by Divers Hands*
EG	*Etudes germaniques*
EHR	*English Historical Review*
EIC	*Essays in Criticism*
EJ	*English Journal*
ELH	*Journal of English Literary History*
ELN	*English Language Notes*
ELR	*English Literary Renaissance*
ELT	*English Literature in Transition (1800–1920)*
ELWIU	*Essays in Literature*
EM	*English Miscellany*
EngR	*English Record*
EnlE	*Enlightenment Essays*
ES	*English Studies*
ESC	*English Studies in Canada*
ESQ	*Emerson Society Quarterly*
ESt	*Erlanger Studien*
ETC	*ETC.: A Review of General Semantics*
ETJ	*Educational Theatre Journal*
Euphorion	*Euphorion: Zeitschrift für Literaturgeschichte*
EUQ	*Emory University Quarterly*
Expl	*Explicator*
FI	*Forum italicum*
FMAS	*Frühmittelalterliche Studien*
FMLS	*Forum for Modern Language Studies*
ForumH	*Forum (Houston)*
FR	*French Review*
FS	*French Studies*
FurmS	*Furman Studies*
FWF	*Far-Western Forum: A Review of Ancient and Modern Letters*
GaR	*Georgia Review*
GL&L	*German Life and Letters*
Goethe	*Goethe: Neue Folge des Jahrbuchs der Goethe-Gesellschaft*
GQ	*German Quarterly*
GR	*Germanic Review*
GRM	*Germanisch-romanische Monatsschrift, neue Folge*
HAR	*Humanities Association Review/Revue de l'association des humanités*
Hermes	*Hermes: Zeitschrift für klassische Philologie*
HINL	*History of Ideas Newsletter*
HJ	*Hibbert Journal*

HLB	*Harvard Library Bulletin*
HLQ	*Huntington Library Quarterly*
HQ	*Hopkins Quarterly*
HR	*Hispanic Review*
HS	*History of Science*
HSL	*Hartford Studies in Literature*
HTR	*Harvard Theological Review*
IFR	*International Fiction Review*
IJAS	*Indian Journal of American Studies*
IJE	*International Journal of Ethics*
IL	*Information littéraire*
IowaR	*Iowa Review*
IPEN	*Indian P.E.N.*
IQ	*Italian Quarterly*
IS	*Italian Studies*
JAAC	*Journal of Aesthetics and Art Criticism*
JAmH	*Journal of American History*
JAmS	*Journal of American Studies*
JBeckS	*Journal of Beckett Studies*
JDSG	*Jahrbuch der deutschen Schiller-Gesellschaft*
JEGP	*Journal of English and Germanic Philology*
JFDH	*Jahrbuch des freien deutschen Hochstifts*
JGE	*Journal of General Education*
JHI	*Journal of the History of Ideas*
JHM	*Journal of the History of Medicine and Allied Sciences*
JIG	*Jahrbuch für internationale Germanistik*
JJQ	*James Joyce Quarterly*
JLN	*Jack London Newsletter*
JML	*Journal of Modern Literature*
JoHS	*Journal of Hellenic Studies*
JP	*Journal of Philosophy*
JPC	*Journal of Popular Culture*
JR	*Journal of Religion*
JRUL	*Journal of the Rutgers University Library*
JWCI	*Journal of the Warburg and Courtauld Institute*
JWGV	*Jahrbuch des Wiener Goethe-Vereins*
KFLQ	*Kentucky Foreign Language Quarterly*
KPAB	*Kentucky Philological Association Bulletin*
KR	*Kenyon Review*
KRQ	*Kentucky Romance Quarterly*
KSJ	*Keats-Shelley Journal*
KSMB	*Keats-Shelley Memorial Bulletin*
KuL	*Kunst und Literatur*
L&P	*Literature and Psychology*
Lang&L	*Language and Literature*
LC	*Library Chronicle*
LE&W	*Literature East and West*
LI	*Lettere italiane*

LiLi	*Zeitschrift für Literaturwissenschaft und Linguistik*
LJGG	*Literaturwissenschaftliches Jahrbuch der Görres-Gesellschaft*
LWU	*Literatur in Wissenschaft und Unterricht*
LY	*Lessing Yearbook*
MAL	*Modern Austrian Literature: Journal of the International Arthur Schnitzler Research Association*
MAQR	*Michigan Alumnus Quarterly Review*
MarkhamR	*Markham Review*
McNR	*McNeese Review*
MD	*Modern Drama*
MedH	*Medical History*
MedJ	*Medizinhistorisches Journal*
Merkur	*Merkur: Deutsche Zeitschrift für europäisches Denken*
MFS	*Modern Fiction Studies*
MHG	*Mitteilungen der E. T. A. Hoffmann-Gesellschaft-Bamburg e.V.*
MiltonQ	*Milton Quarterly*
ML	*Modern Languages*
MLJ	*Modern Language Journal*
MLN	*Modern Language Notes*
MLQ	*Modern Language Quarterly*
MLR	*Modern Language Review*
MLS	*Modern Language Studies*
Mnemosyne	*Mnemosyne: Bibliotheca classica Batava*
ModA	*Modern Age: A Quarterly Review*
Monatshefte	*Monatshefte: Für deutschen Unterricht, deutsche Sprache und Literatur*
Month	*Month*
Mosaic	*Mosaic: A Journal for the Comparative Study of Literature and Ideas*
MP	*Modern Philology*
MQ	*Midwest Quarterly*
MQR	*Michigan Quarterly Review*
MR	*Massachusetts Review*
N&Q	*Notes and Queries*
NCF	*Nineteenth-Century Fiction*
NCFS	*Nineteenth-Century French Studies*
NDH	*Neue deutsche Hefte*
NDL	*Neue deutsche Literatur*
Neophil	*Neophilologus*
NEQ	*New England Quarterly*
NFS	*Nottingham French Studies*
NGS	*New German Studies*
NLH	*New Literary History*
NM	*Neuphilologische Mitteilungen*
NMAL	*Notes on Modern American Literature*
NMQ	*New Mexico Quarterly*
Novel	*Novel: A Forum of Fiction*
NRF	*Nouvelle revue française*
NRs	*Neue Rundschau*
NS	*Neueren Sprachen*

OL	*Orbis Litterarum*
OUR	*Ohio University Review*
PaideiaFS	*Paideia* (Buffalo)
Paideuma	*Paideuma: A Journal Devoted to Ezra Pound Scholarship*
P&R	*Philosophy and Rhetoric*
PAPA	*Publications of the Arkansas Philological Association*
PAPS	*Proceedings of the American Philosophical Society*
PCL	*Perspectives on Contemporary Literature*
PCLS	*Proceedings of the Comparative Literature Symposium*
PCP	*Pacific Coast Philology*
PEGS	*Publications of the English Goethe Society*
Person	*Personalist*
PLL	*Papers on Language and Literature*
PMASAL	*Papers of the Michigan Academy of Science, Arts, and Letters*
PMLA	*Publications of the Modern Language Association of America*
PN	*Poe Newsletter*
PNotes	*Pynchon Notes*
PoeS	*Poe Studies*
PolR	*Polish Review*
PQ	*Philological Quarterly*
PR	*Partisan Review*
PrS	*Prairie Schooner*
PsyR	*Psychoanalytic Review*
PZKA	*Philologus: Zeitschrift für klassische Philologie*
QJS	*Quarterly Journal of Speech*
QQ	*Queen's Quarterly*
QR	*Quarterly Review*
QRL	*Quarterly Review of Literature*
RealM	*Realtà del mezzogiorno*
REI	*Revue des études italiennes*
REL	*Review of English Literature*
RenP	*Renaissance Papers*
RenQ	*Renaissance Quarterly*
RES	*Review of English Studies*
RF	*Romanische Forschungen*
RHL	*Revue d'histoire littéraire de la France*
RJ	*Romantisches Jahrbuch*
RLC	*Revue de littérature comparée*
RM	*Review of Metaphysics*
RMS	*Renaissance and Modern Studies*
RNL	*Review of National Literatures*
RomN	*Romance Notes*
RPh	*Romance Philology*
RPLit	*Res Publica Litterarum: Studies in the Classical Tradition*
RQ	*Riverside Quarterly*
RR	*Romanic Review*
RS	*Research Studies* (Pullman)
RSH	*Revue des sciences humaines*

RSS	*Revue de seizième siècle*
SAB	*South Atlantic Bulletin*
SAQ	*South Atlantic Quarterly*
SatR	*Saturday Review*
SBHT	*Studies in Burke and His Time*
SC	*Stendhal-Club*
Scan	*Scandinavica*
SCB	*South Central Bulletin*
SciAm	*Scientific American*
SciMo	*Scientific Monthly*
ScLJ	*Scottish Literary Journal*
SCN	*Seventeenth-Century News*
Scriblerian	*Scriblerian: A Newsletter Devoted to Pope, Swift, and Their Circle*
SECC	*Studies in Eighteenth-Century Culture*
SEEJ	*Slavic and East European Journal*
SEL	*Studies in English Literature, 1500–1900*
SELit	*Studies in English Literature* (English Literary Society of Japan)
Seminar	*Seminar: A Journal of Germanic Studies*
Serif	*Serif* (Kent, OH)
SFI	*Studi di filologia italiana*
SFr	*Studi francesi*
SFS	*Science-Fiction Studies*
ShakAB	*Shakespeare Association Bulletin*
ShawR	*Shaw Review*
SHR	*Southern Humanities Review*
ShS	*Shakespeare Survey*
SIR	*Studies in Romanticism*
SLitl	*Studies in the Literary Imagination*
SLJ	*Southern Literary Journal*
SM	*Speech Monographs*
SN	*Studia Neophilologica*
SNL	*Satire Newsletter*
SNNTS	*Studies in the Novel*
SoQ	*Southern Quarterly*
SoR	*Southern Review*
SoRA	*Southern Review* (Adelaide)
SP	*Studies in Philology*
SPCT	*Studi e problemi di critica testuale*
Speculum	*Speculum: A Journal of Medieval Studies*
SQ	*Shakespeare Quarterly*
SR	*Sewanee Review*
SS	*Scandinavian Studies*
SSF	*Studies in Short Fiction*
SSL	*Studies in Scottish Literature*
StQ	*Steinbeck Quarterly*
STTH	*Science/Technology, and the Humanities*
SubStance	*SubStance: A Review of Theory and Literary Criticism*
Sudhoffs Archiv	*Sudhoffs Archiv für Geschichte der Medizin und der Naturwissenschaften*

SuF	*Sinn und Form*
Survey	*Survey: A Journal of East and West Studies*
SVEC	*Studies on Voltaire and the Eighteenth Century*
SWR	*Southwest Review*
SZ	*Stimmen der Zeit*
TA	*Theater Annual*
TCL	*Twentieth Century Literature*
Thought	*Thought: A Review of Culture and Idea*
THR	*Travaux d'humanisme et renaissance*
TJQ	*Thoreau Journal Quarterly*
TLS	*Times Literary Supplement* (London)
TMV	*Todd Memorial Volumes*
TQ	*Texas Quarterly*
Trema	*Trema: Travaux et recherches sur le monde anglophone*
TriQ	*TriQuarterly*
TSB	*Thoreau Society Bulletin*
TSL	*Tennessee Studies in Literature*
TSLL	*Texas Studies in Literature and Language*
TWA	*Transactions of the Wisconsin Academy of Sciences, Arts, and Letters*
UDQ	*Denver Quarterly*
UES	*Unisa English Studies*
UKCR	*University of Kansas City Review*
UR	*University Review*
UTQ	*University of Toronto Quarterly*
UWR	*University of Windsor Review*
VLit	*Voprosy literatury*
VN	*Victorian Newsletter*
VP	*Victorian Poetry*
VPN	*Victorian Periodicals Newsletter*
VQR	*Virginia Quarterly Review*
VS	*Victorian Studies*
WascanaR	*Wascana Review*
WB	*Weimarer Beiträge*
WC	*Wordsworth Circle*
WCWN	*William Carlos Williams Newsletter*
WGCR	*West Georgia College Review*
WHR	*Western Humanities Review*
WN	*Wake Newslitter: Studies in James Joyce's* Finnegans Wake
WSA	*Wolfenbütteler Studien zur Aufklärung*
WSCL	*Wisconsin Studies in Comparative Literature*
WSJour	*Wallace Stevens Journal*
WWR	*Walt Whitman Review*
WZUH	*Wissenschaftliche Zeitschrift der Martin-Luther Universität Halle-Wittenberg: Gesellschafts- und sprachwissenschaftliche Reihe*
YCGL	*Yearbook of Comparative and General Literature*
YES	*Yearbook of English Studies*
YFS	*Yale French Studies*
YR	*Yale Review*

YULG	*Yale University Library Gazette*
ZAA	*Zeitschrift für Anglistik und Amerikanistik*
ZDA	*Zeitschrift für deutsches Altertum und deutsche Literatur*
ZDP	*Zeitschrift für deutsche Philologie*
ZDS	*Zeitschrift für deutsche Sprache*

General

Interactions of Literature and Science

1.   Allen, Harrison. "Poetry and Science." *Poet-Lore* 3 (1891): 233–49.
   Illustrates congenial relations between science and poetry in writers such as Shakespeare, Goethe, Kingsley, Tennyson, and Wordsworth.

2.   Ames, Van Meter. "The Novel: Between Art and Science." *KR* 5 (1943): 34–48.
   Reflections on the role of the modern novel in mediating the tension between fine art as pure expression and science as explanation.

3.   Anon. "Nature and Science in Poetry." *Nature* 132 (1933): 293–96.
   Maintains that science is a fitting subject for poetry only if assimilated in a truly artistic manner.

4.   ———. "Science and Literature." *Nature* 85 (1910–11): 446–48.
   Brief remarks on the appropriateness of using scientific data in poetry.

5.   Antokolski, P. "Poesie und Physik." *Sowjetwissenschaft* 6 (1960): 620–23.
   A brief discussion of the schism between contemporary science, especially physics, and literature. The author suggests ways in which the gap between the two might be bridged and cites figures, such as Goethe and Lomonosov, who successfully combined their literary and scientific endeavors.

6.   Arnett, Willard E. "Poetry and Science." *JAAC* 14 (1955–56): 445–52.
   Science and poetry differ primarily in their modes of symbolization and the context of human experience in which and out of which they occur; but their differences should not obscure their affinities.

7.   Arnold, Matthew. "Literature and Science." *Nineteenth Century* 12 (1882): 216–30.
   The first printed appearance of Arnold's Cambridge Rede Lecture, which considers the question of whether natural science or literature and the humanities should predominate in the educational curriculum. In favoring the humanities Arnold conflicted with T. H. Huxley, thus precipitating a nineteenth-century "two cultures" debate.

8.   Ashley Montagu, M. F. "Suggestions for the Better Correlation of Literature
        and Science." *Studies and Essays in the History of Science and Learning Offered
        in Homage to George Sarton on the Occasion of His Sixtieth Birthday, 31 August
        1944.* Ed. M. F. Ashley Montagu. New York: Schuman, 1946. 235–46.
Outlines changes in educational curricula that should be implemented to bring
about closer relations between literature and science.

9.   Balmer, Heinz. "Naturerkenntnis und Dichtung." *Gesnerus* 37 (1980):
        314–20.
Examines passages from works by Shakespeare, Goethe, Schiller, and Meyer con-
cerning gunpowder, the air balloon, the lightning rod, and atmospheric electricity.
The author maintains that the impact of scientific progress on literature has been
especially strong since the Enlightenment. His primary example is the influence of
Scheuchzer's natural history publications on Schiller's *William Tell*.

10.   Barbour, Ian G. *Myths, Models and Paradigms: The Nature of Scientific and
        Religious Language.* London: SCM, 1974. 198 pp.
        Rev. Leroy T. Howe, *Theology Today* 31 (1974–75): 270–72; John A.
        Miles, Jr., *American Academy of Religion Journal* 43 (1975): 376–77.
Primarily a comparison of the function of myths, models, and paradigms in
science and religion, though chapter 2 treats the nature of metaphor, symbol,
parable, and analogy in religious language and suggests a relation between the
literary and scientific uses of language.

11.   Bardach, John E., with Alice Bloch. "There *Is* Poetry in Science." *MQR*
        6 (1967): 107–08.
A discussion of the task of poeticizing scientific data, illustrated by an untitled
poem by Alice Bloch on molecular biology.

12.   Barmeyer, Eike, ed. *Science Fiction: Theorie und Geschichte.* München: Fink,
        1972. 383 pp.
Essays treating the genre, content, literary value, history, and scientific background of science fiction. Martin Schwonke's "Naturwissenschaft und Technik im
utopischen Denken der Neuzeit" (57–76), for example, discusses the influence of
Copernicus's astronomical teachings on such seventeenth-century novels as F. Bacon's
New Atlantis (1628) and Campanella's *Civitas solis* (1623) and comments on the
impact of contemporary science and technology on the modern science fiction novel.
James Blish's "Nachruf auf die Prophetie" (118–28) studies scientific prediction in
science fiction, stressing the topic of nuclear technologies in Heinlein's "Blow-Ups
Happen" and "Solution Unsatisfactory" as well as in Cartmill's "Deadline." Stanislaw
Lem's "Roboter in der Science Fiction" (163–86) examines the function and position
of the robot in modern science fiction. Includes discussion of Leiber's *Silver Eggheads*,
Asimov's *I, Robot*, and Merliss's *Stutterer*. Michael Kandel's "Stanislaw Lem über
den Menschen und Roboter" (304–18) treats the influence of Turing's *Computing
Machinery and Intelligence* (1950) and Asimov's *I, Robot* (1950) on Lem's "Test,"
"Terminus," and "Kyberiade," among other stories.

13.   Battistini, Andrea, ed. *Letteratura e scienza*. Letteratura e problemi 10. Bologna: Zanichelli, 1977. 234 pp.
This anthology of essays on literature and science examines such problems as scientific versus literary language, the style of scientific writing, and various responses to scientific advancement by such writers as Lucretius, Dante, Goethe, Flaubert, and Zola. Includes essays by T. H. Huxley, M. Arnold, Richards, Snow, Leavis, A. Huxley, Nicolson, and others.

14.   Baym, Max I. "Metaphysical Malaise: Science and the Struggle for a Universal Poetics." *BuR* 9 (1960–61): 199–211.
Reflections on the potential roles of science and poetry in the development of a "universal poetics," which, in its understanding of human beings and nature, would resolve the tension between object and subject, reason and feeling.

15.   ———. "On the Relationship between Poetry and Science." *YCGL* 5 (1956): 21–25.
General remarks on the conflict between science and imagination as treated by P. Shelley, Stevens, Wordsworth, and others.

16.   ———. "Science and Poetry." *Encyclopedia of Poetry and Poetics*. Ed. Alex Preminger. Princeton: Princeton UP, 1965. 742–53.
A historical overview of the relations between poetry and science, citing the major theoretical formulations of the relation by Plato, Aristotle, M. Arnold, Richards, and others. Also discusses some of the central literary figures whose works incorporate science, including Dante, Milton, Blake, Hardy, Keats, Meredith, and P. Shelley.

17.   Bernard, Kenneth. "C. P. Snow and Modern Literature." *UR* 31 (1964–65): 231–33.
Maintains that Snow's essay "The Two Cultures: And a Second Look" fails to treat adequately the nature and function of literature in modern science-dominated society.

18.   Blissett, William. "Poetic Wave and Poetic Particle." *UTQ* 24 (1954–55): 1–7.
A discussion of analysis in poetry as analogous to analysis in physics. "Just as the things of physics may be spoken of in two vocabularies, as made up of waves or of particles, so poetry as a 'thing' subject to analysis has been found to have two analogous units, the line and the image."

19.   Bölsche, Wilhelm. *Die naturwissenschaftlichen Grundlagen der Poesie: Prolegomena einer realistischen Ästhetik*. Tübingen: Niemeyer, 1976. 166 pp.
Advocates a realistic literature that abandons metaphysics and adapts itself to new discoveries in the natural and social sciences. An autodidact in the sciences and the author of several novels, Bölsche was most effective as a popularizer of science and as an advocate of a naturalistic aesthetics.

20.   ———. "Naturwissenschaft und Poesie." *Das litterarische Echo* 6 (1903): 1–8.

Examines the split between literature and science in the nineteenth century, citing the attempts by Novalis and Zola to unify the two. Novalis, however, subordinated science to literature, and Zola subordinated literature to science. The author explores the scientific methodology of disciplines such as biology and ethnography in which he finds a creative process that parallels a similar process in the arts. His prime example of the scientist as artist is C. Darwin.

21.   Briggs, E. R. "The Impact of Science upon the Concept of Imagination." *Literature and Science*. Proc. of the Sixth Triennial Congress of the International Federation for Modern Languages and Literatures. Oxford, 1954. Oxford: Blackwell, 1955. 85–90.
Considers the relation between hypothesis and imagination in science and art and analyzes various connotations of the term *imagination* as used by poets, scientists, and philosophers.

22.   Broker, Gulabdas. "Imaginative Literature in the Age of Science." *IPEN* 25 (1959): 299–303.
General remarks on the cognitive and practical achievements of literature and science. Imaginative literature can flourish in an age dominated by science because both science and literature are rooted in humankind's quest for knowledge.

23.   Brown, Bahngrell W. "The Separation of Literature and Science: A Twentieth Century Evil." *SoQ* 3 (1965): 217–24.
Maintains that much scientific literature deserves, by virtue of its high literary merit, to be included in contemporary anthologies of imaginative literature. Such anthologies would help bridge the gap between scientists and humanists.

24.   Brown, Harold I. "Objective Knowledge in Science and the Humanities." *Diogenes* 97 (1977): 85–102.
Evaluates epistemological models based on logical positivism and Popper's *Logik der Forschung* (1935) and develops a theory of objective scientific knowledge by drawing from the epistemology of Feyerabend, Kuhn, and Polanyi. Applications to Borges's story "The Library of Babel" illustrate the theory's epistemological implications. Includes an assessment of the epistemic status of literature, history, and philosophy.

25.   Bukin, W. "Ästhetische Kultur und wissenschaftliches Weltbild." *KuL* 26 (1978): 1029–33.
Discusses the "two cultures" problem as outlined in Snow's 1959 Cambridge Rede Lecture, "The Two Cultures and the Scientific Revolution." Focuses on the interaction between the scientific and aesthetic cultures, their influence on mass culture, and the influence of aesthetic culture on the creative process in science.

26.   Burroughs, John. "The Literary Value of Science." *Macmillan's Magazine* 54 (1886): 184–91.
The value of science lies in its ability ". . . to foster in us noble ideals, and to lead us to new and larger views of moral and spiritual truths." Science will, however, never usurp the humanities as an instrument of culture; rather, the two must interact cooperatively.

27.   ———. "Science and Literature." *North American Review* 199 (1914): 415–24.

Maintains that science is antithetical to, and even destructive of, literary sensibility. "Literature interprets life and nature in terms of our sentiments and emotions; science interprets them in terms of our understanding."

28.   Cadden, John J., and Patrick R. Brostowin. *Science and Literature: A Reader.* Boston: Heath, 1964. 310 pp.

An anthology divided into three sections. The first, spanning the century from T. H. Huxley and M. Arnold to Snow, collects essays that, as a group, chart the emergence of the "two cultures." The second reprints selections from the works of Douglas Bush, Basil Willey, Marjorie Nicolson, Ralph Crum, B. Ifor Evans, and others that outline the interactions between science and literature in specific periods from the Renaissance to the present. The third presents poetry, fiction, and essays by authors discussed in the second section, including Donne, Milton, Swift, Poe, Whitman, Wordsworth, and Frost.

29.   Campbell, Paul N. "Poetic-Rhetorical, Philosophical, and Scientific Discourse." *P&R* 6 (1973): 1–29.

Argues that "poetic, rhetorical, philosophical, and scientific discourse are not processes of similar or equal logical stature, but that a symbological hierarchy is involved in which poetic-rhetorical discourse is the primary form, philosophical discourse the secondary form, and scientific discourse the tertiary form."

30.   Cargill, Oscar. "Science and the Literary Imagination in the United States." *CE* 13 (1951–52): 90–94.

Much of what passes as the influence of science on literary figures is an accommodation to settled beliefs. One should be hesitant about assigning value to literary works that depend on fast-developing, transient trends in science.

30a.   Carlisle, E. Fred. "Literature, Science, and Language: A Study of Similarity and Difference." *Pre/Text* 1 (1980): 39–72.

Defines the common functions of the languages of science and literature, drawing on theoretical work in phenomenology, literary theory, and philosophy of science.

31.   Cherry, Douglas. "The Two Cultures of Matthew Arnold and T. H. Huxley." *WascanaR* 1 (1966): 53–61.

A discussion of the inadequacies of M. Arnold's defense of literature in "Literature and Science" (1882) in the face of the challenge posed to classical education by T. H. Huxley in "Science and Culture" (1880).

32.   Cohen, Joseph W. "Aspects of the Relations between Philosophy and Literature." *University of Colorado Studies.* Series B: Studies in the Humanities 1 (1939–41): 117–67.

Pages 161–66 of this study assess the extent of science's influence on literature. The study maintains that literature, though capable of absorbing scientific themes and concepts indirectly from the general cultural environment, is an inappropriate medium for the expression of scientific thought or for the pursuit of scientific inquiry.

33.   Colomb, Gregory G. "Roman Ingarden and the Language of Art and Science." *JAAC* 35 (1976–77): 7–13.
A discussion of the distinction between a literary work of art and a scientific text as developed in Ingarden's *Literary Work of Art* (1973).

34.   Corday, Michel. "L'image scientifique en littérature." *Revue de Paris* 5 (1904): 837–53.
Examines the reasons behind the increasing literary use of metaphors drawn from scientific fields such as chemistry, botany, and physics.

35.   Cottrell, T. L. "The Scientific Textbook as a Work of Art." *REL* 3.4 (1962): 7–16.
Suggests that, compared with other types of scientific literature, scientific textbooks are the most amenable to literary criticism.

36.   Day Lewis, C. "The Poet's Way of Knowledge." *EDH* ns 33 (1965): 1–17.
Contrasts poetic and scientific cognitive approaches to natural phenomena, concluding that poetry yields a form of knowledge inaccessible to science but as worthwhile as scientific information.

37.   Denbigh, K. G. "The Use of Imagery in Science." *Fortnightly* 178 (1952): 411–18.
Close similarities exist between the poet's use of metaphor and the scientist's use of hypothesis or model. The author outlines the nature of imagery in science, stressing the difficulties of searching for exact images to describe phenomena such as wave-particle complementarity.

38.   Derfer, George. "Science, Poetry, and 'Human Specificity': An Interview with J. Bronowski." *ASch* 43 (1974): 386–404.
Bronowski outlines some elements of his biological theory of "human specificity." The human being, for Bronowski, is the "planning animal," the animal with imagination. Imagination, or the ability to hypothesize, is the fundamental link between scientific and poetic activity. Bronowski's *Science and Human Values* and *Identity of Man* are the primary textual referents in the interview.

39.   Deutsch, Karl W. "Scientific and Humanistic Knowledge in the Growth of Civilization." *Science and the Creative Spirit: Essays on Humanistic Aspects of Science*. Ed. Harcourt Brown. Toronto: U of Toronto P, 1958. 3–51.
Compares the principal aspects of scientific method and knowledge with the humanistic mode of inquiry in the context of their contributions to civilization. Includes discussion of the extent to which each study both serves as a resource for and imposes constraints on the other.

40.   Dingle, Herbert. "The Relations between Science and Literature." *Literature and Science*. Proc. of the Sixth Triennial Congress of the International Federation for Modern Languages and Literatures. Oxford, 1954. Oxford: Blackwell, 1955. 1–11.

Emphasizes the traditionally conflicting relations between science and poetry, showing that the conflict can be reduced to a misunderstanding of the essential and distinct functions of the two disciplines. Includes discussion of "experiment" versus "intuition" and "truth" versus "illusion."

41.   ———. *Science and Literary Criticism*. London: Nelson, 1949. Folcroft: Folcroft, 1974. Norwood: Norwood, 1977. 184 pp.
Traces the history of attempts by such critics as Sainte-Beuve, Taine, Moulton, Robertson, and Richards to formulate a scientific literary criticism. Discusses the obstacles confronting such an endeavor and uses essays on Browning, Swinburne, and Wordsworth to illustrate one possible approach to integrating science into criticism.

42.   Dudley, Fred A. "The Impact of Science on Literature." *Science* 115 (1952): 412–15.
An overview of the twentieth-century trend toward scholarly interest in the influence of science on literature. Cites examples from the poetry of Milton, Tennyson, Wordsworth, and others.

43.   Eastman, Max. "Literature in an Age of Science." *The Writer and His Craft: Being the Hopwood Lectures, 1932–1952*. Ann Arbor: U of Michigan P, 1954. 16–29.
The author links what he sees as the "cult of unintelligibility" in modern poetry to the gradual usurpation by science of literature's traditional role as the purveyor of knowledge.

44.   Elliot, George P. "Science and the Profession of Literature." *Atlantic* Oct. 1971: 105–11.
Rejects the application of scientific principles to the study of literature. "Qualities which are true goods in the realm of science, impersonal objectivity above all, are in most respects inappropriate to the moral, social, and aesthetic realms."

45.   Fagan, Edward R. "Science and English: A Rapprochement through Literature." *EJ* 54 (1965): 357–63.
Notes the importance of teaching English in an interdisciplinary manner and indicates that literature, replete with scientific themes and structures, can serve as a bridge between the sciences and the humanities.

46.   Federman, Donald. "The Measure of All Things: The Conflict of Art and Biology in American Natural History Writing." *DAI* 36 (1975–76): 6682A.
The American nature essay combines artistic and literary qualities with a scientific conceptual orientation based on modern biology.

47.   Fiedler, Leslie A. "Poetry, Science and the End of Man." *TriQ* 1 (1964): 7–14.
"Poetry ideally performs not a single but a double (and apparently contradictory) function in relation to science; it criticizes and collaborates with, attacks and reinforces the other discipline."

48.   Fietz, Lothar. "Cambridge und die Diskussion um das Verhältnis von Literatur und Naturwissenschaft." *Literatur-Kultur-Gesellschaft in England und Amerika: Aspekte und Forschungsbeiträge. Friedrich Schubel zum 60. Geburtstag.* Ed. Gerhard Müller-Schwefe and Konrad Tuzinski. Frankfurt: Diesterweg, 1966. 113–27.

Maintains that the roots of the "two cultures" debate between Snow and Leavis can be found in seventeenth-century essays such as F. Bacon's "Proficiency and Advancement of Learning, Divine and Human," Temple's "Essay upon the Ancient and Modern Learning," and Wotton's "Reflections upon Ancient and Modern Learning." Discusses also three methodologically different approaches to the relations between literature and science as reflected in essays by Marjorie Nicolson, Richard Foster Jones, and Donald Davie.

49.   Fraser, Russell. "The Poet as Middle-Man of Knowledge: On Metaphor, Mysticism, and Science." *MQR* 8 (1969): 49–57.

Outlines the epistemological foundations and presuppositions of science, mysticism, and poetry, stressing how each one relates to particularity and generality in its investigative approach to nature.

50.   ———. "Science and Poetry." *KR* 30 (1968): 384–99.

Compares the perspectives of scientists and poets in regard to the quest for truth. Concludes that the scientist seeks primary, empirically verifiable, and useful knowledge, whereas the poet seeks knowledge that is secondary, superficial, and inconsequential.

51.   Gaspar, Lorand. "Science and Poetry." *Diogenes* 67 (1969): 26–50; *Diogène* 67 (1969): 35–60.

A linguistic analysis of poetic and scientific language, stressing the phonic, semantic, emotive, and metaphoric characteristics of the two branches of language, as well as the possibilities of mutual influence.

52.   Ghiselin, Michael T. "Poetic Biology: A Defense and Manifesto." *NLH* 7 (1975–76): 493–504.

Outlines the importance and utility of metaphorical expression in scientific literature and draws attention to the need for a new branch of literary criticism and aesthetics devoted to science.

53.   Gingerich, Owen. "Circumventing Newton: A Study in Scientific Creativity." *AJPhys* 46 (1978): 202–06.

Examines the nature of scientific creativity and imagination by comparing Newton's achievements in the *Principia* with the creative achievements of artists such as Beethoven and Shakespeare.

54.   Glicksberg, Charles I. "Literary Criticism and Science." *UTQ* 12 (1942–43): 485–96.

Argues that no grounds exist for the belief that science inherently conflicts with poetry; in fact, ". . . literature can secure validity and tap new sources of strength by relating itself intimately to the scientific outlook." Because science provides only empirical data and no criteria of appreciation or evaluative principles, literary criticism retains its autonomous function.

55.   ———. "Literature and Science: A Study in Conflict." *SciMo* 59 (1944): 467–72.

Maintains that the literary critique of science is naive and ill-founded and tries to show that literature can only benefit from an alliance with science—an alliance based on mutual understanding of the limitations and appropriate functions of the two disciplines.

56.   Goldman, Steven Louis. "Present Strains in the Relations between Science, Technology and Society." *Science, Technology, and Human Values* 4.27 (1978–79): 44–51.

Examines the cultural context from which contemporary criticism of science and technology has arisen. The literary forebears of the current attitude include Goethe, Rousseau, Swift, and Thoreau.

57.   Goran, Morris. "Science as Art." *JGE* 18 (1966–67): 281–88.

Scientific activity engages scientists in experiences comparable to those of poets and artists. An appreciation of beauty, order, and symmetry characterizes workers in both fields. Scientists no less than writers must possess and exhibit creativity and imagination.

58.   Gordon, David J. "The Dilemma of Literature in an Age of Science." *SR* 86 (1978): 245–60.

The procedures of scientific and literary knowing are different, as are their uses of language. A poet who absorbs a scientific theory animates and changes it, creating a logical problem between scientific materialism and poetic idealism.

59.   Green, Martin. "A Literary Defense of 'The Two Cultures.' " *KR* 24 (1962): 731–39.

The author finds weaknesses in Leavis's attack on Snow and suggests that Snow has, indeed, made a valuable contribution to the redefinition of culture in a scientific age.

60.   ———. *Science and the Shabby Curate of Poetry: Essays about the Two Cultures*. London: Longmans, 1964. New York: Norton, 1965. 159 pp.

A record of the impact that Snow's "two cultures" theory had on the author, a literary man. Includes a defense of Snow that critically analyzes Leavis's and Trilling's responses to his theory; essays that trace the author's attempt to supplement his literary training with four years of scientific studies, reflections on literary and liberal education, commentary on the nature of science fiction, and a survey of some science nonfiction that helped the author reeducate himself.

61.   Grimaldi, William M. A., SJ. "Science or Literature as a New Humanism?" *Catholic World* 195 (1962): 356–63.

Argues that the study of literature is the best means of overcoming the "confusion in our understanding of man" wrought by the dominance of science in contemporary society.

62.   Haas, W. "Of Living Things." *GL&L* 10 (1956–57): 62–70.
Through a discussion of Goethe's biological studies (stressing his theories of Gestalt, morphology, and metamorphosis), this exercise in the history of ideas attempts to reveal the affinities between biology, comparative philology, and literary criticism.

63.   Hallowes, Kenneth Knight. *The Poetry of Geology*. London: Murby, 1933. 61 pp.
A collection of poems based on geological themes. The author's introduction reflects on the relations between poetry and science and attempts to outline the qualifications of a true poet of science. Hallowes claims that ". . . the mission of a Poet of Science is to *transfigure* the dry and prosaic facts of Science with the magic of his poetic genius till they become interesting to the generality of mankind as well as to the scientific specialist."

64.   Hand, Harry E. "The Paper Curtain: The Divided World of Snow and Leavis Revisited." *Journal of Human Relations* 14 (1966): 351–63.
Reflections on the "two cultures" controversy between Snow and Leavis, tracing the historical background of the division and commenting on the inadequacies of both views. Maintains that both Snow and Leavis lacked insight into the relation between science and the humanities and that signs of increasing cooperation between the two disciplines are beginning to appear.

65.   Hassan, Ihab. *The Right Promethean Fire: Imagination, Science, and Cultural Change*. Urbana: U of Illinois P, 1980. 218 pp.
Rev. William E. Cain, *GaR* 34 (1980): 920–22; Matei Calinescu, *ConL* 21 (1980): 632–38; Jerome Klinkowitz, *MFS* 26 (1980–81): 719–22; Anna Otten, *AR* 39 (1981): 391; Jay Martin, *AL* 54 (1982): 604–06.
This intriguing collage of essays, quotations from writers ranging from Pythagoras to Pynchon, "paracritical" visionary "frames," and snippets of insight concerns the power of imagination, the Promethean fire at the heart of science, technology, literature, criticism, and culture in general. The figure of Prometheus serves as the book's principal image and represents the prophet of imaginative gnosis who foretells the advent of postmodern, transhumanized, planetary humanity.

66.   Hayakawa, S. I. "Poetry and Science." *English Institute Annual, 1942*. New York: Columbia UP, 1943. 163–81.
Suggests that poetry functions as an essential part of the human survival mechanism and is no less important an element of human activity than science is. Poetry and science contribute equally to the health of human beings.

67.   Heissenbüttel, Helmut. "Literatur und Wissenschaft." *Akzente* 12 (1965): 171–91.
Briefly sketches the history of the domains of literature and science and the points of contact regarding their respective modes of representing reality. Discusses the various transformations of reality as caused first by the natural sciences and later by the social sciences. Cites numerous examples to demonstrate the evolution of literary genres corresponding to developments in the sciences.

68.   Holtz, William. "Field Theory and Literature." *CentR* 11 (1967): 532–48.
Applies the field approach characteristic of modern physical, biological, and social sciences to the study of literature and literary criticism, hence suggesting similarities between the sciences and the humanities. Illustrates the method by analyzing Sterne's *Tristram Shandy*.

69.   Hoskins, John P. "Biological Analogy in Literary Criticism." *MP* 6 (1908–09): 407–34; 7 (1909–10): 61–82.
Part 1 explores the principal elements in the formation of new literary types or species and compares this process with biological evolution. The author emphasizes the psychological aspects of variation that are not applicable to the biological analogy, such as individual consciousness, selective imitation, social heredity, and aesthetic invention or constructive imagination. Part 2 concerns factors, such as social utility, that lead to the survival and decay of literary species, stressing that biological processes like natural selection and the struggle for existence are irrelevant to literature. Includes a discussion of the need to place literary criticism on a scientific basis.

70.   Howarth, J. L. "Literature and Science." *BRMMLA* 22.4 (1968): 177–82.
Discusses the problem of compartmentalization in education, particularly the separation of science from literature, in the context of the "two cultures" debate between Snow and Leavis.

71.   Huxley, Aldous. *Literature and Science*. London: Chatto; New York: Harper, 1963. 118 pp.
Rev. *YR* ns 53.2 (1963–64): xxiv–xxviii; Jacques Barzun, *Science* Jan. 1964: 33; Max Black, *SciAm* Mar. 1964: 141–44.
Written in the wake of controversies over Snow's essay "The Two Cultures and the Scientific Revolution" (1959), this essay attempts to mediate between Snow's "bland scientism" and "the one-track, moralistic literarism" of his principal detractor, Leavis. Huxley examines the function, psychology, and language of both literature and science, outlines the history of relations between the two fields, and speculates on ways in which contemporary scholars might use the theories and findings of science in a new literature capable of expressing the totality of human experience.

72.   James, David G. *Skepticism and Poetry: An Essay on the Poetic Imagination*. New York: Barnes; London: Allen, 1937. Westport: Greenwood, 1980. 274 pp.
Compares the roles imagination plays in science and literature. Builds on the distinctions among sensibility, imagination, and reason as found in Kant and Coleridge and contrasts the resulting model of creativity with the ideas of empiricists, such as Richards, who reduce literature to mechanistic states of mind and thus set it against science. Case studies consider the attitudes toward science expressed in the works of Shakespeare, Keats, and Wordsworth.

73.   Jeffares, A. Norman. *Language, Literature and Science: An Inaugural Lecture.*
       Cambridge: Leeds UP, 1959. 24 pp.
    Comments on the changes science wrought on literary style in the seventeenth
and eighteenth centuries, noting especially the impact of the Royal Society's attempt
to foster a plain and accurate style of scientific writing. Among the scientists and
writers discussed are F. Bacon, Newton, Glanvill, Wilkins, and Donne.

74.   Johnson, Francis R. "Literary History and the History of Science." *Literature
       and Science.* Proc. of the Sixth Triennial Congress of the International
       Federation for Modern Languages and Literatures. Oxford, 1954. Oxford:
       Blackwell, 1955. 101–06.
    Discusses the interdependence of literary historians and historians of science.
Histories of science must reflect a literary understanding of the nuances of scientific
terminology; such sensitively written histories are an indispensable tool for the
literary historian's investigation of scientific allusions in literature.

75.   Just, Klaus Günther. "Über Luftfahrt und Literatur." *Antaios* 11 (1970):
       393–411. Rpt. in *Marginalien: Probleme und Gestalten der Literatur.* Bern:
       Francke, 1976. 79–97.
    Examines the representation of human flight in literature, focusing especially on
balloon travel, initiated by the Montgolfier brothers in 1783. Discusses Wieland's
reports about balloon travel, entitled "Die Aeropetomanie" and "Die Aeronauten,"
which appeared in the *Teutschen Merkur* in 1783. Also cites works by Jean Paul,
Verne, and Ringelnatz.

76.   Kahler, Erich. *The Inward Turn of Narrative.* Trans. Richard Winston and
       Clara Winston. Bollingen Series 83. Princeton: Princeton UP, 1973. 214
       pp.
       Rev. Philip Stevick, *CL* 26 (1974): 85–87.
    Maintains that the development of human consciousness has been accompanied
by a process of ever-greater internalization of reality, as reflected in the development
of narrative technique beginning with Homer and culminating, for the purposes of
this study, in Sterne's *Tristram Shandy.* Sees the rise of science and scientific empiricism as one of the decisive factors influencing the process of internalization; thus,
devotes considerable attention to the impact of science on the narrative mode in
authors such as Defoe, Swift, and J. Thomson.

77.   Kreuzer, Helmut, ed. *Literarische und naturwissenschaftliche Intelligenz: Dialog
       über die "zwei Kulturen."* Stuttgart: Klett, 1969. 273 pp.
    A collection of essays reflecting the worldwide impact of the "two cultures" debate
sparked by Snow's essay "The Two Cultures and the Scientific Revolution" (1959)
and Leavis's critical response, *Two Cultures? The Significance of C. P. Snow* (1962).
Includes selections from the works of English, American, and German writers such
as Trilling, Oppenheimer, A. Huxley, Bahrdt, and Steinbuch.

78.   Kurz, Paul Konrad, SJ. "Literatur und Naturwissenschaft." *SZ* 176 (1965):
       1–20. Rpt. as "Literature and Science." *On Modern German Literature.*
       Trans. Sister Mary Frances McCarthy. University: U of Alabama P, 1970.
       56–79.

Reflections on the object, method, goal, and language of both literature and science and an assessment of literature's role in a world dominated by science and technology. Provides a brief history of the interaction between literature and science, citing works by Goethe, Wordsworth, Zola, Broch, A. Huxley, Musil, and others.

79.   Leavis, F. R. *Two Cultures? The Significance of C. P. Snow.* London: Chatto, 1962. 45 pp. New York: Pantheon, 1963. 64 pp.

Leavis's famous scathing appraisal of Snow's "two cultures" theory as outlined in the Cambridge Rede Lecture of 1959 (see item 121). Claims that Snow's exposition of the relations between literary and scientific education is an intellectual embarrassment.

80.   Lepenies, Wolf. "Der Wissenschaftler als Autor: Über konservierende Funktionen der Literatur." *Akzente* 25 (1978): 129–47.

To determine how scientists and writers poeticize scientific findings, examines Humboldt's *Ansichten der Natur*, Buffon's *Histoire naturelle*, and Jean Paul's "Vorschule der Ästhetik" and briefly explores Balzac's, Flaubert's, and Zola's approaches to the question.

81.   McCorquodale, Marjorie K. "Poets and Scientists." *Bulletin of the Atomic Scientists* 21.9 (1965): 18–20.

Suggests a link between poetic and scientific methodology by claiming that poets use a method remarkably similar to phenomenology. Notes similarities and differences between poetry and science, emphasizing that the two must ". . . advance together toward discovery and communication of the unknown."

82.   McKeon, Richard. "Semantics, Science, and Poetry." *MP* 49 (1951–52): 145–59.

Explores the possible applications of dialectical, operational, and circumstantial semantics to an analysis of the commonalities and differences between poetic and scientific language usage.

83.   Main, William W. "Symbol and Object in Science and Literature." *CentR* 2 (1958): 248–60.

Differing perceptions of reality are among the distinguishing features between literature and science: literature tends to view reality as symbolic, while science sees reality as objective. Examines the constitution, structure, and expressive forms of symbol and object and their functions in literary and scientific activity. Includes references to Homer, Shakespeare, and quantum physics.

84.   Manly, John M. "Literary Forms and the New Theory of the Origin of Species." *MP* 4 (1906–07): 577–95.

Compares the Darwinian theory of evolution, the mutation theory of Hugo de Vries, and the origin of new literary forms, thus demonstrating the limitations of biological and physical metaphors when applied to literature. Traces the origin of modern drama and notes how the emergence of this literary form differs from the evolutionary emergence of natural forms.

85.   Medawar, P. B. "Science and Literature." *Encounter* 32.1 (1969): 15–23.

Maintains that science and literature tend to expel each other from territory to which both can legitimately lay claim. Both assert sole grasp on the means to truth, though literature emphasizes imagination at the expense of critical thinking, while science emphasizes criticism over imagination. Both scientism and poetism are equally contemptible intellectual positions to the author.

86.   Menzel, Donald H. "Space—the New Frontier." *PMLA* 77 (1962): 10–17.
An exhortation, written at the brink of the space age, to bridge the gap between the sciences and the humanities. Sees science as a possible inspiration to literature and cites Swift, Poe, Verne, and Wells as examples.

87.   Meyerhoff, Hans. *Time in Literature.* Berkeley: U of California P, 1955. 160 pp.
        Rev. G. Wilson Knight, *MLR* 51 (1956): 577; A. A. Mendilow, *RES* ns 8 (1957): 342–43.
Primarily a comparison of philosophical, psychological, and scientific analyses of time with various aspects of experiential time as rendered in literature. Refers to works by Proust, Joyce, Mann, Wolfe, and others. Also assesses the validity of literary and scientific treatments of time.

88.   Muller, Herbert J. "Scientist and Man of Letters." *YR* ns 31 (1941–42): 279–96.
Science and literature share significant affinities, especially in their uses of imaginative intellect. Any overly sharp distinction between the two fields of inquiry is unjustified.

89.   Murray, Byron D. "C. P. Snow: Grounds for Reappraisal." *Person* 47 (1966): 91–101.
Argues, against Snow, that traditional literary culture *has* included an abundance of authors who were aware of scientific and industrialized culture and who, in fact, composed responses to it. Among the authors who belie the generalizations of the Snow-Leavis-Trilling "two cultures" controversy are Cowper, Crabbe, Goldsmith, G. Eliot, Twain, Whitman, Wordsworth, and Zola.

90.   Myers, Henry. "Literature, Science, and Democracy." *Pacific Spectator* 8 (1954): 333–45.
Literature may be distinguished from other forms of writing, such as scientific writing, by its ability to provide insight into the inner life of human beings. The author examines the social function of literature and comments on the complementary function of science in forming society.

91.   Neubauer, John. "Scientific Law and Poetic Form: A Dialogue on Literature and Science." *YCGL* 24 (1975): 50–55.
Fictional historians of science and literature discuss science's impact on poetic structure and vocabulary and speculate on literature's impact on scientific methodology.

92.   Nicolson, Marjorie. "Resource Letter SL-1 on Science and Literature."
          AJPhys 33 (1965): 175–83.
Provides a brief history of literature-and-science studies and an annotated bibliography of major works in the field. "Intended to guide college physicists to some
of the literature and other teaching aids that may help them improve course contents
in specified fields of physics."

93.   Northrop, F. S. C. "The Functions and Future of Poetry." *Furioso* 1.4
          (1941): 71–82. Rpt. in *The Logic of the Sciences and the Humanities*. New
          York: Macmillan, 1947. 169–90.
Poetry both communicates a sense of the immediately observable world in an
aesthetically pleasing way and serves "as the instrument or handmaid for meta-
phorically and analogically conveying a theoretical doctrine." The challenge to poetry
in the contemporary age is to apprehend, interpret, and articulate the complex,
experimentally verified theories of science and all their moral, philosophical, and
aesthetic implications.

94.   ———. "Literature and Science." *SatR* 5 Aug. 1944: 33–36.
General remarks on the fundamental complementarity of contemporary science
and poetry and the need to integrate the two disciplines to achieve a more enlightened
and humane society.

95.   Oehser, Paul H. "The Lion and the Lamb: An Essay on Science and Poetry."
          AmerSci 43 (1955): 89–96.
A discussion of the affinities and distinctions between scientific and poetic de-
scriptions of phenomena, with selections from the writings of Thoreau, Whitman,
Frost, and other poets.

96.   Perewersew, L. "Kunst und Wissenschaft." *KuL* 14 (1966): 292–95.
Elaborates on the different modes of cognition characteristic of literature and
science, maintaining that separation between the two can only be relative, never
absolute. Traces the apparent separation between art and science to the Romantic
period, discussing also the related debate during the late nineteenth century between
T. H. Huxley and M. Arnold. Includes comments on the influence of "scientific
socialism" on the relations between art and science, as evidenced in the rise of
sciences such as cybernetics, bionics, mathematical linguistics, and semiotics. Among
the writers discussed are Montaigne, R. Descartes, Pascal, Goethe, and Voltaire.

97.   Perrine, Laurence. "The Poet and the Laboratory." *SWR* 58 (1973): 285–
          92. Rpt. in *SWR* 59 (1974): 472–79.
Commentary on the differences between poetic and scientific activity. Author
maintains that science and poetry are, or should be, complementary and affirms the
need for poetry in an age dominated by science.

98.   Platt, Arthur. "The Relations of Poetry and Science." *Nine Essays*. Cam-
          bridge: Cambridge UP, 1927. 162–86.
Far from being antagonistic to poetry, science has always served to heighten the

effect of the world's finest poetry. Discusses the synthesis of science and poetry in Lucretius, Dante, Milton, Goethe, Keats, Tennyson, and others.

99. Priestley, F. E. L. "Science and the Poet." *DR* 38 (1958): 141–53.
An analysis of various ways in which poets incorporate scientific data and concepts into their work. Among the poets discussed are Donne, Akenside, E. Darwin, Bridges, P. Shelley, and Tennyson.

100. Putnam, Hilary. "Literature, Science, and Reflection." *NLH* 7 (1975–76): 483–91.
Contrasts the contribution that literary and scientific knowledge can make to ethical theory.

101. Putt, S. Gorley. "The Snow-Leavis Rumpus." *AR* 23 (1963–64): 299–312.
Expresses partial agreement with both Leavis and Snow and attempts to mediate their "two cultures" dispute.

102. Raimondi, Ezio. "La strada verso Xanadu: Letteratura e scienza." *LI* 28 (1976): 273–304.
A survey of the various approaches of nineteenth- and twentieth-century essayists to the relation between literature and science. Examines the contributions of M. Arnold, Bush, Musil, Richards, and others.

103. Rannit, Aleksis. "The Logic of Poetic Symbols in the Age of Science." *BNYPL* 63 (1959): 466–72.
Discusses the parallels between scientific description of the order relations in the empirical world and poetic symbolization of the order relations of inner experience. Mentions Baudelaire, Perse, Stevens, and Valéry in regard to their contributions to poetic symbology.

104. Renard, Georges. "La littérature et la science." *La nouvelle revue* 113 (1898): 34–54.
Discusses the interrelatedness of science and literature, showing that literature often anticipates scientific discoveries and that science influences literature topically and stylistically. Notes the influence of science on the naturalist novel and on poetry, citing authors such as Cyrano de Bergerac, Diderot, Voltaire, Hugo, Lamartine, and Verne.

104a. Richards, I. A. *Science and Poetry.* London: Paul, 1926. 83 pp. New York: Norton, 1926. 96 pp. 2nd ed., rev. and enl. London: Paul, 1935. 99 pp. Rev. as *Poetries and Sciences.* London: Routledge, 1970. 123 pp. New York: Norton, 1970. 121 pp.
An analysis of the poetic experience and a discussion of the value of poetry in human life, focusing on the challenge science poses to poetry in the twentieth century.

105. Rieser, Max. "Language of Poetic and of Scientific Thought." *JP* 40 (1943): 421–35.

Poetic thought and creation involve valuation of the empirical world, while scientific investigation seeks only to analyze facts without considering their emotive or valuative significance.

106.   Roberts, Catherine. "Nightingales, Hawks, and the Two Cultures." *AR* 25 (1965): 221–38.

Evaluates in the context of the "two cultures" debate the roles poetic and scientific knowledge play in the attainment of human *arete* or excellence.

107.   Romey, William D. "Science as Fiction or Nonfiction? A Physical Scientist's View from a General Semantics Perspective." *ETC* 37 (1980): 201–07.

Asserts that the distinction between fiction and nonfiction often obfuscates more than it clarifies. In particular, maintains that because many "scientific" works contain fictional elements, the distinction is blurred and hence ineffective as a means of literary classification.

108.   Ross, Ronald. "Science and Poetry." *Royal Institution of Great Britain: Proceedings* 23 (1920–22): 206–27.

Stresses the fundamental compatibility of science and poetry, noting that both are in many ways inspired by the same muse and directed toward the same end, the service of humanity. Author supplements his discussion with several of his poems that illustrate an intimacy between the pursuits of science and poetry.

109.   Rothenberg, Albert. *The Emerging Goddess: The Creative Process in Art, Science, and Other Fields*. Chicago: U of Chicago P, 1979. 440 pp.
        Rev. Hugh G. J. Aitken, *Isis* 71 (1980): 665–66; H. J. Eisenman, *Technology and Culture* 21 (1980): 689–91; Colin Martindale, *Contemporary Psychology* 25 (1980): 802–03; Jeffrey Maitland, *JAAC* 39 (1980–81): 206–09.

An examination of the psychodynamics of poetic, artistic, and scientific creativity. Based on in-depth interviews with notable contemporaries and on the writings of earlier figures. Considers Mozart, Beethoven, C. Darwin, Pasteur, Einstein, Kahn, Picasso, Schoenberg, Sessions, and J. Watson.

110.   Rousseau, George S. "Are There Really Men of Both 'Cultures'?" *DR* 52 (1972–73): 351–72.

Evaluates various typical approaches to the "two cultures" problem, emphasizing the impracticability of seeking detailed knowledge in both science and the arts in an age of increasing specialization. Surveys historical personages said to have assimilated knowledge of both "cultures" and reveals, in fact, little verifiable or significant influence of science on art or of art on science. The rift between science and art may be of little practical importance in daily life, and such fragmentation may even signal progress in human civilization.

111.   ———. "Literature and Science: The State of the Field." *Isis* 69 (1978): 583–91.

Maintains that the study of literature and science is stagnant because its students have failed to advance conceptually beyond the methods of the discipline's founders.

Intellectual historians like Marjorie Nicolson created the field of literature and science in the 1940s, but they used simplistic source hunting that adduced influence by listing literary references whose sources were presumably scientific documents. By the 1960s, however, more sophisticated theories of referentiality, such as structuralism, had come to characterize serious literary criticism. Because the literature-and-science field has not yet formulated essential questions of theory, few young scholar-critics are attracted to it as a discipline. Structuralist ideas could lead the field to address serious issues, such as how scientific knowledge can inform authorial consciousness and thus creativity.

112.   ———. "Marjorie Hope Nicolson (1894–)." *Scriblerian* 10 (1977–78): 84–87.
A brief overview of Nicolson's accomplishments in literary history, stressing her contributions to the field of literature and science.

113.   ———, ed. *Organic Form: The Life of an Idea*. London: Routledge, 1972. 108 pp.
Rev. Elinor Shaffer, *MLR* 71 (1976): 110–12.
G. N. Orsini's "Ancient Roots of a Modern Idea" shows that Plato's treatment in the *Phaedrus* of the principle of organic unity in literary compositions forms the basis for later systems of criticism. Philip C. Ritterbush's "Organic Form: Aesthetics and Objectivity in the Study of Form in the Life Sciences" focuses on Goethe's and Coleridge's contributions to the idea of organic form and outlines the idea's gradual acceptance among nineteenth-century scientists, engineers, philosophers, and critics. William K. Wimsatt's "Organic Form: Some Questions about a Metaphor" reappraises the analogy between organic forms in nature and in art. He opposes ". . . the notion that the representation of biological forms in a work of verbal or visual art implies something about the presence of organic or artistic form in that work." This idea, he suggests, rests on a sophism.

114.   Ryan, Steven T. "The Importance of Thomas S. Kuhn's Scientific Paradigm Theory to Literary Criticism." *MQ* 19 (1977–78): 151–59.
Kuhn's paradigm theory applies to change not only in science but also in literary styles and models. For example, the "decadence and exhaustion" characteristic of contemporary literature reflects an artistic response to the pervasive influence of contemporary scientific paradigms. "No writer has ever escaped the paradigms of his age, and we cannot deny science today as the primary shaper of our patterned perception."

115.   Schenck, Hilbert, Jr. "Revisiting the 'Two Cultures.' " *CentR* 8 (1964): 249–61.
Disputes Snow's contention that "scientific culture" contains a "moral component" and, thus, should play a leadership role in society. Claims that traditional, or "literary," culture truly contains the moral component and, hence, should direct cultural developments.

116.   Schirmbeck, Heinrich. *Vom Elend der Literatur im Zeitalter der Wissenschaft*. Abhandlungen der Klasse der Literatur 2. Mainz: Akademie der Wissenschaften und der Literatur; Wiesbaden: Steiner, 1967. 20 pp.

Claims that literature can no longer encompass the great intellectual revolutions as it could in Dante's and even in Goethe's time. Argues that since contemporary poets and writers are alienated from the reality perceived by modern science, their works have become peripheral to the central concerns of culture in our modern, scientific age. Sees the possibility of a common ground for science and literature in behaviorism—the biological and psychological study of behavior.

117.   Seleskovic, M. T. "Natur- und Literaturwissenschaft." *GRM* 13 (1925): 81–94, 161–68.
This discussion of literary and scientific studies tries to ascertain the differences between them that arise from their distinctive objects. Since the one studies literary works and the other studies nature, their methods must be correspondingly different. Literary scholarship can become a systematic discipline by adapting its methodology to the nature of the object it studies and not by imitating science and its methodology.

118.   Settembrini, Ludovico. "A Humanist Delivers an Uninvited Lecture to Scientists." *CentR* 8 (1964): 262–77.
Reflections on the social responsibilities of scientists compared with those of humanists, including literary scholars.

119.   Sewell, Elizabeth. *The Orphic Voice: Poetry and Natural History*. New Haven: Yale UP, 1960. London: Routledge, 1961. New York: Harper, 1971. 463 pp.
        Rev. George Ross Ridge, *CL* 15 (1963): 85–86; Edwin Morgan, *RES* ns 15 (1964): 226–28.
"This study is an explanation of the biological function of poetry in the natural history of mankind as symbolized by the myth of Orpheus in the works of major Western writers from Bacon and Shakespeare to Erasmus Darwin and Goethe to Wordsworth and Rilke." Focuses on the theme that "for the last four hundred years poetry has been struggling to evolve and perfect the inclusive mythology on which language works and all thought in words is carried on, and . . . this type of thinking is the only adequate instrument for thinking about change, process, organisms and life."

120.   Smith, Ralph A. "The Two Cultures Debate Today." *Oxford Review of Education* 4 (1978): 257–65.
An essay in the ecology of social ideas. Author outlines the historical development and reception of the principal ideas generated by the "two cultures" debate, noting especially the impact of Snow's "The Two Cultures and the Scientific Revolution."

121.   Snow, C. P. "The Two Cultures and the Scientific Revolution." *Encounter* 12.6 (1959): 17–24; 13.1 (1959): 22–27. Rpt. New York: Cambridge UP, 1959. 58 pp.
        Rev. Steven Marcus, *Commentary* 29 (1960): 165–68.
The text of Snow's influential 1959 Cambridge Rede Lecture. Snow develops the thesis that "a gulf of mutual incomprehension" exists between literary and scientific intellectuals, and he outlines some educational reforms to remedy this situation.

122. Stanford, Derek. "A Disputed Master: C. P. Snow and His Critics." *Month* ns 29 (1963): 91–94.

Maintains that Snow is neither a "novelist of the Age of Science" nor an adequate expositor of the "two cultures" theory.

123. ———. "Sir Charles and the Two Cultures." *Critic* 21.2 (1962–63): 17–21.

A commentary on Snow's intellectual weaknesses, largely supportive of Leavis's criticisms of Snow in *Two Cultures? The Significance of C. P. Snow*.

124. Starobinski, Jean. "Poetic Language and Scientific Language." *Diogenes* 100 (1977): 128–45.

Maintains that modern science and the corresponding advent of the specialized terminology of the exact sciences brought about the separation of language into scientific and poetic modes. Traces the history of attempts to recover the primordial language underlying both scientific and poetic expression.

125. Stewart, George R., Jr. "Color in Science and Poetry." *SciMo* 30 (1930): 71–78.

Poetry written before the seventeenth century used an extremely limited vocabulary to denote colors. Newton's experiments with prisms, however, as well as biological and botanical studies in the eighteenth century and the chemical research of William Henry Perkin in the nineteenth century, enormously enriched the terminology available to poets for describing colors.

126. Suvin, Darko. "On What Is and Is Not an SF Narration; with a List of 101 Victorian Books That Should Be Excluded from SF Bibliographies." *SFS* 5 (1978): 45–57.

Discusses five literary categories that should not be considered branches of science fiction. Science fiction "is distinguished by the narrative dominance of a fictional novelty (*novum*, innovation) validated both by being continuous with a body of already existing cognitions and by being a 'mental experiment' based on cognitive logic." Also determinative is the presence of some form of scientific cognition "identical to that of a modern philosophy of science."

127. Sweetkind, Morris. "Poetry in a Scientific World." *EJ* 59 (1970): 359–66.

Explores the twentieth-century cultural schism between poetry and science by outlining the principal facets of Snow's assessment in "The Two Cultures and the Scientific Revolution" and by surveying the attitudes toward science expressed by poets such as Donne, Blake, Coleridge, Keats, Poe, Auden, Frost, and Sandburg. Calls for a reevaluation of curricular strategy in dealing with this cultural conflict.

128. Sypher, Wylie. *Literature and Technology: The Alien Vision*. New York: Random, 1968. 257 pp.
Rev. Martin Lebowitz, *YR* ns 58 (1968–69): 149–54; G. S. Rousseau, *Isis* 60 (1969): 396–97; *PR* 37 (1970): 319–22.

The "two cultures" debate should be framed not as a conflict between science and art but as a contamination of both by the pursuit of reductive technique, which suppresses individuality to maximize efficiency and order. Writers such as Mallarmé, P. Shelley, Tennyson, and the aesthetes responded to their perception of the existential emptiness of the world by reifying as "Necessity" a single "Method" or "Style" of composition and by distancing the perceiver from the world as described. Contemporary practice in both the sciences and the arts (such as Heisenberg's and Williams's) marks the healthy return to contingent fact and free mental play and away from the tyranny of subjective theorizing and privative technique.

129.   Telle, Joachim. "Chymische Pflanzen in der deutschen Literatur." *MedJ* 8 (1973): 1–34.

Traces the alchemical idea of palingenesis—namely, the reproduction of a plant from its ashes by chemical (i.e., alchemical) arts—to several Renaissance texts, especially Paracelsus's German-language work *Liber de natura rerum* (1537). Demonstrates the interest in palingenesis, primarily in such seventeenth-century German writings as Harsdörffer's *Frauenzimmer-Gesprächsspiele* (1641–49) and Rist's *Monats-Unterredungen* (1663–68). Notes that the interest in palingenesis continued into the twentieth century, citing as examples Mann's *Doktor Faustus* (1947) and Bernus's novella *Die Blumen des Magiers* (1950).

130.   Thomas, Calvin. "Poetry and Science." *Open Court* 3 (1889–90): 1727–31.

". . . [T]he idea of any radical antithesis between poetry and science is at the bottom untenable. Poetry is in no danger of a general blight from the pressure of the scientific spirit."

130a.   Thompson, Alan R. "Science, Criticism, and Poetry." *American Review* 8 (1937): 513–49.

In the context of the debate between T. H. Huxley and M. Arnold on the relative importance of science and letters, the author asserts that humanists need not fear true scientists such as Huxley but should fear lay partisans who exaggerate the scope of science. Levels criticism against those who claim that science will eventually supersede all traditional disciplines, including literary criticism.

131.   Toulmin, Stephen. "Creativity: Is Science Really a Special Case?" *CLS* 17 (1980): 190–200.

Outlines affinities between creativity in the natural sciences and creativity in the arts, including literature.

131a.   Traschen, Isadore. "Modern Literature and Science." *CE* 25 (1963–64): 248–55.

Discusses parallels and differences in the methods, goals, and visions of reality that characterize modern science and literature.

132.   Triggs, Oscar L. "Literature and the Scientific Spirit." *Poet-Lore* 6 (1894): 113–26.

Discusses differences in the methods, functions, and results of literary and scientific activity, with reflections on the relative value of each. "The study of science, fascinating though it may be, inasmuch as it eliminates the personal equation of the observer, yields no joy comparable to the pleasures of the artistic imagination."

133.   Trilling, Lionel. "Science, Literature and Culture: A Comment on the Leavis-Snow Controversy." *Commentary* 33 (1962): 461–77.
A critical analysis of Snow's "Two Cultures" and Leavis's *Two Cultures? The Significance of C. P. Snow*. Maintains that both Snow and Leavis misapprehend the essential relations between literature and science in contemporary society and distort the concept of culture.

134.   Usinger, Fritz. *Wissenschaft und Dichtung: Zum 25 jährigen Bestehen der Akademie der Wissenschaften und der Literatur in Mainz*. Abhandlungen der Klasse der Literatur 2, 1973–74. Mainz: Akademie der Wissenschaften und der Literatur; Wiesbaden: in Kommission bei F. Steiner, 1974. 18 pp.
A general discussion of the need for greater cooperation and communication between science and literature, both of which seek to ameliorate the human situation in the atomic age.

135.   Waggoner, Hyatt Howe. "Poets, Test-Tubes, and the Heel of Elohim." *UKCR* 12 (1945–46): 272–77.
A discussion of poetic sensibility in an age dominated by scientism. The interest poets have in religious, metaphysical, and axiological themes puts them ahead of most others in the quest for wisdom.

136.   Watts, Nevile. "Poetry and Science." *DubR* 197 (1935): 295–310.
Poetry's status becomes ever more tenuous as science and its by-products increasingly determine the world's values.

137.   Wellek, René. "The Concept of Evolution in Literary History." *For Roman Jakobson: Essays on the Occasion of His Sixtieth Birthday, 11 October 1956*. Comp. Morris Halle et al. The Hague: Mouton, 1956. 653–61.
An overview of the evolutionary theories of Aristotle, Hegel, Spencer, and C. Darwin as assimilated by literary criticism and applied to the development of literary form.

138.   West, Robert H. "Literature and Knowledge." *GaR* 25 (1971): 125–44.
A comparison of the forms of knowledge characteristic of literature and science. Though literature fails scientific tests of what constitutes knowledge, it nevertheless performs a cognitive function equal in importance to that performed by science.

139.   Whyte, Lancelot Law. "Letter from a Scientist to an Artist." *Griffin* 6 (1957): 13–19.
Maintains that science, literature, music, and the other arts are commonly grounded in the ordering capacity of the human mind.

140.   Woodcock, John. "Literature and Science since Huxley." *Interdisciplinary Science Reviews* 3.1 (1978): 31–45.

Summarizes the contribution A. Huxley's *Literature and Science* (1963) made to the "two cultures" debate and surveys recent critical, narrative, fictional, and poetic responses to the topic by authors such as Bellow, Bronowski, A. Clarke, P. Goodman, Koestler, Le Guin, Mailer, Skinner, Snow, Snyder, Vonnegut, and J. Watson.

141.   Yabes, Leopoldo Y. "Literature, Science, and Obscurantism." *DilR* 6 (1958): 299–306.
Maintains that literature and the humanities, by failing to reflect scientific advancement and to keep pace with it, tend toward obscurantism and oppose the expansion of knowledge.

Surveys of Literature and Science

142.   Armytage, W. H. G. *Yesterday's Tomorrows: A Historical Survey of Future Societies*. Toronto: U of Toronto P; London: Routledge, 1968. 288 pp.
        Rev. Giovanni Costigan, *AHR* 74 (1969): 943–44; Sanford A. Lakoff, *Technology and Culture* 11 (1970): 124–27.
Deals in part with the contributions that Newtonianism, Darwinism, religion, and philosophy made to extrapolative fiction by authors such as Bellamy, Bulwer-Lytton, S. Butler, Lasswitz, Verne, and Wells.

143.   Associazione internazionale per gli studi di lingua e letteratura italiana. *Letteratura e scienza nella storia della cultura italiana*. Atti del IX congresso dell'associazione internazionale per gli studi di lingua e letteratura italiana. Palermo, Messina, Catania, 21–25 Apr. 1976. Palermo: Manfredi, 1978. 913 pp.
The proceedings of a conference dealing with various aspects of the interaction between science and Italian arts, especially literature. Includes discussion of authors such as Boccaccio, Calvino, Leopardi, Magalotti, Pirandello, and Svevo. For annotations of relevant essays see items 455, 858, 1775, 1776, 1777, 1826, 1929, 2254, and 2256.

144.   Bailey, J. O. *Pilgrims through Space and Time: Trends and Patterns in Scientific and Utopian Fiction*. New York: Argus, 1947. Westport: Greenwood, 1972. 341 pp.
Briefly reviews a wide range of fiction that uses science and technology to depict innovative societies, including science fiction and fantasy, utopian fiction and satires, stories of the future, and adventure tales. Examines works in many languages from the classical age to about 1940, emphasizing the period since 1870. Chapter 9 covers in detail the use of scientific discoveries.

144a.   Benjamin, Georgiana K. "Science in Modern Romance." *Stanford University Abstracts of Dissertations* 3 (1928): 59–64.
Examines how various authors have adapted scientific ideas for literary uses. Considers the imaginary voyages of Rabelais, Swift, and Voltaire; the utopian novels of S. Butler, Bulwer-Lytton, and Zamyatin; and the "scientific romances" of Verne and Wells.

145. Bridenne, Jean-Jacques. *La littérature française d'imagination scientifique.* Paris: Dassonville, 1952. 294 pp.
Surveys French novels, short stories, and dramas, ranging from the Renaissance to the present, whose themes concern mathematics, mechanics, astronomy, geography, physics, chemistry, natural science, medicine, and archaeology.

146. Brown, Harcourt. "Tensions and Anxieties: Science and the Literary Culture of France." *Science and the Creative Spirit: Essays on Humanistic Aspects of Science.* Ed. Harcourt Brown. Toronto: U of Toronto P, 1958. 91–126.
Briefly traces the history of relations between science and French literature from the sixteenth to the twentieth century, noting how literary resistance to science gradually gave way to the fusion of science with the literary imagination. Treats Fontenelle, Voltaire, Balzac, Baudelaire, Hugo, Saint-Exupéry, Zola, and Camus.

147. Bush, Douglas. *Science and English Poetry: A Historical Sketch, 1590–1950.* New York: Oxford UP, 1950. Westport: Greenwood, 1980. 166 pp.
Rev. William V. O'Conner, *Poetry* 76 (1950): 352–54.
The major topics discussed include the medieval sciences in Shakespeare, Spenser, and other Elizabethans; the impact of the "new science" on Cowley, Donne, Dryden, Greville, and Milton; Newtonianism and Akenside, Cowper, Pope, J. Thomson, and Young; the revolt against rationalism in Blake, Coleridge, Keats, P. Shelley, and Wordsworth; the theory of evolution's influence on Browning, Hardy, Meredith, and Tennyson; and the relations between modern science and modern poetry.

148. Chalke, H. D. "The Impact of Tuberculosis on History, Literature and Art." *MedH* 6 (1962): 301–18.
A brief history of tuberculosis and a survey of poets, artists, and musicians who suffered from the disease. Includes a commentary on some literary sources that provide information on tuberculosis, such as Shakespearean drama, Kingsley's *Yeast* (1848), Smollett's *Roderick Random* (1748), and Swift's *Tale of a Tub* (1689).

149. Crouch, Laura E. "The Scientist in English Literature: Domingo Gonsales (1638) to Victor Frankenstein (1817)." *DAI* 36 (1975–76): 2181A.
Examines the changing portrayal of scientists in English literature from 1638 to 1817. The progression of literary portraits moves from scientists whose work has little effect on society to those, such as Frankenstein, whose research leads to destruction. Considers works by S. Butler, Shadwell, Pope, Swift, M. Shelley, and others.

150. Crum, Ralph B. *Scientific Thought in Poetry.* Diss. Columbia U, 1931. New York: Columbia UP, 1931. New York: AMS, 1966. Folcroft: Folcroft, 1973. 246 pp.
Rev. I. A. Richards, *MLN* 48 (1933): 64–65.
Includes chapters on the science in Lucretius's *De rerum natura*; the impact of the new science on seventeenth-century poetry by S. Butler, Abraham Cowley, Donne, Marvell, Milton, and others; references to Newtonianism in poetry by Akenside, Blake, Johnson, Pope, Swift, J. Thomson, and Young; allusions to mechanism in the poetry of Chénier and Voltaire; E. Darwin's poetic assimilation of data drawn

from biology, botany, and other sciences; Goethe's theories of evolution and morphology; Tennyson's treatment of evolution in *In Memoriam* and other poems; the
impact of science on Browning and Meredith; and Davidson's poetic response to
science.

151.   De Selincourt, Ernest. "The Interplay of Literature and Science during the
        Last Three Centuries." *HJ* 37 (1938–39): 225–45.
A general overview of the influence of science on the theme and style of seven-
teenth-, eighteenth-, and nineteenth-century literature. Specifically discusses Donne,
Milton, Shadwell, Swift, Bridges, Hardy, Tennyson, Wordsworth, and others.

152.   Eddy, Pearl F. "Insects in English Poetry." *SciMo* 33 (1931): 53–73,
        148–63.
Cites entomological allusions in works by Chaucer, Shakespeare, Donne, Coleridge, Dickinson, P. Shelley, Tennyson, Wordsworth, and many others.

153.   Engelhardt, Dietrich von. "Medizin und Literatur in der Neuzeit-Per-
        spektiven und Aspekte." *DVLG* 52 (1978): 351–80.
A study of the relation between medicine and literature in modern times. Central
aspects are the function of medicine for literature, the function of literature for
medicine, and the function of fictionalized medicine for a general understanding of
illness and medicine. Studies the incorporation of a wide range of medical themes
in works by English, French, German, and Russian authors.

154.   Evans, B. Ifor. *Literature and Science*. London: Allen, 1954. Folcroft: Fol-
        croft, 1969. Norwood: Norwood, 1975. Philadelphia: West, 1977. 114
        pp.
Assesses the literary artist's position in modern scientific society by considering
the historical relation between science and literature from the Renaissance to the
twentieth century. Includes chapters on F. Bacon, Donne, Milton, Newton, Swift,
Blake, Coleridge, P. Shelley, Tennyson, Wordsworth, and others. Describes commonalities and differences between scientific and literary activities within a humanistic tradition encompassing both disciplines.

155.   Georlette, R. "La science-fiction dans la littérature française." *Fenêtre ouverte*
        56 (1965): 15–31.
Provides a short history of French science fiction, citing works by Cyrano de
Bergerac, Verne, and several contemporary authors. Discusses the role science fiction
plays in this age of science and technology.

156.   Graham, John. "The Development of the Use of Physiognomy in the
        Novel." Diss. Johns Hopkins U, 1960.
Not seen for annotation.

157.   Green, Roger Lancelyn. *Into Other Worlds: Space-Flight in Fiction, from Lucian
        to Lewis*. London: Abelard, 1958. New York: Arno, 1975. 190 pp.
Outlines the central features of space-voyage literature from ancient times to the
present, including plot, means of conveyance, and details of destination. Discusses

Lucian, Cyrano de Bergerac, F. Godwin, Defoe, Greg, Poe, Verne, E. Burroughs, C. S. Lewis, Wells, and several lesser-known writers.

158.   Grover, Frederick W. "Poetry and Astronomy." *SciMo* 44 (1937): 519–29.
A survey of the astronomical allusions in the poetry of Milton, J. Thomson, Longfellow, Tennyson, Wordsworth, and others. The author emphasizes allusions that he judges both aesthetically pleasing and scientifically accurate.

159.   Keys, Thomas E. "The Plague in Literature." *Bulletin of the Medical Library Association* 32 (1944): 35–56.
Studies several outstanding literary descriptions of the bubonic plague, stressing their contributions to a medical understanding of the disease. Includes accounts by Thucydides, Boccaccio, Chaucer, Jonson, Nashe, Shakespeare, and Defoe.

160.   Linden, Stanton J. "Alchemy and the English Literary Imagination: 1385 to 1633." *DAI* 33 (1972–73): 3591A–92A.
Treats the satirical use of alchemical imagery from Chaucer to Donne. Other authors studied include Barclay, Dunbar, R. Greene, Jonson, Lyly, and Nashe.

161.   Madden, J. S. "Melancholy in Medicine and Literature: Some Historical Considerations." *British Journal of Medical Psychology* 39 (1966): 125–30.
Explains the principal features of the theory of the four humors, outlines the medical aspects of the condition known as "melancholy," and discusses references in literature to both the positive and the negative aspects of melancholy. Cites Bright, Burton, Milton, Keats, Tennyson, Wordsworth, and others.

162.   Meadows, A. J. *The High Firmament: A Survey of Astronomy in English Literature.* Leicester: Leicester UP, 1969. 207 pp.
Rev. William Powell Jones, *Isis* 61 (1970): 121–22.
Broadly surveys the treatment of astronomy in English literature from 1400 to 1900. Author explains the principal features of the Aristotelian, Ptolemaic, Copernican, and Newtonian astronomical systems and comments on the references to them in works by Chaucer, Shakespeare, Milton, Wilkins, Blake, Swift, J. Thomson, Tennyson, Wordsworth, and many others.

163.   Moore, Patrick. *Science and Fiction.* London: Harrap, 1957. Folcroft: Folcroft, 1970. Norwood: Norwood, 1978. 192 pp.
Traces the history of science fiction from its beginnings in Greek literature to the present, stressing examples that exhibit sound literary or scientific characteristics and that treat the theme of interplanetary travel. Examines works by Lucian, Cyrano de Bergerac, F. Godwin, Kepler, Wilkins, Verne, Wells, and others.

164.   Pfeiffer, K. Ludwig. *Wissenschaft als Sujet im modernen englischen Roman.* Konstanzer Universitätsreden 127. Konstanz: Universitätsverlag, 1979. 63 pp.
Investigates changing attitudes toward science as reflected in English literature from the seventeenth to the twentieth century. Discusses the symbiotic relation of

poetic and cosmogonical elements in Donne's "Valediction: Forbidden Mourning"; the satirizing of science in such nineteenth-century works as R. D. Blackmore's *Tommy Upmore* and Peacock's *Gryll Grange*; the influence of sciences such as geology, psychophysiology, and Darwinism on twentieth-century literature, including S. Butler's *Way of All Flesh*, A. Huxley's *Point Counter Point*, and Wells's *World of William Clissold*; and the role of the novel in integrating literature, science, and contemporary life.

165.   Plank, Robert. "The Golem and the Robot." *L&P* 15 (1965): 12–28.
Traces the motif of the synthetic humanoid in folklore and literature, from the golem to the robot. The development leads from magical and biological fiction to scientific and technological fantasy literature and includes such works as Goethe's "Sorcerer's Apprentice," Bulwer-Lytton's "Coming Race," Hoffmann's "Sandman," and M. Shelley's *Frankenstein*.

166.   Priestley, F. E. L. " 'Those Scattered Rays Convergent': Science and Imag-
           ination in English Literature." *Science and the Creative Spirit: Essays on Hu-
           manistic Aspects of Science*. Ed. Harcourt Brown. Toronto: U of Toronto P,
           1958. 53–88.
Priestley's essay, which stresses the cognitive and emotive components of both science and poetry, provides a thorough and wide-ranging summary of the relation between science and literature from the founding of the Royal Society (1662) to the present.

167.   Rehder, Helmut. "Planetenkinder: Some Problems of Character Portrayal
           in Literature." *Graduate Journal* 8 (1968–71): 69–97.
Discusses the allegorical survival of the astrological concept of *Planetenkinder*, or "children of planets," in literature, citing Wittenweiler's *Ring*, Grimmelshausen's *Simplicius Simplicissimus*, and Mann's *Joseph and His Brothers*.

168.   Robertson, J. K. "Science in Literature." *QQ* 58 (1951): 36–55.
Briefly discusses novels and poems that contain scientific material. Among the authors considered are Lucretius, Donne, F. Godwin, Milton, Pope, P. Shelley, Tennyson, Verne, Wells, and Shute.

169.   Robin, P. Ansell. *Animal Lore in English Literature*. London: Murray, 1932.
           Folcroft: Folcroft, 1970. Norwood: Norwood, 1975. Philadelphia: West,
           1976. 196 pp.
Shows that English authors used animal lore for their descriptions of the form and habits of real or imagined animals; for character types or dispositions analogous to human nature; and for similes or metaphors to illustrate aspects of human life. Discusses major sources such as the *Physiologus* and Pliny's *Natural History* and cites the use of animal lore by authors such as Chaucer, Jonson, Lyly, Shakespeare, Spenser, Dryden, Milton, and Pope.

170.   Schwartz, Sheila. "The World of Science Fiction." *EngR* 21.3 (1971):
           27–40.
A brief history of science fiction and its typical themes, stressing the genre's

ability to reflect the contemporary world and scientific advances. Among the authors considered are Cyrano de Bergerac, Poe, M. Shelley, Verne, Wells, Bradbury, and A. Clarke.

171.   Scudder, Vida D. "Science and the Modern Poets." *The Life of the Spirit in the Modern English Poets.* Boston: Houghton, 1895. 5–56.
Shows that modern science has enlarged the sphere of poetry by introducing a world of new subjects and that the change that has transfigured science has also had an impact on modern poetry. Traces basic scientific conceptions from the Renaissance to C. Darwin, citing reflections in the poetry of Chaucer, Cowper, Spenser, E. Darwin, P. Shelley, Browning, Tennyson, and Wordsworth.

172.   Vinge, Louise. *The Five Senses: Studies in a Literary Tradition.* Acta Regiae Societatis Humaniorum Litterarum Lundensis 72. Lund: Gleerup, 1975. 193 pp.
          Rev. John M. Steadman, *CL* 29 (1977): 275–78.
Surveys the use of the five-senses topos as a structural device in literature and science from classical times to the twentieth century. Includes an overview of the scientific and medical sources of the topos, such as Aristotle, Lucretius, Cicero, Lactantius, Pliny the Elder, and Vincent of Beauvais; a study of medieval allegorical representations of the five senses; and discussions of the topos as treated by Palingenius, B. Barnes, Chapman, Davies, Du Bartas, Shakespeare, Spenser, Calderón de la Barca, Cowley, Marino, Marvell, Prior, Pope, Auden, Hopkins, Joyce, and Lindegren.

173.   Ward, Robert. "What Forced by Fire: Concerning Some Influences of Chemical Thought and Practice upon English Poetry." *Ambix* 23 (1976): 80–95.
Cites references to alchemical and chemical matters in English poetry, thus indicating the extent of the interaction between chemistry and poetry over the centuries. Includes references to Southwell, Webster, Donne, Coleridge, Hopkins, Keats, T. S. Eliot, and others.

173a.   Wetzels, Walter D. "Versuch einer Beschreibung popularwissenschaftlicher Prosa in den Naturwissenschaften." *JIG* 3.1 (1971): 76–95.
Examines the rhetorical literary strategies by which authors from the Enlightenment to the present have disseminated complex scientific theories. Includes authors such as Fontenelle, von Helmholtz, and Einstein.

174.   Williams, Raymond. "Utopia and Science Fiction." *SFS* 5 (1978): 203–14.
Focuses on willed and technological transformations of society—including the role science and scientists play in these changes—as characteristic of utopian, dystopian, and science fiction literature. Considers T. More, F. Bacon, Bellamy, Bulwer-Lytton, Morris, A. Huxley, Le Guin, and others.

Antiquity

Studies and Surveys

175.   Amundsen, Darrel W. "Images of Physicians in Classical Times." *JPC* 11 (1977–78): 643–55.
Discusses satirical and disparaging references to the medical profession in classical literature, including works by Lucius Apuleius, Lucian, Pliny the Elder, Xenophon of Ephesus, and others. The attitudes expressed toward physicians parallel those of contemporary civilization.

176.   ————. "Romanticizing the Ancient Medical Profession: The Characterization of the Physician in the Graeco-Roman Novel." *BHM* 48 (1974): 320–37.
Studies the somewhat romanticized depiction of the physician in Lucius Apuleius's *Metamorphoses*, Heliodorus's *Ethiopian Romance*, Xenophon of Ephesus's *Ephesian Tale*, and the anonymous *Apollonius, Prince of Tyre*.

177.   Evans, Elizabeth C. *Physiognomics in the Ancient World*. Transactions of the American Philosophical Society ns 59, pt. 5. Philadelphia: American Philosophical Soc., 1969. 101 pp.
Traces the ancient origins of physiognomy by analyzing physiognomic allusions in philosophical and medical treatises and various literary works, including dramas, epics, satires, fiction, and poetry, from the time of Homer to the end of the fourth century AD.

178.   Gregory, Richard. "The Apotheosis of Astronomy." *Science, Medicine and History: Essays on the Evolution of Scientific Thought and Medical Practice Written in Honour of Charles Singer*. Ed. E. Ashworth Underwood. Vol. 1. New York: Oxford UP, 1953. 75–82. 2 vols. New York: Arno, 1975.
Discusses Greek, Arabian, Hindu, and other ancient astronomical myths and theories and their influence on poets such as Aratus, Vergil, Chaucer, and Dante.

179.   Hough, John N. "Bird Imagery in Roman Poetry." *CJ* 70 (1974–75): 1–13.
Assesses Roman interest in ornithology by statistically analyzing occurrences of bird imagery in the poetry of Lucretius, Ovid, Statius, Vergil, and others.

180.   Kahn, Arthur D. " 'Every Art Possessed by Man Comes from Prometheus':
         The Greek Tragedians and Science and Technology." *Technology and Culture*
         11 (1970): 133–62.
Traces the rapid developments in science and technology in fifth-century Athens
and notes their impact on the Athenian social, economic, and political environment.
Examines the various attitudes toward science and technology in Aeschylus's *Prometheus Bound*, Sophocles's *Antigone*, and Euripides's *Suppliants* and discusses how
technology affected the form and structure of Greek drama in general.

181.   Knowlton, Edgar C. "The Goddess Nature in Early Periods." *JEGP* 19
         (1920): 224–53.
Examines the origin and history of the allegorical figure of Nature from the Greek
classical period to the Renaissance, drawing on works by Aristotle, Plato, Pliny the
Elder, and Seneca. Examines in particular the twelfth-century didactic works of
poetry *De mundi universitate*, by Bernardus Silvestris; *De planctu naturae*, by Alanus
de Insulis; and *Archithrenus*, by Jean de Hauteville.

182.   Olson, Richard. "Science, Scientism and Anti-Science in Hellenic Athens:
         A New Whig Interpretation." *HS* 16 (1978): 179–99.
Suggests parallels between Athenian scientific practices, scientistic attitudes, and
reactionary antiscientistic sentiments and those of the twentieth century. Evidence
for a strong antiscientistic movement appears in writers such as Aristophanes and
Euripides, while the roots of Athenian scientism may be found in texts like Aeschylus's *Prometheus Bound*. Pays considerable attention to Socrates's position in the
conflict between science and antiscience.

Individual Authors

Achilles Tatius (fl. 300 AD)

183.   McLeod, A. M. G. "Physiology and Medicine in a Greek Novel: Achilles
         Tatius' *Leucippe and Clitophon*." *JoHS* 89 (1969): 97–105.
Analyzes how Achilles Tatius artistically adapts Erasistratean medical dogma in
describing the treatment of Leucippe's madness in *Leucippe and Clitophon*.

Aratus (c. 315–240/239 BC)

184.   Effe, Bernd. "Arat—ein medizinischer Lehrdichter?" *Hermes* 100 (1972):
         500–03.
Examines the legends claiming that the ancient Greek poet Arat, known for his
didactic verse on astronomy, also composed didactic medical poetry.

Aristophanes (c. 448–385 BC)

185.   Southard, Gretchen C. "The Medical Language of Aristophanes." *DA* 31
         (1970–71): 4745A.

Studies how Aristophanes comically appropriates medical and anatomical terminology in the light of its usage in Hippocrates.

Claudian (370?–410? AD)

186.   Semple, W. H. "Notes on Some Astronomical Passages of Claudian." *ClassQ* 31 (1937): 161–69; 33 (1939): 1–8.
Notes Claudian's use of Ciceronian astronomy in *Carminum minorum corpusculum* and *De raptu Proserpinae*.

Hesiod (fl. c. 800 BC)

187.   Hershbell, Jackson P. "Hesiod and Empedocles." *CJ* 65 (1969–70): 145–61.
Assesses the extent of the relation between Hesiod's poetry and Empedocles's natural philosophy.

Homer (n.d.)

188.   Mugler, Charles. *Les origines de la science grècque chez Homère: L'homme et l'univers physique*. Paris: Klincksieck, 1963. 242 pp.
Homer's characters are exceptionally sensitive to nuances of light and sound, and their precise observations of natural phenomena afford them an understanding of the physical universe that forms the basis for the cosmic theories of Ionian philosophers and Empedocles. Their belief in a divinely created natural order, however, prevented the development of physics and permitted only astrological speculation.

Lucian (c. 120–c. 200)

189.   Stannard, Jerry. "Lucianic Natural History." *Classical Studies Presented to Ben Edwin Perry by His Students and Colleagues at the University of Illinois, 1924–60*. Illinois Studies in Language and Literature 58. Ed. Burton R. Milligan, John R. Frey, and Philip Kolb. Urbana: U of Illinois P, 1969. 15–26.
Surveys references to natural history in Lucian's writings. Lucian was brilliant at incorporating scientific material into his literary works in an aesthetically effective manner.

190.   Swanson, Roy Arthur. "The True, the False, and the Truly False: Lucian's Philosophical Science Fiction." *SFS* 3 (1976): 228–39.
Discusses Lucian's view of fiction as potentially superior to scientific cognition in the elucidation of truth, noting parallels with the function of contemporary science fiction. "Effective science fiction does not transform science into fantasy, even though it may give the appearance of doing so; it brings us back to the limitations of science by means of fantasy or fiction, just as Lucian brings us back to the limitations of philosophy through satiric fiction and the fantastic voyage." Focuses on Lucian's *True Tales* as philosophical science fiction.

Lucretius (96?–55 BC)

191.   Cox, A. S. "Lucretius and His Message: A Study in the Prologues of the *De rerum natura.*" *Greece and Rome* 2nd ser. 18 (1971): 1–16.
Despite the mass of scientific material incorporated into Lucretius's poem, the work's scientific aspects are subordinated to the theme of Epicurean ethics.

192.   Geer, Russel M. "Lucretian Reflections." *CJ* 49 (1953–54): 114–16.
Concerns the optics of Lucretius's reference to mirrors in *De rerum natura* 4.311–12.

193.   Masson, John. *Lucretius: Epicurean and Poet.* London: Murray; New York: Dutton, 1907. 453 pp.
Provides an exposition of Epicurean atomism as depicted in *De rerum natura* and assesses the extent to which Epicurus's propositions accord with or form the basis of modern chemistry, physics, and theory of evolution. Also includes chapters on the historical roots of Epicureanism, the life and times of Lucretius, Epicurean theology, and Lucretius's transformation of science into poetry.

194.   Minadeo, Richard. *The Lyre of Science: Form and Meaning in Lucretius'* De rerum natura. Detroit: Wayne State UP, 1969. 174 pp.
         Rev. Erling B. Holtsmark, *CJ* 65 (1969–70): 372–75; Lydia Lenaghan, *Classical World* 63 (1969–70): 92.
Stresses the failure of previous scholarship to apprehend the organic unity of theme and form in Lucretius's poem. Maintains that the work's poetic structure is carefully designed and fitted to the expression of Epicurean philosophy and science and examines each of the poem's books to illustrate this thesis.

195.   Schoenheim, Ursula. "The Place of 'Tactus' in Lucretius." *PZKA* 110 (1966): 71–87.
Describes Lucretius's exposition of the Epicurean concept of "tactus," or touch, and considers the idea's role in *De rerum natura*.

196.   Schrijvers, P. H. "La pensée de Lucrèce sur l'origine de la vie (*De rerum natura* V 780–820)." *Mnemosyne* 27 (1974): 245–61.
Examines the scientific theories of spontaneous generation, phylogenesis, and ontogenesis that underlie Lucretius's surrealistic description of the origin of life in *De rerum natura* 5.780–820.

197.   Segal, Charles. "Lucretius, Epilepsy, and the Hippocratic *On Breaths.*" *ClasPhil* 65 (1970): 180–82.
Suggests that Lucretius's description of epilepsy in *De rerum natura* may have been inspired by the Hippocratic medical text *On Breaths*.

198.   Serres, Michel. *La naissance de la physique dans le texte de Lucrèce.* Paris: Minuit, 1977. 237 pp.
Challenges the view that modern physics had its beginnings during the Renaissance and proposes its inception in Lucretius's *De rerum natura*. Argues that this

poem presents a new theory of atoms based not on the conventional system of solids but, rather, on a system of fluids. Lucretius's physics, which was derived from Archimedes's theories on whirlwinds, was heavily influenced by Epicureanism.

199.   Sikes, E. E. *Lucretius: Poet and Philosopher*. Cambridge: Cambridge UP, 1936. New York: Russell, 1971. 187 pp.
        Rev. M. F. Ashley Montagu, *Isis* 27 (1937): 70–72.
Includes an account of Lucretius's Epicurean philosophy and an assessment of his genius and art in transforming Epicurean atomism into poetry. Concentrates on Lucretius's personal, poetic side rather than on the details of atomism.

200.   Slaughter, M. S. "Lucretius—the Poet of Science." *University of Wisconsin Studies in Language and Literature* 3 (1919): 158–70.
Outlines the principal features of the Epicurean science in Lucretius's *De rerum natura* and comments on the breadth of his scientific conceptions and his impressive ability to combine poetic and scientific concerns.

201.   Stehle, Eva. "The Unity of Physics and Ethics in Lucretius." *DAI* 32 (1971): 3279A.
Illustrates the connection between Epicurean physics and ethics by examining pertinent portions of Lucretius's *De rerum natura*.

Petronius (1st cent. AD)

202.   Sage, Evan T. "Medicine in the Romance of Petronius." *AMH* ns 7 (1935): 192–96.
References in the "Satiricon" to the treatment of wounds, the restoration of virility, and other medical matters—including passages that display an almost technical precision—suggest that Petronius's knowledge of the medicine of his time was surprisingly exact.

Solon (c. 638–c. 559 BC)

203.   Phillips, Joanne H. "Early Greek Medicine and the Poetry of Solon." *Clio medica* 15 (1980–81): 1–4.
Claims that Solon's poetry provides valuable commentary on early Greek medicine and on practitioners in the sixth century BC.

Marco Terenzio Varro (116–c. 27 BC)

204.   Salvatore, Armando. *Scienza e poesia in Roma: Varrone e Virgilio*. Esperienze 45. Napoli: Guida, 1978. 162 pp.
A comparative analysis of the scientific, social, and artistic aspects of Varro's *De re rustica* and Vergil's *Georgics*, both of which concern agricultural issues and humankind's relation to nature. Emphasizes the poetic treatment of animal and vegetal life and nature's symbolic value for the two authors.

Vergil (70–19 BC)

205.   Abbe, Elfriede Martha. *The Plants of Vergil's* Georgics. Ithaca: Cornell UP, 1965. 217 pp.
Provides scientific commentary, with illustrations, on the plants referred to in Vergil's *Georgics*. Draws on ancient and medieval botanical texts.

206.   Royds, Thomas Fletcher. *The Beasts, Birds and Bees of Vergil: A Naturalist's Handbook to the* Georgics. Oxford: Blackwell, 1914. 107 pp.
      Rev. D. S. Robertson, *Isis* 2 (1914–19): 205.
Comments on Vergil's zoology, ornithology, and entomology as contained in the *Georgics*.

207.   Salvatore, Armando. *Scienza e poesia in Roma: Varrone e Virgilio*. Esperienze 45. Napoli: Guida, 1978. 162 pp.
See item 204 for annotation.

208.   Sullivan, Francis A. "Volcanoes and Volcanic Characters in Vergil." *ClasPhil* 67 (1972): 186–91.
Assesses the function of volcanic imagery in the *Aeneid* and the scientific accuracy of Vergil's descriptions of the eruptions of Etna.

Middle Ages

Studies and Surveys

209.   Bleker, Johanna. "Die Alchemie im Spiegel der schönen Literatur." *Gesnerus* 28 (1971): 154–67.
Studies critical treatments of alchemy and alchemists in prominent literary works from the fourteenth to the seventeenth century. Discusses Dante's *Divine Comedy*, Petrarch's *De remedis utriusque fortunae* (1360), Chaucer's *Canterbury Tales*, Brant's *Narrenschiff* (1494), and Jonson's *Alchemist* (1610).

210.   Briere, Daniel H. "The Structural and Thematic Uses of Astrology in Spanish Literature of the Late Middle Ages." *DAI* 39 (1978): 2923A.
Examines the role of astrology in Imperial's *Decir a las siete virtudes*, Mena's *Laberinto de Fortuna*, Ruiz's *Libro de buen amor*, and other works.

211.   Collins, Robert A. "The Christian Significance of the Astrological Tradition: A Study in the Literary Use of Astral Symbolism in English Literature from Chaucer to Spenser." *DA* 31 (1970–71): 353A.
Surveys astral symbolism in Chaucer, Henryson, Lydgate, Lyly, R. Greene, and Spenser.

212.   Doob, Penelope B. R. "*Ego Nabugodonosor*: A Study of Conventions of Madness in Middle English Literature." *DA* 31 (1970–71): 1755A–56A.
Discusses astrological, physiological, and psychological theories of the cause of madness as they are reflected in literary works such as *Ywain and Gawain*, *Sir Orfeo*, Geoffrey of Monmouth's *Vita Merlini*, and Hoccleve's poetry.

212a.   ———. *Nebuchadnezzar's Children: Conventions of Madness in Middle English Literature*. New Haven: Yale UP, 1974. 247 pp.
Briefly discusses the medical and physiological aspects of madness, a theme treated in more detail in item 212.

213.   Economou, George D. *The Goddess Natura in Medieval Literature*. Cambridge: Harvard UP, 1972. 213 pp.
Rev. P. M. Kean, *RES* ns 25 (1974): 190–92; D. W. Robertson, Jr., *CL* 26 (1974): 263–65; Chauncey Wood, *JEGP* 74 (1975): 223–25; Charles Witke, *Speculum* 51 (1976): 132–34.
Traces the philosophic sources of the medieval concept of nature to the cosmology of Plato and Aristotle and the thought of Chalcidius, Macrobius, Plotinus, and

others. Studies the treatment of nature in Bernardus Silvestris's *De mundi universitate*, Alain de Lille's *Anticlaudianus* and *De planctu naturae*, Jean de Meun's *Roman de la Rose*, and Chaucer's *Parlement of Foules*.

214.   Galpin, Stanley L. "Centrifugal Force Applied to Fortune's Wheel." *MLN* 29 (1914): 62–63.

Notes that the principle of centrifugal force is applied to the motion of Fortune's wheel in the anonymous fourteenth-century poem *Les échecs amoureux*—an application believed to be unique in French allegorical poetry before 1400.

215.   Garver, Milton S. "Sources of the Beast Similes in the Italian Lyric of the Thirteenth Century." *RF* 21 (1907): 276–320.

Examines the similes drawn from medieval animal lore as used by the Italian lyric poets preceding Dante.

216.   Gregory, Richard. "The Apotheosis of Astronomy." *Science, Medicine and History: Essays on the Evolution of Scientific Thought and Medical Practice Written in Honour of Charles Singer*. Ed. E. Ashworth Underwood. Vol. 1. New York: Oxford UP, 1953. 75–82. 2 vols. New York: Arno, 1975.

See item 178 for annotation.

216a.   Heather, P. J. "Precious Stones in Middle-English Verse of the Fourteenth Century." *Folk-Lore* 42 (1931): 217–64, 345–404.

Studies the *Anglo-Norman Lapidaries* as a major source of knowledge and beliefs about precious stones in medieval England. Quoting copiously from the poets of the time, especially Chaucer, the author cites references to precious stones dealing with their physical qualities, the meanings attached to them, and the customs and beliefs associated with them.

216b.   ———. "The Seven Planets." *Folk-Lore* 54 (1943): 338–61.

Examines the *Early South English Legendary*, a comprehensive account of medieval science, as a source of references to astronomy and astrology in Middle English verse.

217.   Hirth, Wolfgang. "Popularisierungstendenzen in der mittelalterlichen Fachliteratur." *MedJ* 15 (1980): 70–89.

Examines how ancient medical knowledge was popularized by medieval medical texts written in the contemporary vernacular or in a mixture of Latin and Middle High German for the educated laity. Among the popularizing works cited are several didactic poems that appeared in German by the thirteenth century.

218.   Holthausen, F. "Medizinische Gedichte aus einer Stockholmer Handschrift." *Anglia* 18 (1896): 293–331.

This critical edition of a manuscript dating from the fourteenth century contains English language poems of instruction in medical practices.

219.   ———. "Zu den mittelenglischen medizinischen Gedichten." *Anglia* 44 (1920): 357–72.

Supplement to medical poems printed in item 218.

220.   Knowlton, Edgar C. "The Goddess Nature in Early Periods." *JEGP* 19
        (1920): 224–53.
    See item 181 for annotation.

221.   Kuhns, Oscar. "The Literary Influence of Mediaeval Zoology." *Poet-Lore*
        11 (1899): 73–81.
    Medieval bestiaries exerted a wide and lasting influence on literature, as references
to animal lore in Dante, Shakespeare, and Milton demonstrate.

222.   Legge, M. Dominica. " 'To speik of science, craft and sapience' in Medieval
        Literature." *Literature and Science.* Proc. of the Sixth Triennial Congress of
        the International Federation for Modern Languages and Literatures. Oxford,
        1954. Oxford: Blackwell, 1955. 122–26.
    Concerns the use of scientific, pseudoscientific, experimental, and Aristotelian
logical methods in medieval literature.

223.   Lewis, C. S. *The Discarded Image: An Introduction to Medieval and Renaissance
        Literature.* Cambridge, Eng.: Cambridge UP, 1964. 231 pp.
        Rev. Morton W. Bloomfield, *Speculum* 40 (1965): 354–56; S. K. Heninger,
        Jr., *SAQ* 64 (1965): 429.
    Outlines the medieval conception of the universe and considers its effect on
medieval and Renaissance literature. Discusses medieval astronomy, zoology, theology, and philosophy as well as the influence of Boethius, Chalcidius, Cicero,
Claudian, Lucan, Macrobius, and Statius.

224.   Lewis, Gertrud Jaron. *Das Tier und seine dichterische Funktion in* Erec, Iwein,
        Parzival *und* Tristan. Kanadische Studien zur deutschen Sprache und Li-
        teratur 11. Bern: Lang, 1974. 199 pp.
    Examines the symbolic and metaphoric use of the animal in the Arthurian epics
Erec, Iwein, Parzival, and *Tristan,* noting the authors' reliance on the *Physiologus*—
a theological, allegorical, and scientific description of the animal kingdom—as well
as on natural histories by Aristotle and Pliny the Elder.

225.   Linden, Stanton J. "Alchemy and the English Literary Imagination: 1385
        to 1633." *DAI* 33 (1972–73): 3591A–92A.
    See item 160 for annotation.

226.   Meadows, A. J. *The High Firmament: A Survey of Astronomy in English
        Literature.* Leicester: Leicester UP, 1969. 207 pp.
    See item 162 for annotation.

226a.   Neaman, Judith S. "The Distracted Knight: A Study of Insanity in the
        Arthurian Romances." *DA* 29 (1968): 573A.
    Partly concerns the medical background to the depiction of insanity in the Ar-
thurian romances.

227.   Parker, Roscoe E. "Some Relations between the Literature of Science and
        Early English Prose." *Literature and Science.* Proc. of the Sixth Triennial

Congress of the International Federation for Modern Languages and Literatures. Oxford, 1954. Oxford: Blackwell, 1955. 110–14.

Briefly discusses the roles played by the secular prose translations of Chaucer's *Astrolabe*, Bartholomaeus Anglicus's *De proprietatibus rerum*, and Higdon's *Polychronicon* in disseminating scientific information during the fourteenth century.

228.   Raby, F. J. E. "*Nuda natura* and Twelfth-Century Cosmology." *Speculum* 43 (1968): 72–77.

The cosmology of the anonymous twelfth-century poem *Nuda natura* was probably derived from Macrobius's fifth-century work *Commentarium in somnium Scipionis*.

229.   Robin, P. Ansell. *Animal Lore in English Literature*. London: Murray, 1932. Folcroft: Folcroft P, 1970. Norwood: Norwood, 1975. Philadelphia: West, 1976. 196 pp.

See item 169 for annotation.

230.   Said, Rushdi. "Geology in Tenth Century Arabic Literature." *American Journal of Science* 248 (1950): 63–66.

"The Discourses of the Brothers of Purity," a tenth-century classic Arabic work of both scientific and literary interest, contains a discourse on geology that anticipates many later geological theories, including theories of peneplanation, pond evolution, and epicontinental seas.

231.   Schweisheimer, W. "Heilkunde im alten Skandinavien: Die Medizin der *Edda* und der Normannen." *Medizinische Welt* 13 (1962): 618–20.

Working from references in the Germanic epic *Edda*, describes several medical practices and remedies known in Scandinavia between the ninth and eleventh centuries.

232.   Telle, Joachim. "Ein altdeutsches Spruchgedicht nach der 'Turba philosophorum.' " *ZDP* 95 (1976): 416–43.

The author publishes and interprets two alchemical poems written by an anonymous poet-alchemist that follow the tradition of the *Turba philosophorum*.

233.   ———. *Sol und Luna: Literar- und alchemiegeschichtliche Studien zu einem altdeutschen Bildgedicht. Mit Text und Bildanhang*. Schriften zur Wissenschaftsgeschichte 2. Hürtgenwald: Pressler, 1980. 273 pp.

A study of the origin, tradition, and reception of the medieval poem "Sol und Luna." The poem's sources lie in Greek-Arabic alchemical knowledge, promulgated to a great extent by medieval physicians.

233a.   Wedel, Theodore Otto. *The Mediaeval Attitude toward Astrology, Particularly in England*. Yale Studies in English 60. New Haven: Yale UP, 1920. 163 pp.

Provides a history of astrology from Augustine to the fifteenth century and cites references to astrology in Old and Middle English literature. A separate chapter treats Chaucer and Gower.

234.   Yates, Donald. "A Fourteenth-Century Latin Poem on the Art of the
        Physician." 54 (1980): 447–50.
Presents the Latin text and translation of an anonymous fourteenth-century poem
consisting of 35 rhymed hexameters on medicine and its practitioners; also includes
a brief commentary.

235.   Zacher, J. "*Macer Floridus* und die Entstehung der deutschen Botanik."
        ZDP 12 (1881): 189–215.
Macer Floridus, a Latin work of 77 chapters and 2,269 unrhymed hexameters,
describes the medicinal qualities of plants. Its origin is uncertain but its composition
can be situated between 849 and 1112. The work was popular throughout the
Middle Ages, and even Paracelsus wrote a commentary on the first 37 chapters.
Zacher discusses the work's antecedents and its many successors up to the sixteenth
century.

Individual Authors

Albrecht von Scharfenberg (fl. 13th cent.)

236.   Leckie, R. William, Jr. "*Bestia de funde*: Natural Science and the *Jüngerer
        Titurel*." *ZDA* 96 (1967): 263–77.
In the *Jüngerer Titurel* (lines 2785–92), Albrecht describes the healing of Tschio-
natulander's wounds with a salve made from the *bestia de funde*; Leckie traces the
scientific sources of this account, citing such works as the *Physiologus*, Bartholomaeus
Anglicus's *De proprietatibus rerum*, and Vincent de Beauvais's *Speculum naturale*.

237.   ———. " 'Gamaniol, der Vogel': Natural Science and the *Jüngerer Titurel*
        II." *ZDA* 98 (1969): 133–44.
Suggests that Albrecht's description of the *Gamaniol* (a bird subsisting solely on
air) in the *Jüngerer Titurel* (2807–2809) may have derived from Reinbot von Dürne's
rendering of the Saint George legend.

Geoffrey Chaucer, (c. 1340–1400)

237a.   Adams, John F. "Irony in Troilus' Apostrophe to the Vacant House of
        Criseyde." *MLQ* 24 (1963): 61–65.
The significance of *Troilus and Criseyde* 5.540–53 depends largely on the astrological figure appearing throughout the passage.

238.   Aiken, Pauline. "Arcite's Illness and Vincent of Beauvais." *PMLA* 51
        (1936): 361–69.
A probable source of Chaucer's knowledge of medicine in the Knight's Tale is
the medical section of Vincent's *Speculum majus*.

239.   ———. "The Summoner's Malady." *SP* 33 (1936): 40–44.
Chaucer's description of the Summoner's skin disease corresponds exactly to Vin-

cent de Beauvais's description of scabies in his *Speculum doctrinale*, suggesting that Vincent was Chaucer's principal medical source for the characterization.

240.   ———. "Vincent of Beauvais and Chaucer's Knowledge of Alchemy." *SP* 41 (1944): 371–89.

Tries to ascertain the extent of Chaucer's knowledge of alchemy by carefully comparing the alchemical references in the Canon's Yeoman's Tale with the alchemical chapters of Vincent's *Speculum naturale* and *Speculum doctrinale*.

241.   ———. "Vincent of Beauvais and Dame Pertelote's Knowledge of Medicine." *Speculum* 10 (1935): 281–87.

Dame Pertelote in the Nun's Priest's Tale refers to medical theories derived from Vincent's *Speculum naturale* and *Speculum doctrinale*.

242.   ———. "Vincent of Beauvais and the 'Houres' of Chaucer's Physician." *SP* 53 (1956): 22–24.

Suggests that the significance of the term *houres* in the *Canterbury Tales* (Prologue, 415–16) is medical rather than, as is commonly supposed, astrological. Chaucer probably derived this usage from Vincent's *Speculum doctrinale*.

243.   Bashford, H. H. "Chaucer's Physician and His Forbears." *Nineteenth Century* 104 (1928): 237–48.

Provides biographical information on Gilbert the Englishman and John of Gaddesden, the two English physicians Chaucer refers to in the Prologue to his *Canterbury Tales*.

244.   Bloomfield, Morton W. "The Eighth Sphere: A Note on Chaucer's 'Troilus and Criseyde,' V, 1809." *MLR* 53 (1958): 408–10.

Chaucer's sources for a disputed passage from *Troilus* indicate that he located Troilus's final resting place on the eighth rather than the seventh sphere. The sources include the astrology of Boccaccio's *Teseide*—whose source is Dante's *Paradiso* (12.100–54)—and the Hellenistic astrological concept of the ogdoad (eighth sphere).

245.   Bolduan, Nils W. "Chaucer and Matters Medical." *New England Journal of Medicine* 208 (1933): 1365–68.

Cites passages from the *Canterbury Tales* that illuminate Chaucer's opinions on medicine and reveal the general state of medieval medical science.

246.   Bombardier. "Chaucer: Ornithologist." *Blackwood's Magazine* 256 (1944): 120–25.

The descriptions of birds in *The Parlement of Foules* suggest that Chaucer was a good observer of natural phenomena. Only when he relies on authorities such as Pliny does his bird lore tend to be ornithologically inaccurate.

247.   Braddy, Haldeen. "The Cook's Mormal and Its Cure." *MLQ* 7 (1946): 265–67.

John Arderne's *Treatises* and other medieval medical sources clarify the nature of the Cook's mormal, which Chaucer refers to in line 386 of the General Prologue to the *Canterbury Tales*.

248.   Branca, Geraldine S. "Experience versus Authority: Chaucer's Physician and Fourteenth-Century Science." *DAI* 32 (1972): 5731A.
Chaucer's physician in the *Canterbury Tales* represents an allegorical synthesis of theology and science.

248a.   Brooks, Douglas, and Alastair Fowler. "The Meaning of Chaucer's *Knight's Tale*." *Medium Ævum* 39 (1970): 123–46.
The authors suggest astrological and cosmological approaches to the work.

249.   Browne, William H. "Notes on Chaucer's Astrology." *MLN* 23 (1908): 53–54.
Discusses the astrological details of Chaucer's Man of Law's Tale, Knight's Tale, and *Compleynt of Mars*.

250.   Bryant, Joseph A., Jr. "The Diet of Chaucer's Franklin." *MLN* 63 (1948): 318–25.
Chaucer's source of information about the regulation of diet was probably the *Secreta secretorum*, a popular work containing medical data that recalls the writings of Celsus, Hippocrates, and Macrobius.

251.   Camden, Carroll, Jr. "Chaucer and Elizabethan Astrology." *MLN* 45 (1930): 298–99.
The author cites the two allusions to Chaucer he discovered in the text of a debate between John Chamber and Christopher Heydon over the validity of astrological prediction.

252.   ———. "Chaucer and Two Elizabethan Pseudo-Sciences." *PQ* 38 (1959): 124–26.
Three allusions to the *Canterbury Tales* in works of Elizabethan pseudoscience by Hugh Platt, Samuel Rid, and William Vaughan provide evidence of Chaucer's respectable standing among the true and sham scientists of the Elizabethan age. The passages cited concern alchemy and the interpretation of dreams.

253.   ———. "The Physiognomy of Thopas." *RES* 11 (1935): 326–30.
Chaucer burlesqued the typical knightly hero in *Sir Thopas* by characterizing Thopas in accord with the physiognomical conception of the timid and cowardly man.

253a.   Ciavolella, M. "Mediaeval Medicine and Arcite's Love Sickness." *Florilegium* 1 (1979): 222–41.
Maintains that the word *hereos* is the scientific name given to lovesickness in medieval medical treatises. Studies the concept of *hereos* as reflected in Chaucer's Knight's Tale.

254.   Clark, Thomas B. "Forehead of Chaucer's Prioress." *PQ* 9 (1930): 312–14.
Interprets Chaucer's description of the Prioress in the light of popular medieval physiognomical beliefs.

255. Clayton, Margaret. "A Virgilian Source for Chaucer's 'White Bole.' " *N&Q* ns 26 (1979): 103–04.

Chaucer's association of the epithet "white" with Taurus the bull in an astronomical discussion in *Troilus and Criseyde* 2.54–55 may have been derived from Vergil's *Georgic* 1.217–18.

256. Cope, Jackson I. "Chaucer, Venus, and the 'Seventhe Spere.' " *MLN* 67 (1952): 245–46.

Chaucer's apparent reliance on Dante's cosmology in *Troilus and Criseyde* suggests that Troilus's final resting place was on the seventh and not the eighth sphere as had been supposed.

257. Curry, Walter Clyde. "Astrologising the Gods." *Anglia* 47 (1923): 213–43.

Maintains that Chaucer used astrology to shape his heroes' actions in the Knight's Tale. Specifically, he transferred the power of the ancient gods to the planets named for them, so that the real conflict in the tale is between the planets Saturn and Mars in the guise of Lycurgus and Emetreus.

258. ———. *Chaucer and the Mediaeval Sciences.* New York: Oxford UP, 1926. 267 pp. 2nd ed. rev. and enl. New York: Barnes; London: Allen, 1960. 367 pp.

Examines the extent to which medieval science informed the creation of Chaucer's poetic works. Includes chapters on Chaucer's use of medicine, physiognomy, metoposcopy, alchemy, geomancy, the science of dreams, and astrology.

259. ———. "Chaucer's Doctor of Physyk." *PQ* 4 (1925): 1–24.

Reconsiders Chaucer's "Doctor of Physyk" in the light of medieval medical lore with a view toward discovering the sources of the learned physician's "credentials." Curry sketches an overview of medieval astrology and the theory of the four elements and four humors insofar as they pertain to medieval medicine and to Chaucer's creation of the Doctor.

260. ———. "Chaucer's Reeve and Miller." *PMLA* 35 (1920): 189–209.

Shows that Chaucer's characterizations of the Reeve and the Miller follow the specifications of medieval physiognomical lore.

261. ———. "Chaucer's Science and Art." *Texas Review* 8 (1922–23): 307–22.

Outlines the general topics the author will discuss in his proposed study of the influences the medieval sciences exerted on Chaucer. The study will emphasize the artistry, rather than the accuracy, of Chaucer's adaptation of scientific and pseudoscientific material. This preview notes Chaucer's use of physiognomy in characterizations, of dream lore in the Nun's Priest's Tale, and of astrology in the Knight's Tale.

262. ———. "Destiny in Chaucer's *Troilus*." *PMLA* 45 (1930): 129–68.

Treats in part the astrological aspects of Chaucer's portrayal of destiny in *Troilus*.

43 Individual Authors

263. ———. "*Fortuna Maior* [*Troilus*, III. 1420]." *MLN* 38 (1923): 94–96.
Maintains that Chaucer's reference to "Fortuna Maior" is a reference to the sun and not, as was previously supposed, an astrological allusion to the planet Jupiter.

264. ———. "The Malady of Chaucer's Summoner." *MP* 19 (1921–22): 395–404.
Curry attempts to identify the Summoner's malady in the *Canterbury Tales* (A 623–33) by analyzing Chaucer's description of the disease. That it is clearly a type of leprosy called alopecia testifies to Chaucer's accurate knowledge of medicine.

265. ———. "More about Chaucer's Wife of Bath." *PMLA* 37 (1922): 30–51.
Interpreting the Wife of Bath's horoscope in the light of medieval astrological and physiognomical lore not only reveals the subtleties of her character but illuminates Chaucer's method of characterization as well.

266. ———. "O Mars, O Atazir." *JEGP* 22 (1923): 347–68.
Studies how Chaucer used medieval astrology to rationalize his characterizations. Focuses on the *Legend of Hypermnestra* and the Man of Law's Tale.

267. ———. "The Secret of Chaucer's Pardoner." *JEGP* 18 (1919): 593–606.
Interprets the Pardoner's character with reference to various medieval physiognomies that Chaucer may have consulted in creating his characterizations. The Pardoner is a typical example of what physiognomists refer to as a *eunuchus ex nativitate*.

268. ———. "Two Notes on Chaucer." *MLN* 36 (1921): 272–76.
The second of these two notes refers to medieval medical writings to explain the Cook's mormal. A key to understanding the Cook's character lies in recognizing Chaucer's use of popular medical knowledge.

269. Curtiss, Joseph T. "The Horoscope in Chaucer's *Man of Law's Tale*." *JEGP* 26 (1927): 24–32.
Challenges Walter Clyde Curry's earlier interpretation of the astrological significance of the horoscope (see item 266).

270. Damon, S. Foster. "Chaucer and Alchemy." *PMLA* 39 (1924): 782–88.
An analysis of the last 54 lines of the Canon's Yeoman's Tale reveals that Chaucer intended the work to glorify "true" alchemical practices while repudiating "false" alchemy. The lines present in verse the substance of Arnald of Villanova's alchemical text *De lapide philosophorum*.

271. Doob, Penelope B. R. "Chaucer's 'Corones Tweyne' and the Lapidaries." *ChauR* 7 (1972–73): 85–96.
Explicates the expression "Corones tweyne" from Chaucer's *Troilus and Criseyde* (2.1735) by referring to the lapidarian lore in Bartholomaeus Anglicus's *De proprietatibus rerum*, Gower's *Confessio amantis*, and Marbode's *Liber lapidum*.

272.   Drake, Gertrude C. "The Moon and Venus: Troilus's Havens in Eternity."
         PLL 11 (1975): 3–17.
A thorough reexamination of the question concerning Troilus's final resting place.
Demonstrates that Chaucer designated the moon as Troilus's original port of death
and Venus as his eternal abode.

273.   Duncan, Edgar Hill. "Alchemy in Chaucer, Jonson, and Donne." Diss.
         Vanderbilt U, 1941.
Not seen for annotation.

274.   ———. "Chaucer and 'Arnold of the Newe Toun.' " *MLN* 57 (1942):
         31–33.
Though Chaucer cited Arnald's *Rosarium* as the alchemical source of lines 1431–
40 of the Canon's Yeoman's Tale, he actually used Arnald's *De lapide philosophorum*.
Suggests that the greater popularity of the *Rosarium* may have prompted Chaucer's
citation.

275.   ———. "The Literature of Alchemy and Chaucer's *Canon's Yeoman's Tale*:
         Framework, Theme, and Characters." *Speculum* 43 (1968): 633–56.
Among the alchemical treatises that helped to shape Chaucer's work were probably
Arnald of Villanova's *Rosarium* and *De secretis nature* and Geber's *Sum of Perfection*.

276.   ———. "The Yeoman's Canon's 'Silver Citrinacioun.' " *MP* 37 (1939–
         40): 241–62.
Demonstrates the depth and accuracy of Chaucer's alchemical knowledge by analyzing part 1 of the Canon's Yeoman's Tale in the light of the alchemical theory
and practice of the later Middle Ages. Maintains that the processes described by
the Yeoman refer to the citrination of silver. The author relies on the alchemical
tracts known as the *Works of Geber* and the alchemical works of Arnald of Villanova.

277.   Economou, George D. "Januarie's Sin against Nature: The *Merchant's Tale*
         and the *Roman de la rose*." *CL* 17 (1965): 251–57.
Elucidates Chaucer's depiction of Januarie's narcissistic love for May in the Merchant's Tale by referring to Chaucer's use of the optical and mirror imagery of Jean
de Meun's poem *La roman de la rose*.

278.   Emerson, Oliver F. "Chaucer's 'Opie of Thebes Fyn.' " *MP* 17 (1919–
         20): 287–91.
Shows how Chaucer's references to Theban opium in the Knight's Tale (A
1470–74) reflect his considerable knowledge of medicine.

279.   Evers, Jim W. "Some Implications of Chaucer's Use of Astrology in the
         Canterbury Tales." *DAI* 32 (1972): 4561A.
Examines the significance of Chaucer's astrological allusions for the form and
meaning of the *Canterbury Tales*.

279a.   Farnham, Willard. "*The Dayes of the Mone*." *SP* 20 (1923): 70–82.
Comments on Chaucer's knowledge of astrology and prints *The Dayes of the Mone*,

a medieval astrological poem that illustrates the popular understanding of astrology relating to the phases of the moon.

279b. Finkelstein, Dorothee. "The Code of Chaucer's 'Secree of Secrees': Arabic Alchemical Terminology in *The Canon's Yeoman's Tale.*" *Archiv* 207 (1970–71): 260–76.
Examines the medieval alchemists' use of allegory as illustrated in a "code of secrecy" that entered Europe from Arabic sources. This code illuminates the last 53 lines of the Canon's Yeoman's Tale, in which Chaucer cites some of the sources of his alchemical knowledge.

280. Gallacher, Patrick. "Food, Laxatives, and Catharsis in Chaucer's *Nun's Priest's Tale.*" *Speculum* 51 (1976): 49–68.
Examines the theme of reconciliation between the spiritual and physical as expressed in Chaucer's food and purgation imagery in the Nun's Priest's Tale. Philosophic, medical, and scientific antecedents include Plato's *Timaeus*, Hildegard of Bingen's *Causae et curae*, Hugh of Folieto's *De medicina animae*, and Arnald of Villanova's *Speculum introductionum medicalium*.

280a. Gaylord, Alan T. "The Role of Saturn in the *Knight's Tale.*" *ChauR* 8 (1973–74): 171–90.
A reinterpretation of the Knight's Tale that considers the work's astrological elements.

281. Gilliard, Frank D. "Chaucer's Attitude towards Astrology." *JWCI* 36 (1973): 365–66.
The plan and purpose of Chaucer's *Treatise on the Astrolabe* as well as the frequency of astrological allusions in his poetic works suggest that his attitude toward astrology was favorable.

282. Grenberg, Bruce L. "The *Canon's Yeoman's Tale*: Boethian Wisdom and the Alchemists." *ChauR* 1 (1966–67): 37–54.
The contrast between "true" and "false" alchemy in the Canon's Yeoman's Tale parallels and amplifies Chaucer's use of Boethian philosophy to illustrate true and proper goals as opposed to false and improper ones. "With the greatest of artistic skill, through imagery, allusion, irony, and implication, Chaucer brings the Canon's pursuit of false goods to judgment before the courts of Boethian wisdom and true alchemical doctrine."

283. Grennen, Joseph E. "The Canon's Yeoman and the Cosmic Furnace: Language and Meaning in the *Canon's Yeoman's Tale.*" *Criticism* 4 (1962): 225–40.
Explicates the various alchemical significations of lines 1407–08 of the Canon's Yeoman's Tale. The passage reveals the conceptual complexity characteristic of Chaucer's style and technique.

284. ———. "The Canon's Yeoman's Alchemical 'Mass.' " *SP* 62 (1965): 546–60.

Maintains that the two-part structure of the Canon's Yeoman's Tale derives from Chaucer's familiarity with alchemical literature. The work "duplicates the very structure of an alchemical treatise, a first part filled with an enormous mélange of directions and ingredients, and a second part which dissolves into mystic mummery and allegory when it purports to describe the actual transmutation."

285. ————. "Chaucer and the Commonplaces of Alchemy." *C&M* 26 (1965): 306–33.

Identifies and discusses the topoi of alchemical literature on which Chaucer drew, emphasizing their contribution to the meaning of the Canon's Yeoman's Tale. Treats behavioral, preparatory, and procedural topoi.

285a. ————. "Chaucerian Portraiture: Medicine and the Monk." *NM* 69 (1968): 569–74.

Argues that sources such as medieval physiognomies, astrological manuals, and medical treatises illuminate Chaucer's physical characterizations of the Monk.

286. ————. "Chaucer's Characterization of the Canon and His Yeoman." *JHI* 25 (1964): 279–84.

Although Chaucer's characters in the Canon's Yeoman's Tale tend to be depicted unrealistically, they serve his conceptual purposes regarding alchemy and alchemical imagery.

286a. ————. "Chaucer's Monk: Baldness, Venery, and Embonpoint." *AN&Q* 6 (1967–68): 83–85.

On the medical background of Chaucer's portrait of the Monk.

287. ————. "Chaucer's 'Secree of Secrees': An Alchemical 'Topic.' " *PQ* 42 (1963): 562–66.

Suggests that Chaucer used the phrase "secree of secrees" in the Canon's Yeoman's Tale as an ". . . ironical denunciation of the oracular pretensions of alchemical philosophers." The phrase is an example of a formula, or topos, commonly used by alchemists.

288. ————. "Double-Entendre and the Doctor of Phisik." *AN&Q* 1 (1962–63): 131–32.

Points out that the phrase "esy of dispence," which Chaucer used to describe the Doctor of Physic in the *Canterbury Tales* (A 439–44), may have a medical connotation in addition to its common meaning of "slow to spend money."

289. ————. "Hert-Huntyng in the *Book of the Duchess*." *MLQ* 25 (1964): 131–39.

Maintains that Chaucer's reference to "hert-huntyng" in the *Book of the Duchess* (2.1311–13) is rooted in medical lore.

290. ————. "Jargon Transmuted: Alchemy in Chaucer's *Canon's Yeoman's Tale*." *DA* 22 (1961): 859.

Examines the structure and "jargon" of the Canon's Yeoman's Tale from the perspective of its indebtedness to alchemical literature and tradition.

291.   ———. "Saint Cecilia's 'Chemical Wedding': The Unity of the *Canterbury Tales*, Fragment VIII." *JEGP* 65 (1966): 466–81.

Maintains that Chaucer composed the Second Nun's Tale as an adaptation of the legend of Saint Cecilia and intended it to contrast with the alchemical themes of the Canon's Yeoman's Tale.

291a.   ———. "Science and Poetry in Chaucer's *House of Fame*." *AnM* 8 (1967): 38–45.

Traces an episode in *House of Fame* to a medieval medical theory concerning apoplexy.

292.   ———. "Science and Sensibility in Chaucer's Clerk." *ChauR* 6 (1971–72): 81–93.

Examines the physical, logical, and theological scholastic backgrounds of Chaucer's characterization of the Clerk in the Clerk's Tale. "For a knowledgeable audience in Chaucer's day, a large part of the texture of the poem was its resonance of the intellectual style of Oxonian scholasticism—of abstruse theorizing about qualitative change, probably particularly such things as the interest of the Mertonians in the intension and remission of forms or qualities, and the application of physical laws to psychological and moral acts."

293.   Grimm, Florence M. *Astronomical Lore in Chaucer*. University of Nebraska Studies in Language, Literature and Criticism 2. Lincoln: U of Nebraska P, 1919. 96 pp.
          Rev. H. R. Patch, *MLN* 35 (1920): 128; John S. P. Tatlock, *JEGP* 19 (1920): 129–30.

Surveys Chaucer's knowledge of and literary references to astronomical, astrological, and cosmological lore. Treats separately his use of sun, moon, planet, and galaxy imagery and his references to the four elements, the celestial spheres, and heaven, hell, and purgatory.

294.   Hamlin, B. F. "Astrology and the Wife of Bath: A Reinterpretation." *ChauR* 9 (1974–75): 153–65.

A detailed interpretation of the Wife of Bath's horoscope, supplementing studies by Walter Clyde Curry and Chauncey D. Wood. (See items 258 and 336.)

294a.   Hanson, Thomas B. "Criseyde's Brows Once Again." *N&Q* ns 18 (1971): 285–86.

Chaucer's description of Criseyde's brows was based on physiognomy.

295.   ———. "Stylized Man: The Poetic Use of Physiognomy in Chaucer's *Canterbury Tales*." *DA* 31 (1970–71): 1278A.

Among the characters examined for their physiognomic characteristics are Chaucer's Miller, Reeve, Summoner, and Pardoner.

296.   Harrison, Thomas P. *They Tell of Birds: Chaucer, Spenser, Milton, Drayton*. Austin: U of Texas P, 1956. Westport: Greenwood, 1969. 159 pp.
          Rev. Don Cameron Allen, *MLN* 72 (1957): 388.

Surveys the ornithological references in such works as Chaucer's *Parlement of Foules* and *Canterbury Tales*; Spenser's *December, Complaints,* and *Faerie Queene*; Milton's *Paradise Lost* and *Comus*; and Drayton's *Owle, Man in the Moone,* and *Noahs Flood.* Discusses the probable sources of these allusions and tentative comments on the evolving relations between poetry and science over the lifetimes of the cited poets.

297.   Harvey, S. W. "Chaucer's Debt to Sacrobosco." *JEGP* 34 (1935): 34–38.
Maintains that a significant source of information for Chaucer's *Treatise on the Astrolabe* may have been Sacrobosco's *Sperae mundi.* Suggests that Chaucer used similar methods in compiling his literary and scientific works.

298.   Henkin, Leo J. "The Pardoner's Sheep-Bone and Lapidary Lore." *BHM* 10 (1941): 504–12.
Maintains that possible sources for the curative powers Chaucer attributed to the sheep bone in the Pardoner's Prologue (C 350–71) may have been lapidaries such as the French *Lapidaire,* Discorides's *Materia medica,* the *Peterborough Lapidary,* and the *Secreta secretorum.*

298a.   Henning, Standish. "Chauntecleer and Taurus." *ELN* 3 (1965–66): 1–4.
Outlines the relevance of astrology to Chaucer's description of Chauntecleer's catastrophe in the Nun's Priest's Tale.

299.   Hertz, John A. "Chapters toward a Study of Chaucer's Knowledge of Geography." *DA* 19 (1959): 2600–01.
A study of Chaucer's references to geographical matters, coupled with an examination of his cosmography and cosmographical sources, including works by Macrobius, Ovid, Dante, and Vincent de Beauvais.

300.   Herz, Judith Scherer. "*The Canon's Yeoman's Prologue* and *Tale.*" *MP* 58 (1960–61): 231–37.
Notes how the metaphor of alchemy informs the structure and characterization of the Canon's Yeoman's Tale.

301.   Hill, John M. "The *Book of the Duchess,* Melancholy, and That Eight-Year Sickness." *ChauR* 9 (1974–75): 35–50.
Shows, with reference to Burton's *Anatomy of Melancholy,* that the narrator's eight-year sickness is a variety of melancholia identified as "head-melancholy."

302.   Houseman, Percy A. "Science in Chaucer." *SciMo* 38 (1934): 561–64.
Calls attention to the breadth of Chaucer's scientific knowledge in fields such as alchemy, astronomy, astrology, and medicine.

303.   Jennings, Margaret. "Chaucer's *Troilus* and the Ruby." *N&Q* ns 23 (1976): 533–37.
Correlates Chaucer's ruby symbolism in *Troilus and Criseyde* with the medieval lapidary tradition, including such works as the *Third Anglo-Norman Prose Lapidary,* the *Sloane Lapidary,* and the *London Lapidary of King Philip.*

304.   Kohl, Stephan. *Wissenschaft und Dichtung bei Chaucer. Dargestellt hauptsächlich am Beispiel der Medizin.* Frankfurt: Akademische, 1973. 401 pp.

Examines the impact of Chaucer's medical and scientific knowledge on the development of his literary technique. Among the works studied with reference to medicine, alchemy, and astrology are the Canon's Yeoman's Tale, the Miller's Tale, the Franklin's Tale, and *Troilus and Criseyde*.

305.   Kreisler, Nicolai von. "Bird Lore and the Valentine's Day Tradition in Chaucer's *Parlement of Foules*." *ChauR* 3 (1968–69): 60–64.
In addition to drawing on literary tradition and fable, Chaucer may have patterned the ornithology of lines 309–15 of the *Parlement of Foules* after Frederick II of Hohenstaufen's ornithological work *De arte venandi cum avibus*, written between 1244 and 1250.

306.   Laird, Edgar S. "Astrology and Irony in Chaucer's 'Complaint of Mars.' " *ChauR* 6 (1971–72): 229–31.
Renders the adulterous relationship between Venus and Mars in Chaucer's *Complaint of Mars* in terms of astrological allusions to the conjunction of planets and their "aspects."

306a.   ———. "Chaucer's *Complaint of Mars*, Line 145: 'Venus valaunse.' " *PQ* 51 (1972): 486–89.
Explicates the astrological significance of the term *valaunse*.

306b.   Leyerle, John. "Chaucer's Windy Eagle." *UTQ* 40 (1970–71): 247–65.
Sources for the eagle in the *House of Fame* include astronomical lore and natural history.

306c.   Loomis, Dorothy Bethurum. "Constance and the Stars." *Chaucerian Problems and Perspectives*. Ed. Edward Vasta and Zacharias P. Thundy. Notre Dame: U of Notre Dame P, 1979. 207–20.
Maintains that the story of Constance in the Man of Law's Tale serves as a vehicle for Chaucer's expression of his belief in astrology.

307.   Lowes, John Livingston. "The Dragon and His Brother." *MLN* 28 (1913): 229.
Chaucer's use of material from Arnald of Villanova's *De lapide philosophorum* in the Canon's Yeoman's Tale (G 1428–40) suggests that Arnald was an important source of Chaucer's alchemical and medical knowledge.

308.   ———. "The Loveres Maladye of Hereos." *MP* 11 (1913–14): 491–546.
A thorough study of the medical significance of the word *hereos* in the Knight's Tale. Cites allusions to the term in works by Arnald of Villanova, Burton, John of Gaddesden, and many others.

308a.   Luengo, Anthony E. "Magic and Illusion in *The Franklin's Tale*." *JEGP* 77 (1978): 1–16.
Comments on the relation between astrological and stage magic in the Franklin's Tale.

309.   Manly, John Matthews. "On the Date and Interpretation of Chaucer's
         Complaint of Mars." *Harvard Studies and Notes in Philology and Literature* 5
         (1896): 107–26.

Any attempt to date the *Complaint of Mars* by its astronomical and astrological
allusions is hazardous, since Chaucer's descriptions of astrological conjunctions may
be imaginary rather than factual.

309a.   Manzalaoui, Mahmoud. "Chaucer and Science." *Writers and Their Back-
         ground: Geoffrey Chaucer*. Ed. Derek Brewer. Athens: Ohio UP, 1974.
         224–61.

Surveys Chaucer's scientific reading and outlines his literary use of medieval
sciences such as astronomy, astrology, alchemy, and medicine.

310.   Miller, Amanda H. "Chaucer's 'Secte Saturnyn.' " *MLN* 47 (1932): 99–
         102.

Maintains that the phrase "secte Saturnyn" in *The House of Fame* (1.1432) refers
to an astrological theory of the origin of the Jewish religion.

310a.   Muscatine, Charles. "The *Canon's Yeoman's Tale*." *Chaucer Criticism: The
         Canterbury Tales*. Ed. Richard J. Schoeck and Jerome Taylor. Notre Dame:
         U of Notre Dame P, 1960. 259–67.

Partly on the Canon's Yeoman's Tale as a guide to Chaucer's attitude toward
alchemy.

311.   Neaman, Judith S. "Brain Physiology and Poetics in *The Book of the Duchess*."
         RPLit 3 (1980): 101–13.

Studies the relations among the progress and cure of melancholy, the anatomy
and function of the brain, and the chronological structure of Chaucer's *Book of the
Duchess*. Maintains, in particular, that the work is structured on an analogy with
medieval brain physiology, which conceived a tripartite form and function of the
brain consisting of fantasy, rational intellect, and memory.

312.   Nicholls, Albert G. "Medicine in Chaucer's Day." *DR* 12 (1932–33):
         218–30.

Discusses the historical background of Chaucer's references to medical theory and
practice in his description of the "Doctour of Physik" in the *Canterbury Tales*. Also
assesses the extent of Chaucer's medical knowledge.

313.   North, J. D. "Kalenderes Enlumyned Ben They: Some Astronomical Themes
         in Chaucer." *RES* ns 20 (1969): 129–54, 257–83, 418–44.

Analyzes astronomical and astrological allusions in Chaucer's works and establishes
that Chaucer "adopted the habit of referring the action in his tales, usually in a
veiled way, to planetary, solar, and lunar configurations subsisting within his lifetime, and indeed within a few years, at the very most, of the time of composition."
Deduces approximately twenty precise dates from a dozen works.

314.   O'Connor, John J. "The Astrological Background of the *Miller's Tale*."
         Speculum 31 (1956): 120–25.

Interprets Nicholas's scheme to cuckold John in the Miller's Tale in the light of the astrological tradition of the Deluge.

315.   ———. "The Astronomical Dating of Chaucer's *Troilus*." *JEGP* 55 (1956): 556–62.
Reexamines an astronomical allusion that had led scholars to believe that Chaucer wrote the *Troilus* in 1385. The conjunction of Saturn and Jupiter referred to may have been an allusion to an earlier event, not a description of the actual conjunction of 1385.

315a.   O'Neil, W. M. "The Bente Moone." *AUMLA* 43 (1975): 50–52.
Author attempts the astronomical dating of *Troilus and Criseyde*.

316.   O'Neill, Ynez Violé. "A Speculation concerning the Grain in Chaucer's *Prioress's Tale*." *MedH* 12 (1968): 185–90.
Suggests that Chaucer's use of the miraculous grain in the Prioress's Tale may derive from medical sources such as Gilbertus Anglicus's *Compendium medicinae*, John of Gaddesden's *Rosa anglica*, and Bernard of Gordon's *Lilium medicinae*.

317.   Pace, George B. "Physiognomy and Chaucer's Summoner and Alisoun." *Traditio* 18 (1962): 417–20.
Explains the physiognomic significance of the "black brows" characterizing both the Summoner and Alisoun, the young wife in the Miller's Tale. In medieval physiognomic lore black brows indicated a lecherous personality.

318.   Parr, Johnstone. "Chaucer's 'Cherles Rebellying.' " *MLN* 69 (1954): 393–94.
Interprets the phrase "cherles rebellying" in the Knight's Tale (line 2459) as an astrological allusion.

318a.   ———. "The Date and Revision of Chaucer's *Knight's Tale*." *PMLA* 60 (1945): 307–24.
Includes an attempt at astrological dating of the Knight's Tale.

319.   Peavler, James M. "Chaucer's 'Natural' Astronomy." *DAI* 32 (1971): 3264A–65A.
Catalogs and explains references to "natural" astronomy (the observation of stars) in Chaucer's works. Though Chaucer was not an original thinker in astronomical matters, he was an expert on the astronomy of his time.

319a.   Pratt, Robert A. "Albertus Magnus and the Problem of Sound and Odor in the Summoner's Tale." *PQ* 57 (1978): 267–68.
Jankyn's comments on sound and odor (D 2243–86) coincide with Albertus Magnus's scientific speculations on the subject.

320.   Price, Derek J. "Chaucer's Astronomy." *Nature* 170 (1952): 474–75.
Outlines *Equatorie of the Planetis*, an astronomical treatise ascribed to Chaucer.

321.   Root, Robert K., and Henry N. Russell. "A Planetary Date for Chaucer's *Troilus*." *PMLA* 39 (1924): 48–63.

An allusion to a planetary conjunction in the *Troilus* (lines 624–28) suggests that the poem could not have been written earlier than the spring or summer of 1385, though no definite date of composition is thereby established.

322.   Rosenberg, Bruce A. "Swindling Alchemist, Antichrist." *CentR* 6 (1962): 566–80.

Interprets the symbolic significance of the Canon in the Canon's Yeoman's Tale by examining his relation to alchemy and Christian dogma. The Canon is both a fraudulent alchemist and a symbol of the Antichrist. Outlines the central tenets of alchemy.

323.   Rowland, Beryl. "Alison Identified ('The Miller's Tale,' 3234)." *AN&Q* 3 (1964–65): 3–4, 20–21, 39.

Claims that Chaucer's analogy in the Miller's Tale between Alison and a weasel was based on traditional animal folklore.

324.   ———. *Blind Beasts: Chaucer's Animal World*. Kent: Kent State UP, 1971. 198 pp.
        Rev. Paul Piehler, *UTQ* 41 (1971–72): 359–60; David E. Lampe, *ELN* 10 (1972–73): 226–28; D. S. Brewer, *MLR* 68 (1973): 630–34; Edmund Reiss, *Speculum* 49 (1974): 151–53.

Shows that Chaucer derived his animal imagery both from personal observation and from traditions such as fables, the Bible, natural histories, encyclopedias, and manuscript illustrations. He generally used animal imagery to reveal unpleasant aspects of human behavior. Includes separate chapters on Chaucer's use of boar, hare, wolf, horse, sheep, and dog imagery.

325.   ———. "The Physician's 'Historial Thyng Notable' and the Man of Law." *ELH* 40 (1973): 165–78.

Discusses the medical and legal backgrounds of the Man of Law's Tale and the Physician's Tale.

325a.   Rutledge, Sheryl P. "Chaucer's Zodiac of Tales." *Costerus* 9 (1973): 117–43.

Maintains that Chaucer placed far more credence in astrology than previous scholars believed he had. Argues that the twelve astrological signs and seven associated planets "served as the hidden motif of *The Canterbury Tales*."

326.   Schuman, Samuel. "The Circle of Nature: Patterns of Imagery in Chaucer's *Troilus and Criseyde*." *ChauR* 10 (1975–76): 99–112.

Among the prominent images of circularity in *Troilus and Criseyde* are the ring, city walls, seasonal cycles, the wheel of fortune, and astrological and cosmological spheres. The poem's circular motifs focus its themes and unify its structure.

327.   Scott, Forrest S. "The Seventh Sphere: A Note on 'Troilus and Criseyde.' " *MLR* 51 (1956): 2–5.

Discusses the cosmology pertinent to the scholarly dispute over Troilus's final resting place—either the seventh or the eighth sphere.

328.   Smyser, Hamilton M. "A View of Chaucer's Astronomy." *Speculum* 45 (1970): 359–73.
Traces the development of Chaucer's interest in astronomy and astrology and discusses the astrological allusions in *The Complaint of Mars, Troilus and Criseyde*, and other works. Notes that during his *Canterbury* period Chaucer's astrological interests shifted to more exacting astronomical concerns.

328a.   Spargo, John Webster. "The Canon's Yeoman's Prologue and Tale." *Sources and Analogues of Chaucer's* Canterbury Tales. Ed. W. F. Bryan and Germaine Dempster. Chicago: U of Chicago P, 1941. 685–98.
Discusses the alchemical background of Chaucer's work and prints excerpts from several relevant alchemical texts.

329.   Steadman, John M. "Chauntecleer and Medieval Natural History." *Isis* 50 (1959): 236–44.
Beneath the mock-heroic style of Chaucer's Nun's Priest's Tale lies a straightforward description of cocks and hens rooted firmly in medieval natural history. The author notes parallels between Chaucer's descriptions and those found in natural histories by such authors as Bartholomaeus Anglicus, Saint Albertus, Vincent de Beauvais, Neckam, and Pliny the Elder.

330.   Tatlock, John Strong Perry. "Astrology and Magic in Chaucer's *Franklin's Tale.*" *Anniversary Papers by Colleagues and Pupils of George Lyman Kittredge Presented on the Completion of His Twenty-Fifth Year of Teaching in Harvard University, June,* MCMXIII. Boston: Ginn, 1913. 339–50.
Explains the significance of astrology for the success of the Clerk's magical feat in the Franklin's Tale.

331.   Ussery, Huling E. *Chaucer's Physician: Medicine and Literature in Fourteenth-Century England.* Tulane Studies in English 19. New Orleans: Dept. of English, Tulane U, 1971. 158 pp.
Rev. Pearl Kibre, *AHR* 78 (1973): 668–69; Rossell Hope Robbins, *Archiv* 210 (1973): 366–67; C. H. Talbot, *RES* ns 24 (1973): 201–03; Joseph E. Grennen, *Speculum* 49 (1974): 158–59; M. Andrew, *ES* 56 (1975): 154–56.
Examines the medical profession of Chaucer's day and its relation to Chaucer's writing. Stresses the possible influence of contemporary physicians on the characterization of the "Doctour of Phisik" in the *Canterbury Tales* and on the appropriateness of the Physician's Tale to its narrator.

332.   Veazie, Walter B. "Chaucer's Text-Book of Astronomy; Johannes de Sacrobosco." *University of Colorado Studies.* Series B: Studies in the Humanities 1 (1939–41): 169–82.
Discusses the contents of Sacrobosco's *Sphaera,* an astronomy textbook that Chaucer is known to have studied in some detail. Much of Chaucer's *Treatise on the Astrolabe,* for example, is based on Sacrobosco's work.

333.   Walker, Frederic. "Geoffrey Chaucer and Alchemy." *Journal of Chemical Education* 9 (1932): 1378–85.

Because the Canon's Yeoman's Tale describes alchemy and the activities of alchemists in the fourteenth century, it is a valuable document for students of the history of chemistry. Includes an abridged translation of the tale and lists and defines the alchemical terms used.

333a.   Weese, Walter E. " 'Vengeance and Pleyn Correccioun,' *KnT* 2461." *MLN* 63 (1948): 331–33.

Maintains that Johnstone Parr's interpretation of the phrase "pleyn correccioun" (see item 318a) may flaw his astrological dating of the Knight's Tale.

333b.   Williams, George. "What Is the Meaning of Chaucer's *Complaint of Mars?*" *JEGP* 57 (1958): 167–76.

Argues that a supposed astronomical event is the basis for the human action and emotion described in Chaucer's *Complaint*.

334.   Winny, James. "Chaucer's Science." *An Introduction to Chaucer*. By Maurice Hussey, A. C. Spearing, and James Winny. Cambridge: Cambridge UP, 1965. 153–84.

Surveys Chaucer's use of the medieval sciences in his literary works and considers his knowledge of astronomy, alchemy, the theory of humors, the theory of elements, and medicine.

335.   Wood, Chauncey D. "The April Date as a Structural Device in *The Canterbury Tales*." *MLQ* 25 (1964): 259–71.

Illuminates the structural unity of Chaucer's *Canterbury Tales* by explaining the astrological significance of references to the time of year and day throughout the work.

335a.   ———. "Chaucer and Astrology." *Companion to Chaucer Studies*. Ed. Beryl Rowland. London: Oxford UP, 1968. 176–91.

Surveys and summarizes scholarship treating the theme of Chaucer and astrology.

336.   ———. *Chaucer and the Country of the Stars: Poetic Uses of Astrological Imagery*. Diss. Princeton U, 1963. *DA* 25 (1964): 2970. Princeton: Princeton UP, 1970. 318 pp.
         Rev. J. D. North, *RES* ns 22 (1971): 471–74; John M. Steadman, *JEGP* 71 (1972): 113–16.

A thorough examination of Chaucer's attitude toward and literary use of astrology, including a historical survey of the astrological tradition up to his time. Studies in detail the astrological components of *The Complaint of Mars*, the Man of Law's Tale, the Franklin's Tale, and other works.

337.   ———. "Of Time and Tide in the *Franklin's Tale*." *PQ* 45 (1966): 688–711.

Knowledge of the medieval theory of the annual period of the tides clarifies some thematic difficulties concerning magic and astrology in the Franklin's Tale. Wood consulted astronomical texts such as Bede the Venerable's *De temporum ratione*, Isidore of Seville's *De ordine creaturarum*, and William of Auvergne's *De universo*.

338.   Young, Karl. "The 'Secree of Secrees' of Chaucer's Canon's Yeoman." *MLN* 58 (1943): 98–105.

Chaucer's characterization of alchemy as "the secree of secrees" in line 1447 of the Canon's Yeoman's Tale is a translation of a familiar Latin byname for the pseudoscience and not, as was previously supposed, a reference to the pseudo-Aristotelian *Secretum secretorum*.

Dante Alighieri (1265–1321)

339.   Angelitti, Filippo. "Ulisse astronomo e geodeta nella *Divina commedia*." *Giornale dantesco* 9 (1901): 208–13.

Examines astronomical references in the *Divina commedia*, particularly those relating to the tale of Ulysses's travels. While admitting that Dante was primarily a poet, the author cites scientifically accurate observations in the poetry to show that Dante was also a scholar and a scientist.

340.   Anon. "The Astronomy of Dante." *QR* 187 (1898): 490–520.

Even a modest knowledge of pre-Copernican astronomy yields great rewards for the interpreter of astronomical passages in Dante's works. Outlines the basics of Ptolemaic astronomy and other pertinent astronomical theories that help illuminate these difficult sections.

341.   Austin, Herbert D. "Dante and the Mineral Kingdom." *RPh* 4 (1950–51): 79–153.

Compiles Dante's references to various metals, stones, and inorganic substances in the *Divine Comedy*, *Monarchia*, *Convivio*, *Quaestio de aqua et terra*, and other works. Discusses the etymology of Dante's mineralogical terminology and notes his main mineralogical sources: Albertus Magnus, Isidore of Seville, Pliny the Elder, and Uguiccione da Pisa.

342.   ———. "Number and Geometrical Design in the *Divine Comedy*." *Person* 16 (1935): 310–30.

Focuses on the predominance of point, line, and circle imagery in Dante's *Divine Comedy*, noting its aesthetic function in the work and its relation to the Ptolemaic astronomical schema and the religious dogma of the time.

343.   Batard, Yvonne. "Dante et la science de son temps." *Literature and Science*. Proc. of the Sixth Triennial Congress of the International Federation for Modern Languages and Literatures. Oxford, 1954. Oxford: Blackwell, 1955. 114–21.

Assesses Dante's knowledge of medieval science, cosmography, psychology, history, and theology and discusses his poetic assimilation of information from each field.

344.   Boffito, Giuseppe. "Saggio d'un commento scientifico alla *Divina comme-dia.*" *Giornale dantesco* 37 (1934): 3–23.
Examines lines 13–24 of Dante's *Purgatorio* in detail to determine the extent and possible sources of Dante's scientific knowledge.

345.   Bowden, John Paul. "Topics of Medieval Culture: Science." *An Analysis of Pietro Alighieri's Commentary on the* Divine Comedy. New York: Columbia UP, 1951. 77–83.
Briefly surveys the remarks on biology, mathematics, physics, and astronomy in Dante's son's commentary on the *Divine Comedy*.

346.   Capasso, Ideale. "L'astronomia nella *Divina commedia.*" *Physis* 7 (1965): 75–106, 129–201, 261–72; 8 (1966): 23–98. Pisa: Galilaeana, 1967. 211 pp.
The author, a professor of astronomy, has formidably documented the relation between certain astronomical references in the *Divina commedia* and the astronomical phenomena known to Dante. The study stresses Dante's grasp of the astronomical data then available and assesses his accuracy in integrating the information into his work.

347.   Falkenhausen, Friedrich Freih. von. "Dantes Sternglaube." *DDJ* 25 (1943): 25–38.
Passages from the *Divine Comedy* show that Dante shared with his age the Ptol-emaic cosmology and a belief in the stars' influence on the physical and spiritual well-being of human beings. He did not, however, subscribe to contemporary beliefs in the stars' deterministic and predictable influence on human events. His conviction in free will and the possible intervention of God's grace induced him to question the main tenets of astrology.

348.   Freccero, John. "*Paradiso* x: The Dance of the Stars." *DSARDS* 86 (1968): 85–111.
Examines Dante's description of the Heaven of the Sun in *Paradiso* 10 with reference to the Christian and Platonic cosmological traditions that it incorporates. Identifies elements of symbolic cosmology in the description and comments on Dante's use of astronomical terminology and astrological imagery in depicting beat-itude.

349.   Gnudi, Martha Teach. "Might Dante Have Used a Map of Orosius?" *Italica* 15 (1938): 112–19.
Maintains that Dante probably derived the chief general concepts and some details of his geographical knowledge from a map by Orosius.

350.   Gutmann, René A. "Dante et la médecine." *Dante et son temps*. Paris: Nizet, 1977. 165–74.
Establishes that Dante studied medicine in Padua and Bologna and examines the reflection of his medical knowledge in works such as the *Divina commedia* and *Convito*.

351.   Haberling, Wilhelm. "War Dante ein Arzt?" *DDJ* 7 (1923): 59–78.
Drawing primarily on passages from the *Divine Comedy*, the author tries to establish

whether the numerous descriptions of physicians and illnesses support the allegation that Dante was a practicing physician. Concludes that although Dante was well read in the traditional medical texts of antiquity and the Middle Ages and evidently was keenly observant of hospitals and patients, he did not have the firsthand knowledge that a medical practitioner of his time would have had.

352.   Levavasseur, A. "Les pierres précieuses dans la *Divine comédie.*" *REI* ns 4 (1957): 31–100.

Explores Dante's tempered use of precious stones and gems as images or symbols in the *Divine Comedy*. Studies their aesthetic or symbolic function in relation to the significance accorded them in antiquity, Eastern religions, the Judaic tradition, later Christianity, and medieval lapidaries.

353.   Luccio, M. "Teorie cosmogoniche e poesia nell'opera di Dante." *Scientia* 95 (1960): 307–14, 339–46.

Sees Dante as a milestone in the journey toward scientific enlightenment. Examines the scientific content of the *Divina commedia*, drawing comparisons with the theories of modern science.

354.   Mascia, Francesco S. *L'astronomia nella* Divina commedia. Castellammare di Stabia: Molinari, 1968. 86 pp.

Interprets and explains in detail the astronomical allusions in the *Divine Comedy*. A picture of Dante's broad knowledge of science emerges, though the study also notes that Dante, first and foremost a poet, sometimes abandoned scientific accuracy for the sake of poetry.

355.   Mayer, Sharon E. "Dante's Alchemists." *IQ* 12. 47–48 (1969): 185–200.

Dante's portrayal of the sufferings of alchemists in hell, depicted in the *Inferno*, cantos 29 and 30, is based on the vitalistic theory of chemical transformation.

356.   Meiklejohn, M. F. M. "The Birds of Dante." *AnS* 10 (1954): 33–43.

Surveys Dante's descriptions of birds in the *Divine Comedy*, stressing the remarkable clarity and ornithological accuracy of his depictions.

357.   Miller, James L. "Three Mirrors of Dante's *Paradiso.*" *UTQ* 46 (1976–77): 263–79.

Interprets in detail Beatrice's optical experiment in *Paradiso* (2.94–105) and its significance for Dante's metaphoric elaborations of mirror and light imagery in later cantos. Cites Saint Thomas Aquinas and Saint Bonaventure as sources for Dante's "philosophy of mirrors."

358.   Orr, Mary Acworth. *Dante and the Early Astronomers*. London: Gall, 1914. London: Wingate, 1956; Port Washington: Kennikat, 1969. 359 pp.

Traces the development of astronomy from ancient times to the age of Dante and discusses the principal sources of Dante's astronomical knowledge, including Aristotle, Cicero, and Ptolemy. Examines the numerous references to astronomy in Dante's *Convivio*, *Vita nuova*, *Quaestio de aqua et terra*, *Divine Comedy*, and other works.

359.   Preyer, Jacques. *Dante alchimiste: Interprétation alchimique de la* Divine Comédie. i. L'enfer. Paris: Vieux Colombier, 1957. 267 pp.
Provides an introduction to alchemical terminology and belief, discusses the alchemical meaning of the structure of the *Divine Comedy*, and gives a canto-by-canto alchemical interpretation of the *Inferno*.

360.   Stebbins, Frederick A. "Dante in Orbit." *Journal of the Royal Astronomical Society of Canada* 57 (1963): 210–17.
Surveys references to time and astronomy in the *Divine Comedy*. Dante imagines the earth as it would appear to a person in orbit and offers apparently correct solutions to problems of local time, elapsed time, and the international date line.

361.   Tuzet, Hélène. "L'imagination stellaire de Dante." *REI* 6 (1959): 5–22.
Shows that Dante developed an imaginative view of the cosmos based in part on ancient philosophy at a time when the Ptolemaic cosmology prevailed. Suggests that he anticipated the heliocentric system. Cites illustrative passages from the *Paradiso* and *Convivio*.

Rudolf von Ems (c. 1200–c. 1254)

362.   Doberentz, Otto. "Die Erd- und Völkerkunde in der *Weltchronik* des Rudolf von Hohen-Ems." *ZDP* 12 (1881): 257–301, 387–454; 13 (1882): 29–57, 165–223.
The *Weltchronik* is a work of 36,500 verses whose origin can be situated between 1250 and 1254. Doberentz considers it a storehouse of information about the medieval worldview; here he discusses the geographic aspects of the text.

Wolfram von Eschenbach (c. 1170–c. 1220)

363.   Schäfer, Hans-Wilhelm. "Die Planetennamen in Wolframs *Parzival*." *ZDS* 21 (1965): 60–68.
A close analysis of the planetary names in Wolfram's *Parzival* permits the critic to establish Arabic sources for the characterization of Parzival.

364.   Stavenhagen, Lee. "The Science of *Parzival*." *DA* 25 (1965): 7249–50.
Examines the scientific coloring that Wolfram gave to the Grail story in *Parzival* and speculates on the scientific and alchemical influences.

The *Gawain* Poet (fl. c. 1370–90)

365.   Pace, George B. "Physiognomy and *Sir Gawain and the Green Knight*." *ELN* 4 (1966–67): 161–65.
Primarily illustrates the physiognomic significance of Morgan le Fay's "black brows."

365a.   White, Robert B., Jr. "A Note on the Green Knight's Red Eyes (*GGK*, 304)." *ELN* 2 (1964–65): 250–52.
Uses medieval physiognomical theories for interpretation.

366.   Wintermute, Edwin. "The *Pearl*'s Author as Herbalist." *MLN* 64 (1949): 83–84.
The etymology of the word "gromwell," referred to in line 43 of the *Pearl*, suggests that the author of the work may have been a monastic apothecary with a wide knowledge of herbal lore.

John Gower (1330?–1408)

367.   Fox, George G. *The Mediaeval Sciences in the Works of John Gower*. Diss. Princeton U, 1926. Princeton Studies in English 6. Princeton: Princeton UP, 1931. New York: Haskell, 1966. 164 pp.
        Rev. Walter Clyde Curry, *MLN* 48 (1933): 59–61.
Although Gower alludes to various medieval sciences in works such as *Confessio amantis*, *Vox clamantis*, and *Mirour de l'omme*, his scientific knowledge was merely superficial. The author surveys Gower's references to physiology, geography, meteorology, astrology, dream theory, zoology, medicine, alchemy, and other pseudosciences.

Nicholas de Guildford (fl. 1250)

367a.   Cawley, A. C. "Astrology in *The Owl and the Nightingale*." *MLR* 46 (1951): 161–74.
Maintains that lines 1145–330 of *The Owl and the Nightingale* concern astrological prediction and defend astrological doctrine, a point hitherto overlooked by critics.

368.   Hinckley, Henry B. "Science and Folk-Lore in *The Owl and the Nightingale*." *PMLA* 47 (1932): 303–14.
Nicholas drew on natural history works by Aristotle, Neckam, and Pliny the Elder; his own acute zoological observations; and several folklore traditions in creating characters for *The Owl and the Nightingale*.

Robert Henryson (c. 1425–c. 1506)

369.   Fox, Denton. "Henryson's 'Sum Practysis of Medecyne.' " *SP* 69 (1972): 453–60.
Henryson's poem "Sum Practysis of Medecyne" (c. 1475) is related in style, meter, and use of medical and pseudomedical terminology to a tradition of medical burlesques that includes the French *Herberies*, Chaucer's *Canterbury Tales*, and later English plays such as J. Heywood's *Four PP*, the Croxton *Play of the Sacrament*, and the Chester *Adoration of the Shepherds*.

369a.   Hanham, Alison, and J. C. Eade. "Foxy Astrology in Henryson." *Parergon* 24 (1979): 25–29.
Considers the astrological significance of Henryson's idiosyncratic arrangement of the planets in the fourth stanza of his fable "How the Tod Maid Confession to Freir Wolf Waitskaith."

370.   Stearns, Marshall W. "The Planet Portraits of Robert Henryson." *PMLA* 59 (1944): 911–27.

Henryson's descriptions of the seven planets in *Testament of Cresseid* are fundamentally astrological. The likely sources of his astrological information include Albohazen's *Liber de fatis astrorum* (1485) and writings of Ovid, Chaucer, and Lydgate.

John Lydgate (c. 1370–c. 1450)

371.   Dwyer, Richard A. "Arthur's Stellification in the *Fall of Princes*." *PQ* 57 (1978): 155–71.

Explains Lydgate's use of astronomical imagery in his modification of the King Arthur legend in the *Fall of Princes*. Emphasizes the influence of Boethius.

372.   Hagen, Susan K. "*The Pilgrimage of the Life of Man*: A Medieval Theory of Vision and Remembrance." *DAI* 37 (1976): 2853A.

The medieval optical theories of R. Bacon, Grosseteste, and Pecham help elucidate the theories of vision and remembrance in Lydgate's translation of Guillaume de Deguileville's fourteenth-century poem.

373.   Mullett, Charles F. "John Lydgate: A Mirror of Medieval Medicine." *BHM* 22 (1948): 403–15.

Presents Lydgate's writings as a comprehensive illustration of the fifteenth-century worldview. Maintains that his frequent mention of medicine, especially in *The Dance of Death*, reflects a contemporary obsession with pestilence and sudden death. Also treats Lydgate's allusions to astrology as correlated with health.

374.   Parr, Johnstone. "The Astronomical Date of Lydgate's *Life of Our Lady*." *PQ* 50 (1971): 120–25.

Uses the astronomical references in book 4, lines 1–16, of *The Life of Our Lady*, to determine that the poem was composed in 1415–16.

375.   ———. "Astronomical Dating for Some of John Lydgate's Poems." *PMLA* 67 (1952): 251–58.

Attempts to date Lydgate's *Temple of Glas*, *Troy Book*, *Siege of Thebes*, and *Title and Pedigree of Henry VI* by means of the astronomical allusions in the poems.

376.   ———. "The Horoscope of Edippus in Lydgate's *Siege of Thebes*." *Essays in Honor of Walter Clyde Curry*. Vanderbilt Studies in the Humanities 2. Nashville: Vanderbilt UP, 1955. 117–22.

Assesses the technical accuracy of Edippus's horoscope in *The Siege of Thebes* by referring to medieval and Renaissance authorities on astral configurations indicating patricide. Though the arrangement of the stars in the horoscope was generally malevolent, it did not conform to the pattern for patricide specified by these authorities.

Sir John Mandeville (fl. 14th cent.)

377.   Bennett, Josephine Waters. *The Rediscovery of Sir John Mandeville*. New York: MLA, 1954. New York: Kraus, 1971. 436 pp.

Rev. R. M. Wilson, *RES* ns 6 (1955): 305–06; Philip W. Souers, *CL* 8 (1956): 161–64.

Reevaluates the scholarly tradition surrounding Mandeville's *Travels*, a work important for its literary merits and for its place in the history of geographical discovery. Presents evidence that Mandeville is its author and examines the work's influence on Mandeville's contemporaries and on English writers such as T. More, Shakespeare, Spenser, Milton, Defoe, Swift, and Coleridge.

Jean de Meun (d. c. 1305)

378.   Eberle, Patricia J. "The Lovers' Glass: Nature's Discourse on Optics and the Optical Design of the *Romance of the Rose.*" *UTQ* 46 (1976–77): 241–62.

Maintains that the design of Jean's continuation of Guillaume de Lorris's *Romance of the Rose* is based on thirteenth-century optical science. The work is ". . . a complex optical instrument made of a series of optical glasses, an instrument designed to supplement the single perspective offered in Guillaume's dream-vision of love with a multiplicity of perspectives on the subject of love and on the dream-vision itself." Jean's major scientific influences were Seneca, Robert Grosseteste, and Nigel Longchamps.

Bernardus Silvestris (fl. 1136)

379.   Stock, Brian. *Myth and Science in the Twelfth Century: A Study of Bernard Silvester.* Princeton: Princeton UP, 1972. 331 pp.
        Rev. A. G. Keller, *Ambix* 20 (1973): 139–40; Kenelm Foster, *MLR* 69 (1974): 605–07; Richard Lorch, *British Journal for the History of Science* 8 (1975): 180–81; David Luscombe, *History* 60 (1975): 284–85; Winthrop Wetherbee, *Speculum* 50 (1975): 537–40; Chauncey Wood, *JEGP* 74 (1975): 105–08.

Examines Silvestris's *Cosmographia*, a poetic allegory depicting the universe in the light of rediscovered ancient science. Though it is tempting to see the work as a synthesis of literature and "pure" science, Silvestris's originality lies in the poetic presentation of twelfth-century information about the universe available elsewhere in more precise form. In this respect Silvestris resembles the "cosmic" poets of antiquity—Plato, Lucretius, and Manilius—but he should not be considered a scientist.

380.   Wetherbee, Winthrop, ed. and trans. *The Cosmographia of Bernardus Silvestris.* New York: Columbia UP, 1973. 180 pp.

The translator's introduction outlines the cosmological and theological background of Silvestris's work; traces its principal sources; examines its theme, structure, and literary qualities; and comments on Silvestris's role in determining the direction of twelfth-century Scholastic literary and scientific inquiry. Influences include Plato's *Timaeus* and works by Boethius, Chalcidius, Macrobius, and Martianus Capella.

John Skelton (c. 1460–1529)

381.   Colley, John Scott. "John Skelton's Ironic *Apologia*: The Medieval Sciences, Wolsey, and the *Garlande of Laurell*." *TSL* 18 (1973): 19–32.
Skelton's use of astrological and dream lore heightens the ironic and satiric intentions of his *Garlande*. The chief butt of Skelton's satire was Wolsey.

Gottfried von Strassburg (fl. 1210)

382.   Ober, Peter C. "Alchemy and the *Tristan* of Gottfried von Strassburg." *Monatshefte* 57 (1965): 321–35.
Reexamines the "Minnegrotte" scene of Strassburg's *Tristan und Isold* in the light of alchemical symbolism.

Heinrich Wittenweiler (15th cent.)

383.   Zaenker, Karl. "Zur Arzt-Szene in Wittenwilers [sic] *Ring*." *Seminar* 15 (1979): 1–14.
Interprets the didactic portions of the physician's scene in Wittenweiler's *Ring* with reference to the medical literature extant around 1400, including the *Secreta mulierum*, Trotula's *De passionibus mulierum*, and Hartlieb's German translation of the *Secreta secretorum*.

Renaissance

Studies and Surveys

384.   Allen, Don Cameron. *The Legend of Noah: Renaissance Rationalism in Art, Science, and Letters.* Illinois Studies in Language and Literature 33.3–4. Urbana: U of Illinois P, 1949. 221 pp.
        Rev. S. Stein, *MLR* 45 (1950): 526–28; Francis Lee Utley, *MLN* 68 (1953): 240–44.
Outlines the Renaissance and seventeenth-century conflict between reason and faith caused in part by the incursion of rational and scientific methodologies into traditional biblical hermeneutics. Traces the impact of these methodologies on the interpretation of the story of Noah and the Flood, noting the contributions of scientists T. Burnet, J. Ray, Woodward, and Whiston. Literary and artistic treatments of the Noah story also reflect the growing influence of rationalism, which was ". . . successful in freeing the imagination from the manacles of tradition." Studies accounts of the legend by Du Bartas, Hunnis, Sabie, T. Browne, Cowley, Donne, Drayton, and Milton.

385.   ———. *The Star-Crossed Renaissance: The Quarrel about Astrology and Its Influence in England.* Durham: Duke UP, 1941. 280 pp.
        Rev. Francis R. Johnson, *Isis* 34 (1942–43): 377–78; Carroll Camden, *MLN* 58 (1943): 145–47.
This overview of Elizabethan and Jacobean attitudes toward astrology and astrologers includes a survey of English literary responses to the subject in works by R. Greene, Jonson, Shakespeare, Sidney, F. Bacon, Donne, Drayton, and many others.

386.   Arthur, Thomas J. "Anatomies and the Anatomy Metaphor in Renaissance England." *DAI* 39 (1979): 4263A–64A.
Examines literary anatomies such as Lyly's *Euphues: The Anatomy of Wit*, Stubbes's *Anatomie of Abuses*, and Rogers's *Anatomie of the Minde* and relates them to the study of anatomy in the sixteenth- and seventeenth-century medical schools.

387.   Babb, Lawrence. *The Elizabethan Malady: A Study of Melancholia in English Literature from 1580 to 1642.* East Lansing: Michigan State Coll. P, 1951. 206 pp.
        Rev. John W. Draper, *MLR* 47 (1952): 571–72; Paul V. Kreider, *MLN* 68 (1953): 250–52.
Explores the physiological, psychological, and scientific theories behind the al-

lusions to melancholy that abound in Elizabethan and early Stuart literature. Treats the literary depiction of the malcontent, pathological grief, the lover's malady, and other forms of melancholy.

387a.   ———. "Love Melancholy in the Elizabethan and Early Stuart Drama." *BHM* 13 (1943): 117–32.

According to Renaissance medical theory, lovesickness is a physical malady. Demonstrates the widespread adherence to this belief with numerous excerpts from Elizabethan and early Stuart plays.

388.   ———. "Melancholic Villainy in the Elizabethan Drama." *PMASAL* 29 (1943): 527–35.

Outlines the scientific and pseudoscientific background to the common association of villainy and melancholy expressed in Elizabethan drama. Cites passages from Marston, Shakespeare, Tourneur, J. Webster, and others.

389.   ———. "On the Nature of Elizabethan Psychological Literature." *Joseph Quincy Adams Memorial Studies*. Ed. James G. McManaway, Giles E. Dawson, and Edwin E. Willoughby. Washington: Folger Shakespeare Library, 1948. 509–22.

Although modern scholarship has tended to impose a unity on Elizabethan psychological theories that they do not exhibit, it has greatly helped us recognize the figurative use of psychological terms and unravel dramatic character in many Elizabethan plays.

390.   ———. "The Physiological Conception of Love in Elizabethan and Early Stuart Drama." *PMLA* 56 (1941): 1020–35.

Outlines the principal features of the Elizabethan physiological conception of love as treated in scientific works by Melanchthon, W. Vaughan, Walkington, and Wright. The theory appears frequently in the thought and phraseology of Elizabethan and early Stuart dramatists such as Chapman, Ford, Lyly, Marston, Massinger, and Middleton.

391.   ———. "Scientific Theories of Grief in Some Elizabethan Plays." *SP* 40 (1943): 502–19.

Outlines the scientific lore behind the portrayal of grief in Elizabethan drama, focusing especially on the physiological theory of the humors. Cites works by Chapman, Jonson, Lyly, Marston, Massinger, Shakespeare, J. Webster, and others.

392.   Barkan, Leonard. *Nature's Work of Art: The Human Body as Image of the World*. New Haven: Yale UP, 1975. 291 pp.

Rev. Edward William Tayler, *ELN* 13 (1975–76): 297–98; David G. Hale, *RenQ* 29 (1976): 295–97; Kenneth Muir, *JEGP* 75 (1976): 279–80; Robert S. Goetsch, *PrS* 50 (1976–77): 175–76; Elizabeth H. Hageman, *SQ* 28 (1977): 126–27; S. K. Heninger, Jr., *MLR* 72 (1977): 141–43; John M. Steadman, *CL* 29 (1977): 359–61; Sears Jayne, *MP* (1977–78): 300–01.

Presents the concept of the human body as a microcosm and sketches its history from Plato's *Timaeus* to the Renaissance. Discusses Platonic cosmology, the theory of the four elements, astrology, numerology, and natural philosophy. Emphasizes the body's importance in poetic metaphor and imagery, especially during the Renaissance. Separate chapters treat Sidney's *Astrophil and Stella* and Spenser's *Faerie Queene*.

393.   Bercovitch, Sacvan. "Empedocles in the English Renaissance." *SP* 65 (1968): 67–80.
The likelihood that the Empedoclean texts *On Nature* and *Purifications* were available during the Renaissance may account for the many Empedoclean ideas and allusions in the poetry of Shakespeare, Spenser, T. Watson, G. Herbert, Herrick, and Milton.

394.   Bleker, Johanna. "Die Alchemie im Spiegel der schönen Literatur." *Gesnerus* 28 (1971): 154–67.
See item 209 for annotation.

395.   Briggs, K. M. *Pale Hecate's Team: An Examination of the Beliefs on Witchcraft and Magic among Shakespeare's Contemporaries and His Immediate Successors.* New York: Humanities; London: Routledge, 1962. New York: Arno, 1977. 291 pp.
Rev. R. H. Syfret, *RES* ns 14 (1963): 287–88.
Provides a brief history of the witchcraft tradition in England and examines references to witchcraft, magic, alchemy, and astrology in the poetry and drama of Shakespeare's time. Authors discussed include R. Greene, T. Heywood, Jonson, Lyly, Marlowe, Middleton, H. More, Shadwell, Shakespeare, Spenser, and T. Vaughan.

396.   Brown, Harcourt. *Science and the Human Comedy: Natural Philosophy in French Literature from Rabelais to Maupertuis.* Toronto: U of Toronto P, 1976. 221 pp.
Rev. Trevor H. Levere, *UTQ* 46 (1976–77): 443–44; W. H. Barber, *AnS* 34 (1977): 429–31; Robert J. Ellrich, *Isis* 68 (1977): 458–60; E. T. Dubois, *MLR* 73 (1978): 632–33; Rhoda Rappaport, *ECS* 12 (1978–79): 107–10; Dorothy Gabe Coleman, *RenQ* 32 (1979): 636–37.
Relates the scientific revolutions of the sixteenth, seventeenth, and eighteenth centuries to the development of French literature of the period, showing that during this time literature and science were closely integrated. Topics include the differences and similarities of investigative method in the sciences and the humanities; the impact of medicine on Rabelais's works; the influence of science on Pascal's *Pensées*; the scientific background of Molière's medical satires; Voltaire's humanism and the seventeenth-century scientific revolution; and Maupertuis's knowledge of mathematics, physics, and other sciences.

397.   ———. "Tensions and Anxieties: Science and the Literary Culture of France." *Science and the Creative Spirit: Essays on Humanistic Aspects of Science.* Ed. Harcourt Brown. Toronto: U of Toronto P, 1958. 91–126.
See item 146 for annotation.

398.　Bush, Douglas. *Science and English Poetry: A Historical Sketch, 1590–1950.* New York: Oxford UP, 1950. Westport: Greenwood, 1980. 166 pp.
See item 147 for annotation.

399.　Camden, Carroll, Jr. "Elizabethan Almanacs and Prognostications." *Library* 4th ser. 12 (1931): 83–108, 194–207.
Reviews the contents of Elizabethan almanacs, emphasizing their astrological components. Satirical references to almanacs and their prognostications appear in writings by R. Greene, Jonson, Middleton, Nashe, Shakespeare, and others.

400.　————. "The Mind's Construction in the Face." *PQ* 20 (1941): 400–12.
Surveys references to physiognomy and metoposcopy in Elizabethan literature, including works by Chapman, R. Greene, Jonson, Nashe, Shakespeare, Walkington, and J. Webster.

401.　Collins, Robert A. "The Christian Significance of the Astrological Tradition: A Study in the Literary Use of Astral Symbolism in English Literature from Chaucer to Spenser." *DA* 31 (1970–71): 353A.
See item 211 for annotation.

402.　Craig, Hardin. *The Enchanted Glass: The Elizabethan Mind in Literature.* New York: Oxford UP, 1936. 293 pp.
Rev. Douglas Bush, *MLN* 52 (1937): 442–44; B. E. C. Davis, *MLR* 32 (1937): 90–91.
Provides an overview of the scientific, philosophic, and social doctrines informing the Elizabethan worldview as reflected in Elizabethan literature. Covers alchemy, astrology, cosmology, and Elizabethan psychology.

403.　Cruttwell, Patrick. "Physiology and Psychology in Shakespeare's Age." *JHI* 12 (1951): 75–89.
Describes some theories of physiology and psychology current in sixteenth- and early seventeenth-century England and examines their appearance in imaginative works by Davies, Donne, Marlowe, J. Webster, and especially Shakespeare. Draws on Vicary's *Profitable Treatise of the Anatomie of Mans Body* (1548).

404.　Davril, Robert. "The Use of Physiology in the Elizabethan Drama with Special Reference to John Ford." *Literature and Science.* Proc. of the Sixth Triennial Congress of the International Federation for Modern Languages and Literatures. Oxford, 1954. Oxford: Blackwell, 1955. 126–31.
Examines the role played by the physiology of Plato, Aristotle, Hippocrates, and Galen in delineating characters in Elizabethan drama. Contrasts this common use of physiology with Ford's use of Burton's *Anatomy of Melancholy* in *The Lover's Melancholy* and *The Queen.*

405.　Demerson, Guy. "Météorologie et poésie française de la Renaissance." *French Renaissance Studies, 1540–70: Humanism and the Encyclopedia.* Ed. Peter Sharratt. Edinburgh: Edinburgh UP, 1976. 81–94.
Studies the assimilation of meteorological data into sixteenth-century French poetry, including Baïf's "Météores" and Scève's "Microcosme."

406.   Dick, Hugh G. "The Doctrines of the Ptolemaic Astronomy in the Literature of the English Renaissance." Diss. Cornell U, 1938.
Not seen for annotation.

407.   Dunstan, Florence J. "Medical Science in the Picaresque Novels, 1550–1650." Diss. U of Texas, Austin, 1936.
Not seen for annotation.

408.   Fletcher, Robert. *Medical Lore in the Older English Dramatists and Poets (Exclusive of Shakespeare). Read before the Historical Club of the Johns Hopkins Hospital, May 13, 1895.* Baltimore: Friedenwald, 1895. 35 pp. Rpt. from *The Bulletin of the Johns Hopkins Hospital,* May-June 1895.
Discusses references to the status of medicine and physicians, venereal disease, uroscopy, and other medical matters in works by F. Beaumont and J. Fletcher, Chapman, Glapthorne, Herrick, Jonson, Massinger, Middleton, and others.

409.   Forest, Louise C. Turner. "A Caveat for Critics against Invoking Elizabethan Psychology." *PMLA* 61 (1946): 651–72.
Maintains that Elizabethan "psychology" is a construction of modern scholarship, a selective synthesis of concepts drawn from works of psychological lore that are themselves eclectic and contradictory. Claims that analyzing Elizabethan poetry in the light of this theory obscures its imaginative splendor. An appropriate interpretation should invoke the "plain poetical meanings" of the works themselves.

410.   Hall, Michael G. "Renaissance Science in Puritan New England." *Aspects of the Renaissance: A Symposium.* Ed. Archibald R. Lewis. Proc. of a Conference on the Meaning of the Renaissance. Austin: U of Texas P, 1967. 123–36.
Surveys the chief sources of scientific information for New England Puritans, examines the reflection of Renaissance science in New England almanacs, and notes the scientific pursuits of I. Mather, C. Mather, Bradstreet, and others.

411.   Harrison, Thomas P., Jr. "The Literary Background of Renaissance Poisons." *University of Texas Studies in English* 27 (1948): 35–67.
Reviews Renaissance literature devoted to the description and classification of poisons and considers its applications to a study of poisons in Renaissance drama. Gives particular attention to contact poisons, slow poisons, and sleeping potions, emphasizing the use of sleeping potions as a device in dramas by Dekker, Haughton, T. Heywood, Marlowe, Middleton, Shakespeare, Sharpham, and others.

412.   Hellman, C. Doris. "A Poem on the Occasion of the Nova of 1572." *Philosophy and Humanism: Renaissance Essays in Honor of Paul Oskar Kristeller.* Ed. Edward P. Mahoney. New York: Columbia UP, 1976. 306–09.
Comments briefly on a poem by Swiss theologian Rudolph Gualter (1518–86). Links the poem's mention of the nova of 1572 with theological prognostications of doom.

413.   Heninger, S. K., Jr. *A Handbook of Renaissance Meteorology with Particular Reference to Elizabethan and Jacobean Literature.* Durham: Duke UP, 1960.

New York: Greenwood, 1968. 269 pp.
Rev. R. H. Syfret, *RES* ns 12 (1961): 288–89.
The first two divisions of this book discuss Elizabethan meteorology, which encompassed the study of clouds, dew, winds, lightning, comets, rainbows, the Milky Way, and earthquakes. The third division examines the meteorological imagery in works by Chapman, Donne, Jonson, Marlowe, Shakespeare, and Spenser.

414.   ———. *Touches of Sweet Harmony: Pythagorean Cosmology and Renaissance Poetics*. San Marino: Huntington Library, 1974. 446 pp.
Rev. Wayne Shumaker, *JEGP* 74 (1975): 231–33; Dwight J. Sims, *JAAC* 34 (1975–76): 217–19; Howard Baker, *RenQ* 29 (1976): 130–31; Alan Brissenden, *RES* ns 27 (1976): 337–39; Robert M. Schuler, *ELN* 14 (1976–77): 62–67; O. B. Hardison, Jr., *SQ* 28 (1977): 121–26; James V. Mirollo, *CL* 29 (1977): 74–76; Thomas P. Roche, Jr., *MLR* 72 (1977): 381–83.
Assesses the extent of Renaissance knowledge of Pythagoras and surveys Renaissance expositions of Pythagorean beliefs; reconstructs Pythagorean doctrines as known during the Renaissance, including doctrines of number, cosmos, deity, and time, and considers their relation to occult sciences and moral philosophy; and examines the aesthetic assumptions deriving from Pythagorean cosmology and their influence on Renaissance poetry and poetics. Includes chapters on the concept of poet as creator, metaphors as cosmic correspondence, and the poem as a literary microcosm.

415.   Howe, Linda K. "The English Anatomy, 1543–1640: History, Metaphor, Genre." *DAI* 39 (1978): 1590A.
Traces the history of medical anatomy, emphasizing Andreas Vesalius's *De humani corporis fabrica* (1543) and its influence on literary anatomies such as Burton's *Anatomy of Melancholy* (1621) and Donne's *Anatomy of the World* (1611).

416.   Johnson, Francis R. "Elizabethan Drama and the Elizabethan Science of Psychology." *English Studies Today*. Ed. C. L. Wrenn and G. Bullough. Proc. of the International Conference of University Professors of English. Magdalen Coll., Oxford, August 1950. London: Oxford UP, 1951. 111–19.
Reassesses the value of Elizabethan psychology for studying characterization in Elizabethan drama. Concludes that though some knowledge of the science is indispensable to an accurate interpretation of Elizabethan drama, critics should not presuppose a more precise analysis or consistent doctrine in the widely varied body of Elizabethan psychological treatises than is actually there.

417.   ———. "The Progress of the Copernican Astronomy among English Scientists to 1645 and Its Reflection in Literature from Spenser to Milton." Diss. Johns Hopkins U, 1935.
Not seen for annotation.

418.   Lewis, C. S. *The Discarded Image: An Introduction to Medieval and Renaissance Literature*. Cambridge: Cambridge UP, 1964. 231 pp.
See item 223 for annotation.

419.	Linden, Stanton J. "Alchemy and the English Literary Imagination: 1385 to 1633." *DAI* 33 (1972–73): 3591A–92A.
	See item 160 for annotation.

420.	Lyons, Bridget Gellert. *Voices of Melancholy: Studies in Literary Treatments of Melancholy in Renaissance England.* New York: Barnes; London: Routledge, 1971. New York: Norton, 1975. 189 pp.
	Following a brief exposition of Renaissance theories of melancholy and a review of their backgrounds, the author examines various uses of melancholy in Renaissance satire, comedy, and tragedy; studies melancholy in Marston's works and in Shakespeare's *Hamlet*; analyzes the literary aspects of Burton's *Anatomy of Melancholy*, noting the work's relation to other Renaissance treatises on the subject; and concludes with a chapter on melancholy in Milton's *Il Penseroso*.

421.	Maynard, Katharine. "Science in Early English Literature 1550 to 1650." *Isis* 17 (1932): 94–126.
	Outlines the major scientific developments from 1550 to 1650 and notes corresponding changes in the literature of the period. Treats mathematics, astronomy, astrology, alchemy, and cartography in writers such as R. Greene, Jonson, Milton, Nashe, Shakespeare, and Wilkins.

422.	Mazzeo, Joseph A. "Aspects of Wit and Science in the Renaissance." *Microfilm Abstracts* 11 (1951): 114–15.
	Discusses the unity of scientific, philosophic, and poetic imagination in the "metaphysical" poetry of the Renaissance.

423.	Meadows, A. J. *The High Firmament: A Survey of Astronomy in English Literature.* Leicester: Leicester UP, 1969. 207 pp.
	See item 162 for annotation.

424.	Naïs, Hélène. *Les animaux dans la poésie française de la Renaissance.* Paris: Didier, 1961. 718 pp.
	Rev. Don Cameron Allen, *Isis* 53 (1962): 408; Marcel Françon, *MLN* 77 (1962): 327–28.
	The French Renaissance poets' interest in zoology was not scientific but personal and poetic. Du Bartas, Ronsard, and others considered science and poetry incompatible. At a time when science was emerging from the realm of legends, the poets used scientific observations to propound a moral theory.

425.	Oruch, Jack B. "Topography in the Prose and Poetry of the English Renaissance, 1540–1640." *DA* 25 (1964): 2966.
	Discusses the significance of topographical description in works by Daniel, Jonson, Milton, Sidney, Spenser, and others.

426.	Parr, Johnstone. "Cosmological Fortune: Astrology in the Elizabethan and Jacobean Drama." Diss. Vanderbilt U, 1944.
	Not seen for annotation.

427. ———. *Tamburlaine's Malady, and Other Essays on Astrology in Elizabethan Drama*. University: U of Alabama P, 1953. Westport: Greenwood, 1971. 158 pp.
Rev. Carroll Camden, *MLN* 69 (1954): 512–14; C. Doris Hellman, *Isis* 45 (1954): 398–99; J. C. Bryce, *RES* ns 6 (1955): 306–08.

A collection of essays (several previously published) that use Renaissance astrological principles and techniques to interpret the astrological allusions in Elizabethan and Jacobean drama. Includes chapters on Marlowe's *Tamburlaine* and *Doctor Faustus*, Lyly's *Woman in the Moone*, R. Greene's *Scottish Historie of James the Fourth*, Shakespeare's *King Lear*, J. Webster's *Duchess of Malfi*, and Jonson's *Alchemist*. (For annotations of reprinted material see items 482, 491, 492, and 597.)

428. Patrides, C. A. "The Microcosm of Man: Further References to a Commonplace." *N&Q* ns 10 (1963): 282–86.

Catalogs references in Renaissance popular literature to the hierarchical structure of the universe and the relation between the microcosm and the macrocosm.

429. ———. "The Microcosm of Man: Some References to a Commonplace." *N&Q* ns 7 (1960): 54–56.

Cites 55 Renaissance prose works containing allusions to the commonplace analogy between the macrocosm and the microcosm of human beings.

430. Petti, Anthony G. "Beasts and Politics in Elizabethan Literature." *E&S* 16 (1963): 68–90.

Surveys the allegorical use of beast imagery by Elizabethan writers, including R. Greene, Lyly, Nashe, Shakespeare, and Spenser. Among the sources for this imagery are the Bible, Aristotle's *Historia animalium*, Pliny the Elder's *Naturalis historia*, and various physiognomical treatises from Aristotle to Giambattista della Porta.

431. Plattard, Jean. "Le système de Copernic dans la littérature française au XVIᵉ siècle." *Revue du seizième siècle* 1 (1913): 220–37.

Traces the slow dissemination of Copernican heliocentrism in France as reflected in sixteenth-century literature. Shows that the poets of the Pléiade continued to uphold the Ptolemaic system, as did Du Bartas. Not until Montaigne's *Essais* appeared was the Copernican system fully acknowledged.

432. Randolph, Mary C. "The Medical Concept in English Renaissance Satiric Theory: Its Possible Relationships and Implications." *SP* 38 (1941): 125–57.

A ubiquitous and varied use of medical metaphors was a prominent characteristic of English Renaissance satiric theory. A small number of these metaphors either represent satire as having a potentially lethal power or portray the satirist as taking a sadistic and vengeful pleasure in using satire to harm the human body. These may have derived from primitive Celtic incantational and magical verse. A larger number of medical metaphors assign a cathartic effect to satire, partly anticipating the eighteenth-century development of a philosophical satire analyzing the morality of human behavior.

433.   Roberts, David A. "Mystery to Mathematics Flown: Time and Reality in the Renaissance." *CentR* 19 (1975): 136–56.

Sketches the disintegration of the medieval worldview, especially its concept of time, and the ascendency of a mathematically oriented concept of time under the influence of the Copernican revolution. The new temporal concepts and associated changes in the understanding of reality and of humankind's relation to the universe are reflected in Renaissance literature.

434.   Robin, P. Ansell. *Animal Lore in English Literature.* London: Murray, 1932. Folcroft: Folcroft, 1970. Norwood: Norwood, 1975. Philadelphia: West, 1976. 196 pp.

See item 169 for annotation.

435.   ———. *The Old Physiology in English Literature.* New York: Dutton; London: Dent, 1911. 184 pp.

Renaissance writers were generally well acquainted with a tradition of medicine and physiology based largely on the authority of Galen. Cites references to the four elements, anatomy, digestion, the four humors, blood, and other aspects of physiology in works by P. Fletcher, Jonson, Shakespeare, and many other Renaissance authors.

436.   Russell, H. K. "Elizabethan Dramatic Poetry in the Light of Natural and Moral Philosophy." *PQ* 12 (1933): 187–95.

Stresses the affinities between the representation of the bodily passions in Elizabethan drama and Elizabethan theories of physiology and psychology.

437.   ———. "Tudor and Stuart Dramatizations of the Doctrines of Natural and Moral Philosophy." *SP* 31 (1934): 1–27.

Surveys and discusses Tudor and Stuart morality plays and masques whose themes emphasize doctrines drawn from natural philosophy (such as the Empedoclean doctrine of the four elements) and moral philosophy (especially the psychological doctrine of the humors). Works studied include Medwall's *Goodly Interlude of Nature* (c. 1510), the anonymous *A New Interlude and a Merry of the Nature of the Four Elements*, Redford's *Play of Wit and Science* (c. 1530), Tomkis's *Lingua* (1607), and Holyday's *Technogamia: Or, The Marriages of the Arts* (1618).

438.   Schmidt, Albert-Marie. *La poésie scientifique en France au seizième siècle.* Paris: Michel, 1938. 378 pp.

Examines the Pléiade poets' perception of the Aristotelian-Ptolemaic world system, their attitudes toward the astrological trends of their time, and the poetic cosmologies they developed by personally synthesizing various scientific opinions. Analyzes the scientific poetry of Du Bartas, Peletier du Mans, Ronsard, Scève, and others.

438a.   Schuler, Robert M., ed. "Three Renaissance Scientific Poems." *SP* 75.5 (1978): 1–152.

An edition of scientific poetry by Blomfild, Ballista, and Buchanan. Introductions and notes discuss the scientific content in the printed works.

439.   Secret, François. "Littérature et alchimie." *BHR* 35 (1973): 499–531.
Comments on fifteenth- and sixteenth-century French scholarship reflecting an interest in and knowledge of alchemy. Among the doctors, scientists, poets, and scholars studied are Brahe, Bureteau, Fabre, Melissus, and Rossellet.

440.   ———. "Palingenesis, Alchemy and Metempsychosis in Renaissance Medicine." *Ambix* 26 (1979): 81–92.
This historical treatment of the relations among palingenesis, alchemy, and metempsychosis in Renaissance medicine cites allusions to these concepts in poetry such as Joseph du Chesne's *Grand miroir du monde* (1593), and Du Bartas's *Sepmaine de la création du monde* (1584).

441.   Silvette, Herbert. *The Doctor on the Stage: Medicine and Medical Men in Seventeenth-Century England*. Ed. Francelia Butler. Knoxville: U of Tennessee P, 1967. 291 pp. (An earlier version appeared in *AMH* ns 8 [1936]: 520–40; ns 9 [1937]: 62–87, 174–88, 264–79, 371–94, 482–507.) Rev. Larry D. Clark, *QJS* 54 (1968): 196; Seymour L. Gross, *SCN* 26 (1968): 13.
Attempts to determine the position of medicine in seventeenth-century English life by examining the medical metaphors and allusions in the popular literature of the period, especially drama. Topics discussed include uroscopy, bleeding, herbal remedies, charms and potions, syphilis, quacks and quackery, the virtuoso, and medical satire. Among the many authors considered are F. Beaumont and J. Fletcher, S. Butler, Dekker, J. Ford, Jonson, Lyly, Marlowe, Marston, Nashe, Shadwell, Shakespeare, and J. Webster.

442.   Soellner, Rolf. "The Madness of Hercules and the Elizabethans." *CL* 10 (1958): 309–24.
Outlines the classical medical and physiological background of the literary tradition of Hercules's madness, citing works by Euripides, Aristotle, and Seneca. Discusses the vestiges of this tradition in Elizabethan drama by R. Greene, T. Heywood, Marston, and Shakespeare.

443.   Taylor, Donn E. "The Theatre of the Mind: Aesthetic Response and the Renaissance Imagination." *DAI* 38 (1977): 2819A.
Links the characteristic sixteenth-century symbolic and aesthetic models with medieval cosmology and contrasts them with those Renaissance concepts that emerged in conjunction with the acceptance of Copernicanism. Applies the relation between artistic structures and modes of thought typical of Renaissance audiences to an examination of visual art, poetry, and drama, including Shakespeare's *As You Like It* and Spenser's *Faerie Queene*.

444.   Taylor, F. Sherwood. "The Argument of Morien and Merlin: An English Alchemical Poem." *Chymia* 1 (1948): 23–35.
Publishes, with brief commentary, a fragment of the alchemical poem "The Argument between Morien the Father and Merline the Sonne: How the Philosophers' Stone Should Be Wrought" (15th cent.?), included in Elias Ashmole's "Theatrum chemicum britannicum" (1652).

445.   Weidhase, Helmut. "Himmelsauskunft in irdischer Sprache: Materialien
        und Gedanken zum literarisch-publizistischen Kleingenre 'Horoskop.' "
        DU 30.6 (1978): 109–38.
Examines horoscopes within the context of astrological and literary traditions,
citing works by Brant, Fischart, and Grimmelshausen. Astrological forecasts in
contemporary German weekly magazines such as *Der Stern* and *Quick* reveal that the
fascination with horoscopes is as evident today as in ancient and medieval times.

446.   Whittaker, E. J. "Natural History and Literature, 1550–1660." Diss. U
        of Durham, 1977.
Not seen for annotation.

447.   Wilson, John D. "Some Uses of Physiognomy in the Plays of Shakespeare,
        Jonson, Marlowe and Dekker." *DA* 26 (1965–66): 4642.
Most Elizabethans were ambivalent about physiognomy, but the authors cited
articulated its principles imaginatively in their plays.

Individual Authors

Jean Antoine de Baïf (1532–89)

448.   Simpson, Lurline V. "Some Unrecorded Sources of Baïf's *Livre des météores.*"
        PMLA 47 (1932): 1012–27.
Traces the scientific references in Baïf's *Livre des météores* to their sources in
Aristotle, Vergil, Manilius, Hyginus, Seneca, Pliny the Elder, and Pontano.

Remy Belleau (1528?–77)

449.   Martin, Rose-Ann. "Nature and the Cosmos in the Works of Remy Bel-
        leau." *DAI* 36 (1975–76): 1561A.
Belleau's poetry blends elements of science and mysticism drawn from the as-
tronomy, medicine, and natural science of his day. This study emphasizes how
Belleau uses the concept of celestial influence to decipher nature poetically.

John Bellenden (fl. 1533–87)

450.   Eade, J. C. "Astronomical Reference in John Bellenden's 'Propheme of the
        Cosmographe.' " *ScLJ* 6.1 (1979): 69–71.
Attempts to date Bellenden's poem by citing a reference to an eclipse that may
have occurred on 18 December 1526.

William Blomfild (16th cent.)

451.   Schuler, Robert M. "An Alchemical Poem: Authorship and Manuscripts."
        Library 5th ser. 28 (1973): 240–42.
Provides a brief bibliographic history of "Bloomfield's Blossoms," the most fre-

quently copied sixteenth-century alchemical poem; a record of its manuscripts; and evidence demonstrating that its author is William Blomfild.

452.   ————. "Hermetic and Alchemical Traditions of the English Renaissance and Seventeenth Century, with an Essay on Their Relation to Alchemical Poetry, as Illustrated by an Edition of 'Blomfild's Blossoms,' 1557." *DAI* 32 (1972): 3963A–64A.
Studies the relations between Hellenistic material alchemy and the Hermeticism of Hermes Trismegistus as illustrated in Blomfild's poem "Blomfild's Blossoms."

453.   ————. "William Blomfild, Elizabethan Alchemist." *Ambix* 20 (1973): 75–87.
Provides biographical information on the author of the important alchemical poem "Bloomfields Blossoms."

Giovanni Boccaccio (1313–75)

454.   Bloomfield, Morton W. "The Source of Boccaccio's *Filostrato* III, 74–79 and Its Bearing on the MS Tradition of Lucretius, *De rerum natura*." *ClasPhil* 47 (1952): 162–65.
Attempts to establish Lucretius's *De rerum natura* as Boccaccio's source for astrological or cosmological matters.

455.   Cottino-Jones, Marga. "Boccaccio e la scienza." *Letteratura e scienza nella storia della cultura italiana*. Atti del IX congresso dell'associazione internationale per gli studi di lingua e letteratura italiana. Palermo, Messina, Catania, 21–25 Apr. 1976. Palermo: Manfredi, 1978. 356–70.
Outlines the state of science in Boccaccio's time and examines Boccaccio's use of scientific and medical concepts in his *Decamerone* and other works.

456.   Pace, Antonio. "Sage and Toad: A Boccaccian Motif (and a Misinterpretation by Musset)." *Italica* 48 (1971): 187–99.
Alfred de Musset misrepresented the significance of the sage-and-toad motif in his *Simone conte imité de Boccace* (1840), a paraphrase of the tale of Simona and Pasquino from Boccaccio's *Decameron*. The author discusses the medical background of Boccaccio's image.

Sebastian Brant (1457–1521)

457.   Benedek, Thomas G. "The Image of Medicine in 1500: Theological Reactions to *The Ship of Fools*." *BHM* 38 (1964): 329–42.
In Brant's collection of 110 verses, *Das Narrenschiff* (1494), two verses (nos. 38 and 55) concern medical practices. The author translates these verses and compares them with two later works that they inspired: Geiler von Kaysersberg's sermon "Sick Fools" (1498) and Barclay's *The Shyp of Folys of the Worlde* (1509).

George Buchanan (1506–82)

458.   Naiden, James R., ed. *The* Sphera *of George Buchanan (1506–1582): A
        Literary Opponent of Copernicus and Tycho Brahe*. Philadelphia: Allen, 1952.
        184 pp.
Buchanan's *Sphera* contains ". . . extensive attacks upon the fundamental as-
sumptions of Copernicus's *De Revolutionibus* (1543) and upon parts of Tycho Brahe's
De Nova Stella (1572), the two most important astronomical treatises of the century."
The author summarizes the literary and scientific background of the poem, discusses
its place in the tradition of Neo-Latin didactic poetry, traces the stages in its
composition, and appraises its literary merits. Includes an English translation of the
Sphera.

George Chapman (1559?–1634)

459.   Heninger, S. K., Jr. "Chapman's *Hymnus in noctem*, 376–377, and Shake-
        speare's *Love's Labour's Lost*, IV, iii, 346–347." *Expl* 16.8 (1958): item 49.
Notes that the cited passages of Chapman and Shakespeare both refer to the
meteorological aspects of melancholy.

460.   Parr, Johnstone. "The Duke of Byron's Malignant *Caput Algol*." *SP* 43
        (1946): 194–202.
Claims that the motivating force behind the hero's tragedy in Chapman's play
Byron's Conspiracy lies in the unfortunate configuration of Byron's natal horoscope.
Explains the astrological significance of the horoscope, especially its reference to the
Caput Algol, a sign presaging decapitation.

Guillaume de Saluste Du Bartas (1544–90)

461.   Monod, Théodore. "Notes sur le vocabulaire ichthyologique de Du Bartas
        (1578)." *RSH* 117 (1965): 5–27.
Monod, an ichthyologist, examines Du Bartas's ichthyological vocabulary, par-
ticularly in *Cinquiesme jour de la sepmaine ou création du monde* (1578), and discusses
Du Bartas's possible sources.

462.   Whitaker, Virgil K. "Du Bartas' Use of Lucretius." *SP* 33 (1936): 134–
        46.
In Du Bartas's encyclopedic poem *The Divine Weekes and Workes*, the scientific
doctrines that appear to have been derived from Lucretius's *De rerum natura* include
the principle of the conservation of matter and the anthropological notion of the
rise of primitive human beings from savagery.

Nicolò Franco (1515–70)

463.   Schullian, Dorothy M. "Nicolò Franco, Vilifier of Medicine." *BHM* 24
        (1950): 26–37.

Franco's *Pistole vulgari* (1538), written as an invective against the medical practices of his day, illuminates the state of sixteenth-century medicine.

Robert Greene (1558?–92)

464.   Allen, Don C. "Science and Invention in Greene's Prose." *PMLA* 53 (1938): 1007–18.
Studies the sources for the images of natural history in Greene's prose. Emphasizes the distinctions among sources from scientific literature, literary works, and Greene's imagination.

465.   Lievsay, John L. "Greene's Panther." *PQ* 20 (1941): 296–303.
Comments on the scientific accuracy of Greene's panther imagery.

466.   Parr, Johnstone. "Sources of the Astrological Prefaces in Robert Greene's *Planetomachia*." *SP* 46 (1949): 400–10.
Maintains that Greene derived the astrological content of the *Planetomachia* largely from Lucian's *De astrologia* and corrupt versions of treatises by Manilius, Ptolemy, and Pontano.

467.   Sadler, Lynn Veach. "Alchemy and Greene's *Friar Bacon and Friar Bungay*." *Ambix* 22 (1975): 111–24.
Briefly summarizes R. Bacon's alchemical interests and assesses the extent to which the alchemical tradition influenced Greene's characterizations in *Friar Bacon and Friar Bungay* (c. 1589). Maintains that the dominant magical elements of the play overlap with alchemical elements and that study of the alchemical aspects offers additional insight into the verbal texture and larger themes of the work.

468.   Wells, Stanley. "Greene and Pliny." *N&Q* ns 8 (1961): 422–24.
Greene's *Planetomachia* appears to owe much to the anonymous sixteenth-century *Secrets and Wonders of the World*, which abstracts material from Pliny the Elder's *Natural History*.

Christoph von Hirschenberg (16th cent.)

469.   Telle, Joachim. "Der Alchemist im Rosengarten: Ein Gedicht von Christoph von Hirschenberg für Landgraf Wilhelm IV. von Hessen-Kassel und Graf Wilhelm von Zimmern." *Euphorion* 71 (1977): 283–305.
This study of Hirschenberg's alchemical poem "Panegyrici rithmi de rosario philosophico aique eiusdem rosis philosophicis" provides a formal and structural analysis of the work, dates it as 1589 or 1590, and discusses its principal source: Bernard of Trevisan's *De chemia, Hermetische philosophia, de chymico miraculo*, a fifteenth-century alchemical text.

Ben Jonson (1572–1637)

470.   Clancy, James H. "Ben Jonson and the 'Humours.' " *TA* 11 (1953): 15–23.

Summarizes Jonson's use of the Renaissance theory of the physiological humors in his comic characterizations. Focuses on *Every Man Out of His Humour*.

471.   Dale, Leona F. "Health Imagery and Rhetoric in the Major Comedies of Ben Jonson." *DA* 30 (1969–70): 3427A.
Studies the impact of Jonson's use of medical imagery on the characterizations, plot developments, and themes of his comedies.

472.   Duncan, Edgar Hill. "Alchemy in Chaucer, Jonson, and Donne." Diss. Vanderbilt U, 1941.
Not seen for annotation.

473.   ———. "The Alchemy in Jonson's *Mercury Vindicated*." *SP* 39 (1942): 625–37.
Jonson's masque *Mercury Vindicated from the Alchemists at Court* (1615) is, in its details and dramatic conception, a direct satire of alchemical principles and practice. Duncan analyzes its alchemical elements by referring to the alchemical literature available in Jonson's day.

474.   ———. "Jonson's *Alchemist* and the Literature of Alchemy." *PMLA* 61 (1946): 699–710.
The major alchemical speeches of *The Alchemist* take on a richer meaning when read against the background of medieval and Renaissance alchemical treatises available to Jonson. Duncan notes the sources of Jonson's remarkable knowledge of alchemy, including Paracelsus, Ashmole, and Arnald of Villanova.

475.   ———. "Jonson's Use of Arnald of Villa Nova's *Rosarium*." *PQ* 21 (1942): 435–38.
Proposes that a source for three speeches from Jonson's *Alchemist* (2.1.38–40; 2.1.63–68; and 2.3.102–14) may have been Arnald's alchemical treatise *Rosarium philosophorum*.

476.   Fieler, Frank B. "The Impact of Bacon and the New Science upon Jonson's Critical Thought in *Timber*." *RenP* (1960): 84–92.
In attempting to forge an original critical method in *Timber*, Jonson was influenced by F. Bacon's *Advancement of Learning*, which outlines methods for the true transmission of knowledge.

477.   Flachmann, Michael. "Ben Jonson and the Alchemy of Satire." *SEL* 17 (1977): 259–80.
"Jonson's use of the standard terminology of alchemy serves also as a figurative aid in effecting the satiric exposure of the flawed characters in the play [*The Alchemist*] and as a powerful metaphor that explains his conception of the proper relation between a playwright and his audience."

478.   Kernan, Alvin B. "Alchemy and Acting: The Major Plays of Ben Jonson." *SLitI* 6.1 (1973): 1–22.
Studies Jonson's treatment of character development in plays such as *The Alchemist*,

Every Man Out of His Humour, *Volpone*, and *Bartholomew Fair*. By seeking an "alchemical" transformation to higher levels of physical and spiritual existence, his characters reveal the limitations of human nature.

478a.   ———, ed. *Ben Jonson:* The Alchemist. New Haven: Yale UP, 1974. 246 pp.
This edition of Jonson's *Alchemist* contains an appendix entitled "Jonson's Use of Alchemy and a Glossary of Alchemical Terms" (227–39) which covers some central alchemical doctrines and expressions used by Jonson.

479.   Linden, Stanton J. "Jonson and Sendivogius: Some New Light on *Mercury Vindicated from the Alchemists at Court.*" *Ambix* 24 (1977): 39–54.
Views Jonson's masque of 1616 as a profitable work through which to investigate the artistic potential inherent in alchemy. Maintains that in both the design and the execution of *Mercury Vindicated* Jonson relied on *Dialogus mercurii, alchymistae et naturae* (c. 1607), an alchemical treatise by Michael Sendivogius. Examines also the relation between literary and alchemical imagination by closely comparing the treatise with Jonson's masque.

480.   McFarland, Ronald E. "Jonson's *Magnetic Lady* and the Reception of Gilbert's *De magnete.*" *SEL* 11 (1971): 283–93.
Assesses the impact on Jonson's *Magnetic Lady* of William Gilbert's *De magnete* (1600) and of such popularizations of Gilbert's theories as Mark Ridley's *Short Treatise of Magneticall Bodies and Motions* (1613) and William Barlow's *Magneticall Advertisements* (1616).

481.   Nicholl, Charles. *The Chemical Theatre*. London: Routledge, 1980. 292 pp.
See item 593 for annotation.

482.   Parr, Johnstone. "Non-alchemical Pseudo-Sciences in *The Alchemist.*" *PQ* 24 (1945): 85–89. Rpt. in *Tamburlaine's Malady, and Other Essays on Astrology in Elizabethan Drama*. University: U of Alabama P, 1953. Westport: Greenwood, 1971. 107–11.
Notes that in *The Alchemist* the remarks Jonson's character Subtle makes about physiognomy, chiromancy, metoposcopy, and astrology usually have a sound basis in the pseudoscientific literature of the age.

483.   ———. "A Note on Jonson's *The Staple of News.*" *MLN* 60 (1945): 117.
Reveals the astrological significance of Jonson's reference to the star Hercules (3.4.1–3).

484.   Thayer, C. G. "Theme and Structure in *The Alchemist.*" *ELH* 26 (1959): 23–35.
This discussion of *The Alchemist* stresses Jonson's skillful interweaving of an alchemical theme with a complex dramatic structure based in part on the tenets of alchemy.

Thomas Lodge (1558?–1625)

485.   Duncan, Edgar Hill. "Thomas Lodge's Use of Agrippa's Chapter on Alchemy." *Vanderbilt Studies in the Humanities* 1 (1951): 96–105.
Shows that Lodge's verse epistle "The Anatomie of Alchymie," from *A Fig for Momus* (1595), includes material adapted from Agrippa's *De incertitudine et vanitate scientiarum et artium* (1530).

John Lyly (1553–1606)

486.   Willcox, Alice. "Medical References in the Dramas of John Lyly." *AMH* 10 (1938): 117–26.
Cites references to medical lore, especially herbal medicine, in Lyly's *Midas*, *Endymion*, *Loue's Metamorphosis*, and other plays, noting his probable acquaintance with Bartholomaeus Anglicus's *De proprietatibus rerum*.

Christopher Marlowe (1564–93)

487.   Camden, Carroll, Jr. "Marlowe and Elizabethan Psychology." *PQ* 8 (1929): 69–78.
Provides an overview of Marlowe's allusions to the Elizabethan theory of the humors. Examines *Tamburlaine*, *The Jew of Malta*, and *Hero and Leander*.

488.   ———. "Tamburlaine: The Choleric Man." *MLN* 44 (1929): 430–35.
Explains the physiological, psychological, and astrological aspects of Marlowe's description of Tamburlaine's choleric disposition.

489.   Johnson, Francis R. "Marlowe's Astronomy and Renaissance Skepticism." *ELH* 13 (1946): 241–54.
Marlowe probably derived his understanding of astronomy from the astronomical textbooks current in his student days. He tended to embrace an unconventional, skeptical version of Ptolemaic astronomy instead of the orthodox astronomy of his time. Johnson stresses the astronomical allusions in *Doctor Faustus*.

490.   ———. "Marlowe's 'Imperiall Heaven.' " *ELH* 12 (1945): 35–44.
Explains the Renaissance astronomical signification of the term *imperiall heaven*, which appears frequently in *Doctor Faustus* and *Tamburlaine*.

490a.   Lesser, Linda R. "Christopher Marlowe's *Tamburlaine the Great* and Elizabethan Scientific Contexts." *DAI* 37 (1976): 3649A.
Evaluates the role science plays in "fostering important cultural and intellectual attitudes during the Elizabethan age" and examines *Tamburlaine* in the context of these attitudes.

491.   Parr, Johnstone. "The Horoscope of Mycetes in Marlowe's *Tamburlaine 1*." *PQ* 25 (1946): 371–77. Rpt. as "Foolish Mycetes' Unfortunate Horoscope." *Tamburlaine's Malady, and Other Essays on Astrology in Elizabethan Drama*.

University: U of Alabama P, 1953. Westport: Greenwood, 1971. 24–31.
Elucidates Marlowe's characterization of Mycetes in *Tamburlaine* by citing Renaissance astrological authorities such as Ptolemy, Augier Ferrier, Jerome Cardan, and William Lilly.

492. ———. "Tamburlaine's Malady." *PMLA* 59 (1944): 696–714. Rpt. in *Tamburlaine's Malady, and Other Essays on Astrology in Elizabethan Drama.* University: U of Alabama P, 1953. Westport: Greenwood, 1971. 3–23.
Tamburlaine's death is one of the most unsatisfactorily explained aspects of Marlowe's *Tamburlaine.* This discussion suggests that Tamburlaine's inordinate and innate passions precipitated his death and explains in detail the role played in his decease by the medical, psychophysiological, and astrological concepts his physician refers to.

492a. Rickey, Mary E. "Astronomical Imagery in *Tamburlaine.*" *RenP* (1954): 63–70.
Studies how Marlowe uses two orders of astronomical imagery within the controlling metaphors of the play.

Thomas Middleton (1570?–1627)

492b. Holdsworth, R. V. "The Medical Jargon in *A Fair Quarrel.*" *RES* ns 23 (1972): 448–54.
Attempts to resolve some of the difficulties surrounding Middleton's use and misuse of medical terminology in *A Fair Quarrel.*

Michel Eyquem de Montaigne (1533–92)

493. Clark, Carol E. "Montaigne, auteur scientifique?" *KRQ* 20 (1973): 127–42.
Studies allusions in Montaigne's *Essais* to topics of scientific interest and reveals that Montaigne cannot properly be considered scientific in his outlook, though his witticisms and skepticism toward received scientific dogmas helped prepare the ground for a truly scientific worldview.

Sir Thomas More (1478–1535)

494. Adams, Robert P. "The Social Responsibilities of Science in *Utopia, New Atlantis,* and After." *JHI* 10 (1949): 374–98.
Examines the idea, expressed in More's *Utopia* (1516) and F. Bacon's *New Atlantis* (1627), that applied natural science can lead to the unlimited progress of the human race and compares it to the views of contemporary scientists and critics of science regarding the prospects for social advancement through applied science.

495. Frietzsche, Arthur H. "The Impact of Applied Science upon the Utopian Ideal." *BYUS* 3.3–4 (1960–61): 35–42.
Assesses how various attitudes toward applied science influenced the utopian ideal

in three representative imaginary commonwealths: More's *Utopia* (1516), F. Bacon's *New Atlantis* (1627), and Swift's "Voyage to Laputa" from *Gulliver's Travels* (1727).

Giambattista della Porta (1535–1615)

496.   Rienstra, Miller H. "Giovanni Battista Della Porta and Renaissance Science." *DA* 24 (1963): 2450–51.
Stresses Porta's writings in optics, meteorology, geometry, pneumatics, and physiognomy and discusses their connection with his dramatic works.

François Rabelais (c. 1490–1533)

497.   Antonioli, Roland. *Rabelais et la médecine*. Etudes rabelaisiennes 12. Genève: Droz, 1976. 394 pp.
Rev. Laura G. Durand, *RenQ* 31 (1978): 617–19.
Traces Rabelais's medical training and career and explores medicine's contribution to the thoughts and themes of his works. Analyzes in particular the medical themes in *Quart livre*, *Pantagruel*, *Gargantua*, and *Tiers livre*. For Rabelais, medicine was a way of understanding humankind, society, and the universe.

498.   Brown, Harcourt. "Doctor François Rabelais: Pantagruel and Health." *AnS* 27 (1971): 117–34.
Outlines Rabelais's career as a physician and discusses the contribution his medical knowledge made to his literary works. Rabelais's ideal of health pervades his works from *Gargantua* to *Quart livre*.

499.   Francis, K. H. "The Mechanism of the Magnetic Doors in Rabelais, Book v, Chapter 37." *FS* 13 (1959): 293–303.
Explains the mechanical and magnetic principles of Rabelais's magnetic doors. Rabelais derived his information from Francesco Colonna's *Hypnerotomachia poliphili*.

500.   ———. "Some Popular Scientific Myths in Rabelais: A Possible Source." *Studies in French Literature Presented to H. W. Lawton by Colleagues, Pupils and Friends*. Ed. J. C. Ireson, I. D. McFarlane, and Garnet Rees. Manchester, Eng.: Manchester UP; New York: Barnes, 1968. 121–34.
Suggests that the source of Rabelais's references in *Pantagruel* to such scientific myths and curiosities as invisible inks, the properties of an ivy funnel, and garlic's effects on magnets may have been Ringelbergh's *Experimenta*.

501.   Godlewski, Guy. *Des médecins et des hommes: Léonard de Vinci, Rabelais, Vincent de Paul, médecins de Molière, Lavoisier, Cagliostro, Marat, Bichat, Corvisart, Larrey, O'Meara, Antommarchi, Savigny, Bretonneau, Véron, Gérard de Nerval, Claude Bernard*. Paris: L'expansion, 1972. 389 pp.
Studies the relation of medicine to the lives and works of famous men from Leonardo da Vinci to Bernard and profiles Rabelais as a physician and a writer. Shows that Rabelais's medical knowledge added depth to his novels and that his writing, in turn, influenced medicine and eighteenth-century encyclopedists. A

chapter on Molière discusses his portrayal of doctors and the sources from which he drew his characterizations.

502.   Keller, Abraham C. "The Geophysics of Rabelais' Frozen Words." *Renaissance and Other Studies in Honor of William Leon Wiley*. University of North Carolina Studies in the Romance Languages and Literatures 72. Ed. George B. Daniel, Jr. Chapel Hill: U of North Carolina P, 1968. 151–65.
The findings of contemporary geophysics suggest that Rabelais's description of the thawing of frozen words in *Les œuvres*, book 4, chapters 55–56, may have a scientific basis.

503.   Lamont, Rosette C. "The Pantagruelion: An Occult Voyage." *Centerpoint* 3 (1978–80): 51–58.
Describes the alchemical significance and magical properties of the herb Pantagruelion, a central feature of the imaginary voyage of books 4 and 5 of Rabelais's *Œuvres*.

504.   Lapp, John C. "Three Attitudes toward Astrology: Rabelais, Montaigne, and Pontus de Tyard." *PMLA* 64 (1949): 530–48.
Discusses skepticism toward and rejection of astrology in works by Rabelais, Montaigne, and Tyard.

505.   Margarot, Jean. "Rabelais médecin: La médecine dans son œuvre." *BHR* 16 (1954): 25–40.
Traces Rabelais's general education and medical studies and considers his reputation as a physician. Because Rabelais the man and writer is inseparable from Rabelais the doctor, the extent to which medicine directly influenced his works is difficult to establish. Also discusses *Pantagruel* and *Gargantua*.

506.   Sainéan, Lazare. "L'histoire naturelle et les branches connexes dans l'œuvre de Rabelais." *RSS* 3 (1915): 187–277; 4 (1916): 36–104, 203–306; 5 (1918): 28–74; 6 (1919): 84–113; 7 (1920): 1–45, 185–205; 8 (1921): 1–41. Rpt. as *L'histoire naturelle*. . . . Paris: Champion, 1921. 449 pp.
A lexicographical and etymological study of the language of natural history, providing excellent coverage of the scientific knowledge of the age and special attention to Rabelais's works and scientific sources.

507.   Screech, M. A. "Eleven-Month Pregnancies: A Legal and Medical Quarrel a propos of Gargantua, Chapter Three, Rabelais, Alciati and Tiraqueau." *THR* 99 (1969): 93–106.
Examines the legal and medical background for Rabelais's ideas concerning the possibility of eleven-month pregnancies, as treated in chapter 3 of *Gargantua*. Rabelais cited medical writers such as Hippocrates, Macrobius, and Pliny the Elder in addition to various legal authorities.

508.   Slaughter, Donald. "Medicine in the Life of François Rabelais." *AMH* 3rd ser. 1 (1939): 396–401, 438–51.

Primarily discusses Rabelais's medical training, especially his work as a dissectionist; also treats the anatomical, pharmaceutical, and medical references in *Pantagruel* and other writings.

509.   Smith, W. F. "Rabelais' List of Fowls, Fishes, Serpents and Wild Beasts."
        MLR 13 (1918): 431–38.
Rabelais's descriptions of banquets in *Gargantua* reveal his extensive knowledge of the animal kingdom, drawn from sources such as Pliny the Elder, Galen, and Pierre Gilles.

510.   Tilley, Arthur. "Rabelais and Geographic Discovery." 1. "The *Novus orbis*
        of Simon Grynaeus." *MLR* 2 (1906–07): 317–26; 2. "Jacques Cartier."
        MLR 3 (1907–08): 209–17; 3. "The Short Way to Cathay." *MLR* 5
        (1910): 68–77.
Rabelais took a lively interest in the great geographical discoveries of his day; contrary to previous beliefs, certain sections of *Pantagruel* are founded on fact, not fantasy. The three articles trace the authorities that Rabelais used for his geographical descriptions.

John Rastell (d. 1536)

511.   Nugent, Elizabeth M. "Sources of John Rastell's *The Nature of the Four
        Elements*." *PMLA* 57 (1942): 74–88.
Compares passages from Rastell's work with passages from his scientific sources, which include Bartholomaeus Anglicus's *De proprietatibus rerum* (1495), Sacrobosco's *Textus de sphaera* (1511), Reisch's *Margarita philosophica* (1508), and Waldseemüller's *Cosmographiae introductio* (1507).

511a.   Parks, George B. "The Geography of the *Interlude of the Four Elements*."
        PQ 17 (1938): 251–62.
Evaluates the extent of Rastell's geographical knowledge as revealed in his play and concludes that Rastell was largely ignorant of current discoveries and maps. Suggests that he had "grafted on a roughly Ptolemaic knowledge of geography some imperfect knowledge of the new discoveries."

512.   Parr, Johnstone. "John Rastell's Geographical Knowledge of America."
        PQ 27 (1948): 229–40.
Assesses Rastell's geographical knowledge of the New World by comparing the geographical passages of his play *The Nature of the Four Elements* (1518) to various geographical texts available to him, such as Waldseemüller's *Cosmographiae introductio* (1507) and Schöner's *Luculentissima quaedam terrae totius descripto* (1515).

513.   ———. "More Sources of Rastell's *Interlude of the Four Elements*." *PMLA*
        60 (1945): 48–58.
Suggests that the following works be considered as sources for Rastell's play: Schöner's *Luculentissima quaedam terrae totius descripto* (1515), Stobnicza's *Introduction in Claudii Ptholomai cosmographiam* (1512), Pliny the Elder's *Historia naturalis and*

Kalander of Shepherdes, and Hieronymo de Sancto Marco's *Opusculum universalis mundi machina* (1505).

Pierre de Ronsard (1524?–85)

514. Quainton, Malcolm D. "Ronsard's Philosophical and Cosmological Conceptions of Time." *FS* 23 (1969): 1–22.
Augments Isidore Silver's earlier study of Ronsard's verse "Ronsard's Reflections on the Heavens and Time" (*PMLA* 80 [1965]: 344–64). Quainton emphasizes Ronsard's scientific, cosmological, allegorical, and philosophical use of time in poems such as *Hymne du ciel*, *Hymne de l'eternite*, and *Hymne des astres*.

515. Silver, Isidore. "Ronsard's Reflections on Cosmogony and Nature." *PMLA* 79 (1964): 219–33.
Concerns the influence that Hesiod, Thales, Plato, Lucretius, and others had on Ronsard's speculations on cosmogony and nature, as reflected in *Hymne de la philosophie*, *Hymne de l'automne*, *Hymne du ciel*, *Hymne des astres*, *Hymne de la justice*, *Discours d'un amoureaux despere*, and other works.

Maurice Scève (c. 1510–c. 1564)

516. Smith, Jacqueline C. "Structures scientifiques dans la *Délie* de Maurice Scève." *DAI* 38 (1978): 4872A.
Analyzes the language, imagery, and structure of Scève's sixteenth-century poem *Délie* to demonstrate the influence of astronomy, astrology, and cosmology. Maintains that Scève is a precursor of the Renaissance scientific poets because he used science in his poetry to explain humankind's relation to and place in the universe.

William Shakespeare (1564–1616)

517. Allen, Don Cameron. "Shakspere [sic] and the Doctrine of Cosmic Identities." *ShakAB* 14 (1939): 182–89.
Cites references in Shakespeare's plays to the theory of the macrocosm and the microcosm, which was a central aspect of Renaissance psychology, medicine, and physics.

518. Anderson, Ruth L. *Elizabethan Psychology and Shakespeare's Plays*. Diss. U of Iowa, 1927. University of Iowa Humanistic Studies 3.4. University of Iowa Studies 1st ser. 127. Iowa City: U of Iowa, 1927. New York: Haskell, 1964. New York: Russell, 1966. 182 pp.
Interprets numerous well-known passages from Shakespeare's plays in the context of Elizabethan theories of psychology. Uses the theory of the four elements and the associated humors, the "sciences" of physiognomy and astrology, and the popular belief in the correspondence between the microcosm and the macrocosm to explain the thoughts and actions of many of Shakespeare's characters.

519. Aston, Margaret. "The Fiery Trigon Conjunction: An Elizabethan Astrological Prediction." *Isis* 61 (1970): 159–87.

Shakespeare's astrological reference to the conjunction of Saturn and Venus in *2 Henry IV* (2.4.261–65) takes on a satirical cast if one considers the uproar caused by the astrological prediction of 1583 that the fiery trigon conjunction of Saturn and Jupiter would lead to global upheaval.

520.   Babb, Lawrence. "Hamlet, Melancholy, and the Devil." *MLN* 59 (1944): 120–22.
Traces the Renaissance medical and psychological background of Shakespeare's reference to the association of melancholy, the Devil, and delusion in *Hamlet* (2.2.638–40).

521.   Bachrach, A. G. H. "The Icicle on the Dutchman's Beard." *ES* 45 (1964): 97–104.
General remarks on Shakespeare's imaginative response to developments in astronomy, anatomy, and geographical exploration during the Elizabethan age.

522.   Bergeron, David M. "Alchemy and *Timon of Athens*." *CLAJ* 13 (1969–70): 364–73.
Interprets the gold imagery of *Timon of Athens* in the light of alchemical theory and practice. Maintains that alchemy serves as an informing principle of the play and notes its relation to the work's language and structure.

523.   Bishop, David H. "Shylock's Humour." *ShakAB* 23 (1948): 174–80.
Maintains that Shylock's reference to his "humour" in *The Merchant of Venice* (4.1.35–62) is an allusion to the medieval theory of the physiological humors and not merely, as is sometimes supposed, a synonym for *whim* or *caprice*.

524.   Bradford, F. C. "Shakespeare and Bacon as Horticultural Prophets." *MLN* 48 (1933): 108–10.
References to grafting in Shakespeare's *Winter's Tale* and F. Bacon's *Sylva sylvarum* (1627) anticipate scientific references to hybrids by nearly a century.

525.   Camden, Carroll, Jr. "On Ophelia's Madness." *SQ* 15 (1964): 247–55.
The author, after reviewing previous scholarly opinions, diagnoses the cause of Ophelia's madness as "erotic melancholy," a condition not uncommon in the annals of Elizabethan medicine and psychology.

526.   ———. "The Suffocation of the Mother." *MLN* 63 (1948): 390–93.
Provides the medical background of Shakespeare's reference to the disease called "the mother" (suffocation by choking) in *King Lear*.

527.   Campbell, Lily B. *Shakespeare's Tragic Heroes: Slaves of Passion*. Cambridge: Cambridge UP; New York: Barnes, 1930. London: Methuen, 1961. Gloucester: Smith, 1973. 296 pp.
Discusses the Elizabethan moral philosophy of the passions, in part as informed by medical and physiological concepts such as the theory of the four humors. Examines Shakespeare's *Hamlet*, *Othello*, *King Lear*, and *Macbeth* as tragedies, respectively, of grief, jealousy, wrath, and fear.

528. Campbell, Oscar James. "What Is the Matter with Hamlet?" *YR* 32 (1942–43): 309–22.

Examines the dramatic expression of Hamlet's melancholic disposition and speculates on the medical and psychological significance of melancholy for Renaissance audiences.

529. Carney, Linda L. "Alchemy in Selected Plays of Shakespeare." *DAI* 38 (1978): 4176A.

Relates material from primary alchemical texts to passages in *Hamlet*, *Julius Caesar*, *Macbeth*, and *King Lear*.

530. Clark, Cumberland. *Astronomy in the Poets*. Bournemouth: Sydenham, 1922. Folcroft: Folcroft, 1969. Norwood: Norwood, 1975. Philadelphia: West, 1978. 116 pp.

Catalogs Shakespeare's poetic allusions to astronomical and astrological phenomena, examines the astronomy of Milton's *Paradise Lost*, and notes some astronomical references in M. Arnold, Browning, Byron, P. Shelley, and Tennyson.

531. ————. *Shakespeare and Science: A Study of Shakespeare's Interest in, and Literary and Dramatic Use of, Natural Phenomena; with an Account of Astronomy, Astrology, and Alchemy of His Day, and His Attitude towards These Sciences.* Birmingham: Cornish, 1929. New York: Haskell, 1970. 262 pp.

Includes chapters on Shakespeare's allusions to the sun, the moon, eclipses, the planets, the seasons, earthquakes, rainbows, snow, echoes, and many other natural phenomena.

532. Cole, John W. "Romeo and Rosaline." *Neophil* 24 (1939): 285–89.

Examines Romeo's love for Rosaline in the light of the physical and psychological symptoms sixteenth-century medical science attributed to the condition.

533. Cook, Albert S. "Shakespeare, *Oth.* 3.4.74." *MLN* 21 (1906): 247–50.

Glosses Shakespeare's references to the substance "mummy," noting its various medicinal connotations in works by Du Bartas, F. Bacon, T. Browne, Johnson, and others.

534. Cook, Phyllis. "William Shakspere [sic], Botanist." *ShakAB* 15 (1940): 149–65.

Catalogs the plant references in Shakespeare's plays and makes some comments on their dramatic roles. Though Shakespeare probably had no systematic knowledge of botany, he was familiar with a wide variety of plants and usually described them with remarkable accuracy.

535. Cooke, John. "The Astrology of Shakspere [sic]." *Macmillan's Magazine* 51 (1884–85): 462–69.

Cites allusions to astrology in several of Shakespeare's plays. The references attest to Shakespeare's intimate knowledge of the principles of the pseudoscience.

536. Craig, Hardin. "Shakespeare's Depiction of Passions." *PQ* 4 (1925): 289–301.

Examines the physiological basis of the Elizabethan theory of the passions as used in Shakespeare's works.

537.   Darby, Robert H. "Astrology in Shakespeare's 'Lear.' " *ES* 20 (1938): 250–57.
Considers Shakespeare's satirical attack on astrology in *King Lear* in the context of the late-sixteenth- and early-seventeenth-century controversy over the pseudo-science's merits. Gives specific attention to the possibility that King James's condemnation of astrology influenced Shakespeare's attitude.

538.   Dean, John Candee. "The Astronomy of Shakespeare." *SciMo* 19 (1924): 400–06.
Briefly examines Shakespeare's attitude toward astronomy and his knowledge of the astronomical developments of his time.

539.   Draper, John W. "Benedick and Beatrice." *JEGP* 41 (1942): 140–49.
Analyzes the Elizabethan psychological principles informing Shakespeare's portrayal of Benedick and Beatrice's courtship in *Much Ado about Nothing*. Both characters were choleric in nature.

540.   ———. "Cassius and Brutus." *BHM* 13 (1943): 133–43.
In *Julius Caesar* Shakespeare portrays Cassius as choleric and Brutus as sanguine, deriving the main details of these characterizations from Plutarch's *Life of Brutus*.

541.   ———. "The Character of Richard II." *PQ* 21 (1942): 228–36.
Analyzes Richard's character with reference to the Elizabethan theory of the humors and concludes that Richard exemplifies the mercurial humor.

542.   ———. "The Choleric Cassio." *BHM* 7 (1939): 583–94.
In *Othello* Shakespeare used the Renaissance theory of the four humors to achieve coherence and unity in his depiction of Cassio's choleric personality.

543.   ———. "The Date of *A Midsommer Nights Dreame*." *MLN* 53 (1938): 266–68.
Uses astronomical allusions in *A Midsummer Night's Dream* to fix the date of the play as 1595.

544.   ———. "The Date of *Romeo and Juliet*." *RES* 25 (1949): 55–57.
Astrological references in *Romeo and Juliet* imply a composition date of 1596.

545.   ———. "The 'Gracious Duncan.' " *MLR* 36 (1941): 495–99.
Examines Duncan's speech, behavior, and tragic fate in the light of the sanguine humor Shakespeare attributed to his character.

546.   ———. *The* Hamlet *of Shakespeare's Audience*. Durham: Duke UP, 1938. 254 pp.
Analyzes Hamlet's character in the light of the principles of Elizabethan humoral psychology. Draws on works by Bright, Dariot, Walkington, and others.

547. ———. "Hamlet's Melancholy." *AMH* ns 9 (1937): 142–47.
Relates Hamlet's melancholic disposition to the medical and psychological works
extant in Shakespeare's time, including Burton's *Anatomy of Melancholy*, Bright's
Treatise of Melancholy, and Bartholomaeus Anglicus's *De proprietatibus rerum*.

548. ———. "Humor and Tempo in *The Tempest*." *NM* 52 (1951): 205–17.
Assesses Shakespeare's reliance on the principles of Galenic humoral psychology
and notes possible relations to his characters' speech tempos in *The Tempest*.

549. ———. *The Humors and Shakespeare's Characters*. Durham: Duke UP, 1945.
New York: AMS, 1965. 126 pp.
Rev. Una Ellis-Fermor, *RES* 22 (1946): 234–35; Lawrence Babb, *MLN*
62 (1947): 56–57.
Surveys Shakespeare's use of Elizabethan humoral psychology and related aspects
of astrology in his dramatic characterizations. Includes separate chapters on the
sanguine, phlegmatic, choleric, and melancholic types.

550. ———. "The Jealousy of Iago." *Neophil* 25 (1940): 50–60.
Relates Iago's intricate personality to the Elizabethan theory of the humors and
explains that his jealousy resulted in part from his choleric disposition.

551. ———. "Lady Macbeth." *PsyR* 28 (1941): 479–86.
Shows how Lady Macbeth's temperament fits the choleric humor defined by the
Elizabethan theory of the four humors.

552. ———. "Macbeth, 'Infirme of Purpose.' " *BHM* 10 (1941): 16–26.
The Renaissance theory of the four humors suggests that Macbeth's vacillating
temperament is mercurial.

553. ———. "The Old Age of King Lear." *JEGP* 39 (1940): 527–40.
Links Shakespeare's portrayal of Lear's old age with the Elizabethan pseudoscientific
concept of the ages of human life and the psychological theory of the humors.

554. ———. *The* Othello *of Shakespeare's Audience*. Paris: Didier, 1952. 246
pp.
Cites Elizabethan scientific texts and earlier scientific works to explain the humoral
dispositions of the characters in Shakespeare's *Othello*.

555. ———. "Patterns of Humor and Tempo in *King Lear*." *BHM* 21 (1947):
390–401.
Demonstrates a correlation between the humors of the characters in *King Lear* and
the tempos of their speech.

556. ———. "Patterns of Humor and Tempo in *Macbeth*." *Neophil* 31 (1947):
202–07.
Computes and graphs the speech tempos of the major figures in *Macbeth* and
discusses the various tempos in the context of Galenic humoral psychology.

557.   ———. "Patterns of Tempo and Humour in *Othello*." *ES* 28 (1947): 65–74.
Examines the speech tempos of the four major roles in *Othello*—Desdemona, Othello, Iago, and Cassio—and relates them to Galenic humoral psychology.

558.   ———. "Patterns of Tempo in *Measure for Measure*." *West Virginia University Philological Papers* 9 (1953): 11–19.
Correlates the speech tempos and the psychological natures of the characters in *Measure for Measure* in the light of the theory of the four humors.

559.   ———. "The Psychology of Shakespeare's Timon." *MLR* 35 (1940): 521–25.
Shows how Shakespeare used the theory of the four humors to motivate Timon's psychological evolution.

560.   ———. "The Psychology of Shylock." *BHM* 8 (1940): 643–50.
Studies Shakespeare's portrayal of Shylock's melancholic temperament in *The Merchant of Venice*, drawing on Renaissance medical and pseudoscientific treatises such as Dariot's *Judgement of the Starres*, Lemnuis's *Touchstone of Complexions*, and Bright's *Treatise of Melancholy*.

561.   ———. "Shakespeare's *Coriolanus*: A Study in Renaissance Psychology." *West Virginia University Bulletin, Philological Studies* 3 (1939): 22–36.
Demonstrates that Coriolanus manifests the choleric humor and shows how his character develops step by step in accordance with the Renaissance psychological theory of the humors.

562.   ———. "Shakespeare's Orlando Innamorato." *MLQ* 2 (1941): 179–86.
Uses the Elizabethan psychological theory of the humors to interpret Shakespeare's characterization of Orlando.

563.   ———. "Shakespeare's 'Star-Crossed Lovers.' " *RES* 15 (1939): 16–34.
Shakespeare's astrological allusions lend coherence to the plot of *Romeo and Juliet*.

564.   ———. "Signior Brabantio's Humor." *BHM* 18 (1945): 539–43.
Analyzes the character of Brabantio from *Othello*, revealing that the choleric humor dominated his personality.

565.   ———. "Speech-Tempo and Humor in Shakespeare's Antony." *BHM* 20 (1946): 426–32.
Studies the correlation between Antony's phlegmatic character and the tempo of his speech in *Antony and Cleopatra*. The association of character with speech tempo was a commonplace of Elizabethan popular science.

566.   ———. "The Speech-Tempo of Brutus and of Cassius." *Neophil* 30 (1946): 184–86.
Examines how Brutus and Cassius's speech tempos exemplify their physiological and psychological humors.

567.   ———. *The* Twelfth Night *of Shakespeare's Audience.* Stanford: Stanford
        UP; London: Cumberlege-Oxford UP, 1950. 280 pp.
Quoting copiously from Elizabethan scientific literature, the author shows how
Shakespeare's characterizations in *Twelfth Night* were informed by Elizabethan con-
cepts of astrology, psychology, and the humors.

568.   Edgar, Irving I. *Shakespeare, Medicine and Psychiatry: An Historical Study in
        Criticism and Interpretation.* New York: Philosophical Library, 1970; Lon-
        don: Vision, 1971. 382 pp.
Reassesses Shakespeare's medical and psychiatric knowledge and critically surveys
previous scholarship on the subject, most of which made exaggerated claims for his
knowledge of medicine. Discusses Shakespeare's alleged knowledge of the circulation
of the blood; Elizabethan conceptions of physiology as reflected in Shakespeare's
dramas; astrology, medical practice, and the physician in Shakespeare's works and
in Elizabethan England; and the neuropsychiatry and humoral psychophysiology in
Shakespeare's works, especially *King Lear* and *Hamlet.*

569.   Ellis, Oliver Coligny de Champfleur. *Shakespeare as a Scientist. His Philo-
        sophical Background: A Preliminary Study of the Questionings Explicit in His
        Dialogue, and of the Acceptances Implicit in His Vocabulary.* Manchester, Eng.:
        Sherratt, 1933. Folcroft: Folcroft, 1976. Norwood: Norwood, 1977. Phil-
        adelphia: West, 1978. 42 pp. Rpt. from *Manchester Quarterly* July 1933:
        81–118.
Discusses the influence of Empedoclean and Platonic cosmologies on Shakespeare's
natural philosophy.

570.   Ewing, S. Blaine. "Scientists and Shakespeare." *ShakAB* 23 (1948): 5–
        11.
General remarks on scholarly attempts to catalog the scientific elements of Shakespeare's works.

571.   Ficarra, Bernard J. "Surgical References in Shakespeare." *Essays on Historical
        Medicine.* New York: Froeben, 1948. 89–93.
A cursory glance at references to surgery and surgeons in *The Merchant of Venice,
A Midsummer Night's Dream, Hamlet, Richard II, Othello, Henry VI, Part 2* and *Macbeth.*

572.   Fraser-Harris, D. F. "Biology in Shakespeare." *SciMo* 34 (1932): 54–68.
Notes some biological allusions in Shakespeare's works that are of contemporary
physiological or psychological interest, such as references to the causes of sleep, the
effect of drugs, the circulatory and nervous systems, and vision.

573.   Griffiths, Lemuel M. "Shakespere [sic] and the Practice of Medicine."
        AMH os 3 (1921): 50–61.
Assesses Shakespeare's knowledge of medicine and examines allusions in his major
plays to the physician, surgeon, apothecary, tooth drawer, midwife, and nurse.

574.   Guido, Angelina. "The Humor of Juliet's Nurse." *BHM* 17 (1945):
        297–303.

An analysis of the psychological complexities of Juliet's nurse indicates that she was subject primarily to the mercurial humor, with some admixture of the phlegmatic and melancholic humors.

575.   Guthrie, W. G. "The Astronomy of Shakespeare." *Irish Astronomical Journal* 6 (1964): 201–11.
Cites references in Shakespeare's works to geocentrism, the sun, the moon, eclipses, comets, and other astronomical topics.

576.   Hall, Marie Boas. "Scientific Thought." *Shakespeare in His Own Age*. Shakespeare Survey 17. Ed. Allardyce Nicoll. Cambridge: Cambridge UP, 1964. 138–51.
Surveys the central features of the astronomy, astrology, alchemy, medicine, zoology, and cartography of Shakespeare's age and briefly remarks on the reflection of these sciences in Shakespeare's works.

577.   Hankins, John E. "Hamlet's 'God Kissing Carrion': A Theory of the Generation of Life." *PMLA* 64 (1949): 507–16.
Establishes a connection between the phrase "good kissing carrion" (variant reading: "God kissing carrion") in *Hamlet* 2.2.180 and Aristotelian theories of the spontaneous generation of life.

577a.   Hansen, Abby J. D. "Shakespeare and the Lore of Precious Stones." *CollL* 4 (1977): 210–19.
An understanding of the "age-old magical lapidary tradition" from which Shakespeare's descriptions of precious stones derive enhances one's appreciation of his images.

578.   Harrison, John L. "The Convention of 'Heart and Tongue' and the Meaning of *Measure for Measure*." *SQ* 5 (1954): 1–10.
Shakespeare's heart-tongue figure, which symbolizes the relation between the heart's emotive capacity and the brain's expressive power, serves as the unifying dramatic feature of *Measure for Measure* and reflects Renaissance psychological principles.

579.   Harrison, Thomas P. "Flower Lore in Spenser and Shakespeare: Two Notes." *MLQ* 7 (1946): 175–78.
See item 634 for annotation.

580.   ———. "Shakespeare's Birds." *TSL* 3 (1958): 53–62.
Attempts to assess Shakespeare's ornithological knowledge by analyzing his references to birds.

581.   Heninger, S. K., Jr. "Chapman's *Hymnus in noctem*, 376–377, and Shakespeare's *Love's Labour's Lost*, IV, iii, 346–347." *Expl* 16.8 (1958): item 49.
See item 459 for annotation.

582.   ———. "The Heart's Meteors, a Microcosm:Macrocosm Analogy." *SQ* 7 (1956): 273–75.

Shakespeare's comparison of facial expressions to "meteors" in several plays is based on Renaissance meteorological theory and the microcosm-macrocosm analogy.

583.   Hilliard, Addie S. "Shakespeare's Botanical Imagery: Its Meaning to the Elizabethan Audience and Its Dramatic Function in the Plays." *DA* 25 (1964–65): 5906.

Appraises Shakespeare's botanical knowledge, emphasizing the thematic and structural import of the botanical imagery in his plays. Also stresses the probable significance of this imagery for the Elizabethan audience.

584.   Kennedy, William Sloane. "Shakespeare's Astronomy." *Poet-Lore* 13 (1901): 366–79.

Though Shakespeare was probably familiar with the Copernican hypothesis of heliocentrism, the available evidence suggests that he never accepted it. Kennedy proposes alternative readings for three passages sometimes supposed to refer to Copernicanism—*Antony and Cleopatra* 2.7.124, *Coriolanus* 2.2.118, and *Julius Caesar* 1.3.3.

585.   Knoepflmacher, U. C. "The Humors as Symbolic Nucleus in *Henry IV, Part I.*" *CE* 24 (1962–63): 497–501.

Explicates *Henry IV, Part 1*, emphasizing Shakespeare's symbolic use of the Renaissance psychological theory of the humors in the character development and plot structure.

586.   Kocher, Paul H. "Lady Macbeth and the Doctor." *SQ* 5 (1954): 341–49.

Lady Macbeth's encounters with the Doctor of Physick in *Macbeth* acquire dramatic importance if viewed in the light of the religiomedical issues of Shakespeare's age.

587.   Lever, J. W. "Three Notes on Shakespeare's Plants." *RES* ns 3 (1952): 117–29.

Shows that the botanical information in Shakespeare's references to flowers and herbs in *Love's Labour's Lost, Hamlet, Othello, Antony and Cleopatra*, and other plays derives from famous herbals by John Gerard, Henry Lyte, and others.

588.   Macht, David I. "A Physiological and Pharmacological Appreciation of *Hamlet*, Act I, Scene 5, Lines 59–73." *BHM* 23 (1949): 186–94.

The author describes his experiments on the coagulant properties of various drugs known during Shakespeare's time, thus shedding light on Shakespeare's reference in *Hamlet* 1.5.68–70 to the drug hebenon's power to speed coagulation of the blood.

589.   Miller, Donald S., and Ethel H. Davis. "Shakespeare and Orthopedics." *Surgery, Gynecology and Obstetrics* 128 (1969): 358–66.

Surveys Shakespeare's references to orthopedics, including such areas as skeletal defects, amputations and prostheses, bone ache, and gout.

590.   Monsarrat, G. "Notes sur le vocabulaire astronomique et astrologique de Shakespeare." *EA* 13 (1960): 320–30.

Analyzes Shakespeare's astrological and astronomical terminology with reference to Elizabethan astrological treatises and the *New English Dictionary on Historical Principles*.

591.   Muir, Kenneth. "Holland's Pliny and *Othello*." *N&Q* 198 (1953): 513–14.
Suggests that references in *Othello* to mandragora, earthquakes, the Pontic Sea, and "bloody thoughts" may derive from Holland's translation of Pliny the Elder.

591a.   Murray, W. A. "Why Was Duncan's Blood Golden?" *ShS* 19 (1966): 34–44.
Uses Paracelsian medical doctrines to explain Duncan's golden blood in *Macbeth*.

592.   Museus. "The Astronomy of Shakespeare." *Contemporary Review* 94. supp. 10 (1908): 1–6.
Although allusions to astronomical and astrological phenomena abound in Shakespeare's works, none of the references suggests that Shakespeare was acquainted with the new astronomy of Copernicus, Kepler, and Galileo.

593.   Nicholl, Charles. *The Chemical Theatre*. London: Routledge, 1980. 292 pp.
Following a brief exposition of the history of alchemical thought, the author analyzes the alchemical imagery informing Jonson's *Eastward Hoe* and *Alchemist*, Donne's *Songs and Sonets*, and especially Shakespeare's *King Lear*. Claims that *Lear* is a masterpiece of "chemical theatre" and that its structure is deeply alchemical.

594.   Nutt, Sarah M. "The Arctic Voyages of William Barents in Probable Relation to Certain of Shakespeare's Plays." *SP* 39 (1942): 241–64.
Examines passages containing geographical details that Shakespeare may have derived from Gerrit de Veer's narrative account of three voyages undertaken by the explorer William Barents.

595.   O'Brien, Gordon W. "Hamlet IV. v. 156–157." *SQ* 10 (1959): 249–51.
Laertes's speech upon first beholding Ophelia's madness refers to the physiology of the brain and the chemical constitution of tears. The author explains the passage by alluding to Bright's *Treatise of Melancholy* and Bartholomaeus Anglicus's *De proprietatibus rerum*.

596.   O'Sullivan, Mary Isabelle. "Hamlet and Dr. Timothy Bright." *PMLA* 41 (1926): 667–79.
Textual parallels between *A Treatise of Melancholy* and *Hamlet* suggest that Shakespeare may have drawn on Bright's work in characterizing the melancholic Hamlet.

597.   Parr, Johnstone. "Edmund's Nativity in *King Lear*." *ShakAB* 21 (1946): 181–85. Rpt. as "Edmund's Birth under Ursa Major." *Tamburlaine's Malady, and Other Essays on Astrology in Elizabethan Drama*. University: U of Alabama P, 1953. Westport: Greenwood, 1971. 80–84.
Edmund's "rough and lecherous" character can be attributed to the astrological configuration during his birth: he was influenced by the constellation Ursa Major governed by the planets Mars and Venus.

598. Phipson, Emma. *The Animal-Lore of Shakespeare's Time, including Quadrupeds, Birds, Reptiles, Fish and Insects*. London: Kegan, 1883. New York: AMS, 1973. 476 pp.

Catalogs the scientific sources of numerous allusions to natural history made by Shakespeare and other Renaissance dramatists.

599. Pomeranz, Herman. *Medicine in the Shakespearean Plays and Dickens' Doctors*. New York: Powell, 1936. 410 pp.

Surveys allusions to medicine in Shakespeare's major plays, covering such topics as anatomy, physiology, therapeutic methodologies, nervous disorders, quacks and mountebanks, T. Browne and witchcraft, and F. Bacon's reflections on medicine. Briefly discusses other Elizabethan dramatists, including Chapman, J. Ford, Greene, T. Heywood, Jonson, Lyly, and Marlowe. Also reviews the treatment of doctors and medicine in Dickens's major works.

600. ————. "Medicine in the Shakespearean Plays and Era." *Medical Life* 41 (1934): 351–76, 479–532.

After surveying the state of Elizabethan medicine and commenting on various well-known practitioners, empirics, and quacks, such as Napier, Fludd, Dee, and Burton, the author cites references in Shakespeare's plays to anatomy, physiology, herbal remedies, obstetrics, embryology, and other aspects of medicine.

601. Poynter, F. N. L. "Medicine and Public Health." *ShS* 17 (1964): 152–66, 258–59.

Examines common medical practices, medical knowledge, and public health regulations in Elizabethan England to help explain the medical allusions that abound in Shakespeare's works.

602. Reynolds, Lou A., and Paul Sawyer. "Folk Medicine and the Four Fairies of *A Midsummer Night's Dream*." *SQ* 10 (1959): 513–21.

The names and characteristics of the four fairies (Cobweb, Peaseblossom, Mustardseed, and Moth) have their origin in Elizabethan herbal folklore. Interprets the play's magical and supernatural aura in the light of this folk-medicine tradition.

603. Rusche, Harry. "Edmund's Conception and Nativity in *King Lear*." *SQ* 20 (1969): 161–64.

Uses the astrological imagery in *King Lear* to explain Edmund's character.

604. Savage, D. S. "An Alchemical Metaphor in *Hamlet*." *N&Q* 197 (1952): 157–60.

Suggests a textual emendation for *Hamlet* 1.3.36–38 that clarifies the passage's alchemical significance.

605. ————. "Heraldry and Alchemy in Shakespeare's *Hamlet*." *UKCR* 17 (1951): 231–40.

Cites numerous long passages from *Hamlet* that refer to heraldry and alchemy. Although alchemy is traditionally concerned with regeneration, the alchemical references in the play reinforce the theme of degeneration.

606.   Seager, Herbert West. *Natural History in Shakespeare's Time: Being Extracts Illustrative of the Subject As He Knew It.* London: Stock, 1896. New York: AMS, 1971. Chicheley, Bucks, Eng.: Minet, 1972. 358 pp.

An encyclopedia of Shakespeare's references to natural history from *aconitum* to *yew*, with explanatory extracts from the natural history works extant in his time.

607.   Shickman, Allan. "The 'Perspective Glass' in Shakespeare's *Richard II.*" *SEL* 18 (1978): 217–28.

Outlines the background to Shakespeare's use of the optical term *perspective* in *Richard II* (2.2.14–27).

608.   Simpson, Robert R. *Shakespeare and Medicine.* Edinburgh: Livingstone, 1959. 267 pp.

Surveys references to a wide range of medical topics in Shakespeare's plays. Discusses Dr. John Hall, Shakespeare's son-in-law, as a possible source of Shakespeare's considerable knowledge of medicine.

609.   Sisson, C. J. "Shakespeare's Helena and Dr. William Harvey." *E&S* 13 (1960): 1–20.

Explores Elizabethan medical practices and medical ethics to assess the plausibility of Shakespeare's portrayal of Helena as a doctor in *All's Well That Ends Well.* Compares a medical case involving Harvey in 1620 with Helena's medical treatment of the King of France.

610.   Smith, Warren D. "The Elizabethan Rejection of Judicial Astrology and Shakespeare's Practice." *SQ* 9 (1958): 159–76.

After surveying Elizabethan publications that condemn judicial astrology, the author concludes that belief in this pseudoscience was officially denounced by Queen Elizabeth and that Shakespeare shared her attitude. Cites passages from *Macbeth*, *Love's Labour's Lost*, and other plays to support this thesis.

611.   Smith, Winifred. "A Note on *As You Like It*, II, vii, 139f." *MLN* 30 (1915): 94–95.

Compares Shakespeare's treatment of the sevenfold division of human life with aspects of astrology and humoral psychology.

612.   Sondheim, Moriz. "Shakespeare and the Astrology of His Time." *JWCI* 2 (1939): 243–59.

Attempts to determine Shakespeare's attitude toward astrology by carefully analyzing Shakespearean texts and the astrological beliefs common in Renaissance Europe. The available evidence suggests that the poet accepted natural astrology but rejected judicial astrology.

613.   Steadman, John M. "Falstaff's 'Facies Hippocratica': A Note on Shakespeare and Renaissance Medical Theory." *SN* 29 (1957): 130–35.

In *Henry V*, the hostess's prognostication of Falstaff's approaching death is based in part on a medical tradition traceable to Hippocrates's *Prognosticon*.

613a. Stensgaard, Richard K. *"All's Well That Ends Well* and the Galenico-Paracelsian Controversy." *RenQ* 25 (1972): 173–88.

Maintains that the controversy between Galenic and Paracelsian medical methods serves as background to the passage about the "healing of the king" in *All's Well That Ends Well*.

614. Strathmann, Ernest A. "The Devil Can Cite Scripture." *SQ* 15 (1964): 17–23.

Discusses Edmund's denunciation of judicial astrology in *King Lear*.

615. Tabor, Edward. "Plant Poisons in Shakespeare." *Economic Botany* 24 (1970): 81–94.

Briefly describes the herbal poisons referred to in Shakespeare's plays, noting his sophisticated knowledge of the plant lore and botanical concepts of his time.

616. Thomas, Sidney. "The Elizabethan Idea of Melancholy." *MLN* 56 (1941): 261–63.

Challenges the view that Shakespeare based the melancholic characters of Hamlet and Jaques on psychological treatises such as Bright's *Treatise of Melancholy*. Claims that the average Elizabethan's understanding of melancholy derived not from technical works but from sermons and tracts of popular preachers.

616a. Toole, William B. "The Metaphor of Alchemy in *Julius Caesar*." *Costerus* 5 (1972): 135–51.

Maintains that Shakespeare's use of alchemy in *Julius Caesar* is entirely metaphorical and allusive. Claims that Shakespeare "adapts some of the implications of the alchemical process and the philosophy which underlay it as a means of illustrating ironically the significance of the central action and some of the central character relationships in the drama."

617. Wainwright, John W. *The Medical and Surgical Knowledge of William Shakspere* [sic], *with Explanatory Notes*. New York: Wainwright, 1915. 80 pp.

Includes chapters on Shakespeare's references to medicine, surgery, mental and nervous diseases, obstetrics and midwifery, therapeutics, pharmacy and toxicology, anatomy, physiology, hygiene and dietetics, ethics, and medical jurisprudence.

618. Walker, Albert L. "Convention in Shakespeare's Description of Emotion." *PQ* 17 (1938): 26–66.

Suggests that Shakespeare's descriptions of various states of emotion in plays such as *Othello*, *King Lear*, and *Henry VI, Part 3* depended only minimally on a technical knowledge of Elizabethan physiology and psychology. Shakespeare probably appropriated common and conventional physiological and psychological theories—stock material for playwrights of the period. Nonetheless, he put this stock material to creative and lyrical use.

619. Walker, Roy. "The Celestial Plane in Shakespeare." *ShS* 8 (1955): 109–17.

Surveys previous critical attempts to define Shakespeare's attitude toward astrology and cites examples of celestial imagery in *The Rape of Lucrece*, *Othello*, *Macbeth*, and other plays.

620.   Watson, E. M. "Medical Lore in Shakespeare." *AMH* 8 (1936): 249–65.
Assesses Shakespeare's medical and biological knowledge and cites references to the circulation of the blood, neuropsychiatry, psychopathology, disease, pharmacology, and obstetrics in his major plays.

621.   Willard, Bradford. "The Geology of Shakespeare." *SciMo* 65 (1947): 399–404.
Surveys the physiographic, lithological, and mineralogical allusions in Shakespeare's plays, indicating the extent of Elizabethan geological knowledge.

622.   Wilson, J. Dover. "A Note on 'Richard III': The Bishop of Ely's Strawberries." *MLR* 52 (1957): 563–64.
Maintains that the episode in *Richard III* concerning Richard's withered arm and the Bishop of Ely's strawberries (3.4.55–80) may have a medical explanation.

623.   Wilson, William. *Shakespeare and Astrology, from a Student's Point of View.* Boston: Occult, 1903. New York: AMS, 1975. 12 pp.
Exemplifies Shakespeare's adept knowledge of astrology by citing key references from plays such as *Twelfth Night*, *A Midsummer Night's Dream*, *The Tempest*, and *Much Ado about Nothing*.

624.   Yellowlees, Henry. "Medicine and Surgery in the 1955 Season's Plays." *More Talking of Shakespeare.* Ed. John Garrett. London: Longmans, 1959. 172–86.
Treats the medical and psychological aspects of *Titus Andronicus*, *The Merry Wives of Windsor*, *All's Well That Ends Well*, *Twelfth Night*, and *Macbeth*.

625.   Zekman, Theodore N., and Ethel H. Davis. "Shakespeare's Ophthalmologic Vocabulary and Concepts." *American Journal of Ophthalmology* 68 (1969): 1–9.
Cites passages from Shakespeare's sonnets and major plays that refer to ophthalmology. Notes various classes of ophthalmologic vocabulary including "pin and web," "galled eyes," "coffer-lids," and "imperfect sight."

Edmund Spenser (1552?–99)

626.   Albright, Evelyn May. "Spenser's Cosmic Philosophy and His Religion." *PMLA* 44 (1929): 715–59.
Maintains that Lucretius is not, as has been supposed, the source of Spenser's cosmogony and religious convictions. Reexamines the derivation of Spenser's "views on the universe, the creation of the world and of vegetable and animal life, the immortality of the soul, the existence of God, and the relations of God to the universe."

627.   Allen, Don C. "A Note on Spenser's Orology." *MLN* 61 (1946): 555–56.
Notes that a passage from *The Faerie Queene* (5.2.28.1–5) may reflect the influence of Renaissance orological theories.

627a.   Arber, Agnes. "Edmund Spenser and Lyte's *Niewe Herball.*" *N&Q* 160 (1931): 345–47.
Suggests that a source for the enigmatic flower word *cheuisaunce* in Spenser's *Shepheardes Calender* may be Henry Lyte's *Niewe Herball.*

628.   Bennett, Josephine Waters. "Spenser's Garden of Adonis." *PMLA* 47 (1932): 46–80.
Disputes Edwin Greenlaw's contention that the "Garden of Adonis" section of *The Faerie Queene* reflects Lucretian influence (see item 633). Interprets the passage instead as "a single, continuous, and serious allegory, based entirely upon a body of well-known Platonic and Neo-Platonic conceptions about the organization of the universe, and containing no elements of the Lucretian theory of origins."

629.   Camden, Carroll, Jr. "Spenser's 'Little Fish, That Men Call Remora.' " *Rice Institute Pamphlet* 44.1 (1957): 1–16.
Surveys references to the remora in scientific and literary works by Spenser, Aristotle, Plutarch, Batman, Donne, Jonson, and Milton.

630.   De Lacy, Hugh. "Astrology in the Poetry of Edmund Spenser." *JEGP* 33 (1934): 520–43.
Cites decorative, causal, and technical uses of astrology in Spenser's poetry as evidence of his "abiding interest" in the pseudoscience.

631.   Eade, J. C. "The Pattern in the Astronomy of Spenser's *Epithalamion.*" *RES* ns 23 (1972): 173–78.
The astronomical allusions in Spenser's poem correspond to an actual planetary configuration that occurred on 11 June 1594.

632.   Fowler, Alastair. *Spenser and the Numbers of Time.* London: Routledge; New York: Barnes, 1964. 314 pp.
        Rev. Joan Grundy, *MLR* 60 (1965): 92–93; Patricia Thomson, *RES* ns 16 (1965): 414–18.
Explicates the Pythagorean numerology and the related astronomical and astrological symbolism that sustains the structure of Spenser's *Faerie Queene.*

633.   Greenlaw, Edwin. "Spenser and Lucretius." *SP* 17 (1920): 439–64.
Demonstrates that the natural philosophy in the two Mutability Cantos and in the Garden of Adonis passage from *The Faerie Queene* derives largely from Lucretius's *De rerum natura.* Other influences include Plato and Ovid.

634.   Harrison, Thomas P. "Flower Lore in Spenser and Shakespeare: Two Notes." *MLQ* 7 (1946): 175–78.
Notes the influence of Henry Lyte's *Newe Herball* (1578) on Spenser's *Astrophel* and Shakespeare's *Midsummer Night's Dream.*

635.   ———. *They Tell of Birds: Chaucer, Spenser, Milton, Drayton.* Austin: U of
          Texas P, 1956. Westport: Greenwood, 1969. 159 pp.
   See item 296 for annotation.

636.   Hinckley, Henry B. "Theories of Vision in English Poetry." *MLN* 24
          (1909): 125.
   Notes that Spenser's *Faerie Queene* (2.11.26.1–2), Milton's *Samson Agonistes*
(581–85), and Dryden's *Hind and the Panther* (2.74–76) refer to ancient theories of
vision developed by Pythagoras, Plato, Empedocles, and Democritus.

637.   Levinson, Ronald B. "Spenser and Bruno." *PMLA* 43 (1928): 675–81.
   Maintains that the cosmology of both *The Faerie Queene* and the Mutability Cantos
was influenced primarily by Bruno's philosophy and not by Lucretius, whom Edwin
Greenlaw proposes as the source (see item 633).

638.   Marotti, Arthur F. "Animal Symbolism in *The Faerie Queene*: Tradition
          and the Poetic Context." *SEL* 5 (1965): 69–86.
   An introductory study of the tradition of science, pseudoscience, literature, my-
thology, and scripture informing Spenser's use of animal imagery in *The Faerie
Queene*. Authors cited include Aristotle, Lucan, Ovid, Sidney, and Topsell.

639.   Rockwood, Robert J. R. "Alchemical Forms of Thought in Book I of
          Spenser's *Faerie Queene*." *DAI* 34 (1973–74): 3355A–56A.
   Claims that alchemical principles underlie the organization of book 1 of *The Faerie
Queene* and, thus, provide a key to the work's allegory.

640.   Thomson, Patricia. "Phantastes and His Horoscope." *N&Q* ns 13 (1966):
          372–75.
   Discusses the astrological details of Phantastes's horoscope in *The Faerie Queene*
2.9.52. Supplements Alastair Fowler's *Spenser and the Numbers of Time* (see item 632).

641.   Tuve, Rosemond. "A Mediaeval Commonplace in Spenser's Cosmology."
          SP 30 (1933): 133–47.
   Shows that Spenser's concepts of "Mutability," "Dame Nature," and "creation"
derive from a medieval cosmological tradition common to Bartholomaeus Anglicus,
Agrippa, Boethius, Alanus de Insulis, Palingenius, and others.

Lope de Vega (1562–1635)

642.   Halstead, Frank G. "The Attitude of Lope de Vega toward Astrology."
          Diss. U of Virginia, 1937.
   Not seen for annotation.

643.   ———. "The Attitude of Lope de Vega toward Astrology and Astronomy."
          HR 7 (1939): 205–19.
   Careful examination of *La Arcadia*, *Guzman el bravo*, *La Filomena*, and other extant
works reveals that Lope was widely acquainted with pre-Copernican astronomy and
astrology. Halstead maintains, contrary to common critical opinion, that, for the
most part, Lope disapproved of astrology: Lope usually makes astrology the subject
of satirical attack, and his use of astronomical terminology is frequently careless.

Seventeenth Century

Studies and Surveys

644.   Albury, W. R. "Halley's Ode on the *Principia* of Newton and the Epicurean
        Revival in England." *JHI* 39 (1978): 24–43.
    Halley's ode on Newton's *Principia*, printed at the front of the first edition of the
book, served as a model for numerous eighteenth-century poetic works written in
praise of Newtonian science. Albury shows that the ode imitated Lucretius's *De
rerum natura* and suggests that Halley may have used the Lucretian form to guard
against expected attacks from antiscientific Restoration Epicureans such as Temple.

645.   Allen, Don Cameron. *The Legend of Noah: Renaissance Rationalism in Art,
        Science, and Letters*. Illinois Studies in Language and Literature 33.3–4.
        Urbana: U of Illinois P, 1949. 221 pp.
    See item 384 for annotation.

646.   Anderson, Daryll M. "Satires of Science in the Seventeenth and Eighteenth
        Centuries." *DAI* 41 (1980–81): 3114A.
    Studies satirical treatments of the scientific virtuoso in works by S. Butler, Shad-
well, the Scriblerus Club, Johnson, and Swift.

647.   Arthos, John. "Poetic Diction and Scientific Language." *Isis* 32 (1940):
        324–38.
    Many stock words and expressions in late-seventeenth- and early-eighteenth-
century poetry, such as "the liquid air" and "the mineral kinds," originated in the
scientific terminology both of this period and of antiquity. The author traces the
derivation of some expressions to illustrate the methods and principles he will use
in his proposed lexicon of seventeenth- and eighteenth-century poetic diction.

648.   Beum, Robert. "The Scientific Affinities of English Baroque Prose." *EM*
        13 (1962): 59–80.
    The author attributes what he calls the characteristic "asymmetry" of Baroque
prose to the influence of Copernican cosmography and the "new science." Among
the writers studied are F. Bacon, T. Browne, Burton, Jonson, and Milton.

649.   Boas, George. *The Happy Beast in French Thought of the Seventeenth Century*.
        Baltimore: Johns Hopkins P, 1933. New York: Octagon, 1966. 159 pp.
        Rev. Charner M. Perry, *IJE* 43 (1932–33): 477; Harold A. Larrabee, *JP*
        30 (1933): 610–12; C. A. Kofoid, *Isis* 22 (1934–35): 240–41.
    Outlines the seventeenth-century philosophic, scientific, and literary responses to

the doctrine of "theriophily," which posits the natural superiority of beasts over human beings. Focuses on Montaigne's essays, the thoughts of Montaigne's predecessors and disciples, and the works of literary satirists and poets such as Cyrano de Bergerac and La Fontaine.

650.   Brodbar, Harold. "Late Renaissance Astronomy and the 'New Philosophy.' " *ForumH* 3.12 (1963): 19–27.
The astronomical discoveries of Copernicus, Galileo, and Kepler shattered the optimistic Renaissance worldview. Brodbar discusses specifically the impact that Galileo's *Sidereus nuncius* (1610) had on post-Renaissance literature such as Donne's "First Anniversary" (1611) and *Conclave ignatii* (1611) and Campanella's *Civitas solis* (1623).

651.   Brown, Harcourt. "Classical Science and Literary Innovation." *Diogenes* 3 (1953): 50–58.
The intellectual climate of seventeenth-century France fostered a unique, cooperative relationship between literature and science in which each shared principles and methods of investigation with the other as each explored its own territory— science, the natural world; literature, the human world.

652.   ⸺. *Science and the Human Comedy: Natural Philosophy in French Literature from Rabelais to Maupertuis.* Toronto: U of Toronto P, 1976. 221 pp.
See item 396 for annotation.

653.   ⸺. "Tensions and Anxieties: Science and the Literary Culture of France." *Science and the Creative Spirit: Essays on Humanistic Aspects of Science.* Ed. Harcourt Brown. Toronto: U of Toronto P, 1958. 91–126.
See item 146 for annotation.

654.   Bush, Douglas. *Science and English Poetry: A Historical Sketch, 1590–1950.* New York: Oxford UP, 1950. Westport: Greenwood, 1980. 166 pp.
See item 147 for annotation.

655.   ⸺. "Science and Literature." *Seventeenth Century Science and the Arts.* Ed. Hedley Howell Rhys. Princeton: Princeton UP, 1961. 29–62.
Assesses the impact of seventeenth-century astronomy and cosmology on the beliefs, thought, poetic sensibility, and style of Milton, Donne, G. Herbert, Dryden, and other literary figures of the period.

656.   Byard, Margaret M. "Poetic Responses to the Copernican Revolution." *SciAm* 236 (1977): 121–29.
Assesses the extent to which the cosmological elements of post-Copernican English poetry either reflect the astronomical innovations of the Copernican system or adhere to outmoded cosmological concepts. Discusses the poetry of Crashaw, Donne, G. Herbert, Milton, Traherne, and H. Vaughan.

657.   Crouch, Laura E. "The Scientist in English Literature: Domingo Gonsales (1638) to Victor Frankenstein (1817)." *DAI* 36 (1975–76): 2181A.
See item 149 for annotation.

658.   Crum, Ralph B. *Scientific Thought in Poetry*. Diss. Columbia U, 1931. New York: Columbia UP, 1931. New York: AMS, 1966. Folcroft: Folcroft, 1973. 246 pp.
See item 150 for annotation.

659.   Cruttwell, Patrick. "Physiology and Psychology in Shakespeare's Age." *JHI* 12 (1951): 75–89.
See item 403 for annotation.

660.   De Selincourt, Ernest. "The Interplay of Literature and Science during the Last Three Centuries." *HJ* 37 (1938–39): 225–45.
See item 151 for annotation.

661.   Duncan, Carson Samuel. *The New Science and English Literature in the Classical Period*. Diss. U of Chicago, 1913. Menasha: George Banta, 1913. New York: Russell, 1972. 191 pp.
Surveys the principal phases in the development of the "new science," stressing the contributions of Galileo, F. Bacon, R. Descartes, and Harvey and the rise of the Royal Society. Examines the gradual impact of science on English comedy, poetry, and prose, emphasizing the conflict between ancient and modern learning as reflected in the literature of the classical period. The many authors discussed include S. Butler, Cowley, Dryden, Milton, Shadwell, Swift, and Waller. The prevalence of satirical portrayals of science and scientists indicates that the literary figures of the period failed to appreciate or understand the authentic achievements of science.

662.   ———. "The Scientist as a Comic Type." *MP* 14 (1916–17): 281–91.
The rise of the "new science," or experimental philosophy, from 1660 to 1700 and the founding of the Royal Society in 1662 initiated a change in satirical treatments of the scientist in drama. The scientist was no longer depicted as "a vague, peevish pedant, much occupied with physiognomies, dreams, and fantastic ideas" but was portrayed as an experimental philosopher "busied with observation and experimentation, with investigation, with the reconstruction of the natural history of the world." A good example of the new comic type is Sir Nicolas Gimcrack in Shadwell's *Virtuoso* (1676).

663.   Dunstan, Florence J. "Medical Science in the Picaresque Novels, 1550–1650." Diss. U of Texas, Austin, 1936.
Not seen for annotation.

664.   Ellrodt, Robert. "Scientific Curiosity and Metaphysical Poetry in the Seventeenth Century." *MP* 61 (1963–64): 180–97.
Explores the reasons and attitudes behind the scientific imagery in the poetry of Cowley, Donne, G. Herbert, Traherne, H. Vaughan, and others. Discusses four factors that helped form the poets' scientific positions: the utilitarian spirit, intellectual curiosity, reliance on reason, and reliance on faith.

665.   ———. "La vogue de l'image scientifique dans la poésie anglaise du dix-septième siècle." *EA* 14 (1961): 346–47.

Claims that the popularity of scientific imagery in poetry by Donne, G. Herbert, Marvell, Spenser, H. Vaughan, and others was due in part to the English political climate and university system.

666.   Eurich, Nell P. *Science in Utopia: A Mighty Design*. Diss. Columbia U, 1959. Cambridge, MA: Harvard UP, 1967. 332 pp. (Abstract in *DA* 20 [1960]: 4098.)
        Rev. R. L. Colie, *YR* ns 57 (1967–68): 282–85; René Breugelmans, *SCN* 26 (1968): 29–30; Moody E. Prior, *MP* 67 (1969–70): 187–92.

In literary utopias from Mesopotamian and Greek tales to T. More's *Utopia*, authors relied primarily on political, economic, and social reforms to effect society's improvement. In utopias written after the scientific discoveries and theories of Copernicus, Kepler, Galileo, Harvey, and Gilbert, however, science played the central role in providing social blessings. Eurich examines the impact the "new science" had on utopian literature by Andreae, F. Bacon, Campanella, Cowley, Glanvill, and others.

667.   Gorceix, Bernard. "Alchimie et littérature au XVIIᵉ siècle en Allemagne." *EG* 26 (1971): 18–31.

Shows that the surge of interest in alchemy in seventeenth-century Germany had an impact on literature. Analyzes Andreae's *Chymische Hochzeit: Christian Rosencreütz* (1616) and Knorr von Rosenroth's *Conjugium Phoebi et Palladis* (1677), two novels abundant in alchemical symbolism.

668.   Graham, Peter W. "Harvey's *De motu cordis*: The Rhetoric of Science and the Science of Rhetoric." *JHM* 33 (1978): 469–76.

Attributes the continued appeal of *De motu cordis* to Harvey's rhetorical strategy, notably his attention to matters of argument, audience, and language. Aristotle was the principal source of Harvey's scientific and rhetorical principles.

669.   Greenlaw, Edwin. "The New Science and English Literature in the Seventeenth Century." *Johns Hopkins Alumni Magazine* 13 (1925): 331–59.

Studies the seventeenth-century intellectual milieu, specifically the "new science" as a transforming cultural force. Examines works by Spenser, Du Bartas, and Milton to show the revolutionary effect of science on the structure of cosmological poetry.

670.   Guerlac, Henry. "The Poets' Nitre." *Isis* 45 (1954): 243–55.

Considers Mayow's *Tractatus quinque medico-physici* (1674) and its theory of nitroaerial particles in the context of a meteorological tradition that was widely influential in the seventeenth and eighteenth centuries. Views the theory as part of a scientific interregnum ascendant between the collapse of classical natural philosophy and the triumph of Newtonianism. Discusses allusions to the theory in Blackmore's *Creation*, Milton's *Paradise Lost*, Philips's *Cyder*, J. Thomson's *Winter*, and other works.

671.   Harris, Victor. *All Coherence Gone: A Study of the Seventeenth-Century Controversy over Disorder and Decay in the Universe*. Chicago: U of Chicago P, 1949. London: Cass, 1966. 255 pp.
        Rev. Don Cameron Allen, *MLN* 65 (1950): 497–98.

Follows the development of the seventeenth-century idea of mutability and decay in nature as expressed by philosophers, theologians, scientists, and scholars. The chief inaugurators of the controversy were Godfrey Goodman, whose treatise *The Fall of Man: Or, The Corruption of Nature* (1616) defended the theory, and George Hakewill, whose *Apologie of the Power and Providence of God* (1627) denounced it. Other contributors to the debate included F. Bacon, T. Browne, T. Burnet, and Burton. A separate section traces the theory's effect on the literary imagination of Alexander, Davies, T. Heywood, Milton, Spenser, Wilkins, and especially Donne.

672.   Harrison, Charles T. "The Ancient Atomists and English Literature of the Seventeenth Century." *Harvard Studies in Classical Philology* 45 (1934): 1–79.

Surveys both the positive and the negative intellectual responses to the seventeenth-century revival of interest in Democritus, Epicurus, and Lucretius. Comments on Blackmore, T. Browne, Burton, Cudworth, Culpepper, Dryden, Du Bartas, Milton, H. More, and others.

673.   Heggen, Alfred. "Die 'ars volandi' in der Literatur des 17. und 18. Jahrhunderts." *Technikgeschichte* 42 (1975): 327–37.

Seventeenth- and eighteenth-century literature alluded to flying more than to any other scientific and technological discovery. Examines references to flying experiments in works by Cyrano de Bergerac, Restif de la Bretonne, Wieland, and others.

674.   Hinnant, Charles H. "Sir William Temple's Views on Science, Poetry, and the Imagination." *SECC* 8 (1979): 187–203.

In *On Ancient and Modern Learning* Temple expresses his antipathy toward modern science and his championship of ancient learning and natural magic. Hinnant examines the implications of these views for the theory of poetics and imagination Temple outlines in *On Poetry*. "*On Poetry* makes a fundamental contribution to poetic theory at the end of the seventeenth century. If this contribution has been overlooked in the past, it is undoubtedly because our bias against Temple's scientific attitudes has so colored our conception of his views on other subjects as to give a false picture of his thought."

675.   Horne, C. J. "Literature and Science." *From Dryden to Johnson.* Vol. 4 of *The Pelican Guide to English Literature.* Ed. Boris Ford. Baltimore: Penguin, 1957. 188–202. 7 vols. 1954–61.

Outlines the stylistic changes in sixteenth- and seventeenth-century English literature resulting from a growing interest in science. Emphasizes the influence of Newtonianism on the poetic imagination and the impact of the Royal Society, which, founded in 1662, fostered the development of a plain English style. Among the authors whose works reflect a concern for the "new science" are Addison, Akenside, S. Butler, Dryden, Johnson, Pope, Shadwell, and Swift.

676.   Johnson, Francis R. "The Progress of the Copernican Astronomy among English Scientists to 1645 and Its Reflection in Literature from Spenser to Milton." Diss. Johns Hopkins U, 1935.

Not seen for annotation.

677.   Jones, Richard Foster. "The Rhetoric of Science in England of the Mid-Seventeenth Century." *Restoration and Eighteenth-Century Literature: Essays in Honor of Alan Dugald McKillop*. Ed. Carroll Camden. Chicago: U of Chicago P for William Marsh Rice U, 1963. 5–24.
Shows that the Royal Society's statutes opposing a rhetorical and learned style of writing were directed primarily against the literary style of atomists and mechanical philosophers, chiefly Walter Charleton and Sir Kenelm Digby. Contrasts the mechanists' use of similes, metaphors, allegories, and other literary devices with the plain prose style of experimentalist Baconians.

678.   ———. "Science and Criticism in the Neo-Classical Age of English Literature." *JHI* 1 (1940): 381–412. Rpt. in *The Seventeenth Century: Studies in the History of English Thought and Literature from Bacon to Pope*. By Richard Foster Jones et al. Stanford: Stanford UP, 1951. 41–74.
The seventeenth-century revolt of science against the dogmas of ancient scientific authorities such as Aristotle gradually exerted a liberalizing influence on the dogmas of neoclassical literary criticism. The critical revolt against ancient authority permitted progress in the literary field as the corresponding revolt in the sciences permitted scientific progress. Discusses the major contributions of Sir R. Blackmore, Dryden, Gildon, and Young in the struggle to liberate criticism from neoclassicism.

679.   ———. "Science and English Prose Style in the Third Quarter of the Seventeenth Century." *PMLA* 45 (1930): 977–1009. Rpt. in *The Seventeenth Century: Studies in the History of English Thought and Literature from Bacon to Pope*. By Richard Foster Jones et al. Stanford: Stanford UP, 1951. 75–110.
Traces the revolt of scientists and members of the Royal Society against the ornate, luxurious prose characteristic of the Commonwealth. The call for a plain prose style by Boyle, Hobbes, Sprat, Wilkins, and others influenced writers such as Cowley, Dryden, and Glanvill.

680.   ———. "Science and Language in England of the Mid-Seventeenth Century." *JEGP* 31 (1932): 315–31. Rpt. in *The Seventeenth Century: Studies in the History of English Thought and Literature from Bacon to Pope*. By Richard Foster Jones et al. Stanford: Stanford UP, 1951. 143–60.
Explores the origins of the seventeenth-century reformation in English prose style instigated by various scientists. Cites the contributions of F. Bacon, Boyle, Petty, Sprat, Wilkins, and others.

681.   Jucovy, Peter M. "Circle and Circulation: The Language and Imagery of William Harvey's Discovery." *Perspectives in Biology and Medicine* 20 (1976–77): 92–107.
Studies the rhetorical and metaphoric qualities of Harvey's scientific description of the circulation of the blood in *De motu cordis*. One of his dominant images was the Renaissance "Circle of Perfection."

682.   Koppel, Richard M. "English Satire on Science, 1660–1750." *DAI* 40 (1979): 250A–51A.

Surveys both anti- and proscientific satire in the writings of Addison, Arbuthnot, S. Butler, Gay, King, Pope, Shadwell, and Swift.

683. Korninger, Siegfried. *Die Naturauffassung in der englischen Dichtung des 17. Jahrhunderts.* Wiener Beiträge zur englischen Philologie 64. Wien: Braumüller, 1956. 260 pp.

Draws on a wide range of seventeenth-century English writings on nature, and quotes copiously from English poetry to show that the sciences of the time (astronomy, botany, chemistry, zoology, medicine, and geography) had transformed the concept of nature with which English poets were working.

684. Kühlmann, Wilhelm. "Neuzeitliche Wissenschaft in der Lyrik des 17. Jahrhunderts: Die Kopernikus-Gedichte des Andreas Gryphius und Caspar Barlaeus im Argumentationszusammenhang des frühbarocken Modernismus." *JDSG* 23 (1979): 124–53.

Contrasts the modernity motifs in the Copernicus poems of Barlaeus and Gryphius. Shows that when Gryphius wrote his Copernicus poems in 1643 he was already familiar with similar poems composed by Barlaeus in 1634. The analysis of the two sets of poems reveals a significant difference, however, between the late Renaissance perspective of Barlaeus and the early baroque view of Gryphius. The optimism of the earlier writer is replaced by the later author's caution and skepticism. Whereas Barlaeus stresses Copernicus's deed as revolutionary, Gryphius mutes this theme and substitutes praise of the astronomer's fame.

685. Linden, Stanton J. "Alchemy and the English Literary Imagination: 1385–1633." *DAI* 33 (1972–73): 3591A–92A.

See item 160 for annotation.

686. McColley, Grant. "The Ross-Wilkins Controversy." *AnS* 3 (1938): 153–89.

Treats in detail the essential phases in the controversy between science and scriptural literalism, specifically as expressed in Ross's *New Planet No Planet* (1646) and Wilkins's *Discovery of a World in the Moone* (1638) and *Discourse concerning a New Planet* (1640). The controversy, which had an important influence on English thought and poetic art, is reflected in various guises in works by Milton, Pope, Swift, and others.

687. ———. "The Seventeenth-Century Doctrine of a Plurality of Worlds." *AnS* 1 (1936): 385–430.

Traces the historical background of the seventeenth-century doctrine of a plurality of worlds. The concept developed principally through the natural philosophy of Anaximander and Democritus, medieval Scholastic doctrine, the publication of Copernicus's *De revolutionibus*, and Galileo's invention of the telescope. Discusses many advocates and opponents of the doctrine, including Plutarch, Epicurus, Augustine, Aquinas, Bruno, Campanella, Kepler, and Wilkins.

688. McCue, Daniel L., Jr. "Science and Literature: The Virtuoso in English Belles Lettres." *Albion* 3 (1971): 138–56.

An overview of literary satires of the scientific virtuoso from roughly 1675 to 1765. The works discussed include Shadwell's *Virtuoso* (1676), Dryden's *Essay of Dramatic Poesy* (1668), Swift's *Gulliver's Travels* (1726), Pope's *Essay on Man* (1733–34), and Akenside's *Virtuoso* (1737).

689.   Mackenzie, Elizabeth. "The Growth of Plants: A Seventeenth-Century Metaphor." *English Renaissance Studies Presented to Dame Helen Gardner in Honour of Her Seventieth Birthday.* Ed. John Carey. Oxford: Clarendon; New York: Oxford UP, 1980. 194–211.

The scientific sources of metaphors concerning plant growth used by writers such as G. Herbert, Milton, and H. Vaughan include Aristotle, Cicero, Albertus Magnus, Digby, and Grew.

690.   Macklem, Michael. *The Anatomy of the World: Relations between Natural and Moral Law from Donne to Pope.* Diss. Princeton U, 1954. Minneapolis: U of Minnesota P, 1958. 139 pp. (Abstract in *DA* 21 (1961): 3091.)
        Rev. Herbert Weisinger, *MLQ* 21 (1960): 265–67.

Traces the impact of theological, physicotheological, and scientific doctrines of natural and moral law on the literary imagination of poets such as Donne, J. Thomson, E. Young, and Pope. Also treats the views of T. Burnet, Hakewill, Warren, Whiston, and Newton.

691.   Mandel, Siegfried. "From the Mummelsee to the Moon: Refractions of Science in Seventeenth-Century Literature." *CLS* 9 (1972): 407–15.

"Seventeenth-century literature drew freely from underworld and extraterrestrial journeys described in ancient, classical, and medical writings, and it continued certain social and philosophical traditions. At the same time, the sciences also were refracted, in varying degrees, particularly in the literary works of Campanella, Kepler, and Grimmelshausen. Kepler's *Somnium* shows precise scientific thinking, while the journey to the center of the earth in Grimmelshausen's *Simplicissimus* exemplifies the baroque imagination in the fictionalizing of contemporaneous technical information and speculation."

692.   Marsak, Leonard M. "Science and the Public Mind: Some Early Popularizers of Science." *Cahiers d'histoire mondiale* 10 (1966–67): 512–18.

Remarks on the early attempts to establish science in the public consciousness through literary means. Among the works discussed are Cyrano de Bergerac's *Voyages to the Sun, and to the Moon* (c. 1649), F. Bacon's *New Atlantis* (1627), and Fontenelle's *Conversations on the Plurality of Worlds* (1686). Accords special attention to Fontenelle's reflections on the relations between the humanities and science.

693.   Maynard, Katharine. "Science in Early English Literature 1550 to 1650." *Isis* 17 (1932): 94–126.

See item 421 for annotation.

694.   Mazzeo, Joseph Anthony. "Seventeenth-Century English Prose Style: The Quest for a Natural Style." *Mosaic* 6.3 (1972–73): 107–44.

Linguistically analyzes the writing of Addison, F. Bacon, T. Browne, Burton,

Dryden, Milton, and others. Includes an overview of the ways the "new science" and the dictates of the Royal Society modified the seventeenth-century prose style.

695.   Meadows, A. J. *The High Firmament: A Survey of Astronomy in English Literature*. Leicester: Leicester UP, 1969. 207 pp.
        See item 162 for annotation.

696.   Meyer, Gerald D. "Fontenelle and Late Seventeenth-Century Science." *HINL* 4 (1958): 26–33.
Fontenelle's *Entretiens sur la pluralité des mondes* (1686) provided a model for communicating scientific ideas to lay readers. Meyer shows how several English translations of the work influenced such writers as Addison, J. Spence, Temple, and Toland.

697.   ———. *The Scientific Lady in England 1650–1760*. University of California Publications, English Studies 12. Berkeley: U of California P, 1955. 126 pp.
        Rev. Miriam K. Starkman, *MLN* 71 (1956): 451–53.
Published in 1686, *Entretiens sur la pluralité des mondes*, Fontenelle's account of an enlightened French woman's initiation into the secrets of astronomy, quickly became a classic for English women, who adopted Fontenelle's Marchioness of G. as their ideal of "the scientific lady." Of the many popularizations of science between 1650 and 1760, the *Entretiens* was by far the most widely read in England and on the Continent.

698.   Moore, W. G. "Scientific Method in the French Classical Writers." *Literature and Science*. Proc. of the Sixth Triennial Congress of the International Federation for Modern Languages and Literatures. Oxford, 1954. Oxford: Blackwell, 1955. 150–57.
Maintains that the French classical writers' method was analogous to the Galilean-Newtonian scientific method that held sway over the intellectual world during the seventeenth and eighteenth centuries. To support this thesis, the author examines the artistic techniques of La Bruyère, La Rochefoucauld, Molière, Pascal, and J. Racine.

699.   Nicolson, Marjorie Hope. *The Breaking of the Circle: Studies in the Effect of the "New Science" on Seventeenth-Century Poetry*. Evanston: Northwestern UP, 1950. 193 pp. Rev. ed. New York: Columbia UP; London: Oxford UP, 1960. 216 pp.
        Rev. Harcourt Brown, *Isis* 42 (1951): 251–52; Joan Bennett, *RES* ns 3 (1952): 178–80; Herbert Grierson, *MLR* 47 (1952): 390–92.
In the early seventeenth century both poets and scientists used the "Circle of Perfection" as the common metaphor for the correspondences among macrocosm, geocosm, and microcosm. But the seventeenth-century scientific discoveries—Galileo's astronomy, Harvey's demonstration of the circulation of the blood, Kepler's elliptical planetary orbits—tended to weaken the circle's hold on the imagination. In differing ways Donne, G. Herbert, Milton, and Traherne all responded to the image of an infinite, dynamic universe. The Royal Society called for clear and simple language purged of the wit and metaphor of poets.

700.   ———. "Cosmic Voyages." *ELH* 7 (1940): 83–107.

The theme of extraterrestrial space travel, explored in early literature such as Lucian's *True History*, Cicero's *Somnium Scipionis*, and Plutarch's *De facie in orbe lunae*, emerged with renewed force in seventeenth- and eighteenth-century literature, primarily as a result of Galileo's invention of the telescope and the publication of his *Siderius nuncius* (1610). Nicolson examines two modern "moon voyages" and one related scientific work—Kepler's *Somnium*, F. Godwin's *Man in the Moone*, and Wilkins's *Discovery of a New World in the Moone*.

701.   ———. "The Discovery of Space." *Medieval and Renaissance Studies*. Ed. O. B. Hardison, Jr. Proc. of the Southeastern Institute of Medieval and Renaissance Studies. Summer 1965. Chapel Hill: U of North Carolina P, 1966. 40–59.

Shows that the origin of our contemporary sense of the vastness of space lies in the seventeenth century, when the astronomical discoveries of Galileo and the philosophy of Bruno shattered the medieval conception of a closed and finite universe. Traces briefly the impact the new astronomy had on the literary imagination of the time, discussing Milton's *Paradise Lost* as well as the moon voyages written by Cyrano de Bergerac, F. Godwin, and Kepler.

702.   ———. "Early Space-Travellers." *CLC* 9.1 (1959): 9–15.

General remarks on early conceptions of space travel in seventeenth-century literature.

703.   ———. "The Early Stage of Cartesianism in England." *SP* 26 (1929): 356–74.

Reviews the reception of Cartesianism in seventeenth-century England and remarks tentatively on its possible influence on the prose style and literary method of the time. Descartes's contribution to English prose style may be greater than hitherto supposed.

704.   ———. "English Almanacs and the 'New Astronomy.'" *AnS* 4 (1939): 1–33.

Traces the decline of interest in astrology and Ptolemaic astronomy and the concomitant increase in the popularity of Copernicanism as reflected in some 800 English almanacs published between 1600 and 1710. Assesses the impact Galileo's astronomical discoveries had on the acceptance of Copernicanism and examines other aspects of astronomy treated in almanacs, such as novas and comets. The almanacs discussed include works by such compilers as Thomas Bretnor, Nicholas Culpepper, Arthur Hopton, William Lilly, and Vincent Wing.

705.   ———. "The Microscope and English Imagination." *Smith College Studies in Modern Languages* 16.4 (1934–35): 1–92. Rpt. in *Science and Imagination*. Ithaca: Great Seal, 1956. Hamden: Archon, 1976. 155–234.

Provides a short history of the microscope's rise to popularity in England and examines its influence on English thought and literary imagination. The microscope offered poets and dramatists a fertile source of figures of speech, poetic imagery, and themes for satire and irony. Authors studied include R. Blackmore, S. Butler, Cowley, Marvell, Shadwell, and especially Swift, whose *Gulliver's Travels* "could not have been written before the period of microscopic observation, nor by a man who had not felt at once the fascination and the repulsion of the Nature which that instrument displayed."

706. ———. "The 'New Astronomy' and English Literary Imagination." *SP* 32 (1935): 428–62. Rpt. in *Science and Imagination*. Ithaca: Great Seal, 1956. Hamden: Archon, 1976. 30–57.

Surveys seventeenth-century literary responses to the "new astronomy" of Galileo and Kepler, noting poetic and dramatic allusions to "new stars," the telescope, the moon, and the Milky Way. Authors discussed include S. Butler, Cowley, Dryden, P. Fletcher, Jonson, Marvell, Pope, Young, and especially Donne.

707. ———. *Science and Imagination*. Ithaca: Great Seal, 1956. Hamden: Archon, 1976. 238 pp.

Reprints several of Nicolson's studies of the impact the telescope, the microscope, the "new astronomy," and science generally had on the English literary imagination. Includes "The Microscope and English Imagination," "The 'New Astronomy' and English Literary Imagination," "The Telescope and Imagination," "Kepler, the *Somnium*, and John Donne," "Milton and the Telescope," and "The Scientific Background of Swift's *Voyage to Laputa*." For individual annotations see items 705, 706, 708, 854, 907, and 1336.

708. ———. "The Telescope and Imagination." *MP* 32 (1934–35): 233–60. Rpt. in *Science and Imagination*. Ithaca: Great Seal, 1956. Hamden: Archon, 1976. 1–29.

Galileo's invention of the telescope, in 1609, transformed the seventeenth-century conception of the universe, ushering in speculations about the immensity of the universe and the possibility of a plurality of worlds. The astronomical discoveries the new instrument made possible exerted a profound influence on the literary imagination of the time and on philosophical and theological thought. Nicolson traces the chief events leading to Galileo's invention; surveys important astronomical discoveries made by Galileo, Kepler, and others; notes the Italian poets' response to Galileo's findings as published in his *Sidereus nuncius*; and sketches Galileo's influence on English literature.

709. ———. "Two Voices: Science and Literature." *AmerSci* 51 (1963): 454–62.

Outlines some dominant aspects of the relations between science and literature during the seventeenth century. Comments on the invention of the telescope, the microscope, and the hot-air balloon and discusses F. Bacon's *New Atlantis*.

710. ———. *Voyages to the Moon*. New York: Macmillan, 1948. 297 pp. Rev. Mark Graubard, *Isis* 40 (1949): 286–87.

The works of classical writers such as Cicero and Lucian and the discoveries of the "new philosophy" inspired Cyrano de Bergerac, F. Godwin, Kepler, and Wilkins, among others, to contrive a variety of "plausible" methods for sending explorers to the moon. Galileo's *Starry Messenger* of 1610 was especially important in stimulating speculation about curious extraterrestrials that continued, in various permutations, in the fiction of Carroll, Poe, Verne, Wells, and C. S. Lewis.

711.   ———. "A World in the Moon: A Study of the Changing Attitude toward the Moon in the Seventeenth and Eighteenth Centuries." *Smith College Studies in Modern Languages*, 17.2 (1935–36): 1–72.

Explores the ways in which the scientific contributions to lunar theory during the period from Galileo to Newton informed the seventeenth- and eighteenth-century poetic, satiric, religious, and philosophic imagination. Emphasizes the impact of Galileo's *Sidereus nuncius* (1610) and Newton's *Principia* (1687). Among the common literary themes drawn from lunar theory were "borrow'd light," moonspots, the moon's influence on tides, and especially the concept of the moon as a habitable world. Briefly discusses various literary formulations of the "lunar voyage" and "cosmic voyage" themes. The many authors considered include R. Blackmore, Burton, Cyrano de Bergerac, Donne, Dryden, F. Godwin, Jonson, Milton, Pope, Swift, J. Thomson, and Wilkins.

712.   Ogden, H. V. S. "Thomas Burnet's *Telluris theoria sacra* and Mountain Scenery." *ELH* 14 (1947): 139–50.

Discusses the negative responses to Burnet's theory of the origin and utility of mountains, including criticism by J. Beaumont, J. Ray, and Warren. Burnet's detractors were instrumental in inspiring the seventeenth- and eighteenth-century poetic and literary appreciation of mountain scenery.

713.   Oruch, Jack B. "Topography in the Prose and Poetry of the English Renaissance, 1540–1640." *DA* 25 (1964): 2966.

See item 425 for annotation.

714.   Pfeiffer, K. Ludwig. *Wissenschaft als Sujet im modernen englischen Roman*. Konstanzer Universitätsreden 127. Konstanz: Universitätsverlag, 1979. 63 pp.

See item 164 for annotation.

715.   Ray, Don E. "Seventeenth-Century Poetry and Science: Twin Champions against Ignorance." *Proceedings: Pacific Northwest Conference on Foreign Languages, Twenty-First Annual Meeting, April 3–4, 1970*. Ed. Ralph W. Baldner. Victoria, BC: U of Victoria, 1970. 234–47.

Outlines how poets and scientists such as T. Browne, Milton, F. Bacon, and Newton helped advance learning in the seventeenth century. Much of the poetry of the time ". . . synthesized and applied the truths which scientific scrutiny and careful reasoning and discourse revealed."

715a.   Riddell, James Allen. "The Evolution of the Humours Character in Seventeenth-Century English Comedy." *DA* 27 (1966): 1037A–38A.

Examines the interest in humoral psychology among seventeenth-century English playwrights and critics, focusing on Jonson and the comic dramatists of the Restoration.

716.   Ridgely, Beverly S. "A Seventeenth-Century French Poetic Debate on the Copernican Theory: Claude de Chaulne versus Hugues de Lionne." *MLN* 80 (1965): 563–74.

Examines the content and tone of a series of informal letters in verse that Claude de Chaulne exchanged with such persons as Nicolas Foucquet and Hugues de Lionne between 1644 and 1660. Includes two letters exchanged between Claude and Hugues that respectively reject and defend the Copernican hypothesis of heliocentrism, though in a lighthearted and offhand manner. The author maintains that these amateur poets' casual treatment of such a controversial topic provides a clue to the reasons behind a similarly lighthearted poetic treatment of heliocentrism by such poets as Dalibray, Le Pailleur, and La Fontaine. Perhaps abstruse philosophical or scientific ideas must necessarily be treated lightly to be popularly received by the literate public.

717.   ———. "The Impact of the 'Old' and 'New' Astronomies on French Poetry from 1600 to 1650." *DA* 16 (1956): 1140–41.
    When French poetry of the period 1600–50 took up astronomy, it tended to adhere to Aristotelio-Ptolemaic-Christian astronomical principles, reflecting the French intellectual sphere's reluctance to accept the Copernican astronomical system.

718.   Robin, P. Ansell. *Animal Lore in English Literature.* London: Murray, 1932. Folcroft: Folcroft, 1970. Norwood: Norwood, 1975. Philadelphia: West, 1976. 196 pp.
    See item 169 for annotation.

719.   Rosenfield, Leonora Cohen. *From Beast-Machine to Man-Machine: Animal Soul in French Letters from Descartes to La Mettrie.* Diss. Columbia U, 1940. New York: Oxford UP, 1940. 353 pp. Enl. ed. New York: Octagon, 1968. 385 pp.
    Rev. M. F. Ashley Montagu, *Isis* 33 (1941–42): 548–50; George R. Havens, *MLN* 57 (1942): 681–83; L. W. Tancock, *MLR* 37 (1942): 516–17.
    Traces the transition from R. Descartes's doctrine of animal automatism to the doctrine of human automatism that culminated in the philosophy of La Mettrie and notes the scientific, philosophic, theological, and literary components of the controversy that grew up around the doctrines. Poets discussed include pro-Cartesians Polignac and L. Racine and anti-Cartesians La Fontaine, Deshoulières, G. Beaumont, and C. Descartes.

720.   Rousseau, G. S. "Science and the Discovery of the Imagination in Enlightened England." *ECS* 3 (1969–70): 108–35.
    Examines how the Enlightenment's scientific concern with the physiology of imagination influenced the aesthetic sensibility of artists and philosophers from 1650 to 1800. Authors cited include Blake, Smollett, Swift, J. Thomson, S. Coleridge, P. Shelley, and Wordsworth.

721.   Sadler, Lynn Veach. "Relations between Alchemy and Poetics in the Renaissance and Seventeenth Century, with Special Glances at Donne and Milton." *Ambix* 24 (1977): 69–76.
    Examines the impact of alchemy on poetic theory and technique by drawing parallels between the pseudoscience and the art, citing the use of alchemical analogies in treatises on poetry such as Reynolds's *Mythomystes* (1632) and Puttenham's *Arte*

of English Poesie (1589), and surveying alchemical techniques in Donne's "Triple Foole" (1633) and Milton's *Samson Agonistes* (1671).

722.   Secret, François. "Littérature et alchimie à la fin du XVIᵉ et au début du XVIIᵉ siècle." *BHR* 35 (1973): 103–16.

Catalogs references to alchemy in the literary works, correspondence, and treatises of Cyrano de Bergerac, l'Hermite, d'Aubry, F. Helmont, Domayron, and an anonymous alchemist from Orléans.

723.   ———. "Littérature et alchimie au XVIIᵉ siècle: 'L'Ecusson harmonique' de Jacques Sanlecque." *SFr* 16 (1972): 338–46.

Maintains that Sanlecque, known chiefly as an alchemist and as the editor of *Bibliothecae chemicae*, deserves a place in the history of early seventeenth-century French literature, especially for his work *L'imprimeur au lecteur sur l'explication de sa marque typographique ou Ecusson harmonique, en faveur du vin et de l'eau de vie.* Cites numerous passages from that book in examining the alchemical motifs in Sanlecque's typographical coat of arms.

723a.   Shugg, Wallace. "The Beast-Machine in England: A Study of the Impact of the Cartesian Doctrine of Animal Automatism in England from 1645 to 1750." *DA* 28 (1967): 643A.

Chapter 4 discusses the impact of the beast-machine doctrine on English scholars, citing references, allusions, and asides that ridiculed or satirized the doctrine.

724.   Simpson, H. C. "The Vogue of Science in English Literature, 1600–1800." *UTQ* 2 (1932–33): 143–67.

Literature by Cowley, Evelyn, Glanvill, Johnson, Milton, Pope, Swift, J. Thomson, and Wilkins. The impact of seventeenth and eighteenth-century developments in astronomy, physics, and medicine by such scientists as Galileo, Kepler, Newton, and Harvey.

725.   Toulmin, Stephen. "Seventeenth Century Science and the Arts." *Seventeenth Century Science and the Arts.* Ed. Hedley Howell Rhys. Princeton: Princeton UP, 1961. 3–28.

Broadly examines how the scientific revolution affected literature, music, and other arts in the seventeenth century.

726.   Wagman, Frederick Herbert. *Magic and Natural Science in German Baroque Literature: A Study in the Prose Forms of the Later Seventeenth Century.* Diss. Columbia U, 1942. New York University Ottendorfer Memorial Series of Germanic Monographs 29. Columbia University Germanic Studies ns 13. New York: Columbia UP, 1942. New York: AMS, 1966. 178 pp.

Rev. Ernest Manheim, *American Sociological Review* 7 (1942): 889–90; Archer Taylor, *MP* 40 (1942–43): 291–92; Leonard Forster, *MLR* 39 (1944): 84–86; Ludwig Edelstein, *MLN* 60 (1945): 58–61.

Traces the transition in seventeenth-century German thought and literature from magical, supernatural, and pseudoscientific views of natural phenomena to a scientific outlook influenced by Renaissance natural-philosophical doctrines and the discoveries and conceptions of Kepler, Galileo, F. Bacon, R. Descartes, Leibniz, and others. Among the authors considered are Lohenstein, Harsdörffer, Rist, Happel, Francisci, Weise, and Grimmelshausen.

727. Whittaker, E. J. "Natural History and Literature, 1550–1660." Diss. U of Durham, 1977.
Not seen for annotation.

728. Wilson, F. P. "English Letters and the Royal Society in the Seventeenth Century." *Mathematical Gazette* 19 (1935): 343–54.
Describes the foundation, aims, and membership of the Royal Society in 1662 and comments on the various ways contemporary English writers responded to the society's scientific activities. The authors discussed include Aubrey, S. Butler, Cowley, Denham, Dryden, Shadwell, and Waller. Also remarks briefly on the similarity between Solomon's House in F. Bacon's *New Atlantis* and the Royal Society.

729. Youngren, William H. "Generality, Science and Poetic Language in the Restoration." *ELH* 35 (1968): 158–87.
Explores the meaning of the neoclassical demand that poetry concern general, rather than particular, phenomena. Surveys the impact of scientific language and methodology on the critical attitudes toward Restoration poetry.

730. Zacharasiewicz, Waldemar. *Die "Cosmic Voyage" und die "Excursion" in der englischen Dichtung des 17. und 18. Jahrhunderts*. Diss. U Graz, 1966. Wien: Notring, 1969. 204 pp.
Among the scientific sources for the poetic topoi of the "cosmic voyage" and the "excursion" in seventeenth- and eighteenth-century poetry are T. Burnet's *Theoria sacra* (1618), Burton's *Anatomy of Melancholy* (1621), Hakewill's *Apology or Declaration of the Power and Providence of God* (1627), Newton's *Principia*, and the astronomy of the time. The poems examined include Cowley's *Extasie*, Milton's *Paradise Lost*, Mallet's "Excursion," and J. Thomson's *Seasons*.

731. ———. *Die Klimatheorie in der englischen Literatur und Literaturkritik von der Mitte des 16. bis zum frühen 18. Jahrhundert*. Wiener Beiträge zur englischen Philologie 77. Vienna: Braumüller, 1977. 666 pp.
Rev. Hans-Joachim Possin, *Arcadia* 14 (1979): 197–98; Karl Josef Höltgen, *GRM* 30 (1980): 246–49.
Cites references in literature and literary criticism between 1550 and 1710 to the "theory of climate"—the view that the physical, mental, and moral qualities of nations are determined by environmental factors. Among the authors studied are J. Bodin, Greene, Shakespeare, Walkington, Burton, Donne, Dryden, Pope, and Swift.

Individual Authors

Juan Ruiz de Alarcón y Mendoza (1581?–1639)

732. Espantoso-Foley, Augusta M. "The Problem of Astrology and Its Use in Ruiz de Alarcón's *El dueño de las estrellas*." *HR* 32 (1964): 1–11.

Outlines the artistic and dramatic role of astrology in Alarćon's comedy, emphasizing the connections among astrology, fate, free will, and Alarćon's Catholicism.

Francis Bacon (1561–1626)

733.   Adams, Robert P. "The Social Responsibilities of Science in *Utopia*, *New Atlantis*, and After." *JHI* 10 (1949): 374–98.
See item 494 for annotation.

734.   Bierman, Judah. "The *New Atlantis*, Bacon's Utopia of Science." *PLL* 3 (1967): 99–110.
Studies the dialogue and discourse that frame Bacon's description of the college of science at Bensalem in *The New Atlantis*. To clarify Bacon's proposal for creating a utopian, science-based society, Bierman examines the central allegories developed in the supporting dialogue—the myths about the founding and Christianization of Bensalem.

735.   ———. "Science and Society in the *New Atlantis* and Other Renaissance Utopias." *PMLA* 78 (1963): 492–500.
A comparative analysis of the relations between scientific, political, and social institutions in Bacon's *New Atlantis*, T. More's *Utopia*, Andreae's *Christianopolis*, and Campanella's *City of the Sun*.

736.   Blodgett, Eleanor D. "Bacon's *New Atlantis* and Campanella's *Civitas solis*: A Study in Relationships." *PMLA* 46 (1931): 763–80.
Outlines the similarities and differences between the utopias of *Civitas solis* and *The New Atlantis*, noting the possible influence of Campanella's work on Bacon's. Discusses the extent to which both texts reflect the Renaissance preoccupation with empirical science.

737.   Bowman, Sister Mary Antonia, BVM. "The English Prose Style of Sir Francis Bacon." *DA* 24 (1964): 4674–75.
Examines how Bacon's prose style reflects his intention to develop a scientific program to advance learning.

737a.   Cochrane, Rexmond C. "Francis Bacon in Early Eighteenth-Century English Literature." *PQ* 37 (1958): 58–79.
In contrast to the seventeenth century, which widely celebrated Bacon and his advocacy of the "new philosophy," the early eighteenth century focused on the moral and religious implications of the "new science." Bacon's defenders were physicotheological poets and thinkers who subordinated his natural philosophy to his moral philosophy.

738.   Frietzsche, Arthur H. "The Impact of Applied Science upon the Utopian Ideal." *BYUS* 3.3-4 (1960–61): 35–42.
See item 495 for annotation.

738a.   Linden, Stanton J. "Francis Bacon and Alchemy: The Reformation of Vulcan." *JHI* 35 (1974): 547–60.

Shows that Bacon's statements about alchemy in his scientific works represent a considerable advance over the medieval and Renaissance depiction of alchemy and alchemists.

739. McCreary, Eugene P. "Bacon's Theory of Imagination Reconsidered." *HLQ* 36 (1972–73): 317–26.

Explicates Bacon's double view of imagination. On the one hand, imagination serves poetry but interferes with the goals of natural science; on the other hand, because it serves both poetry and the religious impulse, it can act as a "minister of propaganda for science."

740. Prior, Moody E. "Bacon's Man of Science." *JHI* 15 (1954): 348–70.

Discusses the development of Bacon's ideal of the "man of science," touching on his portrayal of the scientist in his utopian *New Atlantis*.

741. Rossi, Paolo. *Francis Bacon: From Magic to Science*. Trans. Sacha Rabinovitch. London: Routledge; Chicago: U of Chicago P, 1968. 280 pp.
Rev. J. L. Kirby, *History Today* 18 (1968): 208–09; J. Bronowski, *Political Science Quarterly* 84 (1969): 151–52; Glen R. Driscoll, *AHR* 74 (1969): 979–80; J. R. Ravetz, *EHR* 84 (1969): 795–96.

Surveys the development of Bacon's philosophy of science and learning and studies his relation to magical and alchemical tradition, his appreciation of mechanical arts, his perspective on history and the failure of traditional knowledge, his interpretation of classical mythology and its relation to his program for scientific reform, his concept of logic and its relation to rhetoric, and his adaptation of rhetorical methods to scientific logic and natural inquiry. Among the many works discussed are *Sylva silvarum*, *De sapientia veterum*, *Novum organum*, and *Valerius terminus*.

742. Sessions, William A. "The Hunt for Pan: A Study in Bacon's Use of the Imagination." *DA* 27 (1966): 1040A.

Sees Bacon's vision of time, society, and science in the light of his poetic imagination.

743. Steadman, John M. "Beyond Hercules: Bacon and the Scientist as Hero." *SLitI* 4.1 (1971): 3–47.

Traces the history of heroic topoi in literature, covering the works of Homer, Lucretius, and Milton, and examines in detail Bacon's adaptation of the heroic theme to his celebration of scientists and scientific activity in *The Advancement of Learning*, *Novum organum*, and *The New Atlantis*.

744. Stephens, James. *Francis Bacon and the Style of Science*. Chicago: U of Chicago P, 1975. 188 pp.
Rev. Robert Adolph, *ELN* 13 (1975–76): 299–300; O. B. Hardison, Jr., *Review of Metaphysics* 30 (1976–77): 140–41; Achsah Guibbory, *JEGP* 76 (1977): 129–31.

Traces Bacon's attempts to develop a philosophical style appropriate for the communication of scientific data. Surveys the rhetorical tradition against which Bacon struggled and examines his debt to Aristotle's *Rhetoric*, his central doctrines regarding the unity of science and style, and his attempts to perfect the aphorism as a means of communication.

745.   ———. "Science and the Aphorism: Bacon's Theory of the Philosophical Style." *SM* 37 (1970): 157–71.

Describes Bacon's theory of the aphorism and its function in his program to advance learning and express scientific truths. Principal sources include Bacon's *Novum organum*, *De augmentis*, and *Advancement of Learning*.

746.   Tillman, James S. "Bacon's Georgics of Science." *PLL* 11 (1975): 357–66.

Bacon appropriated georgic form, themes, and imagery to express his philosophic and scientific hypotheses. Emphasizes his debt to Vergil's *Georgics*.

747.   Vickers, Brian. *Francis Bacon and Renaissance Prose*. Cambridge: Cambridge UP, 1968. 316 pp.
        Rev. Jackson I. Cope, *JEGP* 68 (1969): 178–80; Dominic A. LaRusso, *QJS* 55 (1969): 82–83.

Ascribes Bacon's remarkable influence over seventeenth-century thought to his ability as an imaginative writer. Analyzes Bacon's literary style, covering his general organization and structure, his theory of the aphorism, his use of image and argument, and his relation to the tradition of syntactically structured prose. Bacon's use of Ciceronian sentence structure and poetic imagery conflicts with his espousal of a plain style in the service of the "new science."

748.   Warhaft, Sidney. "Science against Man in Bacon." *BuR* 7 (1957–58): 158–73.

Maintains that, by shifting attention from humanity to the world and external nature, Bacon's scientific program in *The New Atlantis* leads to the erosion of religious, moral, philosophical, and humanitarian values. Many tendencies of his new scientific organon have been realized today.

748a.   Weinberger, J. "Science and Rule in Bacon's Utopia: An Introduction to the Reading of the *New Atlantis*." *American Political Science Review* 70 (1976): 865–85.

"The *New Atlantis* is the key to the unity of Bacon's teaching about science and man. The fundamental Baconian theme is the virtue of science as the highest human activity, and this theme consists in a teaching about the nature and virtue of the conquests facilitated by science."

749.   Whitney, Charles C. "Bacon's Modernity: From Literature to Science." *DAI* 38 (1977): 2148A.

Analyzes Bacon's claim to originality and modernity, noting the unacknowledged sources of his eclectic thought and discussing the influence of literary and poetic models on his idea of science.

750.   Wiener, Harvey. "The *New Atlantis* and Baconian Method." *DAI* 32 (1971): 937A.

Although the scientific features of *The New Atlantis* are generally recognized, the relation of science to theology and poetry in Bacon's utopia must not be overlooked. Nor should his use of induction in structuring his fiction be overemphasized; metaphor (the driving force of which is the power of imagination) is an equal, if not more important, aspect of his literary methodology.

751.   ———. " 'Science or Providence': Toward Knowledge in Bacon's *New Atlantis.*" *EnlE* 3 (1972): 85–92.
Disputes the often expressed view that Bacon severed science from religion. *The New Atlantis*, at least, accords providence a status equal to that of science as a means of attaining knowledge.

752.   Wiley, Margaret L. "Francis Bacon: Induction and/or Rhetoric." *SLitl* 4.1 (1971): 65–79.
Maintains that Bacon's inductive scientific system, outlined in *Novum organum* and *The Advancement of Learning*, is essentially rhetorical. His method of truth-seeking is closely linked to his aphoristic method of literary expression.

Sir Richard Blackmore (c. 1650–1729)

753.   Rosenberg, Albert. *Sir Richard Blackmore: A Poet and Physician of the Augustan Age.* Lincoln: U of Nebraska P, 1953. 175 pp.
This biography stresses the relation between medicine and poetry in Blackmore's life and examines his response to literary satires of his poetic and medical activities written by T. Brown, Dryden, Garth, and others.

Alexander Brome (1620–66)

754.   Dubinski, Roman R. "The Scientific Element in Alexander Brome's Love Poetry." *ESC* 2 (1976): 8–26.
In attempting to treat the psychological complexities of love, Brome's poetry relies on the Baconian scientific method of hypothesis and examination. Poems studied include "The Attempt," "To His Mistress," "The Indifferent," and "Plain Dealing."

Sir Thomas Browne (1605–82)

755.   Howell, Almonte C. "Sir Thomas Browne and Seventeenth-Century Scientific Thought." *SP* 22 (1925): 61–80.
Browne's importance in the history of science lies not in his scientific achievements but in his popularization of scientific thought and the scientific methods of F. Bacon and R. Descartes through such works as *Vulgar Errors*. Howell evaluates Browne's attitude toward Copernicanism.

756.   Huntley, Frank L. *Sir Thomas Browne: A Biographical and Critical Study.* Ann Arbor: U of Michigan P, 1962. 283 pp.

Rev. Joan Bennett, *MLR* 58 (1963): 98–100; C. A. Patrides, *MP* 61 (1963–64): 243–44.

Traces Browne's early life and education, stressing his astronomical and biological interests and his responses to Copernicus's heliocentric theory and Harvey's theory of the circulation of the blood. Undertakes a stylistic and thematic analysis of Browne's major works, including *Religio medici*, *Vulgar Errors*, *The Urn Burial*, and *The Garden of Cyrus*, emphasizing the interplay of science, literature, and theology.

756a.   McCarthy, Paul J. "A Doctor's Language of Devotion: The Occult Sciences in the Works of Sir Thomas Browne." *DAI* 36 (1975): 278A.

Though as a scientist Browne tended to condemn occult studies such as alchemy and astrology, he uses references to these sciences effectively in his devotional works.

756b.   Merton, Egon S. "The Botany of Sir Thomas Browne." *Isis* 47 (1956): 161–71.

Traces Browne's botanical interests, noting plant imagery in *The Garden of Cyrus* and *The Urn Burial*.

757.   ———. *Science and Imagination in Sir Thomas Browne*. New York: King's Crown, 1949. New York: Octagon, 1969. New York: AMS, 1973. 156 pp.
Rev. A. K. Croston, *RES* ns 2 (1951): 285–86.

Examines how Browne's science influenced his philosophic and artistic imagination. Chapter 8 assesses the impact his knowledge of medicine and astronomy had on the *Religio medici*, *The Urn Burial*, and *Christian Morals*.

758.   Merton, Stephen. "Sir Thomas Browne on Astronomy." *HINL* 4 (1958): 83–86.

Brief remarks on Browne's allusions to astronomy in works such as *Religio medici* and *Pseudodoxia*. His "references to astronomy may be taken as a measure of the influence which the new science had upon the intelligent layman of the seventeenth century."

Robert Burton (1577–1640)

759.   Brownlee, A. "Robert Burton an Unhonoured Biologist." *Nature* 219 (1968): 125–27.

Outlines the biological insights in Burton's *Anatomy of Melancholy* (1621), a work admired by Johnson, Keats, Lamb, Osler, and others.

760.   Canavan, Thomas L. "Madness and Enthusiasm in Burton's *Anatomy of Melancholy* and Swift's *Tale of a Tub*." *DAI* 34 (1973): 269A.

Both Burton's *Anatomy* and Swift's *Tale* use elements of the Aristotelian-Galenic medical tradition to characterize madness and enthusiasm.

761.   Dewey, Nicholas. "An Unhonoured Biologist." *Nature* 221 (1969): 394.

Reply to A. Brownlee, item 759. Dewey opposes Brownlee's praise of Burton's biological acumen and maintains that in the *Anatomy of Melancholy* Burton exhibits a superficial and unscientific understanding of biology.

762.   Gardiner, Judith K. "Elizabethan Psychology and Burton's *Anatomy of Melancholy*." *JHI* 38 (1977): 373–88.
This analysis of Burton's *Anatomy* examines Elizabethan psychology to clarify the science's influence on Elizabethan literature.

763.   Goldstein, Leonard. "Science and Literary Style in Robert Burton's 'Cento out of Divers Writers.' " *JRUL* 21 (1957–58): 55–68.
Maintains that Burton's tendency to reinforce the statements and arguments in the *Anatomy of Melancholy* with many relevant citations from earlier thinkers derives from the quantifying aspects of Galileo's scientific method.

764.   Höltgen, Karl J. "Die astrologischen Zeichen in Burtons *Anatomy of Melancholy*." *Anglia* 82 (1964): 485–98.
Maintains that the elucidation of the order and function of the astrological signs in the *Anatomy of Melancholy* helps explain the structure of the work.

765.   Thompson, Roland G. "The Wisdom of the Commonplace in Burton's *Anatomy*: A Study of Its Rhetorical Intentions." *DAI* 32 (1972): 6396A.
This study of the *Anatomy of Melancholy* stresses the social, intellectual, and religious aims underlying Burton's rhetorical and literary use of medical and scientific data.

766.   Vicari, Eleanor P. "Learning and Imagination in Robert Burton." *DAI* 32 (1971): 988A.
Studies Burton's imaginative use and arrangement of diverse materials from natural science, religion, and literature in his *Anatomy of Melancholy*.

Samuel Butler (1612–80)

767.   Nelson, Nicolas H. "Astrology, *Hudibras*, and the Puritans." *JHI* 37 (1976): 521–36.
Reconstructs the debate over the value of astrology that occurred in England during the 1640s and 1650s and, against this background, assesses the role played by Butler's satire of astrology in *Hudibras* (1664), a work that primarily satirized Puritanism.

768.   Wagner, Joseph B. "Samuel Butler's Satire of the Hermetic Philosophers." *DAI* 35 (1974–75): 421A.
Analyzes the full range of Butler's satirical attacks on seventeenth-century hermeticists and the closely allied "new scientists." Examines *Hudibras*, *Characters*, and some minor verse.

Pedro Calderón de la Barca (1600–81)

769.   Lorenz, Erika. "Calderón und die Astrologie." *RJ* 12 (1961): 265–77.
Discusses Calderón's problematic depiction of astrology in such dramatic works as *La vida es sueño* and *El mayor monstruo del mundo*. According to Lorenz, Calderón's

apparent ambivalence toward astrology can be traced to Saint Aquinas, who grants the stars a real, though limited, sphere of influence over human behavior.

Tommaso Campanella (1568–1639)

770.   Blodgett, Eleanor D. "Bacon's *New Atlantis* and Campanella's *Civitas solis*: A Study in Relationships." *PMLA* 46 (1931): 763–80.
See item 736 for annotation.

Thomas Campion (1567–1620)

771.   Lowbury, Edward, et al. *Thomas Campion: Poet, Composer, Physician*. New York: Barnes; London: Chatto, 1970. 195 pp.
Campion, one of many doctor-poets, is uniquely admired not only for writing some of the finest English poems but also for setting his poetry to excellent music. This study examines the range of his poems and considers various influences, including his theories of composition and his practice of medicine, on his creative work.

Thomas Carew (1598?–1639?)

772.   McFarland, Ronald E. "The Rhetoric of Medicine: Lord Herbert's and Thomas Carew's Poems of Green-Sickness." *JHM* 30 (1975): 250–58.
See item 844 for annotation.

Robert Chester (1566?–1640?)

773.   Watson, Elizabeth. "Natural History in *Love's Martyr*." *RMS* 8 (1964): 109–26.
Analyzes Chester's allegorical use of natural history in *Love's Martyr* (1601). The sources of his imagery were Rembert Dodoens's *Nieuwe herball* (1578) and John Maplet's *Greene Forest* (1567).

Abraham Cowley (1618–67)

774.   Hinman, Robert B. *Abraham Cowley's World of Order*. Cambridge: Harvard UP, 1960. 373 pp.
         Rev. Scott Elledge, *MP* 59 (1961–62): 131–33; James Kinsley, *RES* ns 13 (1962): 200–02; Geoffrey Walton, *MLR* 57 (1962): 250.
A highly sympathetic appraisal of Cowley's rank as a poet, stressing his imaginative synthesis of science, faith, and poetry. Includes chapters on Cowley's philosophy, the influence of F. Bacon and Hobbes on his concept of poetry, the harmonious view of the universe expressed in the *Davideis* and *Plantarum*, and his poetic appropriation of scientific data from astronomy, physics, botany, geology, physiology, and meteorology. "No poetic imagination in the seventeenth century was more stimulated than Cowley's by the intellectual energy of the age."

775.   ———. " 'Truth is Truest Poesy': The Influence of the New Philosophy
            on Abraham Cowley." *ELH* 23 (1956): 194–203.
    The new philosophy of F. Bacon, Hobbes, and the Royal Society provided Cowley
with the methods and materials to transform poetry into a "divine science" capable
of bridging the gap between the phenomenal world and the world of God.

Savinien Cyrano de Bergerac (1619–55)

776.   Beichman, Anthony M. "Cyrano de Bergerac and Fontenelle: A Relation-
            ship in the Enlightenment, with Special Reference to the Quarrel of the
            Ancients and the Moderns." *DA* 31 (1970–71): 2373A.
    Examines the intellectual affinities between Cyrano and Fontenelle, particularly
regarding their perspectives on science and scientific progress.

777.   Bourdier, Franck. "Cyrano de Bergerac disciple de Gassendi: Leurs con-
            ceptions sur les êtres vivants." *Histoire et nature* ns 2 (1974): 5–20.
    Provides a brief history of Cyrano's life and a review of the physical theories of
his teacher, Gassendi. A summary of *L'autre monde* shows how Cyrano incorporated
his thoughts about matter and life into his writing.

778.   Bridenne, Jean-Jacques. "Cyrano de Bergerac et la science aéronautique."
            RSH 75 (1954): 241–58.
    Analyzes the interest in aeronautics Cyrano expresses in *Etats de la lune* and *Etats
du soleil* and relates it to the scientific thought of his time.

779.   Lavers, A. "La croyance à l'unité de la science dans *L'autre monde* de Cyrano
            de Bergerac." *CS* 45 (1958): 406–16.
    Studies how Cyrano's *L'autre monde* expresses his views on philosophy and the
unity of science. Among the influences on Cyrano's thought were Campanella, R.
Descartes, and Gassendi.

780.   Spink, J. S. "Form and Structure: Cyrano de Bergerac's Atomistic Con-
            ception of Metamorphosis." *Literature and Science*. Proc. of the Sixth Trien-
            nial Congress of the International Federation for Modern Languages and
            Literatures. Oxford, 1954. Oxford: Blackwell, 1955. 144–50.
    Shows how Cyrano's conception of metamorphosis, expressed in *States and Empires
of the Sun*, combines literary and scientific ideas.

781.   Voisé, Waldemar. "Cyrano de Bergerac entre l'héliocentrisme et le Dar-
            winisme." *Revue de Synthèse* 94 (1973): 53–62.
    Examines Cyrano's scientific thought, focusing on his espousal of heliocentric
astronomy and on his ideas about human evolution, which, the author claims,
anticipate Darwinism. Cyrano incorporated his scientific ideas into *L'autre monde* to
argue his case without incurring the punishments accorded heretics in the seventeenth
century.

782.   Walker, Judy C. "The Unity of Cyrano de Bergerac's Imaginary Voyages."
            DAI 36 (1975–76): 1566A–67A.

One of the unifying features of Cyrano's *Les états et empires de la lune et du soleil* is the work's symbolic and structural use of the archetypal Prometheus myth. The journey to the heavens reflects the spirit of modern science.

Charles Vion Sieur de Dalibray (c. 1600–55)

783.   Ridgely, Beverly S. "Dalibray, Le Pailleur, and the 'New Astronomy' in French Seventeenth-Century Poetry." *JHI* 17 (1956): 3–27.

Surveys French astronomical thought in the first half of the seventeenth century. Examines the sonnets Dalibray wrote between 1640 and 1646 and the poetic "Response" of his friend Le Pailleur, a poet and mathematician. These are among the first French literary works to reflect a knowledge of the "new astronomy" of Copernicanism.

John Donne (1572–1631)

784.   Allen, Don Cameron. "John Donne's Knowledge of Renaissance Medicine." *JEGP* 42 (1943): 322–42.

Surveys Donne's use of medical imagery and terminology and traces his knowledge of medicine to sources in Hippocrates, Galen, and Paracelsus.

785.   Coffin, Charles Monroe. *John Donne and the New Philosophy.* Columbia University Studies in English and Comparative Literature 126. New York: Columbia UP, 1937. Philadelphia: Russell; New York: Humanities, 1958. 311 pp.
         Rev. John T. McNeill, *JR* 17 (1937): 306–09; Francis R. Johnson, *MLN* 53 (1938): 290–93; I. A. Shapiro, *MLR* 33 (1938): 280–81.

Studies the influence Renaissance astronomy had on Donne's thought and poetry from roughly 1601 to 1615 and emphasizes Donne's familiarity with and poetic use of Copernicanism as expounded in the works of Kepler, Galileo, and Gilbert. Includes chapters on Donne's early educational influences; his knowledge of and responses to traditional Aristotelian and Scholastic science; the rise of Copernicanism; and his response to theories of a moving Earth and new stars, the doctrine of the elements, and new concepts of space. Among the works examined are *The First Anniversary*, *The Second Anniversary*, and *Ignatius His Conclave*.

786.   Cognard, Roger A. "The Solstice Metaphor in Donne's 'Lecture upon the Shadow.'" *ELWIU* 7 (1980): 11–20.

Discusses the informing metaphor of Donne's "Lecture"—the comparison of perfect love to the summer solstice. Donne's use of the metaphor attests to an interest in astronomy.

786a.   Crawshaw, Eluned. "Hermetic Elements in Donne's Poetic Vision." *John Donne: Essays in Celebration.* Ed. A. J. Smith. London: Methuen, 1972. 324–48.

Shows that Donne's use of alchemical imagery and terminology in his religious and meditative verse was both serious and precise.

787.   Duncan, Edgar Hill. "Alchemy in Chaucer, Jonson, and Donne." Diss.
        Vanderbilt U, 1941.
    Not seen for annotation.

788.   ———. "Donne's Alchemical Figures." *ELH* 9 (1942): 257–85.
    Discusses the creative adaptation of alchemical imagery in a wide range of Donne's
poetry and traces the probable sources of his alchemical knowledge to works by
Paracelsus, Vincent de Beauvais, John of Rupecissa, and others.

789.   Empson, William. "Donne the Space Man." *KR* 19 (1957): 337–99.
    Assesses the interest in space travel Donne expressed in his poems, notes the
theological implications of such an interest during his time, and discusses his
knowledge of Copernicanism.

790.   Hassel, R. Chris, Jr. "Donne's *Ignatius His Conclave* and the New Astron-
        omy." *MP* 68 (1970–71): 329–37.
    This discussion of *Ignatius His Conclave* focuses on Donne's satirical treatment of
the astronomical theories of Copernicus, Brahe, Galileo, and Kepler.

791.   Hayes, Thomas W. "Alchemical Imagery in John Donne's 'A Nocturnall
        upon S. Lucies Day.' " *Ambix* 24 (1977): 55–62.
    Analyzes the alchemical imagery in Donne's poem. Discusses images of light and
darkness, dryness and wetness, life and death, medieval and Renaissance cosmology,
and other themes related to alchemy.

791a.   Khanna, Urmilla. "Donne's 'A Valediction: Forbidding Mourning'—Some
        Possible Alchemical Allusions." *N&Q* ns 17 (1970): 404–05.
    Cites passages from Paracelsus's alchemical writings that aid in the understanding
of Donne's poem.

792.   Klammer, Enno. "Cosmography in Donne's Poetry." *Cresset* 32.1 (1968–
        69): 14–15.
    Briefly discusses Donne's descriptions of the cosmos and his use of the concept
of the macrocosm and the microcosm as derived from Ptolemaic cosmography.

793.   Lander, Clara. "A Dangerous Sickness Which Turned to a Spotted Fever."
        SEL 11 (1971): 89–108.
    Donne's *Devotions* structurally and rhetorically reflects the typical sufferings of a
victim of typhus, or spotted fever; each of the twenty-three devotions represents a
day of the sickness, and each devotion internally mirrors the daily cycle of the typhus
sufferer.

794.   Levine, Jay A. " 'The Dissolution': Donne's Twofold Elegy." *ELH* 28
        (1961): 301–15.
    Interprets Donne's poem on the basis of its alchemical imagery.

795.   Mahoney, John L. "Donne and Greville: Two Christian Attitudes toward
        the Renaissance Idea of Mutability and Decay." *CLAJ* 5 (1961–62):
        203–12.

The religious doctrine of original sin and the implications of the scientific investigations of Copernicus, Galileo, and Kepler produced the widespread Renaissance belief in the mutability and decay of the world order. The author examines two attitudes toward the concept, reflected in Donne's *Second Anniversary* and Greville's *Treatie of Humane Learning*.

796.   Maxwell, J. C. "Donne and the 'New Philosophy.'" *DUJ* 12 (1951): 61–64.
Disputes the commonly held view that the clash between Ptolemaic and Copernican cosmologies was a major formative influence in Donne's intellectual life. Cites passages from Donne's *Anniversaries*.

797.   Mazzeo, Joseph A. "Notes on John Donne's Alchemical Imagery." *Isis* 48 (1957): 103–23.
Much of Donne's poetic imagery clearly reflects his extensive knowledge of alchemy and the hermetic philosophy, particularly the work of Paracelsus. Mazzeo relates particular passages to alchemical theories such as the macrocosm-microcosm analogy, the balsam theory, and the idea of the quintessence and emphasizes throughout the distinction between physical and spiritual alchemy.

798.   Moody, Peter R. "Donne's *A Lecture upon the Shadow*." *Expl* 20 (1961–62): item 60.
Donne's use of solar and shadow imagery accords with scientific fact.

799.   Morris, William E. "Donne's 'The Sunne Rising,' 30." *Expl* 23 (1964–65): item 45.
Explains the astronomical significance of the word *spheare* in line 30 of Donne's poem.

800.   Murray, W. A. "Donne and Paracelsus: An Essay in Interpretation." *RES* 25 (1949): 115–23.
Refers to the medical treatises of Paracelsus to explicate Donne's "Love's Alchymie" and "A Nocturnall upon S. Lucies Day."

801.   ———. "Donne's Gold-Leaf and His Compasses." *MLN* 73 (1958): 329–30.
Donne's association of gold leaf with a compass in *A Valediction: Forbidding Mourning* suggests an allusion to the then current chemical symbol for gold, possibly encountered in Paracelsian medical and alchemical texts.

802.   Nicholl, Charles. *The Chemical Theatre*. London: Routledge, 1980. 292 pp.
See item 593 for annotation.

803.   Poynter, F. N. L. "John Donne and William Harvey." *JHM* 15 (1960): 233–46.
Several passages in Donne's writings, especially in his *Devotions* and *Sermons*, suggest his familiarity with the medical thought of Harvey. Poynter traces the history of Donne's acquaintance with medicine in general and with Harvey's experiments in particular.

804.   Scott, Robert Ian. "Donne and Kepler." *N&Q* ns 6 (1959): 208–09.
Donne's metaphors alluding to astronomy in *Elegie on the Untimely Death of the Incomparable Prince Henry* (1612) are best understood in the light of Kepler's first law of planetary motion.

805.   Shapiro, I. A. "John Donne the Astronomer: The Date of the Eighth Problem." *TLS* 3 July 1937: 492.
Links Donne's eighth problem of astronomy, "Why Venus-star only doth cast a shadow," with Galileo's 1611 announcement that Venus, like the moon, exhibits phases, thus dating the problem at 1611.

806.   Simpson, David L. "Four Philosophical Poems: Ideas of Order in Donne, Pope, Tennyson, and Eliot." *DAI* 38 (1977): 2781A.
Studies the philosophical cosmology of Donne's *Anniversaries*, Pope's *Essay on Man*, Tennyson's *In Memoriam*, and T. S. Eliot's *Four Quartets*—poems in which elements of science, philosophy, and theology interact.

807.   Titus, O. P. "Science and John Donne." *SciMo* 54 (1942): 176–78.
Notes the impact of the "new science," especially astronomy, on the worldview expressed in Donne's poetry.

Michael Drayton (1563–1631)

808.   Harrison, Thomas P. *They Tell of Birds: Chaucer, Spenser, Milton, Drayton.* Austin: U of Texas P, 1956. Westport: Greenwood, 1969. 159 pp.
See item 296 for annotation.

John Dryden (1631–1700)

809.   Bredvold, Louis I. "Dryden, Hobbes, and the Royal Society." *MP* 25 (1927–28): 417–38.
Attempts to clarify Dryden's position within the intellectual milieu fostered by the Royal Society. An evaluation of Dryden's skepticism, his rejection of Hobbesian materialism, his relations with Boyle and Glanvill, and his knowledge of the new philosophy of motion indicates an essentially sympathetic, though only vaguely scientific, standing with the society.

810.   Cope, Jackson I. "Science, Christ, and Cromwell in Dryden's *Heroic Stanzas*." *MLN* 71 (1956): 483–85.
In the thirty-second poem in the *Heroic Stanzas* Dryden uses a scientific simile associated with the theological "argument from design" to depict Oliver Cromwell.

811.   Dick, Hugh G. "John Dryden's Conception of Tides?" *Isis* 43 (1952): 266.
Maintains that no source has been located for Dryden's theory of the tides in *Annus Mirabilis* (1667).

812.   Eade, J. C. "Don Alonzo 'Gravelled': Astrology in *An Evening's Love*." *SCN* 37 (1979): 80–81.

In *An Evening's Love; Or, The Mock Astrologer*, Dryden uses astrological terminology sparingly but carefully and deliberately, to reveal the pretensions of the mock astrologer Bellamy through the enthusiastic, though somewhat pedantic, astrological questions posed by Don Alonzo.

813.   Gardner, William B. "John Dryden's Interest in Judicial Astrology." *SP* 47 (1950): 506–21.

This chronological investigation of astrological references in Dryden's writings distinguishes four classes of allusions: serious, satirical, humorous, and ornamental.

814.   Griffith, Richard R. "Science and Pseudo-Science in the Imagery of John Dryden." *DA* 17 (1957): 1072–73.

Assesses Dryden's knowledge of the science of metals (comprising metallurgy, chemistry, and alchemy) and the science of the stars (astronomy and astrology) to determine their influences on his life and poetry.

815.   Hinckley, Henry B. "Theories of Vision in English Poetry." *MLN* 24 (1909): 125.

See item 636 for annotation.

816.   Miner, Earl. "Dryden's *Annus Mirabilis*, 653–656." *Expl* 24 (1965–66): item 75.

Explicates the astronomical imagery of lines 653–56.

817.   Ormsby-Lennon, Hugh. "Radical Physicians and Conservative Poets in Restoration England: Dryden among the Doctors." *SECC* 7 (1978): 389–411.

Dryden's allusions to medicine in his plays, essays, and criticism reflect at once an allegiance to the dogma of ancients such as Galen and a general acceptance, tinged with skepticism, of the medical practices of physicians such as Harvey. This essay outlines the medical dispute between the Galenists and the Neoterics and comments on Dryden's literary response to this controversy. Dryden's *Essay on Dramatic Poesy*, *Absalom and Achitophel*, *Astrea Redux*, and *Annus Mirabilis* are among the works referred to.

818.   Osenburg, F. C. "The Prologue to Dryden's *Wild Gallant* Re-examined." *ELN* 7 (1969–70): 35–39.

Discusses the meaning of astrological references in the prologue to Dryden's *Wild Gallant*.

819.   Wasserman, Earl R. "Dryden's Epistle to Charleton." *JEGP* 55 (1956): 201–12.

Though ostensibly treating the "new science" and the activities of the Royal Society, Dryden's epistle "To My Honoured Friend, Dr. Charleton" is more concerned with political and historical matters.

820.   Watson, George. "Dryden and the Scientific Image." *Notes and Records of the Royal Society of London* 18 (1963): 25–35.

Claims that Dryden's works are the single largest corpus of English literature to reflect scientific interest. Cites allusions to astronomy and physics in Dryden's writings.

Phineas Fletcher (1582–1650)

821.   Baldwin, R. G. "Dubious Claims for the Anatomy in *The Purple Island.*" *N&Q* ns 9 (1962): 377–78.

Disputes the claims that Abram B. Langdale makes in *Phineas Fletcher: Man of Science, Letters, and Divinity* for the knowledge of anatomy Fletcher exhibits in *The Purple Island* (see item 822).

822.   Langdale, Abram B. *Phineas Fletcher: Man of Science, Letters, and Divinity.* Columbia University Studies in English and Comparative Literature 125. New York: Columbia UP, 1937. New York: Octagon, 1968. 230 pp. Rev. F. S. Boas, *MLR* 33 (1938): 430–31; Charles A. Kofoid, *Isis* 31 (1939–40): 86–87.

Chapters 11 and 12 discuss the physiological and astronomical elements in Fletcher's long poem *The Purple Island* (1633). Langdale speculates that Fletcher may have been personally acquainted with both F. Bacon and Harvey and that *The Purple Island*, despite vestiges of Galenism, describes the human anatomy with an accuracy that argues for the poem's genesis in the anatomy theater.

823.   Pohlman, Augustus G. "*The Purple Island* by Phenias [sic] Fletcher: A Seventeenth Century Layman's Poetical Conception of the Human Body." *Bulletin of the Johns Hopkins Hospital* 18 (1907): 317–21.

Reprints selections from the first five cantos of *The Purple Island* and argues that these passages reveal Fletcher's adept knowledge of the human body as it was understood in his time. Maintains that Fletcher was not familiar with Harvey's work but that he derived his descriptions of the heart from Galen, Vesalius, Colombo, and others.

John Ford (1586–c. 1640)

824.   Babb, Lawrence A. "John Ford and Seventeenth Century Psychology." *DAI* 40 (1980): 6285A–86A.

This dissertation, completed in 1934, studies how seventeenth-century psychological notions regarding melancholy and the passion of love colored Ford's dramas.

825.   Davril, Robert. "The Use of Physiology in the Elizabethan Drama with Special Reference to John Ford." *Literature and Science.* Proc. of the Sixth Triennial Congress of the International Federation for Modern Languages and Literatures. Oxford, 1954. Oxford: Blackwell, 1955. 126–31.

See item 404 for annotation.

826.   Ewing, S. Blaine. *Burtonian Melancholy in the Plays of John Ford.* Princeton Studies in English 19. Princeton: Princeton UP, 1940. 122 pp.

This detailed study of Ford's indebtedness to Burton's *Anatomy of Melancholy* includes an analytical summary of Burton's work and a play-by-play, character-by-character examination of Ford's use of the material. Assesses Ford's interest in melancholy, his comprehension of the theme, and the impact of melancholy on the characters, action, thought, and mood of his plays.

827.   Sensabaugh, G. F. "John Ford and Elizabethan Tragedy." *PQ* 20 (1941): 442–53.

Discusses the influence that scientific thought—and especially the science in Burton's *Anatomy of Melancholy*—had on Ford's thematic approach to drama. Views *The Broken Heart*, *Love's Sacrifice*, and other plays in relation to the decline of Elizabethan drama.

Galileo Galilei (1564–1642)

828.   Colapietra, Raffaele. "Il pensiero estetico Galileiano." *Belfagor* 11 (1956): 557–69.

Studies Galileo's prose and literary criticism. His critical works on Tasso and Ariosto suggest an opposition between the scientist's demand for verisimilitude, clarity, and precision and the artist's yearning for wonder and fantasy.

829.   Drake, Stillman. "Galileo's Language: Mathematics and Poetry in a New Science." *YFS* 49 (1973): 13–27.

Discusses Galileo's predilection for using nontechnical, poetic language and metaphors to express his scientific theories and notes his views on the limitations of mere logical description. Examines his *Dialogue concerning the Two Chief World Systems—Ptolemaic and Copernican* in this regard.

830.   Vianello, Nereo. "Le postille al Petrarca de Galileo Galilei." *SFI* 14 (1956): 211–433.

Reproduces the 1582 edition of Petrarch's collected poems along with Galileo's annotations and classifies Galileo's comments to show his interests in science, language, and poetry.

Sir Samuel Garth (1661–1719)

831.   Ackerman, Stephen J. "The 'Infant Atoms' of Garth's 'Dispensary.' " *MLR* 74 (1979): 513–23.

Garth's *Dispensary* (1699) is more than a lighthearted mock epic or medical satire. Its physiological and medical allusions reflect a prodigious knowledge of Epicurean atomism.

832.   McCue, Daniel L. "Samuel Garth, Physician and Man of Letters." *Bulletin of the New York Academy of Medicine* 53 (1977): 368–402.

Traces Garth's medical career and summarizes his mock epic *The Dispensary* (1699), commenting on the medical controversies that inspired the work.

833.   Phillips, Steven R. "Sir Samuel Garth, *The Dispensary* (1699): An Old Spelling Edition, with Introduction and Historical Notes." *DA* 30 (1969–70): 3916A.

The introduction to this edition of Garth's *Dispensary* includes a biographical study of Garth, an account of the medical conflict between the College of Physicians and the Society of Apothecaries that inspired the satire, and an assessment of the poem's place in the history of the mock epic.

834.   Sena, John F. "Samuel Garth and the Dispensary: The Project and the Poem." In *Medicine and Literature.* Ed. Enid Rhodes Peschel. New York: Watson Academic, 1980. 28–34.
Examines as the basis of Garth's mock-epic poem *The Dispensary* the seventeenth-century controversy between the Society of Apothecaries and the Royal College of Physicians over establishing a dispensary that would provide free medical treatment for London's poor.

835.   ———. "Samuel Garth's *The Dispensary.*" *TSLL* 15 (1973–74): 639–48.
Evaluates Garth's artistry in composing *The Dispensary*, focusing on his satiric method and rhetorical strategy.

Francis Godwin (1562–1633)

836.   Knowlson, James R. "A Note on Bishop Godwin's *Man in the Moone*: The East Indies Trade Route and a 'Language' of Musical Notes." *MP* 65 (1967–68): 357–61.
Maintains that Godwin's description of the East Indies is based on travel literature such as Richard Hakluyt's *Principal Navigations, Voiages, Traffiques and Discoveries* (1598–1600). Godwin's portrayal of the moon dwellers' language of musical tones may have been influenced by Porta's *De occultis literarum notis* (1606).

Hans Jakob Christoph von Grimmelshausen (1625–76)

837.   Haberkamm, Klaus. *"Sensus Astrologicus": Zum Verhältnis von Literatur und Astrologie in Renaissance und Barock.* Bonn: Bouvier, 1972. 327 pp.
Attempts to clarify passages in Renaissance and baroque literary works by referring to the system of astrology that was prevalent at the time. Although Haberkamm draws on much background literature, the study emphasizes Grimmelshausen's novels, especially *Der abenteuerliche simplicissimus Teutsch, Der seltzame Springinsfeld,* and *Das wunderbarliche Vogelnest.*

838.   Lemke, Gerhard. "Die Astrologie in den Werken Grimmelshausens und seiner Interpreten: Zur Diskussion über den Sternenglauben in der barocken Dichtung." *Argenis* 1 (1977): 63–105.
Long after literary critics had dismissed Grimmelshausen's *Des abenteuerlichen simplicissimus ewigwaehrender Calender* as a vessel of superstition, a reverse movement attempted to reinterpret his complete works in the light of the *Calender*'s astrological content. Both schools of criticism, however, disregard the irony in Grimmelshausen's writings and ignore his critical attitude toward astrology and alchemy.

839.   Philippoff, Eva. " 'Sensus astrologicus' in Grimmelshausens 'Courasche': Ein Beitrag zur astrologischen Aufschlüsselung von Grimmelshausens Werk." *Daphnis* 7 (1978): 531–47.

Maintains that an astrological interpretation of Grimmelshausen's *Die landstörzerin Courasche* is credible if both the author and the work are seen in the context of their time. Analyzes the novel in the light of the Chaldaic planetary series.

840.   Riep, Albert R. "Krankheit, Medizin und Arzt in den Werken Grimmelshausens." *DA* 27 (1966–67): 3061A.
Examines Grimmelshausen's medical references, whose source was probably Paracelsus.

841.   Weydt, Günther. "Planetensymbolik im barocken Roman: Versuch einer Entschlüsselung des 'Simplicissimus Teutsch.' " *DB* 36 (1966): 1–14.
Studies the influence of Grimmelshausen's astrological work *Ewigwährender Kalender* on the structure of his novel *Der abenteuerliche simplicissimus Teutsch* (1669).

Andreas Gryphius (1616–64)

842.   Kühlmann, Wilhelm. "Neuzeitliche Wissenschaft in der Lyrik des 17. Jahrhunderts. Die Kopernikus-Gedichte des Andreas Gryphius und Caspar Barlaeus im Argumentationszusammenhang des frühbarocken Modernismus." *JDSG* 23 (1979): 124–53.
Examines Gryphius's German-language poem "Uber Nicolai Copernici Bildt," contrasting it with two similar poems composed in Latin by Caspar Barlaeus (1584–1648). Attempts to establish the modernity of the two poets within the context of the science and philosophy of their time.

843.   Powell, Hugh. "Andreas Gryphius and the 'New Philosophy.' " *GL&L* 5 (1951–52): 274–78.
Gryphius's argument that fire is not an element, expressed in his disputation "De igne non Elemento," suggests his acceptance of the new cosmology of Copernicus, Brahe, Galileo, and Kepler.

Lord Edward Herbert (1583–1648)

844.   McFarland, Ronald E. "The Rhetoric of Medicine: Lord Herbert's and Thomas Carew's Poems of Green-Sickness." *JHM* 30 (1975): 250–58.
Seventeenth-century medical views on greensickness, or chlorosis, a variety of iron-deficiency anemia, shed light on the metaphoric structure of four poems by Lord Herbert and Thomas Carew that refer to the disease.

George Herbert (1593–1633)

845.   Breiner, Laurence A. "Herbert's Cockatrice." *MP* 77 (1979–80): 10–17.
Maintains that the cockatrice of Herbert's "Sinnes Round" originates in the imagery of alchemical tradition.

846.   Caldwell, Wayne T. " 'Affliction then is ours': George Herbert's *The Temple* as an Anatomy of Religious Melancholy." *DAI* 34 (1973): 4190A.
Herbert used Renaissance psychology and medicine for the themes, imagery, and

didactic purposes of *The Temple* (1633). This work bears a striking resemblance to Burton's *Anatomy of Melancholy* (1621).

847.   Collier, Robert E. "George Herbert and Science: The Significance of Renaissance Learning in *The Temple.*" *DAI* 32 (1971): 912A.
    The many allusions to astronomy, alchemy, and medicine in *The Temple* suggest that Herbert had a thorough grounding in the Renaissance sciences.

848.   Ericson, Edward E. "The Imagery of George Herbert's Poetry." *DA* 28 (1967–68): 227A–28A.
    Astronomy and medicine provided sources for the imagery of *The Temple*.

Johannes Kepler (1571–1630)

849.   Christianson, Gale E. "Kepler's *Somnium*: Science Fiction and the Renaissance Scientist." *SFS* 3 (1976): 79–90.
    Presents biographical information concerning Kepler's scientific studies that sheds light on the content of his *Somnium* and the circumstances surrounding the work's publication. Kepler's vision of travel to the moon and of life on the moon reflects a degree of scientific sophistication.

850.   Hallyn, Fernand. "Le *Songe* de Kepler." *BHR* 42 (1980): 329–47.
    Discusses Kepler's *Somnium* as a literary text containing allegorical representations of science. The section of the *Somnium* devoted to the astronomical observations made by a moon creature is intended as a mirror image of scientific observations made from Earth.

851.   Lear, John. "The Forgotten Moon Voyage of 1609." *SatR* 4 May 1963: 39–44.
    Outlines the scientific details of the lunar voyage Kepler describes in his *Somnium*.

852.   ———. *Kepler's Dream: With the Full Text and Notes of* Somnium, Sive Astronomia Lunaris, *Joannis Kepleri*. Trans. Patricia Frueh Kirkwood. Berkeley: U of California P, 1965. 182 pp.
    The introduction to this translation of Kepler's *Somnium* comments on the astronomical and theological controversies surrounding the work, discusses its biographical elements, and interprets Kepler's footnotes. Lear maintains that the *Somnium* is not a work of fiction but a serious scientific text explicating various aspects of lunar theory. "Kepler's major objective was to spread word of Copernican science in a way that would not arouse enemies of science within the church."

853.   ———. "Life in Hell's Vestibule: Kepler's Ingenious Biography." *SatR* 4 May 1963: 45–46.
    Kepler's *Somnium* is in part an allegorical rendering of his biography.

854.   Nicolson, Marjorie. "Kepler, the *Somnium*, and John Donne." *JHI* 1 (1940): 259–80. Rpt. in *Science and Imagination*. Ithaca: Great Seal, 1956. Hamden: Archon, 1976. 58–79.

Examines the biographical aspects of Kepler's *Somnium*, discusses a probable relation between the work and Donne's *Conclave ignatii*, and assesses the importance of the *Somnium*'s depiction of the first modern scientific moon voyage.

855.   Rosen, Edward. "The Moon's Orbit in Kepler's *Somnium*." *Centaurus* 11 (1965–66): 217–21.

Adduces textual evidence to demonstrate that in the *Somnium* Kepler ascribed a circular orbit to the moon and not, as John Lear suggests, in *Kepler's Dream*, an elliptical orbit (see item 852).

Jean de La Fontaine (1621–95)

856.   Ridgely, Beverly S. "Astrology and Astronomy in the *Fables* of La Fontaine." *PMLA* 80 (1965): 180–89.

Evaluates La Fontaine's poetic treatment of astrological and astronomical ideas, noting his attempts to avoid pedantry, didacticism, and obscurity in his presentation of scientific and pseudoscientific concepts, especially in his *Fables*. Stresses La Fontaine's rejection of judicial astrology in the fables "L'astrologue qui se laisse tomber dans un puits" and "L'horoscope" and points out his allusions to Copernican heliocentrism and other astronomical concepts in "Le loup et le renard," "Un animal dans la lune," and other fables.

857.   ———. " 'Disciple de Lucrèce une seconde fois': A Study of La Fontaine's *Poème du quinquina*." *ECr* 11 (1971): 92–122.

Thoroughly examines the style, structure, and content of La Fontaine's *Poème du quinquina* (1682), which describes the causes and effects of fevers and the use of quinine in treating them. Despite serious poetic flaws, La Fontaine's piece merits critical attention insofar as it reveals his approach to the psychological and aesthetic difficulties of writing learned or scientific poetry in late-seventeenth-century France.

Lorenzo Magalotti (1637–1712)

858.   Basso, Jeannine. "De la science à la littérature: Les *Lettere scientifiche ed erudite* de Lorenzo Magalotti." *Letteratura e scienza nella storia della cultura italiana*. Atti del IX congresso dell'associazione internazionale per gli studi di lingua e letteratura italiana. Palermo, Messina, Catania, 21–25 Apr. 1976. Associazione internazionale per gli studi di lingua e letteratura italiana. Palermo: Manfredi, 1978. 573–81.

Examines Magalotti's *Lettere* as an outstanding example of a synthesis between literature and science. Magalotti, though keenly aware of the differences between the two disciplines, attempted to combine scientific and literary styles in this and other works.

859.   Güntert, Georges. *Un poeta scienziato del seicento: Lorenzo Magalotti*. Firenze: Olschki, 1966. 175 pp.

Magalotti's sensitivity to nature complemented his wish to acquire a scientific understanding of natural phenomena, and his scientific interests were greatly influenced by Galileo. Güntert examines the effect of Magalotti's scientific studies on his poetry, analyzing in particular the importance attributed to sounds in his poems.

Giambattista Marino (1569–1625)

860.   Peters, Susanna N. "The Anatomical Machine: A Representation of the
        Microcosm in the *Adone* of G. B. Marino." *MLN* 88 (1973): 95–110.
    Discusses the anatomical and cosmological imagery of Marino's poem.

Andrew Marvell (1621–78)

861.   Blackmon, Jennings M. "Marvell's Imagery." *DA* 28 (1967–68): 223A.
    Examines five classes of imagery in Marvell's poetry: botanical nature, war, classical lore, science (including scientific apparatus, scientific theory, chemistry, alchemy, astronomy, astrology, cartography, and geometry), and religion.

862.   Cinquemani, A. M. "Marvell's *The Mower against Gardens*, 9–10." *Expl*
        20 (1961–62): item 77.
    Explains the botanical background for the cited lines of Marvell's poem.

863.   Millus, Donald J. "Andrew Marvell, Andreas Vesalius, and a Medieval
        Tradition." *YULG* 47 (1972–73): 216–23.
    "A Dialogue between the Soul and Body" clearly shows that Renaissance anatomical theories influenced Marvell's poetic imagination. A possible source of his anatomical imagery is Vesalius's *De humani corporis fabrica*.

863a.   Wilcher, Robert. "Details from the Natural Histories in Marvell's Poetry."
        N&Q ns 15 (1968): 101–02.
    Cites Conradus Gesner's *Historie of Foure-Footed Beastes* and Philemon Holland's translation of Pliny the Elder as sources for *The Loyall Scot* and *Damon the Mower*.

John Milton (1608–74)

864.   Adamson, J. H. "Kepler and Milton." *MLN* 74 (1959): 683–85.
    Similarities in the writings of Kepler and Milton include a tendency to blend poetic concepts and imagery with scientific theory, a concern with the notion of a harmony of the spheres, and references to "solar mysticism." Adamson notes in particular Milton's allusion in book 8 of *Paradise Lost* (122–25) to Kepler's theory of "attractive virtue" (the notion that the attractive power of the sun accounts for planetary motion).

865.   Allen, Don Cameron. "A Note on *Comus*." *MLN* 64 (1949): 179–80.
    The passage of *Comus* (731–35) that refers to the growth and generation of diamonds can best be understood by reference to the theories of seventeenth-century mineralogists such as Anselm Boetius.

866.   ———. "Two Notes on *Paradise Lost.*" *MLN* 68 (1953): 360–61.
The second note interprets the astrological allegory of Satan's return to Hell (*Paradise Lost* 10.327–29).

867.   Babb, Lawrence. "The Background of *Il Penseroso.*" *SP* 37 (1940): 257–73.
Two competing conceptions of the melancholic humor were prominent in the Renaissance. The first, derived from the medical works of Galen, represented melancholy as a reprehensible condition of the mind, while the second, derived from Aristotle, viewed melancholy as a source of imaginative and creative powers. Babb maintains that Milton's *L'Allegro* and *Il Penseroso* clearly articulate the conflict between the two. A survey of Renaissance commentaries on melancholy by writers such as Bright, Burton, Ficino, and Walkington illuminates the background of Milton's poems.

868.   ———. *The Moral Cosmos of* Paradise Lost. East Lansing: Michigan State UP, 1970. 166 pp.
        Rev. Robert H. West, *MP* 70 (1972–73): 360 64.
Explains the physical milieu of *Paradise Lost* and discusses Milton's use of astronomy, astrology, meteorology, cosmology, physiology, geology, and Renaissance psychology. Includes a chapter assessing Milton's acquaintance with and attitude toward the new astronomy. For the most part, Milton's science was bookish, authoritarian, deductive, and subordinate to his ethical and religious concerns.

869.   Bergel, Lienhard. "Milton's *Paradise Lost,* I, 284–295." *Expl* 10 (1951–52): item 3.
Comments on the poetic function of the moon image in the cited lines of Milton's poem. The lines also allude to Galileo and the telescope.

870.   Boyette, Purvis E. "Sexual Metaphor in Milton's Cosmogony, Physics, and Ontology." *RenP* (1967): 93–103.
Milton uses cosmic imagery drawn in part from Platonism to celebrate the divine creative process in *Paradise Lost.*

871.   Broadbent, J. B. "Milton's Paradise." *MP* 51 (1953–54): 160–76.
Analyzes Milton's description of paradise in *Paradise Lost,* emphasizing the factual geographical elements supporting the description.

871a.   Brockbank, Philip. " 'Within the Visible Diurnal Spheare': The Moving World of *Paradise Lost.*" *Approaches to* Paradise Lost. Ed. Constantinos A. Patrides. London: Arnold, 1968. 199–221.
Recognizes Milton's understanding of astronomy and notes the universal scale and perspective of *Paradise Lost* but argues that Milton seeks to endow the astronomical order with aesthetic and moral validity.

872.   Bundy, Murray W. "Milton's Prelapsarian Adam." *RS* 13 (1945): 163–84.
Analyzes book 8 of *Paradise Lost* and briefly discusses the significance of Milton's reference to Ptolemaic and Copernican astronomy.

873. Carnall, Geoffrey. "Milton's *Paradise Lost*, III, 481–483." *N&Q* 197 (1952): 315–16.

Interprets the astronomical imagery of the cited lines of *Paradise Lost* with reference to Sacrobosco's *Sphaera*.

874. Chambers, A. B. "Chaos in *Paradise Lost*." *JHI* 24 (1963): 55–84.

Thoroughly investigates the concept of "chaos" as presented in *Paradise Lost*. The antecedents for Milton's use of the term include Hesiod, Democritus, Lucretius, and Plotinus, but Milton's usage most nearly resembles the Platonic cosmology of the *Timaeus*.

875. ————. "Milton's Proteus and Satan's Visit to the Sun." *JEGP* 62 (1963): 280–87.

Suggests that Milton's allusion to Proteus in *Paradise Lost* (3.599–605) is best explained by reference to Greek mythology and not, as had been attempted, to pseudoscientific theories. Proper understanding of the reference illuminates the meaning of Satan's visit to the sun.

876. Christopher, Georgia. "Homeopathic Physic and Natural Renovation in *Samson Agonistes*." *ELH* 37 (1970): 361–73.

In Milton's *Samson Agonistes*, Samson's gradual regeneration from spiritual despair is accomplished through homeopathic medicine and "natural renovation," a divinely inspired faith that partially and temporarily restores the human mind and will.

877. Clark, Cumberland. *Astronomy in the Poets*. Bournemouth, Eng.: Sydenham, 1922. Folcroft: Folcroft, 1969. Norwood: Norwood, 1975. Philadelphia: West, 1978. 116 pp.

See item 530 for annotation.

878. Cook, Albert S. "*Paradise Lost* vii.364–66." *MLN* 16 (1901): 202–05.

Milton's allusions to the phases of Venus and to the theory that planets reflect the light of the sun evidence his knowledge of Galileo's astronomical discoveries.

878a. Cope, Jackson I. "Time and Space as Miltonic Symbol." *ELH* 26 (1959): 497–513.

Examines the spatial dimension of *Paradise Lost* "not as a cultural osmosis by which contemporary reality seeps into literature, but as the aesthetic shape of the myth through which Milton created meaning for the boundless space viewed by Galileo." To do so, Cope turns "from the stirring commonplaces of seventeenth-century science to an older tradition of literary 'topoi.' "

879. Cox, Lee. "Natural Science and Figurative Design in *Samson Agonistes*." *ELH* 35 (1968): 51–74.

Describes in detail Milton's use of metaphor and symbol in *Samson Agonistes*, especially his skill in using images from natural science, such as plants and elements, to shape a complex figurative design.

880. Curry, Walter Clyde. "The Genesis of Milton's World." *Anglia* 70 (1951–52): 129–49. Rpt. in *Milton's Ontology, Cosmogony, and Physics*. Lexington: U of Kentucky P, 1957. 92–113.

In *Paradise Lost* Uriel and Raphael give fragmentary reports of the genesis of the world. Curry analyzes and orders these reports, finding elements of Stoic, rabbinical, Neoplatonic, and atomistic philosophy.

881.   ———. "The Lordship of Milton's Sun." In *Milton's Ontology, Cosmogony, and Physics*. Lexington: U of Kentucky P, 1957. 114–43.

Discusses the sun's magnetic and alchemical powers in *Paradise Lost* and explains the physics underlying Milton's depiction of the sun's dominion over the universe.

882.   Duncan, Edgar H. "The Natural History of Metals and Minerals in the Universe of Milton's *Paradise Lost*." *Osiris* 11 (1954): 386–421.

Examines the great variety of mineralogical treatises that were extant in the seventeenth century with a view to reconstructing the "intellectual milieu" of mineralogy. Studies the mineralogical elements of *Paradise Lost* in this light to convey a general sense of the contemporary scientific opinion.

883.   ———. "Satan-Lucifer: Lightning and Thunderbolt." *PQ* 30 (1951): 441–43.

Suggests that J. A. Comenius's physics textbook *Naturall Philosophie Reformed by Divine Light* (1643) is a possible source for Satan's flight through Chaos in *Paradise Lost* 2.927–38.

884.   Fink, Z. S. "*Il Penseroso*, Line 16." *PQ* 19 (1940): 309–13.

Notes that the sources for Milton's description of the face of Melancholy as "o'erlaid with black" (*Il Penseroso* 16) can be found in traditional scientific, astrological, and medical works by Aristotle, Bright, Burton, and Cicero.

885.   ———. "Milton and the Theory of Climatic Influence." *MLQ* 2 (1941): 67–80.

Assesses Milton's response to the idea that northern climates are detrimental to the intellectual capacity of the human mind—an idea dating back to Aristotle's *Politics* and later expressed by J. Bodin and Botero. Fink studies references to the theory in *Mansus*, *The Reason of Church Government*, and *Areopagitica* and notes its effect on Milton's poetic aspirations.

885a.   Gair, W. Reavley. "Milton and Science." *John Milton: Introductions*. Ed. John Broadbent. Cambridge: Cambridge UP, 1973. 120–43.

Outlines Milton's scientific education and examines his debt to seventeenth-century astronomy, astrology, alchemy, and physiology.

886.   Gilbert, Allan H. "Milton and Galileo." *SP* 19 (1922): 152–85.

Many of the abundant allusions to astronomy in *Paradise Lost* suggest that Milton accepted Galileo's astronomical theories, especially those expressed in *Dialogue on the Two Principal Systems of the World*. Much of Milton's astronomical imagery is, however, clearly Ptolemaic; thus, it is unclear to what extent he embraced the conclusions of Copernicanism as conveyed through Galileo's writings.

887.   ———. "Milton's Textbook of Astronomy." *PMLA* 38 (1923): 297–307.

Discusses the structure and content of Sacrobosco's *De Sphaera*, the primary textbook from which Milton derived astronomical information for his poems. Also examines selections from *Paradise Lost*.

888. ———. "The Outside Shell of Milton's World." *SP* 20 (1923): 444–47.
In Milton's cosmology, the outer shell of the universe should not be identified with the primum mobile but should be seen as an adaptation of Saint Basil the Great's concept of the empyrean heaven.

889. Gorecki, John. "Satan among the Stars: *Paradise Lost* x.325–329." *ELN* 15 (1977–78): 274–78.
Interprets the astrological significance of Satan's position between the constellations Centaurus and Scorpius in *Paradise Lost* 10.325–29.

890. Greenlaw, Edwin. "Spenser's Influence on *Paradise Lost*." *SP* 17 (1920): 320–59.
Demonstrates that the principal models for the theme, structure, cosmology, and astronomy of *Paradise Lost* were works by Spenser, such as *Hymnes* and *The Faerie Queene*.

891. Harrison, Thomas P. *They Tell of Birds: Chaucer, Spenser, Milton, Drayton.* Austin: U of Texas P, 1956. Westport: Greenwood, 1969. 159 pp.
See item 296 for annotation.

892. Hinckley, Henry B. "Theories of Vision in English Poetry." *MLN* 24 (1909): 125.
See item 636 for annotation.

893. Hughes, Merritt Y. "Earth Felt the Wound." *ELH* 36 (1969): 193–214.
Milton's treatment in *Paradise Lost* of how Adam's fall affects the physical and spiritual constitution of the universe includes elements of Pythagorean and Aristotelian cosmology, Thomistic metaphysics, Keplerian astronomy, and astrology.

894. Hunter, William B., Jr. "Satan as Comet: *Paradise Lost* ii.708–711." *ELN* 5 (1967–68): 17–21.
Suggests that the cited lines describe a supernova Kepler wrote about and not, as had been supposed, a comet.

895. Kolin, Philip C. "Milton's Use of Clouds for Satanic Parody in *Paradise Lost*." *ELWIU* 5 (1978): 153–62.
Milton derived the complex cloud imagery in *Paradise Lost* from biblical, classical, and poetic sources and from science encyclopedias by Bartholomaeus Anglicus, La Primaudaye, Swan, and others.

896. Konečný, Lubomír. "Young Milton and the Telescope." *JWCI* 37 (1974): 368–73.
Milton's "long and dark Prospective Glass" in *Poem at a Vacation Exercise* may be either an allusion to Galileo's telescope or an image adapted from medieval emblem books.

897.   Le Comte, Edward S. "New Light on the 'Haemony' Passage in *Comus*."
        PQ 21 (1942): 283–98.
Cites possible literary, scientific, and etymological sources for "haemony," Milton's invented plant, including Homer's *Odyssey*, Pliny the Elder's *Naturalis historia*, J. Fletcher's *Faithful Shepherdess*, and Gerard's *Herball*.

898.   Lockwood, Laura E. "A Note on Milton's Geography." *MLN* 21 (1906):
        86.
Confirms the geographical accuracy of Milton's reference to the "Nysian isle" in *Paradise Lost* (4.268–79), citing as evidence the Africae Propriae Tabula map (1590).

899.   Lovejoy, Arthur O. "Milton's Dialogue on Astronomy." *Reason and the
        Imagination: Studies in the History of Ideas, 1600–1800*. Ed. Joseph A.
        Mazzeo. New York: Columbia UP; London: Routledge, 1962. 129–42.
The dialogue on astronomy in books 7 and 8 of *Paradise Lost* suggests both that Milton accepted Copernicanism and the doctrine of a plurality of worlds and that he rejected the two theories. Lovejoy concludes that Milton intended to discourage inquiry into matters ". . . about which it is useless and 'impertinent,' and even sinful, for men to employ their minds."

900.   Low, Anthony. "The Astronomy of *Paradise Lost*." *ELN* 8 (1970–71):
        263–67.
Maintains that the astronomical system in *Paradise Lost* is Ptolemaic.

901.   McColley, Grant. "The Astronomy of *Paradise Lost*." *SP* 34 (1937): 209–
        47.
Maintains that of five basic astronomical hypotheses current in Milton's day, references to four—Copernican heliocentrism, the idea of the earth's diurnal rotation, Ptolemaic geocentrism, and the doctrine of a plurality of worlds—can be found in *Paradise Lost*, indicating that Milton had a broad, though often nontechnical, understanding of seventeenth-century astronomy. Milton ignored the fifth hypothesis—the geoheliocentrism of Brahe—despite its widespread acceptance. McColley outlines the theories and notes Milton's specific references and responses to each.

902.   ———. "Milton's Dialogue on Astronomy: The Principal Immediate
        Sources." *PMLA* 52 (1937): 728–62.
The cosmological elements of the Raphael-Adam dialogue in book 8 of *Paradise Lost* derive from Wilkins's *Discovery of a World in the Moone* (1638) and *Discourse That the Earth May Be a Planet* (1640) and Ross's *New Planet No Planet: Or, The Earth No Wandering Star* (1646). McColley analyzes passages from these works that parallel passages from the astronomical dialogue of book 8 and related portions of books 3 and 9 and briefly assesses Milton's purpose in basing the dialogue on these works.

903.   ———. Paradise Lost: *An Account of Its Growth and Major Origins, with a
        Discussion of Milton's Use of Sources and Literary Patterns*. Chicago: Packard,
        1940. New York: Russell, 1963. 362 pp.
        Rev. Maurice Kelley and T. S. K. Scott-Craig, *MLN* 57 (1942): 295–96.

Primarily discusses Milton's debt to the hexametral literary tradition but also includes a chapter that reveals the direct sources of the dialogue on astronomy in *Paradise Lost*—Wilkins's *Discovery of a World in the Moone* and *Discourse That the Earth May Be a Planet* and Ross's *New Planet No Planet: Or, The Earth No Wandering Star.*

904.   ————. "The Theory of a Plurality of Worlds as a Factor in Milton's Attitude toward the Copernican Hypothesis." *MLN* 47 (1932): 319–25.
Acceptance of Copernican heliocentrism during the seventeenth century often entailed acceptance of the doctrine of a plurality of worlds. Though Bruno, Galileo, Kepler, Wilkins, and H. More associated the two theories, the notions were satirized by Donne, Jonson, and Drummond. Milton apparently followed the tendency of his age in associating the two concepts, but their presentation in *Paradise Lost* indicates that he was cautious and ambivalent about accepting them, possibly because of the theological implications of the plurality-of-worlds doctrine.

905.   Mitchell, Maria. "The Astronomical Science of Milton as Shown in *Paradise Lost*." *Poet-Lore* 6 (1894): 313–23.
Cites examples of Milton's poetic adaptation of astronomical concepts, including Galileo's ideas and theories of eclipses, meteors, comets, and the moon.

906.   Morse, Katherine. "Milton's Ideas of Science as Shown in *Paradise Lost*." *SciMo* 10 (1920): 150–56.
Brief remarks on Milton's allusions to Ptolemaic and Copernican astronomy, astrology, natural history, medicine, and botany.

907.   Nicolson, Marjorie. "Milton and the Telescope." *ELH* 2 (1935): 1–32. Rpt. in *Science and Imagination*. Ithaca: Great Seal, 1956. Hamden: Archon, 1976. 80–109.
Maintains that Milton's interest in the "new astronomy," reflected in *Paradise Lost* but not in his early works, was stimulated by his observations through the telescope. Milton may have first encountered the instrument when he journeyed to Italy in 1638–39 and visited Galileo. Nicolson argues that peculiarities in Milton's mature works, such as his sense of perspective and his portrayal of space, reflect the influence of the telescope on his poetic imagination.

908.   Orchard, Thomas Nathaniel. *The Astronomy of Milton's* Paradise Lost. London: Longmans, 1896. New York: Haskell, 1966. 338 pp.
Briefly sketches the history of astronomy from ancient times to the seventeenth century and then examines passages from *Paradise Lost* that allude to astronomical phenomena. The author also assesses Milton's astronomical knowledge, discusses Galileo's influence on Milton, describes the starry heavens and other celestial objects referred to in *Paradise Lost*, and studies Milton's imaginative assimilation of astronomical themes.

909.   Otten, Charlotte F. "Milton's Haemony." *ELR* 5 (1975): 81–95.
Refers to the herbal literature of the day, including Parkinson's *Theatrum Botanicum* (1640) and Gerard's *Herball* (1597) to assess the scientific accuracy of Milton's description of the plant "haemony" in lines 617–55 of *Comus* (1634).

910.   Pittman, James Hall. "Milton and the *Physiologus.*" *MLN* 40 (1925): 439–40.
Suggests that the source of Milton's descriptions of whales in *Paradise Lost* (1.200–08, 7.410–16) was the Old English version of the *Physiologus*.

911.   Robins, Harry F. "The Crystalline Sphere and the 'Waters Above' in *Paradise Lost.*" *PMLA* 69 (1954): 903–14.
Maintains that Milton's image of the "waters above" in *Paradise Lost* 8.299 originates in theology (Genesis 1.7), not, as has hitherto been supposed, in science. Scholars formerly asserted that the "waters above" were located beneath the primum mobile or the crystalline sphere.

912.   Russo, John Paul. " 'Diffus'd' Spirits: Scientific Metaphor in *Samson Agonistes.*" *PLL* 7 (1971): 85–90.
Milton adapted a physiological metaphor for symbolic purposes in *Samson Agonistes* (90–97, 1139–44). His use of the term *diffused* derives from a tradition of Galenic neurophysiology that is reflected in the physiological literature of the period, such as Burton's *Anatomy of Melancholy* and Charleton's *Natural History of the Passions*.

913.   Sarkar, Malabika. "Satan's Astronomical Journey, *Paradise Lost*, IX.63–66." *N&Q* ns 26 (1979): 417–22.
Interprets the astronomical imagery of Satan's journey in Milton's prelapsarian universe. Details of the Miltonic cosmology may derive from Sacrobosco's *De sphaera*.

914.   Schultz, Howard. *Milton and Forbidden Knowledge*. New York: MLA, 1955. New York: Kraus, 1970. 309 pp.
        Rev. Jackson I. Cope, *MLN* 71 (1956): 529–32; Don Cameron Allen, *MP* 54 (1956–57): 138–39; Kenneth Muir, *RES* ns 8 (1957): 443–44.
Explores the relations between church dogma and various branches of learning, such as philosophy, education, politics, natural science, and pseudoscience. Stresses the influence that the controversies between the church and learning had on Milton's thought.

915.   Stoll, Elmer Edgar. "Criticisms Criticized: Spenser and Milton." *JEGP* 41 (1942): 451–77.
In part, disputes Nicolson's argument that Milton's presumed experiences with the newly invented telescope profoundly affected his poetic imagination (see items 708 and 907).

916.   Stroup, Thomas B. "Implications of the Theory of Climatic Influence in Milton." *MLQ* 4 (1943): 185–89.
Maintains that the theory of climatic influence, which Milton related to the theory of humors outlined in Burton's *Anatomy of Melancholy*, both influenced his interpretation of the universe and affected his perception of his own creative powers. Supplements item 885.

917.   Svendsen, Kester. "Cosmological Lore in Milton." *ELH* 9 (1942): 198–223.
Examines Milton's references to the cosmological phenomena of the so-called

"sublunar vault" and emphasizes that such popular encyclopedias of science like Bartholomaeus Anglicus's *De Proprietatibus Rerum* (c. 1230), Caxton's *Mirrour of the World* (1481), La Primaudaye's *French Academie* (1618), and Swan's *Speculum Mundi* (1643) are useful for the study of Miltonic cosmology.

918.   ———. "Milton and Medical Lore." *BHM* 13 (1943): 158–84.

Examines Milton's use of medical ideas against the background of the common-place, readily available literature of his day, such as Bartholomaeus Anglicus's *De proprietatibus rerum*, Batman's *Batman uppon Bartholome*, and La Primaudaye's *French Academie*.

919.   ———. *Milton and Science*. Cambridge: Harvard UP, 1956. New York: Greenwood, 1969. 304 pp.
        Rev. William B. Hunter, Jr., *MLN* 72 (1957): 620–22; R. H. Syfret, *RES* ns 9 (1958): 322–24.

A comprehensive study of the nature, function, and sources of natural science in Milton's poetry and prose, based largely on revised versions of previously published essays and notes. Chapter 1 surveys the tradition of natural-science encyclopedias as background to an understanding of Milton's use of scientific concepts. Subsequent chapters examine in detail Milton's allusions to cosmology, mineralogy, botany, the animal kingdom, and human physiology and psychology. The final chapters present intensive readings of *The Doctrine and Discipline of Divorce* and *Paradise Lost* and stress the role natural science played in determining the structure, characterization, setting, and tone of the poem.

920.   ———. "Milton and the Encyclopedias of Science." *SP* 39 (1942): 303–27.

A study of the encyclopedias of science extant during Milton's time greatly enhances our understanding of his scientific allusions. The works discussed here are Bartholomaeus Anglicus's *De Proprietatibus Rerum*, Caxton's *Mirror of the World*, Maplet's *Greene Forest or a Naturall Historie*, Batman's *Batman uppon Bartholomew*, La Primaudaye's *French Academie*, and Swan's *Speculum mundi*.

921.   ———. "Milton's 'Aerie Microscope.' " *MLN* 64 (1949): 525–27.

Suggests a possible source for the description of the optical device Milton named an "aerie microscope" (*Paradise Regained* 4.55–60): *A Geometrical Practical Treatize Named Pantometria*, by Leonard Digges and Thomas Digges (1591).

922.   ———. "Milton's *Paradise Lost*, v, 108–111." *Expl* 4 (1945): item 2.

Asserts that Milton's description of "fancy" in *Paradise Lost* 5.108–11 is based on conventional Renaissance physiological and psychological lore.

923.   ———. " 'The Prudent Crane': *Paradise Lost*, VII, 425–431." *N&Q* 183 (1942): 66–67.

Draws on Renaissance encyclopedias of science to suggest a new interpretation of Milton's description of the crane as "prudent" in the cited lines of *Paradise Lost*.

924.   ———. "Satan and Science." *BuR* 9 (1960–61): 130–42.

Studies an association commonly made between Satan and scientific and technological advances, noting especially the reflection of this theme in Milton's *Paradise Lost*.

925.   ———. "Science and Structure in Milton's *Doctrine of Divorce.*" *PMLA* 67 (1952): 435–45.
In *The Doctrine and Discipline of Divorce*, Milton's use of imagery and terminology drawn from astronomical and medical-anatomical lore serves as a structural framework that reinforces the prose argument.

926.   Taylor, Dick, Jr. "The Storm Scene in *Paradise Regained*: A Reinterpretation." *UTQ* 24 (1954–55): 359–76.
Suggests, among other points, that Satan's temptation of Christ in the storm scene of *Paradise Regained* uses false astrological portents. Such a temptation was probably meaningful in Milton's age, given the widespread concern over the interpretation of astrological signs.

927.   Taylor, George C. "Milton on Mining." *MLN* 45 (1930): 24–27.
Chaucer, Shakespeare, Spenser, and Du Bartas express antipathy to the mining of metals. This attitude, which is summarized in a scientific treatise from the Renaissance, the first book of Agricola's *De Re Metallica* (1556), reappears in Milton's poetry.

928.   Thompson, Elbert N. S. "A Forerunner of Milton." *MLN* 32 (1917): 479–82.
H. More's acceptance of Copernican astronomy and his criticism of the Ptolemaic system in *Psychathansia* (1642) anticipate in several respects Milton's views regarding astronomy in *Paradise Lost*.

929.   Tucker, Herbert F., Jr. "Gravity and Milton's Moral Physics." *MiltonQ* 12 (1978): 96–100.
Traces Milton's use of gravity as a physical and metaphysical metaphor in *Paradise Lost*.

930.   Warren, William Fairchild. *The Universe as Pictured in Milton's* Paradise Lost: *An Illustrated Study for Personal and Class Use*. New York: Abingdon, 1915. New York: Gordian, 1968. Folcroft: Folcroft, 1973. 79 pp.
Succinctly describes Milton's geocentric cosmology and provides accompanying diagrams. The appendix reproduces earlier interpretive sketches of Milton's universe by scholars such as David Masson, John A. Himes, Homer B. Sprague, and Thomas N. Orchard.

931.   Whiting, George W. "Milton and Comets." *ELH* 4 (1937): 41–42.
Argues that Milton's comet imagery in *Of Reformation in England* derives from a speech by Lord George Digby and does not, as had been supposed, allude to Galileo's theories.

932.   ———. "Milton's *Taprobane.*" *RES* 13 (1937): 209–12.
Using geographical sources such as Abraham Ortelius's *Theatrum orbis terrarum* (possibly Milton's favorite atlas), the author establishes that "Taprobane" in *Paradise*

Regained (4.74–76) is an allusion to Sumatra and not, as had been supposed, to Ceylon.

Molière (1622–73)

933.   François, Carlo. "Médecine et religion chez Molière: Deux facettes d'une même absurdité." *FR* 42 (1968–69): 665–72.

Maintaining that in the *Malade imaginaire* medicine is a metaphor for the church, François shows the extent to which Molière attacks the heart of Christianity—the creed, the gospels, the Trinity, the Christian view of death and resurrection, the catechism, and various prayers.

934.   Godlewski, Guy. *Des médecins et des hommes: Léonard de Vinci, Rabelais, Vincent de Paul, médecins de Molière, Lavoisier, Cagliostro, Marat, Bichat, Corvisart, Larrey, O'Meara, Antommarchi, Savigny, Bretonneau, Véron, Gérard de Nerval, Claude Bernard.* Paris: L'expansion, 1972. 389 pp.

See item 501 for annotation.

935.   Hall, H. Gaston. "Molière, Satirist of Seventeenth-Century French Medicine: Fact and Fantasy." *Proceedings of the Royal Society of Medicine* 70 (1977): 425–31.

The medical practices with which Molière was acquainted tended to be authoritarian rather than empirical, formalistic to the point of being ritualistic, and rhetorical rather than clinical. Molière satirized these aspects of French medicine in plays such as *L'amour médecin*, *Monsieur de Pourceaugnac*, *Le malade imaginaire*, and *Le médecin malgré lui*.

936.   Livingston, Paisley N. "Comic Treatment: Molière and the Farce of Medicine." *MLN* 94 (1979): 676–87.

Shows how Molière's farcical treatment of medicine in *L'amour médicin*, *Le malade imaginaire*, and other plays had a legitimate therapeutic social function—healing through laughter—that rivaled the pretensions of the medical profession.

937.   McBride, Robert. "The Sceptical View of Medicine and the Comic Vision of Molière." *SFr* 23 (1979): 27–42.

Molière approaches medicine with a "sceptical frame of mind which refuses to condemn it definitively and dogmatically, whilst criticizing amply the present pass to which it has come. It is a frame of mind which is almost never to be equated simply with opposition to the object of ridicule, but rather one which, at one remove from the diversity of opinions and attitudes presented, views the comedy to which they give rise with the eye of a Sceptic beholding the variations which humanity elaborates on a given theme. The subject of medicine and doctors in Molière's theatre would therefore seem to be far more complex than the conventional status which it has long held in comedy would at first suggest; in a particular framework, but in recognizable form, it is used to illustrate a certain sceptical view of life."

938.   Tournemille, Jean. "Molière et l'essai de Montaigne intitulé 'De la ressemblance des enfants aux pères.' " *BSAM* 18 (1956): 42–44.

Montaigne's comments regarding doctors and medicine in such works as "De la ressemblance des enfants aux pères" greatly influenced the view of the medical profession Molière expressed in *Médecin malgré lui*, *Le malade imaginaire*, and other plays.

John Norden (fl. 1600)

939.   McColley, Grant. "An Early Poetic Allusion to the Copernican Theory." *JHI* 3 (1942): 355–57.
Interprets stanza 43 of Norden's *Vicissitudi Rerum* (1600) as a possible allusion to Copernicus's heliocentric theory of the heavens.

Samuel Pepys (1633–1703)

940.   Nicolson, Marjorie Hope. *Pepys' Diary and the New Science*. Charlottesville: UP of Virginia, 1965. 198 pp.
Rev. Dorothy Stimson, *Science* 151 (1966): 1522–23; G. N. Clark, *EHR* 82 (1967): 614; Ernest Tuveson, *JEGP* 66 (1967): 266–69.
In his *Diary* of 1660–69 Pepys recorded observations of numerous experiments and demonstrations at the Royal Society that impressed him and his contemporaries as distinctive innovations of the "new science." Nicolson surveys Pepys's reports on subjects such as blood transfusions, efforts to weigh the air, Petty's "double bottom" boat, and the Duchess of Newcastle's visit to the society. She also discusses satires of the society by S. Butler and Shadwell.

Matthew Prior (1664–1721)

941.   Spears, Monroe K. "Matthew Prior's Attitude toward Natural Science." *PMLA* 63 (1948): 485–507.
Analyzes the antagonism toward science reflected in Prior's writings. Specifically discusses the sources of his scientific knowledge, his critique of scientific "systems," his pessimistic view of the materialistic and deterministic implications of science, and the conflict between science and religion.

Honoré de Bueil, Seigneur de Racan (1589–1670)

942.   Ridgely, Beverly S. "Racan and the Old and New Astronomies." *YFS* 49 (1973): 154–69.
Despite Racan's modest familiarity with the tenets of Copernicanism and his predilection for treating astronomical themes in his poetry, his works neglect contemporary astronomical developments and remain firmly rooted in the old Ptolemaic astronomy. Ridgely examines Racan's "Consolation à Monseigneur de Bellegarde, sur la mort de Monsieur de Termes son frère" in this respect.

Marc Antoinè de Gérard Saint-Amant (1594–1661)

943.   Ridgely, Beverly S. "Saint-Amant and the 'New Astronomy.'" *MLR* 53 (1958): 26–37.

An introduction to a study of the impact that scientific thought had on seventeenth-century French poetry, this essay stresses Saint-Amant's poetic treatment of astronomical ideas such as Copernican heliocentrism, the cause of tides, and the import of sun spots. The "new astronomy" is reflected significantly in three of Saint-Amant's poems—the "Epître à M. le baron de Melay" (1643), the "Epître" to the Baron de Villarnoul (1646), and "La Polonoise." In general, Saint-Amant treated the subject in a casual, nonpedantic, and nondidactic manner to ensure that the French nobility, for whom his poetry was intended, would find his work congenial.

Thomas Shadwell (1642?–92)

944.   Gilde, Joseph M. "Shadwell and the Royal Society: Satire in *The Virtuoso*." *SEL* 10 (1970): 469–90.
"The primary target of satire in *The Virtuoso* is not—as previous commentators have supposed—the experimental scientists of the Royal Society. On the contrary Sir Nicholas Gimcrack and Sir Formal Trifle, Shadwell's two major fools, exhibit specific follies which are best understood in the light of Royal Society strictures against false science and elaborate rhetoric."

945.   Lloyd, Claude. "Shadwell and the Virtuosi." *PMLA* 44 (1929): 472–94.
Discusses Shadwell's satire of science and the Royal Society in *The Virtuoso* as represented by the four virtuosi—Snarl, Sir Samuel Hearty, Sir Formal Trifle, and Sir Nicholas Gimcrack.

Charles Sorel (1597–1674)

946.   Ridgely, Beverly S. "The Cosmic Voyage in Charles Sorel's *Francion*." *MP* 65 (1967–68): 1–8.
Explores the meaning and intention of Sorel's use of cosmic voyages in *Histoire comique de Francion* (1623) and concludes that the voyages are a means of ridiculing and uprooting traditional Aristotelian-Ptolemaic-Christian astronomical beliefs while clearing the way for concepts emerging in the "new astronomy." Ridgely finds corroboration of this thesis in Sorel's *Science universelle* (1668), which explicitly attempts to discredit the "old astronomy."

Edward Taylor (c. 1642–1729)

947.   Clare, Sister M. Theresa. "Taylor's 'Meditation Sixty-Two.' " *Expl* 19 (1960–61): item 16.
Taylor's poem contains references to herbal medicine.

948.   Kehler, Joel R. "Physiology and Metaphor in Edward Taylor's 'Meditation. Can. 1.3.' " *EAL* 9 (1974–75): 315–20.
Examines the complex metaphoric structure of Taylor's "Meditation. Can. 1.3." in the context of the Galenic physiology on which his use of terms such as *spirit* and *mammulary* was probably based.

949.   Sluder, Lawrence Lan. "God in the Background: Edward Taylor as Naturalist." *EAL* 7 (1972–73): 265–71.
The traditional view of Taylor as merely a religious poet is too narrow in that it fails to account for other influences on his poems, principally natural science. Sluder discusses Taylor's interests in natural science and examines the naturalist component of his poem "The Great Bones of Claverack" (1705).

950.   Woodward, Robert H. "Automata in Hawthorne's 'Artist of the Beautiful' and Taylor's 'Meditation 56.' " *ESQ* 31 (1963): 63–66.
See item 1712 for annotation.

Tirso de Molina (1584?–1648)

951.   Halstead, Frank G. "The Attitude of Tirso de Molina toward Astrology." *HR* 9 (1941): 417–39.
Assesses Tirso's understanding of astronomical and astrological thought, emphasizing his dissatisfaction with astrological methodology. Cites passages from several dramatic works.

952.   ———. "The Optics of Love: Notes on a Concept of Atomistic Philosophy in the Theatre of Tirso de Molina." *PMLA* 58 (1943): 108–21.
Notes that passages from Tirso's *Elección por la virtud* (1622) and *Amor médico* (1625) present unique theories of love and its relation to vision that recall the optical principles of Democritean and Epicurean atomism.

Thomas Tomkis (fl. 1614)

953.   Dick, Hugh G. "The Telescope and the Comic Imagination." *MLN* 58 (1943): 544–48.
The publication of *Sidereus nuncius* (1610), in which Galileo reports his invention of the telescope and the astronomical discoveries made through its use, excited a flurry of literary satire and intellectual disdain. Dick examines passages from Tomkis's *Albumazar* (1615) that ridicule Galileo and briefly discusses the history of satire aimed at Galileo's telescope.

Cyril Tourneur (1575?–1626)

954.   Ornstein, Robert. "*The Atheist's Tragedy* and Renaissance Naturalism." *SP* 51 (1954): 194–207.
Discusses D'Amville's naturalist philosophy in Tourneur's *Atheist's Tragedy*, indicating how Tourneur attempted to reconcile religious faith with the developing science of the Renaissance.

955.   Tompkins, J. M. S. "Tourneur and the Stars." *RES* 22 (1946): 315–19.
Briefly discusses the astrological symbolism of Tourneur's *Atheist's Tragedy*.

Thomas Traherne (1637?-74)

956. Hunter, C. Stuart. "Thomas Traherne and Francis Bacon: In Definition of Traherne's Poetic." *HAB* 27 (1976): 1–15.

Explores Traherne's response to Bacon's reflections on poetry, science, and philosophy in *De augmentis scientiarum*, noting especially his rejection of Bacon's materialist principles. Traherne's study of *De augmentis* led to the formation of his organicist worldview and his poetics and also influenced his concept of felicity. Among the poems discussed are "The World," "Hosanna," and "The Circulation."

Henry Vaughan (1622–95)

957. Clough, Wilson O. "Henry Vaughan and the Hermetic Philosophy." *PMLA* 48 (1933): 1108–30.

Attempts to determine the extent to which elements of hermetic philosophy and alchemy enter into Vaughan's poetry. Considers Vaughan's interest in hermetic and alchemical literature, his translation of Henricus Nollius's *Hermetical Physick* (1655), and the influence of his brother Thomas, a known alchemist and hermetist.

958. Farnham, Fern. "The Imagery of Henry Vaughan's 'The Night.' " *PQ* 38 (1959): 425–35.

Contends that the significance of Vaughan's poem "The Night" is greatly enhanced if its imagery is traced not merely to hermetic and alchemical sources but to the Bible.

959. Rudrum, Alan. "The Influence of Alchemy in the Poems of Henry Vaughan." *PQ* 49 (1970): 469–80.

Assesses the extent to which Vaughan's knowledge of the hermetic and alchemical tradition determined his choice of poetic imagery and generally influenced his poetic and religious endeavors.

960. Spitz, Leona. "Process and Stasis: Aspects of Nature in Vaughan and Marvell." *HLQ* 32 (1968–69): 135–47.

Vaughan drew on astronomy, geometry, and physiology to illustrate the relations of humankind to nature and to God in poems such as "The Storm," "Isaacs Marriage," and "The Bee." Marvell's view of nature in poems like "On a Drop of Dew" and "The Garden" stresses the relation between the creative power of the human mind and nature's divine power.

961. Walters, Richard H. "Henry Vaughan and the Alchemists." *RES* 23 (1947): 107–22.

Examines the extent to which Vaughan was influenced by hermetic terminology and by some central hermetic concepts such as the analogy between material transformation and spiritual regeneration.

John Webster (1580?–1634)

962. Parr, Johnstone. "The Horoscope in Webster's *The Duchess of Malfi*." *PMLA* 60 (1945): 760–65. Rpt. as "The Duke of Byron's Malignant Nativity."

Tamburlaine's Malady, and Other Essays on Astrology in Elizabethan Drama. University: U of Alabama P, 1953. Westport: Greenwood, 1971. 85–100.

An analysis of the horoscope read in *The Duchess of Malfi* (2.3.72–80) shows that Webster possessed an adept knowledge of the technicalities of astrology.

Richard Whitlock (b. 1616?)

963.   Bentley, Christopher. "The Rational Physician: Richard Whitlock's Medical Satires." *JHM* 29 (1974): 180–95.

Analyzes the medical satires in Whitlock's *Zootomia* (1654); modeled after Theophrastean characters, they ridiculed mountebanks, astrology, uroscopy, and other aspects of seventeenth-century medicine.

Eighteenth Century

Studies and Surveys

964.   Accame Bobbio, Aurelia. "Note sui rapporti tra poesia e scienza nel settecento." *Convivium* [Bologna] 35 (1967): 522–55.

   Traces the development in the relations between science and poetry during the eighteenth century, noting the changes Newtonianism wrought on poetic themes and style. Among the authors studied are Conti and Foscolo.

965.   ———. *Poesia e scienza nella letteratura del settecento.* Anno accademico 1966–1967. Roma: De Santis, 1967. 272 pp.

   This selection of shorter poems and excerpts from longer poems by Conti, Roberti, Torre de Rezzonico, Mazza, Paradisi, Cassoli, Parini, and Mascheroni is followed by a short essay discussing the impact of seventeenth-century scientific discoveries on literature and on the eighteenth-century understanding of nature. The author provides biographies that emphasize the poets' relations to science and analyzes how the poems included treat scientific material.

966.   Anderson, Daryll M. "Satires of Science in the Seventeenth and Eighteenth Centuries." *DAI* 41 (1980–81): 3114A.

   See item 646 for annotation.

967.   Arntzen, Helmut. "Beobachtung, Metaphorik, Bildlichkeit bei Lichtenberg." *DVLG* 42 (1968): 359–72.

   Shows that the aphorisms of the physicist G. C. Lichtenberg, although scientific insofar as they precisely reflect his scientific observations, display literary qualities, particularly in their use of metaphor.

968.   Arthos, John. *The Language of Natural Description in Eighteenth Century Poetry.* University of Michigan Publications: Language and Literature 24. Ann Arbor: U of Michigan P, 1949. London: Cass; New York: Octagon, 1966. 463 pp.
   Rev. Geoffrey Tillotson, *MLR* 45 (1950): 246–47; J. Butt, *RES* ns 2 (1951): 87–89; W. K. Wimsatt, Jr., *MLN* 66 (1951): 59–61.

   This detailed study of the eighteenth-century poetic terminology in the natural science of the period establishes a relation between the formal elements of this poetic diction, such as epithets, Latinisms, and paraphrasis, and the language of earlier poetic and scientific literature. Poets and scientists cited include Akenside, F. Bacon, Boyle, Du Bartas, Dryden, Harvey, Gilbert, and J. Thomson.

969.   Basile, Bruno. "Scienza e letteratura alla scuola di Fr. Redi: La lettera di
        G. C. Bonomo sopra i pellicelli." *SPCT* 19 (1979): 153–73.
Discusses the changes Redi made in Bonomo's *Osservazioni intorno a' pellicelli del
corpo umano* (1687), an important seventeenth-century scientific work. These linguistic and literary alterations transformed Bonomo's scientific observations into
elegant prose interspersed with literary citations.

970.   Blunden, Edmund. "Physicians and Poetry: A Brief Record." *SELit* 7
        (1927): 1–16.
Briefly describes the careers of several illustrious poet-physicians and presents
excerpts from their poetry. Discusses Akenside, R. Blackmore, E. Darwin, Garth,
Goldsmith, Smollett, H. Vaughan, and others.

971.   Brown, Harcourt. *Science and the Human Comedy: Natural Philosophy in French
        Literature from Rabelais to Maupertuis.* Toronto: U of Toronto P, 1976. 221
        pp.
See item 396 for annotation.

972.   ———. "Tensions and Anxieties: Science and the Literary Culture of
        France." *Science and the Creative Spirit: Essays on Humanistic Aspects of Science.*
        Ed. Harcourt Brown. Toronto: U of Toronto P, 1958. 91–126.
See item 146 for annotation.

973.   Brown, Marshall. "The Eccentric Path." *JEGP* 77 (1978): 104–12.
Shows that references to the "exzentrische Bahn" in writings by Fichte, Goethe,
Hölderlin, Lessing, Novalis, Oken, Tieck, and others derive from Ptolemaic and
Copernican astronomical terminology.

974.   Bush, Douglas. *Science and English Poetry: A Historical Sketch, 1590–1950.*
        New York: Oxford UP, 1950. Westport: Greenwood, 1980. 166 pp.
See item 147 for annotation.

975.   Bush, May Dulaney. "Rational Proof of a Deity from the Order of Nature."
        ELH 9 (1942): 288–319.
Newtonian cosmology and Lockean rationalism provided a basis for the ideas
about nature and its relation to God expressed in eighteenth-century literature. The
physicotheological speculations of the time may have prepared the way for the
Romantic concept of nature. Authors studied include Addison, Akenside, R. Blackmore, I. Browne, Gay, and Needler.

976.   Coleman, William. "The People's Health: Medical Themes in Eighteenth-
        Century French Popular Literature." *BHM* 51 (1977): 55–74.
Though the medical advice in popular eighteenth-century French literature was
corrective rather than preventive and was relatively unsystematic, it sheds light on
the medical awareness of the French population during this period.

977.   Crouch, Laura E. "The Scientist in English Literature: Domingo Gonsales
        (1638) to Victor Frankenstein (1817)." *DAI* 36 (1975–76): 2181A.
See item 149 for annotation.

978.   Crum, Ralph B. *Scientific Thought in Poetry*. Diss. Columbia U, 1931. New York: Columbia UP, 1931. New York: AMS, 1966. Folcroft: Folcroft, 1973. 246 pp.
See item 150 for annotation.

979.   Davie, Donald. *The Language of Science and the Language of Literature, 1700–1740*. Newman History and Philosophy of Science Series 13. New York: Sheed, 1963. 87 pp.
In opposition to views expressed by R. L. Brett, Douglas Bush, and Basil Willey, the author maintains that early-eighteenth-century science was a fertile source of innovative literary metaphors, drawn on frequently by writers such as Arbuthnot, Johnson, Mandeville, Pope, Sterne, Swift, and J. Thomson. Davie concentrates on how scientific terminology passed into literary metaphor.

980.   Dean, Dennis R. "James Hutton and His Public, 1785–1802." *AnS* 30 (1973): 89–105.
When Hutton's geological theory first appeared in 1785, it failed to achieve acceptance. Far from being ignored, however, it was mentioned frequently in scientific and popular works, including E. Darwin's poems.

981.   De Selincourt, Ernest. "The Interplay of Literature and Science during the Last Three Centuries." *HJ* 37 (1938–39): 225–45.
See item 151 for annotation.

982.   Emery, Clark. "Optics and Beauty." *MLQ* 3 (1942): 45–50.
Comments on the poetic use of optical theory in works by eighteenth-century "scientific" poets such as Akenside, J. Thomson, and Young.

983.   ———. "Science and Eighteenth-Century Poetry." Diss. U of Washington, 1940.
Not seen for annotation.

984.   Fabian, Bernhard. "Lukrez in England im siebzehnten und achtzehnten Jahrhundert: Einige Notizen." *WSA* 6 (1980): 107–29.
Examines the influence of Lucretius's *De rerum natura* on sixteenth-, seventeenth-, and eighteenth-century English literature, philosophy, and science. Celebrated by atheists and freethinkers and vilified by defenders of the Christian faith, Lucretius's poem was considered a model for a didactic poetry appropriate for the emerging scientific age. In R. Blackmore's *Creation*, Polignac's *Anti-Lucretius*, and Pope's *Essay on Man* Fabian sees attempts to imitate Lucretius and at the same time replace his Epicurean philosophy. Many viewed Newton as the anti-Epicurus of modernity and yearned for a poet of Lucretius's stature to write a new *De rerum natura* based on Newtonianism.

985.   ———. "Newton und die Dichter im achtzehnten Jahrhundert: Popularisierung durch schöne Literatur." *MedJ* 12 (1977): 309–24.
Reviews the popularization of Newtonian science in the first half of the eighteenth century and discusses some of the best-known versifications of Newtonianism with special attention to Pope's *Essay on Man*.

986.   Fleischmann, Wolfgang B. *Lucretius and English Literature, 1680–1740.*
        Paris: Nizet, 1964. 285 pp.
        Rev. R. L. Colie, *CL* 18 (1966): 177–79.
Assesses the extent to which *De rerum natura* influenced the creative work of
essayists and poets such as Addison, R. Blackmore, Dryden, Garth, Pope, Prior,
Shaftesbury, Steele, Swift, and J. Thomson. A large portion of the book surveys
the editions and translations of Lucretius's poem available to these authors and
appraises previous scholarship concerning Lucretian influence on literature.

987.   Foster, Finley. "Bath: Physicians and Literature." *Bulletin of the Medical
        Library Association* 32 (1944): 2–22.
Outlines the history of the bathing establishment at Bath, England; surveys the
medical literature that assessed the curative powers of the waters of Bath; and
comments on satirical portrayals of the Bath physicians in Smollett's *Peregrine Pickle*
(1751) and *Humphry Clinker* (1771) and Anstey's *New Bath Guide* (1766).

988.   Foster, John Wilson. "The Measure of Paradise: Topography in Eighteenth-
        Century Poetry." *ECS* 9 (1975–76): 232–56.
Traces the rise and decline of topographical, or landscape, poetry, including
Denham's "Cooper's Hill" (1642–55), Dyer's "Grongar Hill" (1726), Jago's "Edge-
Hill" (1767), and Maurice's "Grove-Hill" (1799). The developing sciences of surveying and topography increased their influence on this poetic genre throughout
the eighteenth century, gradually producing an overabundance of scientific precision
and description and an unpoetic result.

989.   Fullard, Joyce. "Satire of the New Science in England, France, and Spain
        during the Enlightenment." *DAI* 36 (1975–76): 2790A.
Paradoxically, the satirical treatment of science by Voltaire, King, and others
stimulated popular interest in scientific activity.

990.   Fusil, Casimir Alexandre. *La poésie scientifique de 1750 à nos jours.* Paris:
        Scientifica, 1917. 320 pp.
Analyzes the reception of science in French poetry from 1750 to 1900. Treats
Voltaire, Hugo, Laforgue, Lahor, Lamartine, and Vigny.

991.   Griggs, Charles I. "Science in English Poetry from Thomson to Cowper."
        Diss. U of Wisconsin, 1937.
Not seen for annotation.

992.   Guerlac, Henry. "An Augustan Monument: The *Opticks* of Isaac Newton."
        The Varied Pattern: Studies in the Eighteenth Century. Publications of the
        McMaster University Association for Eighteenth-Century Studies 1. Ed.
        Peter Hughes and David Williams. Toronto: Hakkert, 1971. 131–63.
Discusses the influence of Newton's *Opticks* on poets, philosophers, and artists,
including Goethe, Hartley, D. Hume, J. Thomson, and Young. Treats the *Opticks*
in its scientific and literary aspects.

993.   Guthke, Karl S. " 'Die Mehrheit der Welten': Geistesgeschichtliche Per-
        spektiven auf ein literarisches Thema im 18. Jahrhundert." *ZDP* 97 (1978):
        481–512.

The notion of a plurality of inhabited worlds, proposed as far back as antiquity, gained a degree of scientific plausibility from Galileo's telescopic observations. Guthke illustrates the prevalence of this doctrine with numerous references to eighteenth-century didactic verse.

994.   Harris, Ronald Walter. *Reason and Nature in the Eighteenth Century*. New York: Barnes, 1969. 439 pp.
         Rev. G. S. Rousseau, *Isis* 61 (1970): 280.
Reviews humanism, politics, economics, religion, and other aspects of eighteenth-century culture; one chapter offers cursory remarks on the impact of science on eighteenth-century poetry and criticism.

995.   Harrison, Thomas P. "Birds in the Moon." *Isis* 45 (1954): 323–30.
Summarizes the theory of bird migration proposed in Charles Morton's *Compendium physicae* and notes references to the idea in works by Dryden, Gay, F. Godwin, Pope, and Wilkins.

996.   Hastings, Hester. *Man and Beast in French Thought of the Eighteenth Century*. Diss. Johns Hopkins U, 1934. Johns Hopkins Studies in Romance Literatures and Languages 27. Baltimore: Johns Hopkins P; London: Milford, Oxford UP, 1936. Portland, ME: Forest City, 1970. New York: Johnson, 1973.
         Rev. Charles A. Kofoid, *Isis* 30 (1939): 532–33.
Surveys the contributions French scientists and philosophers made to the debate over the relationship between human beings and animals. Intended as background to a study of nineteenth-century French animal literature, the work discusses the question of whether animals have souls; the superiority or inferiority of animals to human beings; the antecedents of a humanitarian attitude toward animals; and related issues such as vivesection, vegetarianism, and hunting. Among the chief figures in the debate were Bernardin de Saint-Pierre, Bonnet, Boullier, Buffon, R. Descartes, Helvétius, La Mettrie, Le Roy, Rivarol, Rousseau, and Voltaire.

997.   Heggen, Alfred. "Die 'ars volandi' in der Literatur des 17. und 18. Jahrhunderts." *Technikgeschichte* 42 (1975): 327–37.
See item 673 for annotation.

998.   Heller, John L. "Classical Poetry in the *Systema naturae* of Linnaeus." *Transactions and Proceedings of the American Philological Association* 102 (1971): 183–216.
Identifies passages from classical poetry in the *Systema naturae*. Linnaeus drew chiefly from the works of Vergil, Ovid, and Seneca.

999.   Horne, C. J. "Literature and Science." *From Dryden to Johnson*. Vol. 4 of *The Pelican Guide to English Literature*. Ed. Boris Ford. Baltimore: Penguin, 1957. 188–202. 7 vols. 1954–61.
See item 675 for annotation.

1000.   Jones, William Powell. "The Idea of the Limitations of Science from Prior to Blake." *SEL* 1.3 (1961): 97–114.

Examines physicotheological poems and essays by Prior, Brooke, H. Jones, M. Browne, Smart, Hawkins, Chatterton, Cowper, and Blake. All the works discussed treat the theme of the limitations of science.

1001.   ———. "Newton Further Demands the Muse." *SEL* 3 (1963): 287–306.
Though the influence of Newton's *Opticks* on eighteenth-century poetry was explored by Marjorie Nicolson, Alan McKillop, and others, the influence of his *Principia* has been neglected. Jones traces references to the *Principia* in works by Bowden, Brooke, Glover, Lofft, Mallet, Pope, Roberts, J. Thomson, and many others.

1002.   ———. *The Rhetoric of Science: A Study of Scientific Ideas and Imagery in Eighteenth-Century English Poetry.* Berkeley: U of California P; London: Routledge, 1966. 243 pp.
Rev. R. L. Brett, *RES* ns 18 (1967): 471–72; Morris Golden, *JEGP* 66 (1967): 587–89; G. S. Rousseau, *PQ* 46 (1967): 316–19; Harry P. Kroitor, *MP* 65 (1967–68): 387–88.
A comprehensive survey of eighteenth-century scientific poetry and its scientific background, including separate chapters on physicotheological poetry, moral poetry, and natural history in English poetry. Stresses the influence of Newton and of the new sciences of microscopy and telescopy. Among the many authors considered are Akenside, Baker, R. Blackmore, Brooke, M. Browne, Mallet, Pope, and J. Thomson.

1003.   ———. "Science in Biblical Paraphrases in Eighteenth-Century England." *PMLA* 74 (1959): 41–51.
To introduce a study of scientific influence on eighteenth-century English poetry, the author discusses poetic paraphrases of the Book of Job and other portions of the Bible that were reinterpreted in a scientific light. Jones also examines poetry describing the "creation" and the "last judgment" in scientific terms, including Smart's *Song to David* (1763) and *Jubilate Agno,* Young's *Paraphrase on Part of the Book of Job* (1719), Hughes's *Ode to the Creator of the World* (1713), R. Blackmore's *Creation* (1712), and A. Hill's *Judgement Day* (1721).

1004.   Junker, Christof. *Das Weltraumbild in der deutschen Lyrik von Opitz bis Klopstock.* Germanische Studien 111. Berlin: Ebering, 1932. Berlin: Kraus, 1967. 127 pp.
The transition from the Ptolemaic to the Copernican astronomical system was not fully reflected in German lyric poetry until the eighteenth century. Junker traces references to Copernicanism in poetry from Brockes to Klopstock and examines how the new system affected the poets' conceptions of God, time, eternity, and space. Other poets cited include Gleim, Gryphius, Haller, and Opitz.

1005.   Ketelsen, Uwe-K. *Die Naturpoesie der norddeutschen Frühaufklärung: Poesie als Sprache der Versöhnung Alter Universalismus und neues Weltbild.* Germanistische Abhandlungen 45. Stuttgart: Metzler, 1974. 294 pp.
Studies the reception of the "new science"—especially astronomy from Copernicus to Newton—in the North German nature poetry of the early eighteenth century. Sees in the physicotheological poetry of the time, as represented by Brockes's *Irdisches Vergnügen in Gott,* an effort to reconcile modern science and Lutheran orthodoxy.

1006.   Kleinert, Andreas. *Die allgemeinverständlichen Physikbücher der französischen Aufklärung*. Veröffentlichungen der Schweizerischen Gesellschaft für Geschichte der Medizin und der Naturwissenschaften 28. Aarau: Sauerländer, 1974. 187 pp.
Studies the division that developed between the sciences and the humanities in eighteenth-century France, focusing on the role played by attempted popularizations of science such as Marivetz and Goussier's *Physique du monde* (1780–87) and Algarotti's *Le newtonianisme pour les dames, ou entretiens sur la lumière, sur les couleurs, et sur l'attraction* (1751). Such works tended to distort scientific data in an effort to entertain, though Fontenelle's *Entretiens sur la pluralité des mondes* (1686), which maintained scientific integrity, was a notable exception. Fontenelle's work successfully bridged the gap between belles lettres and the sciences. Kleinert also discusses such scientific works as DuFay's *Mémoires sur l'électricité* (1733) and Voltaire's *Elémens de la philosophie de Newton* (1738).

1007.   Knapp, Lewis M. "Dr. John Armstrong, Littérateur, and Associate of Smollett, Thomson, Wilkes, and Other Celebrities." *PMLA* 59 (1944): 1019–58.
A thorough review of Armstrong's life that discusses his medical career, his few poems (e.g., "The Art of Preserving Health"), and his correspondence with his friends Smollett, J. Thomson, and Wilkes.

1008.   Koppel, Richard M. "English Satire on Science, 1660–1750." *DAI* 40 (1979): 250A–51A.
See item 682 for annotation.

1009.   Link, Viktor. "On the Development of the Modern Animal Story." *DR* 56 (1976): 519–25.
Maintains that the realistic literary depiction of animals and animal behavior occurred first in the late eighteenth century in works such as Kendall's *Crested Wren* (1799), *Sparrow* (1798), and *Keeper's Travels in Search of His Master* (1798) and the anonymous *Hare* (1799) and *Memoirs of Dick, the Little Poney* (1799–1800). Link also briefly discusses late-nineteenth-century developments of the animal story, which were spurred by the influence of Darwinian theory.

1010.   McCue, Daniel L., Jr. "Science and Literature: The Virtuoso in English Belles Lettres." *Albion* 3 (1971): 138–56.
See item 688 for annotation.

1011.   Macklem, Michael. *The Anatomy of the World: Relations between Natural and Moral Law from Donne to Pope*. Diss. Princeton U, 1954. Minneapolis: U of Minnesota P, 1958. 139 pp.
See item 690 for annotation.

1012.   Meadows, A. J. *The High Firmament: A Survey of Astronomy in English Literature*. Leicester: Leicester UP, 1969. 207 pp.
See item 162 for annotation.

1013.   Murdoch, Ruth T. "Newton and the French Muse." *JHI* 19 (1958): 323–34.
Outlines the influence of Newton's *Principia* and *Opticks* on eighteenth-century French poetry.

1014.   Naiden, James R. "Newton Demands the Latin Muse." *Symposium* 6 (1952): 111–22.
Surveys Latin didactic poetry devoted to Newtonianism, originally published primarily in England and Italy until about 1800. Among the poems discussed are I. Browne's "De animi immortalitate" (1754), R. Smith's "Musae etonenses" (1795), Nocet's "Iris" (1729), and Boscovich's "Eclipses of the Sun and Moon" (1760).

1015.   Neubauer, John. "Dr. John Brown (1735–88) and Early German Romanticism." *JHI* 28 (1967): 367–82.
Discusses the influence of Brown's late-eighteenth-century medical theory on Schelling and Novalis. Stresses the interrelations of scientific, literary, and philosophical ideas in the early Romantic period.

1016.   Neubert, Fritz. "Das Weltsystem des Benoît de Maillet." *Archiv* 141 (1921): 79–92.
Maillet's *Telliamed: Ou, Entretiens d'un philosophe indien avec un missionnaire françois*, first published in 1738, was an imaginative cosmogony and cosmology drawing on current scientific thought. Among the poets who eagerly read this work were Goethe and Voltaire.

1017.   Nicolson, Marjorie H. "The Microscope and English Imagination." *Smith College Studies in Modern Languages* 16.4 (1934–35): 1–92. Rpt. in *Science and Imagination*. Ithaca: Great Seal, 1956. Hamden: Archon, 1976. 155–234.
See item 705 for annotation.

1018.   ———. *Mountain Gloom and Mountain Glory: The Development of the Aesthetics of the Infinite*. Ithaca: Cornell UP, 1959. 403 pp.
Rev. Alan D. McKillop, *MP* 57 (1959–60): 206–07; D. C. Allen, *Isis* 51 (1960): 222–23; Jean H. Hagstrum, *MLN* 76 (1961): 48–51; Derek Roper, *RES* ns 12 (1961): 90–91.
In the eighteenth century sublimity became an admired aesthetic response not, as commonly thought, because of a reawakened interest in Longinius but, rather, because men like H. More and Traherne responded with rapture and awe to the limitless space of seventeenth-century astronomy. Later writers regarded mountains, which they considered the most colossal manifestations of nature on Earth, as signs of God's boundless power and diversity; the immense, the infinite, became sublime rather than terrifying or sinful. T. Burnet's *Sacred Theory of the Earth* (1681), with its blend of science, religion, and aesthetics, was the key agent in advancing an "aesthetics of the infinite," which directly influenced writers such as Addison and Swift. Nicolson traces the subsequent tradition of nature poetry describing "mountain glory" from J. Thomson through the Romantics.

1019.   ———. *Newton Demands the Muse: Newton's* Opticks *and the Eighteenth-Century Poets.* History of Ideas Series 2. Princeton: Princeton UP, 1946. Hamden: Archon, 1963. Westport: Greenwood, 1979. 177pp.
Rev. W. J. Bate, *MLN* 62 (1947): 276–77; I. Bernard Cohen, *Isis* 38 (1948): 115–16; Bonamy Dobrée, *RES* 24 (1948): 163–64.

Newton's *Opticks* (1704), written in plain, nontechnical English, deals with the everyday world of light and vision. Consequently, eighteenth-century British poets such as Akenside and J. Thomson responded to the book with much greater interest than they did to the abstract and mathematical arguments of the *Principia* (1687). Newton's explanation of prismatic dispersion appealed to a new school of poets who incorporated colorful, detailed descriptions of nature into their verses. By the end of the century, however, writers such as Blake began to react against the Newtonian implication that secondary (sensuous) qualities were less important than primary (numerable) ones, and Newton's fruitful influence on literature ceased.

1020.   ———. "Ward's 'Pill and Drop' and Men of Letters." *JHI* 29 (1968): 177–96.

Describes various recipes Joshua Ward, an eighteenth-century quack, used for the notorious medicine known as the "pill and drop." Satirical references to the concoction appear in works by C. Churchill, Fielding, Pope, Smollett, Walpole, and others.

1021.   ———. "A World in the Moon: A Study of the Changing Attitude toward the Moon in the Seventeenth and Eighteenth Centuries." *Smith College Studies in Modern Languages* 17.2 (1935–36): 1–72.
See item 711 for annotation.

1022.   Omasreiter, Ria. *Naturwissenschaft und Literaturkritik im England des 18. Jahrhunderts.* Erlanger Beiträge zur Sprach- und Kunstwissenschaft 4. Nürnberg: Carl, 1971. 190 pp.
Rev. Paul H. Meyer, *ECS* 6 (1972–73): 386–89.

Notes the close relation between eighteenth-century developments in science and substantive changes in the literary criticism of the time. For example, critics such as Addison and Johnson viewed poetry as an expression and a function of biological and social constellations; they were strongly influenced in this regard by F. Bacon's *Novum organum*, Newton's *Principia*, T. Burnet's *Sacred Theory of the Earth*, and Sprat's *History*. In literary criticism, Omasreiter documents, scientific terminology replaced generally accepted philosophical terminology—a change that underscores the impact of science on the seemingly unrelated field.

1023.   Pettit, Henry. " 'The Pleasing Paths of Sense': The Subject-Matter of Augustan Literature." *Literature and Science.* Proc. of the Sixth Triennial Congress of the International Federation for Modern Languages and Literatures. Oxford, 1954. Oxford: Blackwell, 1955. 169–74.

Examines Dryden's *Alexander's Feast*, Swift's *Tale of a Tub*, Defoe's *True Relation of the Apparition of Mrs. Veal*, and Pope's *Eloisa to Abelard* from the perspective of their underlying common concern—the nature and significance of human sensation.

1024.   Piper, Herbert W. *The Active Universe*. London: Athlone, 1962. 243 pp.
        Rev. H. A. Smith, *MLR* 58 (1963): 414–15.
The first chapter, "The Two Universes," provides a succinct account of the late-eighteenth-century transition from Newtonian materialism to a vitalistic pantheism. Holbach's summation of atheistic materialism was subverted almost immediately by Volney and others who exploited his implicit pantheism. As S. Coleridge and Wordsworth developed their poetry and literary theory in the 1790s, they were immersed in the mechanistic-vitalistic controversies and were influenced by the radical scientific thought of Priestley and E. Darwin. Piper traces how these controversies over the animate nature of matter affected Coleridge's poetry of the 1790s, including *The Rime of the Ancient Mariner*, and his theory of imagination in *Biographia Literaria*. Piper also contrasts Wordsworth's early response in *The Ruined Cottage* with his mature reexamination in *The Excursion*.

1025.   Priestley, F. E. L. "Newton and the Romantic Concept of Nature." *UTQ*
        17 (1948): 323–36.
Outlines some of the central tenets of Newtonianism that informed the Romantic concept of nature. Refers briefly to several versifiers of Newton and Newtonianism, such as Bally, Foster, Needler, and J. Thomson.

1026.   Richter, Karl. "Die kopernikanische Wende in der Lyrik von Brockes bis
        Klopstock." *JDSG* 12 (1968): 132–69.
With the diffusion and acceptance of the Copernican theory a new German lyric poetry developed in the first half and the middle of the eighteenth century that was in harmony with the new worldview in both form and content. The change from the didactic poetry of Brockes and Haller to the hymns of Klopstock reflects the expanded and more differentiated view of the cosmos revealed by the new astronomy.

1027.   ———. *Literatur und Naturwissenschaft: Eine Studie zur Lyrik der Aufklärung*.
        Theorie und Geschichte der Literatur und der schönen Künste. Texte und
        Abhandlungen 19. München: Fink, 1972. 237 pp.
        Rev. Y. Carbonnel, *EG* 28 (1973): 406–07; Karl S. Guthke, *GR* 50
        (1975): 55–56; Ida M. Kimber, *MLR* 70 (1975): 696; Uwe R. Klinger,
        JEGP 74 (1975): 64–65.
The scientific revolution of the sixteenth and seventeenth centuries, which culminated in Newtonianism, had a decisive impact on the lyric poetry of the German Enlightenment. The didactic poetry of Brockes and Haller, the anacreontic poetry of Hagedorn, and the hymns of Klopstock reveal a linkage between poetry and science that is characteristic of the eighteenth century. Richter sees a transition from a mechanistic to an organismic model of nature in the late eighteenth century, in both science and literature, with Goethe and Herder providing ample evidence of a higher fusion between science and aesthetics.

1028.   Robin, P. Ansell. *Animal Lore in English Literature*. London: Murray, 1932.
        Folcroft: Folcroft, 1970. Norwood: Norwood, 1975. Philadelphia: West,
        1976. 196 pp.
See item 169 for annotation.

1029.   Roger, Jacques. "Les sciences de la vie dans la pensée française du XVIIIe siècle." *IL* 16 (1964): 147–53.

The scientific problem of animal reproduction affected the philosophical view of nature, especially the perception of humanity vis-à-vis nature. Roger cites the major philosopher-authors of the eighteenth century, such as Diderot and Voltaire, who addressed this scientific and philosophic issue. He concludes that the history of ideas—and specifically of scientific ideas—has relevance for the literary historian.

1030.   Rousseau, G. S. "Science and the Discovery of the Imagination in Enlightened England." *ECS* 3 (1969–70): 108–35.

See item 720 for annotation.

1031.   Saine, Thomas P. "Natural Science and the Ideology of Nature in the German Enlightenment." *LY* 8 (1976): 61–88.

Examines aspects of the emergence of a new aesthetic relation between humankind and nature resulting from the "triumph of the Copernican system as crowned by the achievement of Newton in the *Principia*." The Enlightenment "ideology of nature" is reflected in Brockes's "Firmament" (1721) and "Grosse und Kleine" (1724), Klopstock's "Frühlingsfeier" (1759), Huygens's *Cosmotheoros* (1698), Goethe's *Leiden des jungen Werther*, and other works.

1032.   Schatzberg, Walter. *Scientific Themes in the Popular Literature and the Poetry of the German Enlightenment, 1720–1760.* Diss. Johns Hopkins U, 1966. Bern: Lang, 1973. 349 pp. (Abstract in *DA* 27 (1966): 1837A.)
        Rev. Jügen Stenzel, *Germanistik* 14 (1973): 841–42; John T. Brewer, *LY* 6 (1974): 257–58; Markus F. Motsch, *MLN* 90 (1975): 707; Edward P. Harris, *GQ* 49 (1976): 90; James L. Larson, *Isis* 68 (1977): 158.

Discusses the diffusion of the sciences in the German Enlightenment through popular literature such as physicotheological writings, compendiums of science, and periodicals. Explores the variety of literary responses to the sciences by examining the works of fifty poets—most notably, Brockes, Gottsched, Haller, Mylius, and Wieland. The scientific themes in the poetry include cosmogony, astronomy (specifically Newtonianism), earth sciences, plant and animal life, and attitudes toward science and nature.

1033.   Segel, Harold B. "Animal Magnetism in Polish Romantic Literature." *PolR* 7.3 (1962): 16–39.

Discusses the popularity of Franz Mesmer's theory of animal magnetism in eighteenth-century Poland, outlines the main tenets of the idea, and examines its reflection in such Polish literary works as Fredro's *Maiden's Vows* and Mickiewicz's *Konrad Wallenrod* and *Forefathers' Eve*.

1034.   Sena, John F. "The English Malady: The Idea of Melancholy from 1700–1760." *DA* 29 (1968–69): 239A–40A.

Studies the medical and physiological background of melancholy from 1700 to 1760 and notes how contemporary writers such as Smollett used the concept.

1035.   Shackleton, Robert. "Newtonianism and Literature." *Literature and Science.*
         Proc. of the Sixth Triennial Congress of the International Federation for
         Modern Languages and Literatures. Oxford, 1954. Oxford: Blackwell,
         1955. 157–64.
Analyzes the diffusion and popularization of Newtonianism in the eighteenth
century in academic and scientific circles, popular literature, salon society, and
poetry. Cites poems by Glover, Polignac, Smart, J. Thomson, and others.

1035a.   Shugg, Wallace. "The Beast-Machine in England: A Study of the Impact
         of the Cartesian Doctrine of Animal Automatism in England from 1645
         to 1750." *DA* 28 (1967): 643A.
See item 723a for annotation.

1036.   Simpson, H. C. "The Vogue of Science in English Literature, 1600–1800."
         UTQ 2 (1932–33): 143–67.
See item 724 for annotation.

1037.   Spencer, T. J. B. "Lucretius and the Scientific Poem in English." *Lucretius.*
         Ed. D. R. Dudley. London: Routledge; New York: Basic, 1965. 131–
         64.
Lucretius's poetic exposition of Epicurean science and philosophy in *De rerum
natura* served as a model and an inspiration for later attempts to versify science,
especially Newtonianism. Spencer traces the Lucretian influence on philosophico-
scientific poetry by Akenside, R. Blackmore, E. Darwin, Pope, J. Thomson, Byron,
P. Shelley, Tennyson, Wordsworth, and others.

1038.   Stebbins, Sara. *Maxima in Minimis: Zum Empirie- und Autoritätsverständnis
         in der physikotheologischen Literatur der Frühaufklärung.* Frankfurt: Lang, 1980.
         327 pp.
Discusses the impact of science on seventeenth- and eighteenth-century religious
belief as reflected in physicotheological poetry by Brockes, Triller, Zell, and others.

1039.   Stempel, Daniel. "Angels of Reason: Science and Myth in the Enlight-
         enment." *JHI* 36 (1975): 63–78.
Discusses four works in which angels reveal allegorical visions of the universe to
mortals: Addison's Newtonian "Vision of Mirzah," Voltaire's Leibnizian *Zadig,*
Klinger's biologically inspired *Der Faust der Morgenländer,* and Blake's *Marriage of
Heaven and Hell.* Biological science inspired disillusion with the glories of the
Newtonian universe and led to Blake's vision of all that exists.

1040.   Thiersch, Hans. "Die kosmichen Visionen Jean Pauls und die kosmischen
         Vorstellungen in der deutschen Dichtung des 18. Jahrhunderts." Diss. U
         Göttingen, 1963.
Not seen for annotation.

1041.   Thomé, Horst. *Roman und Naturwissenschaft: Eine Studie zur Vorgeschichte der
         deutschen Klassik.* Regensburger Beiträge zur deutschen Sprach- und Lite-

raturwissenschaft: Reihe B, Untersuchungen 15. Bern: Lang, 1978. 507 pp.

Rev. Ernst M. Oppenheimer, *Germanistik* 20 (1979): 474–75.

Discusses the eighteenth-century literary reception of science, emphasizing the influence of the sciences on the development of the German novel. Sees the fusion of science and aesthetics in Wieland's *Agathon* as the last great integration of the Enlightenment. In view of Herder's criticism of Enlightenment science, Goethe's *Werther* and *Wilhelm Meisters Lehrjahre* represent sophisticated syntheses of science and aesthetics.

1042.   Thornton, Linda R. "The Influence of Bernard de Fontenelle upon English Writers of the Eighteenth Century." *DAI* 39 (1978): 1536A.

Discusses the influence of Fontenelle's scientific, literary, and religious writings on writers such as Addison, D. Hume, Johnson, King, Pope, and Prior.

1043.   Todd, Ruthven. "Tracks in the Snow." *Tracks in the Snow: Studies in English Science and Art.* London: Grey Walls, 1946. 1–28.

Discusses the impact of the thought of F. Bacon, R. Descartes, Newton, Locke, and others on the seventeenth- and eighteenth-century intellectual climate. Comments on the incorporation of scientific theories and data into literature such as Smart's *Jubilate Agno* and Blake's *Four Zoas*.

1044.   Turner, Margaret. " 'Natural Philosophy' and Eighteenth-Century Satire." *N&Q* 198 (1953): 296–99.

Comments on satirical references to the "scientific" investigations of eighteenth-century virtuosi made by Addison, T. Brown, Pope, Walpole, and others.

1045.   Wagner, Fritz. *Zur Apotheose Newtons: Künstlerische Utopie und naturwissenschaftliches Weltbild im 18. Jahrhundert.* Bayerische Akademie der Wissenschaften. Philosophisch-Historische Klasse. Sitzungsberichte. Jahrgang 1974, Heft 10. Munich: Beck, 1974. 52 pp. Rpt. in *Isaac Newton im Zwielicht zwischen Mythos und Forschung: Studien zur Epoche der Aufklärung.* Freiburg: Albert, 1976. 106–59.

In part examines the impact of Newton and Newtonianism on such poets as Blake, Haller, Pope, and J. Thomson.

1046.   Wilson, David S. "The Streaks of the Tulip: The Literary Aspects of Eighteenth-Century American Natural Philosophy." *DA* 29 (1968–69): 2689A–90A.

The author defines the literary genre of eighteenth-century American travelogues and natural histories and, in addition, examines the literary qualities of these works, which include Carver's *Travels* (1778), Bartram's *Observations* (1751), and Catesby's *Natural History of Carolina* (1731–43).

Individual Authors

Joseph Addison (1672–1719)

1047.   Jackson, Wallace. "Addison: Empiricist of the Moral Consciousness." *PQ* 45 (1966): 455–59.

An examination of Addison's "On the Pleasures of the Imagination" reveals that his aesthetic theory is founded on empiricist principles consistent with a Newtonian worldview.

John Aikin (1747–1822)

1048.   Jones, William P. "John Aikin on the Use of Natural History in Poetry." *JAAC* 21 (1962–63): 439–43.

Examines Aikin's *Essay on the Application of Natural History to Poetry* (1777) to assess his contributions to clarifying the relation between the two disciplines.

1049.   Plank, Jeffrey. "John Aikin on Science and Poetry." *SBHT* 18 (1977): 167–78.

Examines Aikin's interdisciplinary approach to literary criticism, stressing the influence of medicine and science on his *Essay on the Application of Natural History to Poetry*.

Mark Akenside (1721–70)

1050.   Aldridge, A. O. "Akenside, Anna Seward, and Colour." *N&Q* 193 (1948): 562–63.

Seward's annotations in her copy of Akenside's *Pleasures of the Imagination* indicate that Akenside was consciously interested in the aesthetics of light and color and may have been influenced in this regard by Newtonianism.

1051.   Potter, George R. "Mark Akenside, Prophet of Evolution." *MP* 24 (1926–27): 55–64.

An analysis of *The Pleasures of the Imagination* (2.2.239–77) shows that Akenside had developed a theory of evolution that, though it was based on the old idea of a chain of being, anticipated in some respects the system of evolution developed by Erasmus Darwin and (later) Charles Darwin.

John Arbuthnot (1667–1735)

1052.   Beattie, Lester M. *John Arbuthnot: Mathematician and Satirist*. Harvard Studies in English 16. Cambridge: Harvard UP, 1935. New York: Russell, 1967. 432 pp.
        Rev. Charles Kerby-Miller, *MP* 34 (1936–37): 209–11; Rae Blanchard, *MLN* 52 (1937): 222–23; James R. Sutherland, *MLR* 32 (1937): 458–60.

This critical biography provides a concise introduction to the life and accomplishments of Arbuthnot, a friend and collaborator of Gay's, Pope's, and Swift's. Separate chapters discuss Arbuthnot's writings on mathematics and medicine and his activities as a member of the Royal Society during Newton's ascendancy. The book elucidates Arbuthnot's role in initiating many ideas for the Scriblerian satires, and it sketches the background to the verses directed at Woodward, a collector of fossils who also proposed a theory of the Flood.

1053.   McKillop, Alan D. "The Geographical Chapter in *Scriblerus*." *MLN* 68 (1953): 480–81.

Maintains that the source of Cornelius's knowledge of geography in the *Memoirs of Martinus Scriblerus* is Varenius's *Geographia Generalis*.

1054.   Weidenborner, Stephen S. "The Influence of John Arbuthnot on the Scientific Attitudes Expressed by Pope, Swift, and the Scriblerus Club." *DA* 30 (1969–70): 3440A.

Examines Arbuthnot's role in the Scriblerus Club, emphasizing his contribution to the scientific knowledge of Pope and Swift. Also treats his impact on some of the chief Scriblerian literary productions, including *The Origin of Sciences*, *Gulliver's Travels, Book Three*, and *The Memoirs of Martinus Scriblerus*.

Joel Barlow (1754–1812)

1055.   Ball, Kenneth R. "Joel Barlow's 'Canal' and Natural Religion." *ECS* 2 (1968–69): 225–39.

Reproduces Barlow's previously unpublished poem *The Canal* (1802) and shows that it derives largely from Volney's *Ruins: Or, A Survey of the Revolutions of Empires* (1793), which espouses a materialistic philosophy and a natural religion based on astrology.

William Bartram (1739–1823)

1056.   Fagin, Nathan B. *William Bartram: Interpreter of the American Landscape.* Baltimore: Johns Hopkins P, 1933. 229 pp.
          Rev. Charles A. Kofoid, *Isis* 22 (1934–35): 241–42; Lane Cooper, *MLN* 50 (1935): 54–56.

A study of William Bartram, the American natural historian whose *Travels* (1791) was widely read in the English-speaking world as well as on the Continent. The study seeks to determine Bartram's influence on the development of nature descriptions, specifically those of the American landscape. Part 3 attempts a comprehensive examination of Bartram's influence on literature, including the works of Carlyle, Emerson, P. Shelley, Tennyson, Thoreau, and Wordsworth.

1057.   Gummere, Richard M. "William Bartram, a Classical Scientist." *CJ* 50 (1954–55): 167–70.

Briefly describes and assesses the literary merits of Bartram's botanical and ornithological journal, *Travels through North and South Carolina, Georgia, East and West*

Florida (1791). His literary style exhibits both classical and Romantic characteristics and scientific accuracy.

1058.   Lee, Berta G. "William Bartram: Naturalist or 'Poet'?" *EAL* 7 (1972–73): 124–29.
Discusses the critical dispute over the scientific accuracy of Bartram's description of alligators in *The Travels of William Bartram* (1791).

Giovanni Bianchi [Janus Plancus] (1693–1775)

1059.   Collina, Maria D. *Il carteggio letterario di uno scienziato del settecento: Janus Plancus.* Florence: Olschki, 1957. 172 pp.
Focuses on the literary works of Bianchi, a physician, scientist, and writer. After a brief biography, the author discusses Bianchi's correspondence with the scientists and writers of his time, the scholarly interests of Bianchi's contemporaries, and aspects of literary interest in various Italian cultural centers.

William Blake (1757–1827)

1060.   Ault, Donald. "Incommensurability and Interconnection in Blake's Anti-Newtonian Text." *SIR* 16 (1977): 277–303.
Uses Feyerabend's critique of scientific method and knowledge to "contrast the significance (and narrative form) of the *exclusion* (or temporary suppression) of elements or facts from a field of explanation in Newton and in Blake by contrasting Newton's 'ray theory' of light (as Feyerabend has analyzed it) with some structural properties of Blake's narrative in *The Four Zoas*, Night 1."

1061.   ———. *Visionary Physics: Blake's Response to Newton.* Chicago: U of Chicago P, 1974. 229 pp.
        Rev. Dewey R. Faulkner, *YR* ns 64 (1974–75): 271–74; R. Ravindra, *AJPhys* 43 (1975): 1114–16; Florence Sandler, *WHR* 29 (1975): 301–03; John M. Hill, *ClioI* 5 (1975–76): 385–88; J. D. North, *RES* ns 27 (1976): 517; David Wagenknecht, *MP* 74 (1976–77): 429–31.
"Argues that the developing complexity of Blake's myth turns specific elements of Newton's visionary cosmos inside out and thereby reveals Newton's system (in all its complexity and built-in intellectual crises) to be a 'Satanic' usurpation of the drives of Blake's own 'Human Imagination.' The desperation of Blake's Los in being constrained to construct a countersystem to Newton's own is seen in this context as ironic and potentially dangerous."

1062.   Baine, Rodney M. "Blake's 'Tyger': The Nature of the Beast." *PQ* 46 (1967): 488–98.
Among the influences on Blake's symbolism of the tyger were Buffon, Goldsmith's *Animated Nature*, and Lavater's *Essays in Physiognomy*.

1063.   Curtis, F. B. "Blake and the 'Moment of Time': An Eighteenth Century Controversy in Mathematics." *PQ* 51 (1972): 460–70.

Blake's use of the term *moment* in *Milton* (1804–08) recalls Newton's mathematical use of the term in his theory of fluxions.

1064.   ————. "William Blake and Eighteenth Century Medicine." *BlakeS* 8 (1978–79): 187–99.
An examination of *The Four Zoas*, *An Island in the Moon*, *The Book of Urizen*, and other works suggests that Blake possessed a knowledge of eighteenth-century medicine and anatomy. This study assesses the extent of that knowledge and evaluates the function of anatomical imagery in Blake's verse.

1065.   Doxey, William S. "William Blake and William Herschel: The Poet, and Astronomer, and 'The Tyger.' " *BlakeS* 2.2 (1969–70): 5–13.
Interprets "The Tyger" in the light of astronomy and suggests that William Herschel may have been a source of Blake's knowledge of the science.

1066.   ————. "William Blake, James Basire, and the *Philosophical Transactions*: An Unexplored Source of Blake's Scientific Thought?" *BNYPL* 72 (1968): 252–60.
A descriptive listing of plates from the Royal Society's *Philosophical Transactions* that Blake, as an employee of Basire, may have partially engraved. A study of the plates may elucidate Blake's attitude toward science.

1067.   Essick, Robert N. "Blake's Newton." *BlakeN* 3 (1970–71): 149–62.
Details of Blake's color print "Newton" shed light on the attitude toward Newtonian science revealed in his literary works. "Blake's 'Newton' is part of that great tradition of both pictorial and literary works which explore the mental state resulting from an excessive development of man's abstract reasoning powers to the detriment of his imaginative and spiritual capabilities."

1068.   Goldberg, Jerome E. "William Blake: A Study in the Human Sciences." *DAI* 39 (1979): 4271A–72A.
Examines Blake's rejection of naturalistic philosophy, heathen mythology, and Cartesian ontology and studies the development of his poetry against the background of eighteenth-century natural science.

1069.   Hilton, Nelson. "The Sweet Science of Atmospheres in *The Four Zoas*." *BlakeN* 12 (1978–79): 80–86.
Blake may have derived his distinction between "science" and "sweet science" in *The Four Zoas* from his study of Newton's *Opticks* and Swedenborg's *Wisdom of Angels concerning Divine Love and Divine Wisdom*. These works may also have influenced the cosmogony of *The Four Zoas*.

1070.   Kauvar, Elaine M. "Blake's Botanical Imagery." *DAI* 32 (1971): 3255A–56A.
Among the influences on Blake's botanical imagery were the Bible, alchemy, Boehme, E. Darwin, Paracelsus, and Swedenborg.

1071.   Kreiter, Carmen S. "Evolution and William Blake." *SIR* 4 (1964–65): 110–18.

Maintains that Blake's reference to evolution in *The Book of Urizen* (6.6.6–8) can be traced to the embryological speculations of his friend John Hunter and to Harvey's *De Generatione*.

1072.   Leonard, David Charles. "Erasmus Darwin and William Blake." *ECLife* 4 (1978): 79–81.
Maintains that in *The First Book of Urizen* Blake derived the scientific data for his treatment of the evolutionary theory of recapitulation and embryonic development from E. Darwin's *Economy of Vegetation*.

1073.   Mellor, Anne K. "Physiognomy, Phrenology, and Blake's Visionary Heads." *Blake in His Time*. Ed. Robert N. Essick and Donald Pearce. Bloomington: Indiana UP, 1978. 53–74.
Outlines the physiognomical system of Lavater and the phrenological systems of Gall and Spurzheim, assesses Blake's knowledge of these systems, and studies their impact on three of Blake's portraits known as "Visionary Heads."

1074.   Nurmi, Martin K. "Negative Sources in Blake." *William Blake: Essays for S. Foster Damon*. Ed. Alvin H. Rosenfeld. Providence: Brown UP, 1969. 303–18.
"Blake formed certain of his visionary ideas partly in reaction against philosophical enemies." The author examines Blake's responses to Newton's concept of limits, R. Descartes's theory of vortexes, and T. Burnet's idea of the "mundane shell."

1075.   Parsons, Coleman O. "Tygers before Blake." *SEL* 8 (1968): 573–92.
Blake's characterization of beasts of prey in *Songs of Innocence and Experience*, *Jerusalem*, and other works has analogues in eighteenth-century natural histories and travel books such as Goldsmith's *Animated Nature*, Buffon's *Natural History*, Linnaeus's *Animal Kingdom*, and Smellie's *Philosophy of Natural History*. These and other scientific texts may have nourished Blake's poetic imagination and, thus, may have influenced the animal imagery in his poetry.

1076.   Peterfreund, Stuart. "Blake on Space, Time and the Role of the Artist." *STTH* 2 (1979): 246–63.
With reference to *The First Book of Urizen* (1794), discusses Blake's critique of, and response to, Newtonian conceptions of space and time. Explicates the relation between Blake's spatiotemporal notions and his aesthetic, noting the similarity between Blake's and Einstein's theories of space and time.

1077.   Raine, Kathleen. "Berkeley, Blake, and the New Age." *Thought* 51 (1976): 356–77.
Suggests that Blake's prophecy of a "new age" of immaterialism is closely related to Berkeley's philosophy. Both Berkeley and Blake repudiated the materialism and mechanism of F. Bacon, Newton, and Locke. Raine notes that in *Milton* Blake "set forth existentially what Berkeley had argued discursively—the subjective (or rather mental and imaginative) nature of time and space."

1078.   Sanzo, Eileen. "William Blake and the Technological Age." *Thought* 46 (1971): 577–91.

"Blake's eschatological mythology is in the prophetic tradition—Jerusalem, the salvation of industrial society. Thus in his major prophetic books, *The Four Zoas*, *Milton*, and *Jerusalem*, he fuses the ancient and the contemporary, science and mythology, the primitive and the sophisticated, the industrial and economic with the religious and human."

1079.   Schorer, Mark. "William Blake and the Cosmic Nadir." *SR* 43 (1935): 210–21.
Discusses Blake's antipathy toward the empirical and mathematical aspects of science as represented symbolically by F. Bacon, Locke, and Newton. In opposition to science, Blake championed the cosmic power of imagination.

1080.   Trawick, Leonard. "Blake's Empirical Occult." *WC* 8 (1977): 161–71.
Outlines Blake's relation to various occult traditions, including alchemy, astrology, and cabalism. Maintains that Blake's central ideas are fundamentally incompatible with these traditions—his ontology being radically empirical—though they often serve as allies against the mechanistic, materialistic systems of Newton and Locke.

1081.   White, Harry. "Blake and the Mills of Induction." *BlakeN* 10 (1976–77): 109–12.
Outlines Blake's critique of the logic of empirical science and experimental method. In works such as *The Four Zoas* Blake views this logic as inherently circular and without issue.

1082.   Worrall, David. "William Blake and Erasmus Darwin's *Botanic Garden*." *BNYPL* 78 (1974–75): 397–417.
The poetry Blake wrote between 1791 and 1795, such as *The French Revolution*, *The Book of Los*, *The Book of Urizen*, and *America*, exhibits remarkable parallelisms of imagery with the *Botanic Garden*. This study reveals the main correspondences between Blake's and Darwin's geophysical and biological imagery.

Johann Jakob Bodmer (1698–1783)

1083.   Ibershoff, C. H. "Bodmer and Newton." *MLR* 21 (1926): 192–95.
Cites passages in Bodmer's *Noah* that seem to derive from Newton's *Principia*.

1084.   ———. "Whiston as a Source of Bodmer's *Noah*." *SP* 22 (1926): 522–28.
The chief sources for the astronomical theories Bodmer used to explain the Flood in *Noah* were Whiston's *Astronomical Principles of Religion* and *New Theory of the Earth*.

Barthold Heinrich Brockes (1680–1747)

1085.   Fry, Harold P. "Die 'Betrachtungen über die drey Reiche der Natur' als Schlüssel zu einer neuen Brockes-Deutung." *LY* 11 (1979): 142–64.
Studies Brockes's poem "Betrachtungen über die drey Reiche der Natur" with

reference to its background in the first German physics textbook—Scheuchzer's *Physica oder Natur-Wissenschafft* (1701).

1086.   Ketelsen, Uwe-K. "Naturpoesie als Medium bürgerlicher Ideologiebildung im frühen 18. Jahrhundert: Barthold Heinrich Brockes 'Die kleine Fliege.' " *Naturlyrik und Gesellschaft* 31. Ed. Norbert Mecklenburg. Stuttgart: Klett-Cotta, 1977. 45–55.
Examines Brockes's popular nature poem "Die kleine Fliege" as an example of eighteenth-century scientific poetry influenced by Newton. Ketelsen regards the piece as typical of eighteenth-century physicotheological poetry.

1087.   Martens, Wolfgang. "Über Naturlyrik der frühen Aufklärung (B. H. Brockes)." *Wege der Worte: Festschrift für Wolfgang Fleischhauer. Anlässlich seines 65. Geburtstags und des 40. Jahres seines Wirkens als Professor der deutschen Philologie an der Ohio State University mit Beiträgen von Freunden, Kollegen und Schülern.* Ed. Donald C. Riechel. Köln: Böhlau, 1978. 263–76.
Brockes's nine volumes of didactic verse, *Irdisches Vergnügen in Gott* (1721–47), present nature poetry that is unique for its time. Rationally structured poems describe a multitude of natural phenomena with exacting detail and within a physicotheological frame. By contrast, Goethe's "Metamorphose der Pflanzen" unfolds the inherent, eternal, formative laws of nature.

Richard Owen Cambridge (1717–1802)

1088.   Emery, Clark. "*The Scribleriad's* Electrifying Climax." *PQ* 21 (1942): 438–41.
Concerns Cambridge's use of electrical theory in *The Scribleriad*'s concluding lines, which describe an electrical experiment with a human body.

William Cowper (1731–1800)

1089.   Kroitor, Harry P. "The Influence of Popular Science on William Cowper." *MP* 61 (1963–64): 281–87.
Describes Cowper's attempt to incorporate scientific descriptions of natural events into his poetic imagery. Cites as an example the use of Hamilton's account of earthquakes in Cowper's poem "The Time-Piece."

1090.   ———. "William Cowper and Science in the Eighteenth Century." *DA* 17 (1957): 3018.
Traces Cowper's interest in science to eighteenth-century popular scientific literature and examines the impact of science on his poetic imagination and his view of the relation between science and theology.

George Crabbe (1754–1832)

1091.   Chamberlain, Robert L. "George Crabbe and Darwin's Amorous Plants." *JEGP* 61 (1962): 833–52.

Attempts to dispel a traditional view of Crabbe's poetry that links it stylistically and thematically with E. Darwin's *Botanic Garden*. Chamberlain shows that although Crabbe's treatment of botanical matters in works such as "The Flowers" (1823), "The Library" (1781), and *Tales of the Hall* (1819) occasionally recalls Darwin's poetry, Crabbe's style is antithetical to the excesses of his predecessor.

Erasmus Darwin (1731–1802)

1092. Brandl, Leopold. "Erasmus Darwin, ein englischer Naturdichter des 18. Jahrhunderts." *GRM* 1 (1909): 622–33.

In his didactic poems *The Botanic Garden* and *The Temple of Nature* Darwin attempted to follow the example of Lucretius, whose *De rerum natura* he knew well. Darwin's two poems together constitute a comprehensive view of the natural world as revealed by the late-eighteenth-century natural sciences.

1093. Bush, Clive. "Erasmus Darwin, Robert John Thornton, and Linnaeus' *Sexual System*." *ECS* 7 (1973–74): 295–320.

This discussion of Thornton's artistic achievements in *A New Illustration of the Sexual System of Linnaeus* stresses the artist's debt to the poetic and scientific insights of E. Darwin and examines the extent to which eighteenth-century theories of vision and Linnaeus's classification system influenced Darwin's poetry.

1094. Dean, Dennis R. "Erasmus Darwin's Botanic Terms." *ELN* 10 (1972–73): 27–29.

In annotating James Lee's *Introduction to Biology* (1777), Darwin probably acquired some of the botanic terminology he used in *The Botanic Garden*.

1095. Emery, Clark. "Scientific Theory in Erasmus Darwin's *The Botanic Garden* (1789–91)." *Isis* 33 (1941): 315–25.

Darwin's footnotes to *The Botanic Garden* indicate that the scientific sources of the poem include Cavendish, Franklin, Herschel, Lavoisier, Linnaeus, and Priestley.

1096. Garfinkle, Norton. "Science and Religion in England, 1790–1800: The Critical Response to the Work of Erasmus Darwin." *JHI* 16 (1955): 376–88.

Discusses the hostility between science and religion that sprang up in late-eighteenth-century England in the light of the critical response to Darwin's scientific speculations in *The Botanic Garden* and *Zoonomia*.

1097. Harrison, James. "Erasmus Darwin's View of Evolution." *JHI* 32 (1971): 247–64.

In questioning preformationist embryology and the idea that species are fixed, Darwin posed "unequivocal, evolutionary pronouncements." In fact, he had "in his grasp all, or almost all, the constituent parts of the full theory of evolution by natural selection." Harrison cites Darwin's *Zoonomia*, *Botanic Garden*, and *Temple of Nature*.

1098.   Hassler, Donald M. "David Hume and Erasmus Darwin's *Zoonomia*." *SSL*
        8 (1971): 190–93.
Darwin's attempt to explain nature's complexities produced a comic tension in
even his scientific writing; this rhetorical stance may have been influenced by Hume's
Pyrrhonism.

1099.   ————. *Erasmus Darwin*. New York: Twayne, 1973. 143 pp.
        Rev. David M. Knight, *Isis* 66 (1975): 580.
Primarily reassesses Darwin's accomplishments as a writer, though chapter 1
outlines the scientific, philosophic, and cosmogonic ideas that informed his literary
style. The discussion of Darwin's major works stresses the relation between his
philosophic materialism and his comic view of life.

1100.   ————. "Erasmus Darwin and Enlightenment Origins of Science Fiction."
        SVEC 153 (1976): 1045–56.
Sees the comic rhetorical stance that Darwin, Buffon, and D. Hume took toward
the unimaginable fecundity of nature as an early version of the "meta-comic" narration of perplexing scientific fact and speculation characteristic of science fiction.

1101.   ————. "Erasmus Darwin's Comic Bathos." *Serif* 6 (1969): 15–26.
A summary of the first canto of Darwin's *Economy of Vegetation*, followed by an
analysis of Darwin's overall poetic structures. Hassler finds the encyclopedic organization of Darwin's complex plots and themes, including his scientific ideas, analogous to concepts such as circularity and metamorphosis.

1102.   ————. "The Poems of Erasmus Darwin." *DA* 28 (1967–68): 5017A.
This interpretation of Darwin's poetry focuses on three recurring themes: mythological and scientific evidence for metamorphosis, comic treatment of sex and
marriage, and circles and cyclical movement.

1103.   King-Hele, Desmond. *Doctor of Revolution: The Life and Genius of Erasmus
        Darwin*. London: Faber, 1977. 361 pp.
        Rev. Richard Olson, *AHR* 84 (1979): 1051–52.
Principally a biographical work that emphasizes Darwin's achievements in biology,
botany, chemistry, medicine, and other sciences. The author comments throughout
on Darwin's poetic exposition of scientific concepts in *The Loves of the Plants*, *The
Economy of Vegetation*, and *The Temple of Nature*, which outlines the doctrine of
evolution. He also mentions Darwin's influence on S. Coleridge, Keats, P. Shelley,
and Wordsworth.

1104.   ————. "Erasmus Darwin, Master of Many Crafts." *Nature* 247 (1974):
        87–91.
Discusses thirty-six subjects to which Darwin contributed (including medicine,
botany, poetry, evolution theory, and physical science) and notes his influence on
the English Romantic poets.

1105.   ————, ed. *The Essential Writings of Erasmus Darwin*. London: MacGibbon,
        1968. 223 pp.

An anthology of selections from Darwin's *Botanic Garden, Zoonomia, Phytologia,* and *Temple of Nature* with commentary by King-Hele that provides an overview of Darwin's contributions to both science and poetry.

1106. Logan, James V. *The Poetry and Aesthetics of Erasmus Darwin.* Princeton Studies in English 15. Princeton: Princeton UP, 1936. New York: Octagon, 1972. 162 pp.
Rev. B. E. C. Davis, *MLR* 33 (1938): 286–87.

A study of the aesthetic principles informing Darwin's *Botanic Garden* and *Temple of Nature,* with commentary on Darwin's poetic use of biological and botanical data and his allegorical and ornamental poetic technique. Emphasizes the physiopsychological basis of the aesthetics Darwin outlines in *Zoonomia* and remarks on his scientific and philosophical influences and the literary precedents of his style.

1107. Primer, Irwin. "*Temple of Nature*: Progress, Evolution, and the Eleusinian Mysteries." *JHI* 25 (1964): 58–76.

Discusses Darwin's fascination with Orphic myth and the Eleusinian mysteries and his attempt to blend mythical conceptions of nature with his scientific notions of progress and evolution—an effort reflected primarily in his *Temple of Nature.*

1108. Ross, Robert N. " 'To Charm Thy Curious Eye': Erasmus Darwin's Poetry at the Vestibule of Knowledge." *JHI* 32 (1971): 379–94.

This essay on Darwin's poetic methodology focuses on his attempt to express poetic and scientific abstractions in concrete images. "Darwin thought of poetry as a series of 'emblemmatic exhibitions,' eminently pictorial."

1109. Swinton, W. E. "Physician Contributions to Nonmedical Science: Erasmus Darwin, Evolutionist, Inventor and Poet." *Canadian Medical Association Journal* 115 (1976): 560–64.

This general overview of Darwin's varied activities comments on his personal life, his medical practice, his scientific studies, his achievements as an inventor, and his composition of poems such as *The Botanic Garden* and *The Temple of Nature.*

Daniel Defoe (1660–1731)

1110. Baine, Rodney M. "Daniel Defoe's Imaginary Voyages to the Moon." *PMLA* 81 (1966): 377–80.

Speculates on the authenticity of two imaginary voyages to the moon and on one letter from the "man in the moon" hitherto attributed to Defoe.

1110a. Sena, John F. "Daniel Defoe and 'The English Malady.' " *N&Q* ns 16 (1969): 183–84.

The references to "The English Malady" in *Robinson Crusoe* reflect Defoe's medical knowledge.

Denis Diderot (1713–84)

1111. Berry, David. "Diderot's Optics: An Aspect of His Philosophical and Literary Expression." *Studies in Eighteenth-Century French Literature Presented to Robert Niklaus.* Ed. J. H. Fox, M. H. Waddicor, and D. A. Watts. Exeter: U of Exeter, 1975. 15–28.

"In Diderot's work . . . optics establishes itself as a subject which embraces physics, physiology, psychology, and aesthetics; its laws and terminology are shown to be particularly appropriate for describing human perception and artistic processes; and it helps to underpin Diderot's concern with perceptual, rather than conceptual, knowledge." Berry traces Diderot's interest in the microscope and other optical instruments as reflected in *Le rêve de d'Alembert*, *Lettre sur les aveugles*, and other works.

1112.   Bremner, Geoffrey. "Contradictions in Diderot's Scientific Philosophy and *Le neveu de Rameau.*" *FS* 34 (1980): 153–67.

The contradiction between moral relativism and moral stability in Rameau's character may reflect the contradictions inherent in Diderot's eighteenth-century intellectual background, especially the conflict between the notion of substantial reality and the scientific notion of the universality of matter in motion. Bremner discusses the relation between eighteenth-century science and the problem of the structural and thematic coherence of Diderot's *Neveu de Rameau.*

1113.   Dieckmann, Herbert. "The Metaphoric Structure of the *Rêve de d'Alembert.*" In *The* Rêve de d'Alembert: *Studies by Herbert Dieckmann, Georges May, and Aram Vartanian; with a Discussion Edited by Frederick A. Spear.* Diderot Studies 17.1. Genève: Droz, 1973. 15–24.

Explains the literary devices and the structure of the literary form Diderot used in the *Rêve de d'Alembert* to express scientific and philosophical ideas.

1114.   Immerwahr, Raymond. "Diderot, Herder, and the Dichotomy of Touch and Sight." *Seminar* 14 (1978): 84–96.

Discusses the contrast between touch and vision outlined in Diderot's *Letter on the Blind for the Benefit of the Sighted* (1749), which "documents his well informed interest in the sciences and mathematics, his empirical approach to the psychology of sense perception." Herder later transmitted the dichotomy in his aesthetic works to Goethe and the Romantics. Goethe made creative metaphorical use of the notion in *Wilhelm Meisters Wanderjahre.*

1115.   James, Charles H. "La méthode scientifique-poétique de Diderot et de Buffon." *DAI* 36 (1975–76): 5336A–37A.

Diderot's and Buffon's background in Newtonian physics led them to develop a scientific-poetic method of inquiry based on both experimentation and analogy.

1116.   Mortier, Roland. "Rhétorique et discours scientifique dans *Le rêve de d'Alembert.*" *WSA* 3 (1976): 327–38.

Examines Diderot's integration of scientific discussion and literary dialogue in *Le rêve de d'Alembert*, which he intended as a scientific and philosophical debate accessible to his readers.

1117.   Vartanian, Aram. "The *Rêve de d'Alembert*: A Bio-Political View." *The* Rêve de d'Alembert: *Studies by Herbert Dieckmann, Georges May, and Aram Var-*

tanian; with a Discussion Edited by Frederick A. Spear*. Diderot Studies 17.1. Genève: Droz, 1973. 41–64.

Discusses the relation between Diderot's political views and the materialist biology of his *Rêve de d'Alembert* in the light of three of the work's principal themes: the theory of organism, the definition of matter, and the hypothesis of transformism.

1118.   Vidan, Gabrijela. "Diderot: La construction scientifique et son relais par l'imagination." *SVEC* 155 (1976): 2207–22.

Explores the connection between Diderot's scientific, philosophic, and literary endeavors as reflected in his literary works from 1763 to 1774. Among the works discussed are *Neveu de Rameau* and *Jacques le fataliste*.

1119.   Walker, Eleanor M. "Diderot's *Rêve de d'Alembert*: The Literary and the Scientific Imagination." *DA* 13 (1953): 396.

Analyzes and compares Diderot's literary creativity and scientific imagination as reflected in his *Rêve de d'Alembert*. Shows that the artistic qualities of the work are in harmony with its philosophic and scientific properties.

Henry Fielding (1707–54)

1120.   Hatfield, Glenn W. "Quacks, Pettyfoggers, and Parsons: Fielding's Case against the Learned Professions." *TSLL* 9 (1967–68): 69–83.

Examines Fielding's satire of medical, legal, and clerical abuses in works such as *The Mock Doctor*, *The Coffee House Politician*, *Pasquin*, *Joseph Andrews*, and *Amelia*.

Georg Forster (1754–94)

1121.   Pütz, Peter. "Zwischen Klassik und Romantik: Georg Forsters *Ansichten vom Niederrhein*." *ZDP* 97 (1978): supp. 4–24.

This detailed study of Forster's *Ansichten vom Niederrhein* notes his integration of poetry with sciences such as geology, botany, and zoology and discusses his general literary achievements as an enlightened metaphysician writing between the classic and Romantic periods.

Benjamin Franklin (1706–90)

1122.   Jorgenson, Chester E. "The New Science in the Almanacs of Ames and Franklin." *NEQ* 8 (1935): 555–61.

Jorgenson observes what many have failed to notice—that the almanacs of Nathaniel Ames and Benjamin Franklin reflect the European interest in rationalism, scientific deism, and Newtonianism.

1123.   McKillop, Alan D. "Some Newtonian Verses in *Poor Richard*." *NEQ* 21 (1948): 383–85.

Notes that the verses prefacing Franklin's *Poor Richard Improved* (1748) are adapted from John Hughes's Newtonian poem *The Ecstasy* (1720).

Carl Ignaz Geiger (1756–91)

1124.   Hermand, Jost. Postscript. *Reise eines Erdbewohners in den Mars.* By Carl
          Ignaz Geiger. Stuttgart: Metzler, 1967. 43 pp.
Discusses the influence of baroque air-travel fantasies such as F. Godwin's *Man
in the Moon* (1638) and Cyrano de Bergerac's *Autre monde ou les états et empires de la
lune* (1657) on Geiger's *Reise eines Erdbewohners in den Mars* (1790). Comments on
the air-travel motif in such eighteenth-century novels as Voltaire's *Micromégas* (1752)
and Rousseau's *Nouveau Dédale* (1752) and examines the political, religious, and
social implications of Geiger's novel. Geiger ridiculed the popular air-travel novel
through his depictions of technological triumphs such as air travel by balloon.

Johann Wolfgang von Goethe (1749–1832)

1125.   Adler, J. J. D. "A Study in the Chemistry of Goethe's Novel *Die Wahl-
          verwandtschaften.*" Diss. Westfield Coll., London, 1978.
Not seen for annotation.

1126.   Allemann, Beda. "Zur Funktion der chemischen Gleichnisrede in Goethes
          Wahlverwandtschaften." *Untersuchungen zur Literatur als Geschichte: Festschrift
          für Benno von Wiese.* Ed. Vincent J. Günther, Helmut Koopmann, et al.
          Berlin: Schmidt, 1973. 199–218.
A study of the analogy between the "elective affinities" of chemical elements and
human relationships as depicted in Goethe's *Wahlverwandtschaften.* Through an examination of the novel's plot and structure, Allemann assesses the extent to which
such an analogy holds, emphasizing Goethe's use of irony in portraying the ties
between Charlotte, Hauptmann, Ottilie, and Eduardo.

1127.   Badt, Kurt. "Goethes Wolkengedichte im Zusammenhange mit den Wolk-
          enstudien Constables und anderer zeitgenössischer Maler." *PEGS* 20 (1951):
          21–52.
Reviews Goethe's familiarity with Luke Howard's scientific study of cloud formations and analyzes Goethe's cloud poems in honor of Howard, especially "Howards
Ehrengedächtnis," in which the poet integrates the scientific study of clouds into
his poetic vision by resorting to the principle of metamorphosis. Shows a parallel
between Goethe and the English painter John Constable, who, at about the same
time as Goethe, pursued his fascination with clouds as both artist and scientist.

1128.   Bapp, Karl. "Goethe und Lukrez." *Goethe* 12 (1926): 47–67.
Although Goethe dropped the project of a great nature poem, he did not cease
treating nature and his own philosophical concepts of nature in poetic form. Citing
Goethe's *Farbenlehre, Versuch einer Witterungslehre,* and several poems, this essay discusses Goethe's interest in Knebel's translation of Lucretius's *De rerum natura,* Goethe's
attitude toward Lucretius, and Lucretius's influence on Goethe.

1129.   Bartscherer, Agnes. *Paracelsus, Paracelsisten und Goethes* Faust: *Eine Quellen-
          studie.* Dortmund: Ruhfus, 1911. 333 pp.
Claims that the main source of *Faust* was Goethe's early reading of the mystical

and cabalist writings of Paracelsus, Agrippa, Welling, Johann Baptist van Helmont, G. Arnold, and others. Bartscherer discusses alchemy and astrology in *Faust* and demonstrates that many verses derive from specific passages in Paracelsus's writings.

1130. Böckmann, Paul. "Naturgesetz und Symbolik in Goethes *Wahlverwandt-schaften*." *JFDH* (1968): 166–90.

Discusses Goethe's assimilation of contemporary scientific knowledge into his *Wahlverwandtschaften*. The novel raises the question of whether the chemical laws of the mutual attraction and repulsion of elements are applicable to human relationships.

1131. Bölsche, Wilhelm. "Goethes *Wahlverwandtschaften* im Lichte moderner Naturwissenschaft." *Die Gesellschaft* (Leipzig) 5.3 (1889): 1330–40.

Claims that *Die Wahlverwandtschaften* is a masterful example of a literary work being adapted to contemporary scientific knowledge. By using the psychophysiological knowledge of his time Goethe produced the first realistic novel.

1132. Brady, Ronald H. "Towards a Common Morphology for Aesthetics and Natural Science: A Study of Goethe's Empiricism." *DAI* 33 (1973): 4465A–66A.

Goethe's theory of morphology in the *Metamorphosis of Plants* may point toward a common morphology of appearances for natural and artistic forms.

1133. Brednow, Walter. "Die Basalte—zu einem Gedicht Goethes." *Leopoldina: Mitteilungen der deutschen Akademie der Naturforscher* 3rd ser. 20 (1974): 227–44.

Goethe's famous verses beginning with "Amerika, du hast es besser" conclude with the enigmatic line "Und keine Basalte." Brednow outlines the role basaltic rock played in the Vulcanist-Neptunist controversy represented by Thales and Anaxagoras's discussion in the "Klassische Walpurgisnacht" in *Faust II*, explores Goethe's familiarity with the current mineralogical and geological literature, and explains Goethe's comment about basalt within that context.

1134. ———. "Symbol und Symbolik in der Biologie Goethes." *Goethe* 28 (1966): 236–62.

Examines Goethe's understanding of symbolic representations of science in poetry. Draws on his autobiographical *Dichtung und Wahrheit*, the didactic poems "Metamorphose der Pflanzen" and "Howards Ehrengedächtnis," and the "Klassische Walpurgisnacht" in *Faust II*.

1135. Buchwald, Eberhard. "Wissen und Weisheit in der Naturkunde." *Goethe* 25 (1963): 97–114.

This study of the similarities and differences between science and wisdom focuses on Goethe's transcendence of mere factual knowledge in his scientific endeavors toward achieving a deeper, philosophical view of life and an attitude of wisdom. Cites *Farbenlehre, Faust*, and other works.

1136. Cameron, Dorothy. "Goethe—Discoverer of the Ice Age." *Journal of Glaciology* 5 (1964–65): 751–54.

The reflections on glaciology Goethe interspersed throughout *Wilhelm Meister* suggest that he was the first to formulate a theory of an ice age.

1137.   Castle, Eduard. "Zur Geschichte der Ausgaben der naturwissenschaftlichen Schriften Goethes." *Archiv* 163 (1933): 172–82.
Of special interest is the account of Johann Eckermann's involvement in Goethe's scientific work and his editorial assistance with those writings that were published after Goethe's death.

1138.   Cooper, W. A. "A Paracelsian Passage in Goethe's *Ephemerides.*" *MLN* 25 (1910): 168–70.
Ephemerides contains several quotations from Paracelsus, one of which may be the source for Goethe's conception of anatomy in *Urfaust* (367–72).

1139.   Denker, Rolf. "Luftfahrt auf montgolfierische Art in Goethes Dichten und Denken." *Goethe* 26 (1964): 181–98.
Examines Goethe's lifetime interest in human attempts at flight, specifically the Montgolfier brothers' balloon travel in 1783. Draws on many of Goethe's works, including *Werther*, *Faust*, and *Wilhelm Meisters Lehrjahre*, as well as his correspondence, to demonstrate his fascination with flying.

1140.   Dürler, Josef. *Die Bedeutung des Bergbaus bei Goethe und in der deutschen Romantik.* Wege zur Dichtung. Züricher Schriften zur Literaturwissenschaft 24. Frauenfeld: Huber, 1936. 245 pp.
Discusses the scientific aspects of mining and their depiction in the poetic works of Goethe, Novalis, Jean Paul, Tieck, Hoffmann, Brentano, Arnim, and Eichendorff. Goethe's mineralogical and geological references in works such as *Kunst und Altertum*, *Wilhelm Meisters Wanderjahre*, and *Die Wahlverwandtschaften* served as the principal sources of Romantic ideas about the nature and importance of mining.

1141.   Emmerich, Liberata. "Goethe and the Earth Sciences." *Mineral Industries* 19.2 (1949): 1–4.
This brief history of Goethe's studies in geology, mineralogy, and mining makes passing references to some allusions to the earth sciences in *Faust II* and *Wilhelm Meisters Wanderjahre*.

1142.   Fairley, Barker. "Goethe's Attitude to Science." *BJRL* 20 (1936): 297–311.
Goethe's holistic perspective on nature informed both his poetic endeavors and his approach to science. His conflict with Newtonian optics, for example, was related to his concept of wholeness. Both the ruling idea and the goal of Goethe's science and poetry were the same; he thus practiced poetic science and scientific poetics.

1143.   Fink, Karl J. "Atomism: A Counterpoint Tradition in Goethe's Writings." *ECS* 13 (1979–80): 377–95.
Traces the development of Goethe's interest in atomism from Lucretius to Newton, R. Descartes, and Leibniz and views Goethe's underlying principle of the science of humankind as emerging jointly from this tradition and the opposing tradition

of Neoplatonism. Discusses a resulting contrapuntal principle of chance and purpose in relation to *Wilhelm Meisters Lehrjahre*.

1144. Fuller, Thomas D. "Alone in His Time: Goethe's Theory of Color." *Synthesis* 2.3 (1974): 5–17.

Outlines the central features of Goethe's color theory as expressed in the *Farbenlehre* and examines his grounds for disagreement with Newton's *Opticks*. Both Goethe's color theory and his anti-Newtonian sentiments are reflected in his poetry.

1145. Gausewitz, Walter. "Optic and Acoustic Phenomena in the Poetic Works of Goethe and Schiller." *University of Wisconsin Summaries of Doctoral Dissertations* 1 (1935–36): 323–24.

Compares and statistically analyzes occurrences of acoustic and optic terminology in the poetic works of Goethe and Schiller.

1146. Goebel, Julius. "Cabala and Alchemy in Goethe's *Faust*." *PAPA* 35 (1904): lxii-lxiii.

This abstract notes that the sources for the first soliloquy of *Faust* can be found in the alchemistic and cabalistic literature that Goethe is known to have studied.

1147. Gould, Robert. "Book v of *Dichtung und Wahrheit*: A Morphological Analysis." *FMLS* 8 (1972): 120–31.

Maintains that Goethe's construction of book 5 of *Dichtung und Wahrheit* may have been based on his scientific concept of morphology. Gould examines the parallels between Goethe's morphological principles and his reflections on public ceremonies, love between young people, and human nature.

1148. ———. "The Critical Reception of *Die Wahlverwandtschaften* in the French Press: An Unknown Review of *Ottilia: Ou, Le pouvoir de la sympathie*." *Seminar* 9 (1973): 28–35.

"French press reviews of the first translations of Goethe's *Die Wahlverwandtschaften* are all negative in tone, their criticism being directed primarily at the scientific elements in the novel and at its immorality. These characteristics (and others) are shared by a review in the *Gazette de France* of 17 April 1810, which, however, does not appear in the standard bibliographical reference works. Of all contemporary discussions in French, this review is the most vituperative, to the point that it becomes anti-intellectual."

1149. ———. "Elective Affinities: An Investigation of the Influence of Goethe's Scientific Thinking on *Die Wahlverwandtschaften*." *DA* 31 (1970–71): 6548A–49A.

Treats the relation between Goethe's characterizations of Eduard, Charlotte, and Ottilie in *Die Wahlverwandtschaften* and the principles of organic development in his scientific works. Goethe's novelistic treatment of human relations is closely connected with his concept of affinity and the principles of morphology.

1150. Grappin, Pierre. "Goethe en Alsace: Nature et sciences de la nature." *Revue d'Allemagne* 3.1 (1971): 187–97.

Seeks to contribute to an understanding of Goethe's dual role as poet and geologist by examining his intellectual and scientific development during the 1770–71 school year in Strasbourg; uses testimony from *Dichtung und Wahrheit.*

1151.   Gray, Ronald D. *Goethe the Alchemist: A Study of Alchemical Symbolism in Goethe's Literary and Scientific Works.* Cambridge: Cambridge UP, 1952. 312 pp.
         Rev. Stuart Atkins, *MLR* 49 (1954): 101–03; Heinrich Meyer, *MLN* 69 (1954): 55–57; Heinrich Schneider, *Isis* 45 (1954): 117–19; Heinrich Henel, *GR* 30 (1955): 149–55.
Discusses Goethe's alchemical studies and his gradual turn away from alchemy toward science; Boehme's contributions to the systematization of alchemical symbolism; and Goethe's use of alchemical symbols in his theories of plant metamorphosis and color, his anatomical, geological, and meteorological works, and his literary works. Separate chapters relate alchemy to Goethe's *Märchen* and to his center and circle, the homunculus, and male and female imagery.

1152.   Hagen, Benno von. "Die Anatomie im Leben und Schaffen Goethes." *Anatomischer Anzeiger* 109 (1960): 74–85.
This discussion of Goethe's interest in and study of anatomy—including his discovery of the intermaxillary bone—briefly treats the anatomy and medicine in *Wilhelm Meisters Wanderjahre.*

1153.   Hahn, Karl-Heinz. " 'Die Wissenschaft erhält ihren Werth, indem sie nützt.' Über Goethe und die Anfänge der technisch-wissenschaftlichen Welt." *Goethe* 96 (1979): 243–57.
Examines Goethe's interest in the scientific and technological developments that led to the industrial revolution in the early nineteenth century. Hahn sees Faust's utopian project at the end of *Faust II* as an expression of Goethe's affirmative, though controversial, espousal of technological progress.

1154.   Haile, H. G. "Faust 2069: 'Feuerluft' was the Common Term for Oxygen." *GQ* 41 (1968): 39–41.
Goethe's use of the term *Feuerluft* may indicate his knowledge of Karl Wilhelm Scheele's experiments with air.

1155.   Henel, Heinrich. "Goethe and Science." *Literature and Science.* Proc. of the Sixth Triennial Congress of the International Federation for Modern Languages and Literatures. Oxford, 1954. Oxford: Blackwell, 1955. 216–21.
Insofar as Goethe rejected in principle the use of complicated experimental apparatus and mathematics as tools for investigating nature, he cannot be considered a scientist in the strict sense of the word. However, his sensitive, diligent, and passionate study of the natural world is recognized as a unique and important contribution to the understanding of nature. Goethe's approach to science can perhaps best be characterized as "poetic phenomenology"—a reverent, thoughtful, and holistic questioning of the phenomena that constitute our experience of the world.

1156.   ———. "Type and Proto-Phenomenon in Goethe's Science." *PMLA* 71 (1956): 651–68.

Explains Goethe's idiosyncratic approach to science, including his rejection of mathematics and experimental methods and apparatus. Examines in detail his concept of morphological "types" and his symbolic theory of the protophenomenon in the light of their relation to his overall scientific and poetic goals.

1157.   Hennig, John. "Goethe's Interest in British Meteorology." *MLQ* 10 (1949): 321–37.

Maintains that James Boyd's study *Goethe's Knowledge of English Literature* (1932) fails to consider how Goethe's interest in English science affected his appreciation of English literature and, thus, requires supplementation. The essay traces in particular Goethe's interest in British meteorology, stressing his relations with the meteorologist Luke Howard, and comments on works such as "Howards Ehrengedächtnis" that reflect Goethe's knowledge of the science.

1158.   ———. "A Note on Goethe's Relations with Luke Howard." *MLQ* 12 (1951): 446–50.

Provides background and publication data on Goethe's "Howards Ehrengedächtnis," a poem written as a tribute to the British meteorologist Luke Howard.

1159.   Hippe, Robert. "Der kosmologische Mythos am Ende des 8. Buches von *Dichtung und Wahrheit*." *Goethe* 96 (1979): 75–83.

Discusses the cosmological myth at the end of book 8 of Goethe's *Dichtung und Wahrheit*, citing several sources for Goethe's cosmology, especially Welling's *Opus mago-cabalisticum et theosophicum* (1721). Also refers to the depiction of Goethe's cosmology in "Die Metamorphose der Pflanzen," "Die Metamorphose der Tiere," "Grenzen der Menschheit," and *Faust*.

1160.   Hölscher-Lohmeyer, Dorothea. "Die Einheit von Naturwissenschaft und poetischer Aussage bei Goethe: Anmerkungen zu seinem Gedichtzyklus *Die Weissagungen des Bakis*." *FMAS* 12 (1978): 356–89.

Maintains that Goethe's literary productivity was decidedly shaped by his widening scientific studies. Using the cycle of poems entitled *Die Weissagungen des Bakis*, Hölscher-Lohmeyer attempts to show Goethe's tendency to combine the language of nature with that of poetry.

1161.   Hoppe, Günther. "Goethes Ansichten über Meteorite und sein Verhältnis zu dem Physiker Chladni." *Goethe* 95 (1978): 227–40.

Examines the influence that the physicist Ernst Florens Friedrich Chladni and his theory of meteorites had on Goethe and comments on references to meteorites in *Gott, Gemüth und Welt*, a collection of poems, and *Faust II*.

1162.   Jantz, Harold. "Faust's Vision of the Macrocosm." *MLN* 68 (1953): 348–51.

The "powers of heaven" (*Himmelskräfte*) alluded to in Goethe's *Faust* (447–53) refer to astrological powers and not, as is usually supposed, to angels.

1163.   ———. "Goethe, Faust, Alchemy, and Jung." *GQ* 35 (1962): 129–41.

Jung's misguided attempt in *Psychology and Alchemy* to interpret Goethe's *Faust* as an alchemical drama is typical of revisionist excesses in *Faust* scholarship. Jantz surveys several apparently faulty interpretations of the work and urges a return to the text itself, unencumbered by presuppositions about what *Faust* should mean.

1164.   Jockers, Ernst. "Morphologie und die Klassik Goethes." *Goethe und die Wissenschaft: Vorträge gehalten anlässlich des Internationalen Gelehrtenkongresses zu Frankfurt am Main im August 1949.* Frankfurt: Klostermann, 1951. 63–81.
Goethe's classicism is a living unity that integrates his views on nature, art, and morality. Jockers maintains that the basic structures Goethe developed in his scientific work emerge also in his literary creations and in his views on ethics.

1165.   Keller, Werner. " 'Die antwortenden Gegenbilder': Eine Studie zu Goethes Wolkendichtung." *JFDH* (1968): 191–236.
Discusses Goethe's often stated conviction concerning the unity of poetry and science. Examines "Howards Ehrengedächtnis," Goethe's cycle of poems on cloud formations, within the framework of eighteenth-century didactic poetry and Goethe's unique contribution to that genre.

1166.   King, Ronold. "Goethe and the Challenge of Science in Western Civilization." *Goethe on Human Creativeness and Other Goethe Essays.* Ed. Rolf King, with Calvin Brown and Erich Funke, assoc. eds. Athens: U of Georgia P, 1950. 223–52.
A study of Goethe's life and work would more than satisfy the modern educational need to help the specialist in the humanities or the sciences understand the interrelatedness of all knowledge. Goethe is perhaps the outstanding literary figure whose sympathies for the universal and the eternal in nature—as reflected in his poetry and in his science—would enable the student of literature to appreciate the complementarity of the sciences and the humanities.

1167.   Klickstein, Herbert S. "Johann Wolfgang Goethe and Chemistry." *LC* 16 (1949–50): 18–27.
Traces the development of Goethe's interest in alchemy and chemistry. Goethe used these sciences imaginatively in works such as *Faust*, *Wilhelm Meister*, and *Die Wahlverwandtschaften.*

1168.   Kreuzer, Leo. "Wie herrlich leuchtet uns die Natur? Der Naturwissenschaftler Goethe—Porträt eines Verlierers." *Mein Gott Goethe. Essays.* Reinbeck bei Hamburg: Rowohlt, 1980. 30–46. (An earlier version appeared in *Akzente* 25 [1978]: 381–90.)
Goethe abjured the modern (i.e., Baconian) way of science, which does violence to nature, and favored an empirical but organismic approach. That approach was central to both his scientific and poetic productivity. It is also the basis of his political conservatism and it is the reason why his science soon became obsolete. Now, however, we may find his holistic approach to nature, which integrates the empirical, the aesthetic, and the ethical, a necessity as we try to overcome the perpetual alienation from nature for which modern, Baconian science is responsible.

1169. Kuczynski, Jürgen. "Goethe über die Beziehungen von Kunst und Wissenschaft." *WB* 18 (1972): 142–51.

Proceeding from the Marxist-Leninist position that both art and science are means to grasp the world, the author examines numerous passages from Goethe's works on the differences and similarities between the practices of art and science. Demonstrates that though Goethe highly esteems his work as a scientist, he frequently elevates art above science in his pursuit of a complementarity between the two. Concludes that contemporary Marxists who excel in the scientific perception of reality should avoid one-sidedness by cultivating artistic perception as well.

1170. Kuhn, Dorothea. *Empirische und ideelle Wirklichkeit: Studien über Goethes Kritik des Französischen Akademiestreites.* Neue Hefte zur Morphologie 5. Graz: Böhlau, 1967. 319 pp.
  Rev. Ulrich K. Goldsmith, *MLN* 84 (1969): 829–31; H. B. Nisbet, *MLR* 64 (1969): 939–40.

Explores the unity of Goethe's scientific and poetic productivity by analyzing the background to his last completed work—his review essay of Etienne Geoffroy Saint-Hilaire's *Principes de philosophie zoologique.* Kuhn claims that the essay form enabled Goethe to articulate the profound significance of the famous dispute between Geoffroy Saint-Hilaire and Georges Cuvier about scientific method. Drawing on Goethe's *Tasso,* she contrasts the empirical type oriented toward reality and the ideal type oriented toward imagination and intuition and uses that typology to clarify the controversy between the two French scientists.

1171. ———. "Grundzüge der Goetheschen Morphologie." *Goethe* 95 (1978): 199–211.

Citing Goethe's most significant scientific essays, Kuhn gives a chronological account of the development of Goethe's concept of morphology. She demonstrates that the term *morphology* encompassed Goethe's fundamental scientific ideas, such as metamorphosis, type, continuity, and unity in diversity, as well as polarities such as empiricism and idea, analysis and synthesis, and mechanism and vitalism. She concludes with a depiction of Goethe's morphology in the poem "Dauer im Wechsel" (1803).

1172. ———. "Über den Grund von Goethes Beschäftigung mit der Natur und ihrer wissenschaftlichen Erkenntnis." *JDSG* 15 (1971): 157–73.

The understanding of human beings as the highest development of nature is the source of Goethe's interest in the scientific study of nature. In his later years Goethe explored that source. By holding that human beings are the proper study of humankind, he was not opposing subject to object any more than he ever opposed poetry to science. As a human being, the microcosm, is a compendium of the world, so is nature, the macrocosm, the key to understanding humankind. Poetry and science can mirror each other because humankind and nature are a unity and not a duality.

1173. Laine, Barry. "By Water and by Fire: The Thales-Anaxagoras Debate in Goethe's *Faust.*" *GR* 50 (1975): 99–110.

Goethe resolves the dialectic tension between Vulcanist and Neptunist imagery in *Faust* in a synthesis that illuminates the work's thematic unity.

1174.   Lange, Victor. "Goethe: Science and Poetry." *YR* ns 38 (1948–49): 623–39.
This overview of Goethe's scientific and literary productions stresses the interrelations between science and poetry in Goethe's personal and intellectual life.

1175.   Loeb, Ernst. *Die Symbolik des Wasserzyklus bei Goethe.* Paderborn: Schöningh, 1967. 204 pp.
    Rev. Stuart Atkins, *Erasmus* 20 (1968): 550–53; Hans Albert Maier, *JEGP* 68 (1969): 343–45; Elizabeth Boa, *MLR* 65 (1970): 217–18.
In focusing on Goethe's water symbolism, this study explores the basic principles of his concept of nature, drawing heavily on his scientific activity. Includes illustrative references to poetry from all periods of Goethe's creativity, with special attention to *Faust II.*

1176.   Loesche, Martin. *Grundbegriffe in Goethes Naturwissenschaft (und ihr Niederschlag in Faust).* Leipzig: Seemann, 1944. 131 pp.
Discusses Goethe's scientific studies, his interest in the Urphenomenon, his attempts to establish the unity behind multiplicity, and his understanding of metamorphosis and coming into being. Compares Goethe's conceptions with those of Kant and traces the influence of Goethe's scientific studies and Kant's philosophy on *Faust.*

1177.   Lohmeyer, Dorothea. *Faust und die Welt. Der zweite Teil der Dichtung. Eine Anleitung zum Lesen des Textes.* München: Beck, 1975. 427 pp.
    Rev. N. Horton Smith, *Erasmus* 29 (1977): 338–40.
Analyzes *Faust II* in the light of Goethe's post-1780 scientific studies, stressing their impact on his conceptions of nature, life, and reality.

1178.   Lohmeyer, Karl. "Das Meer und die Wolken in den beiden letzten Akten des *Faust.*" *Goethe* 13 (1927): 106–33.
Discusses Goethe's meteorological interests as reflected in *Faust,* especially through references to cloud types and cloud formations. Also treats Goethe's interest in the sea.

1179.   Macey, Samuel L. "On the Relationship between Eduard and Ottilie in Goethe's *Wahlverwandtschaften.*" *Seminar* 7 (1971): 79–84.
The complex relations among Eduard, Ottilie, Hauptmann, and Charlotte in Goethe's *Wahlverwandtschaften* can be explained in purely chemical terms; for example, Eduard's interaction with Hauptmann parallels the interaction of lime ($CaCO_3$) with sulphuric acid (H_2SO_4).

1180.   Matthaei, Rupprecht. "Die Farbenlehre in *Faust.*" *Goethe* 10 (1947): 59–148.
For at least forty years Goethe worked simultaneously on *Faust* and *Die Farbenlehre.* This study shows how *Faust* reflects the development of *Die Farbenlehre.*

1181.   Mayer, Hans. "Der Famulus Wagner und die moderne Wissenschaft." *Gestaltungsgeschichte und Gesellschaftsgeschichte.* Literatur-, kunst- und musikwissenschaftliche Studien. Ed. Helmut Kreuzer. Stuttgart: Metzler, 1969. 176–200.

Maintains that the distinct change in the portrayal of Faust's assistant, Wagner, from *Faust I* to *Faust II* reflects a change in Goethe's attitude toward science. Links the problem concerning Faust's salvation or damnation to contemporary questions about the moral responsibility of the scientist.

1182. Maync, Harry. "Goethe, Chamberlain und die Wissenschaft." *GRM* 5 (1913): 646–59.

An analysis of Houston Stewart Chamberlain's 851-page monograph on Goethe, which appeared in 1912. Maync shares Chamberlain's conviction that Goethe must be understood in the totality of his poetic-scientific nature but vigorously rejects Chamberlain's personal biases and ideological distortions.

1183. Mehra, Marlis H. "Die Bedeutung der Formel 'offenbares Geheimnis' in Goethes Spätwerk." *DAI* 37 (1976): 2909A.

Illuminates the relations between Goethe's science and poetry by studying his frequently used formula "offenbares Geheimnis," which appears in both his scientific and his poetic works.

1184. Müller, Günther. "Die Gestaltfrage in der Literaturwissenschaft und Goethes Morphologie." *Morphologische Poetik. Gesammelte Aufsätze.* Tübingen: Niemeyer, 1968. 146–224.

Shows that Goethe's thesis about the vertical and spiral tendencies of plants, expounded in his essay "Die Metamorphose der Pflanzen," is reflected also in his literary works. The morphological tendency called "the force to lead" (*Führkraft*) is manifested in the plot and structure of Goethe's works, while the so-called "erectile force" (*Schwellkraft*) is represented in his literary portrayal of landscapes, mood, emotion, and contemplative activity.

1185. ———. "Gestaltung-Umgestaltung in *Wilhelm Meisters Lehrjahre.* Die Metamorphose der Menschen." *Morphologische Poetik. Gesammelte Aufsätze.* Tübingen: Niemeyer, 1968. 419–510.

Maintains that the structure, form, and depiction of character development in *Wilhelm Meisters Lehrjahre* reflect Goethe's theory of the process of metamorphosis in plants, expressed in "Die Metamorphose der Pflanzen." Emphasizes the correspondences in the development of plants and human beings.

1186. ———. "Goethes Elegie 'Die Metamorphose der Pflanzen.' Versuch einer morphologischen Interpretation." *Morphologische Poetik. Gesammelte Aufsätze.* Tübingen: Niemeyer, 1968. 356–87.

Examines the poetic aspects of Goethe's elegy but notes that the poem, as an organic entity of form and content, reflects the morphological theory Goethe expressed in "Versuch die Metamorphose der Pflanzen zu erklären."

1187. ———. "Goethes Morphologie in Ihrer Bedeutung für die Dichtungskunde." *Goethe und die Wissenschaft: Vorträge gehalten anlässlich des Internationalen Gelehrtenkongresses zu Frankfurt am Main im August 1949.* Frankfurt: Klostermann, 1951. 23–34.

Müller examines how Goethe's concept of morphology functions in his scientific works and develops a thesis about the applicability of that concept to a theory of literary criticism. Such an extension of the concept of morphology from the sphere of nature to the sphere of the spirit is consistent, he maintains, with Goethe's holistic thought.

1188.   Müller-Seidel, Walter. "Naturforschung und deutsche Klassik: Die Jenaer Gespräche im Juli 1794." *Untersuchungen zur Literatur als Geschichte: Festschrift für Benno von Wiese.* Berlin: Schmidt, 1973. 61–78.
Discusses the first meeting between Goethe and Schiller, on 20 July 1794; their subsequent famous conversation concerning Goethe's theory of the metamorphosis of plants; and details of their developing relationship through correspondence.

1189.   Overbeck, Gertrud. "Goethes Lehre von der Metamorphose der Pflanzen und ihre Widerspiegelung in seiner Dichtung." *PEGS* 31 (1960–61): 38–59.
Juxtaposes Goethe's essay "Versuch die Metamorphose der Pflanzen zu erklären" and his didactic elegy "Die Metamorphose der Pflanzen" and concludes that the poem is a literary manifestation of Goethe's scientific concept of metamorphosis.

1190.   Petzsch, Hans. "Die Leben und Wirken C. W. Hufelands in Thüringen im Spiegel des Faustwerkes seines Patienten, Freundes und Gönners J. W. v. Goethe." *Deutsches medizinisches Journal* 14 (1963): 67–73.
Traces the medical career of C. W. Hufeland, Goethe's physician from 1783 to 1793, and explores parallels between Hufeland's medical publications and passages in Goethe's *Faust*.

1191.   Plath, Margarethe. "Der Goethe-Schellingsche Plan eines philosophischen Naturgedichts: Eine Studie zu Goethes *Gott und Welt.*" *Preussische Jahrbücher* 106 (1901): 44–74.
Around 1800, Goethe and Schelling had planned the composition of a comprehensive epic poem that would encompass their conception about nature. Though this work was never realized, the common ground between the two writers is reflected in Schelling's philosophical works about nature and Goethe's cycle of poems entitled *Gott und Welt.* The cycle contains some of Goethe's finest nature poetry, such as "Die Metamorphose der Pflanzen," "Proömion," "Eins und Alles," and "Dauer im Wechsel."

1192.   Pörksen, Uwe. "Zur Metaphorik der naturwissenschaftlichen Sprache: Dargestellt am Beispiel Goethes, Darwins und Freuds." *NRs* 89 (1978): 64–82.
Warns of the dangers of using metaphoric language drawn from or applied to the sciences, especially of borrowing linguistic formulations from the social realm to explain natural processes and using scientific terminology to describe social phenomena. Claims that Goethe was aware of the problem when he chose a chemical metaphor to describe human relations in his novel *Die Wahlverwandtschaften* and shows that he used the metaphor deliberately and maintained the polarity between the natural and the human spheres.

1193.   Prange, Klaus. "Das anthropologisch-pädagogische Motiv der Naturauffassung Goethes in dem Lehrgedicht 'Metamorphose der Pflanzen.' " *LWU*
8 (1975): 123–33.
Includes a detailed literary-structural analysis of Goethe's "Die Metamorphose
der Pflanzen" and a discussion of Goethe's understanding of the harmony between
knowledge and experience in "Die Metamorphose der Tiere." Also treats the anthropological and pedagogical significance of Goethe's view of nature and comments
on the apparent conflict between the objective-scientific and the subjective-poetic
approaches to nature.

1194.   Raphael, Alice. "Alchemistic Symbols in Goethe's 'Walpurgis Night's
Dream.' " *Yearbook of Comparative Criticism* 1 (1968): 181–98.
Examines Goethe's symbolic representation of alchemical concepts such as *medi-
tatio, imaginatio, elevation,* and the *tria prima* in "Walpurgis Night's Dream" from
Faust.

1195.   Rehder, Helmut. "Goethes Metamorphose der Insekten." *Monatshefte* 45
(1953): 255–67.
Reviews Goethe's entomological studies and notes the absence of entomology in
his two major poems on metamorphosis. Cites numerous passages in *Faust* where
insects are represented, concluding that the repeated poetic association of insects
with the Mephistophelian element is inconsistent with Goethe's objective scientific
study of insects.

1196.   Richter, Karl. "Morphologie und Stilwandel: Ein Beitrag zu Goethes Lyrik."
JDSG 21 (1977): 192–215.
Maintains that Goethe's views on morphology and its central thesis concerning
metamorphosis can illuminate the synthesis between literature and science in the
poet's creative work. Examines that synthesis especially in "Die Metamorphose der
Pflanzen," "Trilogie zu Howards Wolkenlehre," and selected poems from the *West-
östlicher Divan.*

1197.   Riley, Thomas A. "Goethe and Parker Cleveland." *PMLA* 67 (1952):
350–74.
Discusses Goethe's enthusiasm for geological and mineralogical study and his
admiration for the work of the American geologist Parker Cleveland. Emphasizes
the importance of Cleveland's *Elementary Treatise of Mineralogy and Geology* (1816)
for Goethe and examines the geologic elements of Goethe's poem *The United States*
(1830).

1198.   Rittersbacher, Karl. *Der Naturforscher Goethe in Selbstzeugnissen: Ein Beitrag
zur Erkenntnis seiner Naturanschauung.* Freiburg: Kommenden, 1968. 292
pp.
To understand Goethe's view of nature, one cannot merely study his scientific
texts but must consider his poetic works as well. This volume juxtaposes excerpts
from Goethe's scientific essays and aphorisms with passages from *Faust II, Dichtung
und Wahrheit,* and other works.

1199.   Rosenfeld, Emmy. "Goethe und der Mailänder Naturforscher Giuseppe de Cristoforis." *LJGG* 20 (1979): 107–38.

Briefly describes Goethe's interest in geological and mineralogical studies as expressed, for example, in the "Klassische Walpurgisnacht" of *Faust II*. Provides a short biography of De Cristoforis, the founder of the museum of natural science in Milan and a collector of minerals, and publishes three letters to Goethe in which De Cristoforis describes some mineral samples that he sent to Goethe.

1200.   Rotermund, H-M. "Zur Kosmogonie des jungen Goethe." *DVLG* 28 (1954): 472–86.

To explain Goethe's cosmogony in book 8 of *Dichtung und Wahrheit*, Rotermund draws on Welling's *Opus mago-cabbalisticum et theosophicum* (1721), which Goethe had studied in his youth.

1201.   Salm, Peter. *The Poem as Plant: A Biological View of Goethe's Faust*. Cleveland: Case Western Reserve UP, 1971. 149 pp.
        Rev. Horst S. Daemmrich, *JAAC* 30 (1971–72): 407; Robert P. Bareikis, *PQ* 51 (1972): 686; Ulrich K. Goldsmith, *MLJ* 56 (1972): 515; Ludwig W. Kahn, *GR* 48 (1973): 60–61; Wolfgang Leppman, *CL* 25 (1973): 278–79; Helmut Rehder, *JEGP* 72 (1973): 591–93.

Uses Goethean science to interpret *Faust*. Specifically, attempts to sustain an analogy between the structure of *Faust* and the principles of polarity, metamorphosis, and heightening developed in Goethe's plant morphology and color theory. Demonstrates that *Faust* is a poetic representation of Goethe's *Urpflanze*.

1202.   Schiff, Julius. "Goethe und die Astrologie." *Preussische Jahrbücher* 210 (1927): 86–96.

Examines Goethe's attitude toward astrology and outlines its role in his works, especially in his poetry. Cites poems such as "Planetentanz" and "Urworte Orphisch."

1203.   Schmidt, Karl. *Betrachtungen über Goethes Weltschau: Ein Versuch mit Berücksichtigung des modernen naturwissenschaftlichen Weltbildes*. Zürich: Europa, 1958. 335 pp.

This general study of Goethe's worldview reflects on his idiosyncratic approach toward science, his rejection of Newtonianism, and the depiction of science in his poetry, especially in *Faust I* and *II*.

1204.   Schmidt, Peter. *Goethes Farbensymbolik. Untersuchungen zu Verwendung und Bedeutung der Farben in den Dichtungen und Schriften Goethes*. Philologische Studien und Quellen 26. Berlin: Schmidt, 1965. 258 pp.
        Rev. Edmund Papst, *MLR* 62 (1967): 563–65.

Examines Goethe's use of color in his poetry and prose, with numerous references to his color theory, and classifies his allegorical and symbolic uses of color.

1205.   ———. "Das Motiv des Seismos in der klassischen Walpurgisnacht des *Faust II*." *Zeitschrift für geologische Wissenschaften* 5 (1977): 395–402.

Focuses on the figure of Seismos, in the "Klassische Walpurgisnacht" in *Faust*

II, as an expression of Goethe's interest in geological and geophysical matters. Examines the sources the poet may have used for the seismological passages.

1206.   Schneider, Mark A. "Goethe and the Structuralist Tradition." *SIR* 18 (1979): 453–78.
An examination of Goethe's scientific and literary writings, including *The Metamorphosis of Plants*, *The Theory of Colors*, and *Elective Affinities*, suggests that Goethe was developing a methodology that anticipated structuralist criticism.

1207.   Schöne, Albrecht. "Über Goethes Wolkenlehre." *Der Berliner Germanistentag 1968: Vorträge und Berichte.* Ed. Karl H. Borck and Rudolf Henss. Heidelberg: Winter, 1970. 24–41.
Traces the development of Goethe's meteorological studies from "Howards Terminologie" (1817) to "Versuch einer Witterungslehre" (1823–25) and discusses his incorporation of these scientific findings into poetic works such as *Faust II*, "Howards Ehrengedächtnis," and "Zahme Xenien."

1208.   Scott, D. F. S., ed. *Luke Howard (1772–1864): His Correspondence with Goethe and His Continental Journey of 1816.* York: Sessions-Ebor, 1976. 99 pp.
Briefly discusses Howard's influence on Goethe's meteorological studies, comments on Howard's autobiographical letter to Goethe, and reprints a translation of Goethe's poem to Howard, "Howards Ehrengedächtnis." Also includes the complete text of Howard's notes concerning his Continental journey of 1816.

1209.   Solotusski, I. "Faust und die Physiker." *KuL* 14 (1966): 276–91.
Calling for the depiction of more scientists in literature, Solotusski examines the figure of the modern physicist in the light of Goethe's characterization of Faust as a scientist. This essay discusses Grekova's "Hinter der Kontrollbude," S. Lewis's *Arrowsmith*, Leonov's *Skutarewski*, and Granin's *Gewitter entgegen* as illustrations of the scientist in literature.

1210.   Stahl, E. H. "Nature and Art in Goethe's Science and Poetry." *Literature and Science.* Proc. of the Sixth Triennial Congress of the International Federation for Modern Languages and Literatures. Oxford, 1954. Oxford: Blackwell, 1955. 221–28.
Concerns Goethe's distinction between scientific and poetic descriptions of natural phenomena. Goethe best exemplifies the connections and differences between his own science and poetry in a poetic version of the *Metamorphosis of Plants* that he wrote in 1798.

1211.   Staiger, Emil. "Goethes Wolkengedichte." *Spätzeit: Studien zur deutschen Literatur.* Zürich: Artemis, 1973. 57–78.
Examines how Luke Howard's essay "On the Modification of Clouds, and on the Principle of Their Production, Suspension, and Destruction" influenced Goethe's didactic poems on clouds, which appeared as a cycle in *Zur Naturwissenschaft überhaupt* (1822). Emphasizes Goethe's synthesis of a scientific description of clouds with their mythological, psychological, and poetic aspects.

1212. Steer, A. G., Jr. *Goethe's Science in the Structure of the* Wanderjahre. Athens: U of Georgia P, 1979. 170 pp.
Rev. Jane K. Brown, *GQ* 53 (1980): 480–81; Alan P. Cottrell, *JEGP* 80 (1981): 97–98.

Steer applies ideas central to Goethe's scientific studies to this analysis of the structure of the *Wanderjahre*. He emphasizes the importance of the concepts of metamorphosis, archetype (*Urform*), family, series, polarity, and enhancement (*Steigerung*) for an understanding of the work's titled and untitled narrative insertions as well as its numerous aphorisms, maxims, and reflections.

1213. ———. "The Wound and the Physician in Goethe's *Wilhelm Meister*." *Studies in German Literature of the Nineteenth and Twentieth Centuries. Festschrift for Frederic E. Coenan*. University of North Carolina Studies in the Germanic Languages and Literatures 67. Ed. Siegfried Mews. Chapel Hill: U of North Carolina P, 1970. 11–23.

One of the features of both the *Lehrjahre* and the *Wanderjahre* that suggest the unity of the two is Goethe's depiction of physical and psychological wounds and his portrayal of the role physicians played in the treatment of these wounds.

1214. Tietzel, Manfred. "Sympathy for the Devil: Die literarische Figur des Wissenschaftlers aus der Sicht der modernen Wissenschaftslehre." *Zeitschrift für allegemeine Wissenschaftstheorie* 11 (1980): 254–75.

This comparative study of Goethe's *Faust*, Brecht's *Leben des Galilei*, and Dürrenmatt's *Physiker* focuses on the differing depictions of scientists in these works and on the attitudes expressed toward scientific method, the validity of scientific data, the value of science, and the impact of science on human life.

1215. Trunz, Erich. "Goethe als Sammler." *Goethe* 89 (1972): 13–61.

Describes Goethe as a collector in areas such as botany, mineralogy, zoology, and anatomy. Goethe's interest in collecting is reflected in his literary works, such as *Wilhelm Meisters Lehrjahre*, *Wilhelm Meisters Wanderjahre*, *Die Wahlverwandtschaften*, and the novella "Der Sammler und die Seinigen," and in his autobiographical works, especially *Dichtung und Wahrheit*.

1216. Wachsmuth, Andreas B. *Geeinte Zwienatur: Aufsätze zu Goethes naturwissenschaftlichem Denken*. Beiträge zur deutschen Klassik 19. Berlin: Aufbau, 1966. 352 pp.

Includes six essays on the depiction of science in Goethe's literary works. "Goethe und die Magie" (26–56) and "Die Magia naturalis im Weltbilde Goethes" (157–79) treat Goethe's use of alchemy in *Faust* and his relations with chemist-botanist Friedrich C. Oetinger and chemist-physician Johann K. Dippel. "Goethes naturwissenschaftliches Denken im Spiegel seiner Dichtungen seit 1790" (246–66) considers Goethe's use of botany, mineralogy, anatomy, and morphology in *Wilhelm Meisters Lehrjahre* and *Faust*. "Goethes Naturforschung und Weltanschauung in ihrer Wechselbeziehung" (140–56) provides an account of Goethe's development as a scientist and discusses the scientific aspects of "Die Metamorphose der Pflanzen," *Die Wahlverwandtschaften*, and other works. "Goethes Farbenlehre und ihre Bedeutung für seine Dichtung und Weltanschauung" (180–200) focuses on Goethe's optical studies and color theory and their relation to the worldview reflected in his poetry. "Goethe und die Medizin" (290–98) surveys Goethe's medical studies and their reflection in *Faust* and *Wilhelm Meisters Wanderjahre*.

1217. ———. "Goethes naturwissenschaftliche Erfahrungen und Überzeugungen in dem Roman *Wilhelm Meisters Wanderjahre*." *WB* 4 (1960): 1091–107.

Although many scientific themes are evident in the *Wanderjahre*, Goethe's geological interests, specifically represented in the figure of Jarno-Montan, predominate.

1218. Wattenberg, Diedrich. "Goethe und die Sternenwelt." *Goethe* 31 (1969): 66–111.

Surveys Goethe's interests in astronomy and cites numerous references to astronomical motifs in *Wilhelm Meisters Wanderjahre* and various poems.

1219. Weiland, Werner. "Goethes glückliches Gleichnis von der Ergänzung der Wissenschaft durch Religion und Kunst." *Goethe* 96 (1979): 146–58.

Analyzes Goethe's response of 21 April 1819 to Carl Ernst Schubart's reflections on the relations among poetry, religion, and science. Focusing on Goethe's cryptic schematic chart, Weiland reveals the complexity and profundity of Goethe's thought on the interconnections linking these three fundamental realms. The poems "Zueignung" and "Epirrhema" offer examples of Goethe's principle of unity.

1220. Wells, Larry D. "Organic Structure in Goethe's 'Novelle.' " *GQ* 53 (1980): 418–31.

Contends that the thematic structure of Goethe's "Novelle" is informed by morphological concepts relevant to plant growth, including polarity, prefiguration and anticipation, metamorphosis, *Steigerung*, expansion and contraction, and centricity.

Johann Christoph Gottsched (1700–66)

1221. Schatzberg, Walter. "Gottsched as Popularizer of Science." *MLN* 83 (1968): 752–70.

Examines Gottsched's considerable efforts to popularize the new sciences through his translations of scientific texts, his popular account of science, *Erste Gründe der gesammten Weltweisheit* (1731), and his occasional poetry, which frequently draws on Copernican astronomy for its imagery.

Albrecht von Haller (1708–77)

1222. Jackson, Philip H. " 'Air and Angels,' The Origenist Compromise in Haller's *Über den Ursprung des Übels*." *GL&L* 32 (1978–79): 273–92.

Maintains that Haller uses elements of Origenist cosmogony, angelology, and eschatology to reconcile the opposing claims of religion and science in his *Über den Ursprung des Übels*.

1223. Jones, Howard M. "Albrecht von Haller and English Philosophy." *PMLA* 40 (1925): 103–27.

Maintains that the philosophical content of Haller's *Alpen, Gedanken über Vernunft, Aberglauben und Unglauben, Die Falschheit menschlicher Tugenden*, and *Über den Ursprung des Übels* was influenced primarily by Newtonianism and not, as had been supposed, by Shaftesbury's philosophy.

1224.   Price, Lawrence M. "Albrecht von Haller and English Theology." *PMLA* 41 (1926): 942–54.

Provides an overview of the scientific, philosophical, and theological influences on Haller's philosophical poetry, emphasizing S. Clarke, King, Newton, and Shaftesbury.

1225.   Shteir, Ann B. "Albrecht von Haller's Botany and 'Die Alpen.' " *ECS* 10 (1976–77): 169–84.

Reviews Haller's contributions to botanical research and examines his poem *Die Alpen* from the perspective of his interest in and knowledge of botany. G. Lessing's criticism of *Die Alpen* in *Laokoon* (1766) and Haller's response to this criticism round out the article.

1226.   Toellner, Richard. "Decora Merenti. Glory, Merit and Science: Haller Spellbound by the Newtonian Star." *Janus* 67 (1980): 171–85.

Outlines Haller's early scientific training; his scientific achievements, especially in physiology; and the extent of Newton's influence on his scientific thought. Briefly remarks on Haller's verse in praise of Newton, such as *Gedanken über Vernunft, Aberglauben und Unglauben*.

1227.   Wiswall, Dorothy R. "A Comparison of Selected Poetic and Scientific Works of Albrecht von Haller." *DAI* 40 (1979): 884A–85A.

Examines the parallels between Haller's poetic and scientific works, noting similarities in content, vocabulary, and style.

Johann Gottfried von Herder (1744–1803)

1228.   Nisbet, H. B. *Herder and the Philosophy and History of Science.* Modern Humanities Research Association: Dissertation Series 3. Cambridge: Modern Humanities Research Assn., 1970. 358 pp.
Rev. Edgar B. Schick, *JEGP* 71 (1972): 67–72; Albert R. Schmitt, *GR* 48 (1973): 157–60.

This useful background study provides a detailed examination of Herder's philosophy of science (including an explanation of his logical, metaphysical, and physical concept of "*Kraft*"), an analysis of his various investigative methodologies (including empirical, analogical, dialectical, and mathematical systems), and a review of his principal reflections on the physical and biological sciences. The volume concludes with a discussion of Herder's understanding of the role science plays in the acquisition of knowledge, stressing the interrelation of the sciences with poetry, art, and aesthetic values and the relation of science to education, history, and religion.

1229.   Schick, Edgar B. "Art and Science: Herder's Imagery and Eighteenth-Century Biology." *GQ* 41 (1968): 356–68.

Herder frequently used botanical metaphors to characterize human physiology. Schick surveys this imagery and notes Herder's influence on Goethe's view of the relations between natural science and poetry. Among the works discussed are Herder's *Vom Erkennen und Empfinden der menschlichen Seele* (1778) and Goethe's *Versuch einer allgemeinen Vergleichungslehre* (1792).

1230. —————. *Metaphorical Organicism in Herder's Early Works: A Study of the Relation of Herder's Literary Idiom to His World-View*. The Hague: Mouton, 1971. 135 pp.
Rev. Joe K. Fugate, *JEGP* 72 (1973): 89–90; H. B. Nisbet, *MLR* 68 (1973): 456–57; Friedhelm Radandt, *MP* 71 (1973–74): 448–50.

This study of the poetic aspects of Herder's early prose examines his application of organistic imagery from zoology and botany to his writings on language, literature, aesthetic criticism, the creative thinker, education, and humankind's historical and cultural growth.

John Hill (1707?–75)

1231. Emery, Clark. "'Sir' John Hill versus the Royal Society." *Isis* 34 (1942–43): 16–20.

A brief exposition of Hill's satires of the Royal Society, *A Review of the Works of the Royal Society of London* (1751) and *Lucine sine Concubitu, a Letter Humbly Addressed to the Royal Society* (1750).

Jean Paul (1763–1825)

1232. Haas, Margarete. "Ein Traum über das All bei Jean Paul und Dostojewski." *Archiv* 164 (1933): 1–6.

At the end of Jean Paul's novel *Der Komet*, in his "Traum über das All," his spirit journeys throughout the universe observing planets, suns, and galaxies. Evidence shows that Dostoyevski had this dream voyage in mind when he wrote his "Dream of a Curious Fellow" (1877).

1233. Thiersch, Hans. "Die kosmischen Visionen Jean Pauls und die kosmischen Vorstellungen in der deutschen Dichtung des 18. Jahrhunderts." Diss. U Göttingen, 1963.
Not seen for annotation.

Samuel Johnson (1709–84)

1234. Atkinson, A. D. "Dr. Johnson and Newton's *Opticks*." *RES* 2 (1951): 226–37.

Newton's *Opticks* was a dominant influence on, and source of information for, the sections of Johnson's *Dictionary* that deal with the science of optics; there are 461 quotations from Newton's work in the dictionary.

1235.   ———. "Dr. Johnson and Some Physico-Theological Themes." *N&Q* 197
         (1952): 16–18, 162–65, 249–53.
Examines the sources for references in Johnson's *Dictionary* to physicotheological
themes such as chaos, creation, the Flood, and mountains. Sources include works
by T. Burnet, Derham, Hale, J. Ray, and Woodward.

1236.   Bernard, F. V. "The Hermit of Paris and the Astronomer in *Rasselas*."
         JEGP 67 (1968): 272–78.
Suggests that Johnson modeled the character of the learned astronomer in *Rasselas*
(1759) after Louis Morin, the botanist-physician, whose biography Johnson had
translated in 1741.

1237.   Brown, John J. "Samuel Johnson and Eighteenth-Century Science." Diss.
         Yale U, 1943.
Not seen for annotation.

1238.   Fisher, S. T. "Johnson on Flying." *TLS* 4 Nov. 1965: 988.
In the chapter of *Rasselas* entitled "A Dissertation on the Art of Flying," Johnson
was able to develop a fairly sophisticated account of the properties of an artificial
satellite by drawing on his grasp of the principles of mechanics outlined in Wilkins's
Mathematical Magick (1648).

1239.   Fox, Robert C. "Dr. Johnson, Bishop Wilkins, and the Submarine." *N&Q*
         ns 5 (1958): 364, 368.
Johnson's speculations on submarine navigation published in the *Rambler* of 19
March 1751 owe much to his study of Wilkins's *Mathematical Magick* (1648).

1240.   ———. "The Imaginary Submarines of Dr. Johnson and Richard Owen
         Cambridge." *PQ* 40 (1961): 112–19.
Notes references to submarines in issue 105 of Johnson's *Rambler* (19 Mar. 1751)
and in book 4 of Cambridge's *Scribleriad* (1751) that have been overlooked by
historians of the submarine.

1241.   Kolb, Gwin J. "Johnson's 'Dissertation on Flying' and John Wilkins'
         Mathematical Magick." *MP* 47 (1949–50): 24–31.
Analyzes the structure of "A Dissertation on the Art of Flying" in Johnson's
Rasselas, emphasizing his indebtedness to the principles of mechanics outlined in
Wilkins's *Mathematical Magick*.

1242.   Landa, Louis A. "Johnson's Feathered Man: 'A Dissertation on the Art of
         Flying' Considered." *Eighteenth-Century Studies in Honor of Donald F. Hyde*.
         Ed. W. H. Bond. New York: Grolier, 1970. 161–78.
Maintains that Johnson's "Dissertation" in *Rasselas* reflects the eighteenth-century
intellectual ferment surrounding the ethical, scientific, religious, and social implications of ideas about the possibility of human flight. The artist in *Rasselas* represents
the "new science," and his failure to construct a workable flying apparatus suggests
Johnson's skeptical attitude toward science as a mode of inquiry. For Johnson, as

for Pope, Locke, and many others, the proper study for humankind is the moral, ethical, or humanistic dimension of human being.

1243.   Lawrence, Robert G. "Dr. Johnson and the Art of Flying." *N&Q* ns 4 (1957): 348–51.

John Wilkins's *Mathematical Magick* (1648) and Robert Cadman's fatal flying experiment in 1740 are the two principal influences on Johnson's interest in and attitude toward flying, expressed in part in *Rasselas*.

1244.   Mitchell, Stephen O. "Samuel Johnson and the New Philosophy: The Effects of the New Philosophy on Johnson's Thought." *DA* 22 (1961): 3203–04.

Describes Johnson's confrontation with the epistemology and scientific materialism of Galileo, Newton, and R. Descartes and, with this conflict in mind, examines his *Dictionary*, *Lives of the Poets*, and essays.

1245.   Moore, Thurston M. "Samuel Johnson and the Literature of Travel." *DA* 28 (1967–68): 237A–38A.

Documents the travel literature with which Johnson was familiar and ascertains its influence on his work. The travel literature discussed includes references to geography, topography, and natural history.

1246.   Pettit, Henry. "Dr. Johnson and the Cheerful Robots." *WHR* 14 (1960): 381–88.

Discusses aspects of Johnson's intellectual activity and shows how the dramatization of science in *Rasselas* reflects Johnson's views on the application of knowledge to life.

1247.   Schwartz, Richard B. "Dr. Johnson and the Satiric Reaction to Science." *SBHT* 11 (1969–70): 1336–47.

Johnson deplored the satiric attitude toward science and scientists expressed by S. Butler, King, Swift, and others, though it is sometimes assumed that his treatment of virtuosos in his *Rambler*, *Idler*, and *Adventurer* essays suggests a similarly disparaging attitude toward science. Schwartz shows that Johnson's ostensible criticism of the virtuosos is offset by a tone of general sympathy, praise, and encouragement.

1248.   ———. *Samuel Johnson and the New Science*. Madison: U of Wisconsin P, 1971. 188 pp.
Rev. G. S. Rousseau, *Isis* 63 (1972): 582–84; M. C. Jacob, *AHR* 78 (1973): 686–87; Paul J. Korshin, *JEGP* 72 (1973): 137–40; Donald A. Cress *RM* 27 (1973–74): 158–59.

Attempts to dispel the popular image of Johnson as indifferent or hostile to the science of his time. Surveys Johnson's experiences with and writings on science, analyzes his view of the Baconian scientific tradition, and discusses both the satiric opposition and the physicotheological support that science encountered in Johnson's time. Draws on Johnson's *Rambler* essays, his *Dictionary*, *Life of Barretier*, *Life of Boerhaave*, and other works.

1249. ———. "Samuel Johnson's Attitudes toward Science." *DA* 28 (1967–68): 3156A.
Johnson's enthusiasm for science, particularly the utilitarian science of the Baconian tradition, is evident in his writings in various literary genres. Works studied include *Rasselas*, *Lives of the Poets*, and *Journey to the Western Islands of Scotland*.

1250. Wimsatt, W. K., Jr. "Johnson on Electricity." *RES* 23 (1947): 257–60.
Assesses the extent to which Johnson's entry on electricity in the original folio version of his *Dictionary* (1755) reflects the advances in electrical theory resulting from the experiments of Benjamin Franklin and Stephen Gray.

Abraham Gotthelf Kästner (1719–1800)

1251. Dyck, Martin. "Mathematics and Literature in the German Enlightenment: Abraham Gotthelf Kästner (1719–1800)." *SVEC* 190 (1980): 508–12.
Briefly sketches Kästner's career in mathematics and its influence on the theme, style, and organization of his literary works.

Louis-Guillaume de La Follie (1739–80)

1252. Mohler, Nora M., and Marjorie H. Nicolson. "The First 'Electrical' Flying Machine." *Essays Contributed in Honor of President William Allen Neilson.* Smith College Studies in Modern Languages 21.1–4. Ed. Caroline B. Bourland, et al. Northampton: Smith Coll., 1939–40. 143–58.
Briefly traces the reflection of science in seventeenth- and eighteenth-century literature concerning "cosmic voyages." Specifically, discusses La Follie's *Philosophe sans prétention* (1775), which contains the first description of an electrical "flying chariot," to demonstrate the impact of electrical theory on the technology of literary flying machines.

Gotthold Ephraim Lessing (1729–81)

1253. Dyck, Martin. "Lessing and Mathematics." *LY* 9 (1977): 96–117.
Following a discussion of Lessing's background in mathematics, Dyck examines Lessing's literary works from the perspective of the mathematical principles that inform his imaginative thought and literary style.

Mikhail Vasilyevich Lomonosov (1711–65)

1254. Markovitch, Milan. "Lomonossov, homme de lettres et homme de science russe du XVIIIᵉ siècle." *Literature and Science.* Proc. of the Sixth Triennial Congress of the International Federation for Modern Languages and Literatures. Oxford, 1954. Oxford: Blackwell, 1955. 212–16.
Lomonosov distinguished himself as a scientific polymath and founded the University of Moscow. A native of the Arctic, he was led to scientific inquiry through religious reverence inspired by polar nights and vast seascapes. While his scientific

discoveries no longer have significance, his great legacy lies, according to Markovitch, in advancing science as a major subject for poetry.

1255.   Smith, M. N. "Old Russian Literature—Michael Vasilievich Lomonosov (1711–1765)." *SCB* 28 (1968): 126–28.

These biographical notes on Lomonosov emphasize his influence in Russia as both a man of letters and a scientist. Poems such as *Epistle on the Use of Glass* and *Meditations on the Divine Majesty* exemplify his broad intellectual interests.

Novalis (1772–1801)

1256.   Bluth, Karl Theodor. *Medizingeschichtliches bei Novalis: Ein Beitrag zur Geschichte der Medizin der Romantik*. Abhandlungen zur Geschichte der Medizin und der Naturwissenschaften. Berlin: Ebering, 1934. Nendeln, Liechtenstein: Kraus, 1977. 59 pp.

This examination of the medical aspects of Novalis's fragments stresses his concepts of the organism and of sickness and discusses his influence on John Brown's *Elementa medicinae* (1788).

1257.   Cardinal, Roger. "Werner, Novalis and the Signature of Stones." *Deutung und Bedeutung: Studies in German and Comparative Literature Presented to Karl-Werner Maurer*. Ed. Brigitte Schludermann, Victor G. Doerksen, Robert J. Glendinning, and Evelyn Scherabon Firchow. The Hague: Mouton, 1973. 118–33.

The analogical and intuitive scientific method practiced by the geologist Abraham Gottlob Werner (1749–1817) influenced the way Novalis approached nature, drawing him to see "spiritual meanings in the structure of Nature, and to interpret factual discoveries in terms of mental or spiritual values." Cardinal examines the analogies and associations that Novalis drew from his own mineralogical research and mining experience, as reflected in *Die Lehrlinge zu Sais* and *Heinrich von Ofterdingen*.

1258.   Dyck, Martin. *Novalis and Mathematics: A Study of Friedrich von Hardenberg's Fragments on Mathematics and Its Relation to Magic, Music, Religion, Philosophy, Language, and Literature*. University of North Carolina Studies in the Germanic Languages and Literatures 27. Diss. U of Cincinnati, 1956. Chapel Hill: U of North Carolina P, 1960. New York: AMS, 1969. 109 pp. (Abstract in *DA* 16 (1956): 2160–61.)
        Rev. C. Truesdell, *Isis* 52 (1961): 606–07; Ralph Tymms, *MLR* 60 (1965): 307–08.

Surveys Novalis's mathematical studies, discusses the philosophical and mathematical sources of his fragments on mathematics, and studies his attempts to project mathematical concepts into fields other than the physical sciences. "In his fragments on mathematics, Novalis is concerned with an extension of this science beyond its usual domain and with its elucidation in broad contexts of art, life, and thought, and not with strict mathematical research."

1259.   Hamburger, Käte. "Novalis und die Mathematik: Eine Studie zur Erkenntnistheorie der Romantik." *Romantik Forschungen.* DVLG Buchreihe 16. Ed. Paul Kluckhohn and Erich Rothacker. Halle: Niemeyer, 1929. 113–84. Rpt. in *Philosophie der Dichter Novalis, Schiller, Rilke.* Stuttgart: Kohlhammer, 1966. 11–82.

Claims that for Novalis mathematics has a symbolic significance and plays a key role in his Romantic quest for the unity of all disciplines. The epistemology of the Marburg Neo-Kantian school shows that in his theoretical grasp of mathematics Novalis approaches the understanding of the discipline held by modern mathematicians.

1260.   Hegener, Johannes. *Die Poetisierung der Wissenschaften bei Novalis dargestellt am Prozess der Entwicklung von Welt und Menschheit: Studien zum Problem enzyklopädischen Welterfahrens.* Bonn: Bouvier, 1975. 521 pp.

Rev. Martin Dyck, *Seminar* 12 (1976): 191–92; Günter Strenzke, *Aurora* 36 (1976): 181–82; Heinrich Schipperges, *Sudhoffs Archiv* 61 (1977): 397–98.

Demonstrates the unity of poetry and thought within Novalis's comprehensive encyclopedic system, which includes sciences such as chemistry, physiology, physics, medicine, and mathematics. Draws on Novalis's philosophical and literary works, with special attention to *Heinrich von Ofterdingen* and *Die Lehrlinge zu Sais.*

1261.   Hiebel, Frederick. "Goethe's *Maerchen* in the Light of Novalis." *PMLA* 63 (1948): 918–34.

Elements of mysticism, alchemy, natural philosophy, and Romantic physiology underlie Novalis's attempts to interpret Goethe's *Maerchen,* a fairy tale.

1262.   Loosen, Renate. "Die 'Kugel' der Wissenschaften: Zur Idee der Enzyklopädie bei Novalis." *Scheidewege* 2 (1972): 262–81.

A discussion of Novalis's project to construct a true encyclopedia of knowledge that would synthesize religion, poetry, philosophy, and science and overcome the modern fragmentation of learning, illuminating the original order of the world.

1263.   Mahoney, Dennis F. *Die Poetisierung der Natur bei Novalis. Beweggründe, Gestaltung, Folgen.* Abhandlungen zur Kunst-, Musik- und Literaturwissenschaft, 286. Bonn: Bouvier, 1980. 125 pp.

Rev. Ansgar Hillach, *Germanistik* 22 (1981): 170; Bernard Ajac, *Critique* 38 (1982): 915–21; R. Leroy, *CollG* 15 (1982): 373–74.

A study of Novalis's use of philosophic and scientific theory to facilitate his presentation of his concept of nature in *Die Lehrlinge zu Sais* and *Heinrich von Ofterdingen.* Among the sources of influence discussed are works by Fichte, Kant, Schelling, Baader, and Ritter. Evaluates the contributions of Copernicus, Kepler, Galileo, and Newton to eighteenth- and nineteenth-century ideas of nature.

1264.   Moser, Walter. "Poetik der Enzyklopädie: Untersuchung des 'Allgemeinen Brouillon' für die Enzyklopädie von Novalis." *Akten des VI. Internationalen Germanisten-Kongresses, Basel 1980.* Ser. A, 8.4. Bern: Lang, 1980. 422–31.

Examines how "Das allgemeine Brouillon" reflects Novalis's conception of a complex, multidimensional net of interrelations among all the humanities and sciences that would achieve an encyclopedic or universal science, the science of all sciences.

1265.   Neubauer, John. "Apprenticeship in Science." *Novalis*. Boston: Twayne, 1980. 44–63.
Sketches the course of Novalis's education in science, including geology, mining, mathematics, physics, and medicine.

1266.   ———. *Bifocal Vision: Novalis' Philosophy of Nature and Disease*. University of North Carolina Studies in the Germanic Languages and Literatures 68. Chapel Hill: U of North Carolina P, 1971. 194 pp.
Rev. Robert P. Artigiani, *PQ* 51 (1972): 742; James M. McGlathery, *JEGP* 71 (1972): 429–32; Elizabeth Stopp, *MLR* 68 (1973): 458–60; Jean Théodoridès, *Isis* 67 (1976): 641–42.
Outlines the background of Novalis's philosophy of science and examines his interest in medicine, physiology, and psychology as revealed in his scientific notebooks. Influences include Baader, J. Brown, Eschenmayer, Hemsterhuis, Kant, and Schelling. Neubauer maintains that Novalis's scientific and empirical interests developed independently of his poetic interests and that the two pursuits tended to contradict each other. His attempts to ". . . construct a synthesis, to give a poetic, moral, and religious meaning to the empirical world" in his encyclopedia, "Das allgemeine Brouillon," and in *Die Lehrlinge zu Sais* ultimately failed.

1267.   ———. "Novalis und die Ursprünge der romantischen Bewegung in der Medizin." *Sudhoffs Archiv* 53 (1969–70): 160–70.
Seeks to demonstrate that Novalis has been mistakenly considered a major influence on German Romantic medicine. Shows that principal thinkers of the "Naturphilosophie" movement, such as Schelling, developed their key concepts before becoming acquainted with Novalis. In general, Novalis should be dissociated from the Romantic movement in medicine and judged, instead, on the basis of the overall philosophy of science emerging from his various remarks.

1268.   Schmidt, Heinz Dieter. "Friedrich von Hardenberg (Novalis) und Abraham Gottlob Werner." Diss. U Tübingen, 1951.
Not seen for annotation.

1269.   Schueler, H. J. "Cosmology and Quest in Novalis' 'Klingsohrs Märchen.' " *GR* 49 (1974): 259–66.
Demonstrates that Novalis used the Ptolemaic cosmological schema as a device for organizing the imagery of the "Märchen" in the ninth chapter of *Heinrich von Ofterdingen*. Notes also that a traditional quest myth structure informs the action of the fairy tale.

1270.   Smith, Gary A. "The Romantic View of Science in Novalis' Notes and Fragments." *DA* 31 (1970–71): 1813A.
Examines the scientific and philosophical foundations of Novalis's view of science and presents his principal opinions concerning science generally, scientific method, mineralogy, physics, and chemistry.

1271.   Wagner, Lydia Elizabeth. *The Scientific Interest of Friedrich von Hardenberg (Novalis)*. Ann Arbor: Edwards, 1937. 117 pp.

Shows that Novalis was interested in all the sciences of his time and assesses the impact of this interest on his life and art. Traces the development of his involvement in medicine, physiology, anatomy, geology, chemistry, physics, astronomy, and other sciences.

1272.   Wetzels, Walter D. "Klingsohrs Märchen als Science Fiction." *Monatshefte* 65 (1973): 167–75.

Interprets "Klingsohrs Märchen" from the ninth book of *Heinrich von Ofterdingen* as reflecting elements of Novalis's knowledge of physics. Wetzels classifies the fairy tale as a form of science fiction because it refers to discoveries in the fields of electricity and galvanism.

Cardinal Melchior de Polignac (1661–1742)

1273.   Fleischmann, Wolfgang Bernard. "Zum *Anti-Lucretius* des Kardinals de Polignac." *RF* 77 (1965): 42–63.

Polignac's *Anti-Lucretius*, which consists of nine books of hexameter verse, follows the tradition of Latin didactic poetry since the Renaissance and uses Lucretius, Vergil, Ovid, and Manilius as models. In the first five books scientific subject matter appears in Polignac's polemic against the cosmologies of Lucretius, Gassendi, and especially Newton. The last four books are predominantly didactic; the eighth book defends Copernican astronomy.

Alexander Pope (1688–1744)

1274.   Fabian, Bernhard. "Newtonische Anthropologie: Alexander Popes *Essay on Man*." *Deutschlands kulturelle Entfaltung: Die Neubestimmung des Menschen*. Studien zum achtzehnten Jahrhundert 2–3. Ed. Bernhard Fabian, Wilhelm Schmidt-Biggemann, and Rudolf Vierhaus. München: Kraus, 1980. 117–33.

Interprets the worldview expressed in Pope's *Essay on Man*, stressing its relation to Newtonianism and the concept of a chain of being. Maintains that the Newtonian anthropology of Pope's poem permitted the development of a view of humanity that provided agreement with macrocosmic principles, an explanation of human nature in relation to the cosmos, and a measure for social and ethical behavior.

1275.   ———. "Pope and Lucretius: Observations on *An Essay on Man*." *MLR* 74 (1979): 524–37.

Opposing the traditional reading of Pope's *Essay* as Horatian in style and tone, Fabian suggests a Lucretian perspective on the poem and shows convincing stylistic parallels between the *Essay* and *De rerum natura*. External evidence also suggests that Pope's poetic design was Lucretian in form, though Newtonian and anti-Epicurean in cosmological thrust.

1276.   ———. "Pope und die goldene Kette Homers." *Anglia* 82 (1964): 150–71.

In his translation of the *Iliad* Pope reinterpreted the chain of being in the light of Newtonianism, incorporating the latest scientific theories into what was once a primarily metaphysical conception.

1277.   Kinsley, William. "Physico-Demonology in Pope's 'Dunciad' IV, 71–90." *MLR* 70 (1975): 20–31.

Pope drew much of the imagery and terminology for the cited passage of the *Dunciad* from Newton's *Principia*.

1278.   Knoepflmacher, U. C. "The Poet as Physician: Pope's *Epistle to Dr. Arbuthnot.*" *MLQ* 31 (1970): 440–49.

This study of the *Epistle* emphasizes Pope's analogy between the therapeutic art of the physician and the art of the poet.

1279.   Nicolson, Marjorie, and G. S. Rousseau. *"This long disease, my life": Alexander Pope and the Sciences.* Princeton: Princeton UP, 1968. 315 pp.
        Rev. Lawrence C. McHenry, Jr., *ECS* 3 (1969): 136–39; Patricia M. Spacks, *JEGP* 68 (1969): 525–29; R. Harré, *RES* ns 21 (1970): 219–21.

Provides a medical case history of Pope and discusses the medical themes in his works, including the circulation and transfusion of blood, animalitarianism, and the "Mummius" episode in *The Dunciad*. A large central section examines the impact of astronomy on Pope's poetic imagination, noting especially Whiston's lectures on astronomy in 1715. The final section traces Pope's interest in other sciences, such as Newtonian optics, microscopy, and geology.

1280.   Priestley, F. E. L. "Pope and the Great Chain of Being." *Essays in English Literature from the Renaissance to the Victorian Age Presented to A. S. P. Woodhouse, 1964.* Ed. Millar MacClure and F. W. Watt. Toronto: U of Toronto P, 1964. 213–28.

Shows that Pope's conception of the great chain of being in *An Essay on Man* differs fundamentally from the traditional conception described in King's *De Origine Mali* (1702). King treats the idea from an a priori, ontological perspective, whereas Pope derives it from empirical, a posteriori grounds in accordance with a Newtonian view of nature.

1281.   Rousseau, George S. "Poiesis and Urania: The Relation of Poetry and Astronomy in the English Enlightenment." *Actes du XIIe Congres International d'Histoire des Sciences, Paris 1968*. Vol. 3B: *Science et Philosophie XVIIe et XVIIIe Siècles*. Paris: Blanchard, 1971. 113–16.

The effect of science on literature is not ". . . in any sense linear, direct, or simple." A case in point is Pope, who acquired his knowledge of Newtonianism from Whiston's lectures and not from Newton's works.

1282.   ———. " 'To Thee, whose Temple is all Space': Varieties of Space in *The Dunciad.*" *MLS* 9.3 (1978–79): 37–47.

Discusses Pope's poetic transformation of the Newtonian concepts of attraction, impulse, energy, and space in *The Dunciad*, stressing the distinctions between varieties of space in the poem, such as literal, poetic, Newtonian, and metaphysical space.

1283.   Schneider, Michael. "Of Mystics and Mechanism: The Reception of New-
        tonian Physics in Eighteenth Century English Poetry." *Synthesis* [Cam-
        bridge] 1.1 (1972): 14–26.
This study of Newton's impact on eighteenth-century poetry focuses on Pope's
treatment of physicotheology in *An Essay on Man* and on Blake's responses to
Newtonian empiricism in such works as *The Four Zoas* and *Jerusalem*.

1284.   Sherburn, George. "Pope and 'The Great Shew of Nature.' " *The Seventeenth
        Century: Studies in the History of English Thought and Literature from Bacon to
        Pope by Richard Foster Jones and Others Writing in His Honor.* Stanford: Stanford
        UP, 1951. 306–15.
Discusses Whiston's influence on Pope's concepts of nature and the universe.

1285.   Simpson, David L. "Four Philosophical Poems: Ideas of Order in Donne,
        Pope, Tennyson, and Eliot." *DAI* 38 (1977): 2781A.
See item 806 for annotation.

1286.   Zoellner, Robert H. "Poetic Cosmology in Pope's *An Essay on Man.*" *CE*
        19 (1957–58): 157–62. (Reply by John M. Aden, *CE* 19 [1957–58]:
        358.)
Examines the metaphoric and linguistic "texture" of the four cosmological elements of *An Essay on Man*: the chain of being, the Newtonian system of planets
and spheres, humankind's place in the chain of being, and balance in the universe.

L'Abbé Antoine-François Prévost (1697–1763)

1287.   Vernière, Paul. "L'abbé Prévost et les réalités géographiques, à propos de
        l'épisode américain de 'Cleveland.' " *RHL* 73 (1973): 626–35.
Examines Prévost's use of geography books and maps in the composition of the
"American episode" in the novel *Cleveland* (1731), citing geography texts by Robert
Beverley, Gonzalez de Barcia, François Coréal, Pierre van der Aa, and others and
maps by Nicolas Swanson (1713), Guillaume Delisle (1718), and J. B. Nolin (1720).
Vernière concludes that Prévost balanced his literary imagination with historical
truth and geographical exactitude.

Nicolas Edme Restif de la Bretonne (1734–1806)

1288.   Chinard, Gilbert. "An Eighteenth-Century Interpretation of the 'Struggle
        for Existence.' Rétif de la Bretonne's *Ecole des pères.*" *PAPS* 102 (1958):
        547–54.
Outlines Restif's cosmogony and his biological interpretation of the development
and function of human society as expressed in *Ecole des pères*, which responds to and
imitates Rousseau's *Emile*.

1289.   Fletcher, Dennis, ed. "Nicolas Edmé Restif de La Bretonne, *Le généographe.*"
        SVEC 170 (1977): 125–234.
The introduction to this edition of Restif's *Généographe* surveys the likely sources
of the work's antimechanistic cosmology, including Thales, Anaximander, Anaxa-

goras, Pythagoras, Plato, Aristotle, Cicero, Ficino, Campanella, Bruno, and Gassendi.

Jean Jacques Rousseau (1712–78)

1290.   Fellows, Otis. "Buffon and Rousseau: Aspects of a Relationship." *PMLA* 75 (1960): 184–96.
Traces the historical development of the personal and intellectual relationship between Rousseau and Buffon. Stresses the influence of Buffon's *Histoire naturelle* on Rousseau's essays and novels.

1291.   Scott, David. "Rousseau and Flowers: The Poetry of Botany." *SVEC* 182 (1979): 73–86.
Rousseau's interest in flowers was primarily botanical, though his descriptions of flowers in works like *Les rêveries* suggest a poetic sensibility comparable to that of Romantic poets such as Wordsworth.

Friedrich von Schiller (1759–1805)

1292.   Dewhurst, Kenneth, and Nigel Reeves. *Friedrich Schiller: Medicine, Psychology, and Literature, with the First English Edition of His Complete Medical and Psychological Writings*. Berkeley: U of California P; Oxford: Sanford, 1978. 413 pp.
Rev. R. W. Pickford, *British Journal of Aesthetics* 19 (1979): 276–77; Jeffrey Barnouw, *GQ* 53 (1980): 116–18; Margaret C. Ives, *MLR* 75 (1980): 449–50.
Maintains that Schiller's medical and psychological writings " . . . extend unashamedly across medicine, psychology, psychiatry, philosophy, theology and even literature with scant regard to the distinctions between subjects of today" and that their importance for elucidating his literary works has been underestimated. Includes a biography of Schiller's medical years; accounts of conflicting eighteenth-century medical theories and of the emergence of psychology from philosophy, psychosomatic medicine, and neural pathology; and an appraisal of the formative influence of medicine, and especially psychology, on Schiller's poetry, drama, and narrative, philosophical, and aesthetic works.

1293.   Düsing, Wolfgang. "Kosmos und Natur in Schillers Lyrik." *JDSG* 13 (1969): 196–220.
In early poems like "Die Freundschaft" and "Der Eroberer" Schiller drew on the new astronomy of Copernicus and Newton for his cosmological metaphors. During his classical period he made a clear distinction between the artist's and the scientist's approaches to nature and the cosmos. In poems such as "Menschliches Wissen" and "An die Astronomen" Schiller rejected the scientist's quantifying method.

1294.   Hill, Harold C. "Astrology and Friendship: The Net of Commitment in *Wallenstein*." *MLN* 91 (1976): 467–77.
The astrological element of Schiller's *Wallenstein* symbolizes both the metaphysical order of the universe and humankind's relations with the greater whole.

1295.   May, Walther. "Schillers Verhältnis zur Natur und ihrer Wissenschaft."
        Preussische Jahrbücher 123 (1906): 451–62.
Schiller rejected science as too materialistic and opposed abstract formulas and
the objective mathematical analysis of nature. The spirit of exact scientific research
was alien to him and incompatible with his pantheism. May compares Goethe's and
Schiller's attitudes toward science and nature, mentions their exchange of ideas, and
cites Schiller's *Anthologie vom Jahre 1782*, his medical treatises, and his philosophical
letters.

1296.   Richards, David B. "Mesmerism in *Die Jungfrau von Orleans.*" *PMLA* 91
        (1976): 856–70.
Traces Schiller's acquaintance with the principles of mesmerism and discusses
their application in *Die Jungfrau*.

1297.   Waldeck, Marie-Luise. "Shadows, Reflexions, Mirror-Images and Virtual
        'Objects' in 'Die Künstler' and Their Relation to Schiller's Concept of
        'Schein.' " *MLR* 58 (1963): 33–37.
Speculates about the derivation of Schiller's aesthetic term *Schein*. Schiller's use
of the term in "Die Künstler" suggests an origin in the science of optics.

1298.   Wells, George A. "Astrology in Schiller's *Wallenstein.*" *JEGP* 68 (1969):
        100–15.
Measures the extent to which astrological explanations are used to interpret the
behavior of Wallenstein in Schiller's trilogy.

Christopher Smart (1722–71)

1299.   Adams, Francis D. "*Jubilate Agno* and the 'Theme of Gratitude.' " *PLL* 3
        (1967): 195–209.
Concerns in part Smart's attempt, in the "a posteriori" portion of *Jubilate Agno*,
to construct a divine physics opposing Newtonian physics.

1300.   Friedman, John B. "The Cosmology of Praise: Smart's *Jubilate Agno.*"
        PMLA 82 (1967): 250–56.
Analyzes Smart's cosmology in *Jubilate Agno* with reference to his treatment of
four main personages in the poem: the psalmist David; the musician Orpheus;
Newton; and Smart's cat, Jeoffry. Contrasts the poem's imagery with the quasi-
scientific tenor of the period.

1301.   Greene, D. J. "Smart, Berkeley, the Scientists and the Poets: A Note on
        Eighteenth-Century Anti-Newtonianism." *JHI* 14 (1953): 327–52.
Explores Smart's anti-Newtonian sentiments as anticipating the Romantic revolt
against Newtonianism. A comparison of passages from Smart's *Jubilate Agno* with
passages from Berkeley's *First Dialogue between Hylas and Philonus* and other works
reveals striking epistemological similarities. Greene stresses the importance of Berke-
lean idealism in shaping resistance to the epistemological and ontological principles
of Newton, R. Descartes, and Locke and thus clearing a way for the validation of
poetic endeavor in an age dominated by scientism.

1302.   Kuhn, Albert J. "Christopher Smart: The Poet as Patriot of the Lord."
         ELH 30 (1963): 121–36.

Studies Smart's religious motives for composing *Jubilate Agno*, commenting briefly
on the relation between his prophetic mission and his use of physicotheological
analogies in the work.

1303.   Williamson, Karina. "Smart's *Principia*: Science and Anti-Science in *Jubilate
         Agno*." *RES* ns 30 (1979): 409–22.

The scientific material in Smart's *Jubilate Agno* is secondhand, undisciplined, and
outdated, yet it contains the basic plan for his projected, but never completed,
Principia.

Tobias George Smollett (1721–71)

1304.   Jones, Claude E. "Tobias Smollett (1721–1771)—The Doctor as Man of
         Letters." *JHM* 12 (1957): 337–48.

Provides biographical information on Smollett, stressing his medical training,
and surveys his contributions to medical literature. Comments on his allusions to
medical practice and belief; his portrayal of physicians, apothecaries, and surgeons;
and the medical imagery and terminology in novels such as *Humphry Clinker*, *Roderick
Random*, and *Peregrine Pickle*.

1305.   Moss, Harold Gene. "The Surgeon's Mate: Tobias Smollett and *The Ad-
         ventures of Roderick Random*." *Medicine and Literature*. Ed. Enid Rhodes
         Peschel. New York: Watson, 1980. 35–38.

In five episodes in the middle ten chapters of *Roderick Random* the protagonist
confronts a series of biological threats. Smollett may have based these incidents on
his experiences as a physician.

1306.   Rousseau, George S. "Doctors and Medicine in the Novels of Tobias Smol-
         lett." *DA* 27 (1966–67): 2160A.

Discusses Smollett's use of science and medicine in shaping the structure and
content of his novels and examines *Sir Launcelot Greaves*, *Humphry Clinker*, and other
works in this light.

1307.   ———. "Matt Bramble and the Sulphur Controversy in the xviiith Cen-
         tury: Medical Background of *Humphry Clinker*." *JHI* 28 (1967): 577–89.

Finds the medical context of Smollett's *Humphry Clinker* in the eighteenth-century
scientific controversy over the definition of sulfur, which was discussed in medical
treaties such as Lucas's *Cursory Remarks* (1764) and *Essay on Waters* (1756).

1308.   ———. "Smollett's 'Acidum Vagum.' " *Isis* 58 (1967): 244–45.

Smollett's reference to the "vague acid" in *The Adventures of Sir Launcelot Greaves*
(1760–62) has precedents in eighteenth-century chemical texts such as Boerhaave's
Elementa Chemiae (1732).

1309.   Sena, John F. "Smollett's Matthew Bramble and the Tradition of the
         Physician-Satirist." *PLL* 11 (1975): 380–96.

Maintains that Smollett's Matthew Bramble is not an autobiographical character. "Rather, Bramble is a fictive creation, a consciously drawn satiric persona derived from a literary tradition which reached its apogee in the Renaissance and continued to be popular throughout the eighteenth century. Bramble is a physician-satirist, a satiric persona who describes and responds to reality in medical terms."

Laurence Sterne (1713–68)

1310.   DePorte, Michael V. *Nightmares and Hobbyhorses: Swift, Sterne, and Augustan Ideas of Madness*. San Marino: Huntington Library, 1974. 164 pp.
See item 1324 for annotation.

1311.   Furst, Daniel C. "Sterne and Physick: Images of Health and Disease in *Tristram Shandy*." *DAI* 35 (1974–75): 3738A.
Establishes the coherence of Sterne's medical imagery in *Tristram Shandy* by comparing it with the eighteenth-century medical theories of Boerhaave and Cheyne.

1312.   Greenberg, Bernard L. "Laurence Sterne and Chambers' *Cyclopaedia*." *MLN* 69 (1954): 560–62.
Suggests that Sterne consulted E. Chambers's *Cyclopaedia* for various details of *Tristram Shandy*, including references to the nose, the brain, and the cesarean operation.

1313.   Holtz, William. "Field Theory and Literature." *CentR* 11 (1967): 532–48.
See item 68 for annotation.

1314.   Landa, Louis A. "The Shandean Homunculus: The Background of Sterne's 'Little Gentleman.' " *Restoration and Eighteenth-Century Literature: Essays in Honor of Alan Dugald McKillop*. Ed. Carroll Camden. Chicago: U of Chicago P for William Marsh Rice U, 1963. 49–68.
Sterne's description of the homunculus in *Tristram Shandy* is based on the work of such late-seventeenth-century biologists as Graff, Harvey, Leeuwenhoek, Malpighi, and Swammerdam. Landa outlines the views on embryology reflected in the theory of preformation and in the controversy between the ovists and the animalculists.

1315.   New, Melvyn. "Laurence Sterne and Henry Baker's *The Microscope Made Easy*." *SEL* 10 (1970): 591–604.
Sterne's concept of time and duration was influenced by his interest in microscopic science. New examines Sterne's treatment of the concept in *Tristram Shandy* with reference to Baker's *Microscope Made Easy* (1742).

1316.   Rodgers, James S. "Ideas of Life: *Tristram Shandy* and Contemporary Medicine and Physiology." Diss. U of East Anglia, 1978.
Not seen for annotation.

1317.   ———. " 'Life' in the Novel: *Tristram Shandy* and Some Aspects of Eighteenth-Century Physiology." *ECLife* 6 (1980): 1–20.

Suggests that the development of character and narrative technique in *Tristram Shandy* parallels developments in eighteenth-century physiology and natural history. Especially relevant is the contemporary scientific shift from mechanist and vitalist theories of life to an organicist conception. *"Tristram Shandy* and the nascent life sciences evolve out of shared preconceptions about the constitution of knowledge and the characteristics of life."

Jonathan Swift (1667–1745)

1318. André, Robert. "Les instruments d'optique du doyen." *NRF* 160 (1966): 677–88.

Comments on Swift's fascination with optical instruments such as microscopes and magnifying lenses and discusses their power to transform our perception of reality. Sees a reflection of this power in *Gulliver's Travels*, where Swift examines reality from different perspectives, as if through lenses that enlarge or reduce reality.

1319. Ashley Montagu, M. F. "Tyson's *Orang-outang, sive homo sylvestris* and Swift's *Gulliver's Travels*." *PMLA* 59 (1944): 84–89.

Suggests that in creating *Gulliver's Travels* Swift probably drew information from Tyson's *Orang-outang, sive homo sylvestris* (1699), which presents anatomical observations of apes, chimpanzees, and monkeys.

1320. Bracher, Frederick. "The Maps in *Gulliver's Travels*." *HLQ* 8 (1944–45): 59–74.

The maps in *Gulliver's Travels* were based on the work of the cartographer Herman Moll. Bracher discusses Swift's role in including the maps in his text, his interest in maps generally, and the possible identity of the producer of the maps.

1321. Canavan, Thomas L. "Madness and Enthusiasm in Burton's *Anatomy of Melancholy* and Swift's *Tale of a Tub*." *DAI* 34 (1973): 269A.

See item 760 for annotation.

1322. Canseliet, Eugene. "L'hermetisme dans la vie de Swift et dans ses 'voyages.' " *CS* 44 (1957): 15–30.

Swift's names for people and places in *Gulliver's Travels* commonly have hidden meanings, the key to which lies in the terminology and formulas of alchemical and cabalistic literature.

1323. Cobb, Joann P. "Jonathan Swift and Epistemology: A Study of Swift's Satire on Ways of Knowing." *DAI* 36 (1975–76): 3647A.

Studies Swift's *Tale of a Tub* and *Gulliver's Travels* as representative of his attacks on scientific method and on the epistemologies of R. Descartes, Hobbes, Locke, and Berkeley.

1324. DePorte, Michael V. *Nightmares and Hobbyhorses: Swift, Sterne, and Augustan Ideas of Madness*. San Marino: Huntington Library, 1974. 164 pp.
Rev. Leo Braudy, *YR* ns 64 (1974–75): 620–26; T. R. Steiner, *JEGP* 74 (1975): 245–47; Patricia Meyer Spacks, *MP* 73 (1975–76): 305–10; Lodwick Hartley, *SAQ* 75 (1976): 136–37.

Examines various theories of mental disorder formulated by English philosophers and physicians from 1660 to 1760 and discusses how the works of Swift and Sterne engage the issues raised by the abnormal psychology of the period. Focuses on Swift's *Tale of a Tub* and Sterne's *Tristram Shandy*.

1324a.   Eddy, William A. Gulliver's Travels: *A Critical Study*. Princeton: Princeton UP; London: Oxford UP, 1923. 216 pp.
Cites numerous sources for *Gulliver's Travels*, including several with scientific content, such as the imaginary voyages of Cyrano de Bergerac, Rabelais, Defoe, and Holberg.

1325.   Frietzsche, Arthur H. "The Impact of Applied Science upon the Utopian Ideal." *BYUS* 3.3–4 (1960–61): 35–42.
See item 495 for annotation.

1326.   Gingerich, Owen. "The Satellites of Mars: Prediction and Discovery." *Journal for the History of Astronomy* 1 (1970): 109–15.
Discusses Swift's prediction in *Gulliver's Travels* of the existence of two martian satellites and comments on the circumstances surrounding Asaph Hall's actual discovery of the moons in 1877.

1327.   Gould, S. H. "Gulliver and the Moons of Mars." *JHI* 6 (1945): 91–101.
Discusses Swift's prediction in the "Voyage to Laputa" of two moons around Mars and examines the astronomical accuracy of his description and its relation to Newton's *Principia*.

1328.   Griffith, George W. "Jonathan Swift's Relation to Science." *DA* 31 (1970–71): 1229A.
Studies the historical scientific context of Swift's criticism and satire of science.

1329.   Hawkins, Sherman H. "Swift's Physical Imagery: The Medical Background and the Theological Tradition." *DA* 21 (1961): 3451.
Examines the Pauline "body of sin" and the satire of illnesses such as "Spleen" and "Melancholy" in *Gulliver's Travels* and *A Tale of a Tub*.

1330.   Hill, John M. "Corpuscular Fundament: Swift and the Mechanical Philosophy." *EnlE* 6 (1975): 37–49.
Examines Swift's satiric critique of mechanical philosophy in the Academy of Lagado section of *Gulliver's Travels*, with special reference to Boyle's version of corpuscular theory.

1330a.   Hönncher, E. "Quellen zu Dean Jonathan Swift's *Gulliver's Travels* (1727)." *Anglia* 10 (1887): 397–427.
Studies Cyrano de Bergerac's imaginary voyages to the moon and the sun as major sources of Swift's *Gulliver's Travels*.

1330b.   Hübener, Gustav. "Die Entstehung von *Gulliver's Travels* und die 'Curiosity'-Kultur." *Neophil* 7 (1921): 35–57.
Suggests that the seventeenth-century vogue of science and of scientists as collectors of "curiosities" was a source of *Gulliver's Travels*.

1331. Kiernan, Colin. "Swift and Science." *Historical Journal* 14 (1971): 709–22.

Maintains that Swift's criticism of Newtonian science was aimed at the uselessness and the moral degeneracy of Newton's system. Swift attempted to steer a middle course between the extreme mechanism of Newtonianism and the extreme organicism of Paracelsian science, and his naturalistic explanation of the universe tended to undergird his religious beliefs.

1332. LaCasce, Steward. "Swift on Medical Extremism." *JHI* 31 (1970): 599–606.

Examines Gulliver's pronouncements on medicine in the context of the controversy over ancient and modern learning. Gulliver may have represented for Swift "the epitome of the eighteenth-century medical extremist."

1333. Leonard, David C. "Swift, Whiston, and the Comet." *ELN* 16 (1978–79): 284–87.

Argues that Whiston's *New Theory of the Earth* (1696), rather than Halley's conclusion to his *Synopsis* (1705), is the probable source for the Laputans' dread of comets in book 3 of *Gulliver's Travels*.

1333a. McGowan, Joseph P. "Gulliver's Third Voyage: Survey and Revaluation." *DA* 27 (1966): 1376A–77A.

Studies the history of the third voyage's critical reputation. Chapters 2 and 3 examine scholarship devoted to the literary and scientific sources of the voyage.

1334. Merton, Robert C. "The 'Motionless' Motion of Swift's Flying Island." *JHI* 27 (1966): 275–77.

Explains the physics underlying Swift's flying island in the "Voyage to Laputa" and speculates on his satirical intentions in creating the image.

1335. Moog, Florence. "Gulliver Was a Bad Biologist." *SciAm* 179.5 (1948): 52–55.

Outlines the physical and biological impossibilities in Swift's description of the Lilliputians and Brobdingnagians in *Gulliver's Travels*.

1335a. Moore, John R. "The Geography of *Gulliver's Travels*." *JEGP* 40 (1941): 214–28.

Examines the five maps that describe the imaginary voyages of *Gulliver's Travels* and argues that Swift's incredible geography—yet another attack on false learning—indicates that "his contempt for natural science carried over into the field of geography."

1336. Nicolson, Marjorie, and Nora M. Mohler. "The Scientific Background of Swift's *Voyage to Laputa*." *AnS* 2 (1937): 299–334. Rpt. in *Science and Imagination*. Ithaca: Great Seal, 1956. Hamden: Archon, 1976. 110–54.

"The mathematicians who feared the sun and comet, the projectors of the Grand Academy, the Flying Island—these came to Swift almost entirely from contemporary science. The sources for nearly all the theories of the Laputans and the Balnibarians are to be found in the work of Swift's contemporary scientists and particularly in the *Philosophical Transactions of the Royal Society*."

1337.   ———. "Swift's 'Flying Island' in the *Voyage to Laputa*." *AnS* 2 (1937): 405–30.
Demonstrates that details of the structure and mechanism of Swift's flying island were drawn from contemporary science. The episode combines theories of magnetism involving lodestones, contemporary interest in "flying chariots," speculations about the world in the moon, and other scientific elements.

1338.   Olson, Robert C. "The Scientific Milieu of Jonathan Swift." Diss. U of Colorado, 1952. Abstract in *University of Colorado Studies* gen. ser. 29.1 (1952): 206–09.
Analyzes Swift's relation to the science of his day, emphasizing developments in cosmology and physiology and their impact on his satire of science and medicine in *Gulliver's Travels* and *A Tale of a Tub*.

1339.   Ong, Walter J., SJ. "Swift on the Mind: Satire in a Closed Field." *MLQ* 15 (1954): 208–21. Rpt. in *Rhetoric, Romance, and Technology*. Ithaca: Cornell UP, 1971. 190–212.
Partly concerns how the scientific and mechanistic ideas of Swift's day influenced his view of the cognitive function of poetry.

1340.   Owens, Robert R. "Jonathan Swift's Hostility to Science." *DA* 16 (1956): 115–16.
Examines two aspects of Swift's evaluation of science: the utility of science and the relation between science and truth.

1341.   Phillips, Mabel. "Jonathan Swift's Relations to Science." *DA* 29 (1968): 236A.
This overview of the great and varied influence of the scientific movement on Swift and his works analyzes his satire of science, scientific method, and astrology in *A Tale of a Tub*, *The Battle of the Books*, and *Gulliver's Travels*.

1342.   Potter, George R. "Swift and Natural Science." *PQ* 20 (1941): 97–118.
Contends that the satire of science in the third voyage of *Gulliver's Travels* is artistically ineffective because of Swift's casual and superficial understanding of natural science. Provides an overview of his scientific sources and activities.

1343.   Probyn, Clive T. "Swift and the Physicians: Aspects of Satire and Status." *MedH* 18 (1974): 249–61.
Discusses Swift's contemptuous satirical attacks on the medical profession—especially surgical practices—in *Gulliver's Travels* and *A Tale of a Tub*. Emphasizes the conflict between medicine and morality as reflected in the character of Gulliver.

1344.   ———. "Swift's Anatomy of the Brain: The Hexagonal Bite of Poetry." *N&Q* ns 21 (1974): 250–51.
Swift derived his imagery of the brain's anatomy for *A Tale of a Tub* from Wotton's *Reflections upon Ancient and Modern Learning* (1694).

1345.   Sena, John F. "Swift, the Yahoos and 'The English Malady.' " *PLL* 7
         (1971): 300–03.
Swift's description of the Yahoos' medical disorder, the spleen, a common disease
in Augustan England, was based on popular contemporary medical theories.

1346.   Starkman, Miriam K. "Quakers, Phrenologists, and Jonathan Swift." *JHI*
         20 (1959): 403–12.
Examines the structure and content of Americanus's *Tale of a Tub: Part Second*
(1826), a defense of Quakerism that attacks the abuses of contemporary religion and
learning and criticizes the new pseudoscience of phrenology. Compares Americanus's
tract with its literary model, Swift's *Tale of a Tub* (1704).

1347.   ————. *Swift's Satire on Learning in* A Tale of a Tub. Diss. Columbia U,
         1950. Princeton: Princeton UP, 1950. New York: Octagon, 1968. 159
         pp.
         Rev. Harold Williams, *RES* ns 5 (1954): 86–87.
Maintains that *A Tale of a Tub* is best understood in the light of the seventeenth-
century controversy over ancient and modern learning. In the *Tale*, Swift gives vent
to his predominantly ancient temper and satirizes perceived abuses in modern philosophy, science, criticism, and religion. Starkman analyzes how the book's structure
is determined by the satire on learning and examines Swift's satiric repudiation of
Epicureanism, occultism, Hobbism, modern logic, and aspects of the "new science"
such as Baconian utilitarianism, Cartesian universalism, and scientific societies.

1348.   Steensma, Robert C. "The Influence of Sir William Temple on the Mind
         and Art of Jonathan Swift." *DA* 31 (1970–71): 1815A–16A.
Temple's influence on Swift's scientific ideas is discernible in the *Battle of the
Books*, *A Tale of a Tub*, and *Gulliver's Travels*.

1349.   Todd, Dennis. "Laputa, the Whore of Babylon, and the Idols of Science."
         SP 75 (1978): 93–120.
Swift's attacks on science in the "Voyage to Laputa" episode of book 3 of *Gulliver's
Travels* involve complex allusions to the historical Babylon and its idols as well as
references to the idols of science outlined by F. Bacon.

1350.   Tuveson, Ernest. "Swift and the World-Makers." *JHI* 11 (1950): 54–74.
Discusses Swift's satire of the physicotheological theories of T. Burnet, Temple,
and others in the 1690s.

James Thomson (1700–48)

1351.   Cronk, Gertrude G. "Lucretius and Thomson's Autumnal Fogs." *AJP* 51
         (1930): 233–42.
Assesses the influence of Lucretian theory and principle on Thomson's description
of autumnal fogs in "Autumn," especially lines 707–35.

1352.   Drennon, Herbert. "James Thomson's Contact with Newtonianism and
         His Interest in Natural Philosophy." *PMLA* 49 (1934): 71–80.

Traces Thomson's educational background at the University of Edinburgh to assess his interest in Newton and the work of natural scientists such as F. Bacon and Boyle and to determine their influence on his poetry.

1353.   ———. "James Thomson's Ethical Theory and Scientific Rationalism."
          PQ 14 (1935): 70–82.
Examines the ethical theory in Thomson's poetry, emphasizing the influence of scientific rationalists such as Barrow, Bentley, S. Clarke, and Wollaston.

1354.   ———. "Newtonianism in James Thomson's Poetry." *ESt* 70 (1936):
          358–72.
An analysis of poems such as *The Seasons*, *Liberty*, and *To the Memory of Sir Isaac Newton* reveals that the foundation of Thomson's theological orientation and philosophy of life was the scientific rationalism characteristic of Newtonianism.

1355.   ———. "Scientific Rationalism and James Thomson's Poetic Art." *SP* 31
          (1934): 453–71.
Maintains that Thomson's poetic theory and practice is a logical extension of the scientific principles established by Newton and other adherents of the "new science." Thomson's view of nature in the preface to the second edition of *Winter* (1726) accords with the mood and intent of scientific rationalism, and his scientific orientation toward natural phenomena, reflected repeatedly in *The Seasons*, dominates his artistic perspective.

1356.   Haas, Rudolf. "Newton und Thomson: Naturwissenschaft und Dichtung
          in der englischen Lyrik des 18. Jahrhunderts." *Wege zur englischen Lyrik in
          Wissenschaft und Unterricht: Interpretationen.* Heidelberg: Quelle, 1962. 49–
          71.
Eighteenth-century English lyric poets conceived of heaven and the celestial bodies in anthropocosmical terms. Haas examines in particular Thomson's attempt to poeticize science and discusses *The Seasons* as a poetic study of light influenced by Newton's optics.

1357.   Hamilton, Horace E. "Travel and Science in Thomson's 'Seasons.' " *DA*
          30 (1969–70): 4945A–46A.
Traces the geographical and scientific sources of Thomson's poetry.

1358.   McKillop, Alan Dugald. *The Background of Thomson's* Seasons. Minneapolis:
          U of Minnesota P; London: Milford–Oxford UP, 1942. Hamden: Archon,
          1961. 191 pp.
          Rev. J. C. Bryce, *MLR* 38 (1943): 258–59; Hoxie N. Fairchild, *MLN*
          58 (1943): 643–44; James R. Sutherland, *RES* 19 (1943): 218–20.
Focuses on the philosophic and scientific background of *The Seasons* and discusses its interaction with Thomson's religious views, especially his understanding of physicotheology. Treats Thomson's poetic use of astronomy, botany, microscopic science, meteorology, Newtonian optics, and the literature of geography and travel.

1359.   Potter, George R. "James Thomson and the Evolution of Spirits." *ESt* 61
          (1926–27): 57–65.

Thomson's theory of spiritual evolution in *The Seasons* was based on a synthesis of Pythagorean metampsychosis with the conception of a chain of being. Contrary to what some have supposed, the theory bears no relation to later evolutionary hypotheses by C. Darwin and others, though Thomson may have "caught a dim speculative glimpse" of the concept of organic evolution.

Voltaire (1694–1778)

1360.   Barber, W. H. "The Genesis of Voltaire's *Micromégas*." *FS* 11 (1957): 1–15.
Analyzes *Micromégas* and attempts to establish, on the basis of internal evidence such as Voltaire's criticisms of Leibniz, that the work was written in 1752 and not, as had been supposed, in 1739. It contains "in addition to the scientific elements basic to the original conception, which had their origin in Voltaire's scientific preoccupations of the 1730s, a body of new material, allusions, attitudes and ideas, closely bound up with his activities and outlook at the time he was writing."

1361.   ———. "Voltaire's Astronauts." *FS* 30 (1976): 28–42.
Analyzes Voltaire's depiction of astronauts and astral voyages in *Traité de métaphysique*, *Discours en vers sur l'homme*, *Le voyage du baron de Gangan*, and *Micromégas*, with a view toward demonstrating the Newtonian and Copernican influence on this imagery.

1362.   Brown, Harcourt. "Science and the Human Comedy: Voltaire." *Daedalus* 87.1 (1958): 25–34.
Assesses the impact of the seventeenth-century scientific revolution on Voltaire's humanism.

1363.   Engstrom, Alfred G. "Lucretius and Micromégas." *Romance Studies Presented to William Morton Dey on the Occasion of His Seventieth Birthday by His Colleagues and Former Students*. Ed. Urban T. Holmes, Jr., Alfred G. Engstrom, and Sturgis E. Leavitt. Chapel Hill: U of North Carolina P, 1950. 59–60.
Voltaire's inspiration for his characterizations of the giant, Micromégas, and the dwarf-giant from Saturn in *Micromégas* may have come from Lucretius's speculations about similar creatures in *De rerum natura* 1.199–202.

1364.   Epstein, Julia L. "Voltaire's Myth of Newton." *PCP* 14 (1979): 27–33.
Voltaire popularized the myth linking a falling apple with Newton's discovery of gravity; he may have understood the apple myth as a metaphoric reversal of the consequences of original sin.

1365.   Folkierski, Wladyslaw. "Voltaire contre Fontenelle ou la présence Copernic." *Literature and Science*. Proc. of the Sixth Triennial Congress of the Federation for Modern Languages and Literatures. Oxford, 1954. Oxford: Blackwell, 1955. 174–84.
Voltaire's alleged critique of Fontenelle in *Micromégas* (1752) actually takes over

Fontenelle's popularized exposition of Copernican heliocentricity in the *Entretiens sur la pluralité des mondes* (1686). The close textual relation between these two works has been obscured by Voltaire's satiric approach to the *person* of Fontenelle in *Micromégas*. In fact, *Micromégas* offers an initial example of a literary imagination seizing Copernican theories, two hundred years after their promulgation.

1366.   Fontius, Martin. *Voltaire in Berlin. Zur Geschichte der bei G. C. Walther veröffentlichten Werke Voltaires.* Neue Beiträge zur Literaturwissenschaft 24. Berlin: Rütten, 1966. 257 pp.

On pages 69–90 the author examines the circumstances under which Voltaire's *Micromégas* was published, elucidates the novel's philosophico-ideological background, and shows the work to be a reflection of the early-eighteenth-century philosophical controversy over Newton's law of attraction. Voltaire, while ridiculing the French secretary of the Academy of Sciences—Bernard de Fontenelle—who endorsed Cartesian physics, supports Newton's thesis that attraction is a fundamental law of nature.

1367.   Kahane, Ernest. "Micromégas et l'anticipation scientifique." *Europe* 37.361–62 (1959): 129–36.

Maintains that Voltaire's *Micromégas* exhibits characteristics that could qualify it as science fiction, such as its references to astronomy, geometry, and physics and its attempt to be scientifically plausible. Unlike science fiction, though, *Micromégas* does not try to predict future technologies, but it does display a faith in human inventiveness.

1368.   Kiernan, C. "Voltaire and Science: A Religious Interpretation." *Journal of Religious History* 4 (1966): 14–27.

"As well as employing science to prove the truth of his Deist belief in a God who created the universe in its present form and who had thereafter supervised its functioning, Voltaire always had in mind the importance of science for instruction, to reduce ignorance. As a popularizer of science, Voltaire continued a tradition introduced by Fontenelle of forging a link between science and literature, of writing about science in a manner comprehensible to non-scientists, a trend which has continued from that time."

1369.   Perkins, Merle L. "Concepts of Necessity in Voltaire's *Poème sur le désastre de Lisbonne.*" *KFLQ* 3 (1956): 21–28.

Discusses aspects of pessimism and optimism regarding humankind's fate and the human condition in Voltaire's poem. Emphasizes his concept of hope in relation to mechanical and providential necessity.

1370.   Redshaw, Adrienne M. "Voltaire and Lucretius." *SVEC* 189 (1980): 19–43.

Traces Voltaire's attitude toward the literary, scientific, philosophical, and ethical aspects of *De rerum natura.*

1371.   Vartanian, Aram. "Voltaire's Quarrel with Maupertuis: Satire and Science." *ECr* 7 (1967): 252–58.

Voltaire's attitude toward science is revealed in his satirical attack on Maupertuis and experimentalism in the *Histoire du Docteur Akakia*.

1372. Wade, Ira O. *Voltaire and Candide: A Study in the Fusion of History, Art, and Philosophy*. Princeton Publication in Modern Language 11. Princeton: Princeton UP, 1959. Port Washington: Kennikat, 1972. 369 pp.
Rev. W. H. Barber, *MLR* 56 (1961): 427–29; William F. Bottiglia, *MLN* 76 (1961): 171–74; Roger B. Oake, *CL* 13 (1961): 176–78; C. D. Rouillard, *MP* 60 (1962–63): 145–49.

A detailed analysis of *Candide*'s religious, philosophical, and scientific background. Of special importance is Voltaire's relation to the eighteenth-century controversy regarding the physical and metaphysical systems of R. Descartes, Newton, and Leibniz. Wade also remarks on Voltaire's response to Pope's *Essay on Man*; the genesis of *Candide* and its relation to Voltaire's earlier works, such as *Scarmentado* and *Le poème sur le désastre de Lisbonne*; the composition and publication of *Candide*; and *Candide*'s structure, plot, meaning, and characterization.

1373. ———. *Voltaire's* Micromégas: *A Study in the Fusion of Science, Myth, and Art*. Princeton Publication in Modern Language 10. Princeton: Princeton UP, 1950. 190 pp.
Rev. Emile Malakis, *MLN* 66 (1951): 347–48.

Maintains that *Micromégas* fuses elements of seventeenth-century physics, astronomy, and biology with elements of speculative metaphysics. Surveys Voltaire's scientific reading from 1734 to 1739 and traces the philosophic and scientific traditions that culminated in his *Eléments de la philosophie de Newton* and *Traité de métaphysique*. Major influences include Galileo, Newton, Leeuwenhoek, Pascal, and Leibniz. Wade also considers the literary tradition from which *Micromégas* arose, especially its relation to Swift's *Gulliver's Travels*.

1374. ———. "Voltaire's Quarrel with Science." *BuR* 8 (1958–59): 287–98.

Comments on Voltaire's view of the limitations of science and its relation to metaphysics, religion, and morality as reflected in *Candide*, *Traité de métaphysique*, and *Eléments de la philosophie de Newton*.

1375. Waldinger, Renée. "Voltaire and Medicine." *SVEC* 58 (1967): 1777–1806.

Preoccupied with his ill health, Voltaire consulted numerous medical books and sought out the medical doctors and practices of his day. Waldinger suggests that Voltaire's medical considerations are indirectly responsible for his literary works.

1376. Walters, Robert L. "Voltaire and the Newtonian Universe: A Study of the *Eléments de la philosophie de Newton*." *DA* 16 (1956): 540.

The impact of Newtonian science on Voltaire's intellectual growth is reflected in the *Eléments de la philosophie de Newton*, Voltaire's attempt to popularize Newtonian philosophy.

Nineteenth Century

Studies and Surveys

1377. Abel, Richard M. "Scientific Imagination and the American Novel." *DAI* 39 (1979): 7400A.

Analyzes the interaction of scientific imagination and artistic expression in American literature and culture between 1870 and 1920. Concentrates on the work of William Dean Howells.

1378. Abrams, M. H. "Science and Poetry in Romantic Criticism." In *The Mirror and the Lamp: Romantic Theory and the Critical Tradition*. New York: Oxford UP, 1953. New York: Norton, 1958. 298–335.

Focusing primarily on the views of Coleridge, Keats, P. Shelley, and Wordsworth, Abrams examines the range of attitudes expressed in Romantic criticism toward the relations of science and poetic sensibility. He discusses critical reactions to positivism and Newtonianism and comments on the relative truth values of science and poetry.

1379. Alcorn, John. *The Nature Novel from Hardy to Lawrence*. Diss. New York U, 1966. New York: Columbia UP; London: Macmillan, 1977. 139 pp. (Abstract in *DA* 29 (1968–69): 251A–52A.)

Rev. R. P. Draper, *CritQ* 19.3 (1977): 91–92; William R. Siebenschuh, *Thought* 52 (1977): 219–21; Romey T. Keys, *NCF* 32 (1977–78): 351–53; Dale Kramer, *MFS* 23 (1977–78): 628–32; Roger Bowen, *SAQ* 77 (1978): 252–53; William Myers, *VS* 22 (1978–79): 355–57.

Traces the development of "naturism" in English fiction, a movement the author defines as strongly influenced by C. Darwin and characterized by a view of the world in which "biology replaces theology as the source both of psychic health and of moral authority." The "naturist" writers studied include Hardy, S. Butler, Carpenter, T. E. Lawrence, Hudson, Kipling, Wells, E. M. Forster, Douglas, and D. H. Lawrence.

1380. Altick, Richard D. "Four Victorian Poets and an Exploding Island." *VS* 3 (1959–60): 249–60.

Discusses the responses of Tennyson, Bridges, Hopkins, and Swinburne to the explosion of Krakatoa in 1883. Notes Tennyson's and Hopkins's lifelong interests in astronomy and remarks that a letter Hopkins wrote to Swinburne about the brilliant sunsets resulting from the explosion contains "a delicate blending of scientific description and aesthetic perception."

1381.   Angenot, Marc. "Science Fiction in France before Verne." *SFS* 5 (1978): 58–66.
Surveys French authors who initiated and helped to define the genre of science fiction before Verne published his first scientific adventure novel, in 1862. Among the works discussed are Restif de la Bretonne's *Les posthumes* (1802), F. Bodin's *Le roman de l'avenir* (1834), J. Geoffroy's *Napoléon apocryphe* (1836), Boitard's *Etudes astronomiques* (1839), and Defontenay's *Star* (1854).

1382.   Appleman, Phillip [sic] D. "Darwin and the Literary Critics." *DA* 15 (1955): 1618.
Examines the impact of the *Origin of Species* on the work of the Victorian literary critics Symonds, Pater, and Stephen.

1382a.   Armytage, W. H. G. "Extrapolators and Exegetes of Evolution." *Extrapolation* 7 (1965): 2–17.
Examines numerous literary treatments of evolution theory, including works by Bulwer-Lytton, S. Butler, and London.

1383.   ———. *Yesterday's Tomorrows: A Historical Survey of Future Societies*. Toronto: U of Toronto P; London: Routledge, 1968. 288 pp.
See item 142 for annotation.

1384.   Asker, David B. D. "The Modern Bestiary: Animal Fiction from Hardy to Orwell." *DAI* 39 (1979): 7338A.
Studies the renewed attention to medieval bestiary art in representative fiction from 1870 to 1945, including works by Hardy, Kipling, Wells, D. H. Lawrence, and Orwell. C. Darwin's *Origin of Species* serves as the thematic point of departure and accounts in part for the "revival in the fortunes of Bestiary art."

1385.   Badt, Kurt. *Wolkenbilder und Wolkengedichte der Romantik*. Berlin: Gruyter, 1960. 117 pp.
Focuses on the representation of cloud formations in early-nineteenth-century poetry and painting to demonstrate the impact of science on the art and literature of that period. Examines Goethe's cloud poems in honor of the English meteorologist Luke Howard, discusses the treatment of meteorological themes in the works of Wordsworth and Constable, and points out the significance of meteorology in Stifter's prose.

1386.   Bailey, J. O. *Pilgrims through Space and Time: Trends and Patterns in Scientific and Utopian Fiction*. New York: Argus, 1947. Westport: Greenwood, 1972. 341 pp.
See item 144 for annotation.

1387.   Beach, Joseph Warren. *The Concept of Nature in Nineteenth-Century English Poetry*. New York: Macmillan, 1936. New York: Pageant, 1956. New York: Russell, 1966. 618 pp.
Rev. Irwin Edman, *JP* 33 (1936): 696–97; Adele B. Ballman, *MLN* 52 (1937): 609–11.

Examines the religious, metaphysical, and scientific doctrines and presuppositions informing the nineteenth-century concept of nature in English poetry and in some American poetry. Focuses on Wordsworth's concept of nature but includes separate chapters on M. Arnold, Browning, Carlyle, Hardy, Meredith, Swinburne, Tennyson, Whitman, P. Shelley's naturalism, and the influence of S. Coleridge and evolution theory on Emerson's nature poetry.

1388.   Bell, Ian F. A. "Divine Patterns: Louis Agassiz and American Men of Letters. Some Preliminary Explorations." *JAmS* 10 (1976): 349–81.
Explores Agassiz's major scientific concerns and cites allusions to the geologist in works by H. Adams, Emerson, Holmes, H. James, W. James, Longfellow, Pound, and Whittier.

1389.   Bender, Bert A. "Let There Be (Electric) Light! The Image of Electricity in American Writing." *ArQ* 34 (1978): 55–70.
Discusses how H. Adams, Hawthorne, Melville, Whitman, O'Neill, Stevens, and others used electricity as metaphor for either salvation or damnation.

1390.   Black, Joel D. "The Second Fall: The Laws of Digression and Gravitation in Romantic Narrative and Their Impact on Contemporary Encyclopaedic Literature." *DAI* 39 (1979): 7331A–32A.
Studies the relation between rhetorical digressions and thematic allusions to Newton's law of gravitation in works by Hegel, Hölderlin, Jean Paul, Kleist, and Sterne.

1391.   Blinderman, Charles S. "The Great Bone Case." *Perspectives in Biology and Medicine* 14 (1970–71): 370–93.
Identifies T. H. Huxley's initiation of the theory of human evolution and discusses how the debate on the concept appeared in popular fiction and the press as well as in intellectual and scientific periodicals.

1392.   Boia, Lucian. "Le roman astronomique: (Seconde moitié du xixᵉ siècle—début du xxᵉ siècle)." *Synthesis* 7 (1980): 145–63.
The progress of astronomy had a tremendous impact on literature from the middle of the nineteenth century to the beginning of the twentieth. The popularization of the science by Camille Flammarion, founder of the Société Astronomique de France, played an important role in the evolution of the astronomical novel. Boia traces the genre's development from 1865 to 1914 and cites, among other works, Flammarion's *Urania*, *Fin du monde*, and *Stella*; Verne's *De la terre à la lune* and *Autour de la lune*; and Wells's *War of the Worlds*, *First Men in the Moon*, and *In the Days of the Comet*.

1393.   Bredeson, Robert C. "Landscape Description in Nineteenth-Century American Travel Literature." *AQ* 20 (1968): 86–94.
Concerns the travel writer's problem of combining scientifically exact description with a sense of grandeur. Discusses literature by Curtis, Greeley, Ludlow, B. Taylor, and others.

1393a.   Brightfield, Myron F. "The Medical Profession in Early Victorian England, As Depicted in the Novels of the Period (1840–1870)." *BHM* 35 (1961): 238–56.

Surveys numerous novels published between 1840 and 1870 and selects excerpts that represent physicians attempting to heal the sick.

1394. Brown, Harcourt. "Tensions and Anxieties: Science and the Literary Culture of France." *Science and the Creative Spirit: Essays on Humanistic Aspects of Science.* Ed. Brown. Toronto: U of Toronto P, 1958. 91–126.
See item 146 for annotation.

1395. Bump, Jerome. "Science, Religion, and Personification in Poetry." *CVE* 7 (1978): 123–37.
Associates the decline of pastoral poetry from Marvell's "Garden" to M. Arnold's "Lines Written in Kensington Gardens" with the gradual intrusion of abstract scientific sensibility into a poetic worldview that saw both humankind and God personified in nature. The modern nature poets' scientific resistance to the pathetic fallacy was overcome by Hopkins, who by ". . . refusing to limit himself to the models fashionable in Victorian science resurrected a sense of a universe animated by powerful cosmic forces."

1396. Burne, Glenn S. "Remy de Gourmont: A Scientific Philosophy of Art." *WHR* 13 (1959): 71–79.
Discusses the scientific roots of Gourmont's aesthetics, including positivist psychology and the laws of selection and heredity. Gourmont influenced writers such as Pound, T. S. Eliot, and Murry.

1397. Burroughs, John. "Science and the Poets." *Cosmopolitan* 5 (1888): 127–30.
Briefly assesses the extent to which science informs the work of poets such as Carlyle, Emerson, Keats, Tennyson, and Whitman.

1398. Burstein, Janet. "Victorian Mythography and the Progress of the Intellect." *VS* 18 (1974–75): 309–24.
The mythographic writings of Clodd, Grote, Pater, and others reflect the Victorian preoccupation with evolutionary speculation and scientific rationalism that influenced attitudes toward the study of myth.

1399. Bush, Douglas. *Science and English Poetry: A Historical Sketch, 1590–1950.* New York: Oxford UP, 1950. Westport: Greenwood, 1980. 166 pp.
See item 147 for annotation.

1400. Cameron, Alex J. "The Image of the Physician in the American Novel 1859 to 1925." *DAI* 33 (1973): 6342A–43A.
Concerns the depiction of the physician as a scientific servant to humankind's spiritual needs.

1401. Cannon, Walter F. "The Normative Role of Science in Early Victorian Thought." *JHI* 25 (1964): 487–502.
Maintains that natural science, especially Newtonian studies, provided the norm of truth in early Victorian thought. Treats in part Wordsworth's changing relation to science and Newtonianism.

1402.   Carter, Ann R. "Songs of the Body Electric: A Model for the Poetic Imagination in Emerson, Whitman, and Hart Crane." *DAI* 39 (1978): 1562A–63A.
Discusses the impact of electricity as a symbol for the creative self in American Romantic poetry.

1403.   Christensen, John M. "New Atlantis Revisited: Science and the Victorian Tale of the Future." *SFS* 5 (1978): 243–49.
Briefly examines several futuristic fantasies published in England between 1870 and 1900. Informed by the metaphor of Darwinian evolution, they tended to reflect a growing disenchantment with science and its social implications. Works studied include F. Hume's *Year of Miracle*, Wells's *Time Machine*, Cobbe's *Age of Science*, Nisbet's *Great Secret*, and Clowes's *Great Peril*.

1404.   Clareson, Thomas D. "The Emergence of American Science Fiction, 1880–1915: A Study of the Impact of Science upon American Romanticism." *DA* 16 (1956): 962.
Maintains that science fiction directly reflects the scientific discoveries and intellectual interests of its age. Examines the emergence of the genre in America in the light of the contemporary psychology, geology, astronomy, chemistry, physics, and political science.

1405.   Clark, Cumberland. *Astronomy in the Poets*. Bournemouth: Sydenham, 1922. Folcroft: Folcroft, 1969. Norwood: Norwood, 1975. Philadelphia: West, 1978. 116 pp.
See item 530 for annotation.

1406.   Clark, Harry H. "The Influence of Science on American Literary Criticism, 1860–1910, including the Vogue of Taine." *TWA* 44 (1955): 109–64.
Surveys major critical essays by J. Burroughs, Stedman, Howells, H. James, Twain, Payne, and others, stressing the relation between these works and Zola's naturalism, Taine's literary theory, and the evolutionary theories of C. Darwin and Spencer. A large section cites the responses of American literary critics to Taine's critical tenets.

1407.   Clarke, I. F. "Science Fiction: Past and Present." *QR* 295 (1957): 260–70.
Surveys thematic developments in science fiction from the nineteenth to the twentieth century, noting especially the influence of Darwinism. The authors considered include Hay, Bulwer-Lytton, Hudson, Wells, and A. Huxley.

1408.   Cohen, I. Bernard. "Maxwell's Poetry." *SciAm* 186.3 (1952): 62–63.
Reproduces some untitled and previously unpublished verses by the nineteenth-century physicist James Clerk Maxwell. The poems satirize the British Association for the Advancement of Science.

1409.   Conner, Frederick William. *Cosmic Optimism: A Study of the Interpretation of Evolution by American Poets from Emerson to Robinson*. Gainesville: U of Florida P, 1949. New York: Octagon, 1973. 458 pp.
Rev. Harry Hayden Clark, *AL* 22 (1950–51): 189–92.

Provides a historical survey of the philosophic, religious, and scientific background of the concept of evolutionary cosmic optimism and traces the development of evolutionary meliorism in Emerson, Poe, Whitman, Bryant, Longfellow, J. Lowell, Lanier, Holmes, Robinson, and several minor poets.

1410. Connolly, Francis X. "Newman and Science." *Thought* 38 (1963): 107–21.

Maintains that Newman was a man of "two cultures" who successfully bridged the gap between the sciences and the humanities. Traces the development of Newman's scientific interests and of his view that science, literature, and theology are coordinate rather than antagonistic modes of inquiry. Among the works that reflect this attitude are *Essay on the Development of Christian Doctrine*, *The Idea of a University*, and "Christianity and Scientific Investigation."

1411. Cowley, Malcom. "Naturalism in American Literature." *Evolutionary Thought in America*. Ed. Stow Persons. New Haven: Yale UP, 1950. New York: Braziller, 1956. Hamden: Archon, 1968. 300–33.

Outlines the central features of American naturalism and its impact on American literature generally. Influences include C. Darwin, T. H. Huxley, Spencer, and Zola. Discusses works by S. Crane, Norris, London, Dreiser, and others.

1412. Crouch, Laura E. "The Scientist in English Literature: Domingo Gonsales (1638) to Victor Frankenstein (1817)." *DAI* 36 (1975–76): 2181A.

See item 149 for annotation.

1413. Crum, Ralph B. *Scientific Thought in Poetry*. Diss. Columbia U, 1931. New York: Columbia UP, 1931. New York: AMS, 1966. Folcroft: Folcroft, 1973. 246 pp.

See item 150 for annotation.

1414. Culler, A. Dwight. "The Darwinian Revolution and Literary Form." *The Art of Victorian Prose*. Ed. George Levine and William Madden. New York: Oxford UP, 1968. 224–46.

Maintains that the chief source of C. Darwin's influence on literature, specifically literary form, lies in his dramatic reversal of orthodox thinking about design and adaptation in nature. His turnabout in the realm of evolutionary thought parallels the literary concept of peripeteia, and his discovery "of the true explanation of adaptations in the natural world is analogous to what in comedy we also call a 'discovery' (or recognition scene or *anagnorisis*)." Culler examines Darwin's influence on satiric structure in S. Butler's *Erewhon*, Shaw's *Man and Superman*, and works by Carroll, Pater, and Wilde.

1415. Daiches, David. "Literature and Science in Nineteenth-Century England." *The Modern World*. 1972. Vol. 5 of *Literature and Western Civilization*. Ed. David Daiches and Anthony Thorlby. London: Aldus, 1972–76. 441–59.

Provides an overview of both the symbiosis and the conflict between literature and science in nineteenth-century England. Discusses the Romantic response to science in works by S. Coleridge, Keats, P. Shelley, and Wordsworth; examines the schism between science and religion arising from the influence of Victorian geologists and biologists, especially Lyell and C. Darwin, as reflected in works by Tennyson, Hardy, S. Butler, Shaw, and others; and includes an account of an early stage of the "two cultures" controversy in the debate over education between T. H. Huxley and M. Arnold.

1415a.   Davies, John D. *Phrenology, Fad and Science: A Nineteenth-Century American Crusade*. New Haven: Yale UP, 1955. 203 pp.
"Phrenology and Literature," chapter 10 of this history of phrenology (118–25), describes the use of phrenology by American authors such as Melville, Whitman, and Poe.

1416.   Dean, Dennis R. "Geology and English Literature: Crosscurrents, 1770–1830." *DA* 29 (1968–69): 1864A.
Traces the interrelations between Romantic geological investigation and Romantic literature. Examines geological passages in the writings of Blake, S. Coleridge, E. Darwin, Scott, and Wordsworth.

1417.   ———. "Hitchcock's Dinosaur Tracks." *AQ* 21 (1969): 639–44.
The discovery of fossil tracks in the Connecticut River valley in Massachusetts, described in geologist Edward Hitchcock's *Report on the Geology, Mineralogy, Botany and Zoology of Massachusetts* (1833), elicited the interest of several literary personages, as evidenced by references to the event in works by Holmes, Longfellow, J. Lowell, Melville, Thoreau, and others.

1418.   ———. "The Influence of Geology on American Literature and Thought." *Two Hundred Years of Geology in America*. Ed. Cecil J. Schneer. Hanover: UP of New England, 1979. 289–303.
Ambitiously surveys American literary responses to geology. Includes such figures as Byles, Irving, Bryant, Cooper, Poe, Longfellow, Emerson, Thoreau, Whitman, Melville, Holmes, Twain, H. Adams, Frost, Jeffers, Auden, and Ammons.

1419.   DeBakey, Lois E. "The Physician-Scientist as Character in Nineteenth-Century American Literature." *DA* 24 (1964): 3333–34.
Studies Hawthorne, Holmes, Howells, Jewett, Melville, and Mitchell. Their works reflect "the accomplishments and problems of the medical profession with varying degrees of accuracy."

1420.   De Selincourt, Ernest. "The Interplay of Literature and Science during the Last Three Centuries." *HJ* 37 (1938–39): 225–45.
See item 151 for annotation.

1421.   Drachman, Julian M. *Studies in the Literature of Natural Science*. Diss. Columbia U, 1930. New York: Macmillan, 1930. 487 pp.
           Rev. G. R. Potter, *MLN* 46 (1931): 332–33; Charles A. Kofoid, *Isis* 27 (1937): 89–90.
Surveys and analyzes the literary aspects of nineteenth-century scientific writings. Excludes from consideration popularized science, science fiction, and poetry and

novels influenced by science. Discusses the scientific writings of R. Chambers, Cuvier, C. Darwin, T. H. Huxley, Lyell, H. Miller, Paley, Spencer, and many others, particularly works relating to evolutionary theory.

1422.   Dürler, Josef. *Die Bedeutung des Bergbaus bei Goethe und in der deutschen Romantik*. Wege zur Dichtung. Züricher Schriften zur Literaturwissenschaft 24. Frauenfeld: Huber, 1936. 245 pp.
See item 1140 for annotation.

1423.   Dufour, Louis. *Les écrivains français et la météorologie: De l'âge classique à nos jours*. Brussels: Inst. Royal Météorologique de Belgique, 1966. 122 pp.
Assesses the extent to which the treatment of meteorology in French literature reflects scientific progress and developments and concludes that literary interest in meteorology has been primarily nonscientific. Refers to Bernardin de Saint-Pierre, Chateaubriand, Flaubert, Gautier, Gide, Hugo, Maupassant, Nerval, Proust, Saint-Exupéry, Saint-Simon, Stendhal, Verne, and Zola.

1424.   Dyck, Martin. "Relativity in Physics and in Fiction." *Studies in German Literature of the Nineteenth and Twentieth Centuries. Festschrift for Frederic E. Coenen.* Ed. Siegfried Mews. University of North Carolina Studies in the Germanic Languages and Literatures 67. Chapel Hill: U of North Carolina P, 1970. 174–85.
Briefly treats space-time relations in literary criticism, Goethe's *Faust*, Tolstoy's *War and Peace*, and Mann's *Magic Mountain*.

1425.   Eddy, Willard O. "The Scientific Bases of Naturalism in Literature." *WHR* 8 (1953–54): 219–30.
Traces the roots of literary naturalism to deterministic concepts of causality— concepts that also underlie the mechanistic interpretation of nature characteristic of modern science. Notes especially the influence D. Hume's philosophy had on naturalism.

1426.   Ehrlich, Carol. "Evolutionism and the Female in Selected American Novels 1885–1900." *DAI* 35 (1974–75): 399A.
In the novels of Howells, Holmes, Crane, Dreiser, and others, the theory of evolution through natural selection serves either to support or to reject sexual stereotypes of women.

1427.   Forsyth, R. A. "The Myth of Nature and the Victorian Compromise of the Imagination." *ELH* 31 (1964): 213–40.
Describes the transition from the Romantic mythopoeic view of nature held by poets such as S. Coleridge, P. Shelley, and Wordsworth to the scientific, technologically oriented view of nature and truth that developed in the Victorian age under the influence of Darwinian thinking and other scientific innovations. Depicts this period as abdicating belief in imaginative truth and espousing faith in empirically verifiable facts. Stresses the impact of this approach on Tennyson and other Victorian poets.

1428.   ————. "The Victorian Self-Image and the Emergent City Sensibility."
          UTQ 33 (1963–64): 61–77.
Traces Victorian responses to the encroachment of science, technology, and in-
dustrialism on values and on the rural landscape. Cites G. Eliot, W. Barnes, J.
Thomson (B.V.), Hardy, Tennyson, and others.

1429.   Fox, Arthur W. "The Influence of Science upon Poetry and Fiction."
          Manchester Quarterly 42 (1916). 208–28.
Assesses the benefits and drawbacks of assimilating science and the scientific spirit
into Victorian poetry and fiction. Though judicious use of science in literature can
lead to a higher spiritual unity of the two disciplines, literature's tendencies to
embrace the materialistic basis of science and to exalt the intellectual at the expense
of the emotional should be avoided.

1430.   Francke, Kuno. "The Evolutionary Trend of German Literary Criticism."
          International Monthly 2 (1900): 612–46.
Studies the influence of evolution on metaphysical, sociologico-historical, philological, and psychological stages of German literary criticism. Discusses pre-Darwinian ideas in German criticism from Herder to Hegel, Riehl's and Burckhardt's
critical views, and Volkelt's evolutionary critical method.

1431.   Frost, Alan J. "James Cook and the Early Romantic Imagination." *DA*
          31 (1970–71): 1797A.
Analyzes the process by which the explorational voyages of James Cook came to
influence the Romantic imagination of poets such as S. Coleridge, Southey, and
Wordsworth.

1432.   Fusil, Casimir Alexandre. *La poésie scientifique de 1750 à nos jours*. Paris:
          Scientifica, 1917. 320 pp.
See item 990 for annotation.

1433.   Gainor, Mary E. "Thunder on the Horizon: Hostility to Science in English
          Literature from 1860–1900." Diss. Harvard U, 1974.
Not seen for annotation.

1434.   Gale, Barry G. "Darwin and the Concept of a Struggle for Existence: A
          Study in the Extrascientific Origins of Scientific Ideas." *Isis* 63 (1972):
          321–44.
Traces the metaphor of a struggle for existence in the works of E. Darwin,
Lamarck, R. Chambers, Lyell, and Malthus. The idea was critical both in the
development of a scientific theory and in extrascientific contexts such as economics
and literature.

1435.   Gattégno, Jean. *La Science-Fiction*. "Que sais-je?" Le point des connaissances
          actuelles, 1426. Paris: PUF, 1971. 125 pp.
Reviews the development of science fiction, discussing the major international
contributors, such as Verne, Wells, Poe, E. Burroughs, and Asimov. Examines the
recurring themes that characterize the genre, including human biological and in-

tellectual evolution and the creation of a new society, voyages to other worlds, extraterrestrial beings, and the manipulation of time. Also considers science fiction as ideology, the literary status of the genre, and the dosage of science in current science fiction.

1436. George, Nadine F. "Popular Science and Philosophy in France, 1850–1875." *DAI* 35 (1974–75): 1005A.

Investigates popular literary journalism concerning three areas of scientific thought: cosmogony, theories of matter and motion, and the origin and development of life.

1437. Gerber, Gerald E. "Science vs. Poetry: The Beginnings of the Ideological Significance of a Modern Literary Idea." *DA* 25 (1964–65): 3553.

The historical foundations of the conflict between poetic and scientific ways of thinking are reflected in nineteenth-century literary criticism, particularly the critical writings of Emerson, Poe, and Wordsworth.

1438. Gibbons, Tom H. *Rooms in the Darwin Hotel: Studies in English Literary Criticism and Ideas, 1880–1920.* Nedlands, Austral.: U of Western Australia P, 1973. 164 pp.
Rev. Karl Beckson, *VS* 18 (1974–75): 494–96.

Studies how evolutionist ideas current in 1880–1920 influenced the religious, political, and aesthetic beliefs expressed in the literary criticism of Ellis, Symons, and Orage. The final chapter argues that ". . . orthodox twentieth-century modernism is deeply indebted to the occult symbolist aesthetic that flourished in the evolutionary climate" of the period under consideration.

1439. Gode-von Aesch, Alexander. *Natural Science in German Romanticism.* Diss. Columbia U, 1941. Columbia University Germanic Studies ns 11. Ed. Robert Herndon Fife. New York: Columbia UP, 1941. New York: AMS, 1966. 302 pp.
Rev. Francis R. Johnson, *Isis* 34 (1942–43): 172–73; Ernst Rose, *GR* 18 (1943): 75–76.

Studies the interconnections among poetry, science, and philosophy in German Romanticism, treating such topics as the renewed interest in poetry modeled after Lucretius's *De rerum natura*; the Romantic conception of the unity of organic nature; the problem of evolution; Romantic anthropomorphism; the Romantic concept of nature's infinitude; type and organism; the relation between ego and cosmos; vitalism, mesmerism, and physiognomics; and cosmic poetry. The poets, philosophers, and scientists discussed include J. Brown, Carus, Chénier, Goethe, Herder, Hölderlin, Humboldt, Le Sage, G. Lessing, Novalis, Ritter, Schelling, Schiller, F. Schlegel, Schubert, and Wieland.

1440. Grabo, Carl. "Science and the Romantic Movement." *AnS* 4 (1939): 191–205.

Surveys advances made by eighteenth-century scientists such as Herschel, E. Darwin, and Davy in geology, chemistry, astronomy, botany, and other fields, briefly commenting on the relations between these sciences and the English Romantic literary movement.

1441.   Graham, John. "Lavater's *Physiognomy* in England." *JHI* 22 (1961): 561–72.
Traces the publication history of Lavater's *Essays on Physiognomy* and the rise of its popularity in England during the late eighteenth and early nineteenth centuries. Discusses the work's impact on English literature of this period, including I. Disraeli's *Flim-Flams!*, C. Smith's *Desmond*, and Planché's *Lavater, the Physiognomist: Or, Not a Bad Judge*.

1442.   Habben, Dorothy E. "The Reputation of Sir Francis Bacon among the English Romantics." *DAI* 38 (1977): 804A.
The Romantics' interest in Bacon's scientific and literary achievements flourished with the appearance of Montagu's edition of his works in 1825.

1443.   Haley, Bruce. *The Healthy Body and Victorian Culture*. Cambridge: Harvard UP, 1978. 296 pp.
Rev. Max Byrd, *YR* 68 (1978–79): 612–18; George Levine, *AHR* 84 (1979): 1381; Carl Woodring, *WHR* 33 (1979): 161–63; John Morton Osborne, *VS* 23 (1979–80): 134–35.
Outlines the medical and psychophysiological background of the Victorian obsession with mental and physical health and studies the concept of health as related to Victorian literary criticism and as reflected in literature by Carlyle, Kingsley, and Meredith.

1444.   Hall, Jason Y. "Gall's Phrenology: A Romantic Psychology." *SIR* 16 (1977): 305–17.
Explains the principal features of Franz Joseph Gall's theory of phrenology and notes both its enthusiastic reception by later Romantic writers, such as Balzac, Vigny, Sand, C. Brontë, Baudelaire, Melville, Whitman, and Poe, and its rejection by early Romantics, including the Danish poet Staffeldt, the natural philosopher Steffens, and A. Schlegel.

1445.   Hastings, Harry W. "The Scientific Spirit in the English Novel from 1850 to 1900." Diss. Harvard U, 1916.
Not seen for annotation.

1446.   Haugrud, Raychel A. "Tyndall's Interest in Emerson." *AL* 41 (1969–70): 507–17.
The stylistic details of Tyndall's scientific writings reflect his great admiration for Emerson. Tyndall's "On the Scientific Use of the Imagination" (1870) and "Matter and Force" (1867) exhibit literary and poetic qualities.

1447.   Henkin, Leo J. *Darwinism in the English Novel, 1860–1910: The Impact of Evolution on Victorian Fiction*. New York: Corporate, 1940. New York: Russell, 1963. 303 pp.
Rev. M. F. Ashley-Montagu, *Isis* 33 (1941–42): 343–44; H. V. Routh, *RES* 23 (1947): 87–88.
Examines the impact of evolution theory on religion and on the romance of science as reflected in Victorian fiction. The authors considered include R. D. Blackmore,

S. Butler, Collins, Gissing, Kingsley, Bulwer-Lytton, Meredith, Corelli, Reade, and Wells.

1448. Hillegas, Mark R. "The Cosmic Voyage and the Doctrine of Inhabited Worlds in Nineteenth-Century English Literature." *DA* 17 (1957): 2001–02.

Nineteenth-century scientific and technological innovations and a widening gulf between science and theology contributed to a pronounced realism that was reflected in the literary cosmic voyage. Works studied include Verne's *From the Earth to the Moon* and Wells's *First Men in the Moon*.

1449. Hoeges, Dirk. *Literatur und Evolution. Studien zur französischen Literaturkritik im 19. Jahrhundert. Taine, Brunetière, Hennequin, Guyau*. Heidelberg: Winter, 1980. 213 pp.

In the nineteenth century the orientation of literary criticism changed from a sociohistorical outlook to a perspective determined principally by C. Darwin's *Origin of Species*. Hoeges explains this development in the writings of Brunetière, Hennequin, Guyau, and Taine, emphasizing 1888 to 1890, the apogee of Taine's criticism.

1450. Irvine, William. "The Influence of Darwin on Literature." *PAPS* 103 (1959): 616–28.

Surveys the impact of Darwinism on the Victorian worldview, on literary critics such as Brunetière and Taine, and on authors such as T. H. Huxley, Meredith, Hardy, and S. Butler.

1451. Johnson, William B., and Thomas D. Clareson. "The Interplay of Science and Fiction: The Canals of Mars." *Extrapolation* 5 (1963–64): 37–39. (Followed by "A Checklist to Articles on the Martian 'Canal' Controversy," William B. Johnson, 40–48.)

Discusses how Schiaperelli's 1877 discovery of the "canals" of Mars affected the contemporary literary imagination.

1452. Kapitza, Peter. *Die frühromantische Theorie der Mischung: Über den Zusammenhang von romantischer Dichtungstheorie und zeitgenössischer Chemie*. Münchener Germanistische Beiträge 4. München: Hueber, 1968. 204 pp.

Reviews the history of chemistry in the eighteenth and early nineteenth centuries, with special attention to the chemical handbooks and monographs of the time and concludes that certain chemical concepts and terms are central to the views of poetry and the creative process held by Novalis and the Schlegel brothers.

1453. ———. "Physik der Poesie: Zu einem naturwissenschaftlichen Begriffsmodell im ästhetischen Programm der Frühromantik." *LJGG* 12 (1971): 97–112.

Discusses the application of scientific concepts such as "neutralization," drawn from chemistry, and "indifference," drawn from magnetism, to early Romantic aesthetics, particularly in Novalis, Schelling, and the two Schlegels.

1454.   Kearns, Michael S. "Anatomy of the Mind: Mid-Nineteenth-Century Psychology and the Works of Nathaniel Hawthorne, Charlotte Brontë, Charles Dickens and Herman Melville." *DAI* 41 (1980): 2613A.

Provides an account of the psychological dispositions and presuppositions of the cited authors, emphasizing their attitudes toward physiognomy, phrenology, and mesmerism. Brontë's *Jane Eyre*, Dickens's *Our Mutual Friend*, and Melville's *Typee* are among the works examined.

1455.   Kelly, Alfred H. "Between Poetry and Science: Wilhelm Bölsche as Scientific Popularizer." *DAI* 37 (1976): 532A–33A.

The nonfiction works of the German author Wilhelm Bölsche were instrumental in disseminating Darwinian ideas to the general public. This dissertation examines *Mittagsgöttin* (1891), *Das Liebesleben in der Natur* (1898–1902), and other works.

1456.   Knight, D. M. "The Physical Sciences and the Romantic Movement." HS 9 (1970): 54–75.

Broadly assesses how the Romantic worldview influenced physics and chemistry during the Romantic period and how scientific discoveries affected Romantic poets. Also discusses Hegel's philosophy of science.

1457.   Kragness, Sheila I. "Doctors and Medical Science in the Contemporary French Drama, 1887 to 1939." Diss. U of Minnesota, 1948.

Not seen for annotation.

1458.   Macandrew, Ronald M. "Science in Spanish Poetry from Cabanyes (1808–1833) to Núñez de Arce (1833–1909)." *PQ* 9 (1930): 57–60.

Through the influence of Locke and Hobbes, science and scientific data emerged as factors in Spanish poetry. In the nineteenth century, science divided Spanish poetry into camps—one saw in science the death of poetry, and the other viewed science as the means to truth and as a principal goal of poetic activity.

1459.   Meadows, A. J. *The High Firmament: A Survey of Astronomy in English Literature.* Leicester: Leicester UP, 1969. 207 pp.

See item 162 for annotation.

1460.   Milch-Breslau, Werner. "Zum Problem der Krankheit in der Dichtung der deutschen Romantik." *Sudhoffs Archiv* 23 (1930): 213–35.

Briefly surveys Romantic medical theories by J. Brown, Fichte, Herder, Kant, and Schelling and assesses Romantic medicine's influence on Romantic poetry, finding it minimal. Attempts to establish the true medical sources of poets such as Jean Paul, Hoffmann, and Novalis.

1461.   Miles, Elton. "The Influence of Darwinism on American Literary Criticism." *The Impact of Darwinian Thought on American Life and Culture: Papers Read at the Fourth Annual Meeting of the American Studies Association of Texas at Houston, Texas, December 5, 1959.* Austin: U of Texas P, 1959. 27–36.

This overview of the development of Darwinian literary criticism stresses the contributions of Perry and Howells and the influence of Zola and Taine.

1462.   Millhauser, Milton. "The Literary Impact of *Vestiges of Creation.*" *MLQ* 17 (1956): 213–26.
Although it is difficult to gauge the influence R. Chambers's *Vestiges of the Natural History of Creation* (1844) had on literature, implicit and explicit references to the work can be found in the writings of Agassiz, Emerson, Landor, H. Miller, Tennyson, Whewell, Whitman, and others.

1463.   Mitchell, Robert L. "From Heart to Spleen: The Lyrics of Pathology in Nineteenth-Century French Poetry." *Medicine and Literature.* Ed. Enid Rhodes Peschel. New York: Watson, 1980. 153–59.
Maintains that Baudelaire, Rimbaud, and Corbière were among the first French poets to introduce medical terminology into their works, thus spurring a lexical and imaginative revolution in nineteenth-century French poetics.

1464.   Nettesheim, Josefine. "Die aufklärerische Volksbildungsliteratur und ihre Wirkung auf die Dichtung in den ersten Jahrzehnten des 19. Jahrhunderts." *JWGV* 70 (1966): 115–30.
Traces the popularization of science in eighteenth- and nineteenth-century encyclopedias and other general-interest works and examines the ensuing impact on the themes, metaphors, and terminology of nineteenth-century literature. Discusses topics such as magnetism, galvanism, and mesmerism as assimilated by authors such as Benn, Chamisso, Hoffmann, Jean Paul, and Stifter.

1465.   ———. *Poeta doctus oder die Poetisierung der Wissenschaft von Musäus bis Benn.* Berlin: Duncker, 1975. 184 pp.
Includes essays on Chamisso's scientific studies, Hoffmann and magnetism, Holz's scientifically oriented poetic theory, Poe's use of astronomy, and the motif of balloon travel in Poe and Stifter. See items 1577, 1717, 1724, 1856, and 1857 for individual annotations.

1466.   ———. "Ursprung und Sinn der Wissenschaftskunst in der Lyrik. Vom Einfluss der Naturwissenschaften und der Technik auf die Entwicklung der Dichtungstheorie (Lyrik)." *LJGG* ns 3 (1962): 315–33.
Traces the impact of science and technology on poetic theory from Wordsworth's Preface to the second edition of the *Lyrical Ballads* (1800) to Holz and T. S. Eliot. Cites Holz's *Phantasus* and Eliot's "Love Song of J. Alfred Prufrock" and *Four Quartets.*

1467.   Neubauer, John. "The Mines of Falun: Temporal Fortunes of a Romantic Myth of Time." *SIR* 19 (1980): 475–95.
The geological curiosity involving the petrified body of a Falun miner, buried in an underground explosion in 1720, inspired a rich literary tradition. The author discusses versions of the event in works by Schubert, Hebel, Arnim, Hoffmann, and Hofmannsthal.

1468.   O'Hanlon, R. "Changing Scientific Concepts of Nature in the English Novel 1850–1920, with Special Reference to Joseph Conrad." Diss. Oxford U, 1977.
Not seen for annotation.

1469.   Oldroyd, D. R. "Darwinism and Literature." *Darwinian Impacts: An Introduction to the Darwinian Revolution*. Atlantic Highlands: Humanities; Milton Keynes: Open UP, 1980. 309–32.

Sketches the principal nineteenth-century literary responses to Darwinism by authors such as R. Browning, Bulwer-Lytton, S. Butler, Hardy, Meredith, Shaw, Swinburne, Tennyson, Verne, and Wells. Also briefly discusses the alleged link between Darwinism and Zola's literary naturalism.

1470.   Outram, Dorinda. "The Language of Natural Power: The 'Eloges' of Georges Cuvier and the Public Language of Nineteenth-Century Science." *HS* 16 (1978): 153–78.

Cuvier's *éloges* of natural philosophers helped define the relations between science and politics in the nineteenth century. By adapting language typical of the pastoral to his literary eulogies of scientists, Cuvier promoted the ideal of science as value-free and politically unthreatening.

1471.   Paul, Fritz. *Heinrich Steffens. Naturphilosophie und Universalromantik*. München: Fink, 1973. 252 pp.

Compares and analyzes the scientific writings of Steffens and the literary works of the Jena circle of Romantic poets, including F. Schlegel, A. Schlegel, Tieck, Novalis, and Goethe. Though Steffens's scientific work contributed little to science itself, his *Beyträge zur innern Naturgeschichte der Erde* (1801), an original study and his first publication on natural philosophy, earned the recognition and respect of the Romantics. His poetic treatment of natural science and the correspondences between his theory of nature and creation and the Romantic literary and poetic theory proved influential.

1472.   Payne, William Morton. "American Literary Criticism and the Doctrine of Evolution." *International Monthly* 2 (1900): 26–46, 127–53.

Defines "evolutionary" literary criticism and explains its importance in the history of criticism. Assesses the extent to which the principle of evolution informs American literary criticism in general and the critical works of J. Lowell, Whitman, Stedman, and Lanier in particular.

1473.   Perkins, George. "Death by Spontaneous Combustion in Marryat, Melville, Dickens, Zola, and Others." *Dickensian* 60 (1964): 57–63.

Citing Marryat's *Jacob Faithful*, Melville's *Redburn*, Dickens's *Bleak House*, and Zola's *Docteur Pascal*, Perkins argues that scientists and literary figures were taken in by circumstantial details surrounding stories that have little or no basis in fact.

1474.   Peterson, Audrey C. "Brain Fever in Nineteenth-Century Literature: Fact and Fiction." *VS* 19 (1975–76): 445–64.

Examines eighteenth- and nineteenth-century medical sources such as Huxham's *Essay on Fevers* (1750) and Buchan's *Domestic Medicine* (1828) to show that the brain fever suffered by, for example, Catherine Linton in *Wuthering Heights* and Emma Bovary in *Madame Bovary* was not a fictional invention but a severe and prolonged fever that physicians and lay people believed was brought on by emotional shock or excessive intellectual activity. Discusses references to brain fever in works by Dickens, Dostoyevsky, Doyle, and Meredith.

1475. Petitpas, Harold M. "Newman's Universe of Knowledge: Science, Literature, and Theology." *DR* 46 (1966–67): 494–507.
This study of Newman's philosophy of liberal education in *The Idea of a University* outlines his concept of the functions of three branches of knowledge—science, literature, and theology—and the essential relations among them.

1476. Pfeiffer, K. Ludwig. *Wissenschaft als Sujet im modernen englischen Roman.* Konstanzer Universitätsreden 127. Konstanz: Universitätsverlag, 1979. 63 pp.
See item 164 for annotation.

1477. Pizer, Donald. "Evolutionary Ideas in Late Nineteenth-Century English and American Literary Criticism." *JAAC* 19 (1960–61): 305–10. Rpt. in *Realism and Naturalism in Nineteenth-Century American Literature.* Carbondale: Southern Illinois UP, 1966. New York: Russell, 1976. 77–87.
Outlines the critical model used by literary critics in the late nineteenth century. This "developmental" theory of literature, based on the evolutionary systems of Spencer and Taine, is reflected in the criticism of Perry, Garland, Payne, Symonds, Posnett, Howells, Pellew, and others.

1478. ———. *Realism and Naturalism in Nineteenth-Century American Literature.* Carbondale: Southern Illinois UP, 1966. New York: Russell, 1976. 176 pp.
Rev. Clara M. Kirk, *Criticism* 8 (1966): 398–401; Kenneth Graham, *RES* ns 18 (1967): 351–52.
Collects previously published essays that treat various aspects of realism and naturalism in the fiction of Norris, Garland, and Crane or that examine the influence of evolution on the literary criticism of Howells and Perry.

1479. Proffitt, Edward. "Science and Romanticism." *GaR* 34 (1980): 55–80.
Maintains that science and Romanticism are not, as is commonly supposed, antithetical to one another; rather, both are oriented toward a nondogmatic, empirical, and humanistic mode of inquiry. One essential difference, however, is Romanticism's emphasis on an organic, interactive epistemological model and its rejection of the mechanistic metaphysics grounding the scientific epistemological perspective. Romantic poets such as S. Coleridge, Keats, P. Shelley, and Wordsworth had good reason to criticize the mechanistic basis of science, as current developments in physics, biology, ecology, linguistics, and psychoanalytic psychology demonstrate.

1480. Raymond, George R. "The Reaction against Science in the French Novels of the 1880s." Diss. Yale U, 1954.
Not seen for annotation.

1481. Rees, Garnet. "The Influence of Science on the Structure of the Novel in the Nineteenth Century (Balzac, Flaubert, Zola)." *Literature and Science.* Proc. of the Sixth Triennial Congress of the International Federation for Modern Languages and Literatures. Oxford, 1954. Oxford: Blackwell, 1955. 255–61.

The biology of Geoffroy Saint-Hilaire contributed significantly to Balzac's descriptive techniques. The structure of Flaubert's novels owes much to the objective, dispassionately critical spirit and method of science. Though both the content and the method of science also influenced Zola, he overemphasized them artlessly in his works.

1482.   Reimer, Howard J. "Darwinism in Canadian Literature." Diss. McMaster U, 1975.
Not seen for annotation.

1482a.   Roos, David A. "Matthew Arnold and Thomas Henry Huxley: Two Speeches at the Royal Academy, 1881 and 1883." *MP* 74 (1976–77): 316–24.
The speeches considered here concern Arnold and Huxley's conflict over the roles of science and literature in education.

1483.   Root, Winthrop H. "The Naturalistic Attitude toward Aesthetics." *GR* 13 (1938): 56–64.
Traces attempts by Bölsche, Conrad, Welten, Alberti, and others to develop a scientific aesthetics based on the principles of naturalism outlined in Zola's *Roman expérimental*.

1484.   Roppen, Georg. *Evolution and Poetic Belief: A Study in Some Victorian and Modern Writers*. Oslo Studies in English 5. Oslo: Oslo UP, 1956. Folcroft: Folcroft; Darby: Darby, 1969. Norwood: Norwood, 1976. 474 pp.
Studies the poetic or creative function of evolution in its "transition from idea to belief, from conceptual framework material to personal and intuitive symbol or vision, expressive of profound emotional attachments." Examines the various guises of evolution theory reflected in literature—as part of the Platonic tradition in Tennyson and Browning, as a cult of life and humankind in Swinburne and Meredith, as naturalism in Hardy, and as optimism and utopianism in S. Butler, Wells, and Shaw.

1485.   Rousseau, G. S. "Science and the Discovery of the Imagination in Enlightened England." *ECS* 3 (1969–70): 108–35.
See item 720 for annotation.

1486.   Schmidt, Günter. *Die literarische Rezeption des Darwinismus: Das Problem der Vererbung bei Emile Zola und im Drama des deutschen Naturalismus*. Sitzungsberichte der sächsischen Akademie der Wissenschaften zu Leipzig 117.4. Berlin: Akademie, 1974. 209 pp.
Outlines the development of Darwinism and its formative influence on naturalist literature, especially drama. Discusses Zola's role in founding the genre of literary naturalism and assesses the impact of Darwinism on Hauptmann's *Vor Sonnenaufgang*, Voss's *Mutter Gertrud*, and Kirchbach's *Waiblinger*.

1487.   Schmidt, Peter. "Gesundheit und Krankheit in romantischer Medizin und Erzählkunst." *JFDH* (1966): 197–228.
Surveys Romantic medical concepts such as Mesmer's idea of animal magnetism and Schelling's and J. Brown's theories and discusses the role medicine played in

the Romantic view of the poet as a "transcendental doctor" capable of restoring organic harmony. Treats works by Arnim, Hoffmann, Tieck, and Novalis.

1488.   Schwartz, Sheila. "The World of Science Fiction." *EngR* 21.3 (1971): 27–40.
See item 170 for annotation.

1489.   Senseman, Wilfred M. "Demi-science and Fiction: The Utilization of the Pseudo-Scientific in Some English Novels of the Period from 1790–1840." *Microfilm Abstracts* 10.3 (1950): 150–51.
Studies the role played by astrology, alchemy, physiognomy, and phrenology in works by C. Brontë, Bulwer-Lytton, Scott, M. Shelley, and others.

1490.   Sewell, Elizabeth. "Science and Literature: Two Strands of the Imagination over One Hundred Years." *Commonweal* 84 (1966): 218–21. (See replies by D. E. Carr and Joseph F. Jackson, 448–49.)
In the nineteenth century, reflection on the nature and methodology of thinking and imagination was largely the province of poets, while in the twentieth century it is primarily scientists who make significant contributions in this area. To illustrate this point, Sewell cites Whitman's "Passage to India," Hugo's *Légende des siècles*, Poincaré's *Science et méthode*, Polanyi's *Man in Thought*, and other works.

1491.   Shaffer, Elinor. "Schelling and Romantic Science: The Frontier between Disciplines." *Language and Literature in the Formation of National and Cultural Communities*. Proc. of the Thirteenth Congress of the Fédération Internationale des Langues et Littératures Modernes and the Seventh Congress of the Australasian Universities Language and Literature Association, Sydney Univ., 25–29 Aug. 1975. Ed. Robert D. Eagleson, et al. Sydney: Australasian Univ. Lang. and Lit. Assn., 1976. 191–93.
Brief remarks on Schelling's program to develop a conceptual basis for both science and literature by reanimating mythology through the power of the idea of organicism.

1492.   Smith, Sheila M. "Blue Books and Victorian Novelists." *RES* ns 21 (1970): 23–40.
Examines the influence of scientific methods and data on the works of Victorian novelists, including Dickens's *Hard Times*, Kingsley's *Yeast*, and B. Disraeli's *Sybil*. Stresses the impact of the government statistical reports known as "blue books."

1493.   Snelders, H. A. M. "Romanticism and Naturphilosophie and the Inorganic Natural Sciences 1797–1840: An Introductory Survey." *SIR* 9 (1970): 193–215.
Primarily studies the influence of German Romantic thought on scientists, briefly referring to the scientific works of the poets Arnim and Novalis. A competent scientist, Arnim combined experimental findings with speculative reflection. In contrast to Arnim, who kept his scientific work separate from his literary work, Novalis refers to mathematics, natural science, and medicine in many of his aphorisms.

1494.   Stein, Robert. "Naturwissenschaftliche Romantiker." *Sudhoffs Archiv* 15 (1923): 121–25.
Briefly refers to poets generally categorized as Romantics who were also actively engaged in scientific studies. Mentions primarily Novalis, Arnim, Görres, Kleist, Chamisso, and Stifter.

1495.   Stevens, Neil E. "The Botany of the New England Poets." *SciMo* 12 (1921): 137–49.
Assesses the scientific significance of allusions to botany, horticulture, mycology, phytopathology, ecology, and wood technology in Holmes, Longfellow, J. Lowell, and Whittier.

1496.   Stevenson, Lionel. *Darwin among the Poets*. Chicago: U of Chicago P, 1932. New York: Russell, 1963. 357 pp.
Traces the influence of the evolution theory on the English poets Bridges, Browning, Hardy, Kipling, Masefield, Meredith, Noyes, Tennyson, and Watson.

1497.   ———. "Darwin and the Novel." *NCF* 15 (1960–61): 29–38.
Ideas contained in several works of fiction written between 1855 and 1859 prepared the reading public for understanding and accepting C. Darwin's theory of evolution in *The Origin of Species* (1859). These ideas concern social and physical change, religious controversy, the infinitude of space and time, the indifference of nature's mechanical processes, the relation between human behavior and that of the lower animals, and the concept of biological evolution in R. Chambers's *Vestiges of the Natural History of Creation*. Works discussed include Kingsley's *Two Years Ago*, G. Eliot's *Scenes of Clerical Life*, and Meredith's *Ordeal of Richard Feverel*.

1498.   Stoll, Elmer E. "Criminals in Shakespeare and in Science." *MP* 10 (1912–13): 55–80.
The scientific spirit of observation enabled poets of the nineteenth and twentieth centuries to develop a more differentiated view of the criminal than the one we find in Shakespeare, where a duality of good and evil prevails. This essay contrasts Shakespeare's depiction of criminals with Zola's, Ibsen's, and Hardy's portraits.

1499.   Stooke, David E. "The Portrait of the Physician in Selected Prose Fiction of Nineteenth-Century American Authors." *DAI* 37 (1977): 5130A.
Studies the literary depiction of herbalists, scientist-physicians, psychiatrists, and surgeons in the prose works of Cable, Crane, Hawthorne, Holmes, Howells, Jewett, and Melville.

1500.   Suderman, Elmer F. "Popular Fiction (1870–1900) Looks at Darwin and the Nature of God." *Challenges in American Culture*. Ed. Ray B. Browne, Larry N. Landrum, and William K. Bottorff. Bowling Green: Bowling Green U Popular P, 1970. 142–49.
The influence of Darwinism on theological questions about the nature of God, especially whether God is transcendent or immanent, is reflected in popular novels by H. Adams, Woolley, Savage, and others.

1501. Tatar, Maria M. *Spellbound: Studies on Mesmerism and Literature.* Princeton: Princeton UP, 1978. 293 pp.
Rev. Max Byrd, *YR* ns 68 (1978–79): 612–18; Michael Steig, *NCF* 33 (1978–79): 505–08; Marjorie Gelus, *GQ* 52 (1979): 569–70; Sander L. Gilman, *SIR* 18 (1979): 489–91; Michael Hays, *GR* 54 (1979): 171–72; J. M. McGlathery, *JEGP* 78 (1979): 405–06; Keith Schuchard, *SNNTS* 11 (1979): 376–77; M. Kay Flavell, *MLR* 75 (1980): 836–37; Oskar Seidlin, *MLN* 95 (1980): 715–16.

Traces the impact of mesmerist ideas on literature, with special reference to Kleist, Hoffmann, Balzac, and Hawthorne and to the reshaping of the mesmerist tradition in twentieth-century writers such as H. James, D. H. Lawrence, and Mann. Includes an introductory appraisal of Mesmer's historical significance and an assessment of mesmerism in the context of eighteenth- and nineteenth-century science, psychology, and philosophy.

1502. Trudgian, Helen. "Claude Bernard and the 'groupe de Médan.' " *Literature and Science.* Proc. of the Sixth Triennial Congress of the International Federation for Modern Languages and Literatures. Oxford, 1954. Oxford: Blackwell, 1955. 273–76.

Concerns the influence of Bernard's *Introduction à l'étude de la médecine expérimentale* (1865) on the naturalism of Zola and his disciples in the "Medan group," such as Maupassant, Huysmans, Céard, Hennique, and Alexis.

1503. Turner, Frank Miller. *Between Science and Religion: The Reaction to Scientific Naturalism in Late Victorian England.* New Haven: Yale UP, 1974. 273 pp.
Rev. William H. Brock, *VS* 18 (1974–75): 372–74; James Hall, *RM* 28 (1974–75): 765–66; Lawrence F. Barmann, *JMH* 47 (1975): 553–56; J. H. Brooke, *British Journal for the History of Science* 8 (1975): 262–64; W. F. Cannon, *AHR* 80 (1975): 409–10; R. Harré, *RES* ns 26 (1975): 500–02.

"This study deals with six late nineteenth-century Englishmen who abandoned the Christian faith but then found it impossible to accept in its stead the scientific naturalism that proved so attractive to many of their contemporaries." Examines the views of the poet and critic Frederic W. H. Myers and the novelist Samuel Butler.

1504. Turner, John M. "The Response of Major American Writers to Darwinism, 1859–1910." Diss. Harvard U, 1956.
Not seen for annotation.

1505. Tytler, Graeme D. C. "Character Description and Physiognomy in the European Novel (1800–1860) in Relation to J. C. Lavater's *Physiognomische Fragmente.*" *DA* 31 (1971): 4798A–99A.

Lavater's book reawakened a European interest in physiognomy that, when combined with the prominence of phrenology, may account for the stylistic tendencies of the European novel, especially its emphasis on physical portraiture.

1506.   Umbach, William E. "The Reflection of Natural Science in German Literature from 1830 to 1859." *Microfilm Abstracts* 10.3 (1950): 153–54.
Examines evidence suggesting that German writers such as Büchner, Hebbel, Immermann, Keller, and Stifter shared an interest in natural science.

1507.   Vadé, Yves. "Comte, les poètes et les nombres." *Romantisme* 21–22 (1978): 105–16.
Argues that Comte's disdain for contemporary poets, including Lamartine and Hugo, resulted not from the conflict between science and literature and their respective powers to comprehend the universe but, rather, from two different applications of the concept of numbers. Discusses numbers in Lamartine, Hugo, Baudelaire, Nerval, Rimbaud, and Mallarmé.

1508.   Walcutt, Charles Child. "From Scientific Theory to Aesthetic Fact: The 'Naturalistic' Novel." *QRL* 3 (1946–47): 167–79.
Suggests a critical approach to naturalistic novels that accounts for the dialectic tension between scientific determinism and its antithesis. Stresses the aesthetic intentions in the use of scientific concepts by writers such as Dreiser, Norris, and Zola.

1509.   Warren, F. M. "Cabanis, the Medical School, and French Realism." *TMV* 2 (1930): 251–54.
Notes that the physiological theories expressed in Cabanis's *Rapports du physique et du moral de l'homme* (1802) influenced Baudelaire, Flaubert, Gautier, Sainte-Beuve, Stendhal, Taine, and Zola.

1510.   Weiss, Sydna S. "Scientists in Late Nineteenth and Twentieth Century German Literature: Their Projects, Personalities, and Problems." *DAI* 36 (1975–76): 2233A.
Discusses scientists in four categories: alchemists and early historical scientists (e.g., Hoffmann's *Klein Zaches*), scientists as creators (e.g., Hamerling's *Homunculus*), scientists as seekers of knowledge (e.g., Schirmbeck's *Ärgert dich dein rechtes Auge*), and scientists and society (e.g., Döblin's *Berge, Meere und Giganten*).

1511.   Welsh, Alexander. "Theories of Science and Romance, 1870–1920." *VS* 17 (1973–74): 135–54.
This comparative analysis of the functions of invention, hypothesis, and fictions in physics and literature cites scientists and authors such as Balzac, H. James, Kelvin, Maxwell, Poincaré, Stevenson, Wilde, and Zola.

1512.   Wetzels, Walter D. "Aspects of Natural Science in German Romanticism." *SIR* 10 (1971): 44–59.
Analyzes the complex interactions between German Romanticism and the natural sciences. Describes the physical and metaphysical components of Schelling's *Naturphilosophie*; the attempts by Novalis and F. Schlegel to bring about a fusion of all knowledge, especially of science and art; and the efforts of Ritter to develop a genuinely "Romantic" science.

1513.   ———. *Johann Wilhelm Ritter: Physik im Wirkungsfeld der deutschen Romantik*. Berlin: de Gruyter, 1973. 139 pp.

Examines how Ritter developed as a physicist while he was connected with the circle of Romantic poets and scientists that included Tieck, Brentano, Arnim, Novalis, Herder, and Goethe. Discusses Ritter's scientific adaptation of the concept of the "Weltseele" and treats some works, such as his *Das elektrische System der Körper* and *Physisch-Chemische Abhandlungen in chronologischer Folge*, that may have influenced his contemporaries.

1514.   Woodring, Carl. "Nature and Art in the Nineteenth Century." *PMLA* 92 (1977): 193–202.

The Romantic concept of nature underwent gradual transformation during the nineteenth century under the influence of Comte's positivism, French materialism, Darwinism, and the objectivity inspired by developments in photography. Woodring notes responses to this change in literature by S. Butler, J. Conrad, Dickens, Dreiser, Zola, and others.

1515.   Wright, C. J. "The 'Spectre' of Science: The Study of Optical Phenomena and the Romantic Imagination." *JWCI* 43 (1980): 186–200.

Shows that while many Romantics accepted scientific explanations for optical phenomena such as the rainbow, the glory (a body or shadow surrounded by a halo), mirages, and specters and interpreted them in the light of natural philosophy, others ignored this rationalist approach as not conducive to the love of beauty. Cites references to optical phenomena in works by Beddoes, C. Brontë, Hogg, Keats, Wordsworth, and others.

Individual Authors

Henry Adams (1838–1918)

1516.   Glicksberg, Charles I. "Henry Adams and the Repudiation of Science." *SciMo* 64 (1947): 63–71.

Discusses Adams's attempt to attain a unified vision of the truth through an intellectual synthesis of religious belief and the empirical facts revealed by scientific investigation. This struggle is reflected in his novel *Esther* and in *Mont-Saint Michel and Chartres*.

1517.   Hahn, Herbert F. "*The Education of Henry Adams* Reconsidered." *CE* 24 (1962–63): 444–49.

A reconsideration of Adams's *Education* reveals that his negative, despairing view of a world dominated by scientific, utilitarian values is of secondary importance to his larger purpose of presenting an alternative set of values with which to countenance the implications of a scientific worldview.

1518.   Hamill, Paul J., Jr. "Autobiography as Intellectual History: Science and Symbolism in Henry Adams, Hans Zinsser and Norbert Wiener." *DAI* 32 (1972): 4610A–11A.

The autobiographies of Adams, Zinsser, and Wiener incorporate metaphors drawn from scientific concepts such as linear momentum, evolution, and feedback responsiveness. The metaphors reflect the authors' ideologies of science and society and hence provide a record of intellectual history.

1519.   ———. "The Future as Virgin: A Latter-Day Look at the Dynamo and the Virgin of Henry Adams." *MLS* 3 (1973): 8–12.
The dynamo and the virgin, Adams's metaphors for the electronic age, may still be viable symbols for computer-age attempts to construct images of the future.

1519a.   Jordy, William H. *Henry Adams: Scientific Historian*. New Haven: Yale UP, 1952. 327 pp.
Analyzes Adams's attempts to develop a scientific theory of history based largely on the second law of thermodynamics. From this endeavor Adams derived images of degradation, diffusion, and energy loss for his *Education of Henry Adams*.

1520.   Levenson, J. C. "Henry Adams and the Culture of Science." *Studies in American Culture: Dominant Ideas and Images*. Ed. Joseph J. Kwiat and Mary C. Turpie. Minneapolis: U of Minnesota P, 1960. 123–38.
Underscores the principal aspects of Adams's attitude toward the role of science in American culture, stressing his warnings against the abuse of technology. Discusses *The Education of Henry Adams* in this regard.

1521.   Mane, Robert. "Henry Adams et la science." *EA* 16 (1963): 1–10.
Documents Adams's shift from faith in the potential powers of science to anguish over science's capacity to produce global destruction. Links his fears of a nuclear disaster to his belief in the theory of catastrophe posited by leading geologists.

1522.   Mindel, Joseph. "The Uses of Metaphor: Henry Adams and the Symbols of Science." *JHI* 26 (1965): 89–102.
Examines the shortcomings in Adams's use of metaphors derived from science for the formulation of his theory of history. In works such as *History of the United States of America* and *Degradation of the Democratic Dogma*, the chief metaphors are based on the first and second laws of thermodynamics, evolution, the phase rule, and historical geology.

1523.   Munford, Howard M. "Henry Adams: The Limitations of Science." *SoR* ns 4 (1968): 59–71.
Fastening on the provisional and subjective nature of scientific concepts, Adams developed a dynamic theory of history that calls attention to the limits of its own method. Munford discusses *The Education of Henry Adams*, *Esther*, *History of the United States*, and other works.

1523a.   Wasser, Henry. "Science and Religion in Henry Adams's *Esther*." *MarkhamR* 2.2 (1970): 24–26.
Maintains that *Esther* reflects Adams's attempt to come to terms with the nineteenth-century conflict between religion and science.

1524.   ———. "The Thought of Henry Adams." *NEQ* 24 (1951): 495–509.

Traces Adams's intellectual development—especially his conception of history—and shows how his thought and writings were influenced by other thinkers and scientists, including C. Darwin, Gibbs, Kelvin, and Lyell.

1525.   Wilson, Larman C. "Henry Adams and the Second Law of Thermodynamics." *TQ* 7.3 (1964): 29–33.

Outlines the principal features of Adams's adaptation of the second law of thermodynamics to his theories of history, life, and society in *Mont-Saint-Michel and Chartres: A Study of Thirteenth Century Unity* and *The Education of Henry Adams: A Study of Twentieth Century Multiplicity.*

Tirso Aguimana de Veca (19th cent.)

1526.   Dendle, Brian J. "A Romantic Voyage to Saturn: Tirso Aguimana de Veca's *Una temporada en el más bello de los planetas.*" *SIR* 7 (1967–68): 243–47.

Aguimana's novel (1870), which reflects a concern with science and deistic rationalism, may be viewed as a romantic precursor to the literary genre of science-fiction adventure typified by the works of Verne and Wells.

Ludwig Joachim von Arnim (1781–1831)

1527.   Beckers, Gustav. "Phänomene des 'Tierischen Magnetismus' in Achim von Arnims Novelle 'Die Majoratsherren.' " *Akten des VI. Internationalen Germanisten-Kongresses, Basel 1980.* Ser. A, 8.4. Bern: Lang, 1980. 453–59.

Elucidates Arnim's "Die Majoratsherren" by drawing on the theory of animal magnetism as propagated by Franz Mesmer and, especially, Jung-Stilling.

1528.   Darmstaedter, Ernst. "Achim von Arnim und die Naturwissenschaft." *Euphorion* 32 (1931): 454–76.

In his university years Arnim devoted himself intensively to natural science, quickly mastering the major writings in physics and chemistry. His numerous publications deal primarily with electricity and magnetism and his theoretical work *Versuch einer Theorie der elektrischen Erscheinungen* (1799) reveals a thorough knowledge of the many writings on electricity as well as an independence of thought. During his European journey in 1801–04, his literary interests gained the ascendancy, though his correspondence during those years indicates his continuing concern with scientific matters.

1529.   Riley, Helene M. "Scientist, Sorcerer, or Servant of Humanity: The Many Faces of Faust in the Work of Achim von Arnim." *Seminar* 13 (1977): 1–12.

Examines the influence of science and pseudoscience on the actions of the Faustian characters in Arnim's *Gräfin Dolores*, *Kronenwächter*, and *Auch ein Faust*. "Although he was himself trained in methods of scientific research, Arnim viewed the purely rational approach to the solution of existential problems as invalid."

Matthew Arnold (1822–88)

1530. Dudley, Fred A. "Matthew Arnold and Science." Diss. U of Iowa, 1939.
Not seen for annotation.

1531. ———. "Matthew Arnold and Science." *PMLA* 57 (1942): 275–94.
This overview of Arnold's attempt to make poetry an integrative force between scientism and religion is framed in the broader context of his defense of literature and classicism in an age dominated by scientific concerns.

1532. Mackie, Alexander. *Nature Knowledge in Modern Poetry: Being Chapters on Tennyson, Wordsworth, Matthew Arnold, and Lowell as Exponents of Nature-Study.* London: Longmans, 1906. 132 pp.
See item 1946 for annotation.

1532a. Pitman, Ruth. "On Dover Beach." *EIC* 23 (1973): 109–36.
This analysis of Arnold's "Dover Beach" discusses its geological aspects, especially the influence of Lyell's theories.

Jane Austen (1775–1817)

1533. Brogan, Howard O. "Science and Narrative Structure in Austen, Hardy, and Woolf." *NCF* 11 (1956–57): 276–87.
Theoretical assumptions based on Newtonianism, Darwinism, and contemporary physics inform, respectively, the narrative structures of Austen's *Pride and Prejudice*, Hardy's *Mayor of Casterbridge*, and Woolf's *To the Lighthouse*.

Honoré de Balzac (1799–1850)

1533a. Baldensperger, F. "Balzac at the Paris Zoo." *VQR* 15 (1939): 97–104.
Traces Balzac's naturalistic preoccupations to his early acquaintance with the Muséum d'Histoire Naturelle.

1534. Borel, Jacques. *Médecine et psychiatrie balzaciennes. La science dans le roman.* Paris: Corti, 1971. 156 pp.
Rev. H. J. Hunt, *FS* 28 (1974): 92–93.
Shows that mental and physical pathology played a considerable role in Balzac's works, informing especially the development and resolution of his novels' plots. Outlines Balzac's medical background and discusses the medical theories grounding his literary depiction of illness.

1535. Demetz, Peter. "Balzac and the Zoologists: A Concept of the Type." *The Disciplines of Criticism: Essays in Literary Theory, Interpretation, and History.* Ed. Demetz et al. New Haven: Yale UP, 1968. 397–418.
Balzac's concept of the type is both traditional, or "romantic," and scientific, or "realistic." Demetz discusses the concept as outlined in Balzac's *Comédie humaine* and comments on similar ideas developed earlier by Buffon, Herder, Geoffroy Saint-Hilaire, and others.

1536.　Fess, Gilbert M. *The Correspondence of Physical and Material Factors with Character in Balzac*. Diss. U of Pennsylvania, 1924. Publications of the University of Pennsylvania Series in Romanic Languages and Literatures 10. Menasha: Banta, 1924. 108 pp.

Examines the influence of theories of physiognomy, phrenology, mesmerism, and pre-Darwinian evolution on Balzac's literary characterizations.

1537.　Françon, Marcel. "Balzac e la scienza del suo tempo." *Convivium* 23 (1955): 627–30.

Examines the many references to science and scientists in Balzac's novels and discusses the sources from which Balzac drew the scientific content of his work.

1538.　Le Yaouanc, Moïse. *Nosographie de l'humanité balzacienne*. Paris: Maloine, 1959. 523 pp.
　　　　Rev. W. G. Moore, *MLR* 56 (1961): 618–19.

Assesses the medical knowledge revealed in Balzac's novels, noting that its sources range from personal contacts and observations to the study of medical texts. Balzac exploited the maladies of his day for dramatic purposes.

1539.　Luce, Louise Fiber. "Honoré de Balzac and the *Voyant*: A Recovered Alchemical Discourse." *ECr* 18.2 (1978): 13–23.

Examines the extent to which the rhetorical structures of Balzac's *Massimilla Doni* and *La peau de chagrin* are informed by doctrines of alchemy drawn from the *Corpus hermeticum*.

1540.　Scheel, Hans L. "Balzac als Physiognomiker." *Archiv* 198 (1961): 227–44.

Using the studies of Johann Caspar Lavater and Franz Joseph Gall and, to a large extent, his own observations, Balzac developed in his novels a complex system of physiognomy reflecting the character, fate, and social class of individuals and their epochs.

1541.　Wirtz, Dorothy. "Animalism in Balzac's *Curé de Tours* and *Pierrette*." *RomN* 11 (1969–70): 61–67.

In *Curé de Tours* and *Pierrette* Balzac criticized and satirized a class of society that he termed the "célibataire" (priests, spinsters, and bachelors) by portraying its members with animal-like characteristics. He based his satire in part on the zoological system of Geoffroy Saint-Hilaire.

Charles Baudelaire (1821–67)

1541a.　Boon, Pierre. "*Correspondances* et le magnetisme animal." *PMLA* 86 (1971): 406–10.

Examines evidence suggesting that the occult science of animal magnetism was a chief source of Baudelaire's *Correspondances*.

1542.　Cottrell, Robert D. "Baudelaire's *Elévation* and the Ptolemaic System." *RomN* 15 (1973–74): 426–29.

Shows that the world system described in the opening stanzas of Baudelaire's *Elévation* is Ptolemaic.

Thomas Lovell Beddoes (1803–49)

1543.   Potter, George R. "Did Thomas Lovell Beddoes Believe in the Evolution of Species?" *MP* 21 (1923–24): 89–100.
A careful examination of Beddoes's *Death's Jest-Book* and other works indicates that Beddoes was interested in the paleontological and biological discoveries of his age. He seemed to be moving toward a belief in evolution, yet he remained rooted in the great-chain-of-being tradition.

Giuseppe Gioacchino Belli (1791–1863)

1544.   Almansi, Guido. "Belli e la scienza." *IQ* 80 (1980): 45–52.
Many of Belli's poems and essays treat scientific themes, though his scientific discussions show little originality. Almansi discusses Belli's overall attitude toward science—which is sometimes favorable and sometimes openly hostile and mocking.

Robert Bridges (1844–1930)

1545.   Eaker, J. Gordon. "Robert Bridges' Concept of Nature." *PMLA* 54 (1939): 1181–97.
Submits that Bridges was not uninterested in the findings of geology and the theory of biological evolution and that he accommodated scientific discoveries in his concept of nature as a benevolent universal mind made manifest in the external world. Cites *The Testament of Beauty*, "The Tapestry," "Morning Hymn," "A Hymn of Nature," and "Wintry Delights" to support this analysis.

1546.   Lipscomb, Herbert C. "Lucretius and *The Testament of Beauty*." *CJ* 31 (1935–36): 77–88.
Traces similarities of theme and poetic style in Lucretius's *De rerum natura* and Bridges's *Testament of Beauty*. Both poems are philosophic and scientific, with Lucretius's poem focusing on atomism and Bridges's on Darwinian evolution.

Charlotte Brontë (1816–55)

1547.   Jack, Ian. "Physiognomy, Phrenology and Characterization in the Novels of Charlotte Brontë." *BST* 15 (1966–70): 377–91.
Assesses the role Brontë's knowledge of physiognomy and phrenology played in the characterizations of *The Professor*, *Jane Eyre*, *Villette*, and *Shirley*. Briefly summarizes Lavater's system of physiognomy and Gall's theory of phrenology.

Robert Browning (1812–89)

1548.   Fisher, Charles. "The Idea of Evolution in Browning's Poetry." *Temple Bar* 118 (1899): 534–39.

Cites passages from Browning's poetry to illustrate his optimistic interpretation of evolution theory.

1549. Hegner, Anna. *Die Evolutionsidee bei Tennyson und Browning.* Diss. Freiburg U, 1931. Wertheim: Bechstein, 1931. 34 pp.
See item 1939 for annotation.

1550. Schneck, Jerome M. "Robert Browning and Mesmerism." *Bulletin of the Medical Library Association* 44 (1956): 443–51.
Examines the extent to which Browning incorporated references to hypnosis and its antecedents, mesmerism and animal magnetism, into his poem "Mesmerism."

1551. White, Frances Emily. "Browning's 'Mesmerism' from a Scientific Point of View." *Poet-Lore* 4 (1892): 261–66.
Suggests that Browning's poem "Mesmerism" inadequately depicts the mesmeric processes.

William Cullen Bryant (1794–1878)

1552. Glicksberg, Charles I. "William Cullen Bryant and Nineteenth-Century Science." *NEQ* 23 (1950): 91–96.
Outlines Bryant's cautious but favorable attitude toward scientific research of the period (such as medical studies) and his moderate views on the compatibility of science with religion and poetry.

1553. Ringe, Donald A. "William Cullen Bryant and the Science of Geology." *AL* 26 (1954–55): 507–14.
Suggests that Lyell's *Principles of Geology* (1830–33) and other geologic literature of the period 1835–47 influenced Bryant's poetry. Examines "The Fountain" and "A Hymn of the Sea."

Georg Büchner (1813–37)

1554. Jens, Walter. "Poesie und Medizin: Gedenkrede für Georg Büchner." *NRs* 75 (1964): 266–77.
Studies the influence of Büchner's medical background on his writings, including *Dantons Tod*, *Leonce und Lena*, and *Woyzeck*.

1555. Majut, R. "Georg Büchner and Some English Thinkers." *MLR* 48 (1953): 310–22.
Among the English scientists that appear to have influenced Büchner's works are T. H. Huxley and the physiologists Monro, J. Shaw, and Bell. Also considers Büchner's relation to the English thinkers Carlyle, Paine, Hobbes, and H. More.

1556. Mette, Alexander. "Medizin und Morphologie in Büchners Schaffen." *SuF* 15 (1963): 747–55.

The influence of medicine and psychology on Büchner's writings is apparent not only in his chosen literary themes but also in his precise, factual language. Among the works examined are *Woyzeck*, *Lenz*, *Leonce und Lena*, and *Dantons Tod*.

1557.   Müller-Seidel, Walter. "Natur und Naturwissenschaft im Werk Georg Büchners." *Festschrift für Klaus Ziegler*. Ed. Eckehard Catholy and Winfried Hellmann. Tübingen: Niemeyer, 1968. 205–32.
Examines *Woyzeck*, *Dantons Tod*, and *Lenz* to study the influence of Büchner's medical background on his use of language and his understanding of history, humankind, and nature.

1558.   Pross, Wolfgang. "Die Kategorie der *Natur* im Werk Büchners." *Aurora* 40 (1980): 172–88.
Claims that the history of science can clarify the function of the concept of nature in Büchner's works. Traces the tensions in the analogy between social and biological nature from the seventeenth century to Büchner's time and illustrates with quotations from *Dantons Tod*, *Woyzeck*, and *Lenz*.

1559.   ———. "Naturgeschichtliches Gesetz und gesellschaftliche Anomie: Georg Büchner, Johann Lucas Schönlein und Auguste Comte." *Literatur in der sozialen Bewegung. Aufsätze und Forschungsberichte zum 19. Jahrhundert*. Ed. Alberto Martino. Tübingen: Niemeyer, 1977. 228–59.
Rejects the view that Büchner's scientific works have no bearing on his literary, social, and political interests. Contrasts his approach to nature in his scientific treatises with his approach to history and society in his dramas. Maintains that his understanding of social order is derived from concepts that social scientists have borrowed from physiology.

Samuel Butler (1835–1902)

1560.   Breuer, Hans-Peter. "Samuel Butler's 'The Book of the Machines' and the Argument from Design." *MP* 72 (1974–75): 365–83.
S. Butler's "Book of the Machines" from *Erewhon* (1872) was primarily a satire of J. Butler's analogical reasoning in *The Analogy of Religion Natural and Revealed to the Constitution and Course of Nature* (1736) and not a repudiation of C. Darwin's argument in *The Origin of Species* (1859).

1561.   Bryan, Daniel V. "Samuel Butler: Creative Evolution in Literature." *DA* 13 (1953): 1191–92.
Expounds Butler's theory of creative evolution in *The Way of All Flesh* and discusses its historical significance.

1562.   Carey, Glenn O. "Samuel Butler's Theory of Evolution: A Summary." *ELT* 7 (1964): 230–33.
Traces the major stages in the development of Butler's evolution theory, noting especially his growing dissatisfaction with Darwinism. Discusses *Life and Habit*, *Evolution, Old and New*, *Unconscious Memory*, *Luck, or Cunning*, and other works.

1563. Coleman, Brian. "Samuel Butler, Darwin and Darwinism." *Journal of the Society for the Bibliography of Natural History* 7 (1974–76): 93–105.
This overview of Butler's dispute with C. Darwin regarding evolution theory cites works such as *Erewhon*, *Evolution, Old and New*, and *Life and Habit*.

1564. Gounelas, Ruth. "Samuel Butler, Homeopathy, and the Unity of Opposing Principles." *AUMLA* 53 (1980): 25–41.
Butler's espousal of homeopathic medicine entailed the view that mind and matter are interdependent and not separate. Gounelas traces Butler's attempts to formulate a theory of the unity of the physical and the spiritual, examining such works as *Unconscious Memory*, *Erewhon*, *Life and Habit*, and *Evolution, Old and New*.

1565. Hartog, Marcus. "Samuel Butler and Recent Mnemic Biological Theories." *Scientia* 15 (1914): 38–52.
Comments on the rhetorical effectiveness of Butler's literary treatment of biological theory in *Life and Habit* and other works.

1566. Jones, Joseph. *The Cradle of Erewhon: Samuel Butler in New Zealand*. Austin: U of Texas P, 1959. 224 pp.
Studies Butler's experiences in New Zealand in an attempt to describe the milieu from which his novel *Erewhon* emerged. Includes chapters on the geography of Butler's portrait of the New Zealand countryside and on the ethnology in the novel, emphasizing his debt to the Maori tribe and tradition.

1567. Lothamer, Eileen E. "The Religious Evolution of Samuel Butler." *DA* 25 (1964–65): 5260.
Traces Butler's attempts to construct a religious belief compatible with contemporary scientific developments such as evolution theory. Comments on Butler's "scientific" works, including *Life and Habit*, *Evolution, Old and New*, and *Unconscious Memory*.

1568. MacDonald, W. L. "Samuel Butler and Evolution." *North American Review* 223 (1926–27): 626–37.
Outlines the evolution theory presented in Butler's *Life and Habit* and in "The Book of the Machines," from *Erewhon*.

1569. Willey, Basil. *Darwin and Butler: Two Versions of Evolution*. Hibbert Lectures 1959. London: Chatto; New York: Harcourt, 1960. 116 pp.
After outlining C. Darwin's evolution theory and its bearing on religion, surveying pre-Darwinian evolution theories, and examining the views of evolution Darwin's contemporaries held, Willey discusses Butler's criticism of Darwinism in works such as *Erewhon*, *Evolution, Old and New*, and *Life and Habit*.

George Gordon, Lord Byron (1788–1824)

1570. Bostetter, Edward E. "Masses and Solids: Byron's View of the External World." *MLQ* 35 (1974): 257–71.

Locke's separation of senses into primary and secondary sensations—the external world and the inner world—was scorned by most Romantics, who extolled the secondary sensations as the realm of visionary experience superior to the external world. This essay maintains that Byron was the only major Romantic poet who wrote within the empirical tradition and viewed the external world as the ultimate reality. Bostetter examines Byron's *Don Juan*, *Manfred*, *Cain*, *Island*, and other works.

1571.   Goldstein, Stephen L. "Byron's *Cain* and the Painites." *SIR* 14 (1975): 391–410.
Byron's imaginative use of geological, biological, and astronomical theory in *Cain* undermined traditional orthodox religious views of creation and cosmology.

1572.   Hassler, Donald M. "Byron and Erasmus Darwin." *BSUF* 20.3 (1979): 75–80.
Assesses the impact of Darwin's diffuse literary style, which incorporates a vast array of scientific ideas, on Byron's poetic strategy in *Don Juan*.

Luigi Capuana (1839–1915)

1573.   Norman, Hilda L. "The Scientific and the Pseudo-Scientific in the Works of Luigi Capuana." *PMLA* 53 (1938): 869–85.
Although Capuana's early enthusiasm for Zola's naturalism accounts for his reputation as a literary naturalist, he soon abandoned that phase of his writing in favor of scientific and pseudoscientific ideas, perhaps derived from the writings of Wells and Poe. Norman reviews scientific, medical, occult, and fantastic themes in Capuana's *Spiritismo?*, *Mondo occulto*, *Coscienze*, *Rassegnazione*, and other works.

Thomas Carlyle (1795–1881)

1574.   Gridgeman, Norman. "Thomas Carlyle, Geometer." *New Scientist* 44 (1969): 466–67.
Though Carlyle was interested principally in literature and history, he made minor contributions to geometry and commented enthusiastically on Newton's *Principia*. He was, however, generally unsympathetic to science.

1574a.   Moore, Carlisle. "Carlyle and Goethe as Scientist." *Carlyle and His Contemporaries: Essays in Honor of Charles Richard Sanders*. Ed. John Clubbe. Durham: Duke UP, 1976. 21–34.
Maintains that the attitude toward science Carlyle expressed in his literary works was largely shaped by his study of Goethe's writing, both literary and scientific. Goethe was instrumental in Carlyle's effort to unite science, poetry, and religion.

1575.   Sigman, Joseph T. "Idea and Image in Thomas Carlyle's *Sartor Resartus*." *DA* 29 (1968–69): 240A.
Traces the philosophical background of Carlyle's *Sartor Resartus* to the epistemology and ethics of Locke, Leibniz, D. Hume, Kant, and Fichte. In *Sartor Resartus* "Carlyle constructs a world which defeats the theological pretensions of Enlight-

enment empirical science. Replacing the anachronistic Newtonian universe with the seemingly absurd chaos of history, he proceeds, through the carefully controlled development of a series of key images, to develop a vision which discovers meaning in the chaos."

1576. Turner, Frank M. "Victorian Scientific Naturalism and Thomas Carlyle." *VS* 18 (1974–75): 325–43.
Carlyle's natural supernaturalism and social criticism in works such as *Sartor Resartus* were the intellectual springboard for later developments in the scientific naturalism of Galton, T. H. Huxley, Spencer, Tyndall, and others.

Adalbert von Chamisso (1781–1838)

1577. Nettesheim, Josefine. "Adalbert von Chamissos botanisch-exotische Studien, Peter Schlemihl und die Lieder von 'armen' Leuten und Verbrechern." *Marginalien zur poetischen Welt: Festschrift für Robert Mühlher zum 60. Geburtstag.* Ed. Alois Eder, Hellmuth Himmel, and Alfred Kracher. Berlin: Duncker, 1971. 197–217. Rpt. in *Poeta doctus oder die Poetisierung der Wissenschaft von Musäus bis Benn.* Berlin: Duncker, 1975. 57–76.
Outlines Chamisso's scientific and botanical studies and examines their impact on the view of nature reflected in his poetry. Cites works such as "Die alte Waschfrau" and "Zweites Lied von der alten Waschfrau."

Anton Pavlovich Chekhov (1860–1904)

1578. Kovalevsky, Pierre. "Antoine Tchékhov, écrivain et médecin." *Literature and Science.* Proc. of the Sixth Triennial Congress of the International Federation for Modern Languages and Literatures. Oxford, 1954. Oxford: Blackwell, 1955. 283–87.
Essentially a capsule biography of Chekhov, this essay emphasizes the writer's continued and sustained interest in medicine and literature.

1579. Scielzo, Caroline A. G. "The Doctor in Chekhov's Works." *DAI* 37 (1977): 5879A–80A.
Examines the influence of Chekhov's medical training on his fictional portrayals of physicians. In general, his descriptions integrate medical accuracy with aesthetic refinement.

Arthur Hugh Clough (1819–61)

1580. Palmer, Francis W. "The Bearing of Science on the Thought of Arthur Hugh Clough." *PMLA* 59 (1944): 212–25.
Concerns Clough's dedication to reason, objectivity, and a scientific outlook. Discusses the treatment of pre-Darwinian evolutionary theory in his poem *Natura Naturans* (1849).

Samuel Taylor Coleridge (1772–1834)

1581.   Abrams, Meyer Howard. "Coleridge's 'A Light in Sound': Science, Meta-
         science, and Poetic Imagination." *PAPS* 116 (1972): 458–76.
Lines 26–33 of "The Eolian Harp" shed light on Coleridge's attempt to develop
a metascientific countermetaphysic to the metaphysical foundations of modern science. Abrams stresses Coleridge's views about Newton's *Opticks* as well as the influence of Schelling's *Naturphilosophie* and Boehme's philosophy.

1582.   Coburn, Kathleen. "Coleridge, a Bridge between Science and Poetry: Re-
         flections on the Bicentenary of His Birth." *Proceedings of the Royal Institution
         of Great Britain* 46 (1973): 45–63.
Traces the development of Coleridge's friendship with the chemist Humphry
Davy, stressing the impact Coleridge's lively interest in chemistry had on his poetics.

1583.   Corrigan, Timothy J. "*Biographia Literaria* and the Language of Science."
         JHI 41 (1980): 399–419.
Describes Coleridge's attempt in the *Biographia Literaria* to express his theories
of life and poetry in the scientific language of biology and chemistry.

1584.   Haeger, Jack H. "Coleridge's 'Bye Blow': The Composition and Date of
         Theory of Life." *MP* 74 (1976–77): 20–41.
Examines Coleridge's letters and notebooks, the testimony of his daughter, Sara,
and the style and conceptual content of *Theory of Life* and concludes that Coleridge
began to write this biological work for his friend, the physician James Gillman, in
about 1817.

1585.   ———. "The Scientific Speculations of Samuel Taylor Coleridge: Manu-
         script Transcriptions and a Commentary." *DAI* 32 (1971): 2642A.
Examines Coleridge's synthesis of philosophical and scientific speculation in works
such as *Biographia Literaria*, *Treatise on Method*, and *Theory of Life*.

1585a.   Harris, John. "Coleridge's Readings in Medicine." *WC* 3 (1972): 85–95.
Surveys Coleridge's study of texts in fields such as physiology, hygiene, pathology,
and pharmacopoeia.

1586.   Levere, Trevor H. "Coleridge and Romantic Science." *Science, Technology,
         and Culture in Historical Perspective*. Ed. Louis A. Knafla, Martin S. Staum,
         and T. H. E. Travers. Calgary: U of Calgary P, 1976. 81–104.
Outlines the scope, method, assumptions, laws, contents, and sources of the
Romantic science underlying Coleridge's philosophy. According to Levere, Romantic
science ". . . dealt with synthesis, unification, reality, unity, organicism and ra-
tionality in its highest sense" and provided a fertile source of metaphor for Coleridge.
Levere emphasizes Coleridge's interest in chemistry.

1587.   ———. "Coleridge, Chemistry and the Philosophy of Nature." *SIR* 16
         (1977): 349–79.
Traces Coleridge's scientific education, stressing his relations with Davy and

Beddoes and noting their influence on his lifelong interest in chemistry. Also examines the development of Coleridge's philosophy of nature and its basis in the science of his time.

1588. ———. "S. T. Coleridge and the Human Sciences: Anthropology, Phrenology, and Mesmerism." *Science, Pseudoscience, and Society.* Ed. Marsha P. Hanen, Margaret J. Osler, and Robert G. Weyant. Waterloo: Wilfred Laurier UP, 1980. 171–92.
Outlines the extent to which Coleridge's knowledge of anthropology, phrenology, and mesmerism informs his theory of nature and humankind in *Theory of Life.*

1589. ———. "S. T. Coleridge: A Poet's View of Science." *AnS* 35 (1978): 33–44.
"This paper is concerned with Coleridge's view of science as at once a branch of knowledge and a creative activity, mediating between man and nature, and thereby complementing poetry. Coleridge was well-informed about contemporary science. He stressed the symbolic status of scientific language, the role of scientific genius, and the need in science to rely upon reason rather than the unqualified senses. Kepler and, more recently, John Hunter and Humphry Davy provided his favorite instances of scientific genius, while chemistry—Davy's, not Lavoisier's—was poetic. Science and poetry could both rely on reason, the power of language, and faithfulness to nature."

1590. Male, Roy R., Jr. "The Background of Coleridge's *Theory of Life.*" *University of Texas Studies in English* 33 (1954): 60–68.
Treats Coleridge's contribution to the debate over the electrovital analogy initiated by Galvani, Abernethy, and W. Lawrence.

1590a. Miller, Craig. "Coleridge's Concept of Nature." *JHI* 25 (1964): 77–96.
Considers study of Coleridge's scientific theories important because many of his writings are devoted to the sciences and because "in nearly all his works Coleridge utilizes for illustrative purposes concepts and imagery drawn from the sciences."

1591. Needham, Joseph. "S. T. Coleridge as a Philosophical Biologist." *Science Progress* 20 (1926): 692–707. Rpt. as "S. T. Coleridge as a Philosophic Biologist." *The Sceptical Biologist.* New York: Norton, 1930. 154–68.
Coleridge's *Theory of Life* contains several interesting points for the historian of biology, such as its anticipation of the idea of emergent evolution, but the work fails to adhere to the rigors of scientific method.

1592. Potter, George R. "Coleridge and the Idea of Evolution." *PMLA* 40 (1925): 379–97.
Coleridge was deeply influenced by the strains of evolutionary thought in the writings of Bruno, Hunter, Geoffroy Saint-Hilaire, E. Darwin, Lyell, and Oken; but since this thought conflicted with his religious beliefs, he was never completely won over by evolutionary theories. Pertinent passages in his writings evidence his ambivalence.

1593.   Snyder, Alice D. "Coleridge's Cosmogony: A Note on the Poetic 'World-View.' " *SP* 21 (1924): 616–25.
Coleridge's cosmogony, gleaned here from his notebooks and his marginalia in scientific texts, anticipates in some respects the evolutionary cosmogony that would dominate the later nineteenth century.

1594.   Wells, G. A. "Coleridge and Goethe on Scientific Method in the Light of Some Unpublished Coleridge Marginalia." *GL&L* ns 4 (1950–51): 101–14.
Investigates the similarities and differences between Goethe's and Coleridge's conceptions of scientific method. Both believed in the conceptual interpenetration of the particular and the universal, though Goethe preferred the particular as the point of departure in scientific inquiry, while Coleridge opted for the universal.

William Wilkie Collins (1824–89)

1595.   MacEachen, Dougald B. "Wilkie Collins' *Heart and Science* and the Vivisection Controversy." *VN* 29 (1966): 22–25.
Outlines the vivisection controversy in Victorian England and briefly examines Collins's propagandistic novel *Heart and Science*, which attacks science in general and the practice of vivisection in particular.

James Fenimore Cooper (1789–1851)

1596.   Clark, Harry H. "Fenimore Cooper and Science." *TWA* 48 (1959): 179–204; 49 (1960): 249–82.
Discusses Cooper's familiarity with the science of Newton, F. Bacon, Buffon, Laplace, and Lyell; the relation between his religious ideas and science; his interest in astronomy; his concepts of heredity and ethnology; his attitude toward the practical utility of applied science; and the influence of science on the themes and structures of his fiction. Among the works covered are *The Crater*, *Monikins*, *Mercedes of Castile*, *Notions of the Americans*, and *The Last of the Mohicans*.

Marie Corelli (1855–1924)

1597.   Huff, Chester C., Jr. "The Novels of Marie Corelli: Their Themes and Their Popularity as an Index to Popular Taste." *DA* 31 (1971): 4718A–19A.
Among the themes studied is Corelli's attempt to reconcile science and religion. Her novels were read and praised by Meredith, Tennyson, Wilde, and others.

Stephen Crane (1871–1900)

1598.   Fitelson, David. "Stephen Crane's *Maggie* and Darwinism." *AQ* 16 (1964): 182–94.
The ideology that informs the naturalism of Crane's *Maggie* is based on Darwinistic determinism.

1599.   Gibson, Donald B. "The Fiction of Stephen Crane." *DA* 23 (1963): 2525.
Studies Crane's use of scientific themes, especially the implications of Darwinism, in works such as *Maggie* and *The Red Badge of Courage*.

1600.   Osborn, Neal J. "Optograms, George Moore, and Crane's 'Silver Pageant.' " *AN&Q* 4 (1965–66): 39–40.
Cites scientific experiments in optograms (pictures in the eyes) and G. Moore's *Confessions of a Young Man* as possible influences on Crane's portrayal of the artist Gaunt in "The Silver Pageant."

1601.   Smith, Allen N. "Stephen Crane and the Darwinian Revolution." *DAI* 35 (1974–75): 6160A–61A.
Maintains that Crane was the first major American writer to abandon the materialistic determinism characteristic of the first stage of the Darwinian revolution and to develop instead the relativistic and nihilistic outlook characteristic of the second stage. An examination of Crane's peculiar type of naturalism, as reflected in *Maggie* and *The Red Badge of Courage*, forms the basis of this study.

Charles Robert Darwin (1809–82)

1602.   Campbell, John A. "Darwin and the *Origin of Species*: The Rhetorical Ancestry of an Idea." *SM* 37.1 (1970): 1–14.
Darwin's synthesis of the rhetorical legacies of Lyell's *Principles of Geology*, Paley's *Natural Theology*, and R. Chambers's *Vestiges of the Natural History of Creation* largely accounts for the success of his *Origin of Species*.

1603.   Gaull, Marilyn. "From Wordsworth to Darwin: 'On the Fields of Praise.' " *WC* 10 (1979): 33–48.
See item 2047 for annotation.

1604.   Grove, Richard S. "A Re-examination of Darwin's Argument in *On the Origin of Species*." *DA* 30 (1969–70): 4411A–12A.
Analyzes the rhetorical strategy in Darwin's *Origin* and assesses the logical validity and scientific accuracy of his argument.

1605.   Hyman, Stanley Edgar. "Darwin the Dramatist." *CentR* 3 (1959): 364–75.
The rhetorical effectiveness of Darwin's *Origin of Species* depends largely on its dramatic use of metaphor and on its dramatic structure. In these and other respects the work deserves to be classified as literature rather than as mere prosaic science.

1606.   ———. "The 'Origin' as Scripture." *VQR* 35 (1959): 540–52.
As a work of literature, Darwin's *Origin of Species* has the structure of tragic drama and the texture of poetry. It is comparable to sacred writing in its genealogical concerns, prophetic qualities, emphasis on personal testimony, and depiction of the workings of the unknowable "god" of natural selection.

1607.   ———. "The Whole Round World." *NMQ* 29 (1959): 277–91.
Examines passages from Darwin's *Voyage of the Beagle* that prefigure scientific tenets expressed in the *Origin of Species* and comments briefly on the literary qualities of the *Voyage*, especially Darwin's concern for the poetry of landscape.

1608.   Scheick, William J. "Epic Traces in Darwin's *Origin of Species*." *SAQ* 72 (1973): 270–79.
In three ways the *Origin of Species* reflects the epic tradition, with which Darwin was familiar from his schooling. The *Origin* expresses epic mystery through the personifying power of natural selection, epic heroism through the travails of its flora and fauna, and the elevated tone of the epic through its descriptive imagery. Throughout, the agony of the universal struggle for life pervades the *Origin*, reaching mythic proportions in the discovery of unity and cohesion in the universe.

1609.   Tallmadge, John. "From Chronicle to Quest: The Shaping of Darwin's 'Voyage of the Beagle.' " *VS* 23 (1979–80): 325–45.
Explains Darwin's strategies in composing and organizing the *Voyage of the Beagle*, a popular travel journal of lasting literary and scientific interest.

Alphonse Daudet (1840–97)

1609a.   Carter, Boyd G. "Alphonse Daudet and Darwinism." *MLQ* 6 (1945): 93–98.
Discusses Daudet's negative response, in works such as *L'immortel*, to the social and moral implications of Darwinian evolution.

Charles Dickens (1812–70)

1610.   Axton, William F. "Religious and Scientific Imagery in *Bleak House*." *NCF* 22 (1967–68): 349–59.
Explores Dickens's conceptual synthesis of pre-Darwinian evolutionary theory and the religious imagery of creation in *Bleak House*.

1611.   Baker, William. "*Hard Times* and *Orr's Circle of the Sciences*." *DSN* 8 (1977): 78.
Dickens's reference in *Hard Times* (bk. 1, ch. 3) to the textbooks edited by William Somerville Orr, entitled *Orr's Circle of the Sciences* (1854), was intended "to indicate to his readers precisely the nature of the ideology that Gradgrind is trying to impose upon his own children and those under his care."

1612.   Fehr, Bernhard. "Dickens und Malthus." *GRM* 2 (1910): 542–55.
Carlyle introduced Dickens to the scientific concepts of the political economist Robert Malthus. Offended by Malthus's "facts and figures," Dickens wrote *The Chimes* as a satire on Malthusian population theories.

1613.   Kaplan, Fred. *Dickens and Mesmerism: The Hidden Springs of Fiction*. Princeton: Princeton UP, 1975. 250 pp.
        Rev. Richard J. Dunn, *SNNTS* 8 (1976): 223–33; G. W. Kennedy, *VS* 20 (1976–77): 343–45; T. J. Cribb, *RES* ns 28 (1977): 514–15; Sam Pickering, *SR* 85 (1977): 651–60; Branwen B. Pratt, *L&P* 27.1 (1977): 35–38; Edwin M. Eigner, *MLR* 73 (1978): 416–17.

Outlines the history of mesmerism in nineteenth-century Britain, traces Dickens's growing interest in the pseudoscience, and discusses his mesmeric sessions with Madame de la Rue. Kaplan sees mesmerism as an important aspect of Dickens's fiction. He explains scenes from various novels in the light of the relationship between mesmeric operator and subject, and he claims that mesmerism is both a significant image and a central organizing principle in Dickens's art.

1614.   Metz, Nancy A. "The Artistic Reclamation of Waste in *Our Mutual Friend*." *NCF* 34 (1979–80): 59–72.

The themes and characterizations of *Our Mutual Friend* reflect Dickens's interest in the chemistry of the regenerative process and in Victorian popular science generally, which was the focus of his journal, *Household Words*.

1615.   ———. "Science in *Household Words*: 'The Poetic . . . Passed into our Common Life.' " *VPN* 11 (1978): 121–33.

Examines the range of scientific and technical issues presented in Dickens's magazine, *Household Words*, and assesses his attitude toward science and scientists, noting especially his view of the importance of science as an influence on the imaginative faculties of the creative artist.

1616.   Peyrouton, N. C. "Boz and the American Phreno-Mesmerists." *DiS* 3 (1967): 38–50.

Briefly discusses Dickens's favorable attitude toward phrenology and mesmerism and his relations with the phreno-mesmerists Collyer, Elliotson, O. Fowler, and L. Fowler. Surveys the results of the Fowlers' reading of Dickens's cranium, which took place around 1842.

1617.   Pomeranz, Herman. *Medicine in the Shakespearean Plays and Dickens' Doctors*. New York: Powell, 1936. 410 pp.
        See item 599 for annotation.

1618.   Potter, George R. "Mr. Pickwick, Eminent Scientist, and His Theory of Tittlebats." *PQ* 2 (1923): 48–55.

A comparison between Dickens's satire of science in the *Pickwick Papers* and J. Hill's satire of the Royal Society in his *Review of the Works of the Royal Society* (1751) suggests that Dickens may have been influenced by Hill's work, though no definite connection has yet been established.

1619.   Sloane, David E. E. "Phrenology in *Hard Times*: A Source for Bitzer." *DSN* 5 (1974): 9–12.

Dickens's characterization of George Bitzer in *Hard Times*, with its frequent allusions to mathematics and phrenology, may have been drawn from George Combe's description of the phrenologist and mathematician George Parker Bidder in *Lectures on Phrenology* (1854).

1620.   Wiley, Elizabeth. "Four Strange Cases." *Dickensian* 58 (1962): 120–25.
Dickens's inspiration for the episode in *Bleak House* that involves death by spontaneous combustion may have come in part from a French medical report of 1783. Wiley also describes the theme of spontaneous combustion in C. Brown's *Wieland*, Marryat's *Jacob Faithful*, and Melville's *Redburn*.

Emily Dickinson (1830–86)

1621.   Patterson, Rebecca. "Emily Dickinson's Geography: Latin America." *PLL* 5 (1969): 441–57.
Assesses the extent to which Dickinson's knowledge of Latin America's physical geography affected the metaphors and imagery of poems 137, 247, 397, 427, and 498.

1622.   Witherington, Paul. "Dickinson's 'Faith is a Fine Invention.' " *Expl* 26 (1967–68): item 62.
Dickinson's reference to the microscope in "Faith" is ambiguous. It suggests both the potential intensification of awareness through science and the danger of distorted vision through reliance on scientific apparatus that narrows the perceptual field.

Sir Arthur Conan Doyle (1859–1930)

1623.   Blackburn, Julian. "A Note on Sherlock Holmes and Radioactivity." *Baker Street Journal* 23 (1973): 32–33.
Holmes's allusions to his research on the properties of radioactive substances in *The Adventure of the Empty House*, *The Adventure of the Devil's Foot*, and other works seem to anticipate results later obtained in the field by Becquerel and P. Curie.

1624.   Kissane, James, and John M. Kissane. "Sherlock Holmes and the Ritual of Reason." *NCF* 17 (1962–63): 353–62.
Analyzes Doyle's *Hound of the Baskervilles*, discussing Holmes's "scientific" deductive method and its role in Doyle's dramatization of the struggle between reason and superstition characteristic of nineteenth-century "scientism."

1625.   Rose, Phyllis. "Huxley, Holmes, and the Scientist as Aesthete." *VN* 38 (1970): 22–24.
Discusses Doyle's adaptation of T. H. Huxley's concept of scientific method. "The adventures of Sherlock Holmes may be read as a corrective commentary on, perhaps, a parody of Huxley's oversimplification of science."

Annette von Droste-Hülshoff (1797–1848)

1626.   Lobdell, William Y., Jr. "The Animal World of Annette von Droste-Hülshoff." *DA* 29 (1968–69): 3103A.

Surveys Droste-Hülshoff's zoological imagery and discusses her interest in natural science and her use of scientific fact in her poetry.

1627.   Nettesheim, Josefine. *Annette Droste zu Hülshoff: Naturwissenschaftliches Lexikon Lyrik und Epik.* Münster: Regensberg, 1973. 71 pp.
Demonstrates that Droste-Hülshoff was thoroughly imbued with the modern, enlightened learning of her time. Provides a lexicon of the scientific terms in her lyric and epic works and discusses their sources and poetic usage.

1628.   ———. *Die geistige Welt der Dichterin Annette Droste zu Hülshoff.* Münster: Regensburg Münster, 1967. 211 pp.
Rev. Elisabeth Stopp, *MLR* 64 (1969): 949–50.
Maintains that the intellectual climate of Droste's age, including the scientific currents of magnetism, mesmerism, and galvanism, is fully reflected in her writing. Analyzes works such as "Das Vermächtnis des Arztes," "Die Judenbuche," "Der Rosstäuscher," "Der Hünenstein," and "Die Mergelgrube."

1629.   ———. "Wissen und Dichtung in der ersten Hälfte des 19. Jahrhunderts am Beispiel der geistigen Welt Annettes von Droste-Hülshoff." *DVLG* 32 (1958): 516–53.
Droste's writings bear the imprint of her age and reflect contemporary scientific developments in fields such as galvanism, magnetism, and electricity. A comparative study of her story "Die Judenbuche," her epic poem "Das Vermächtnis des Arztes," and her ballad "Der Rosstäuscher" reveals how her attempt to assimilate contemporary knowledge determines the complexity of these works.

George Eliot (1819–80)

1630.   Adam, Ian. "A Huxley Echo in *Middlemarch*." *N&Q* ns 11 (1964): 227.
Cites a reference to physiological reality in *Middlemarch* that was probably derived from T. H. Huxley's "Physical Basis of Life."

1631.   Beer, Gillian. "Plot and the Analogy with Science in Later Nineteenth-Century Novelists." *CCrit* 2 (1980): 131–49.
Argues that the plot techniques and narrative structures of works by Eliot, Hardy, and Zola are based on analogies to scientific method. Stresses the influence of Lyell's *Principles of Geology*, C. Darwin's *Origin of Species*, and Bernard's *Le médecine expérimentale*.

1632.   Collins, Kenny K. "Experimental Method and the Epistemology of *Middlemarch*." *DAI* 37 (1977): 5843A.
"The narrator of *Middlemarch* employs an experimental method codified in Claude Bernard's *Introduction à l'étude de le médecine expérimentale* (1865), and implies an empirical epistemology advocated in George Henry Lewes's *Problems of Life and Mind* (1873–79) and *Principles of Success in Literature* (1865)."

1633.   Feltes, N. N. "Phrenology: From Lewes to George Eliot." *SLitI* 1.1 (1968): 13–22.

Summarizes the development of Lewes's views on phrenology, expressed in successive editions of his *Biographical History of Philosophy* (1845–46). Lewes distinguished between the materialism of phrenology proper and the practice of cranioscopy. While ridiculing cranioscopy, he saw phrenology as the bridge between supernatural and positivist psychology, an opinion echoed in Eliot's allusions to phrenology and psychology in novels such as *Daniel Deronda* and *Middlemarch*.

1634.   Greenberg, Robert A. "Plexuses and Ganglia: Scientific Allusion in *Middlemarch*." *NCF* 30 (1975–76): 33–52.
An examination of the notebooks Eliot compiled before writing *Middlemarch* reveals that the sources of the novel's complex and carefully refined scientific allusions include Davy's *Elements of Agricultural Chemistry* (1814), Lewes's *Physiology of Common Life* (1859–60), and Bichat's *Traité sur les membranes* (1800) and *Anatomie générale* (1801).

1635.   Halstead, Frank G. "George Eliot: Medical Digressions in *Middlemarch*, and Eliot's State of Health." *BHM* 20 (1946): 413–25.
Discusses Eliot's references in *Middlemarch* to Bichat's medical ideas, especially the tissue theory he expounded in *General Anatomy Applied to Physiology and Medicine*, and comments on the state of Eliot's health as revealed through her personal correspondence.

1636.   Hudson, Stewart M. "George Henry Lewes' Evolutionism in the Fiction of George Eliot." *DA* 31 (1970–71): 6059A.
Explicates Lewes's evolutionary philosophy, psychology, and biology and demonstrates its influence on Eliot's fiction.

1637.   Hulme, Hilda M. "*Middlemarch* as Science-Fiction: Notes on Language and Imagery." *Novel* 2 (1968–69): 36–45.
Among the sources of the scientific language and imagery in Eliot's *Middlemarch* were the writings of Bichat, the French anatomist and surgeon (including *Recherches physiologiques sur la vie et la mort*), Lewes's *Physiology of Common Life*, and Spencer's *First Principles*.

1638.   Kitchel, Anna T. "Scientific Influences in the Work of Emile Zola and George Eliot." Diss. U of Wisconsin, 1921.
Not seen for annotation.

1639.   Levine, George. "George Eliot's Hypothesis of Reality." *NCF* 35 (1980–81): 1–28.
Discusses Eliot's *Middlemarch* and *Daniel Deronda* from the perspective of her hypothesis that an ideal reality provides a scientific means of comprehending the sensible, empirically verifiable world. Emphasizes Lewes's influence on Eliot's notion of an extrasensible world.

1640.   Lothamer, Eileen. "Science and Pseudo-Science in George Eliot's 'The Lifted Veil.'" *Extrapolation* 17 (1975–76): 125–32.

Summarizes "The Lifted Veil," which alludes to phrenology, extrasensory perception, and science, to illustrate Eliot's "religion of humanity."

1641. Mason, Michael Y. *"Middlemarch* and Science: Problems of Life and Mind." *RES* ns 22 (1971): 151–69.
Projects the influence of Lewes, Mill, Whewell, and others on the development of Eliot's view of empiricism and science in *Middlemarch*.

1642. Newton, K. M. "George Eliot, George Henry Lewes, and Darwinism." *DUJ* 66 (1973–74): 278–93.
Though Eliot accepted Darwin's theory of evolution as valid, she was disturbed by many of its moral and social implications. Eliot's complex attitude toward Darwinism was influenced by Lewes's ideas on the subject, and her ambivalence is evident in the themes and characterizations of novels such as *Felix Holt, Romola, Daniel Deronda,* and *Middlemarch.*

1643. Paris, Bernard J. "George Eliot, Science Fiction, and Fantasy." *Extrapolation* 5 (1963–64): 26–30.
Treats the relations between Eliot's realistic fiction, which is based in part on science and positivistic cosmology and epistemology, and the literary genres of science fiction and fantasy. "Science fiction . . . is separated from the fairy-tale and allied to fiction such as George Eliot's by its attempt to do justice to the laws of nature; and it is separated from truly mature fiction such as George Eliot's and allied to the fairy-tale by its self-indulgence, its use of science to transcend reality."

1644. Wolf, Emily V. "George Eliot's Liberal Menagerie: Natural History, Biology, and Value in the Early Novels." Diss. Harvard U, 1969.
Not seen for annotation.

Ralph Waldo Emerson (1803–82)

1644a. Allen, Gay Wilson. "A New Look at Emerson and Science." *Literature and Ideas in America: Essays in Memory of Harry Hayden Clark.* Ed. Robert Falk. Athens: Ohio UP, 1975. 58–78.
Examines Emerson's first professional lectures (1833–34), of which the first four were almost entirely on science. Maintains that these works—with their focus on astronomy, geology, and, to a lesser extent, biology and chemistry—help elucidate his book *Nature* (1836), in which he attempts to "spiritualize science."

1645. Baym, Nina. "From Metaphysics to Metaphor: The Image of Water in Emerson and Thoreau." *SIR* 5 (1965–66): 231–43.
Water imagery is common in Emerson and pervasive in Thoreau but the two thinkers used it for different metaphoric ends, reflecting their diverse metaphysical and cosmological views.

1646. Beach, Joseph Warren. "Emerson and Evolution." *UTQ* 3 (1933–34): 474–97.

Outlines the process by which Emerson arrived at his transcendental version of evolution theory. His opinions on evolution were informed not by great scientific evolutionists like Lamarck and C. Darwin but by second-rate, popular, and dubious authorities on the subject such as S. Coleridge, Abernethy, Bell, and Oegger.

1647.   Cameron, Kenneth Walter. "Emerson and Hydrostatics—the Siphars."
            ESQ 48 (1967): 93–98.
In writing "Organ" (1822), later published as "An Extract from Unpublished Travels in the East" (1829), young Emerson probably referred to an article on hydrostatics in the *Encyclopedia Britannica*. Cameron reprints both Emerson's story and the relevant portion of the article.

1648.   ———. "Emerson, Cosmology, and Thomas Bassnett's *Outlines*." *ATQ* 36
            (1977): 61–63.
Examines evidence that Emerson consulted Bassnett's *Outlines of a Mechanical Theory of Storms, Containing the True Laws of Lunar Influence* (1854), which adduced new theories of planetary movements and laws of gravitation. This essay reprints excerpts from Bassnett's book as well as F. B. Sanborn's one-paragraph review in the January 1855 *Harvard Magazine*.

1649.   ———. "Emerson, Thoreau, and the Society of Natural History." *AL* 24
            (1952–53): 21–30.
See item 1973 for annotation.

1650.   Clark, Harry Hayden. "Emerson and Science." *PQ* 10 (1931): 225–60.
This broad outline of Emerson's scientific interests and influences during his formative years (up to 1838) focuses on his study of astronomy and evolution theory and its bearing on his turn against ecclesiasticism and toward faith in a depersonalized oversoul.

1651.   Conroy, Stephen S. "Emerson and Phrenology." *AQ* 16 (1964): 215–17.
Notes Emerson's cautious interest in phrenology, which he refers to in several essays, including "Experience" and "Fate."

1652.   Francis, Robert L. "The Architectonics of Emerson's *Nature*." *AQ* 19 (1967):
            39–52.
This analysis of the structure of *Nature* emphasizes the stylistic tension between Emerson's poetic aspirations and the demands of his scientific naturalism.

1653.   Haig, Robert L. "Emerson and the 'Electric Word' of John Hunter." *NEQ*
            28 (1955): 394–97.
Maintains that in the "electric word" passage of "Poetry and Imagination" Emerson incorrectly attributes the phrase "arrested and progressive development" to the British anatomist and surgeon John Hunter. Haig argues that, contrary to the common assumption, the passage should not be cited as evidence of Emerson's acceptance of evolution.

1654.   Hopkins, Vivian C. "Emerson and Bacon." *AL* 29 (1957–58): 408–30.

Traces the development of Emerson's interest in and admiration for F. Bacon, noting Baconian influence on Emerson's works, such as *Nature, English Traits*, and various essays.

1655.   Lindner, Carl M. "Newtonianism in Emerson's *Nature.*" *ESQ* 20 (1974): 260–69.

In *Nature*, replete with metaphors and images derived from Newtonianism, Emerson's thinking is at a transitional stage between the Enlightenment view that nature is static and stable and the Romantic view that nature is organic and developmental.

1656.   Neufeldt, Leonard N. "The Science of Power: Emerson's Views on Science and Technology in America." *JHI* 38 (1977): 329–44.

Discusses Emerson's understanding of the implications, both positive and negative, of the machine and of the power of invention in nineteenth-century America. In his essay "Works and Days," Emerson calls for a balanced, spiritual appropriation and manipulation of technology.

1657.   Obuchowski, Peter A. "Emerson, Evolution, and the Problem of Evil." *HTR* 72 (1979): 150–56.

The theory of spiritual evolution Emerson expresses in "The Over-Soul," "Inspiration," and other essays is bound up with his philosophical solution to the problem of evil.

1658.   Panek, LeRoy Lad. "Imagery and Emerson's 'Compensation.'" *ESQ* 69 (1972): 218–21.

An analysis of the language of "Compensation" discloses that the essay is controlled by patterns of imagery drawn from commerce, law, and physics. Panek maintains that the image cluster involving scientific concepts is particularly appropriate, for "Emerson's view of compensation could be stated in terms, say, of the Law of Conservation of Energy, or other similar physical concepts."

1659.   Sanford, Charles L. "Emerson, Thoreau, and the Hereditary Duality." *ESQ* 54 (1969): 36–43.

Outlines the conceptual difficulties Emerson and Thoreau faced in their attempt to reconcile idealism and realism, poetry and science. Cites Emerson's *Nature* and "Over-Soul" and Thoreau's *Walden*, "Wild Apples," "Succession of Forest Trees," and other works.

1660.   Shepard, Grace F. "Emerson and Natural Science." *Education* 59 (1938–39): 590–94.

Cites passages from Emerson's *Journals* and *Essays* that reveal his poetic appreciation for natural science.

1661.   Shurr, William H. "Emerson and Lucretius on Nature: Questions of Method and Matter." *ATQ* 38 (1978): 153–65.

Juxtaposes Emerson's *Nature* and Lucretius's *De rerum natura*. Concerning the nature of reality, the American idealist and the classical materialist are at opposite poles, but they are remarkably alike with respect to mental processes, methodology, and the possibilities of human knowledge. Biographical and textual evidence suggests that the Roman poet exerted a powerful influence on Emerson's early work.

1662.   Strauch, Carl F. "Emerson's Sacred Science." *PMLA* 73 (1958): 237–50.
Neoplatonism, Swedenborg, R. Chambers, Schelling, Goethe, Oken, and S. Coleridge are among the influences on Emerson's acceptance of a skeptical science united with a religious impulse. Strauch examines Emerson's "Song of Nature," "Fate," *English Traits*, and journal entries from 1843–45 to illustrate Emerson's imaginative dialectic confrontation of opposites such as science and religion, skepticism and faith, evolution and emanation.

1662a.   ———. "The Sources of Emerson's 'Song of Nature.' " *HLB* 9 (1955): 300–34.
Argues that "Song of Nature" is "the crown of Emerson's subjective evolutionary humanism, making a synthesis of ancient fable and modern science." Surveys the extensive studies Emerson undertook in astronomy, biology, and geology between 1836, when he read Lyell's *Principles of Geology*, and 1859, when he wrote the poem.

1662b.   Thompson, Frank T. "Emerson and Etienne Geoffroy St. Hilaire." *Symposium* 5 (1951): 216–29.
Examines Emerson's familiarity with Geoffroy Saint-Hilaire's thought and concludes that Emerson sided with Geoffroy Saint-Hilaire in his famous scientific controversy with Georges Cuvier. To Emerson, Geoffroy Saint-Hilaire belonged to the "poets in science," whereas Cuvier was one of the "men of severe science."

Gustave Flaubert (1821–80)

1663.   Seznec, Jean. "Saint Antoine et les monstres: Essai sur les sources et la signification du fantastique de Flaubert." *PMLA* 58 (1943): 195–222.
Flaubert sought in literature freedom from the monsters that haunted him since childhood. The sources for the final version of his conte are bestiaries, natural histories, and Spinoza, not Flaubert's imagination. The meaning of these monsters is scientific and philosophical, rather than religious or moral. Science is the final temptation that dissolves mind into matter.

1664.   ———. "Science et religion chez Flaubert d'après les sources de la *Tentation de Saint-Antoine*." *RR* 33 (1942): 360–65.
Flaubert's revisions of the episode concerning the gods and the episode concerning the monsters in *Tentation de Saint-Antoine* reveal his intellectual evolution from religion to science. Seznec argues that the monster episode in the final version reflects Flaubert's preoccupation with Spinozism and transformism.

Theodor Fontane (1819–98)

1665.   Faucher, Eugène. "Fontane et Darwin." *EG* 25 (1970): 7–24, 141–54.
A thorough understanding of Fontane's novels depends on a knowledge of their Darwinian elements. Faucher studies C. Darwin's influence on the characterization and themes of Fontane's novels, including *Irrungen Wirrungen* and *Effi Briest*.

Ugo Foscolo (1778–1827)

1666.   Reynolds, Barbara. " 'L'altissimo a Pallade': A Point of Astronomy in Foscolo's *Le grazie.*" *IS* 12 (1957): 57–67.

Foscolo's reference to the asteroid Pallas in *Le grazie* combines elements of ancient mythology with contemporary astronomical data. Reynolds outlines the astronomical background of the reference.

Hamlin Garland (1860–1940)

1667.   Fujii, Gertrude S. "The Veritism of Hamlin Garland." *DA* 31 (1970–71): 2914A.

Traces Garland's literary creed of "veritism" to the evolutionary thought of Spencer and Taine.

1668.   Harder, Hyla H. "The Influence of Scientific Theories of Expression on Garland's *Main-Travelled Roads.*" *DAI* 34 (1973): 1279A–80A.

Garland's *Main-Travelled Roads* was profoundly influenced by C. Darwin's *Expression of the Emotions in Man and Animals*, Mategazza's *Physiognomy and Expression*, and M. Brown's *Synthetic Philosophy of Expression*.

Edmond Goncourt (1822–96) and Jules Goncourt (1830–70)

1669.   Ricatte, Robert. "Les romans des Goncourt et la médecine." *RSH* 69 (1954): 27–43.

An examination of the medical sources available to Edmond Goncourt and Jules Goncourt reveals the degree to which these novelists reproduced medical detail and departed from scientific exactitude for literary purposes. As the first nineteenth-century writers to incorporate technical medical information into their novels, they interwove their characters' physiological and psychological traits. The novels studied include *Soeur Philomène*, *Renée Mauperin*, *Germinie Lacerteux*, *Madame Gervaisais*, *La fille Elisa*, *La Faustin*, and *Chérie*.

Edmund Gosse (1849–1928)

1670.   Ross, Frederic R. "Philip Gosse's *Omphalos*, Edmund Gosse's *Father and Son*, and Darwin's Theory of Natural Selection." *Isis* 68 (1977): 85–96.

Discusses Gosse's partially fictionalized biography of his father, Philip, stressing his portrayal of an alleged meeting between Philip Gosse and C. Darwin and the circumstances surrounding the publication of *Omphalos*. The work attempted to reconcile scriptural and evolutionary views of human development.

Kenneth Grahame (1859–1931)

1671.   Lowe, Elizabeth C. "Kenneth Grahame and the Beast Tale." *DAI* 37 (1977): 5817A.

Studies Grahame's *Wind in the Willows* as an example of a beast tale whose animal imagery exhibits the effects of Romanticism, Darwinism, and industrialism. Compares it to earlier beast tales and sees it as a forerunner of twentieth-century naturalist and ethological literature.

Thomas Hardy (1840–1928)

1672.   Bailey, J. O. "Evolutionary Meliorism in the Poetry of Thomas Hardy."
         SP 60 (1963): 569–87.
Traces the development of Hardy's poetry from its pessimistic stage (1862–86), which was influenced by C. Darwin, T. H. Huxley, Spencer, and Mill; through its middle stage (1886–1908), which reflected the metaphysics of Schopenhauer and Hartmann and concerned the existence of an unconscious will; to its final stage, which expressed a view of natural law that Hardy termed "evolutionary meliorism." This concept entails the hope that the gradual evolution of human consciousness will improve the circumstances of life.

1673.   ———. "Hardy's 'Imbedded Fossil.' " *SP* 42 (1945): 663–74.
Sees Hardy's use of scientific terms and descriptions from geology, biology, and astronomy as deepening and enriching the artistic and emotional impact of his novels.

1674.   Beer, Gillian. "Plot and the Analogy with Science in Later Nineteenth-
         Century Novelists." *CCrit* 2 (1980): 131–49.
See item 1631 for annotation.

1675.   Brogan, Howard O. "Early Experience and Scientific Determinism in Twain
         and Hardy." *Mosaic* 7.3 (1973–74): 99–105.
See item 1991 for annotation.

1676.   ———. "Science and Narrative Structure in Austen, Hardy, and Woolf."
         NCF 11 (1956–57): 276–87.
See item 1533 for annotation.

1677.   Dove, John Roland. "Thomas Hardy and the Dilemma of Naturalism: A
         Study of Hardy's Lyric Poetry." *NS* ns 16 (1967): 253–68.
Hardy's attempts to overcome the limits of naturalism by invoking transcendent values met with perpetual frustration. The metaphysical pathos resulting from his failure is reflected in his treatment of love, death, and evolutionary meliorism in poems such as "God's Funeral," "Afterwards," "Nature's Questioning," and "There Seemed a Strangeness."

1678.   Ebbatson, J. R. "The Darwinian View of *Tess*: A Reply." *SoRA* 8 (1975):
         247–53.
Maintains that Hardy's interpretation of Darwinian evolution was more complex and balanced and less pessimistic than Peter Morton's analysis of *Tess* allows (see item 1685).

1679. Gallivan, Patricia. "Science and Art in *Jude the Obscure.*" *The Novels of Thomas Hardy.* Ed. Anne Smith. New York: Barnes; London: Vision, 1979. 126–44.
Discusses Hardy's interest in the physiological psychology of Maudsley's *Natural Causes and Supernatural Seemings*; Hardy used scientific theories found in the work to support the complex symbols and metaphors in *Jude*.

1680. Glicksberg, Charles I. "Hardy's Scientific Pessimism." *WHR* 6 (1951–52): 273–83.
Hardy's interpretation of the insights contributed by nineteenth-century science accounts for the pessimistic tenor of his philosophy, expressed poignantly in his poetry. This essay discusses *Wessex Poems and Other Names*, *Poems of the Past and the Present*, *Time's Laughingstocks*, and other poetry collections.

1681. Gose, Elliott B., Jr. "Psychic Evolution: Darwinism and Initiation in *Tess of the d'Urbervilles.*" *NCF* 18 (1963–64): 261–72.
Hardy's *Tess* is thematically organized around a synthesis of concepts drawn from Darwinism and nineteenth-century anthropological studies such as Frazer's *Totemism* (1887).

1682. Ingham, Patricia. "Hardy and *The Wonders of Geology.*" *RES* ns 31 (1980): 59–64.
Brings to light Hardy's reading in geology and its effect on his writings—in particular, on *A Pair of Blue Eyes*.

1683. Johnson, Bruce. " 'The Perfection of Species' and Hardy's *Tess.*" *Nature and the Victorian Imagination.* Ed. U. C. Knoepflmacher and G. B. Tennyson. Berkeley: U of California P, 1977. 259–77.
Examines the Darwinian basis of Hardy's characterization of Tess. Hardy's interpretation of Darwinism emphasized the relatedness of all creatures and creative evolution rather than the survival of the fittest.

1684. Morton, Peter R. "*Tess* and August Weismann: Unholy Alliance?" *SoRA* 8 (1975): 254–56.
Finds unpersuasive J. R. Ebbatson's attempt ". . . to mitigate the deterministic quality of neo-Darwinian thought as perceived by Hardy" (see item 1678).

1685. ———. "*Tess of the D'Urbervilles*: A Neo-Darwinian Reading." *SoRA* 7 (1974): 38–50.
This interpretation of *Tess* describes Hardy's aesthetic use of data drawn from theories of heredity, degeneration, and sexual selection and "asserts the novel's rigid determinism, its total pessimism and its fidelity to one coherent scientific vision of the world."

1686. Newton, William. "Chance as Employed by Hardy and the Naturalists." *PQ* 30 (1951): 154–75.
Compares in some detail Hardy's treatment of fictional events as haphazard, accidental, and coincidental with the deterministic or scientific approach used by naturalists such as Zola.

1687.   ———. "Hardy and the Naturalists: Their Use of Physiology." *MP* 49
         (1951–52): 28–41.
Attempts to clarify Hardy's intellectual relation to the dicta of French naturalism,
especially the notion of the physiological basis of emotion, character, and thought.
Stresses his use and modification of these principles in many of his novels.

1688.   Sampson, Edward C. "Telling Time by the Stars in *Far from the Madding
         Crowd.*" *N&Q* ns 14 (1967): 63–64.
Explains the procedure by which Farmer Oak tells time by the stars in *Far from
the Madding Crowd*. The discussion reveals something of Hardy's knowledge of
astronomy.

1689.   Scott, Nathan A., Jr. "The Literary Imagination and the Victorian Crisis
         of Faith: The Example of Thomas Hardy." *JR* 40 (1960): 267–81.
Briefly traces the influence of C. Darwin's *Origin of Species* and of *Essays and Reviews*
(1860), an anthology of theological scholarship edited by Benjamin Jowett, on the
Victorian religious worldview. Many prominent features of the Victorian crisis of
faith are reflected in Hardy's novels, several of which Scott discusses in this regard,
though he stresses analysis of *The Return of the Native*.

1690.   Sherman, George Witter. "Thomas Hardy and the Lower Animals." *PrS*
         20 (1946): 304–09.
Hardy's compassion for the lower animals, evident in works such as *Tess of the
d'Urbervilles* and *The Dynasts*, was spurred by reflection on the ethical consequences
of C. Darwin's *Origin of Species*.

1691.   Sullivan, Thomas R. "A 'Way to the Better': Hardy's Two Views of
         Evolution." *DA* 29 (1968–69): 276A.
Discusses Hardy's contrasting views of evolution. His novels represent both evolutionary meliorism and evolution as purposeless, compassionless natural law.

1692.   Van Valkenburgh, Lee H. "The Darkening Vision of Thomas Hardy: A
         Study of Four Major Novels." *DA* 31 (1970–71): 2944A.
Discusses the impact of Darwinian science and the discoveries of natural scientists
on Hardy's worldview in *The Return of the Native*, *The Mayor of Casterbridge*, *Tess of
the d'Urbervilles*, and *Jude the Obscure*.

Nathaniel Hawthorne (1804–64)

1693.   Baym, Nina. "The Head, the Heart, and the Unpardonable Sin." *NEQ*
         40 (1967): 31–47.
In the context of a discussion of Hawthorne's moral "head-heart" distinction,
Baym explores his satiric criticism of science and scientists in "The Birthmark" and
"The Great Carbuncle."

1694.   Boewe, Charles. "Rappaccini's Garden." *AL* 30 (1958–59): 37–49.
Hawthorne's understanding of hybridization and of the biological tradition of his
time is reflected in his symbolic references to flowers in "Rappaccini's Daughter."

1695.   Bunge, Nancy L. "A Thematic Analysis of Forty Short Stories by Nathaniel Hawthorne." *DA* 31 (1971): 4707A.

Discusses the theme of the relations between scientists and artists in stories such as "The Snow Image" and "The Prophetic Pictures."

1696.   Burns, Shannon. "Alchemy and 'The Birth-Mark.' " *ATQ* 42 (1979): 147–58.

Elucidates the symbolic complexity of Hawthorne's "Birthmark" by referring to the alchemical practices of the character Aylmer and by paying special attention to Aylmer's philosophical understanding of the alchemical principle of the duality of spirit and matter.

1697.   Fairbanks, Henry G. "Hawthorne and the Machine Age." *AL* 28 (1956–57): 155–63.

Seeks to qualify the commonly expressed critical generalization that Hawthorne was hostile toward science, scientists, technology, and progress. An examination of Hawthorne's stories and novels, including "Ethan Brand," "The Celestial Railroad," *Septimius Felton*, and *The House of the Seven Gables*, suggests that he was not opposed to science or technology per se but that he sought to curb the overardent and inappropriate use of science by those who desire totalitarian control over human beings and nature.

1698.   Franklin, H. Bruce. "Hawthorne and Science Fiction." *CentR* 10 (1966): 112–30.

Discusses Hawthorne's "Birthmark," "Rappaccini's Daughter," *Septimius Felton*, and other works as examples of early science fiction and notes that the use of science in these works was usually well-grounded in nineteenth-century science.

1699.   ———. "Science Fiction as an Index to Popular Attitudes toward Science: A Danger, Some Problems, and Two Possible Paths." *Extrapolation* 6 (1964–65): 23–31.

See item 2115 for annotation.

1700.   Gatta, John, Jr. "Aylmer's Alchemy in 'The Birthmark.' " *PQ* 57 (1978): 399–413.

Discusses Hawthorne's use of alchemical symbolism as reflected in the character of Aylmer in "The Birthmark." Makes some attempt to trace Hawthorne's knowledge of alchemy to works by Paracelsus, R. Bacon, Agrippa, Chaucer, and others.

1701.   Grant, William E. "Nathaniel Hawthorne and Empirical Psychology." *DAI* 32 (1971): 2686A–87A.

Although Hawthorne generally distrusted the empirical pseudosciences of physiognomy, phrenology, and mesmerism, analysis of his writings suggests that he occasionally used their principles and results.

1702.   Heilman, R. B. "Hawthorne's 'The Birthmark': Science as Religion." *SAQ* 48 (1949): 575–83.

Hawthorne's language and imagery in "The Birthmark" indicate that Aylmer's spiritual shortcomings stem from his deification of science.

1702a.   Hennelly, Mark. "Hawthorne's *Opus Alchymicum*: 'Ethan Brand.' " *ESQ* 22
         (1976): 96–106.
Attempts to resolve some interpretive difficulties concerning "Ethan Brand" by
viewing the work in the light of metallurgy and alchemy.

1703.   Hosmer, Elizabeth R. "Science and Pseudo-Science in the Writings of
         Nathaniel Hawthorne." Diss. U of Illinois, 1948.
Not seen for annotation.

1704.   Hull, Raymona E. "Hawthorne and the Magic Elixir of Life: The Failure
         of a Gothic Theme." *ESQ* 18 (1972): 97–107.
Traces Hawthorne's knowledge and literary use of the philosophers' stone, the
alchemical symbol of the elixir of life, emphasizing its role in the artistic failure of
his last works, *Septimius Felton* and *The Dolliver Romance*.

1705.   Kesterson, David B. "Hawthorne and Nature: Thoreauvian Influence?"
         ELN 4 (1966–67): 200–06.
Hawthorne's aesthetic, though unscientific, interest in nature developed well
before the beginning of his friendship with Thoreau in 1842. No evidence of an
appreciable Thoreauvian scientific influence on Hawthorne's attitude toward nature
can be found.

1706.   Marks, Alfred H. "Hawthorne's Daguerreotypist: Scientist, Artist, Re-
         former." *BSTCF* 3.1 (1961): 61–74.
Outlines the science of the daguerreotype as it existed during Hawthorne's time,
examines the social and philosophical significance of the invention, and discusses
the importance of the role played by the daguerreotypist Holgrave in *The House of
the Seven Gables*.

1707.   Meikle, Jeffrey L. "Hawthorne's Alembic: Alchemical Images in *The House
         of the Seven Gables*." *ESQ* 26 (1980): 173–83.
Attempts to show that Hawthorne consciously structured his romance as an
"alchemical drama." Hawthorne was aware that the esoteric operations of alchemy
involved more than transmuting base metals into gold or discovering the elixir of
life. Thus in composing *The House of the Seven Gables*, a story of human enlightenment
and regeneration, he drew on the spiritual as well as the mundane level of the
medieval science.

1708.   Rosenberry, Edward H. "Hawthorne's Allegory of Science: 'Rappaccini's
         Daughter.' " *AL* 32 (1960–61): 39–46.
This interpretation of "Rappaccini's Daughter" finds in the figure of Beatrice the
work's unifying symbol—an allegory concerning the ethical implications and inherent dangers of science.

1709.   Stoehr, Taylor. "Hawthorne and Mesmerism." *HLQ* 33 (1969–70): 33–
         60.
Briefly traces the reception of mesmerism in nineteenth-century New England
and explores Hawthorne's references to the pseudoscience in *The Blithedale Romance*

and *The House of the Seven Gables*, both of which used it as a metaphor for problems associated with the writer's art and for the question of moral guilt and innocence.

1710.   ———. *Hawthorne's Mad Scientists: Pseudoscience and Social Science in Nineteenth-Century Life and Letters*. Hamden: Archon, 1978. 313 pp.
Rev. Lawrence Buell, *NEQ* 52 (1979): 284–86; Jeffrey L. Meikle, *Isis* 70 (1979): 635–36; David B. Kesterson, *AL* 51 (1979–80): 119–21; Howard P. Segal, *JAmH* 66 (1979–80): 141–42; C. S. B. Swann, *JAmS* 14 (1980): 330–31; George Guffey, *NCF* 35 (1980–81): 567–69.
Examines the principles of mesmerism, physiognomy, phrenology, homeopathy, and social sciences such as associationism, spiritualism, feminism, and prison reform. Stresses Hawthorne's acquaintance with these fields and notes their impact on his literary manner and narrative technique. Also provides a brief literary history of the "mad scientist" genre, emphasizing Hawthorne's treatment of this theme.

1711.   ———. "Physiognomy and Phrenology in Hawthorne." *HLQ* 37 (1973–74): 355–400.
Traces Hawthorne's acquaintance with the two pseudosciences and discusses his reliance on physiognomy in developing characterizations.

1711a.   Uroff, M. D. "The Doctors in 'Rappaccini's Daughter.' " *NCF* 27 (1972–73): 61–70.
Hawthorne's presentation of the doctors in "Rappaccini's Daughter" suggests that his alleged opposition toward science may be better described as an antipathy toward the misuse of science, specifically medicine.

1711b.   Van Leer, David M. "Aylmer's Library: Transcendental Alchemy in Hawthorne's 'The Birthmark.' " *ESQ* 22 (1976): 211–20.
Evaluates the import of references to pre-Newtonian science, alchemy, and alchemists in "The Birthmark" for an understanding of the work as a whole. Stresses the tale's relation to K. Digby.

1712.   Woodward, Robert H. "Automata in Hawthorne's 'Artist of the Beautiful' and Taylor's 'Meditation 56.' " *ESQ* 31 (1963): 63–66.
Attempts to identify the sources from which Hawthorne and E. Taylor may have drawn their descriptions of automata. Possibilities include works by Wilkins, T. Browne, W. Godwin, and Burton.

William Hazlitt (1778–1830)

1713.   Hassler, Donald M. "The Discovery of the Future and Indeterminacy in William Hazlitt." *WC* 8 (1977): 75–79.
Hazlitt took a positive approach to indeterminacy because he thought it allowed for creativity and newness. He criticized Newtonian mechanics for being deterministic.

James A. Herne (1839–1901)

1714.   Waggoner, Hyatt H. "The Growth of a Realist: James A. Herne." *NEQ* 15 (1942): 62–73.

Herne's plays *Margaret Fleming* and *Shore Acres* reflect his reading of Spencer, C. Darwin, and other scientific writers.

E. T. A. Hoffmann (1776–1822)

1715.   Holbeche, Yvonne Jill Kathleen. *Optical Motifs in the Works of E. T. A. Hoffmann.* Göppinger Arbeiten zur Germanistik 141. Göppingen: Kümmerle, 1975. 248 pp.
Rev. Christoph E. Schweitzer, *MHG* 23 (1977): 70–71.

Systematically studies the optical themes in Hoffmann's writings, including references to telescopes, microscopes, eyeglasses, and mirrors. Shows that these motifs ". . . are related to central preoccupations of his work, particularly the problems of perception and identity, and that they have important artistic functions in individual works." Discusses *Der goldne Topf*, *Der Sandman*, *Klein Zaches*, and five other works.

1716.   Leitherer, Hans. "E. T. A. Hoffmann und die Alchimie." *MHG* 7 (1960): 24–26.
Comments on Hoffmann's familiarity with alchemical processes and refers to his literary use of alchemy in the eighth and twelfth vigils of *Der goldne Topf*.

1717.   Nettesheim, Josefine. "E. T. A. Hoffmanns Phantasiestück *Der Magnetiseur*: Ein Beitrag zum Problem 'Wissenschaft' und Dichtung." *JWGV* 71 (1967): 113–27. Rpt. in *Poeta doctus oder die Poetisierung der Wissenschaft von Musäus bis Benn.* Berlin: Duncker, 1975. 39–56.
Outlines the evolution and later corruption of Mesmer's theory of mesmerism and discusses *Der Magnetiseur* as Hoffmann's successful attempt to deal with the complexities of magnetism in literary form.

1718.   Tatar, Maria M. "Mesmerism, Madness, and Death in E. T. A. Hoffmann's *Der goldne Topf*." *SIR* 14 (1975): 365–89.
Der goldne Topf contains a large vocabulary drawn from nineteenth-century psychology. Tatar studies Hoffmann's allusions to contemporary concepts of mesmerism and madness in his depiction of the mental state of his hero.

Oliver Wendell Holmes (1809–94)

1719.   Adkins, Nelson F. " 'The Chambered Nautilus': Its Scientific and Poetic Backgrounds." *AL* 9 (1937–38): 458–65.
Among the scientific and poetic antecedents of Holmes's poem "The Chambered Nautilus" are Roget's *Animal and Vegetable Physiology Considered with Reference to Natural Theology*, H. Coleridge's "To the Nautilus," and Barnard's "Launch of the Nautilus."

1720.   Boewe, Charles. "Reflex Action in the Novels of Oliver Wendell Holmes."
        AL 26 (1954–55): 303–19.
The thematic basis of Holmes's three novels, *Elsie Venner*, *The Guardian Angel*,
and *A Moral Antipathy*, is a theory of physiological psychology that Holmes learned
from the physiologist Marshall Hall.

1721.   Clark, Harry Hayden. "Dr. Holmes: A Re-interpretation." *NEQ* 12 (1939):
        19–34.
Maintains that Holmes's conservatism in matters of social, political, and literary
theory was offset by his radicalism in religious and philosophic thought. Stresses
the relation between these areas and Holmes's predilection for scientific rationalism
and Darwinian thought, remarking on his assessment of the limitations of the
ultrarealism of writers such as Flaubert and Zola.

1722.   Kurth, Rosaly T., and Donald J. "Oliver Wendell Holmes, M.D.
        (1809–1894): Medical and Literary Knowledge Intertwined." *New York
        State Journal of Medicine* 80 (1980): 121–24.
Briefly describes Holmes's medical career and notes the impact of medicine on
his literary work as well as the influence of his literary imagination on his medical
writings.

1723.   Phillips, Goldwina N. "Oliver Wendell Holmes: Literary Journalist: A
        Study of the Interpreter of Science for Nineteenth Century America." *DA*
        26 (1966): 6049.
Discusses Holmes's familiarity with sciences such as anthropology, botany, physiology, psychology, and psychiatry and his popularization of this knowledge in his
literary works.

Arno Holz (1863–1929)

1724.   Nettesheim, Josefine. "Arno Holz—'Phantasus' (1898–1929), eine dich-
        terische Inkarnation des Neo-Darwinismus." *Poeta doctus oder die Poetisierung
        der Wissenschaft von Musäus bis Benn*. Berlin: Duncker, 1975. 128–37.
Holz based his ontological and sociological-positivistic worldview on his readings
of Comte, C. Darwin, Lamarck, Mill, Wordsworth, and others. He called for an
identification of the sciences and poetry and developed a theory of poetry that finds
full expression in his monumental poem *Phantasus*.

Gerard Manley Hopkins (1844–89)

1725.   Giovannini, Margaret. "Hopkins' 'God's Grandeur.' " *Expl* 24 (1965–66):
        item 36.
Construes the word *grandeur* in Hopkins's poem as a scientific term referring to
extension in space.

1726.   Zaniello, Thomas A. "Hopkins' 'Eurydice' and a Victorian Meteorological
        Report." *AN&Q* 17 (1978–79): 89–90.

Hopkins may have based his poem "The Loss of the Eurydice" on a meteorological report entitled "The Eurydice Squall," written by W. Clement Ley and published in *Symon's Monthly Meteorological Report* (Apr. 1878).

1727. ————. "The Scientific Background of Hopkins' 'Loss of the Eurydice': Two Documents." *HQ* 7 (1980–81): 15–28.

Reproduces meteorological documents by W. Clement Ley and Ralph Abercromby that may have provided source material for Hopkins's description of the storm in "The Loss of the Eurydice."

William Dean Howells (1837–1920)

1728. Clark, Harry Hayden. "The Role of Science in the Thought of W. D. Howells." *TWA* 42 (1953): 263–303.

Shows that Howells was indebted deeply to science, particularly Darwinism, for his literary theory and criticism, his novels, and his social and political attitudes. Among the novels that reflect his knowledge of science are *Dr. Breen's Practice*, *A Hazard of New Fortunes*, and *An Imperative Duty*.

1729. Miles, Elton R. "William Dean Howells: The Impact of Science." Diss. U of Texas, Austin, 1952.

Not seen for annotation.

1730. Pizer, Donald. "The Evolutionary Foundation of W. D. Howells's *Criticism and Fiction*." *PQ* 40 (1961): 91–103. Rpt. in *Realism and Naturalism in Nineteenth-Century American Literature*. Carbondale: Southern Illinois UP, 1966. New York: Russell, 1976. 37–52.

Surveys the use of evolutionary concepts in the literary criticism of the 1880s and assesses the extent to which Howells's attitudes toward criticism and fiction stem from his belief in using evolution theory to interpret literature.

1731. ————. "Evolutionary Literary Criticism and the Defense of Howellsian Realism." *JEGP* 61 (1962): 296–304.

Outlines Garland's, Perry's, and Pellew's views regarding the relation among evolutionary progress, realism, scientific method, and democracy as reflected in their literary criticism and their defense of Howells's literary realism.

William Henry Hudson (1841–1922)

1732. Colwell, Mary Lou M. "The Human Position: Hudson and the Darwinian Revolution." *DA* 31 (1970–71): 2377A.

Studies Hudson's attempt to adapt the theories of naturalists and scientists— including C. Darwin, Lamarck, Mendel, Bates, and Belt—to his fictional purposes. Examines *The Purple Land That England Lost*, *A Crystal Age*, *Green Mansions*, and *A Hind in Richmond Park*.

Victor-Marie Hugo (1802–85)

1733.   Grant, Elliott M. "Victor Hugo, Vesuvius and Etna." *Smith College Studies in Modern Languages* 11.4 (1929–30): 33–61.
Maintains that the explanation for Hugo's frequent use of volcanic metaphors and similes can be found in the geological, archeological, artistic, and literary events of the early nineteenth century.

(Friedrich Wilhelm Karl Heinrich) Alexander von Humboldt (1769–1859)

1734.   Hentschel, Cedric. "Zur Synthese von Literatur und Naturwissenschaft bei Alexander von Humboldt." *Alexander von Humboldt: Werk und Weltgeltung.* Ed. Heinrich Pfeiffer. München: Piper, 1969. 31–95.
Illustrates the symbiotic relation between literature and science in Humboldt's writing by analyzing his only volume of poetry, *Die Lebenskraft oder der rhodische Genius*; his biological treatises, *Ansichten der Natur*; and his five-volume work *Kosmos*, in which his geologicoscientific terminology manifests aesthetic overtones.

Thomas Henry Huxley (1825–95)

1735.   Blinderman, Charles S. "T. H. Huxley's Popularization of Darwinism." *DA* 17 (1957): 2287–88.
Evaluates Huxley's popularization of Darwinism in science, philosophy, religion, and ethics.

1736.   ———. "T. H. Huxley's Theory of Aesthetics: Unity in Diversity." *JAAC* 21 (1962–63): 49–55.
Huxley sought a mechanistic unifying principle not only in his research in comparative anatomy and paleontology but also in botany, music, architecture, and literary style. Thus both his scientific and his literary endeavors expressed the mechanistic worldview.

1737.   Gardner, Joseph H. "A Huxley Essay as 'Poem.' " *VS* 14 (1970–71): 177–91.
Careful examination of Huxley's essay "On the Physical Basis of Life" reveals a poetic or artistic use of metaphor that transcends mere scientific description or rhetoric.

1738.   Routh, James E. "Huxley as a Literary Man." *Century* 41 (1901–02): 392–98.
As a scientist, Huxley was clear, precise, informed, and informative; as a literary man, he brought to the popularization of science a "nimble wit," a "frank earnestness," a "frank pugnacity," and an "easy adaptability." Thus, he turned "the pure biology of Darwin into the channels of humane letters."

Henrik Ibsen (1828–1906)

1739. Sprinchorn, Evert. "Science and Poetry in *Ghosts*: A Study of Ibsen's Craftmanship." *SS* 51 (1979): 354–67.

Ibsen abandoned verse for prose in response to a deterministic view of heredity and environment drawn from science, yet his characters are not completely determined. In *Ghosts* he pits free will against determinism, allowing for tragic resolution in the play.

Henry James (1843–1916)

1740. Clark, Harry H. "Henry James and Science: *The Wings of the Dove*." *TWA* 52 (1963): 1–15.

Maintains that the plot, structure, and characterization of James's *Wings of the Dove* are informed by the principles and themes of social Darwinism, especially the struggle-for-existence motif and the concept of the hereditary and environmental factors in personal development.

1741. Purdy, Strother B. *The Hole in the Fabric: Science, Contemporary Literature, and Henry James*. Pittsburgh: U of Pittsburgh P, 1977. 228 pp.
        Rev. Christof Wegelin, *MFS* 24 (1978): 261–63; Quentin Anderson, *AL* 50 (1978–79): 124–26; Martha Banta, *NCF* 33 (1978–79): 243–48; Kenny Marotta, *ELN* 16 (1978–79): 65–69.

Maintains that James's novels have four conceptual foci that later gained new significance through modern scientific research by writers such as Barth, Beckett, Borges, Fowles, Grass, Ionesco, Nabokov, and Vonnegut. These foci are supernatural horror, disoriented time, psychological eroticism, and confrontations with nothingness.

1742. Sullivan, Jeremiah J. "Henry James and Hippolyte Taine: The Historical and Scientific Method in Literature." *CLS* 10 (1973): 25–50.

"Hippolyte Taine's theory of literature and critical method enjoyed a vogue in America during the latter half of the nineteenth century. Henry James was familiar with Taine's work from the middle of the 1860s on. He usually distrusted but occasionally admired Taine's objective and analytical method of criticism, his view of the novelist as historian of race, milieu, and moment, his habit of generalization (particularly as to type), and his emphasis (pre-Zola) on the aesthetic use of scientific method. James followed Taine in his own essay on Balzac, in his use of types in *The American*, *The Bostonians*, and 'A Bundle of Letters,' in his art criticism, in his historical method of criticism in *Hawthorne*, and in the manner and style of his writing of *The American Scene*, which was influenced by the 'scientific' method of Taine."

Alfred Jarry (1873–1907)

1743. Stillman, Linda K. "Physics and Pataphysics: The Sources of *Faustroll*." *KRQ* 26 (1979): 81–92.

Explores the relation between Jarry's invented science of pataphysics and genuine research in physics during the late nineteenth century and examines the pataphysical elements of Jarry's *Gestes et opinions du docteur Faustroll, pataphysicien, roman néo-scientifique*.

Henry Arthur Jones (1851–1929)

1744.   Bailey, James Osler. "Science in the Dramas of Henry Arthur Jones." *Booker Memorial Studies: Eight Essays on Victorian Literature in Memory of John Manning Booker, 1881–1948*. Ed. Hill Shine. Chapel Hill: U of North Carolina P, 1950. 154–83.

"Jones created characters in terms of their heredity, employed numerous scientists as spokesmen in his dramas, and treated themes meditated in the light of his knowledge of science." This essay discusses *The Middleman*, *Michael and His Lost Angel*, *The Physician*, and several other works.

John Keats (1795–1821)

1745.   Barnard, John. "Sun-Spots in Keats's Epistle 'To My Brother George.' " *KSMB* 31 (1980): 57–60.

Keats may have derived his sunspot imagery in "To My Brother George" from Bonnycastle's *Introduction to Astronomy* (1786).

1746.   Bruère, Richard T. "Pliny the Elder, Diaper, and Keats." *ClasPhil* 61 (1966): 107.

Maintains that the source for Keats's lunar imagery in *Endymion* (3.66–68) is the sixth eclogue of Diaper's *Nereides* (37–42) and not, as has hitherto been supposed, Pliny's *Natural History*.

1747.   Fairchild, Hoxie N. "Keats and the Struggle-for-Existence Tradition." *PMLA* 64 (1949): 98–114.

Shows how the unromantic view of nature as a struggle for existence influenced Keats's thought and poetry. Examines the tradition of this idea (with which Keats was very likely familiar) from Lucretius's *De rerum natura* to E. Darwin's *Temple of Nature*.

1748.   Gittings, Robert. "John Keats, Physician and Poet." *Journal of the American Medical Association* 224 (1973): 51–55.

Provides biographical information about Keats's experiences as a medical student, emphasizing the tension in his last years between his competing ambitions in medicine and poetry.

1749.   Hagelman, Charles W., Jr. "Keats's Medical Training and the Last Stanza of the 'Ode to Psyche.' " *KSJ* 11 (1962): 73–82.

Maintains that Keats's imagery in the final stanza of the *Ode to Psyche* was based on his knowledge of cerebral anatomy and was probably derived from his study of Green's *Outlines to a Course of Anatomy* (1815).

1750.   Martin, John S. "Keats's New Planet." *N&Q* ns 8 (1961): 23.
Keats's allusion to a new planet in "On First Looking into Chapman's Homer" may refer not only to the discovery of Uranus but also to the discovery of the asteroids Ceres, Pallas, Juno, and Vesta. Keats probably derived his information from Bonnycastle's *Introduction to Astronomy*.

1751.   Pettit, Henry. "Scientific Correlatives of Keats' *Ode to Psyche*." *SP* 40 (1943): 560–66.
Relates Keats's poetic treatment of the myth of Psyche to his knowledge of medicine, physiology, and psychology.

1751a.   Sinson, Janice C. *John Keats and* The Anatomy of Melancholy. London: Keats-Shelley Memorial Assn., 1971. 41 pp.
Establishes Keats's intense personal interest in Burton's *Anatomy* and reveals its presence in a number of his poems, including the four odes. Argues that in "To a Nightingale" Keats borrows heavily from the *Anatomy*, especially from the section on medicinal physics.

1752.   Sperry, Stuart M., Jr. "Keats and the Chemistry of Poetic Creation." *PMLA* 85 (1970): 268–77.
Keats's understanding of the process of poetic creation was based in large part on an analogy with the process of chemical reaction. Sperry demonstrates that the words Keats used most frequently to refer to poetry or the creative process, such as *abstract*, *spiritual*, *essence*, *intensity*, *distillation*, and *ethereal*, were derived from chemistry and other sciences, including Newtonian physics.

1753.   Wagenblass, John H. "Keats and Lucretius." *MLR* 32 (1937): 537–52.
Surveys the phrasal and conceptual similarities between Keats's poetry and Lucretius's *De rerum natura*. Among other areas, Lucretian influence is apparent in Keats's attitude toward science and in his references to atomism in poems such as *Lamia*, *Endymion*, and *Hyperion*.

1754.   Ward, Aileen. "Keats and Burton: A Reappraisal." *PQ* 40 (1961): 535–52.
Assesses the accuracy of previous attempts to demonstrate Burton's influence on Keats. Though *The Anatomy of Melancholy* appears to have influenced Keats's poetry far less than hitherto supposed, the work did help shape his ideas and attitudes during the autumn of 1819.

1755.   Woodruff, Bertram L. "Keats's Wailful Choir of Small Gnats." *MLN* 68 (1953): 217–20.
Keats may have derived his imagery of "wailing gnats" in lines 27–29 of "To Autumn" from *An Introduction to Entomology* (1815) by the naturalists W. Kirby and W. Spence.

Charles Kingsley (1819–75)

1756.   Blinderman, Charles S. "Huxley and Kingsley." *VN* 20 (1961): 25–28.
   T. H. Huxley's correspondence with Kingsley tends to obscure the ideological differences between the two regarding the relations between science and religion. In *The Water-Babies* Kingsley ridicules Huxley's interpretation of science through the character of Professor Pttmllnsprts.

1757.   Hanawalt, Mary W. "The Attitude of Charles Kingsley toward Science." Diss. U of Iowa, 1936.
   Not seen for annotation.

1758.   ———. "Charles Kingsley and Science." *SP* 34 (1937): 589–611.
   Nineteenth-century science played a prominent role in shaping Kingsley's philosophy of art. His lifelong interest in science, including Darwinism, geology, medicine, and botany, is reflected in the themes of novels such as *Two Years Ago*, *The Water-Babies*, *Alton Locke*, and *Yeast*.

1759.   Johnston, Arthur. "*The Water Babies*: Kingsley's Debt to Darwin." *English* 12 (1958–59): 215–19.
   Examines Kingsley's *Water-Babies* for aspects of theme and plot that evidence the influence of C. Darwin's *Origin of Species*. The novel espouses a "moral Darwinism."

Rudyard Kipling (1865–1936)

1760.   Beatty, William K. "Some Medical Aspects of Rudyard Kipling." *Practitioner* 215 (1975): 532–42.
   Traces Kipling's interests in medicine, noting his friendship with various physicians, and cites medical descriptions from several poems and short stories.

Heinrich von Kleist (1777–1811)

1761.   Schmidt, Herminio. *Heinrich von Kleist: Naturwissenschaft als Dichtungsprinzip*. Bern: Haupt, 1978. 150 pp.
   Rev. Marjorie Gelus, *GQ* 52 (1979): 121–22.
   A detailed study of the dramatic and narrative works in which Kleist reveals that for him science and art, physics and poetry, formed a unified worldview. Specifically, the scientific studies of electrical phenomena by Franklin, Galvani, and Volta directly influenced Kleist's *Penthesilea*, *Das Käthchen von Heilbronn*, and other works.

1762.   ———. "Heinrich von Kleists Dichtungsprinzip unter besonderer Berücksichtigung der Naturwissenschaft, Mathematik und Musik." *DAI* 37 (1976): 1001A.
   Discusses the influence of science, music, and mathematics on Kleist's poetic technique and examines the reflection of the laws of electricity in his dramas and novellas, such as *Penthesilea* and *Das Käthchen von Heilbronn*.

Sidney Lanier (1842–81)

1763.   Anderson, Charles R. Introduction. *Poems and Poem Outlines*. Ed. Charles
         R. Anderson. Vol. 1 of *The Centennial Edition of the Works of Sidney Lanier*.
         10 vols. Baltimore: Johns Hopkins P, 1945. xxi–xc.
Pages lxvi–lxxxi of this introduction outline the impact of the nineteenth-century
conflict between science and religion on Lanier's poetry. Anderson discusses Lanier's
response to Darwinism and examines his theory of the applicability of science to
poetry as treated in his *Science of English Verse* (1880).

1764.   ———. "Lanier and Science: Addenda." *MLN* 66 (1951): 395–98.
Presents four new fragments or "poem outlines" by Lanier that bear on the
controversy between science and religion. Supplements Anderson's earlier study on
the subject (see item 1763).

1765.   Beaver, Joseph. "Lanier's Use of Science for Poetic Imagery." *AL* 24
         (1952–53): 520–33.
Analyzes and evaluates Lanier's figurative and verbal use of chemistry, biology,
astronomy, geology, and evolution theory.

1766.   Graham, Philip. "Lanier and Science." *AL* 4 (1932–33): 288–92.
Notes that Lanier's early dedication to science resulted from his friendship with
James Woodrow, who held the chair of science at Oglethorpe College, and discusses
the impact of science on Lanier's literary works, including *Tiger-Lilies* and *The Science
of English Verse*.

1767.   Havens, Elmer A. "Sidney Lanier's Concept and Use of Nature." *DA* 25
         (1964–65): 7268.
Studies Lanier's doctrine of etherealization—a theory of philosophical idealism
grounded in scientific evolutionism—as it affects his concept of nature and as it
appears in works such as *The English Novel*, *Tiger-Lilies*, *The Science of English Verse*,
and *Shakspere and His Forerunners*.

1768.   Svendsen, Kester. "Lanier's Cone of Night: An Early Poetic Common-
         place." *AL* 26 (1954–55): 93–94.
Lanier used the image of the "cone of night," a common figure in poetry by
Marlowe, Milton, and others. The image was described fully in scientific texts such
as Caxton's *Mirrour of the World*, Bartholomaeus Anglicus's *De proprietatibus rerum*,
and La Primaudaye's *French Academie*.

Kurd Lasswitz (1848–1910)

1769.   Bölsche, Wilhelm. "Naturwissenschaftliche Märchen." *Neue deutsche Rund-
         schau* 9 (1898): 504–14.
Bölsche criticizes Verne's novels, such as *Voyage au centre de la terre* and *Voyage
autour du monde en quatre-vingts jours*, for their scientific inaccuracies. By contrast,
he sees Lasswitz's *Auf zwei Planeten* as the prototype of the scientific novel because
it is based on the most current astronomical findings.

1770.   Fischer, William B. "German Theories of Science Fiction: Jean Paul, Kurd Lasswitz, and After." *SFS* 3 (1976): 254–65.

Jean Paul's reflections on the relations among science, fantasy, and literature anticipate later formulations of the aesthetics of science fiction. Lasswitz was, however, the first real German theorist of science fiction; his aesthetic writings explore the implications of science for the concept of imagination, the standards of plausibility as applied to fiction, and the content and stylistic techniques of imaginative literature. Later German contributors to science-fiction criticism include Bölsche, Lindau, Lampa, Debus, and Flechtner.

1771.   Hillegas, Mark R. "The First Invasions from Mars." *MAQR* 66 (1959–60): 107–12.

Schiaperelli's 1877 discovery of the "canals" of Mars produced a flurry of speculation about both the possibility of life and an advanced civilization on the planet and the possibility of an invasion from Mars. Hillegas studies two Martian romances that reflect these themes—Lasswitz's *Auf zwei Planeten* and Wells's *War of the Worlds*.

1772.   Just, Klaus Günther. "Ein schlesischer Raumfahrtsroman der Jahrhundertwende. Kurd Lasswitz: *Auf zwei Planeten*." *Schlesische Studien*. Ed. Alfons Hayduk. München: Delp, 1970. 129–33.

Examines Lasswitz's novel *Auf zwei Planeten* (1897) as an early example of space fiction. The work reflects the dichotomy between an absolute belief in progress and an equally strong skepticism concerning science and technology.

1773.   Kretzmann, Edwin M. J. "German Technological Utopias of the Pre-war Period." *AnS* 3 (1938): 417–30.

Studies Lasswitz's *Bilder aus Zukunft* and *Auf zwei Planeten* and Atlas's *Die Befreiung*. The novels portray utopian societies founded on technological innovations and convey a belief in the power of science to ameliorate social conditions.

Charles-Marie-René Leconte de Lisle (1818–94)

1774.   Charleton, D. G. "Positivism and Leconte de Lisle's Ideas on Poetry." *FS* 11 (1957): 246–59.

Outlines the relation of Parnassian poets such as Leconte de Lisle to science and the positivistic aesthetics of Auguste Comte. Also assesses the similarities between Leconte de Lisle's aesthetic principles, especially his emphasis on the ideal in poetry, and symbolist poetics.

Giacomo Leopardi (1798–1837)

1775.   Corsinovi, Graziella. "Note per un'analisi del rapporto tra Leopardi e la scienza." *Letteratura e scienza nella storia della cultura italiana*. Atti del IX congresso dell'associazione internazionale per gli studi di lingua e letteratura italiana. Palermo, Messina, Catania, 21–25 Apr. 1976. Associazione internazionale per gli studi di lingua e letteratura italiana. Palermo: Manfredi, 1978. 655–62.

Shows that science influenced not only the contents of Leopardi's literary works but his cognitive methodology and his overall worldview. Corsinovi traces this influence through Leopardi's entire corpus.

1776.   Frattini, Alberto. "Letteratura e scienza in Leopardi." *Letteratura e scienza nella storia della cultura italiana*. Atti del IX congresso dell'associazione internazionale per gli studi di lingua e letteratura italiana. Palermo, Messina, Catania, 21–25 Apr. 1976. Associazione internazionale per gli studi di lingua e letteratura italiana. Palermo: Manfredi, 1978. 663–75.

Discusses Leopardi's skeptical attitude toward science and examines his concept of poetry as a mediator between science and humankind. Cites works such as *Storia dell'astronomia*, *Saggio sopra gli errori degli antichi*, and *Zibaldone*.

1777.   Sole, Antonino. "Note sul valore della scienza in Leopardi." *Letteratura e scienza nella storia della cultura italiana*. Atti del IX congresso dell'associazione internazionale per gli studi di lingua e letteratura italiana. Palermo, Messina, Catania, 21–25 Apr. 1976. Associazione internazionale per gli studi di lingua e letteratura italiana. Palermo: Manfredi, 1978. 676–99.

Outlines Leopardi's attitudes toward science and its relation to literature in works such as *Storia dell'astronomia*, *Operetti morali*, and *Zibaldone*. Discusses science's impact on Leopardi's literary style and language.

Mikhail Yurevich Lermontov (1814–41)

1778.   Heier, Edmund. "Lavater's System of Physiognomy as a Mode of Characterization in Lermontov's Prose." *Arcadia* 6 (1971): 267–82.

Briefly discusses the principles of descriptive and predictive physiognomy by referring specifically to the physiognomic system in Lavater's *Physiognomische Fragmente zur Beförderung der Menschenkenntnis und Menschenliebe* (1775–78). Examines how Lermontov's method of characterization in *Princess Ligovskaja*, *The Strange Man*, and *A Hero of Our Time* was influenced by Lavater's system and also by the use of physiognomy in various French novels, including works by Balzac, Chateaubriand, Hugo, Musset, and Senancour.

Sir George Steuart Mackenzie (1780–1848)

1779.   Dean, Dennis R. "Scott and Mackenzie: New Poems." *PQ* 52 (1973): 265–73.

Mackenzie's unsuccessful play *Helga* (1812) included previously unknown verses by Walter Scott and Henry Mackenzie, recovered here from a local newspaper. The play's failure was attributed in part to its references to the prevalent Huttonian-Wernerian geological controversy.

Stéphane Mallarmé (1842–98)

1780.   Mehlman, Jeffrey. "Mallarmé/Maxwell: Elements." *RR* 71 (1980): 374–80.

Outlines correspondences between Maxwell's formulation of the second law of thermodynamics in *Theory of Heat* (1871) and Mallarmé's themes in his *Poésies*.

Alessandro Manzoni (1785–1873)

1781. Roedel, Reto. "La scienza e *I promessi sposi.*" *Literature and Science*. Proc. of the Sixth Triennial Congress of the International Federation for Modern Languages and Literatures. Oxford, 1954. Oxford: Blackwell, 1955. 264–69.

Although in *I promessi sposi*, as in other works, Manzoni is a discrete skeptic about science—or any other sphere of human knowledge—he venerated truths he considered divine in origin. Nevertheless, he was dedicated to the study of science, as he believed it was the human task to pry into nature's secrets to learn relative truths necessary for earthly existence.

1782. Suter, Rufus. "Manzoni and Seventeenth-Century Science." *Isis* 56 (1965): 208–09.

Briefly discusses Manzoni's spoof of the peripatetic scientist in his novel *I promessi sposi*.

Herman Melville (1819–91)

1783. Aspiz, Harold. "The 'Lurch of the Torpedo-Fish': Electrical Concepts in *Billy Budd*." *ESQ* 26 (1980): 127–36.

In *Billy Budd*, Melville creates a "master metaphor" of scientific as well as pseudoscientific ideas about electricity, which permeate the novel's themes and language. The image of the torpedo fish unifies three quasi-electrical concepts—vitalism, mesmerism, and electrospiritualism.

1784. ———. "Phrenologizing the Whale." *NCF* 23 (1968–69): 18–27.

Discusses Ishmael's physiognomic and phrenological investigations of the whale in chapters 79 and 80 of Melville's *Moby-Dick*.

1785. Corey, James R. "Herman Melville and the Theory of Evolution." *DA* 29 (1968–69): 3093A.

Discusses the evolutionary writings of Lyell, C. Darwin, and R. Chambers in relation to Melville's *Mardi*, "Encantadas," and *Moby-Dick*.

1786. Foster, Elizabeth S. "Another Note on Melville and Geology." *AL* 22 (1950–51): 479–87.

Questions Tyrus Hillway's suggestions about Melville's sources of geological knowledge (see item 1796).

1787. ———. "Melville and Geology." *AL* 17 (1945–46): 50–65.

Passages from *Mardi* and *Moby-Dick* indicate that Melville had a remarkably accurate knowledge of contemporary geology, especially the theories of Hutton, Werner, and Lyell.

1788.   Frank, Max. *Die Farb- und Lichtsymbolik im Prosawerk Hermann Melvilles*.
         Beihefte zum Jahrbuch für Amerikastudien 19. Heidelberg: Winter, 1967.
         157 pp.
This study of the symbolic use of color in Melville's major novels includes a short
chapter that traces his educational and scientific background. Frank suggests that
Goethe's and Newton's color theories may have influenced Melville's color symbolism.

1789.   Franklin, H. Bruce. "The Island Worlds of Darwin and Melville." *CentR*
         11 (1967): 353–70.
Compares C. Darwin's description of the Galapagos Islands in *The Voyage of the
Beagle* and Melville's in "The Encantadas, or Enchanted Isles." Notes that Melville
relied on Darwin's work for his imagery and symbols.

1790.   Hillway, Tyrus. "Melville and Nineteenth-Century Science." *DA* 29
         (1968–69): 3578A.
Discusses and classifies all allusions to science in Melville's works. Melville's
scientific interests centered on nineteenth-century geology and zoology.

1791.   ———. "Melville and the Spirit of Science." *SAQ* 48 (1949): 77–88.
Discusses the influence of science, especially Darwinism, on Melville's concept
of nature in *Mardi*, *White-Jacket*, *Moby-Dick*, and other works.

1792.   ———. *Melville and the Whale*. Stonington: Stonington, 1950. Folcroft:
         Folcroft, 1969. Norwood: Norwood, 1977. 12 pp.
Discusses Melville's indebtedness to sources of cetological information for *Moby-
Dick*. Among the books with which Melville was familiar were Linnaeus's *Systema
natura* (1776), Goldsmith's *Animated Nature*, and Beale's *Natural History of the Whale*
(1839).

1793.   ———. "Melville as Amateur Zoologist." *MLQ* 12 (1951): 159–64.
Analyzes Melville's attempts at zoological classification and description in *Mardi*.
Despite their literary effectiveness, his forays into zoology remain amateurish and
unscientific.

1794.   ———. "Melville as Critic of Science." *MLN* 65 (1950): 411–14.
Melville's criticism of science's esotericism, inhumanity, exaggerated claims, and
destructive power is reflected primarily in early works such as *Omoo*, *Redburn*, *White-
Jacket*, and *Clarel*.

1795.   ———. "Melville's Education in Science." *TSLL* 16 (1974–75): 411–25.
Charts the course of Melville's scientific learning, citing major sources of his
scientific knowledge and providing a list of books from which he borrowed information for his novels. Among the works that Melville probably read, though sometimes only cursorily, are C. Darwin's *Journal of Researches*, Goldsmith's *Animated
Nature*, R. Chambers's *Vestiges of the Natural History of Creation*, and Beale's *Natural
History of the Sperm Whale*.

1796.   ———. "Melville's Geological Knowledge." *AL* 21 (1949–50): 232–37.
Augments an earlier study by Elizabeth S. Foster (see item 1787). Notes that additional sources of Melville's geological information may be J. Forster's *Observations Made during a Voyage round the World* (1778), Goldsmith's *Animated Nature*, and R. Chambers's *Vestiges of the Natural History of Creation*.

1797.   ———. "Melville's Use of Two Pseudo-Sciences." *MLN* 64 (1949): 145–50.
Melville alludes to phrenology and physiognomy in works such as *Pierre*, *Mardi*, *White-Jacket*, and *The Confidence Man*, and in *Moby-Dick* he undertakes a phrenological investigation of the whale's skull. On the whole, though, he never believed in the pretensions of either pseudoscience and treated both in a playful, half-serious manner.

1798.   Karcher, Carolyn L. "Melville's 'The Gees': A Forgotten Satire on Scientific Racism." *AQ* 27 (1975): 421–42.
Outlines the principal features of Melville's burlesque of ethnology.

1799.   Lease, Benjamin. "Two Sides to a Tortoise: Darwin and Melville in the Pacific." *Person* 49 (1968): 531–39.
Compares the descriptions of the Galapagos archipelago and Tahiti in C. Darwin's *Beagle* journal and in Melville's "Encantadas" and *Omoo*. The striking contrast in perspective illustrates some differences between poetic and scientific imagination.

1800.   Leonard, David Charles. "The Cartesian Vortex in *Moby-Dick*." *AL* 51 (1979–80): 105–09.
Melville probably derived the Cartesian vortex imagery in *Moby-Dick* from his reading of the Cartesian sections of E. Chambers's *Cyclopaedia: Or, An Universal Dictionary of Arts and Sciences*.

1801.   ———. "Descartes, Melville, and the Mardian Vortex." *SAB* 45.2 (1980): 13–25.
The structure of *Mardi* reflects the Cartesian vortical system of physics, which Melville probably researched in E. Chambers's *Cyclopaedia*. Melville's affinity with Cartesian rationalism and physics ". . . alienated him from the main currents of nineteenth century transcendental thought."

1802.   Ward, J. A. "The Function of the Cetological Chapters in *Moby-Dick*." *AL* 28 (1956–57): 164–83.
Views *Moby-Dick* as Melville's allegory for the quest after total knowledge. Shows how Melville carries out this allegory by carefully interweaving scientific descriptions of the whale with poetic attempts to grasp the whale's significance.

1802a.   Werge, Thomas. "Melville's Satanic Salesman: Scientism and Puritanism in 'The Lightning-Rod Man.' " *C&L* 21.4 (1972): 6–12.
Maintains that Melville uses religious language and imagery in "The Lightning-Rod Man" to represent the sharp distinction between a religious perception of the universe and the faith in and reliance on commercial science, which the lightning rod symbolizes.

281

1802b. Wright, Nathalia. "Melville and 'Old Burton,' with 'Bartleby' as an Anatomy of Melancholy." *TSL* 15 (1970): 1–13.
"Bartleby the Scrivener" reflects Melville's thematic and stylistic debt to Burton's *Anatomy of Melancholy*.

George Meredith (1828–1909)

1803. Buchen, Irving H. *"The Ordeal of Richard Feverel*: Science versus Nature." *ELH* 29 (1962): 47–66.
Discusses the relation between the forces of nature and science in Meredith's novel, especially with respect to Sir Austin Feverel's "system" for the education of Richard.

1804. ———. "Science, Society, and Individuality: *The Egoist*." *UR* 30 (1963–64): 185–92.
Outlines the cosmic, social, and psychological dimensions of Willoughby's devotion to science in Meredith's *Egoist*. Willoughby's laboratory at Patterne Hall represents his "great scientific experiment in social and scientific perfectibility."

1805. Coslett, A. T. "The Relation of Scientific Thought and Poetry in the Poems of George Meredith." Diss. Oxford U, 1977.
Not seen for annotation.

1806. Cunliffe, J. W. "Modern Thought in Meredith's Poems." *PMLA* 27 (1912): 1–25.
Examines Meredith's use of the principles of Darwinian evolution in poems such as "The Woods of Westermain," "Manfred," and "Earth's Secret." Briefly discusses Tennyson and Browning in relation to evolution.

1807. Fehr, Bernhard. "George Meredith (1828–1909), der Dichter der Evolution." *NS* 18 (1910–11): 65–82.
Argues that Meredith's concept of human evolution was influenced by C. Darwin, Spencer, and Carlyle and discusses *Richard Feverel*, *Diana of the Crossways*, *The Egoist*, and other works in this light. Meredith believed that humankind's continued evolution demands a thorough understanding of nature and involves a harmony among body, mind, and soul.

1808. Graber, Terry H. " 'Scientific' Education and Richard Feverel." *VS* 14 (1970–71): 129–41.
Views Sir Austin Feverel's scientific system for educating his son, Richard, in Meredith's *Ordeal of Richard Feverel*, against the background of nineteenth-century educational theories, most notably those of Spencer.

1809. Reynolds, George F. "Two Notes on the Poetry of George Meredith." *University of Colorado Studies* 15 (1925–27): 1–12.
The second note treats Meredith's enthusiasm for the doctrine of evolution and assesses the extent to which the theory inspired his poetry.

1810. Robinson, Erwin Arthur. "The Influence of Science upon George Meredith." *Ohio State University Abstracts of Doctors' Dissertations* 21 (1937): 295–306.

The principles of biological evolution appear in each of Meredith's later novels. Robinson studies the extent to which evolution informed Meredith's philosophy and influenced his fictional works, including *The Egoist* and *Diana of the Crossways*.

1811. ———. "Meredith's Literary Theory and Science: Realism versus the Comic Spirit." *PMLA* 53 (1938): 857–68.

Discusses Meredith's critical rejection of realism and his views on the limits of scientific inquiry. Correlates his theory of literature in the *Essay on Comedy* with the philosophy of evolution that underlies his philosophy and artistry.

1812. Whidden, R. W., and John P. Kirby. "Meredith's *Meditation under Stars*." *Expl* 4 (1945): item 19.

Suggests that the theme of Meredith's poem arose from a common nineteenth-century question: "Is there life on stars or celestial bodies other than Earth?"

Jules Michelet (1798–1874)

1813. Orr, Linda. *Jules Michelet: Nature, History, and Language*. Ithaca: Cornell UP, 1976. 215 pp.

Rev. Frank Paul Bowman, *FR* 50 (1976–77): 929–30; Hans Kellner, *History and Theory* 16 (1977): 217–29; Bettina L. Knapp, *SIR* 16 (1977): 401–05; Charles Rearick, *AHR* 82 (1977): 651–52; Hayden White, *Criticism* 19 (1977): 361–63; Michael D. Biddiss, *History* 63 (1978): 72; Walter D. Gray, *Review of Politics* 40 (1978): 292–94; Stephen Wilson, *Historical Journal* 21 (1978): 721–35.

Treats the unique use of language in Michelet's popular natural-history works, *L'oiseau*, *L'insecte*, *La mer*, and *La montagne* and notes their literary qualities.

Silas Weir Mitchell (1829–1914)

1814. Earnest, Ernest. "Weir Mitchell as Novelist." *ASch* 17 (1948): 314–22.

Mitchell was not only a prominent physician but a fairly active literary man, producing a dozen novels as well as other works. Earnest discusses such works as *Roland Blake*, *Constance Trescot*, and *Circumstances* to explain how Mitchell used his impressive physiological, neurological, psychological, and medical knowledge in his novels.

Charles Nodier (1780–1844)

1815. Porter, Laurence M. "Charles Nodier and Saint-Martin." *RomN* 14 (1972–73): 283–88.

Notes that both Nodier and Louis-Claude de Saint-Martin adopted the cosmology Charles Bonnet proposed in *Palingénésie philosophique* (1770). Bonnet ". . . attempted to reconcile orthodox Christian doctrine with the evolutionist theories of eighteenth-century science."

Frank Norris (1870–1902)

1816.   Pehowski, Marian F. "Darwinism and the Naturalistic Novel: J. P. Jacobsen, Frank Norris and Shimazaki Tōson." *DA* 34 (1973): 785A–86A.
Maintains that the naturalistic novels of Jacobsen, Norris, and Tōson exemplify C. Darwin's impact on literature and show the literary naturalists' common dependence on the evolutionary worldview.

1817.   Pizer, Donald. "The Concept of Nature in Frank Norris' *The Octopus.*" *AQ* 14 (1962): 73–80.
The natural cycle of reproduction, growth, and death, typified by the wheat plant, represents a sort of divine energy that shapes the characters of Norris's *Octopus*. This essay traces American evolutionary theism as a surrogate for a traditional deity.

1818.   ————. "Evolutionary Ethical Dualism in Frank Norris' *Vandover and the Brute* and *McTeague.*" *PMLA* 76 (1961): 552–60.
Although Norris was not a philosophical naturalist, he did try to reconcile dualism with materialistic evolution. His short story "Lauth" and his novels *Vandover* and *McTeague* dramatize how the energy of the struggle for existence directs the emergence of animal nature.

1819.   Tatum, Stephen. "Norris's Debt in 'Lauth' to Lemattre's 'On the Transfusion of Blood.' " *ALR* 11 (1978): 243–48.
Norris's story "Lauth" (1893) may have been influenced by Gustave Lemattre's essay "On the Transfusion of Blood" (1873). Norris's story resembles the essay in details of the medical procedure of blood transfusion, in the concern that animal blood may cause reversion in a human recipient, and in the treatment of the question regarding the features distinguishing humans from animals.

Giovanni Pascoli (1855–1912)

1820.   Getto, Giovanni. "Giovanni Pascoli Poeta Astrale." *Studi per il centenario della nascita di Giovanni Pascoli publicati nel cinquantenario della morte.* Convegno bolognese. 28–30 Mar. 1958. Spec. issue of *L'archiginnasio: Bollettino della Biblioteca Communale di Bologna.* Vol. 3. Bologna: Commissione per i testi di lingua, 1962. 35–73. 3 vols.
Pascoli suffered from a spiritual vertigo that stemmed directly from his comprehension of a universe rendered limitless by contemporary science. The scientific ideas about the physical universe that pervade Pascoli's poetry changed what had been for him a stable and comforting heaven and earth into a threatening and alien space.

1821.   Vischi, Luciano. "Fonti scientifiche pascoliane." *Studi per il centenario della nascita di Giovanni Pascoli publicati nel cinquantenario della morte.* Convegno bolognese. 28–30 Mar. 1958. Spec. issue of *L'archiginnasio: Bollettino della*

Biblioteca Communale di Bologna. Vol. 2. Bologna: Commissione per i testi di lingua, 1962. 205–11. 3 vols.

In some poems Pascoli displays a detailed knowledge of contemporary scientific observations of various animals. In particular, several contain accurate and verbatim accounts of animals described in the work of the biologist Luis Paolucci.

Thomas Love Peacock (1785–1866)

1822.   Rudinsky, Norma L. "Source of Asterias's Paean to Science in Peacock's *Nightmare Abbey.*" *N&Q* ns 22 (1975): 66–68.

Asterias appears to be a caricature of the French scientist Pierre Denys de Montfort. Montfort's *Histoire naturelle des mollusques* is the direct source of several references to science in *Nightmare Abbey*.

Benito Pérez Galdós (1843–1920)

1823.   Gordon, M. "The Medical Background to Galdós' *La desheredada.*" *AGald* 7 (1972): 67–77.

Galdós used concepts drawn from the medical and psychological theorists Manuel Tolosa Latour and José María Esquerdo for his characterizations in *La desheredada*. Gordon examines in detail the background to Galdós's character Mariano Rufete and discusses Galdós's position in the literary tradition stemming from Zola's naturalism.

1824.   Willey, Jack R. "The Médico as a Literary Personage in the Works of Benito Pérez Galdós." *DA* 30 (1969–70): 3482A.

Examines Galdós's portrayal of doctors and medicine in works such as *Episodios nacionales*, *Novelas y cuentos*, and *Dramas*.

Thomas Sergeant Perry (1845–1928)

1825.   Pizer, Donald. "Evolution and Criticism: Thomas Sergeant Perry." *TSLL* 3 (1961–62): 348–59. Rpt. in *Realism and Naturalism in Nineteenth-Century American Literature.* Carbondale: Southern Illinois UP, 1966. New York: Russell, 1976. 53–66.

Describes Perry's application of evolution theory to his literary criticism in the 1880s, including *English Literature in the Eighteenth Century* and *A History of Greek Literature*. Perry's conception of evolutionary "laws" is largely Spencerian.

Luigi Pirandello (1867–1936)

1826.   Chinatti, Luigi. "Pirandello e la scienza." *Letteratura e scienza nella storia della cultura italiana.* Atti del IX congresso dell'associazione internazionale per gli studi di lingua e letteratura italiana. Palermo, Messina, Catania, 21–25 Apr. 1976. Associazione internazionale per gli studi di lingua e letteratura italiana. Palermo: Manfredi, 1978. 813–19.

Pirandello was profoundly skeptical toward science, which he saw as superficial and incapable of yielding true wisdom or metaphysical knowledge. Chinatti cites Pirandello's essay "Rinunzia," his novel *Il fu Mattia Pascal*, and the short stories "Canta l'epistola" and "Donna Mimma."

Edgar Allan Poe (1809–49)

1827.   Alterton, Margaret. *Origins of Poe's Critical Theory*. Diss. U of Iowa, 1922. University of Iowa Humanistic Studies 2.3. Iowa City: U of Iowa P; New York: Russell, 1925. 191 pp.
        Rev. Killis Campbell, *MLN* 41 (1926): 208.
Poe's critical theory was influenced by natural science as well as by British periodicals, law, drama, the fine arts, and philosophy. Alterton emphasizes Poe's attempts to base his literary principles on astronomical laws, noting his debt to the *Philosophical Transactions of the Royal Society of London*.

1828.   Autrey, Max L. "Edgar Allan Poe's Satiric View of Evolution." *Extrapolation* 18 (1976–77): 186–99.
Examines Poe's de-evolutionary satire in *Eureka*, "Loss of Breath," "Four Beasts in One; The Homo-Cameleopard," "The System of Dr. Tarr and Prof. Fether," "Hop-Frog," and other tales. Poe alludes to the evolutionary theories of Cuvier, Lyell, E. Darwin, Comte, and others.

1829.   Bailey, J. O. "The Geography of Poe's 'Dream-Land' and 'Ulalume.' " *SP* 45 (1948): 512–23.
Poe's poems are influenced by the "hollow earth" theory in Seaborn's novel *Symzonia*, particularly in Seaborn's representation of Belzubia, a land of dreams. Poe may also imaginatively transform details in Mercator's "Nautical Chart of the World" (1569).

1830.   ———. "Sources for Poe's *Arthur Gordon Pym*, 'Hans Pfaall,' and Other Pieces." *PMLA* 57 (1942): 513–35.
Poe derived much of his thematic material for the scientific and cosmic-voyage elements of *Pym*, "Pfaall," "MS. Found in a Bottle," and *Eureka* from Seaborn's *Symzonia* (1820) and Tucker's *Voyage to the Moon*.

1830a. Barker, Christine R. "Edgar Allan Poe and Fritz Usinger: Two Cosmologies." *NGS* 3 (1975): 165–71.
Maintains that among Poe's readers the German poet and critic Fritz Usinger has been one of the few to stress the importance of *Eureka*. Usinger recognizes that Poe's cosmological theories resemble his own efforts to show how "scientific discoveries have altered man's relationship to the rest of the universe."

1831.   Basore, John W. "Poe as an Epicurean." *MLN* 25 (1910): 86–87.
Poe's attempt in "Mesmeric Revelation" to define spirit as "unparticled matter" may have been based on the principles of Epicurean physics.

1832.   Beaver, Harold, ed. *The Science Fiction of Edgar Allan Poe*. New York: Penguin, 1976. 421 pp.

The introduction outlines Poe's relation to nineteenth-century mathematical and electrochemical advances and comments on his role in the development of the science-fiction genre. Included in the anthology are works such as *Eureka*, "Mesmeric Revelation," "The System of Dr. Tarr and Prof. Fether," and "A Tale of the Ragged Mountains."

1832a.   Bierly, Charles E. "*Eureka* and the Drama of the Self: A Study of the Relationship between Poe's Cosmology and His Fiction." *DA* 18 (1958): 228–29.

Studies the relations between the cosmology of Poe's *Eureka* and the thought and attitude of his other works.

1833.   Brooks, Curtis M. "The Cosmic God: Science and the Creative Imagination in *Eureka*." *Poe as a Literary Cosmologer: Studies on* Eureka*: A Symposium*. Ed. Richard P. Benton. Hartford: Transcendental, 1975. 60–68.

This study of *Eureka* examines Poe's scientific and materialistic explanation of the origin of spirit, thought, and imagination. Brooks also remarks on Poe's early views on science and cosmology in "The Island of the Fay" and "Mesmeric Revelation."

1834.   Buranelli, Vincent. *The Wizard from Vienna: Franz Anton Mesmer*. New York: Coward, 1975. London: Owen, 1976. 256 pp.

This biography of Mesmer, the discoverer of animal magnetism and hypnotism, includes one brief chapter on Poe's references to mesmerism in "A Tale of the Ragged Mountains," "Mesmeric Revelation," and "The Facts in the Case of M. Valdemar."

1835.   Butler, David W. "Usher's Hypochondriasis: Mental Alienation and Romantic Idealism in Poe's Gothic Tales." *AL* 48 (1976–77): 1–12.

Poe's characterization of Usher's mental disorder in *The Fall of the House of Usher* reflects nineteenth-century medical and romantic notions of the correspondence between insanity and creative activity.

1836.   Falk, Doris V. "Poe and the Power of Animal Magnetism." *PMLA* 84 (1969): 536–46.

Examines Poe's use of the theories of animal magnetism and mesmerism in "The Facts in the Case of M. Valdemar," "A Tale of the Ragged Mountains," and "Mesmeric Revelation."

1837.   Finholt, Richard D. "The Vision at the Brink of the Abyss: 'A Descent into the Maelstrom' in the Light of Poe's Cosmology." *GaR* 27 (1973): 356–66.

In "A Descent into the Maelstrom," the psychological dialectic between chaos and control, terror and lucidity, matches the dialectical principles that govern the cosmos. At the moment of lucidity, the hero's thoughts vibrate with those of the "Universal Mind" and thereby sustain his survival. Poe fully developed the cosmological vision informing the tale in *Eureka* and "Mesmeric Revelation."

1838.   Hall, Thomas. "Poe's Use of a Source: Davy's Chemical Researches and 'Von Kempelen and His Discovery.' " *PN* 1.1–2 (1968): 28.

Poe adapted a passage from Davy's *Researches, Chemical and Philosophical* (1839) for his story "Von Kempelen and His Discovery."

1839.   Hoagland, Clayton. "The Universe of *Eureka*: A Comparison of the Theories of Eddington and Poe." *Southern Literary Messenger* 1 (1939): 307–13.
Presents parallel texts from Poe's *Eureka* (1848) and Eddington's *Expanding Universe* (1933). Poe's work seems to anticipate several aspects of Eddington's theory of the universe.

1840.   Holt, Palmer C. "Notes on Poe's 'To Science,' 'To Helen,' and 'Ulalume.' " *BNYPL* 63 (1959): 568–70.
Poe derived the imagery of his sonnet "To Science" (1829) directly from Bernardin de Saint-Pierre's *Studies in Nature* (1808).

1841.   Hungerford, Edward. "Poe and Phrenology." *AL* 2 (1930–31): 209–31.
Traces the development of Poe's interest in phrenology and examines his allusions to phrenological principles in "The Business Man," "Some Words with a Mummy," "Colloquy of Monos and Una," "The Black Cat," "The Fall of the House of Usher," and other works.

1842.   Kennedy, Susan A. "Mark Twain and Edgar Allan Poe: The Development of the Grotesque Absurd." *DAI* 39 (1978): 1785A.
See item 1997 for annotation.

1843.   Kirkland, Joseph M. "Poe's Universe: A Critical Study of *Eureka*." *DAI* 37 (1976): 970A.
This thorough study emphasizes the scientific, aesthetic, and literary qualities of *Eureka*, the book in which Poe expounds his theory of the universe.

1844.   Kremenliev, Elva B. "The Literary Uses of Astronomy in the Writings of Edgar Allan Poe." *DA* 24 (1964): 4176.
Studies Poe's incorporation of astronomical theory and data into his poetry, prose fiction, and criticism, emphasizing the cosmological aspects of his astronomical interests, especially in *Eureka*.

1845.   Laser, Marvin. "The Growth and Structure of Poe's Concept of Beauty." *ELH* 15 (1948): 69–84.
Reviews the development of Poe's aesthetic, showing that it was strongly influenced by his study of phrenology as well as by the thought of S. Coleridge and P. Shelley.

1846.   Laverty, Carroll D. "Poe in His Place—in His Time." *ESQ* 31 (1963): 23–25.
Poe's use of scientific and pseudoscientific material shows that he was very much a product of his time. Laverty cites references to medicine, phrenology, botany, and other sciences in "The Fall of the House of Usher" and "The Thousand-and-Second Tale of Scheherazade."

1847. ———. "Science and Pseudo-Science in the Writings of Edgar Allan Poe."
Diss. Duke U, 1951.
Not seen for annotation.

1848. Leeds, Fredric M. "The Mountains of the Moon in 'Eldorado.' " *PoeS* 10
(1977): 44.
This brief note suggests that Poe derived his reference to the mountains of the
moon from a remark by Ptolemy reported in Charles Anthon's *Classical Dictionary*.

1849. Lemonnier, Léon. "Edgar Poe et le roman scientifique français." *La grande
revue* 133 (1930): 214–23.
Maintains that Poe modernized the "roman de voyages" by incorporating positivism, industrialism, and physics in works such as "L'aventure sans pareille d'un
certain Hans Pfaall" and "Le canard au ballon." As the originator of the scientific
novel, Poe had a considerable effect on Verne and Rosny. To demonstrate Poe's
influence, Lemonnier shows that Verne's fiction evolved from the fantastic to the
scientific in *Cinq semaines en ballon*, *Vingt mille lieues sous les mer*, *Tour du monde en
quatre-vingt jours*, and *Voyage au centre de la terre* and that Rosny's *Mort de la terre* and
Cataclysme maintain a scientific structure embellished with the introduction of the
"marvelous."

1850. Lind, Sidney E. "Poe and Mesmerism." *PMLA* 62 (1947): 1077–94.
Discusses "A Tale of the Ragged Mountains," "Mesmeric Revelation," and "The
Facts in the Case of M. Valdemar" in relation to nineteenth-century theories of
mesmerism and to Poe's main source, *Facts in Mesmerism*, by Chauncey Hare Townshend.

1851. Ljungquist, Kent. "Poe's 'The Island of the Fay': The Passing of Fairyland."
SSF 14 (1977): 265–71.
Poe's "Sonnet—to Science" constitutes a preface to the initial publication of his
sketch "The Island of the Fay"; thus juxtaposed, the two works suggest the challenge
science poses to the exotic realm of fairyland.

1852. Mabbott, Thomas Ollive. "The Astrological Symbolism of Poe's 'Ulalume.' " *N&Q* 161 (1931): 26–27.
In "Ulalume," implied astrological references to Venus in the evening and before
dawn suggest, with Satanic overtones, a love affair that has proved to be pure evil.
Poe may have been influenced by the astrological symbolism in Spenser's minor
poems.

1853. Maddison, Carol Hopkins. "Poe's *Eureka*." *TSLL* 2 (1960–61): 350–67.
"Poe . . . derived his hypothesis of the perfect unity of the universe from his
aesthetic theory, under the stimulation of current scientific and philosophic thought.
He examined natural phenomena for the verification of this hypothesis, using the
method that he had elaborated in his ratiocinative tales, a method that was ultimately
that of science."

1853a.   Meister, John G. H. "The Descent of the Irrelative One: The Metaphysics
         and Cosmology of Edgar Allan Poe's *Eureka.*" *DAI* 30 (1969): 2490A.
Partly concerns Poe's knowledge of eighteenth- and nineteenth-century science
as background to his cosmology.

1854.   Monteiro, George. "Edgar Poe and the New Knowledge." *SLJ* 4 (1971–
         72): 34–40.
Interprets Poe's repudiation of science in "Sonnet—to Science." The lyric voice
that presents the conflict between poetry and science represents the triumph of poetic
imagination over the influence of science.

1855.   Murphy, Christina J. "The Philosophical Pattern of 'A Descent into the
         Maelström.' " *PoeS* 6 (1973): 25–26.
Notes that the principles of attraction and repulsion central to Poe's cosmological
prose poem *Eureka* also play an important role in "A Descent into the Maelstrom,"
operating both on physical or literal and psychological or symbolic levels.

1856.   Nettesheim, Josefine. "Adalbert Stifter—'Der Kondor' und Edgar Allan
         Poe—'The Balloon Hoax.' " *Poeta doctus oder die Poetisierung der Wissenschaft
         von Musäus bis Benn.* Berlin: Duncker, 1975. 116–27.
Examines the motif of balloon travel in Stifter's novella "Der Kondor" and Poe's
story "The Balloon Hoax." While Stifter's work concerns the human aspects of such
travel, Poe's story reflects an interest in science as well as an inclination toward the
fantastic and the sensational.

1857.   ———. "Edgar Allan Poes Universumsdichtung *Eureka*: Ein Beitrag zum
         Thema: Wissenschaft und Dichtung." *JWGV* 76 (1972): 136–54. Rpt.
         in *Poeta doctus oder die Poetisierung der Wissenschaft von Musäus bis Benn.*
         Berlin: Duncker, 1975. 94–115.
Discusses Poe's attempts to unify literature, science, and philosophy in the astronomical prose poem *Eureka* and examines his extension of the Kant-Laplace nebular
hypothesis over metaphysical as well as physical processes. Among the influences
on Poe are Humboldt's *Kosmos*, Novalis, Schelling, and mesmerism.

1858.   Nordstedt, George. "Poe and Einstein." *Open Court* 44 (1930): 173–80.
Maintains that in the prose poem *Eureka* Poe anticipates several aspects of Einstein's
relativity theory, such as speculations concerning the extent and shape of the observable universe.

1859.   O'Donnell, Charles. "From Earth to Ether: Poe's Flight into Space." *PMLA*
         77 (1962): 85–91.
Concerns Poe's attempts to dramatize the tension between spirit and body, self
and universe, in "The Narrative of A. Gordon Pym," "Mesmeric Revelation," and
Eureka.

1860.   Oelke, Karl E. "The Rude Daughter: Alchemy in Poe's Early Poetry."
         DAI 33 (1972): 2388A.

Traces the development of Poe's acquaintance with alchemy and examines the alchemical imagery that informs his poems of 1831.

1861. Olney, Clarke. "Edgar Allan Poe—Science-Fiction Pioneer." *GaR* 12 (1958): 416–21.
Maintains that Poe originated the conventions and form of the science fiction genre with, for example, his method of rational extrapolation from contemporary scientific knowledge. Briefly discusses his use of balloon flight, alchemy, and mesmerism in tales such as "The Balloon Hoax," "Von Kempelen and His Discovery," and "Mesmeric Revelation."

1862. Petersen, Pam. "Mesmerism, Popular Science, and Poe." *Proceedings of the Sixth National Convention of the Popular Culture Association.* Ed. Michael T. Marsden. Bowling Green: Bowling Green State U Popular P, 1976. 251–62.
Outlines the mesmeric techniques Mesmer used in the eighteenth century and comments on the public reception of the pseudoscience. Examines Poe's literary adaptation of mesmeric principles in "A Tale of the Ragged Mountains," "The Facts in the Case of M. Valdemar," "Mesmeric Revelation," and "The Tell-Tale Heart."

1863. Phillips, Elizabeth. "Mere Household Events: The Metaphysics of Mania." *Edgar Allan Poe: An American Imagination—Three Essays.* Port Washington: Kennikat, 1979. 97–137.
Poe exploited contemporary medical and psychological works by Benjamin Rush, D. Meredith Reese, and Isaac Ray in his study of the relations between alcoholism and mania. References to concepts derived from these works appear in tales such as "Berenice," "The Fall of the House of Usher," and "The Man of the Crowd." Phillips assesses the extent to which Poe's personal experiences with alcohol and insanity influenced his fiction.

1864. Pollin, Burton R. "Poe's Use of Material from Bernardin de Saint-Pierre's *Etudes.*" *RomN* 12 (1970–71): 331–38.
Details in Poe's "MS. Found in a Bottle" may derive from the discussion of polar caps and oceanic currents in Bernardin de Saint-Pierre's *Etudes de la nature* (1784). Poe may also have relied on Bernardin de Saint-Pierre for touches in "A Descent into the Maelstrom" and "The Thousand-and-Second Tale of Scheherezade."

1865. Posey, Meredith Neill. "Notes on Poe's 'Hans Pfaall.' " *MLN* 45 (1930): 501–07.
Suggests that two sources of the astronomical information in "Hans Pfaall" were J. Herschel's *A Treatise on Astronomy* (1834) and Rees's *Cyclopedia* (1819).

1866. Ramachandran, Meera. "Naturalism in the Grotesque: A New Look at Poe's *Eureka* and His Tales of the Grotesque." *IJAS* 6 (1976): 30–43.
Maintains that in significant respects the scientific reasoning and principles behind the theory of cosmic evolution in Poe's *Eureka* anticipated the movement of literary naturalism. Shows how Poe's "naturalism" operates in his treatment of the grotesque

themes of "The Cask of Amontillado," "The Tell-Tale Heart," "William Wilson," "The Fall of the House of Usher," and other tales.

1867.   Sharp, Roberta I. "The Problem of Knowledge in Poe's Scientific Prose." *DAI* 38 (1977): 1395A–96A.

Poe held a skeptical and satirical attitude toward science, though he often used scientific elements in his tales to achieve bizarre dramatic effects. This study explores his use of scientific and pseudoscientific principles in works such as *Eureka* and examines his reliance on "mystification" to acquire knowledge beyond the limits of the scientific sphere.

1868.   Sloane, David E. E. "Gothic Romanticism and Rational Empiricism in Poe's 'Berenice.' " *ATQ* 19 (1973): 19–26.

Suggests that "Berenice" is a fictional rendition of the theme of Poe's "Sonnet— to Science." This short story embodies a grotesque rejection of American empirical science while ". . . it burlesques the violation of the female principle of beauty in the European Gothic novel."

1869.   Smith, Herbert F. "Usher's Madness and Poe's Organicism: A Source." *AL* 39 (1967–68): 379–89.

Argues that Poe derived the scientific assumptions grounding "The Fall of the House of Usher" from R. Watson's *Chemical Essays* (1781–87). In particular, Poe used Watson's arguments for the organic relatedness of all matter and the concept of vegetable sentience.

1870.   St. Armand, Barton Levi. "The Dragon and the Uroboros: Themes of Metamorphosis in *Arthur Gordon Pym*." *ATQ* 37 (1978): 57–71.

The narrative events and major images in *Pym* come from alchemy. The transformation of characters is analogous to alchemical transmutations.

1871.   ———. "Poe's 'Sober Mystification': The Uses of Alchemy in 'The Gold-Bug.' " *PoeS* 4 (1971): 1–7.

Poe used alchemy to fuse the disparate elements of his narrative; thus, the study of the alchemical details of "The Gold-Bug" enhances appreciation of the work's coherence and plausibility. Among the alchemical symbols discussed is Poe's use of a tulip tree to represent the mystery of transmutation.

1872.   Stern, Madeleine B. "Poe: 'The Mental Temperament' for Phrenologists." *AL* 40 (1968–69): 155–63.

Because of Poe's interest in phrenology, phrenologists were eager to examine the structure of his phrenological temperament. This essay describes the results of the phrenological studies done on Poe both before and after his death.

1873.   Turner, Arlin. "Sources of Poe's 'A Descent into the Maelstrom.' " *JEGP* 46 (1947): 298–301.

Details of Poe's tale derive from the *Encyclopedia Britannica* (3rd ed., 1797) and from an anonymous story in *Le magasin universel* (1836); Poe's borrowings reflect his method of claiming scientific accuracy by citing spurious authorities.

1874. Walker, I. M. "The 'Legitimate Sources' of Terror in 'The Fall of the House of Usher.' " *MLR* 61 (1966): 585–92.

Poe's depiction of Roderick Usher's mental derangement is based on the psychological and scientific theories of Benjamin Rush, Isaac Ray, and Thomas Upham. For example, Upham's *Elements of Mental Philosophy* (1837) details the psychological impact of a gas known as febrile miasma; this is the same gas that Poe describes as rising from the tarn around the house of Usher and leading ultimately to Roderick's psychological collapse.

1875. Warfel, Harry R. "Poe's Dr. Percival: A Note on 'The Fall of the House of Usher.' " *MLN* 54 (1939): 129–31.

Poe's acknowledged use of volume 5 of R. Watson's *Chemical Essays* (1787) provides a clue to the identification of "Dr. Percival," referred to in a note to "The Fall of the House of Usher" in connection with the scientific theory of vegetable sentience. The reference was probably to the physician and author Thomas Percival.

1876. Wolfe, Charles K. "Poe and the Romance of Science." *Romantist* 2 (1978): 37–39.

Considers Poe a precursor of modern science fiction because of his enthusiasm for science and his incorporation of scientific themes and data into works such as "The Unparalleled Adventure of One Hans Pfaall," "MS. Found in a Bottle," "The Balloon Hoax," and *Eureka*.

Aleksandr Sergeyevich Pushkin (1799–1837)

1877. Gustafson, Richard F. "The Upas Tree: Pushkin and Erasmus Darwin." *PMLA* 75 (1960): 101–09.

Demonstrates that the source of Pushkin's description of the legendary poisonous Upas tree was Darwin's *Loves of the Plants*, which incorporates a spurious scientific report about the tree by a certain "Dr. Foersch."

Arthur Rimbaud (1854–91)

1878. Bouvet, Alphonse. "Rimbaud et l'alchimie." *RSH* 126 (1967): 233–37.

Rimbaud's use of colors and hues in the poem "Voyelles" demonstrates a knowledge of alchemical literature, including Berthelot's *Collection des anciens alchimistes* (1888) and *Origines de l'alchimie* (1885).

1879. Meltzer, Françoise. "On Rimbaud's 'Voyelles.' " *MP* 76 (1978–79): 344–54.

Concerns the extent to which alchemical symbolism, color symbolism, astrology, and other mystical symbol codes enter into Rimbaud's sonnet.

John Ruskin (1819–1900)

1880. Bidney, Martin. "Ruskin, Dante, and the Enigma of Nature." *TSLL* 18 (1976–77): 290–305.

Ruskin's conflict between a Dantean and a Wordsworthian perspective on nature is evidenced in his "poetic" works of science, *Prosperina* and *Deucalion*.

1881. Rosenberg, John D. "The Geopoetry of John Ruskin." *EA* 22 (1969): 42–48.

Reviews Hélène Lemaître's *Pierres dans l'œuvre de Ruskin* (1965), stressing her study of the poetic and humanistic aspects of Ruskin's naturalist and geological writings.

Charles Augustin Sainte-Beuve (1804–69)

1882. Dresden, S. "La méthode critique de Sainte-Beuve et la science." *Literature and Science*. Proc. of the Sixth Triennial Congress of the International Federation for Modern Languages and Literatures. Oxford, 1954. Oxford: Blackwell, 1955. 269–73.

Affirms that the influence of "moral physiology" and history can be discerned in Sainte-Beuve's earliest writings but has been overlooked because of his multiple and personal methodologies. Although Sainte-Beuve could never be affected by science to the extent that Hippolyte Taine was, he frequently indicated how the sciences with which he was familiar aided his critical analysis.

1883. Smith, Horatio. "Sainte-Beuve on Science and Human Nature: Jouffroy, Le Play, Proudhon." *MLN* 57 (1942): 592–602.

Sainte-Beuve's literary criticism of Jouffroy, Le Play, and Proudhon stresses the shortcomings of their attempts to comment scientifically on human psychology. In general, he maintains that they need greater scientific rigor coupled with heightened artistic integrity.

Solomon Schindler (1842–1915)

1884. Segal, Howard P. "*Young West*: The Psyche of Technological Utopianism." *Extrapolation* 19 (1977–78): 50–58.

Examines Schindler's novel *Young West*, an 1894 sequel to Bellamy's *Looking Backward*, in which technology and science play major roles in creating a utopia.

Karl Wilhelm Friedrich Schlegel (1772–1829)

1885. Hudgins, Esther. "Das Geheimnis der *Lucinde*-Struktur: Goethes 'Die Metamorphose der Pflanzen.' " *GQ* 49 (1976): 295–311.

Shows the influence of Goethe's elegy "Die Metamorphose der Pflanzen" on the structure of Schlegel's novel *Lucinde*. Schlegel applied Goethe's concept of the metamorphosis of plants to his own theory of the Romantic novel and composed *Lucinde* in accordance with the principles of metamorphosis described in Goethe's poem.

Mary Shelley (1797–1851)

1886. Buchen, Irving H. "*Frankenstein* and the Alchemy of Creation and Evolution." *WC* 8 (1977): 103–12.

Maintains that Shelley's *Frankenstein* treats the tension between the cosmic creative force of myth and the evolutionary force of history. Its theme also concerns the relation between alchemy and science and the consequences of that pairing for society.

1887.   Cottom, Daniel. "*Frankenstein* and the Monster of Representation." *Sub-Stance* 9.3 (1980): 60–71.

"It is because man cannot escape into objectivity through science that scientific instruments become symbols of violent disorder in *Frankenstein*. . . . The language of science, the tools of science, and the product of science are all as one because, as Victor regards them, all are representations of man as something other than himself. That is to say, they are representations of man as a representation—as a victim of instruments foreign to himself."

1888.   Crouch, Laura E. "Davy's *A Discourse, Introductory to a Course of Lectures on Chemistry*: A Possible Scientific Source of *Frankenstein*." *KSJ* 27 (1978): 35–44.

Shelley read Davy's chemistry book while she was writing *Frankenstein*. His work seems to be the source of both the scientific ideas presented in the novel and the scientific optimism that shaped the character of the young Frankenstein.

1889.   Cude, Wilfred. "Mary Shelley's Modern Prometheus: A Study in the Ethics of Scientific Creativity." *DR* 52 (1972–73): 212–25.

Treats Shelley's *Frankenstein* as a study in the conflict between morality and scientific creativity as well as an examination of the social consequences of, and the social responsibility for, scientific research.

1890.   Roth, Nancy. "Early Electromedicine and the Frankenstein Myth." *Medical Instrumentation* 12 (1978): 248.

Shelley's inspiration for *Frankenstein* may have come in part from reports of the electrical experiments of Galvani, Volta, and Bichat.

1891.   Thomsen, Christian W. "Die Verantwortung des Naturwissenschaftlers in Mary Shelleys *Frankenstein* und Heinar Kipphardts *In der Sache J. Robert Oppenheimer*: Zur literarischen Gestaltung eines Problems." *LWU* 4 (1971): 16–26.

Compares how Shelley's *Frankenstein* and Kipphardt's *In der Sache J. Robert Oppenheimer* handle the problem of scientists' social responsibility for their creations. Includes a brief history of literary works depicting scientists, such as Jonson's *Alchemist* (1610), W. Godwin's *Caleb Williams* (1794), Wells's *Island* (1896), Brecht's *Leben des Galilei* (1938–39), and Zuckmayer's *Kalte Licht* (1955).

1892.   Vasbinder, Samuel H. "Scientific Attitudes in Mary Shelley's *Frankenstein*: Newtonian Monism as a Basis for the Novel." *DAI* 37 (1976): 2842A.

The importance of the scientific aspects of *Frankenstein* has hitherto been under-estimated. This study attempts to redress the shortcomings of previous criticism by examining the extent of Shelley's scientific knowledge, stressing her background in Newtonianism and the elements of "new science" in her novel.

1893.   Wheeler, Wayne B. "The Horror of Science in Politics: Prophecy and the Crisis of Human Values in Mary Shelley's *Frankenstein* and Aldous Huxley's *Brave New World*." *DAI* 40 (1979): 2246A.

Deals in part with Shelley's and Huxley's approaches to "the fate of the individual in his confrontation with the forces of scientific technology and modern society."

Percy Bysshe Shelley (1792–1822)

1894.   Ebeling, Elizabeth. "A Probable Paracelsian Element in Shelley." *SP* 32 (1935): 508–25.
Examines Shelley's use of the Paracelsian cosmological theories of the archeus, the macrocosm and microcosm, and the "evestrum" in *Prometheus Unbound*.

1895.   Grabo, Carl H. "Astronomical Allusions in Shelley's *Prometheus Unbound*." *PQ* 6 (1927): 362–78.
Shows that Shelley was indebted to W. Herschel for the astronomical ideas expressed in *Prometheus Unbound*. Includes a summary of Herschel's astronomical theories.

1896.   ———. "Electricity, the Spirit of the Earth, in Shelley's *Prometheus Unbound*." *PQ* 6 (1927): 133–50.
Examines Shelley's poetic expression of chemical, geological, and electrical concepts in *Prometheus Unbound*. Shelley's chief scientific sources include Davy, Beccaria, and E. Darwin.

1897.   ———. *The Meaning of* The Witch of Atlas. Chapel Hill: U of North Carolina P, 1935. New York: Russell, 1971. 158 pp.
         Rev. Adele B. Ballman, *MLN* 52 (1937): 144–46.
This detailed explication of Shelley's poem stresses his synthesis of elements of Egyptian and Greek myth, Neoplatonism, and the scientific theories of electricity, magnetism, and meteorology.

1898.   ———. *A Newton among Poets: Shelley's Use of Science in* Prometheus Unbound. Chapel Hill: U of North Carolina P, 1930. New York: Cooper Square-Gordian, 1968. 208 pp.
         Rev. A. Koszul, *MLN* 48 (1933): 50–53.
Shelley's extensive reading in science informs many images in his poetry, including those of volcanoes, atmospheric electrical displays, comets, and meteors in *Prometheus Unbound*. Shelley was familiar with E. Darwin's verse accounts of botany, geology, and electricity, with W. Herschel's astronomy, with Newton's physics and metaphysics, and with Davy's electrochemical experiments. Most important, like many scientists of his day, Shelley believed that electricity was the vital spark of life, and thus in his masterpiece he described Asia and other spirits as electrical.

1899.   ———. Prometheus Unbound: *An Interpretation*. Chapel Hill: U of North Carolina P, 1935. New York: Gordian, 1968. 205 pp.
In *Prometheus Unbound* Shelley tried to fuse revolutionary social philosophy, Neoplatonism, and scientific speculation and to reconcile materialism and idealism, physics and metaphysics, science and religion. Among the aspects of science that inform his symbolism are geology, electrical theory, gravitation, magnetism, and evolution theory.

1900.   Jeffrey, Lloyd N. " 'The Birds within the Wind': A Study in Shelley's Use of Natural History." *KSJ* 18 (1969): 61–80.

Surveys the ornithological imagery and symbology of Shelley's poetry and discusses possible scientific and scholarly sources.

1901. ———. "Cuvierian Catastrophism in Shelley's *Prometheus Unbound* and 'Mont Blanc.' " *SCB* 38 (1978): 148–52.
Much of the imagery of *Prometheus Unbound* 4.287–318 and "Mont Blanc" suggests Shelley's familiarity with Cuvier's *Recherches sur les ossements fossiles de quadrupèdes* (1812).

1902. ———. "Reptile-Lore in Shelley: A Study in the Poet's Use of Natural History." *KSJ* 7 (1958): 29–46.
Discusses the probable literary and scientific sources of Shelley's poetic allusions to reptiles, including works by Pliny the Elder, Ovid, Vergil, Dante, Shakespeare, Spenser, Milton, S. Coleridge, Cuvier, and Keats.

1903. ———. *Shelley's Knowledge and Use of Natural History.* Salzburg Studies in English Literature: Romantic Reassessment 48. Ed. James Hogg. Salzburg: Institut für englische Sprache und Literatur, U Salzburg, 1976. 144 pp.
Catalogs Shelley's poetic references to reptiloids, birds, mammals, and insects and comments on the sources of his knowledge of natural history, which, in addition to folkloristic, mythological, biblical, and literary works, include the writings of Aristotle, Pliny the Elder, Buffon, and Cuvier.

1904. ———. "Shelley's 'Plumèd Insects Swift and Free.' " *KSJ* 25 (1976): 103–21.
Surveys the entomological allusions in Shelley's poetry. His use of insect lore, which was generally figurative and symbolic rather than scientific, was drawn from sources such as folklore, the Bible, the classics, and possibly Cuvier's natural history writings.

1905. King-Hele, Desmond. "The Influence of Erasmus Darwin on Shelley." *KSMB* 13 (1962): 30–36.
Maintains that by "forecasting the future triumphs of science, Darwin helped to inspire Shelley with enthusiasm for scientific progress, and with his poems he gave Shelley the idea of bringing science into poetry." Notes the influence of Darwin's *Botanic Garden* and *Temple of Nature* on Shelley's *Queen Mab*, *Prometheus Unbound*, *Adonais*, and other poems.

1906. Male, Roy R., Jr., and James A. Notopoulos. "Shelley's Copy of Diogenes Laertius." *MLR* 54 (1959): 10–21.
Reproduces the marginalia in Shelley's copy of *Lives of the Philosophers*, which indicate Shelley's early interest in science and philosophy.

1907. Reisner, Thomas A. "Some Scientific Models for Shelley's Multitudinous Orb." *KSJ* 23 (1974): 52–59.
Among the scientific sources of Shelley's image of the "multitudinous orb" in *Prometheus Unbound* (4.236–79) may be works by Laplace and Euler.

1908.   Turner, Paul. "Shelley and Lucretius." *RES* ns 10 (1959): 269–82.
Surveys Shelley's poems and cites passages that imply the influence of Lucretian imagery. Covers *Queen Mab*, *The Daemon of the World*, *The Revolt of Islam*, and *Swellfoot the Tyrant*.

1909.   White, Harry. "Shelley's Defence of Science." *SIR* 16 (1977): 319–30.
In his *Defence of Poetry* Shelley introduces a distinction between abstract, analytic knowledge (the result of strictly rational processes) and empirical, synthetic knowledge (the result of imaginative and poetic processes). He argues that rational procedures alone can yield neither existential nor scientific knowledge and require the prior use of the poetic faculty, which, because of its power of synthetic apprehension, can provide meaningful information concerning the empirical world. Shelley's distinction, derived principally from D. Hume's philosophy, grounds scientific procedures in poetic activity, allowing him to defend science without abandoning poetry while clarifying the relation between science and poetry.

Langdon Smith (1858–1908)

1910.   Gardner, Martin. "When You Were a Tadpole and I Was a Fish." *AR* 22 (1962–63): 332–40.
Broadly discusses the Darwinian basis of Smith's poem "Evolution" and notes the work's wide popular appeal.

Stendhal (1783–1842)

1911.   Dufour, L. "Stendhal et la météorologie." *SC* 8 (1966): 281–324.
Documents Stendhal's precise references to the weather and cogent observations of atmospheric conditions in his *Journal* and *Correspondence*. Attributes his keen interest in meteorology to the fact that his physical and emotional health was extremely sensitive to weather conditions.

1912.   Théodoridès, Jean. "Buffon jugé par Stendhal." *SC* 10 (1967–68): 193–202.
Cites references to Georges Buffon in the works of Stendhal, including *Vie de Henri Brulard*, *Mélanges de littérature*, *Les pensées*, *Racine et Shakespeare*, *Courrier anglais*, *Souvenirs d'égotisme*, and *Mémoires d'un Touriste*. Stendhal's negative opinion of Buffon was based not on a critique of the naturalist's scientific theories but rather on an analysis of his writing style and on suppositions about his personality.

1913.   ———. "Le physiologiste Magendie jugé par Stendhal." *SC* 2 (1960): 228–34.
Contrasts Stendhal's praise for the physiologist François Magendie in *Courrier anglais* and *Racine et Shakespeare* with his later accusations of charlatanism in *Souvenirs d'égotisme*. Links his reversal of attitude to Magendie's medical stand on contagious diseases.

1914.   ———. *Stendhal du côté de la science*. Aran: Grand-Chêne, 1972. 303 pp.
Rev. Carrol F. Coates, *FR* 46 (1972–73): 1015–16; William Coleman,
Isis 65 (1974): 423.

Discusses Stendhal's keen interest in mathematics, optics, astronomy, meteorology, chemistry, mineralogy, geology, botany, zoology, and medicine. Notes the influence of his scientific preoccupations on his writings, including *Vie de Henri Brulard*, *La chartreuse de Parme*, and *Le rouge et le noir*.

1915.   ———. "Stendhal et les savants de son temps." *Première journée du Stendhal Club*. Collection stendhalienne 7. Lausanne: Grand-Chêne, 1965. 147–58.

Examines Stendhal's interest in mathematics, astronomy, chemistry, and other natural sciences as revealed in his journal and novels. Discusses his friendship with several scientists and outlines his criticisms of scientists he disliked.

Robert Louis Stevenson (1850–94)

1916.   Strathdee, R. B. "Robert Louis Stevenson as a Scientist." *AUR* 36 (1955–56): 268–75.

This biographical survey of Stevenson's education in science and engineering notes his achievements in theories of illumination and in meteorology. His scientific interests are evident in works such as *Treasure Island*.

Adalbert Stifter (1805–68)

1917.   Banitz, Erhard. "Das Geologenbild Adalbert Stifters." *Gestaltung Umgestaltung: Festschrift zum 75. Geburtstag von Hermann August Korff*. Ed. Joachim Müller. Leipzig: Koehler, 1957. 206–38.

Discusses Stifter's interest in science, specifically geology, as represented in works such as *Der Nachsommer*. Stifter's model for the novel's main character, Heinrich Drendorf, was the geologist Friedrich Simony. Banitz analyzes the work and demonstrates that Stifter was familiar with the developments in the geological thought and research of his time.

1917a.   Gillespie, Gerald. "Space and Time Seen through Stifter's Telescope." *GQ* 37 (1964): 120–30.

Maintains that Stifter found scientific instruments such as the telescope both fascinating and dreadful. Links the predominance of spatial imagery in his works to the impact of his telescopic observation of the solar eclipse of 8 July 1842.

1918.   Heim, Hans Harro J. "Die Naturwissenschaft im Werk Adalbert Stifters." Diss. U Köln, 1952.

Not seen for annotation.

1919.   Lachinger, Johann. "Der Umgang des Menschen mit der Natur in Stifters Werk." *LJGG* 20 (1979): 139–53.

Examines Stifter's view of nature within the context of his scientific interests and religious convictions. The scientists—surveyors, mineralogists, botanists, meteorologists—in Stifter's short stories and novels are never concerned with the utilitarian aspects of their fields; instead, purely scientific, theoretical, and universal matters inspire them. Beyond that, Stifter's attitudes toward nature are grounded in a religious belief in its divine origin.

1920.   Nettesheim, Josefine. "Adalbert Stifter—'Der Kondor' und Edgar Allan Poe—'The Balloon Hoax.' " *Poeta doctus oder die Poetisierung der Wissenschaft von Musäus bis Benn.* Berlin: Duncker, 1975. 116–27.
See item 1856 for annotation.

1921.   Selge, Martin. *Adalbert Stifter. Poesie aus dem Geist der Naturwissenschaft.* Studien zur Poetik und Geschichte der Literatur 45. Stuttgart: Kohlhammer, 1976. 120 pp.
This study of the relations between Stifter's poetic imagination and his scientific thought also evaluates his aesthetic achievement in the literary depiction of scientific topoi. Chapter 1 provides a historical overview of the relations between literature and science, with particular reference to Haller. Chapter 2 analyzes the poetic function of scientific concepts and methods in Stifter's work, focusing on paradigmatic short stories such as "Der Condor," "Der Hochwald," "Die Schwestern/Zwei Schwestern," "Der arme Wohltäter/Kalkstein," and "Der Kuss von Sentze."

1922.   Umbach, William E. *Natural Science in the Work of Adalbert Stifter.* University of Kentucky Library Occasional Contributions 15. Lexington: U of Kentucky Library, 1950. 7 pp.
"The significance of Natural Science for the work of Stifter lies in his gradual perception of the importance of the minute, in his meticulous and detailed portrayal of natural phenomena, and in the calm and dispassionate character of his mature works." Umbach notes references to natural science in *Nachsommer*, *Narrenburg*, *Condor*, *Bunte Steine*, and other works.

1923.   Weidinger, Rosemarie. "Adalbert Stifter und die Naturwissenschaften." Diss. U of Frankfurt, 1952.
Not seen for annotation.

1924.   ———. "Adalbert Stifter und die Naturwissenschaften." *ASILO* 3 (1954): 129–38; 4 (1955): 1–13.
Reprints pages 6–42 of the author's 1952 dissertation. Examines Stifter's education in the natural sciences and shows how his scientific knowledge emerges in his literary works, including *Julius*, *Feldblumen*, *Das Haidedorf*, and *Der Hochwald*.

Bram Stoker (1847–1912)

1925.   Blinderman, Charles S. "Vampurella: Darwin and Count Dracula." *MR* 21 (1980): 411–28.
Ascertains parallels between Darwinian materialism, alleged to have emphasized carnality rather than spirituality, and Stoker's Count Dracula, a materialistic savior.

Johan August Strindberg (1849–1912)

1926. Ekenvall, Asta. "Strindberg och kvinnans fysiologi." *BLM* 38 (1969): 457–64.

Comments on Strindberg's interest in commonly accepted late-nineteenth-century biological, physiological, craniological, and evolutionary hypotheses.

1927. Mercier, Alain. "Auguste Strindberg et les alchemistes français: Hemel, Vial, Tiffereau, Jollivet-Castelot." *RLC* 43 (1969): 23–46.

Traces Strindberg's introduction to, integration into, and eventual alienation from a group of French alchemists during the period 1894–1902. A study of their influence on Strindberg's personal and literary life may contribute to a better understanding of his *Le chemin de Damas*.

1928. Sprinchorn, Evert. " 'The Zola of the Occult': Strindberg's Experimental Method." *MD* 17 (1974): 251–66.

Strindberg's attempts to effect a transition ". . . between natural science on one side and occultism and religion on the other" involved a series of psychological experiments on himself during the years 1894 to 1898. His experience of self-imposed psychological disorders as well as the influence of Kierkegaard and Swedenborg had a decisive impact on plays such as *To Damascus*.

Italo Svevo (1861–1928)

1929. Moloney, Brian. "Scienza e pseudoscienza nei romanzi di Italo Svevo." *Letteratura e scienza nella storia della cultura italiana*. Atti del IX congresso dell'associazione internazionale per gli studi di lingua e letteratura italiana. Palermo, Messina, Catania. 21–25 Apr. 1976. Associazione internazionale per gli studi di lingua e letteratura italiana. Palermo: Manfredi, 1978. 807–12.

Examines allusions to Darwinism, embryology, anatomy, and rejuvenation theories in Svevo's *Corto viaggio sentimentale*, *Mio ozio*, and *Rigenerazione*. His overall attitude toward science was marked by an acute awareness of its limitations.

Alfred, Lord Tennyson (1809–92)

1930. Allen, Katharine. "Lucretius the Poet, and Tennyson's Poem 'Lucretius.' " *Poet-Lore* 11 (1899): 529–48.

Outlines Tennyson's debt to Lucretius and *De rerum natura*. Aspects of Tennyson's "Lucretius" can be traced to elements of Lucretius's life and character, his philosophy and religion, his attitude toward nature, and his scientific theories.

1931. Appleman, Philip. "The Dread Factor: Eliot, Tennyson, and the Shaping of Science." *ColF* ns 3.4 (1974): 32–38.

See item 2296 for annotation.

1932. Emery, Clark. "The Background of Tennyson's 'Airy Navies.' " *Isis* 35 (1944): 139–47.

Tennyson's allusion to flying machines in *Locksley Hall* was probably based on a distillation of information garnered from a variety of literary and scientific sources, including works by Wilkins, Johnson, Cowper, and E. Darwin.

1933. Gibson, Walker. "Behind the Veil: A Distinction between Poetic and Scientific Language in Tennyson, Lyell, and Darwin." *VS* 2 (1958–59): 60–68.

This study of the grammatical structure of Tennyson's "scientific" poetry and of Lyell's and C. Darwin's scientific prose reveals two distinctive approaches to the task of penetrating the world's veil of mystery in the search for truth.

1934. Gliserman, Susan. "Early Victorian Science Writers and Tennyson's 'In Memoriam': A Study in Cultural Exchange." *VS* 18 (1974–75): 277–308, 437–59.

Examines the transmission and interpretation of scientific facts and theories in Tennyson's *In Memoriam* as an example of the relation between literary and scientific culture in the early Victorian period. Explores in depth Tennyson's apparent use of scientific and philosophic works by Roget, Whewell, Lyell, R. Chambers, Arnott, Nichol, J. Herschel, and Babbage.

1935. ———. "Literature as Historical Document: Tennyson and the Nineteenth-Century Science Writers, 1830–1854." *DAI* 34 (1973–74): 4201A.

Attempts to define what kind of historical document a literary work is by examining the changes in Tennyson's apprehension and poetic assimilation of scientific data from 1830 to 1854.

1936. Golffing, Francis. "Tennyson's Last Phase: The Poet as Seer." *SoR* ns 2 (1966): 264–85.

In his late poetry Tennyson develops his vision of an evolved human species capable of integrating science with humanism. This analysis studies the works that express Tennyson's mature utopian views, including "The Dawn," "Mechanophilus," "The Making of Man," and "The Dreamer."

1937. Harrison, James. "Tennyson and Embryology." *HAB* 23 (1972): 28–32.

Argues that Tennyson used embryological imagery as an analogy for physical and spiritual evolution in poems such as *The Palace of Art*, *The Princess*, *Maud*, and *In Memoriam*.

1938. ———. "Tennyson and Evolution." *DUJ* 64 (1971): 26–31.

Sections 54, 55, and 56 of *In Memoriam* indicate that Tennyson conceived a form of genuinely biological evolution well before he read C. Darwin.

1939. Hegner, Anna. *Die Evolutionsidee bei Tennyson und Browning*. Diss. U Freiburg, 1931. Wertheim: Bechstein, 1931. 34 pp.

Contrasts the receptivity toward science in general and toward C. Darwin's evolution theory in particular in the works of Tennyson and Browning.

1940.   Hough, Graham. "The Natural Theology of *In Memoriam*." *RES* 23 (1947): 244–56. Rpt. in *Selected Essays*. Cambridge: Cambridge UP, 1978. 110–25.

In Memoriam expresses a theological argument in scientific guise. Hough traces Tennyson's natural theology to its probable origins in Lyell's *Principles of Geology*, R. Chambers's *Vestiges of the Natural History of Creation*, and S. Coleridge's *Aids to Reflection*.

1941.   Laird, Robert G. "Tennyson and 'The Bar of Michael Angelo': A Possible Source for *In Memoriam* LXXXVII." *VP* 14 (1976): 253–55.

Tennyson's image of the "bar of Michael Angelo" in section 87 of *In Memoriam* is an allusion to an aspect of phrenology. Laird argues that Tennyson may have derived it from Combe's *A System of Phrenology* (1825).

1942.   Leonard, David Charles. "Chambers' 'Mental Constitution of Animals' from *Vestiges of the Natural History of Creation* and Tennyson's 'Poems 54–56' from *In Memoriam*." *UES* 14 (1976): 34–37.

Close comparison of passages from Chambers's *Vestiges* and Tennyson's *In Memoriam* demonstrates Tennyson's belief in a theory of mutability and recapitulation and suggests implications for the poem as a whole.

1943.   Libera, Sharon M. "John Tyndall and Tennyson's 'Lucretius.'" *VN* 45 (1974): 19–22.

Notes that Tennyson's friendship and discussions with the physicist John Tyndall, a leading advocate of Lucretian materialism, informed his critique of Lucretianism in the poem "Lucretius."

1944.   Lockyer, Sir Norman. "Tennyson as a Student and Poet of Nature." *Tennyson and his Friends*. Ed. Hallam Lord Tennyson. London: Macmillan, 1911. 285–91.

Lockyer presents some personal recollections of Tennyson's interest in meteorology and astronomy (e.g., Tennyson's meeting with Urbain Le Verrier) and suggests that Tennyson's poetry projects a cosmogony that reflects the scientific thought of his time.

1945.   Lodge, Sir Oliver. "The Attitude of Tennyson towards Science." *Tennyson and His Friends*. Ed. Hallam Lord Tennyson. London: Macmillan, 1911. 280–84.

Tennyson's faith did not blind him to the revelations of science during his lifetime. If, as the philosopher Henry Sidgwick wrote in 1860, Tennyson is "the Poet of Science," it is not only because his descriptions of natural phenomena agree with the latest findings of science but also because he can perceive the divine unity underlying the facts of nature.

1946.   Mackie, Alexander. *Nature Knowledge in Modern Poetry: Being Chapters on Tennyson, Wordsworth, Matthew Arnold, and Lowell as Exponents of Nature-Study*. London: Longmans, 1906. 132 pp.

Cites Tennyson's allusions to botany, entomology, ornithology, and geology and discusses Wordsworth, M. Arnold, and J. Lowell as naturalists, stressing their references to birds.

1947.   Mattes, Eleanor B. In Memoriam: *The Way of a Soul: A Study of Some Influences That Shaped Tennyson's Poem.* New York: Exposition, 1951. 128 pp.
Interprets successive stages in the composition of *In Memoriam* in the light of the religious, philosophic, and scientific ideas of Victorian England. Chapter 6 presents evidence that Tennyson read Lyell's *Principles of Geology* (1830–33) in 1837 and notes that this reading is reflected in the doubts about humankind's special place in nature that Tennyson expresses in section 56 of the poem. Chapter 8 argues that Tennyson arrived at a more optimistic view of change in nature by reading Herschel's *Preliminary Discourse on the Study of Natural Philosophy* (1830) and R. Chambers's *Vestiges of the Natural History of Creation* (1844). Section 118 and the Epilogue of *In Memoriam* reflect particularly Herschel's and Chambers's transcendental views of change.

1948.   Metzger, Lore. "The Eternal Process: Some Parallels between Goethe's *Faust* and Tennyson's *In Memoriam.*" *VP* 1 (1963): 189–96.
Both Goethe and Tennyson developed theories of the metamorphosis of body and spirit effected by the natural force of divine love. Metzger discusses the preevolutionary theories of change in *Faust* and *In Memoriam.*

1949.   Millhauser, Milton. " 'Magnetic Mockeries': The Background of a Phrase." *ELN* 5 (1967–68): 108–13.
Traces the phrase "magnetic mockeries" in section 120 of *In Memoriam* to scientific works dealing with electricity and magnetism.

1950.   ———. "A Plurality of After-Worlds: Isaac Taylor and Alfred Tennyson's Conception of Immortality." *HSL* 1 (1969): 37–49.
I. Taylor's *Physical Theory of Another Life* (1836) and the scientific speculations of Whewell, Brewster, R. Chambers, and others concerning the existence of a plurality of worlds combined to shape Tennyson's belief in the immortality of the individual. This essay discusses *In Memoriam,* "De Profundis: The Two Greetings," "The Ring," "Akbar's Dream," and other poems.

1951.   ———. "Tennyson's *Princess* and *Vestiges.*" *PMLA* 69 (1954): 337–43.
Suggests that R. Chambers's *Vestiges of the Natural History of Creation* (1844) may have significantly influenced Tennyson's *Princess* and the evolutionary sections of *In Memoriam.*

1952.   ———. "Tennyson, *Vestiges,* and the Dark Side of Science." *VN* 35 (1969): 22–25.
Cites evidence that Tennyson obtained a copy of R. Chambers's *Vestiges of the Natural History of Creation* soon after its publication in 1844 and notes its impact on sections 118 and 120 of *In Memoriam.*

1953.   Mooney, Emory A., Jr. "A Note on Astronomy in Tennyson's *The Princess.*" *MLN* 64 (1949): 98–102.

Discusses Tennyson's reference, in canto 4 of *The Princess,* to the Laplacean "nebular hypothesis" of the sun's origin.

1954. ———. "Tennyson and Modern Science." Diss. Cornell U, 1938.
Not seen for annotation.

1955. Pipes, B. N., Jr. "A Slight Meteorological Disturbance: The Last Two Stanzas of Tennyson's 'The Poet.' " *VP* 1 (1963): 74–76.
Briefly analyzes the poetic problems in lines 49–56 of "The Poet." Tennyson attempted a simile between the meteorological phenomena of thunder and lightning and the impact of "Freedom's words" on the world.

1956. Potter, George R. "Tennyson and the Biological Theory of Mutability in Species." *PQ* 16 (1937): 321–43.
Reassesses the claim that Tennyson believed in the mutability of species before the publication of C. Darwin's *Origin of Species* and examines evidence for the sources of his scientific conceptions. Analyzes poems such as "The Two Voices," *The Palace of Art*, and *In Memoriam* and names S. Coleridge, Sedgwick, Lyell, Owen, and Agassiz as principal scientific influences on his thought.

1957. Rice, William N. "The Poet of Science." *The Poet of Science and Other Addresses.* New York: Abingdon, 1919. 11–45.
Tennyson may be considered "the poet of science" not only because his poetic descriptions of natural phenomena are factually accurate but because his poems draw on the findings and theories of nineteenth-century science. Rice examines references to astronomy, embryology, geology, entomology, and evolution theory in poems such as *The Palace of Art*, *In Memoriam*, "The Two Voices," and "By an Evolutionist."

1958. Rutland, William R. "Tennyson and the Theory of Evolution." *E&S* 26 (1940): 7–29.
Shows that the theory of cosmic process or evolution Tennyson refers to in *The Palace of Art, The Princess, In Memoriam, Maud,* and other poems derives from astronomical concepts such as Laplace's nebular hypothesis and the ideas about embryology and geology espoused by Lyell, R. Chambers, and other nineteenth-century scientists.

1959. Sait, James E. "Tennyson, Mesmerism, and the Prince's 'Weird Seizures.' " *YES* 4 (1974): 203–11.
Maintains that Tennyson's portrayal of the Prince's seizures in *The Princess* was based on his knowledge of mesmerism.

1960. Shannon, Edgar F., Jr. "Tennyson's 'Balloon Stanzas.' " *PQ* 31 (1952): 441–45.
Tennyson's reference to hot-air balloons in "The Dream of Fair Women" (1832) may represent the earliest example of scientific and mechanical references in his poetry.

1961. Shaw, W. David. "Imagination and Intellect in Tennyson's 'Lucretius.' " *MLQ* 33 (1972): 130–39.

In "Lucretius" Tennyson attempts to resolve the post-Romantic conflict between facts and values, intellect and imagination, science and the humanities. Shaw explores the relations among Lucretius's Epicureanism, positivism, spirituality, and theology as presented in Tennyson's poem.

1962.   Simpson, David L. "Four Philosophical Poems: Ideas of Order in Donne, Pope, Tennyson, and Eliot." *DAI* 38 (1977): 2781A.
See item 806 for annotation.

1963.   Tietze, Frederick I. "Tennyson: Science and the Poetic Sensibility." Diss. U of Wisconsin, 1953.
Not seen for annotation.

1964.   Wickens, G. Glen. "The Two Sides of Early Victorian Science and the Unity of 'The Princess.' " *VS* 23 (1979–80): 369–88.
The plot of Tennyson's *Princess* is organized around the distinction between the teleological Christian interpretation of science and the idea of science as mechanistic materialism. His characters ". . . act out the tension and resolution of these two sciences."

1965.   Wilner, Ortha L. "Tennyson and Lucretius." *CJ* 25 (1929–30): 347–66.
Examines the extent to which Tennyson's poem "Lucretius" reflects the great moral and scientific doctrines of Lucretius's *De rerum natura* and thus gives ". . . a true impression of Lucretius, the poet, the scientist, the moralist."

1966.   Young, Robert S. "Tennyson and Swinburne and the Metaphor of Love: The Quest for Spiritual Values in Nineteenth Century England." *DAI* 38 (1977): 2820A.
Concerns Tennyson's responses in *Idylls of the King* and Swinburne's in *Tristram of Lyonesse* to the mechanistic biological naturalism of the nineteenth century. Emphasizes how they used the metaphor of love to redress the spiritual malaise of the times.

Francis Thompson (1859–1907)

1967.   Wilson, W. G. "Francis Thompson's Outlook on Science." *Contemporary Review* 192.1103 (1957): 263–66.
Briefly comments on Thompson's interpretation of science in poems such as *The Nineteenth Century*, *Contemplation*, and *New Year's Chimes*.

James Thomson (B.V.) (1834–82)

1968.   Forsyth, R. A. "Evolutionism and the Pessimism of James Thomson (B.V.)." *EIC* 12 (1962): 148–66.
Thomson's lifelong struggle to face the religious implications of evolution theory drove him ever deeper into pessimism. Forsyth traces the main stages in Thomson's loss of religious faith as reflected in poems such as "The Doom of a City" and "The City of Dreadful Night."

Henry David Thoreau (1817–62)

1969.   Adams, Raymond. "Thoreau's Mock-Heroics and the American Natural History Writers." *SP* 52 (1955): 86–97.
Thoreau's cultivation of a mock-epic, mock-heroic style in his writings on nature (e.g., *Walden* and *A Week on the Concord and Merrimack Rivers*) and his tendency to "magnify" the microcosm until it achieved macrocosmic proportions decisively influenced the form and content of subsequent American natural-history literature. This study explores some of Thoreau's more poignant imagery and traces its sources in classical literature, especially Homer.

1970.   ———. "Thoreau's Science." *SciMo* 60 (1945): 379–82.
Although Thoreau's *Walden*, "Natural History of Massachusetts," "Winter Walk," and other essays venture into traditionally scientific areas, his writings are best classified as the work of a poet-naturalist, or a romanticist of nature, and not that of a scientist.

1971.   Baym, Nina. "From Metaphysics to Metaphor: The Image of Water in Emerson and Thoreau." *SIR* 5 (1965–66): 231–43.
See item 1645 for annotation.

1972.   ———. "Thoreau's View of Science." *JHI* 26 (1965): 221–34.
Traces the development of Thoreau's interest in and gradual disillusionment with natural science, stressing the conflict between science and his poetic and transcendentalist ideals. Discusses his literary use of the large body of scientific material collected in his late journals.

1973.   Cameron, Kenneth Walter. "Emerson, Thoreau, and the Society of Natural History." *AL* 24 (1952–53): 21–30.
Briefly comments on Emerson's and Thoreau's association with the Boston Society of Natural History and publishes a record of Thoreau's borrowings from the society's library.

1974.   ———. "Henry Thoreau and the *Entomology* of Kirby and Spence." *ESQ* 38 (1965): 138–42.
Surveys Kirby and W. Spence's *Introduction to Entomology* and reprints selections dealing with the behavior of ants. These passages were a fertile source for Thoreau's treatment of the theme in *Walden*.

1975.   Cook, Reginald Lansing. *Passage to Walden*. Boston: Houghton, 1949. 238 pp. 2nd ed. New York: Russell, 1966. 253 pp.
This examination of Thoreau's relation to nature contains a chapter, "The Anatomy of Nature" (173–204), that explores his indictment of science on several counts and discusses the interactions between poet-naturalists like Thoreau and scientific naturalists. "Thoreau did not aim at being a scientist. Nor did he expect to be evaluated scientifically. He aimed at being a human being who realized as completely as possible . . . the correspondence of nature and himself."

1976.   Deevey, Edward S., Jr. "A Re-examination of Thoreau's 'Walden.' " *Quarterly Review of Biology* 17 (1942): 1–11.

Shows on the basis of contemporary limnological knowledge that the limnological observations of Walden Pond that Thoreau set down in *Walden* contain important, scientifically accurate material. Also comments on the scientific value of Thoreau's observations in botany, biology, and other sciences.

1977.   Griffin, David. "The Science of Henry David Thoreau." *Synthesis* [Cambridge] 1 (1973): 5–22.

Attempts to define Thoreau's attitude toward science and its relation to his poetic endeavors and transcendental philosophy. Analyzes the allusions to science in Thoreau's *Journals* and his treatment of scientific topics in works such as "The Succession of Forest Trees." In general, his poetic inclinations guided and determined his approach to science.

1978.   Kaiser, Mary I. " 'Conversing with the Sky': The Imagery of Celestial Bodies in Thoreau's Poetry." *TJQ* 9.3 (1977): 15–28.

Argues that Thoreau took a transcendental approach to astronomy and astronomers. The "heavenly imagery" that pervades his verse reveals that he regarded celestial phenomena such as stars, planets, comets, the moon, and the sun as symbols of spiritual meaning.

1979.   Kim, Kichung. "Thoreau's Science and Teleology." *ESQ* 18 (1972): 125–33.

Since Thoreau rebuked the scientists of his day for their failure to deal with "the higher law," he might have been expected to support the idealistic school of scientific thought represented by Agassiz. He subscribed, however, to the empirical school represented by A. Gray, C. Darwin's American disciple. All the same, Thoreau believed that the study of nature should not culminate in naturalistic explanations; it should make nature significant to human beings by moving toward transcendent illumination. In the last analysis, Thoreau advocated a mythopoeic vision of nature.

1980.   Lebeaux, Richard. "Thoreau's Scientific Phase: Thoreau and John Russell." *Concord Saunterer* 15.2 (1980): 1–5.

Reproduces a letter (dated 31 May 1856) from Thoreau to John Russell, an eminent amateur botanist from Salem, Massachusetts. This letter, considered in conjunction with certain journal entries written from 1853 to 1858, suggests that Thoreau experienced a "scientific phase," a period during which he feared that his deepening immersion in science might cause the loss of his poetic vision.

1981.   McDowell, Robin S. "Thoreau in the Current Scientific Literature." *TSB* 143 (1978): 2.

Shows that Thoreau's natural observations, including some in *Walden*, have been cited in scientific journals 27 times between 1964 and 1976.

1982.   McIntosh, James. *Thoreau as Romantic Naturalist: His Shifting Stance toward Nature*. Ithaca: Cornell UP, 1974. 310 pp.
         Rev. Sherman Paul, *JEGP* 73 (1974): 458–59; Joan Burbick, *American*

Academy of Religion Journal 43 (1975): 345–48; Mason I. Lowance, *NEQ* 48 (1975): 426–29; Elizabeth A. Meese, *Criticism* 17 (1975): 95–97; Judith Saunders, *SIR* 14 (1975): 458–60; Charles R. O'Donnell, *AL* 47 (1975–76): 124–25.

Defines Thoreau's place in the Romantic tradition, noting especially his affinities with Goethe and Wordsworth. Maintains that Thoreau used a "programmed inconsistency" of viewpoints to illustrate the diversity and complexity of nature and focuses on these varied and often conflicting perspectives. "Thoreau is a romantic in that he is continually fascinated by the relation of the poetic mind to the external world. He is a 'romantic naturalist' in that he regards man's communication with nature as spiritual, not as destructive of the human spirit."

1982a.   McLean, Albert F., Jr. "Thoreau's True Meridian: Natural Fact and Metaphor." *AQ* 20 (1968): 567–79.

Examines the development of Thoreau's interest in terrestrial magnetism. Cites references to the science in *Walden* and *Journals*.

1983.   Nichols, William W. "Science and the Art of *Walden*: Experiment and Structure." *ESQ* 50 supp. (1968): 77–84.

Thoreau used experimental method as a central structural principle in *Walden*. "The principle is revealed in a pattern which moves from a factual level, usually emphasizing sensory experience and careful observation, to a more abstract level, often approaching allegory or parable."

1984.   ———. "Science and the Development of Thoreau's Art." *DA* 27 (1966–67): 3056A–57A.

Examines Thoreau's involvement in scientific studies and observations and assesses its impact on his development as a literary artist.

1985.   Quick, Donald G. "Thoreau as Limnologist." *TJQ* 4.2 (1972): 13–20.

Thoreau's interest in water levels, his precise description of flora and fauna, and his fascination with the bottomlessness of Walden Pond reflect his pioneering effort in limnology, the study of lakes in the broader context of ecology. Quick examines especially Thoreau's limnological references in *Walden*.

1986.   Sanford, Charles L. "Emerson, Thoreau, and the Hereditary Duality." *ESQ* 54 (1969): 36–43.

See item 1659 for annotation.

1987.   Schneider, Richard J. "Reflections in Walden Pond: Thoreau's Optics." *ESQ* 21 (1975): 65–75.

Explores the relation between Thoreau's interest in optical phenomena (mirages, visual illusions, and, in particular, water reflections) and his role as poet-seer. Throughout his life Thoreau sought to resolve for himself a fundamental epistemological problem—the complex interplay between mind and nature. As part of this effort he studied the physics of light and reflection.

1988.   Smith, George W., Jr. "Thoreau and Bacon: The Idols of the Theatre." *ATQ* 11 (1971): 6–12.

Suggests that, despite his avowed rejection of Baconianism, Thoreau may have unknowingly adhered to many Baconian principles in his investigation of nature. This essay outlines Thoreau's methodological parallels with Baconianism and examines his relation to Bacon's theory of the idols of thought, especially the idols of the theater and the errors of perception due to the worship of traditional philosophy.

1989.   Stoller, Leo. "A Note on Thoreau's Place in the History of Phenology." *Isis* 47 (1956): 172–81.
Analyzes sections of Thoreau's journals to assess his contributions to the science of phenology.

1990.   Taylor, Horace. "Thoreau's Scientific Interests As Seen in His Journal." *McNR* 14 (1963): 45–59.
This assessment of the depth and intensity of Thoreau's scientific interests is based on the references in his journal to botany, geology, scientific methodology, and the work of Linnaeus and C. Darwin. Thoreau's scientific naturalism complemented in many ways his poetic endeavors.

Mark Twain (1835–1910)

1990a.   Baetzhold, Howard G. "Mark Twain on Scientific Investigation: Contemporary Allusions in 'Some Learned Fables for Good Old Boys and Girls.' " *Literature and Ideas in America: Essays in Memory of Harry Hayden Clark.* Ed. Robert Falk. Athens: Ohio UP, 1975. 128–54.
Examines Twain's satires on scientific investigations, stressing his early burlesque of science, "Some Learned Fables for Good Old Boys and Girls." Argues that this insect fable—in the spirit of Swift—alludes to contemporary scientific expeditions and to scientific theories such as those of Cuvier and C. Darwin.

1991.   Brogan, Howard O. "Early Experience and Scientific Determinism in Twain and Hardy." *Mosaic* 7.3 (1973–74): 99–105.
The combination of folk superstition, Protestantism, and nineteenth-century scientific ideas produced an element of scientific determinism in the works of Twain and Hardy.

1992.   Cummings, Sherwood P. "Mark Twain and Sciences." Diss. U of Wisconsin, 1951.
Not seen for annotation.

1993.   ———. "Mark Twain's Acceptance of Science." *CentR* 6 (1962): 245–61.
Characterizes Twain's attitude toward science as alternately critical and enthusiastic and illustrates his ambivalence by citing examples from works such as *A Tramp Abroad*, "What Paul Bourget Thinks of Us," "A Dog's Tale," *The Mysterious Stranger*, and *What Is Man?*

1994.   ———. "Science and Mark Twain's Theory of Fiction." *PQ* 37 (1958): 26–33.

Twain consistently emphasized the importance of portraying fictional characters in the light of the formative influences of their biological and social environments. His attitude was shaped by his study of C. Darwin and Taine as well as by his general attraction to the naturalistic theory of scientific determinism.

1995. Gribben, Alan. "Mark Twain, Phrenology and the 'Temperaments': A Study of Pseudoscientific Influence." *AQ* 24 (1972): 45–68.
Twain cultivated a mild interest in phrenology from age nineteen onward. The principal source for many of his phrenological allusions is Weaver's *Lectures on Mental Science according to the Philosophy of Phrenology* (1852).

1996. Jones, Alexander E. "Mark Twain and the Determinism of *What Is Man?*" *AL* 29 (1957–58): 1–17.
Briefly explores the sources of Twain's philosophy of determinism in Calvinism and nineteenth-century ideas of evolution and discusses his references to determinism in *What Is Man?*

1997. Kennedy, Susan A. "Mark Twain and Edgar Allan Poe: The Development of the Grotesque Absurd." *DAI* 39 (1978): 1785A.
Examines Twain's and Poe's parallel visions of the grotesque, or the absurd, aspects of the human condition in a world vastly changed by science and technology.

1998. Lindborg, Henry J. "A Cosmic Tramp: Samuel Clemens's *Three Thousand Years among the Microbes*." *AL* 44 (1972–73): 652–57.
Twain rejected the philosophic and scientific theories of pantheism and hylozoism in *Three Thousand Years among the Microbes* (1905). Two key scientific works influenced his philosophic position: Saleeby's *Cycle of Life* (1904) and Conn's *Life of the Germ* (1897).

1999. Waggoner, Hyatt Howe. "Science in the Thought of Mark Twain." *AL* 8 (1936–37): 357–70.
The study of Twain's *Notebook, Letters,* and *Autobiography* discloses his knowledge of evolution theory and sciences such as geology and astronomy. Science was a principal factor shaping Twain's pessimistic philosophy in works like *What Is Man?*

2000. Wigger, Anne P. "The Source of Fingerprint Material in Mark Twain's *Pudd'nhead Wilson* and *Those Extraordinary Twins*." *AL* 28 (1956–57): 517–20.
Twain incorporated into the plot of *Pudd'nhead Wilson* scientifically established information on the process of fingerprinting drawn from Galton's *Finger Prints* (1892).

2000a. Wilson, James D. " 'The Monumental Sarcasm of the Ages': Science and Pseudoscience in the Thought of Mark Twain." *SAB* 40.2 (1975): 72–82.
Attempts to explain Twain's view of legitimate science by examining his satiric treatments of phrenology, Christian Science, and paleontology.

Jules Verne (1828–1905)

2001.   Chesnaux, Jean. "Science, machines et progrès chez Jules Verne." *Pensée* 133 (1967): 62–85.
Examines several aspects of Verne's literary use of science and scientific themes, including the central role scientific theory played in Verne's plots, his depiction of scientists, and his views on the relation between human beings and nature.

2002.   Harth, Helene. "Literatur im Dienste des Fortschritts? Die Ästhetisierung von Technik und Wissenschaft in Jules Vernes *Voyages extraordinaires*." *Die Literatur und die Naturwissenschaften*. Literaturmagazin 6. Ed. Nicolas Born and Heinz Schlaffer. Reinbeck bei Hamburg: Rowohlt, 1976. 30–44.
Maintains that the literary project of Verne's novels was not only a summation of the sciences of his time but also a glorification of scientists and the entire scientific enterprise. Sees Verne as a popular encyclopedist of the exact sciences in the service of technological and industrial progress.

2003.   Huet, Marie-Hélène. *L'histoire des voyages extraordinaires: Essai sur l'œuvre de Jules Verne*. Paris: Minard, 1973. 206 pp.
Looks at Verne's works as a historical commentary on the politics and scientific progress of his century. Verne's depiction of machines offers a vision of the future by illustrating the resources of science and the possibilities afforded by technology.

2004.   Kagarlitski, J. "Wells and Jules Verne." *VLit* 6 (1962): 116–33. (Text in Russian.)
See item 2520 for annotation.

2005.   Kylstra, Peter H. "Some Backgrounds of Jules Verne." *Janus* 57 (1970): 156–62.
Surveys the nineteenth-century innovations in electrical technology that Verne used imaginatively in his novels.

2006.   Messac, Régis. "Voyages modernes au centre de la terre." *RLC* 9 (1929): 74–104.
Ancient legends and modern scientific ideas merge in fictional trips to the center of the earth. Even before Verne wrote his *Journey to the Centre of the Earth*, Dante, Cyrano de Bergerac, Holberg, Mouhy, and others had considered such trips in their works. Verne's contribution lies in his rejection of the theory of fire at the earth's center.

2007.   Mustière, Philippe. "Jules Verne et le roman-catastrophe." *Europe* 56.595–96 (1978): 43–47.
Maintains that the prophetic and catastrophic element of Verne's *Voyages extraordinaires* represents his response to the scientific and technological advances of his day. For Verne, the world seemed poised on the brink of disaster.

2008.   Parsons, Coleman O. "Lunar Craters in Science and Fiction: Kepler, Verne, and Wells." *N&Q* 164 (1933): 346–48.

Notes references to Kepler's theory of lunar craters in Verne's *Autour de la lune* and Wells's *First Men in the Moon*.

2009.   Suvin, Darko. "Communication in Quantified Space: The Utopian Liberalism of Jules Verne's Science Fiction." *Cliol* 4 (1974–75): 51–71.
Describes Verne's liberal, Saint-Simonian view of human social progress, stressing the importance of science and technology in his utopian vision of the future. Discusses *Journey to the Centre of the Earth, From the Earth to the Moon, The Mysterious Island*, and other novels.

Edith Wharton (1862–1937)

2010.   Schriber, MarySue. "Darwin, Wharton, and 'The Descent of Man': Blueprints of American Society." *SSF* 17 (1980): 31–38.
Wharton's "Descent of Man" echoes themes developed in C. Darwin's *Descent of Man and Selection in Relation to Sex* (1871). The story "testifies to Wharton's sharp insights into the cultural and intellectual condition of American society at the turn of the century."

Walt Whitman (1819–92)

2011.   Arvin, Newton. *Whitman*. New York: Macmillan, 1938. New York: Russell, 1969. 320 pp.
Chapter 4 reviews the scientific and philosophic influences on Whitman over the course of his lifetime and assesses the extent to which he fulfilled his wish to be a poetic spokesman for the insights and achievements of modern science.

2012.   Aspiz, Harold. " 'The Body Electric': Science, Sex, and Metaphor." *WWR* 24 (1978): 137–42.
Whitman used metaphors linking sexuality with electricity in *Leaves of Grass*. His concepts of electricity can be traced to books on mesmerism and electromagnetism that he is known to have read.

2012a.   ———. "Educating the Kosmos: 'There Was a Child Went Forth.' " *AQ* 18 (1966): 655–66.
Shows that Whitman's treatment of child development and education in "There Was a Child Went Forth" is closely linked to the phrenological theories of Spurzheim and others.

2012b.   ———. "A Reading of Whitman's 'Faces.' " *WWR* 19 (1973): 37–48.
Uses phrenological and physiognomical tenets to interpret Whitman's poem.

2012c.   ———. "Unfolding the Folds." *WWR* 12 (1966): 81–87.
Interprets Whitman's "Unfolded Out of the Folds" in relation to theories of physiology, phrenology, and primitive eugenics.

2013.   Beaver, Joseph. *Walt Whitman—Poet of Science*. Diss. New York U, 1950.
New York: King's Crown, 1951. New York: Octagon, 1974. 178 pp.
Rev. Alice L. Cooke, *MLN* 67 (1952): 204–06; Floyd Stovall, *AL* 24
(1952–53): 99–100.
This comprehensive survey of Whitman's poetic use of astronomy, physics, chemistry, electricity, and evolution theory maintains that Whitman was the first American poet to ". . . embody scientific concepts in his work in a poetic manner."

2014.   ———. "Walt Whitman, Star-Gazer." *JEGP* 48 (1949): 307–19.
Maintains that Whitman's knowledge of astronomy was more extensive and detailed than hitherto suspected and that his observations of astronomical phenomena
were more accurate than previously supposed. His descriptions of celestial objects,
particularly planets, frequently have a factual basis.

2015.   Brinton, Daniel G. "Walt Whitman and Science." *Conservator* 6 (1895):
20–21.
Briefly remarks on Whitman's poetic, though unscientific, references to botany,
astronomy, and zoology and notes the significance of evolution theory in his thought.

2016.   Bucke, Richard Maurice. "*Leaves of Grass* and Modern Science." *In Re Walt
Whitman*. Ed. Horace L. Traubel, Richard Maurice Bucke, and Thomas
B. Harned. Philadelphia: McKay, 1893. 249–51.
Notes that though Whitman appears to have had no technical knowledge of
zoology, physiology, or evolution theory, his works display a remarkable intuitive
insight into these and other sciences.

2017.   Burroughs, John. *Whitman: A Study*. Boston: Houghton, 1896. New York:
Ames, 1969. 268 pp.
The chapter on Whitman and science (249–56) notes that while science significantly enlarged his poetic imagination, he drew on science for images and illustrations less frequently than did poets like Tennyson.

2018.   Cleary, Ann. "The Prism and Night Vision: Walt Whitman's Use of Color
in 'Song of Myself.' " *WWR* 26 (1980): 92–100.
Awareness of the scientific aspects of Whitman's use of color enhances the appreciation of "Song of Myself."

2019.   Cooke, Alice Lovelace. "Whitman's Indebtedness to the Scientific Thought
of His Day." *University of Texas Studies in English* 14 (1934): 89–115.
A knowledgeable reader and editor of scientific material, Whitman exploited
contemporary astronomy, geology, and, to a lesser extent, botany, chemistry, physics, and the pseudosciences of phrenology and physiognomy. His knowledge of
science helped him retain perspective on the challenges to religion in his day.

2019a. Dressman, Michael R. "Goodrich's *Geography* and Whitman's Place Names."
WWR 26 (1980): 64–67.
Notes Whitman's reliance on Goodrich's *Geography* for the geographical details
of *Leaves of Grass*.

2020. Dugdale, Clarence. "Whitman's Knowledge of Astronomy." *University of Texas Studies in English* 16 (1936): 125–37.

This assessment of the depth of Whitman's astronomical knowledge surveys its probable sources, including a period of study with the astronomer Henry Whitall. Whitman's main interests in astronomy lay in observing and naming large stars and great constellations and in finding a stimulus to the imagination rather than a source of scientific exactitude.

2020a. Emmanuel, Lenny. "Whitman's Fusion of Science and Poetry." *WWR* 17 (1971): 73–82.

Whitman embraced science, assimilating its results into his poetry, and he "created a peculiar fusion of poetry and science as a result of recognizing a commonality to both—the search for truth."

2021. Gershenowitz, Harry. "Whitman and Lamarck Revisited." *WWR* 25 (1979): 121–23.

Shows how the Lamarckian evolutionary concepts of the "life-force" and the inheritance of acquired characteristics influenced Whitman's poetry, including "Says" and "Starting from Paumanok."

2022. Hungerford, Edward. "Walt Whitman and His Chart of Bumps." *AL* 2 (1930–31): 350–84.

Whitman's poetry is unmistakably informed by his interest in phrenology, which began in 1846 and climaxed in 1849, when the poet had his "bumps" read at Fowler and Wells's "Phrenological Cabinet" in New York. Hungerford reproduces Whitman's phrenological chart and discusses its role in his personal and poetic development.

2023. Kepner, Diane. "From Spears to Leaves: Walt Whitman's Theory of Nature in 'Song of Myself.'" *AL* 51 (1979–80): 179–204.

Whitman formulated a theory of nature, or being, that attempted to reconcile the precepts of scientific materialism and mystical idealism. He drew his principles from Emerson's *Nature*.

2024. Killingsworth, Myrth J. "Another Source for Whitman's Use of 'Electric.'" *WWR* 23 (1977): 129–32.

Maintains that Whitman drew the term *electric* from contemporary medical science rather than, as Cynthia Sulfrudge had suggested, from physics (see item 2035).

2025. Labianca, Dominick A., and William J. Reeves. "'A March in the Ranks Hard-Prest, and the Road Unknown': A Chemical Analysis." *AN&Q* 15 (1976–77): 110–11.

The dramatic tension of Whitman's description of surgery in "A March in the Ranks Hard-Prest, and the Road Unknown" is heightened through the image of potentially explosive ether being used as an anaesthetic in the presence of surrounding torchlight.

2026. Leonard, David C. "Lamarckian Evolution in Whitman's 'Song of Myself.'" *WWR* 24 (1978): 21–28.

"Song of Myself" contains the most strongly evolutionary poetry in *Leaves of Grass*, bespeaking Whitman's knowledge of Lamarck's four laws of development. The expanding universe parallels humankind's expanding horizons.

2027.   Lindfors, Bernth. "Whitman's 'When I Heard the Learn'd Astronomer.' "
        WWR 10 (1964): 19–21.
Briefly analyzes the theme and structure of Whitman's poem, emphasizing its treatment of the conflict between scientific perception and poetic, mystical intuition.

2028.   McGhee, Richard D. "Concepts of Time in Whitman's Poetry." *WWR*
        15 (1969): 76–85.
The various concepts of time evident in Whitman's poetry were determined in part by his mystical orientation and in part by his response to the modern technological meaning of time.

2029.   Magee, John D. "Whitman's Cosmofloat." *WWR* 10 (1964): 43–46.
Common themes in Whitman's poems—including "Whispers of Heavenly Death," "To Think of Time," and "Crossing Brooklyn Ferry"—are the notion of a nebulous primeval "float" from which matter originally cohered and the idea of "kosmos," or the architectural structure of the universe. Magee coins the term *cosmofloat* to encompass these themes and assesses the concept's role in Whitman's poetry.

2030.   Maria, Sister Flavia, C. SJ. " 'Song of Myself': A Presage of Modern
        Teilhardian Paleontology." *WWR* 15 (1969): 43–49.
Whitman's "Song of Myself" presages the ideas of the paleontologist Pierre Teilhard de Chardin. Like Teilhard, Whitman drew simultaneously on mysticism and science. This essay stresses the resemblances between the two men's thoughts about space and time.

2031.   Moore, William L. "L. of G.'s Purport: Evolution—the Cumulative."
        1980: Leaves of Grass at 125. Eight Essays. Supp. to *WWR*. Ed. William
        White. Detroit: Wayne State UP, 1980. 45–57.
Evidences parallels between Whitman's intuitional grasp of the principles of evolution and the evolutionist Pierre Teilhard de Chardin's scientific theories.

2031a. Morsberger, Robert E. "Whitman's Hermit Thrush: An Ornithological
        Note." *WWR* 20 (1974): 111–13.
Briefly notes the ornithological accuracy of Whitman's depiction of the hermit thrush in "When Lilacs Last in the Dooryard Bloom'd."

2032.   Murphy, Robert Cushman. "The Poet through a Naturalist's Eyes." *WWR*
        13 (1967): 39–44.
Citing Whitman's poetic allusions to astronomy and natural history, Murphy maintains that it is a mistake to see in Whitman's poetry a trend of antiscientific sentiment. Whitman's depiction of nature, indeed, often lends his poetry its peculiar charm.

2033.   Pfeifer, Edward J. "The Theory of Evolution and Whitman's 'Passage to
        India.' " *ESQ* 42 (1966): 31–35.

Evolution theory is subtly and deeply incorporated into "Passage to India." Primarily concerned with the social applications of evolution, Whitman probably derived his evolutionary principles in part from Spencer's *First Principles*.

2034. Reiss, Edmund. "Whitman's Debt to Animal Magnetism." *PMLA* 79 (1963): 80–88.
Whitman's frequent poetic portrayal of an attractive force pervading and uniting the universe may reflect his interest in animal magnetism. Reiss surveys poems such as "I Am He That Aches with Love," "I Sing the Body Electric," "Song of Myself," and "A Hand Mirror" and cites passages that suggest an association with the theory.

2034a. Rizzo, Patrick V. "Whitman and a Cosmic Connection." *WWR* 26 (1980): 67–69.
Suggests an astrophysical interpretation for a line from section 31 of "Song of Myself."

2035. Sulfrudge, Cynthia. "Meaning in Whitman's Use of 'Electric.'" *WWR* 19 (1973): 151–53.
Briefly discusses Whitman's adaptation of the term *electric* from physics and other sources.

2036. Tanner, James T. F. "The Lamarckian Theory of Progress in *Leaves of Grass*." *WWR* 9 (1963): 3–11.
Attempts to assess the Lamarckian influence on Whitman's thought by exploring his use of evolution theory in *Leaves of Grass*. Reviews previous critical attempts to locate the sources of his allusions to evolution.

2037. ———. "Walt Whitman: Poet of Lamarckian Evolution." *DA* 26 (1966): 5446.
Whitman's intellectual allegiance to Lamarckian evolutionary principles is evident in his poetic construction of theories of the superman, political evolution, and aesthetics.

2038. White, Courtland Y. "A Whitman Ornithology." *Cassinia* 35 (1945): 12–22.
Though Whitman refers to 78 species of birds in his poetry, his descriptions were generally vague and ornithologically inadequate or incorrect. White assesses Whitman's ornithological knowledge, much of which was most likely derived from Giraud's *Birds of Long Island* (1844).

2039. Winwar, Frances. "Walt Whitman's 'Dark Lady.'" *UR* 9 (1943): 191–96.
Challenges Edward Hungerford's phrenological interpretation of passages from Whitman's notebooks of 1868–70 that refer to the poet's resolve to stop pursuing a certain mysterious woman, designated cryptically by the numbers 16 and 164 (see item 2022).

2039a. Wrobel, Arthur. "A Poet's Self-Esteem: Whitman Alters His 'Bumps.'" *WWR* 17 (1971): 129–35.

Provides information on Whitman's manipulation of the results of his several phrenological readings. Maintains that the readings influenced Whitman's poetic aspirations.

2039b. ———. "Walt Whitman and the Fowler Brothers: Phrenology Finds a Bard." *DA* 29 (1968–69): 2232A–33A.
Traces the development of Whitman's interest in phrenology, stressing the influence of the phrenologists Lorenzo Fowler and Orson Fowler, and examines the reflection of this interest in his literary works.

2039c. ———. "Whitman and the Phrenologists: The Divine Body and the Sensuous Soul." *PMLA* 89 (1974): 17–23.
Shows that Whitman's phrenological sources inform his synthesis of materialism and spiritualism and shed light on this dualism.

William Wordsworth (1770–1850)

2040. Averill, James H. "Wordsworth and 'Natural Science': The Poetry of 1798." *JEGP* 77 (1978): 232–46.
Wordsworth's *Recluse* and *Lyrical Ballads* reflect his deep involvement with natural science around 1798. Averill discusses some probable sources of Wordsworth's scientific knowledge, including E. Darwin's *Zoonomia*.

2041. Black, M. H. "On Six Lines of Wordsworth." *MLR* 59 (1964): 339–43.
Analyzes the passage of Wordsworth's *Prelude* that refers to the bust of Newton at Cambridge (3.58–63) and suggests that Wordsworth's poetic worldview conflicted with the dominant, Newtonian, rational concept of nature.

2042. Bonacina, L. C. W. "Wordsworth's Responses to Natural Scenery." *Nature* 165 (1950): 621–25.
Examines Wordsworth's prose work on geography ("Guide through the District of the Lakes in the North of England") and the geographical allusions in poems such as *The Prelude*, *The Excursion*, and *Descriptive Sketches* and concludes that Wordsworth was not nearly as antagonistic toward science as has hitherto been supposed. In fact, his outlook on nature narrows the gap between science and the humanities.

2043. Coombe, D. E. "The Wordsworths and Botany." *N&Q* 197 (1952): 298–99.
Briefly discusses William and Dorothy Wordsworth's acquisition of a botany text and its usefulness for Wordsworth's poetry.

2044. Cooper, Lane. "A Glance at Wordsworth's Reading." *MLN* 22 (1907): 83–89, 110–17.
Partly concerns Wordsworth's acquaintance with Bartram's *Travels* and other works of travel literature.

2045. Dodd, George. "Wordsworth and Hamilton." *Nature* 228 (1970): 1261–63.
Describes the 20-year correspondence between Wordsworth and the mathema-

tician and physicist W. R. Hamilton. The friendship nourished both Wordsworth's scientific interests and Hamilton's poetic aspirations.

2046.   Garstang, Walter. "Wordsworth's Interpretation of Nature." *Nature* 117 supp. 1 (1926): 1–8.

Includes commentary on the scientific elements of Wordsworth's poetry and on the basic differences between scientific and poetic investigations of nature. For Wordsworth, nature was "a universal symphony, a harmony of infinitely varied elements, appealing to man through every sense and gateway to the heart."

2047.   Gaull, Marilyn. "From Wordsworth to Darwin: 'On the Fields of Praise.' " *WC* 10 (1979): 33–48.

Explores Wordsworth's interest in the geological controversies of his time, his friendship with the geologist Adam Sedgwick, and his influence through Sedgwick on C. Darwin's narrative technique in *The Origin of Species*. Focuses on Darwin's debt to Wordsworth's poem *The Excursion*.

2048.   Hedetoft, Ulf. "Wordsworth and Science." *Lang&L* 1 (1971): 7–24.

Wordsworth's interest in science is reflected in the scientific perspective informing his treatment of various conflicts and polarities that underlie his poetry. Among the contraries examined here are objectivity/subjectivity, idealism/realism, matter/spirit, and time/eternity. The essay emphasizes *The Prelude*.

2049.   Jeffrey, Lloyd N. "Wordsworth and Science." *SCB* 27 (1967): 16–22.

Briefly remarks on the attitude toward science Wordsworth expresses in *The Prelude, The Excursion*, and other works. Wordsworth recognized that science has a legitimate role as the observer and interpreter of the physical world, but he repudiated science's materialistic and mechanistic tendencies.

2050.   Kadambi, Shantha. "The Newtonian Wordsworth." *DA* 31 (1970–71): 6555A.

Examines the relation between Wordsworth's acceptance of Newtonianism and his theory of poetry.

2051.   Mackie, Alexander. *Nature Knowledge in Modern Poetry: Being Chapters on Tennyson, Wordsworth, Matthew Arnold, and Lowell as Exponents of Nature-Study*. London: Longmans, 1906. 132 pp.

See item 1946 for annotation.

2052.   Pittman, Charles L. "A Biographical Note on Wordsworth." *Bulletin of Furman University* 29.3 (1946): 31–53.

Charts the course of Wordsworth's friendship, beginning in 1827, with the scientist W. R. Hamilton. Hamilton exercised considerable influence on the change in Wordsworth's conception of the relation between poetry and science, sparking the poet's renewed interest in science and its appropriateness as a subject for poetry. Wordsworth's attempts to incorporate scientific knowledge into his later poems were largely the result of his association with Hamilton; and this effort may have contributed to the decline of his poetic imagination in later years.

2053.   ———. "An Introduction to a Study of Wordsworth's Reading in Science."
         FurmS 33.5 (1950): 27–60.
This chronological survey of Wordsworth's scientific reading before 1795 relates
his study of Euclid, Newton and Newtonianism, and E. Darwin to poems such as
The Prelude and *The Excursion*. An appendix lists the scientific works found in
Wordsworth's library in 1829.

2054.   ———. "A Study of Changes in Wordsworth's Conception of the Rela-
         tionship of Poetry and Science." Diss. U of North Carolina, 1939.
Not seen for annotation.

2055.   Potter, George Reuben. "Wordsworth and the *Traité élémentaire de chimie*
         of Lavoisier." *PQ* 17 (1938): 312–16.
Wordsworth's critique of analytical science in book 4 of *The Excursion* contains
an apparent reference to Lavoisier's *Traité*, which Wordsworth may have become
acquainted with through his friendship with the chemist Humphry Davy.

2056.   Robertson, William B. "The Relation of Wordsworth to Science." Diss.
         Cornell U, 1932.
Not seen for annotation.

2057.   Sharrock, Roger. "The Chemist and the Poet: Sir Humphry Davy and the
         Preface to *Lyrical Ballads*." *Notes and Records of the Royal Society of London*
         17 (1962): 57–76.
Comments on the relationships between Davy, S. Coleridge, and Wordsworth
and examines the impact of Davy's knowledge of chemistry on the two poets. Davy's
Introductory Discourse, presented to the Royal Institution in 1802, responds to the
challenges posed to science by Coleridge's epistemology and by Wordsworth's distinction between reason and understanding in the Preface to *Lyrical Ballads*. The
third edition of *Lyrical Ballads* responds, in turn, to Davy's lecture. Sharrock shows
that Davy's *Discourse* had a moderating influence on Wordsworth's view of science
and imagination.

2058.   ———. "Wordsworth on Science and Poetry." *REL* 3.4 (1962): 42–50.
Compares Wordsworth's remarks on science and poetry in his Preface to the third
edition of *Lyrical Ballads* with remarks on the subject made by the chemist Humphry
Davy in his *Introductory Discourse*.

2059.   Smyser, Jane Worthington. "Wordsworth's Dream of Poetry and Science:
         The Prelude, V." *PMLA* 71 (1956): 269–75.
Suggests that Wordsworth's dream of two books—one embracing all scientific
knowledge, the other, all imaginative knowledge—in book 5 of *The Prelude* may
be based on René Descartes's dreams, as recounted by Wordsworth's "philosophic
friend" Michel Beaupuy.

2060.   Watson, R. Spence. "Wordsworth's Relation to Science." *Littel's Living
         Age* 162 (1884): 295–301.
The view that Wordsworth was antagonistic to science is a grave misconception.

Drawing mainly on *The Excursion*, Watson shows that Wordsworth acknowledged the benefits of science but issued cogent warnings about overspecialization.

2061.   Wigglesworth, V. B. "Wordsworth and Science." *Nature* 153 (1944): 367–68.
Although Wordsworth appears generally antagonistic toward science, his attitude toward nature may be akin to the "mystical" tendencies of modern sciences such as physics.

Giacomo Zanella (1820–88)

2062.   Tursi, Joseph. "Giacomo Zanella and Science." *FI* 2 (1968): 102–11.
Examines the attitude toward science expressed in Zanella's poetry, stressing the conflict between religion and science and the rejection of Darwinian evolution. Among the poems discussed are *La veglia*, *A mia madre*, *Microscopio e telescopio*, and *Milton e Galileo*.

Emile Zola (1840–1902)

2063.   Beer, Gillian. "Plot and the Analogy with Science in Later Nineteenth-Century Novelists." *CCrit* 2 (1980): 131–49.
See item 1631 for annotation.

2064.   Duncan, Phillip A. "Zola's Machine-Monsters." *RomN* 3.2 (1961–62): 10–12.
Zola's grotesque machine imagery in *Les Rougon-Macquart*, *L'assommoir*, *La bête humaine*, and other works does not accurately reflect his view of the value of science and technology and its role in furthering human progress. His apparent dread of the machine was stimulated by purely literary considerations.

2065.   Gauthier, E. Paul. "New Light on Zola and Physiognomy." *PMLA* 75 (1960): 297–308.
Examines Zola's application of physiognomical theory to characterization in novels such as *La fortune des Rougon* and *La bête humaine*. His knowledge of physiognomy may have derived from works by Lavater and C. Darwin.

2066.   Gerhardi, Gerhard C. "Zola's Biological Vision of Politics: Revolutionary Figures in *La fortune des Rougon* and *Le ventre de Paris*." *NCFS* 2 (1973–74): 164–80.
The biological vision grounding Zola's writings is manifested in *La fortune des Rougon* and *Le ventre de Paris* in the characters Silvère and Florent. Gerhardi studies the biological motivations of their revolutionary activities—motivations that are both sexual and gastronomic.

2067.   Kitchel, Anna T. "Scientific Influences in the Work of Emile Zola and George Eliot." Diss. U of Wisconsin, 1921.
Not seen for annotation.

2068.   Kuczynski, Jürgen. "Zola—Wissenschaft und Kunst." *Gestalten und Werke.*
        Soziologische Studien zur englischsprachigen und französischen Literatur. Berlin:
        Aufbau, 1971. 389–417.
Analyzes Zola's conception of naturalism as a translation into literature of his
theories of heredity and society. Zola was the first to call for an interaction of literary
realism and scientific data. He was also the first to attempt to synthesize the scientist's
worldview with the artist's vision by controlling artistic perception through scientific
knowledge.

2069.   Martineau, Henri. *Le roman scientifique d'Emile Zola. La médecine et les* Rou-
        gon-Macquart. Paris: Baillière, 1907. 272 pp.
Surveys the scientific background of Zola's age and examines his scientific interests
and his chief scientific theories, especially his theory of heredity. Analyzes his
references to disease and doctors in *Les Rougon-Macquart* and discusses the role of
heredity in the work.

2070.   ———. "La valeur scientifique des romans d'Emile Zola." *Revue critique*
        des idées et des livres 20 (1913): 423–29.
Maintains that because Zola failed to comprehend scientific method and never
possessed the precision or exactitude required of a scientist, his literary works are
of little scientific value.

2071.   Muller, A. "La médecine et les médecins dans l'œuvre d'Emile Zola." Diss.
        U de Dijon, 1977.
Not seen for annotation.

2072.   Rhodes, S. A. "The Source of Zola's Medical References in *La débâcle.*"
        MLN 45 (1930): 109–11.
Zola's minute descriptions of surgical procedures in *La débâcle* were derived from
Farabeuf's *Précis de manuel opératoire* (1885).

2073.   Rostand, Jean. "L'oeuvre de Zola et la pensée scientifique." *Europe*
        46.468–69 (1968): 360–69.
Zola considered himself more a scientist than a man of letters. His literary theory,
developed in *Le roman expérimental*, was based on the conviction that the naturalist
writer is not merely an observer but an experimentalist. This essay examines Zola's
notion of heredity and his familiarity with other ideas of heredity espoused by
Bernard, C. Darwin, and Haeckel.

2074.   Virtanen, Reino. "Claude Bernard and Literature." *Claude Bernard and His*
        Place in the History of Ideas. Lincoln: U of Nebraska P, 1960. 117–28.
Studies the influence of the physiologist Claude Bernard on French literature,
focusing on Zola's debt to Bernard in works such as the essay *Le roman expérimental*
and the novel *Le docteur Pascal.* Also comments briefly on Bernard's influence on
Paul Bourget.

Twentieth Century

Studies and Surveys

2075.   Abel, Richard M. "Scientific Imagination and the American Novel." *DAI* 39 (1979): 7400A.
See item 1377 for annotation.

2076.   Abraham, Pierre, Charles Dobzynski, Pierre Gamarra, et al. "Entretien sur la science-fiction." *Europe* 139–40 (1957): 3–20.
Explores the multiple characteristics of science fiction, including its concept of time, the roles of principal characters and of science, the element of the rational, the idea of conflict, and the genre as ideology and as escapist literature.

2077.   Aldridge, Alexandra B. "Scientising Society: The Dystopian Novel and the Scientific World View." *DAI* 39 (1978): 3560A–61A.
Analyzes the antiscientific attitudes in dystopian novels such as Wells's *When the Sleeper Wakes*, Zamyatin's *We*, and A. Huxley's *Brave New World*.

2077a. Angus, Douglas. "Modern Art and the New Physics." *WHR* 16 (1962): 103–12.
Sees a parallelism between modern physics and modern art and literature. Claims that abstractionism in painting and montage techniques in literature correspond to the radical shift from Newtonian mechanics to quantum physics.

2078.   Armytage, W. H. G. *Yesterday's Tomorrows: A Historical Survey of Future Societies*. Toronto: U of Toronto P; London: Routledge, 1968. 288 pp.
See item 142 for annotation.

2079.   Asker, David B. D. "The Modern Bestiary: Animal Fiction from Hardy to Orwell." *DAI* 39 (1979): 7338A.
See item 1384 for annotation.

2080.   Bailey, J. O. *Pilgrims through Space and Time: Trends and Patterns in Scientific and Utopian Fiction*. New York: Argus, 1947. Westport: Greenwood, 1972. 341 pp.
See item 144 for annotation.

2081.   ———. "Shaw's Life Force and Science Fiction." *ShawR* 16 (1973): 48–58.

Examines Shaw's concept of the life-force and creative evolution, drawn from Buffon, Lamarck, and S. Butler, and relates it to similar themes in science fiction by Wells, Bellamy, E. Burroughs, Stapledon, and others.

2082.   Barraford, Nora M. "The Secular Supernatural." *DAI* 37 (1977): 5841A.
Broadly studies the impact of natural science, astrology, alchemy, and cabalism on the mythic and fantastic qualities of science fiction.

2083.   Barthell, Robert J. "Science Fiction: A Literature of Ideas." *Extrapolation* 13 (1971–72): 56–63.
"The condition of the science fiction hero will remain that of a poorly drawn character within a weak literary style. His condition is the result of the technical and scientific nature of this literature; a literature concerned with technical problems for technical people who find intellectual stimulation in science and technology itself."

2084.   Beach, Joseph W. "American Letters between Wars." *CE* 3 (1941–42): 1–12.
Among the factors shaping the thematic tendencies of American literature from 1920 to 1940 were Darwinism and Victorian naturalism.

2085.   Bender, Bert A. "Let There Be (Electric) Light! The Image of Electricity in American Writing." *ArQ* 34 (1978): 55–70.
See item 1389 for annotation.

2086.   Berger, Harold L. "Anti-Utopian Science Fiction of the Mid-Twentieth Century." *DAI* 32 (1971): 420A.
Explores the dominant features of the dystopian vision of errant scientism in twentieth-century science fiction.

2087.   Biasin, Gian Paolo. "$\frac{4}{3}\pi r^3$ (spazio scientifico, spazio letterario)." *Letteratura e scienza nella storia della cultura italiana*. Atti del IX congresso dell'associazione internazionale per gli studi di lingua e letteratura italiana. Palermo, Messina, Catania, 21–25 Apr. 1976. Associazione internazionale per gli studi di lingua e letteratura italiana. Palermo: Manfredi, 1978. 860–72.
See item 2254 for annotation.

2088.   Bizzel, Patricia. "Thomas Kuhn, Scientism, and English Studies." *CE* 40 (1979): 764–71.
Argues that the theory of paradigmatic change in scientific revolutions, which the historian of science Thomas Kuhn expounds in *The Structure of Scientific Revolutions*, can be applied to the shift from traditional philological studies to the contemporary literary view that language is a "social product and embodiment of ideology."

2089.   Boia, Lucian. "Le roman astronomique: (Seconde moitié du XIXᵉ siècle— début du XXᵉ siècle)." *Synthesis* 7 (1980): 145–63.
See item 1392 for annotation.

2090.   Bork, Alfred M. "Randomness and the Twentieth Century." *AR* 27
        (1967–68): 40–61.
    Maintains that randomness is one of the distinguishing features of the twentieth
century. Illustrates this concept's pervasiveness and its impact on various disciplines
with examples from physics, biology, art, music, and literature such as Joyce's
Finnegans Wake and *Ulysses* and W. Burroughs's *Naked Lunch*. Traces current interest
in randomness to nineteenth-century kinetic principles and statistical thermodynamics and to the evolution theories of C. Darwin and Wallace.

2091.   Bowman, John S. "The Agony and the Entropy." *Harvard Magazine* 81.2
        (1978–79): 14–16.
    Notes in contradiction to C. P. Snow's "two cultures" theory that the second law
of thermodynamics, or entropy, has been enthusiastically adopted as a literary theme,
though often without a proper scientific grounding. Cites examples in works by
Pynchon, Nemerov, Gaddis, and others.

2092.   Brown, Harcourt. "Tensions and Anxieties: Science and the Literary Cul-
        ture of France." *Science and the Creative Spirit: Essays on Humanistic Aspects
        of Science*. Ed. Harcourt Brown. Toronto: U of Toronto P, 1958. 91–126.
    See item 146 for annotation.

2093.   Bryant, Jerry H. *The Open Decision: The Contemporary American Novel and
        Its Intellectual Background*. New York: Free, 1970. 415 pp.
        Rev. R. A. Christmas, *WHR* 25 (1971): 276–77; Maurice Beebe, *AL* 43
        (1971–72): 488–89.
    The background to this study of the intellectual outlook reflected in post-World
War II American fiction includes aspects of contemporary physics, such as relativity
theory and quantum mechanics, modern developments in psychology and sociology,
and central concepts of existentialism.

2094.   Buck, Philo M., Jr. "Science, Literature, and the Hunting of the Snark."
        CE 4 (1942–43): 1–11.
    Interprets the figure of the snark in Carroll's "Hunting of the Snark" as an allegory
of the possibilities for good and evil that modern science poses to culture. Traces
this theme in the literature of T. S. Eliot, O'Neill, Proust, Santayana, and others.

2095.   Bush, Douglas. *Science and English Poetry: A Historical Sketch, 1590–1950*.
        New York: Oxford UP, 1950. Westport: Greenwood, 1980. 166 pp.
    See item 147 for annotation.

2096.   Caillois, Roger. "Science Fiction." *Diogenes* 89 (1975): 87–105.
    Similarity of theme and social function indicates that the literary genres of fairy
stories, fantastic stories, and science fiction form more or less a continuous developmental whole. This article explores the principal themes of technological domination and scientific innovation that characterize science fiction.

2097.   Cameron, Alex J. "The Image of the Physician in the American Novel
        1859 to 1925." *DAI* 33 (1973): 6342A–43A.
    See item 1400 for annotation.

2098.   Carter, Paul A. "Rockets to the Moon 1919–1944: A Dialogue between
         Fiction and Reality." *AmerS* 15.1 (1974): 31–46.
Developments in the science and technology of space travel, beginning with
Goddard's speculations on rocket propulsion in 1919, were often anticipated or
reflected in science fiction. Carter briefly traces the history of rocket experiments
and their relation to fiction by Wells, Pendray, Manning, Gail, Asimov, and others.

2099.   Charbon, Rémy. *Die Naturwissenschaften im modernen deutschen Drama.* Zü-
         rich: Artemis, 1974. 282 pp.
         Rev. Manfred Stöckler, *LJGG* 20 (1979): 310–12.
Examines the implications and consequences of atomic weaponry and technology
as reflected in twentieth-century German drama and framed by the "two cultures"
debate. Among the works considered are Frisch's *Chinesische Mauer*, Zuckmayer's
Kalte Licht, Jahnn's *Trümmer des Gewissens*, and Schneider's *Richard Waverly*. The
study includes detailed interpretations of Brecht's *Leben des Galilei*, Dürrenmatt's
Physiker, and Kipphardt's *In der Sache J. Robert Oppenheimer* and comments on the
relation between the two opposing tendencies apparent in these dramas—the awareness of biological, historical, and social determinants versus the increasing awareness
of humankind's capacity for autonomous control of its destiny.

2100.   Christofides, C. G. "Gaston Bachelard's Phenomenology of the Imagina-
         tion." *RR* 52 (1961): 36–47.
Describes Bachelard's phenomenological aesthetics, which emphasize the creative
force of archetypal imagery for both scientists and poets.

2101.   Clareson, Thomas D., "The Emergence of American Science Fiction,
         1880–1915: A Study of the Impact of Science upon American Romanti-
         cism." *DA* 16 (1956): 962.
See item 1404 for annotation.

2102.   ———, ed. "Science Fiction: The New Mythology." *Extrapolation* 10
         (1968–69): 69–115.
A transcript of the taped proceedings of an MLA forum on science fiction, held
in New York in December 1968. Darko Suvin contributes an overview of Soviet
science fiction; Isaac Asimov discusses the relation between science fiction and science, focusing on science fiction as a vehicle for scientific visions of the future; and
Frederik Pohl examines science fiction as a form of social commentary.

2103.   Clarke, I. F. "Science Fiction: Past and Present." *QR* 295 (1957): 260–
         70.
See item 1407 for annotation.

2103a.   Clement, Hal. "Hard Sciences and Tough Technologies." *The Craft of
         Science Fiction.* Ed. Reginald Bretnor. New York: Harper, 1976. 37–53.
Argues that the use of scientific facts and theories in fiction must be consistent
with what is known. Concludes that the authors of "hard" science fiction, a recognizable field within a field, have a fair amount of scientific knowledge and ability
and write for those who take scientific knowledge seriously.

2104.   Creed, Walter G. "On Reading Einstein." *Four Quarters* 29.1 (1979–80):
         25–36.
All too often critics and scholars who approach the subject of the relation between
Einstein's theories and modern literature have relied on secondary expositions of his
thought instead of consulting his actual texts. Creed reviews the wide range of
Einstein's writings, briefly commenting on their contents, in an effort to correct
this situation.

2105.   Dean, Dennis R. "The Influence of Geology on American Literature and
         Thought." *Two Hundred Years of Geology in America*. Ed. Cecil J. Schneer.
         Hanover: UP of New England, 1979. 289–303.
See item 1418 for annotation.

2106.   Dodge, Stewart C. "The Use of Evolutionary Theory by American Poets:
         1900–1950." *DA* 19 (1958): 1077.
Considers the use of evolutionary theory in the poetry of Robinson, Frost, T. S.
Eliot, Jeffers, Crane, Williams, and Stevens.

2107.   Donley, Carol C. "Modern Literature and Physics: A Study of Interrela-
         tionships." *DAI* 36 (1975–76): 3684A.
Examines some central themes of physics, art, literature, and philosophy and
studies the interrelations between physics and Woolf's *The Waves*, Faulkner's *Absalom, Absalom!*, and Williams's *Paterson*.

2108.   Durrell, Lawrence. "Space Time and Poetry." *A Key to Modern British Poetry*.
         Norman: U of Oklahoma P; London: Nevill, 1952. 24–48.
Argues that developments in twentieth-century science concerning the relation
between subject and object challenged conventional ideas about matter and causality,
postulated a new understanding of space and time, and deeply influenced the experimental work of writers such as T. S. Eliot, Joyce, and Woolf.

2109.   Dyck, Martin. "Relativity in Physics and in Fiction." *Studies in German
         Literature of the Nineteenth and Twentieth Centuries. Festschrift for Frederic E.
         Coenen*. Ed. Siegfried Mews. University of North Carolina Studies in the
         Germanic Languages and Literatures 67. Chapel Hill: U of North Carolina
         P, 1970. 174–85.
See item 1424 for annotation.

2110.   Eoff, Sherman H. *The Modern Spanish Novel: Comparative Essays Examining
         the Philosophical Impact of Science on Fiction*. New York: New York UP, 1961.
         London: Owen, 1962. 280 pp.
Analyzes the ways in which popularized scientific ideas merge with philosophical
or religious concepts to define the underlying thematic contexts of Spanish fiction.
Spanish authors of the mid–nineteenth century, such as Pereda, assumed an orderly
clockwork universe ruled by a benevolent personal God. Successive scientific revolutions in biology in the nineteenth century and in physics in the twentieth displaced
that belief. Separate essays examine how Spanish and other European authors responded to these changes in science, combining the implications of the scientific

theories with various philosophical assumptions. For example, principles of naturalism inform the work of Pardo Bazán and Blasco Ibáñez; Pérez Galdós accepts evolution more optimistically; Unamuno and Sender respond to the new-found freedoms of modern physics and existentialism.

2111.   Fasel, Ida. "Spatial Form and Spatial Time." *WHR* 16 (1962): 223–34.
Examines the thematic and structural uses of temporality and spatiality by authors such as Flaubert, Proust, T. S. Eliot, Joyce, and Faulkner, briefly referring to the possible influence of modern physics on literary treatments of space and time.

2112.   Finkelstein, Sidney. "The World of Science Fiction." *Masses and Mainstream*
          8 (1955): 48–57.
Broadly discusses how common themes in contemporary science fiction reflect socioeconomic and political concerns, including the role of science and scientists in society.

2113.   Folsom, James K. "Magic and Technology as Opposing Values in Science
          Fiction." *Iowa State Journal of Research* 54 (1979): 257–65.
Assesses the relative importance of the metaphors of magic and technology in science fiction. Maintains that magic more adequately expresses the spirit of the scientific quest for knowledge than does technology, which tends to play a surprisingly antiscientific role.

2114.   Foster, Steven M. "Ambiguous Gifts: The Impress of Science on Contem-
          porary Anglo-American Poetry." *DA* 26 (1965–66): 2749.
Discusses relativity and T. S. Eliot's *Waste Land*; the gestalt configurations of Stevens; Crane's use of probability theory derived from quantum mechanics; Auden's appropriation of themes drawn from physics, biology, and geology; and the relevance of modern physics for contemporary literature generally.

2115.   Franklin, H. Bruce. "Science Fiction as an Index to Popular Attitudes
          toward Science: A Danger, Some Problems, and Two Possible Paths."
          Extrapolation 6 (1964–65): 23–31.
Focuses on science fiction as both an unconscious revelation of popular attitudes toward science and a conscious evaluation of those attitudes; illustrates the role of evaluation by analyzing Hawthorne's "Birthmark."

2116.   Fredericks, Sigmund C. "Greek Mythology in Modern Science Fiction:
          Vision and Cognition." *PCLS* 11 (1980): 89–105.
This study of the mythological content and significance of science fiction and fantasy maintains that science fiction bridges the gap between mythic and scientific realms. Fredericks discusses this idea in relation to three kinds of fictional encounters: human-superhuman, human-machine, and human-alien. He sees science fiction's contemporary mythological function as testing social values and views of human nature by comparing them with those of imaginary civilizations.

2117.   Friedman, Alan J. "Contemporary American Physics Fiction." *AJPhys* 47
          (1979): 392–95.

Examines the metaphorical use of principles of contemporary physics in the works of Pynchon, Gaddis, Coover, McElroy, DeLillo, and Pirsig.

2118. ————. "The Novelist and Modern Physics: New Metaphors for Traditional Themes." *Journal of College Science Teaching* 4 (1975): 310–12.
Briefly discusses the influence of modern physics on literary metaphors, citing works by Pynchon and Nabokov.

2119. ————. "Physics and Literature in This Century: A New Course." *Physics Education* 8 (1973): 305–08.
Describes an interdisciplinary course, taught at Hiram College, that was designed to convey a sense of the significance of physics for contemporary English literature. Students were required to read Hardy's *Mayor of Casterbridge*, Durrell's *Alexandria Quartet*, Nabokov's *Ada*, and Pynchon's *Crying of Lot 49*, among other works.

2120. Fullmer, J. Z. "Contemporary Science and the Poets." *Science* 119 (1954): 855–59.
Briefly examines selections from the poetry of T. S. Eliot, MacLeish, and Frost in an attempt to assess the influence of contemporary science on modern poetry.

2121. Gattégno, Jean. *La Science-Fiction*. "Que sais-je?" Le point des connaissances actuelles 1426. Paris: PUF, 1971. 125 pp.
See item 1435 for annotation.

2122. Gibbons, Tom H. *Rooms in the Darwin Hotel: Studies in English Literary Criticism and Ideas, 1880–1920*. Nedlands, Austral.: U of Western Australia P, 1973. 164 pp.
See item 1438 for annotation.

2123. Glass, Bentley. "The Scientist in Contemporary Fiction." *SciMo* 85 (1957): 288–93.
Describes the portrayal of scientists in selected works of twentieth-century literature, including writing by Wells, S. Lewis, Hutchinson, Hilton, and Snow.

2124. Glicksberg, Charles I. "Depersonalization in the Modern Drama." *Person* 39 (1958): 158–69.
Shows how the dramatic works of Strindberg, Pirandello, Lenormand, and O'Neill portray the multidimensional, disintegrated personality characteristic of the modern age. Attributes modern metaphysical uncertainty to factors such as Freudian psychoanalysis, the theories of relativity and indeterminacy, and the decline of religious faith.

2125. Goldstein, Laurence. " 'The End of All Our Exploring': The Moon Landing and Modern Poetry." *MQR* 18 (1979): 192–217.
Analyzes the largely negative responses to the Apollo 11 moon landing by poets such as Eastlake, Auden, Ackerman, and Dickey.

2126. Granin, D. "Wissenschaftlich-technische Revolution, Persönlichkeit, Literatur." *KuL* 26 (1978): 1123–40.

Partly concerns the influence of the scientific and technological revolution on Russian science fiction. Also discusses the literary depiction of scientists and analyzes the "rationalization" of modern literature under the influence of the scientific revolution.

2127.   Griffiths, John. *Three Tomorrows: American, British and Soviet Science Fiction*.
        Totowa: Barnes; London: Macmillan, 1980. 217 pp.
Following a definition of science fiction and a short history of its evolution, Griffiths examines a number of social trends and ideas in the science fiction of English, American, and Soviet writers—mainly of the last 20 to 30 years. He stresses the role of science in science fiction, notes the genre's relation to scientific and political movements, and discusses utopias and dystopias, cybernetics, and alien civilizations.

2128.   Gröger, Erika. "Der bürgerliche Atomwissenschaftler im englisch-ameri-
        kanischen Roman von 1945 bis zur Gegenwart." *ZAA* 16 (1968): 25–48.
Studies aspects of the development and use of the atomic bomb as reflected in the English and American novel. Stresses novels that depict the inner conflicts nuclear physicists faced in relation to their product, such as Snow's *New Men*, Master's *Accident*, and Wilson's *Meeting at a Far Meridian* and *Live with Lightning*.

2129.   Hagopian, John, et al. "Contemporary Science and the Poets Reconsid-
        ered." *Science* 120 (1954): 951–55.
This series of communications by J. Hagopian, H. M. Hirsch, A. Adams, and J. Z. Fullmer focuses on controversies over the extent to which contemporary science has influenced or is reflected in contemporary poetry (see item 2120).

2130.   Handy, William J. "Science, Literature and Modern Criticism." *TQ* 1.2
        (1958): 147–56.
The theoretical orientation of the literary critics Ransom, Tate, and Brooks has its roots in Kantian aesthetic principles and tends to emphasize the nonlogical cognitive function of literary language along with the limitations of scientific cognition. These scholars see literature as a form of knowledge outside the purview of science and necessary for a unified understanding of human reality.

2131.   Hartwick, Harry. *The Foreground of American Fiction*. New York: American
        Book, 1934. New York: Gordian, 1967. 447 pp.
        Rev. Fred B. Millett, *AL* 7 (1935): 105–06.
This study of the social, economic, religious, philosophic, and literary forces shaping late-nineteenth- and early-twentieth-century American fiction includes a section that discusses the scientific sources of the literary naturalism in works by Crane, Norris, London, Dreiser, Anderson, Hemingway, and Faulkner.

2132.   Heidtmann, Horst. "A Survey of Science Fiction in the German Democratic
        Republic." *SFS* 6 (1979): 92–99.
Broadly correlates typical themes in East German science fiction with GDR socioeconomic and political concerns from 1945 to 1977. Considers motifs such as industry and technology, space travel, urbanization and pollution, scientism, and utopia.

2133. Hiersche, Anton. *Sowjetliteratur und wissenschaftlich-technische Revolution*. Berlin: Akademie, 1976. 243 pp.

Examines the relation between the literature and the scientific and technological revolutions in socialist countries. Focusing on literary aesthetics, discusses such issues as the relation between scientific and artistic cognitive processes and the role of literature in the formation of socialist personalities. Traces the change in literary attitudes toward science in the 1950s and 1960s from a focus on the domination of nature through science to a vision of the alliance of nature and humankind against science.

2134. Hirsch, Walter. "American Science Fiction, 1926–1950. A Content Analysis." *DA* 17 (1957): 3113–14.

Analyzes the sociopolitical and scientific content of 300 science fiction stories, a random sample of those published between 1926 and 1950.

2135. ———. "The Image of the Scientist in Science Fiction: A Content Analysis." *American Journal of Sociology* 63 (1957–58): 507–12.

Analyzes 300 science fiction stories, a random sample of those published in America between 1926 and 1950. Some of the questions asked were, How many main characters are scientists? What are the prominent characteristics of villains and heroes? What is the social role of scientists? How might the depiction of scientists in science fiction affect the reading public's attitudes toward science as a career?

2136. Huntington, John. "Science Fiction and the Future." *CE* 37 (1975–76): 345–52.

The scientific basis of most science fiction is conservative rather than boldly visionary and tends to treat the present instead of the future. An attitude of either heady optimism or despairing pessimism toward science underlies many science fiction works.

2137. Hyman, Stanley Edgar. "After the Great Metaphors." *ASch* 31 (1961–62): 236–58.

The scientific metaphors of C. Darwin, Marx, Frazer, and Freud pervade twentieth-century literature, appearing in the work of writers such as Ashley-Montagu, N. Brown, Camus, T. S. Eliot, Golding, Malamud, Marcuse, and Sartre.

2138. Isaacs, Leonard. *Darwin to Double Helix: The Biological Theme in Science Fiction*. London: Butterworths, 1977. 64 pp.

Examines the literary response to C. Darwin's evolution theory and contemporary ideas of genetics and development in works by Bulwer-Lytton, Wells, Stapledon, A. Huxley, Le Guin, and others. Emphasizes how these two advances influenced the portrayal of the biological future of humankind.

2139. Ivasheva, Valentina V. *On the Threshold of the Twenty-First Century: The Technological Revolution and Literature*. Trans. Doris Bradbury and Natalie Ward. Moscow: Progress, 1978. 211 pp.

Examines tendencies in world literature that can be traced to the technological and scientific explosion in the post–World War II era. Topics include the documental tendency in contemporary literature, the rapid increase in the popularity of science fiction, and the widespread incorporation of philosophy into literature. Also discusses the impact of the modern physical concepts of space and time on literary theme and structure, the influence of discoveries in human sciences such as biology and physiology on literature, and the predilection in modern literature for psychophysical themes and themes centering on personality disorders. Makes some attempt to analyze the differences between Western and non-Western literary responses to science and technology. Among the wide variety of authors treated are Asimov, Baldwin, A. Clarke, Dabrowska, Dürrenmatt, T. S. Eliot, Franke, Grass, Hüser, Joyce, and Mailer.

2139a. Jaki, Stanley L. "A Hundred Years of Two Cultures." *UWR* 11.1 (1975): 55–79.
Puts into historical perspective both Matthew Arnold's 1882 Rede lecture, "Literature and Science," and C. P. Snow's 1959 Rede lecture, "The Two Cultures," showing the longevity of the crisis over the split in modern culture.

2140.   Jelly, Oliver. "Fiction and Illness." *REL* 3.1 (1962): 80–89.
Since Flaubert's *Madame Bovary*, fiction has tended to exhibit a prominent clinical element and a preponderance of disease imagery. This essay surveys examples of the clinical theme in Braine, Gide, Mann, Proust, and others.

2141.   Juin, Hubert. "Science-fiction et littérature." *Europe* 35.139–40 (1957): 53–63.
Examines how science fiction as a literary genre, expresses humankind's position in the modern world of high technology and fast-paced scientific development.

2142.   Kirsch, Edgar. "Die Welt der Chemie und die deutsche Dichtung." *WZUH* 14 (1965): 163–74.
Provides an overview of the theme of chemistry in early twentieth-century German literature, including works by Becher, Kaiser, Lask, H. Mann, and F. Wolf. These works typically concern the relations among science, technology, and society.

2143.   Koutaissoff, Elisabeth. "The Scientific Theme in Post-War Soviet Literature." *Literature and Science*. Proc. of the Sixth Triennial Congress of the International Federation for Modern Languages and Literatures. Oxford, 1954. Oxford: Blackwell, 1955. 313–18.
The post–World War II Russian novel integrates scientific, industrial, and technological themes into its structure, conveying a sense of realism characteristic of Soviet culture, in which art, science, and industrial productivity work together toward a common social goal. Among the works discussed here are Kozhevnikov's *Living Water* and Shaginyan's *Diary of a Writer*.

2144.   Kragness, Sheila I. "Doctors and Medical Science in the Contemporary French Drama, 1887 to 1939." Diss. U of Minnesota, 1948.
Not seen for annotation.

2145.   Kügler, Hans. "Dichtung und Naturwissenschaft: Einige Reflexionen zum Rollenspiel des Naturwissenschaftlers in: B. Brecht, *Das Leben des Galilei*, F. Dürrenmatt, *Die Physiker*, H. Kipphardt, *In der Sache J. Robert Oppen-*

heimer." *Weg und Weglosigkeit: Neun Essays zur Geschichte der deutschen Literatur im zwanzigsten Jahrhundert.* Heidenheim: Heidenheimer, 1970. 209–35.
Studies representative dramas by Brecht, Dürrenmatt, and Kipphardt to explore the problematic roles in which scientists, specifically physicists, find themselves in the atomic age. As literary persons cast doubts on the elitist claims of science, so must they recognize the limitations of literature to influence the politically powerful.

2146. Kurman, George. "Entropy and the 'Death' of Tragedy: Notes for a Theory of Drama." *CompD* 9 (1975–76): 283–304.
Suggests a link between the decline of tragedy and the changing applications of entropy from pre-Socratic thought to contemporary information theory.

2147. Kuznetsov, Boris. "Einstein and Dostoevski." *Diogenes* 53 (1966): 1–16.
Maintains that Dostoyevsky was an important source of inspiration for Einstein, "directing and augmenting his attraction for research into a scientific, social and moral harmony."

2148. Lang, Leonard A. "The Impact of Classical Science on American Literature: The Creation of an Epic American Hero in Science Fiction." *DAI* 39 (1978): 3665A.
Maintains that between the late 1930s and the early 1960s the genre of science fiction produced a hero figure that synthesized American and scientific values. Studies the works of Asimov and Sturgeon in this regard.

2149. Lepenies, Wolf. "Abenteuer und Verhängnis der Wissenschaft: Zu den Autobiographien von Erwin Chargaff und Freeman Dyson." *Merkur* 34 (1980): 831–39.
Primarily a comparison between the autobiographies *Das Feuer des Heraklit*, by the biochemist Erwin Chargaff, and *Disturbing the Universe*, by the theoretical physicist and astronomer Freeman Dyson, this study focuses on these scientists' attitude toward the development of modern science. For both, literature serves to further the understanding of those problems that science fails to solve.

2150. McDonald, Daniel. "Science, Literature, and Absurdity." *SAQ* 66 (1967): 42–49.
Maintains that the findings of modern science have contributed decisively to the breakdown of commonsense notions of reality—a breakdown reflected in modern absurdist literature by writers such as Albee, Ionesco, and Beckett.

2151. McQuarie, Donald. "Utopia and Transcendence: An Analysis of Their Decline in Contemporary Science Fiction." *JPC* 14 (1980–81): 242–50.
Antiscientific and antitechnological sentiments combined with ". . . the larger failure of a mass socialist movement and party to emerge and successfully develop in American political life" accounts partly for the twentieth-century decline in the science-fiction utopia, a genre linking ". . . scientific plausibility, optimism concerning the attainment of utopia, and definite, if sometimes vague, socialist sympathies."

2152.   Mandel, Oscar. "Sore Literature and Contented Science." *SAQ* 64 (1965): 308–15.
Contrasts the relatively optimistic attitude of contemporary scientists toward the state of world civilization with the pessimism of contemporary literary figures, including Beckett, Camus, T. S. Eliot, and Kafka.

2153.   Manna, Gennaro. "Aspetti della narrativa contemporanea: Letteratura e scienza." *RealM* 6 (1966): 365–69.
Discusses the decreasing frequency of scientific observation in contemporary literature, maintaining that hitherto modern writers have sought to imitate too closely the objective, scientific approach. Cites Mann's *Magic Mountain* and *Buddenbrooks* as examples of novels that incorporate scientific description into their narratives.

2154.   Marx, Leo. "Reflections on the Neo-Romantic Critique of Science." *Daedalus* 107.2 (1978): 61–74.
Traces the widespread literary critique of science and rationalism in the 1960s and 1970s to its roots in nineteenth-century Romanticism, noting the contributions of Emerson and Carlyle. Discusses particularly Roszak's *Making of a Counter-Culture: Reflections on the Technocratic Society* (1969).

2155.   Metzner, Joachim. "Die Bedeutung physikalischer Sätze für die Literatur." *DVLG* 53 (1979): 1–34.
Examines the relation between literature and science by tracing the second law of thermodynamics, or entropy, through twentieth-century culture, citing examples from the following German and American novelists: Barth, Barthelme, Bellow, Broch, Eich, Elkin, Kafka, Mailer, Percy, Pynchon, Sack, and Updike.

2156.   Meyerhoff, Hans. *Time in Literature*. Berkeley: U of California P, 1955. 160 pp.
See item 87 for annotation.

2157.   Mills, Gordon. "The Influence of Darwinism on the Style of Certain American Writers." *The Impact of Darwinian Thought on American Life and Culture*. Papers Read at the Fourth Annual Meeting of the American Studies Association of Texas. Houston, 5 Dec. 1959. Austin: U of Texas P, 1959. 11–26.
Suggests links between Darwinism, Beard's theory of history writing, and the technical theories of fiction and poetry espoused by Hemingway and Stein.

2158.   Muller, Herbert J. *Science and Criticism: The Humanistic Tradition in Contemporary Thought*. New Haven: Yale UP; New York: Braziller; London: Milford-Oxford UP, 1943. 303 pp.
Rev. William M. Sale, Jr., *YR* ns 33 (1943–44): 151–53; Charles L. Stevenson, *JP* 41 (1944): 21–23.
Outlines the major developments in the social sciences, psychology, physics, and biology that bear on literary criticism. One section discusses the relation between literary criticism and contemporary physics; another reviews the relevance of science for twentieth-century literature and literary studies.

2159.   Nelson, Norman E. "Science and the Irresponsible Imagination." *YR* ns
        43 (1953–54): 71–88.
Maintains that several fundamental concepts of modern physics, such as Einstein's
theory of relativity and Heisenberg's uncertainty principle, have been grossly mis-
understood in the popular mind and put to unseemly and exaggerated use in modern
literature.

2160.   Nettesheim, Josefine. "Ursprung und Sinn der Wissenschaftskunst in der
        Lyrik. Vom Einfluss der Naturwissenschaften und der Technik auf die
        Entwicklung der Dichtungstheorie (Lyrik)." *LJGG* ns 3 (1962): 315–33.
See item 1466 for annotation.

2161.   O'Hanlon, R. "Changing Scientific Concepts of Nature in the English
        Novel 1850–1920, with Special Reference to Joseph Conrad." Diss. Oxford
        U, 1977.
Not seen for annotation.

2162.   Ong, Walter J., SJ. "Evolution, Myth, and Poetic Vision." *CLS* 3 (1966):
        1–20.
Maintains that the temporal and historical paradigms operative in contemporary
poetry rarely reflect the implications of evolution and its impact on the temporal
and historical consciousness. Poets tend to stress either a cyclic conception of time
and history or the significance of the present moment isolated from the past and
the future. Ong discusses the poetics of time and history in Durrell, T. S. Eliot,
Hopkins, Joyce, D. H. Lawrence, Pound, Williams, Yeats, and others.

2163.   Pagetti, Carlo. *Il senso del futuro: La fantascienza nella letteratura americana.*
        Biblioteca di studi americani 20. Rome: Storia e Letteratura, 1970. 323 pp.
An analysis of the works of Verne and Wells shows how science affects literary
genres such as science fiction. Verne used science as a firm basis for his narrative
and stayed well within the realm of scientific possibility, while Wells's scientific
machinery was endowed with fantastical elements that distanced his works from the
logic of Verne. The major distinction between the two writers lies in their goals;
Verne was a storyteller who made science an integral element of his tales, while
Wells used science in his depiction of imaginary worlds to achieve moral and didactic
ends. These two approaches influenced American science fiction in its exploration
of utopias and dystopias throughout the twentieth century.

2164.   Parker, Helen N. "Biological Themes in Modern Science Fiction." *DAI*
        38 (1978): 7347A.
Examines biological themes such as evolution, genetics, manipulative biology,
and exobiology in representative science fiction from the late nineteenth century to
the present. Includes such authors as Asimov, Brunner, F. Herbert, A. Huxley, Le
Guin, and Weinbaum.

2165.   Parrinder, Patrick. "The Black Wave: Science and Social Consciousness in
        Modern Science Fiction." *Radical Science Journal* 5 (1977): 37–61.

One of the central themes of contemporary science fiction is ". . . the questioning of scientific activity itself, distinguishing between its fundamentally progressive role for mankind and the distortions it undergoes in the current economic and political system." Parrinder outlines recent literary and ideological developments in science fiction, focusing discussion on Lem's *Solaris*, A. Strugatskii and B. Strugatskii's *Far Rainbow*, and Le Guin's *Dispossessed*.

2166.   ———. "Science Fiction and the Scientific World-View." *Science Fiction: A Critical Guide*. Ed. Patrick Parrinder. London: Longman, 1979. 67–88.
Examines the transition from Wells's vision of scientists as technocrats who rationally order society to contemporary science fiction's portrayal of scientists as helpless agents of government or corporations.

2167.   Peacock, Ronald. "Abstraction and Reality in Modern Science, Art and Poetry." *Literature and Science*. Proc. of the Sixth Triennial Congress of the International Federation for Modern Languages and Literatures. Oxford, 1954. Oxford: Blackwell, 1955. 324–30.
Elucidates the parallels between abstraction in science and abstraction in art and poetry and draws general conclusions regarding the relation between science and the arts.

2168.   Pearson, Norman H. "The American Poet in Relation to Science." *AQ* 1 (1949): 116–26. Rpt. with slight modifications in *The American Writer and the European Tradition*. Ed. Margaret Denny and William H. Gilman. Minneapolis: U of Minnesota P for U of Rochester, 1950. 154–67.
Contends that the twentieth-century dominance of science and scientific language has forced poets to infuse new life into poetry and to reinvent poetic language and metaphor in order to assimilate the influence of science. Discusses Cummings, T. S. Eliot, Frost, Pound, Williams, and others.

2169.   Perlis, Alan D. "Science, Mysticism, and Contemporary Poetry." *WHR* 29 (1975): 209–18.
The relation to nature expressed in contemporary poetry suggests an alliance with science that belies I. A. Richards's formulation, in *Science and Poetry* (1926), of the separation between poetry and science. "If science left Richards, and generations preceding him, bereft of belief, it has given contemporary poets not only a handle on belief, but the terms with which to articulate belief as well."

2170.   Petrucciani, Mario. *Scienza e letteratura nel secondo novecento: La ricerca letteraria in Italia tra algebra e metafora*. Civiltà letteraria del novecento: Saggi 28. Milan: Mursia, 1978. 113 pp.
Systematically explores the relations between science and literature in Italy. The study examines works ranging from Vittorini's journal *Politecnico* to the writing of Gadda and Sinisgalli to the neo-avant-garde and electronic poetry. Petrucciani emphasizes three major issues: Debenedetti's attempted parallel between human beings and nuclear particles; Calvino's artistic use of cybernetics, molecular biology, and astrophysics; and Levi's "chemical" novel, *The Periodic Table*.

2171. Pfeiffer, K. Ludwig. *Wissenschaft als Sujet im modernen englischen Roman.* Konstanzer Universitätsreden 127. Konstanz: Universitätsverlag, 1979. 63 pp.
See item 164 for annotation.

2172. Plank, Robert. "Heart Transplant Fiction." *HSL* 2 (1970): 102–12.
The portrayal of the medical procedure of organ transplants has been surprisingly rare in twentieth-century imaginative literature. Plank surveys examples of such occurrences and discusses two nineteenth-century works that anticipate heart transplants: Hauff's *Das Kalte Herz* and Hawthorne's *Ethan Brand.*

2173. Porush, David. "Technology and Postmodernism: Cybernetic Fiction." *Sub-Stance* 27 (1980): 92–100.
Cybernetics, defined here as ". . . the science that compares complex computers to the neurophysiology of the human brain in an attempt to advance the study of both," informs the treatment of the relation between human beings and technology in postmodernist fiction by Barth, Barthelme, Beckett, Coover, and Pynchon.

2174. Purdy, Strother B. *The Hole in the Fabric: Science, Contemporary Literature, and Henry James.* Pittsburgh: U of Pittsburgh P, 1977. 228 pp.
See item 1741 for annotation.

2175. Quiñonez, Sister Lora A. "The Concept of Man in Representative Dystopian Novels." *DA* 30 (1969–70): 2038A–39A.
Studies A. Huxley's *Brave New World,* C. S. Lewis's *Out of the Silent Planet,* Orwell's *1984,* Vonnegut's *Player Piano,* and other dystopian novels that attempt to define the concept of humankind in the face of technology, scientific mentality, and alienation.

2176. Reimer, Howard J. "Darwinism in Canadian Literature." Diss. McMaster U, 1975.
Not seen for annotation.

2177. Richter, Karl. "Fortschritt ohne Zukunft: Literarische Prognosen in 'Physikerdramen' der Moderne." *Berichte zur Wissenschaftsgeschichte* 2 (1979): 125–34.
Prognostications about the world in an age of science are made in a number of dramas in which physicists are major characters, including Brecht's *Leben des Galilei,* Dürrenmatt's *Physiker,* and Kipphardt's *In der Sache J. Robert Oppenheimer.* This essay contrasts prognostications in the literary, scientific, and religious realms, concluding with a call for an interdisciplinary approach to present and future world crises.

2178. Rivers, James C. "Astronomy and Physics in British and American Poetry, 1920–1960." *DA* 28 (1967): 1826A.
Surveys the use of astronomy and physics in the poetry of Auden, Jeffers, MacLeish, and others.

2179.   Robinson, G. S., W. T. Williams, D. M. A. Mercer, and A. R. Manser. "Science in Science Fiction." *Advancement of Science* 22 (1965–66): 195–207.

Four papers on science fiction's adaptation of scientific ideas, including relativity theory with respect to modes of space travel, biological theory with respect to alien biologies, communications theory, and sociological theory.

2100.   Rottensteiner, Franz. "Einsteins Theorien in der Literatur." *Kürbiskern* 1 (1980): 88–101.

Analyzes how Einstein's theories were received and treated in literature, especially in science fiction. Discusses stories and novellas by Lenz and Roth, Dürrenmatt's play *Die Physiker*, the science fiction subgenre of space opera, and the science fiction theory of space warps.

2181.   Rueckert, William. "Literature and Ecology: An Experiment in Ecocriticism." *IowaR* 9.1 (1978): 71–86.

Attempts to apply the principles of biological ecology to the reading, teaching, and criticism of literature.

2182.   Sadler, Frank O. "Science and Fiction in the Science-Fiction Novel." *DAI* 36 (1975–76): 883A.

Relativity theory, the principle of indeterminacy, probability theory, and other principles of modern mathematical physics have effected change in the form and structure of the science-fiction novel. Sadler examines Delany's *Einstein Intersection*, Aldiss's *Report on Probability A*, and Vonnegut's *Slaughterhouse-Five*.

2183.   Samuelson, David N. "Studies in the Contemporary American and British Science Fiction Novel." *DA* 30 (1969–70): 1181A.

Includes discussions of the scientific basis of science fiction and the dramatization of scientific and quasi-scientific ideas in A. Clarke's *Childhood's End*, Asimov's *Caves of Steel*, Sturgeon's *More Than Human*, W. Miller's *Canticle for Leibowitz*, Budrys's *Rogue Moon*, and Ballard's *Crystal World*.

2184.   Sanders, Scott. "The Left-Handedness of Modern Literature." *TCL* 23 (1977): 417–36.

Suggests that modernist literature, in its emphasis on myth, intuition, and the unconscious, can be seen as a rebellion against the dominance of scientific rationalism in industrial society.

2185.   Sapiro, Leland. "The Faustus Tradition in the Early Science Fiction Story." *RQ* 1 (1964–65): 3–18, 43–57, 118–25.

Claims that the tendency for scientists to be destroyed by their own inventions in early science fiction stories (such as those published in Hugo Gernsback's magazine *Amazing Stories*) represents an unconscious recapitulation of the Faustus tradition. The modern reappearance of this theme largely entails a protest against Newtonianism.

2185a.   Schmidt, Stanley. "The Science in Science Fiction." *Many Futures, Many Worlds: Theme and Form in Science Fiction*. Ed. Thomas D. Clareson. Kent: Kent State UP, 1977. 27–49.

Examines several definitions of science fiction to determine the relation between science and fiction in the genre. Classifies scientific speculations in science fiction around the concepts of extrapolation and innovation. Sees a broad spectrum in science fiction ranging from works in which science serves only as background to works in which science is central.

2186.   Scholes, Robert. *Structural Fabulation: An Essay on Fiction of the Future*. Notre Dame: U of Notre Dame P, 1975. 111 pp.
        Rev. Willis E. McNelly, *America* 132 (1975): 485–86; Thomas Remington, *North American Review*, 260.4 (1975): 53–55; Jerome Klinckowitz, *MFS* 22 (1976–77): 322–24.

Chapter 2, "The Roots of Science Fiction," shows that contemporary science fiction represents a shift in fictional fabulation from a historical to a structural orientation that bases itself on developments in modern science and their consequences for human beings. "Structural fabulation is neither scientific in its methods nor a substitute for actual science. It is a fictional exploration of human situations made perceptible by the implications of recent science."

2187.   ———, and Eric S. Rabkin. *Science Fiction: History, Science, Vision*. New York: Oxford UP, 1977. 258 pp.
        Rev. Thomas J. Remington, *North American Review* ns 14.3 (1977): 85–87; George Guffey, *NCF* 34 (1979–80): 112–17.

The second part of this survey of science fiction examines how the sciences have provided theme and content for a variety of science fiction works. The topics examined are the scientific method, physics and astronomy, computers, thermodynamics, biology, psychology, and pseudoscience.

2188.   Schumacher, Ernst. "Schöne Literatur im Zeitalter der Wissenschaft." *NDL* 8 (1960): 115–29.

Examines the unique function of literature in an age of science. Uses Brecht's *Leben des Galilei* as a model of a literary work that depicts the role of science as subject matter for literature and that examines the function of literature in representing the revolutionary nature of science for contemporary society.

2189.   Schwartz, James M. "Loren Eiseley: The Scientist as Literary Artist." *GaR* 31 (1977): 855–71.

Loren Eiseley's works invalidate the alleged polarity between science and literature. His writings reveal a scientist-artist's confrontation with the self and with the world. *The Immense Journey, The Invisible Pyramid*, and *The Night Country*, among other works, display a penetrating insight into the "unexpected universe" of human beings.

2190.   Schwartz, Sheila. "Science Fiction: Bridge between the Two Cultures." *EJ* 60 (1971): 1043–51.

Analyzes works by Boulle, Orwell, Shute, Wyndham, and others to illustrate the themes, concerns, and importance of science fiction as a literary genre that bridges the gap between the strictly literary and the strictly scientific views of the world.

2191.   ———. "The World of Science Fiction." *EngR* 21.3 (1971): 27–40.
See item 170 for annotation.

2192.   Sewell, Elizabeth. "Science and Literature: Two Strands of the Imagination over One Hundred Years." *Commonweal* 84 (1966): 218–21. (See replies by D. E. Carr and Joseph F. Jackson, 448–49.)
See item 1490 for annotation.

2193.   Snow, C. P. "Science, Politics, and the Novelist: Or, The Fish and the Net." *KR* 23 (1961): 1–17.
Snow maintains that the abundance of stream-of-consciousness novels, coupled with the tendencies of the New Criticism, has inadvertently narrowed the range of the modern novel's topical province. Subjects such as politics and the experience of being a scientist cannot, he says, be adequately encompassed by the restrictive form of the modern English-language novel—a problem that demands a remedy. He discusses Joyce, Proust, Tolstoy, and other novelists.

2194.   Solotusski, I. "Faust und die Physiker." *KuL* 14 (1966): 276–91.
See item 1209 for annotation.

2195.   Spencer, Sharon. *Space, Time and Structure in the Modern Novel*. New York: New York UP, 1971. Chicago: Swallow, 1974. 251 pp.
Rev. J. H. Matthews, *CL* 25 (1973): 285–86.
This analysis of the structure of the modern architectonic novel stresses works by authors whose conception of space and time reflects an awareness of the speculations of modern science. Among the authors studied are Broch, Butor, Döblin, Dos Passos, Fuentes, Musil, Nin, Robbe-Grillet, Stein, and Woolf.

2196.   Stavrou, C. N. "Darwinism in American Drama." *The Impact of Darwinian Thought on American Life and Culture*. Papers Read at the Fourth Annual Meeting of the American Studies Association of Texas. Houston, 5 Dec. 1959. Austin: U of Texas P, 1959. 37–50.
Maintains that American drama has incorporated the principles of Darwinian naturalism in only a minor way, far less striking than the adaptation of Darwinism by the American novel. The course of American drama may be seen in part as a repudiation of the worldview arising from Darwinism and nineteenth-century science and rationalism.

2197.   Steininger, Alexander. "Scientists in Soviet Literature." *Survey* 52 (1964): 157–65.
Comments on the social and political elements of the portrayal of science and the scientist in Soviet literature. Among the works discussed are Kaverin's "Piece of Glass," Grekova's "Behind the Control Room," Golovanov's "Forge of Thunder," Granin's *Seekers*, and Gor's "University Quay."

2198. Stephan, Alexander. "Die wissenschaftlich-technische Revolution in der Literatur der DDR." *DU* 30.2 (1978): 18–34.

Traces the GDR's changing attitude toward the scientific-technological revolution from unlimited enthusiasm in the twenties to severe criticism of its antihumanism in the late fifties and the sixties. Outlines the shift in literature from a full espousal of the revolution's goals to a call for literary independence and a return to lyricism. Cites C. Wolf's path from *Der geteilte Himmel* to *Unter den Linden* as representative of this development.

2199. Stewart, David H. "Hephaestus and Athena: Science and Humanism Once More." *WHR* 24 (1970): 99–121.

This discussion of the main terminology, components, and personalities in the evolving dispute between science and the humanities includes topics like physics, pataphysics, utopia, and antiliterature and covers authors and scientists such as Snow, Richards, Heisenberg, Ionesco, and Lorenz.

2200. Suvin, Darko. "Science Fiction and The Genological Jungle." *Genre* 6 (1973): 251–73.

These notes toward the construction of a heuristic model for science fiction discuss naturalistic fiction, fantasy, myth, the folktale, the pastoral, and science fiction in relation to science, philosophy, and socioeconomic life.

2201. Talbot, Joanne H. "The Theme of 'The Scientist's Responsibility in the Nuclear Age' in Contemporary German Drama." *DA* 29 (1968–69): 2284A–85A.

Studies Brecht's *Leben des Galilei*, Zuckmayer's *Das Kalte Licht*, Kipphardt's *In der Sache J. Robert Oppenheimer*, Dürrenmatt's *Physiker*, and Jahnn's *Trümmer des Gewissens (Der staubige Regenbogen)*.

2202. Tatar, Maria M. *Spellbound: Studies on Mesmerism and Literature.* Princeton: Princeton UP, 1978. 293 pp.

See item 1501 for annotation.

2202a. Taylor, John. "Scientific Thought in Fiction and in Fact." *Science Fiction at Large: A Collection of Essays, by Various Hands, about the Interface between Science Fiction and Reality.* Ed. Peter Nicholls. London: Gollancz, 1976. 57–72.

Defines science fiction as fiction that explores the hypothetical possibilities of existing scientific theories. Discusses works that exemplify this definition, such as Wells's *Time Machine* and Blish's *Cities in Flight*.

2203. Teeuwissen, W. John. "The *Anatomy of Criticism* as Parody of Science." *SHR* 14 (1980): 31–42.

Maintains that Frye's *Anatomy of Criticism* is best understood as a highly personalized Menippean satire of science that uses the modern physics concept of complementarity and the biological methods of taxonomy and dissection as models for literary criticism.

2203a.   Thiele, Joachim. "Formen der Verwendung naturwissenschaftlicher Be-
         griffe in literarischen Texten." *Muttersprache* 78 (1968): 333–41.
Attempts a selected survey of scientific terms and concepts in German poetry and
prose since 1920, citing examples from Benn, Holz, Mann, Musil, Rilke, and
others.

2204.   Tucker, Frank H. "Patterns in German Science Fiction." *Extrapolation* 19
         (1977–78): 149–55.
This brief survey of typical themes in German science fiction, including scientific
utopias, atomic disasters, and the integrity of the individual, cites authors such as
Daumann, Dominik, H. Franke, Plischke, and Scheer.

2205.   Turner, John M. "The Response of Major American Writers to Darwinism,
         1859–1910." Diss. Harvard U, 1956.
Not seen for annotation.

2206.   Van Benschoten, Virginia A. K. "The Influence of Scientific and Socio-
         Scientific Ideologies on Some Examples of the Modern American Popular
         Novel." *DA* 21 (1961): 3792–93.
Studies the influence of Darwinism, Marxism, and Freudianism on twentieth-
century American best-sellers, sentimental and historical fiction, and detective stories
such as Hammett's *Maltese Falcon*.

2207.   Vietta, Silvio. "Wissenschaft, Literatur und Dunkelfelder der Erkenntnis."
         Akzente 26 (1979): 90–97.
Maintains that the source of new knowledge since the end of the nineteenth
century has been science rather than literature or philosophy. Uses Kraus's novel
Die letzten Tage der Menschheit to study the possibilities of portraying our rationalist-
technological civilization in contemporary literature.

2208.   Waggoner, Hyatt H. *The Heel of Elohim: Science and Values in Modern
         American Poetry*. Norman: U of Oklahoma P, 1950. 235 pp.
         Rev. Norman Holmes Pearson, *AL* 24 (1952–53): 397–99.
Studies the work of Robinson, Frost, T. S. Eliot, Jeffers, MacLeish, and H. Crane
against the background of modern science and scientific philosophies, such as positivism and materialistic naturalism. Specifically at issue is the response of these
poets to the dominant role science played in shaping modern values. The author
discusses throughout the book the tension between "scientific fact" and "poetic fact"
and poetry's function in revealing and determining values.

2209.   Walsh, Chad. "Attitudes toward Science in the Modern 'Inverted Uto-
         pia.' " *Extrapolation* 2 (1960–61): 23–26.
Comments on the portrayal of science and technology as an evil, antihuman force
in dystopian literature such as E. Waugh's "Love among the Ruins," A. Huxley's
Brave New World, Orwell's *1984*, and Vonnegut's *Player Piano*.

2210.   Warrick, Patricia S. *The Cybernetic Imagination in Science Fiction*. Diss. U of
         Wisconsin, Milwaukee, 1977. Cambridge: MIT P, 1980. 282 pp.

Rev. T. D. Clareson, *Extrapolation* 21 (1980): 185–86; Thomas C. Holy-oke, *AR* 38 (1980): 387; David M. Miller, *MFS* 26 (1980–81): 731–33.

The author undertakes to write a history of science fiction works concerning artificial intelligence; to analyze the subgenre for its recurrent images and patterns, stressing the scientific developments producing these; and to enter a critical judgment on the literary value of science fiction.

2211. Weber, Ronald. "The View from Space: Notes on Space Exploration and Recent Writing." *GaR* 33 (1979): 280–96.

Unpoetic astronauts are incapable of describing space in appropriately evocative language. Major writers such as Auden, Bellow, and Updike, however, do treat space in their works, seeing the earth in a new perspective and counterpointing the potential promise of space with the mundane concerns of the earthbound.

2212. Weimar, Karl S. "The Scientist and Society: A Study of Three Modern Plays." *MLQ* 27 (1966): 431–48.

Examines the scientist's responsibility to society and the problem of communication among the sciences, the arts, and society as reflected in Brecht's *Leben des Galilei*, Zuckmayer's *Das Kalte Licht*, and Dürrenmatt's *Physiker*.

2213. Weiss, Sydna S. "Scientists in Late Nineteenth and Twentieth Century German Literature: Their Projects, Personalities, and Problems." *DAI* 36 (1975–76): 2233A.

See item 1510 for annotation.

2214. Wetzels, Walter. "Relativitätstheorie gemeinverständlich: Techniken pop-ulärwissenschaftlicher Didaktik am Beispiel Albert Einsteins." *LiLi* 10 (1980): 14–24.

Outlines the literary and nonliterary devices Einstein used in his attempt to popularize his *Special Theory of Relativity*; notes especially his efforts to transform complex mathematical concepts into language comprehensible to the layperson.

2215. Yourgrau, Wolfgang. "On the New Physics and Modern Literature." *UDQ* 1 (1966–67): 29–41.

Traces the breakdown of belief in causality and determinism in the face of contemporary physical, chemical, and biological theory and comments on the role of creative literature in disseminating scientific concepts and in clarifying their social implications.

2216. Zander, Arlen R. "Science and Fiction: An Interdisciplinary Approach." *AJPhys* 43 (1975): 9–12.

Describes the objectives, structure, and developmental problems of an interdisciplinary course taught at East Texas State University. The theme of the course centers on the cross-fertilization between physics and science fiction. A typical reading list includes Allen's *Science Fiction: The Future*, Bronowski's *Science and Human Values*, Heinlein's *Stranger in a Strange Land*, F. Herbert's *Dune*, and A. Clarke's *Childhood's End*.

2217.   Ziolkowski, Theodore. "The Telltale Teeth: Psychodontia to Sociodontia."
         PMLA 91 (1976): 9–22.
This survey of odontological imagery in literature from ancient mythology to the
present notes the changes in cultural attitudes toward teeth. Ziolkowski emphasizes
the psychological and sociological connotations of dental motifs in twentieth-century
literature and comments on the portrayal of the dentist in contemporary works.
Authors discussed include Bellow, Benn, Grass, G. Greene, Koestler, Mann, and
Pynchon.

Individual Authors

Richard Adams (1920–)

2218.   Flanagan, Dennis. "To Each Generation Its Own Rabbits." *Wilson Library
         Bulletin* 49 (1975): 152–56.
Maintains that Adams's *Watership Down* is "a significant expression of the current
state of relations between the literary culture and the scientific culture" and succeeds
in merging the "two cultures" of C. P. Snow. Adams's novel is based on a large
body of scientific knowledge.

Dámaso Alonso (1898–)

2219.   Pérez Firmat, Gustavo. "Cosmology and the Poem: Dámaso Alonso's 'Sueño
         de las dos ciervas.' " *HR* 46 (1978): 147–71.
Examines Alonso's frequent and varied use of the metaphor of an "exploding
universe," which is based on the big bang theory of the physicist Georges Lemaître.
Treats poems such as "Ese muerto," "A Pizca," and "En el día de los difuntos" and
discusses in detail Alonso's "Sueño de las dos ciervas," in which the metaphor plays
a central role.

Antonin Artaud (1895–1948)

2220.   Demaitre, Ann. "The Theater of Cruelty and Alchemy: Artaud and *Le
         grand œuvre.*" *JHI* 33 (1972): 237–50.
Demonstrates that Artaud's dramaturgical methodology, developed in *Le théâtre
et son double*, parallels alchemical practices and principles. Stresses his dramaturgical
use of the alchemical concepts of *solutio, conjuntio, mortificatio, albedo,* and *rubedo.*

Isaac Asimov (1920–)

2221.   Portelli, Alessandro. "The Three Laws of Robotics: Laws of the Text, Laws
         of Production, Laws of Society." *SFS* 7 (1980): 150–56.
Examines the literary, social, and political implications of the three laws Asimov
devised to order his robot stories. He designed the laws to offset typically anti-

scientific depictions of robots in science fiction. Among the works discussed are his *Caves of Steel*, *Naked Sun*, and *I, Robot*.

2222. Wages, Jack D. "Isaac Asimov's Debt to Edgar Allan Poe." *PoeS* 6 (1973): 29.

"Asimov's science fiction mysteries contain the kind of minute scientific explanation that is the hallmark of Poe's science fiction, in combination with most of the elements of Poe's detective stories."

John Balderston (1889–1954)

2223. Stone, Edward. "From Henry James to John Balderston: Relativity and the '20's." *MFS* 1.2 (1955): 2–11.

Discusses how the popularization of Einstein's theory of relativity in the 1920s influenced the "time element" of Balderston's play *Berkley Square*. Balderston also derived thematic material for this play from H. James's time fantasy *The Sense of the Past*.

Pío Baroja y Nessi (1872–1956)

2224. Templin, E. H. "Pío Baroja and Science." *HR* 15 (1947): 165–92.

Outlines Baroja's knowledge of medicine, biology, physics, geology, astronomy, and the social sciences as revealed in his writings.

John Barth (1930–)

2225. Vitanza, Victor J. "The Novelist as Topologist: John Barth's *Lost in the Funhouse*." *TSLL* 19 (1977): 83–97.

"The particular method that Barth employs to create new forms from old fictions is that of the mathematician, specifically, the topologist, who is concerned with ways in which surfaces can be twisted, bent, pulled, stretched, or otherwise reformed from one shape into another. This new form that Barth creates in the novel is analogous to the Moebius strip, a topological form that he uses as the structure of 'Frame-Tale,' the first section of *Funhouse*, and as the organizing principle of the entire novel."

Samuel Beckett (1906–)

2226. Duggan, Brother I. Pius. "Relativity, Quantum Theory, and the Novels of Samuel Beckett." *DAI* 32 (1971): 2637A.

The principles of modern physics play a dominant role in the cosmology underlying Beckett's fiction. Relativity, chaos, uncertainty, and randomness figure prominently in his themes.

2227. Rabinovitz, Rubin. "Time, Space, and Verisimilitude in Samuel Beckett's Fiction." *JBeckS* 2 (1977): 40–46.

Beckett questions the reality of time and space. He is aware of Einstein's theories and Heisenberg's uncertainty principle, both of which contradict positivist assertions and demonstrate that our usual assumptions about reality are wrong. This essay treats *Watt*, *Molloy*, *Murphy*, *Malone Dies*, and other works.

2228.   Stein, William B. "Beckett's *Whoroscope*: Turdy Ooscopy." *ELH* 42 (1975): 125–55.
Analyzes *Whoroscope* to explore the intricacies of Beckett's satire of R. Descartes's astronomy, embryology, physiology, and philosophy.

Saul Bellow (1915–)

2229.   Held, George. "Men on the Moon: American Novelists Explore Lunar Space." *MQR* 18 (1979): 318–42.
See item 2384 for annotation.

2230.   Lycette, Ronald L. "Saul Bellow and the American Naturalists." *Discourse* 13 (1970): 435–49.
Bellow's novels, including *Mr. Sammler's Planet*, *The Dangling Man*, and *Augie March*, are characterized by a thematic concern with the environmental and biological influences on human beings—themes that also pervade the naturalism of writers such as Dos Passos, Dreiser, Farrell, and Norris.

2231.   Weinstein, Norman. "*Herzog*, Order and Entropy." *ES* 54 (1973): 336–46.
The protagonist of Bellow's *Herzog* was profoundly influenced by science and technology, and his search for order is guided by the principle of entropy.

Gottfried Benn (1886–1956)

2232.   Casper, M. Kent. "The Circle and the Centre: Symbols of Totality in Gottfried Benn." *GL&L* ns 26 (1972–73): 288–97.
Outlines Benn's neurological and biological theories of creative activity and discusses his use of circle imagery to symbolize a totalist perspective on the world. Among the works discussed are the poems "Verlorenes Ich," "Fragmente," and "Gesänge" and the essay "Strömungen."

2233.   Maniak, Beatrice H.-K. "Der Begriff 'Naturwissenschaft' in Benns frühen Werken." *DAI* 37 (1976): 1578A.
Examines Benn's integration of science—especially physiology and medicine—into his early works, such as "Gespräch," "Nocturno," "Ithaka," and "Gehirne."

2234.   Miller, Gerlinde F. "Die Bedeutung des Entwicklungsbegriffs für Menschenbild und Dichtungstheorie bei Gottfried Benn." *DAI* 40 (1980): 4616A.
Benn's rejection of C. Darwin's concept of evolution led him to search for new

insight into human origins and the source of creativity and to establish a theory of poetry.

Jorge Luis Borges (1899–1986)

2235. Franklin, Allan, and Paul M. Levitt. "Borges and Entropy." *Review* 1 (1975): 54–56.
   Maintains that entropy is a central theme of Borges's stories "Tlön, Uqbar, Orbis Tertius," "The Lottery in Babylon," "The Library of Babel," and "The God's Script."

Bertolt Brecht (1898–1956)

2236. Adler, Meinhard. *Brecht im Spiel der technischen Zeit. Naturwissenschaftliche, psychologische und wissenschaftstheoretische Kategorien im Werk Bertolt Brechts: Ein Beitrag zur Literaturpsychologie.* Berlin: Nolte, 1976. 292 pp.
   Includes a chapter that examines the impact of science on Brecht's literary work, especially *Leben des Galilei.* Among the works that most influenced Brecht are Jeans's *Mysterious Universe*, Eddington's *Nature of the Physical World*, and F. Bacon's *Novum Organum.*

2237. Hye, Allen E. "Bertolt Brecht and Atomic Physics." *STTH* 1 (1978): 157–68.
   Brecht's understanding of atomic physics allowed him to move beyond the Marxist view of science and humankind toward a study of humankind based on theories such as relativity and quantum mechanics. Hye examines the impact of contemporary science on Brecht's dramatic themes and form in works such as *Leben des Galilei* and *Schweyk im zweiten Weltkrieg.*

2238. Jevons, F. R. "Brecht's Life of Galileo and the Social Relations of Science." *Technology and Society* 4.3 (1968): 26–29.
   Treats scientific method, the popularization of science, science and authority, and the impact of science on society in Brecht's *Leben des Galilei.*

2239. Knopf, Jan. "Bertolt Brecht und die Naturwissenschaften: Reflexionen über den Zusammenhang von Natur- und Geisteswissenschaften." *BrechtJ* (1978): 13–38.
   Discusses modern physics, specifically quantum mechanics, and shows from Brecht's *Arbeitsjournal* that the poet eagerly pursued developments in this field. Maintains that the impact of Brecht's scientific interests on his literary work can be seen in his drama *Das Leben des Galilei* and in his novel *Die Geschäfte des Herrn Julius Cäsar.*

2240. Ley, Ralph. "Brecht: Science and Cosmic Futility." *GR* 40 (1965): 205–24.
   Traces the development of Brecht's conception of the metaphysical and existential implications of the scientific revolution, including his shift in outlook after reading Marx. Examines *Mann ist Mann, Im Dickicht der Städte*, and other plays in this light.

2241.   Mittenzwei, Werner. "Brecht und die Naturwissenschaften." *Brecht 73*. Ed. Werner Hecht. Berlin: Henschelverlag, 1973. 151–96.

Brecht took an active interest in the developments of modern physics, especially the new understanding of causality that emerges from quantum mechanics. He saw his scientific studies as an extension of his efforts to apply Marx's historical materialism to literature and theater. His *Leben des Galilei* and his fragment *Leben des Einstein* reveal his thinking about the new possibilities that accompany transformations in science.

2242.   Schroer, Dietrich. "Brecht's *Galileo*: A Revisionist View." *AJPhys* 48 (1980): 125–30.

Traces the history and metamorphosis of Brecht's play *Galileo* (1938–56), interprets his intent in writing it, and stresses the unhistorical, symbolic, and inappropriate ways that scientists and writers have used the figure of Galileo.

2243.   Schumacher, Ernst. " 'Leben des Galilei' und Leben und Werk Brechts." *WB* 11 (1965): 846–64.

Compares Brecht's depiction of Galileo and his historical situation in *Leben des Galilei* with Brecht himself and his attempt to transform contemporary dramaturgy. As Galileo developed a new scientific method so Brecht developed a non-Aristotelian theater appropriate for the scientific age.

2244.   Tietzel, Manfred. "Sympathy for the Devil: Die literarische Figur des Wissenschaftlers aus der Sicht der modernen Wissenschaftslehre." *Zeitschrift für allegemeine Wissenschaftstheorie* 11 (1980): 254–75.
         See item 1214 for annotation.

James Bridie (1888–1951)

2245.   Greene, Anne. "Bridie's Concept of the Master Experimenter." *SSL* 2 (1964–65): 96–110.

Discusses *The Sunlight Sonata*, *A Sleeping Clergyman*, and *The Queen's Comedy* and relates Bridie's treatment of evil to his attempt to synthesize the Calvinist concept of God with the Huxleian concept of evolution through the figure of a "Master Experimenter."

Hermann Broch (1886–1951)

2246.   Denninger, Eric. "Hermann Broch le scientifique." *Revue d'Allemagne* 6.1 (1974): 91–103.

Shows how Broch integrated science into literary works such as *Die unbekannte Grösse*, in which he explores the theme of relativity theory. The essay "Notizen zu einer systematischen Ästhetik" provides a good example of Broch's ability to fuse literary form with scientific exactitude and methods.

2247.   Schlant, Ernestine. "Hermann Broch and Modern Physics." *GR* 53 (1978): 69–75.

Assesses the quality of Broch's knowledge of modern physics—especially relativity and quantum mechanics—through a historical review of his studies in this field. Includes some discussion of Broch's application of modern physics to his writings.

2248. Walter-Echols, Elizabeth. "Relativity and Totality: Science as Structure and Imagery in Selected Texts from Hermann Broch." *DAI* 38 (1977): 2154A.
Broch incorporated elements of science, including relativity theory, atomic theory, and thermodynamics, in *Die Schlafwandler* and *Die Schuldlosen*.

2249. ———. "Science as Metaphor in Hermann Broch's *Die Schuldlosen*." *KPAB* (1979): 27–36.
The tea-party scene in the story "Erkaufte Mutter" from Broch's novel *Die Schuldlosen* is a composite image of modern reality based on both Einstein's relativity theory and aspects of impressionism. The scene attests to Broch's awareness of developments in contemporary science.

2250. Ziolkowski, Theodore. "Hermann Broch and Relativity in Fiction." *WSCL* 8 (1967): 365–76.
Assesses the extent to which Broch incorporated the principles of relativity into the structure and content of his novels. Analyzes *The Sleepwalkers* most extensively, with some discussion of *The Unknown Quantity* and *The Innocents*.

John Brunner (1934–)

2250a. Slocum, Robert R. *"Sic Parvis Magna*: Science, Technology, and Ecology in John Brunner's Science Fiction." *The Happening Worlds of John Brunner: Critical Explorations in Science Fiction*. Ed. Joe DeBolt. Port Washington: Kennikat, 1975. 147–66.
Studies Brunner's use of science and technology, his treatment of ecological issues, his characterization of scientists, and his depiction of the interactions between science and society in novels such as *The Sheep Look Up*, *The Jagged Orbit*, and *Stand on Zanzibai*.

Mikhail Afanasévich Bulgakov (1891–1940)

2251. Burgin, Diana L. "Bulgakov's Early Tragedy of the Scientist-Creator: An Interpretation of *The Heart of a Dog*." *SEEJ* 22 (1978): 494–508.
Discusses the complexity of the character of the professor in *The Heart of a Dog* and examines the relation of the novel's main themes to the Faust and Frankenstein traditions of the scientist-creator.

Michel Butor (1926–)

2252. Meakin, D., and E. Dand. "Alchemy and Optimism in Butor's *L'emploi du temps*." *FMLS* 15 (1979): 264–78.

A balanced interpretation of Butor's *L'emploi du temps* requires a recognition and understanding of the work's alchemical references and imagery. This essay surveys the principal alchemical metaphors and analyzes their role in the structural unity of the novel.

2253.   O'Donnell, Thomas D. "Michel Butor and the Tradition of Alchemy." *IFR* 2 (1975): 150–53.
Butor's preoccupation with the concept of transforming individuals and society through literature is rooted in alchemical tradition. In *Portrait of the Artist as a Young Monkey* Butor provides his readers with a key for deciphering the alchemical symbolism of his works.

Italo Calvino (1923–)

2254.   Biasin, Gian Paolo. "$\frac{4}{3}\pi r^3$ (spazio scientifico, spazio letterario)." *Letteratura e scienza nella storia della cultura italiana*. Atti del IX congresso dell'associazione internazionale per gli studi di lingua e letteratura italiana. Palermo, Messina, Catania, 21–25 Apr. 1976. Associazione internazionale per gli studi di lingua e letteratura italiana. Palermo: Manfredi, 1978. 860–72.
Surveys scientific, literary, and philosophic concepts of space and examines the reflection in literature of non-Euclidean geometry, relativity theory, the idea of spherical space, and cybernetics. Stresses the use of space in Calvino's *Cosmicomiche*, *Ti con zero*, and other works.

2255.   Illiano, Antonio. "Per una definizione della vena cosmogonica di Calvino: Appunti su *Le cosmicomiche* e *Ti con zero*." *Italica* 49 (1972): 291–301.
Shows that Calvino's creation of fantastic and absurd worlds in his novels owes much to abstract scientific and philosophic concepts drawn from Bruno, Galileo, Kant, and others.

2256.   Napoletano, Francesca Bernardini. "Letteratura e scienza, linguaggio poetico e linguaggio scientifico ne *Le cosmicomiche* e in *Ti con zero* di Italo Calvino." *Letteratura e scienza nella storia della cultura italiana*. Atti del IX congresso dell'associazione internazionale per gli studi di lingua e letteratura italiana. Palermo, Messina, Catania, 21–25 Apr. 1976. Associazione internazionale per gli studi di lingua e letteratura italiana. Palermo: Manfredi, 1978. 852–59.
Shows that Calvino recognizes the potential contributions of science to literary language and that his novels successfully integrate scientific method and terminology.

2257.   Petrucciani, Mario. "Calvino: 'Una geometria dei sentimenti e dei destini.' " *Scienza e letteratura nel secondo novecento. La ricerca letteraria in Italia tra algebra e metafora*. Turin: Mursia, 1978. 83–91.
Examines Calvino's conception of the interactions among science, philosophy, and literature. Views Calvino as a writer influenced by cybernetics, molecular biology, and astrophysics. Cites his novels *Cosmicomiche* and *Ti con zero*.

Paul Celan (1920–70)

2258.   Lyon, James K. "Paul Celan's Language of Stone: The Geology of the Poetic Landscape." *CollG* 3–4 (1974): 298–317.
Views Celan's use of technical terms from mining, geology, paleontology, geography, geomorphology, mineralogy, and petrology as ciphers of the poetic process.

Arthur C. Clarke (1917–)

2259.   Samuelson, David N. "*Childhood's End*: A Median Stage of Adolescence?" *SFS* 1 (1973–74): 4–17.
Discusses the flaws in the style, plot, characterization, and narrative structure of Clarke's *Childhood's End*, treating in part the failings in his attempted critique of science and scientism.

Paul-Louis-Charles-Marie Claudel (1868–1955)

2260.   Jones, Tobin H. "The Alchemical Language of Paul Claudel's *L'annonce faite à Marie*." *Symposium* 27 (1973): 35–45.
Suggests that alchemical imagery and traditional Christian allegory supplement each other in Claudel's play and that alchemy makes the work more universally intelligible and strengthens its message.

Joseph Conrad (1857–1924)

2261.   Bender, Todd K. "Scientific Models of Reality and Literary Impressionism in Joseph Conrad." *STTH* 1 (1978): 229–39.
Discusses F. Ford's claim that Conrad was a "literary impressionist" in the light of D. Hume's impressionist psychology, Comte's scientific positivism, Bergson's response to Comte, and the physiology of Helmholtz—all of which contributed to the rise of impressionism in painting. Explains the connection between artistic impressionism and the literary impressionism of Conrad and Ford.

2262.   Jacobs, Robert G. "H. G. Wells, Joseph Conrad, and the Relative Universe." *Conradiana* 1.1 (1968): 51–55.
The inspiration for Conrad's literary use of scientific themes such as the relativity of time can be traced to his meeting with Wells in 1896 and to Wells's scientific romances, especially *The Time Machine* and *The Invisible Man*. Wells's influence is especially evident in Conrad's *Heart of Darkness* and *Lord Jim*.

2263.   Karl, Frederick R. "Conrad, Wells, and the Two Voices." *PMLA* 88 (1973): 1049–65.
This survey and analysis of letters exchanged between Conrad and Wells beginning in 1896 reveals the aesthetic schism dividing the two novelists. The split arises over Wells's predilection for scientific and logical modes of novelistic expression versus Conrad's metaphoric and poetic naturalism. Karl views their relationship as an

exemplification of the conflict between science and art discussed later in C. P. Snow's 1959 Rede lecture, "The Two Cultures and the Scientific Revolution."

2264.   Kleiner, Elaine L. "Joseph Conrad's Forgotten Role in the Emergence of Science Fiction." *Extrapolation* 15 (1973–74): 25–34.

Discusses Conrad's and F. Ford's efforts to create in their joint novel *The Inheritors* (1901) a future-oriented literary genre capable of reflecting cultural and social change and decline. Includes comments on the author's conception of social evolution in a post-Darwinian age.

2265.   O'Hanlon, R. "Changing Scientific Concepts of Nature in the English Novel 1850–1920, with Special Reference to Joseph Conrad." Diss. Oxford U, 1977.

Not seen for annotation.

2266.   Renner, Stanley. "The Garden of Civilization: Conrad, Huxley, and the Ethics of Evolution." *Conradiana* 7 (1975–76): 109–20.

Conrad's evolutionary imagery in *Almayer's Folly*, *The Nigger of the "Narcissus,"* *Heart of Darkness*, and *Victory* closely parallels T. H. Huxley's evolution theory in the "Prolegomena" to *Evolution and Ethics* (1894). Central to Huxley's theory are an elaborate analogy between civilization and a garden and an emphasis on self-assertion as the motive force behind the struggle for existence in nature, both of which Conrad's works reflect.

2267.   Walton, James. "Conrad and Naturalism: *The Secret Agent*." *TSLL* 9 (1967–68): 289–301.

Although in *The Secret Agent* Conrad used a descriptive style reminiscent of Zola's naturalism to depict, for example, the complexities of female psychology, his style borders on satirizing naturalism and the scientistic attitude.

Robert Coover (1932–)

2268.   Friedman, Alan J. "Robert Coover's *Universal Baseball Association* and Modern Physics." *Trema* 1 (1976): 147–55.

Shows that the dominant metaphor of Coover's novel—probability or randomness—parallels the worldview inspired by contemporary quantum theory. The work's central character, J. Henry Waugh, faces a dilemma in relation to his game, the Universal Baseball Association, similar to that Einstein faced in relation to quantum theory.

2268a.   Hansen, Arlen J. "The Dice of God: Einstein, Heisenberg, and Robert Coover." *Novel* 10 (1976–77): 49–58.

Explores the relation between the language problems arising from the results of contemporary physics and Coover's handling of names and statistics in *The Universal Baseball Association*.

Hart Crane (1899–1932)

2269. Cowan, James C. "The Theory of Relativity and *The Bridge*." *HSL* 3 (1971): 108–15.
Crane's description of the curvature of the Brooklyn Bridge in *The Bridge* suggests parallels with Einstein's theory of relativity, especially its principle of the curvilinear path of light through world space.

2270. Morgan, John H. "Science and Technology as Sources of Literary Metaphor in Hart Crane's 'For the Marriage of Faustus and Helen' and *The Bridge*." *DAI* 40 (1979): 2064A.
"In the construction of myth-artifice [Crane] aimed at a wholism expressive of both spiritual and material realities, in the latter instance leading to use of scientific theory and technological artifact as sources for symbol and metaphor especially related to 'energy' as fundamentum."

2271. Waggoner, Hyatt Howe. "Hart Crane's Bridge to Cathay." *AL* 16 (1944–45): 115–30.
In his poetry, Crane attempted to synthesize the insights of both religious mysticism and science, though his scientific knowledge was inadequate for the task. At the same time, however, he tended to distinguish radically between poetic and scientific truth, obscuring the relations between them. Waggoner discusses Crane's ambiguous attitude toward science, referring to such works as *The Bridge* and *White Buildings*.

E. E. Cummings (1894–1962)

2272. Mattfield, Mary S. "Cummings' 'Let's, from Some Loud Unworld's Most Rightful Wrong.' " *Expl* 26 (1967–68): item 32.
The cited poem combines Cummings's customary rejection of scientism with a mature philosophical outlook.

Samuel R. Delany (1942–)

2273. Sadler, Frank. "Relativity and the Universe of Fiction." *WGCR* 9 (1977): 8–33.
Examines Delany's *Einstein Intersection* to explore the relation between mathematical physics and the form and content of fiction. The novel's literary and philosophical center is the intersection between the Einsteinian world of relativity and the Gödelian world of mathematics.

Alfred Döblin (1878–1957)

2274. Brown, Barry A. "Alchemical Themes and Gnostic Myth in Alfred Döblin's Novel *Wallenstein*." *DAI* 41 (1980): 684A–85A.
Identifies and explicates the fictional structure of Döblin's historical novel. The work's functional aspects are rooted in gnostic mythification and alchemical imagery.

Norman Douglas (1868–1952)

2275.   Flory, Evelyn A. "Norman Douglas and the Scientific Spirit." *ELT* 14 (1971): 167–77.
Douglas's knowledge of geology, zoology, and botany played a modest though important role in both his fiction and his other literary works. This essay traces his development as a scientist during his early years, comments on his scientific and quasi-scientific writing, and discusses the scientific components of works such as *Old Calabria, Unprofessional Tales, Fountains in the Sand,* and *Alone.*

2276.   ———. "Norman Douglas: The Role of Nature." *DA* 30 (1969–70): 3456A.
Douglas's interest in and knowledge of natural science are reflected in his literary productions.

Theodore Dreiser (1871–1945)

2277.   Katope, Christopher G. "*Sister Carrie* and Spencer's *First Principles.*" *AL* 41 (1969–70): 64–75.
Discusses the influence of Spencer's *First Principles* on Dreiser's naturalism in *Sister Carrie.* The novel incorporates Spencer's laws of evolution, force, and motion.

2278.   McAleer, John J. "Dreiser's 'Notes on Life': Responses to an Impenetrable Universe." *LC* 38 (1972): 78–91.
Discusses the principal themes Dreiser refers to in his notebooks entitled "Notes on Life." The findings of science, especially physical science, often served as points of departure for his entries, though he frequently blended science with philosophic and religious reflections.

Robert Duncan (1919–)

2279.   Cohn, Jack R., and Thomas J. O'Donnell. "An Interview with Robert Duncan." *ConL* 21 (1980): 513–48.
Duncan comments on his career as a poet and on some details of his poetry, briefly referring to his use of Darwinism and to the concept of DNA as an analogy for a linguistic code.

2280.   Simmons, Kenith L. "Old Maids and the Domination of the Sea: Robert Duncan, Stan Brakhage and Robert Kelly on the Self in Context." *DAI* 40 (1979): 1461A–62A.
Uses modern physics and A. N. Whitehead's philosophy of organicism to illustrate the notion that the world constitutes an organic system with no definitive divisions. Emphasizes the relation of this concept to the thematic concerns of Duncan's *Roots and Branches,* Kelly's *Common Shore,* and the films of Brakhage, also noting their relation to the "projective poetics" of Olson.

Lawrence Durrell (1912–)

2280a. Baldanza, Frank. "Lawrence Durrell's 'Word Continuum.' " *Crit* 4.2 (1960–61): 3–17.

Notes how the structure and metaphors in *The Alexandria Quartet* reflect the thoughts about the impact of modern science on literature that Durrell expressed in his lectures on modern poetry.

2281. Bork, Alfred M. "Durrell and Relativity." *CentR* 7 (1963): 191–203.

Durrell's interest in the theory of relativity, explicit in *A Key to Modern British Poetry* (1952), informs the structure, themes, narrative point of view, and handling of time in *The Alexandria Quartet*.

2282. Brown, Sharon L. "Lawrence Durrell and Relativity." *DA* 26 (1966): 7310.

Examines the literary devices in *The Alexandria Quartet* that express Durrell's understanding of both Einstein's theory of the relativity of time and space and the corresponding relativity of human knowledge and action.

2283. Cartwright, Michael P. "*The Alexandria Quartet*: A Comedy for the Twentieth Century: Or, Lawrence Durrell, the Pardoner and His Miraculous Pig's Knuckle." *DA* 31 (1970–71): 5391A.

Modern physics and psychology provided the model for some of the literary innovations of theme and structure Durrell used in works such as *The Black Book*, *An Irish Faustus*, and *The Alexandria Quartet*.

2284. Creed, Walter G. "Contemporary Scientific Concepts and the Structure of Lawrence Durrell's *Alexandria Quartet*." *DA* 30 (1969–70): 1165A.

Maintains that Durrell was unsuccessful in his attempt to translate Einstein's theory of relativity and the theories of other scientists and philosophers into an innovative literary form.

2285. ———. *The Muse of Science and* The Alexandria Quartet. Norwood: Norwood, 1977. Folcroft: Folcroft, 1978. 110 pp.
Rev. George Blake, *MFS* 24 (1978–79): 310–14.

Assesses the extent to which Durrell maintains fidelity to science as muse in *The Alexandria Quartet*. Examines his ideas of time and space, causality and identity, and truth and reality as influenced primarily by relativity theory, quantum mechanics, and other aspects of contemporary physics.

2286. Dawson, Carl. "From Einstein to Keats: A New Look at *The Alexandria Quartet*." *FWF* 1 (1974): 109–28.

Appraises Durrell's claim that *The Alexandria Quartet* is based on Einstein's relativity proposition. Maintains that relativity theory, though not irrelevant to Durrell's work, plays a subordinate role in the *Quartet*. "For all Durrell's professions of having written an Einsteinian, relativistic novel, in fact the *Quartet* expresses an almost anachronistically traditional sense of art and life."

2287. Drescher, Horst W. "Raumzeit: Zur Struktur von Lawrence Durrells *Alexandria Quartet*." *NS* 70 (1971): 308–18.

Claims that Durrell tried to apply Einstein's concept of a space-time continuum in his *Alexandria Quartet*. The first three novels allegedly correspond to three-dimensional space, and the fourth novel introduces the time element. Drescher points out that Durrell recognized that he had confused Bergson's concept of time with Einstein's.

2288.   Franklin, Steve. "Space-Time and Creativity in Lawrence Durrell's *Alexandria Quartet*." *PCL* 5 (1979): 55–61.
Claims that Durrell's *Alexandria Quartet* is largely an attempt to reconcile science and art. Focuses on his treatment of space and time as influenced by Einstein's relativity theory.

2289.   Friedman, Alan Warren. "A 'Key' to Lawrence Durrell." *WSCL* 8 (1967): 31–42.
Draws on Durrell's comments in *A Key to Modern British Poetry* (1952) to explain his experiments with narrative in *The Alexandria Quartet*. Maintains that the scientific concepts of relativity and indeterminacy underlie his emphasis on the subjective.

2290.   Lebas, Gérard. "The Mechanisms of Space-Time in *The Alexandria Quartet*." *Caliban* 6.1 (1970): 79–97.
Appraises the success of Durrell's various devices and techniques for blending the temporal and spatial components of *The Alexandria Quartet*. Focuses on the "mechanisms [Durrell] has employed to transform Alexandria into the 'gravitational field' of action, to distort reality, to dissolve time, and to derive his creation from the 'Relativity Proposition.' "

2291.   Lewis, Nancy W. "Lawrence Durrell's *Alexandria Quartet* and the Rendering of Post-Einsteinian Space." *DAI* 37 (1977): 7143A–44A.
Demonstrates Durrell's literary use of relativity theory with a view to determining his overall conception of the structure of reality.

2292.   Wedin, Warren. "The Unity of a Continuum: Relativity and *The Alexandria Quartet*." *DAI* 32 (1971): 1535A–36A.
Explores the meaning of Durrell's critical theory in *A Key to Modern British Poetry*, which emphasizes the literary "translation" of scientific themes and principles. Discusses Durrell's own "translation" of relativity theory into *The Alexandria Quartet*.

Friedrich Dürrenmatt (1921–)

2293.   Morley, Michael. "Dürrenmatt's Dialogue with Brecht: A Thematic Analysis of *Die Physiker*." *MD* 14 (1971–72): 232–42.
Explores Dürrenmatt's response in *Die Physiker* to the view of science and the social responsibility of the scientist that Brecht reveals in *Leben des Galilei*.

2294.   Tietzel, Manfred. "Sympathy for the Devil: Die literarische Figur des Wissenschaftlers aus der Sicht der modernen Wissenschaftslehre." *Zeitschrift für allgemeine Wissenschaftstheorie* 11 (1980): 254–75.
See item 1214 for annotation.

George Alec Effinger (1947–)

2295.   Sklepowich, Edward A. "The Fictive Quest: Effinger's *What Entropy Means to Me.*" *Extrapolation* 18 (1977): 107–15.
Briefly reviews Effinger's novel, which parodies the entropy theme.

T. S. Eliot (1888–1965)

2296.   Appleman, Philip. "The Dread Factor: Eliot, Tennyson, and the Shaping of Science." *ColF* ns 3.4 (1974): 32–38.
Shows that, far from being antithetical to poetry, science often serves as the occasion for its creation. Specifically discusses Tennyson's response to science in *In Memoriam* and Eliot's in *The Waste Land*.

2296a.   Foster, Steven. "Relativity and *The Waste Land*: A Postulate." *TSLL* 7 (1965): 77–95.
Examines the popularization of Einstein's theory of relativity and the likelihood of Eliot's familiarity with the idea. Maintains that *The Waste Land* resembles Einstein's theory in that it is a "mathematical and symbolic scheme of forces, pressures, tensions, oscillations, and waves. It does not adhere to any classical structure by the character of its rhythms, stanzaic pattern, vocabulary, or general style."

2297.   McMorris, M. N. "Time and Reality in Eliot and Einstein." *Main Currents in Modern Thought* 29 (1972–73): 91–99.
Discusses Eliot's acquaintance with Einstein's theory of relativity and establishes concordances between Einstein's thought and Eliot's treatment of time in *The Waste Land*, *The Four Quartets*, and other poems.

2298.   Simpson, David L. "Four Philosophical Poems: Ideas of Order in Donne, Pope, Tennyson, and Eliot." *DAI* 38 (1977): 2781A.
See item 806 for annotation.

2299.   Waggoner, Hyatt H. "T. S. Eliot and 'The Hollow Men.' " *AL* 15 (1943–44): 101–26.
Traces the intellectual and cultural tradition from which Eliot's assessment of modern science and scientific values emerged. Specifically, the influence of his close study of Bradley, Bergson, and Hulme informed his tendency toward scientific culture. Waggoner cites passages from *The Waste Land*, "The Hollow Men," *The Rock*, and other works.

2300.   Wasson, Richard. " 'Like a Burnished Throne': T. S. Eliot and the Demonism of Technology." *CentR* 13 (1969): 302–16.
Sigfried Giedion's account of the relation between technology and the formation of symbol systems in *Mechanization Takes Command* frames this discussion of the impact of technology's devaluation of symbol on the form, structure, and theme of Eliot's "Game of Chess." Eliot's formal use of technology, when juxtaposed against the attitudes of most technologists, casts light on the "two cultures" dispute.

James Thomas Farrell (1904–79)

2301.   Farrell, James T. "Farrell Looks at His Writing." *TCL* 22 (1976): 11–
        18.
Farrell describes his motivation for writing, his method, some of his central
themes, and the major influences on his work, such as Freud's theories and Zola's
concept of heredity as affecting the formation of character.

2302.   Mitchell, Richard. "James T. Farrell's Scientific Novel." *DA* 24 (1964):
        5413.
Mitchell attempts to define an "experimental method of literary critique"—a
kind of "literary naturalism"—which he then uses to explicate the scientific qualities
of Farrell's trilogy, *Studs Lonigan*.

William Faulkner (1897–1962)

2303.   Beidler, Peter G. "A Darwinian Source for Faulkner's Indians in 'Red
        Leaves.' " *SSF* 10 (1973): 421–23.
Faulkner may have drawn on C. Darwin's *Beagle* journal for information about
Indians and for the title "Red Leaves."

2303a. Franklin, Rosemary. "Animal Magnetism in *As I Lay Dying*." *AQ* 18
        (1966): 24–34.
The theme of animal magnetism pervades Faulkner's novel, and the pseudoscience
is central to an understanding of Cash Bundren's list of reasons for his method of
constructing his mother's coffin.

2304.   Gidley, Mick. "Another Psychologist, a Physiologist and William Faulk-
        ner." *ArielE* 2 (1971): 78–86.
Maintains that Faulkner's treatment of determinism in relation to the physiology
and sexual behavior of his characters may have been influenced by Havelock Ellis's
Little Essays of Love and Virtue (1922) and Louis Berman's *Glands Regulating Personality*
(1921). Also comments on Faulkner's relation to Freudian psychology.

2305.   Ringold, Francine. "The Metaphysics of Yoknapatawpha County: 'Airy
        Space and Scope for Your Delirium.' " *HSL* 8 (1975–76): 223–40.
Examines ideas and concepts central to the space-time continuum theory Faulkner
used in *Absalom, Absalom!* The work is an "artistic testimony of concepts espoused
systematically by Bergson, Einstein, and Minkowski."

2306.   Ryan, Steven T. "Faulkner and Quantum Mechanics." *WHR* 33 (1979):
        329–39.
The fictional structures of *The Sound and the Fury*, *As I Lay Dying*, *Light in August*,
and *Absalom, Absalom!* depend on Faulkner's use of varying, though complementary,
character descriptions, which, nevertheless, do not sharply define his characters.
Such complementarity of perspective resembles the paradigm of quantum mechanics
developed by Bohr and Heisenberg between 1925 and 1928.

Lawrence Monsanto Ferlinghetti (1919–)

2307.   Ianni, L. A. "Lawrence Ferlinghetti's Fourth Person Singular and the Theory of Relativity." *WSCL* 8 (1967): 392–406.

In the novel *Her* and in a number of poems, Ferlinghetti explores a "relational" epistemology based on the philosophical implications of relativity theory.

Thomas Hornsby Ferril (1896–)

2308.   Richards, Robert F. "Science, Ferril, and Poetry." *PrS* 21 (1947): 312–18.

This critical commentary on Ferril's poetry notes his synthesis of scientific insight with poetic sensibility. Among the works discussed are *Westering*, *Fort Vasquez*, and *Something Starting Over*.

Francis Scott Fitzgerald (1896–1940)

2309.   Scott, Robert I. "A Sense of Loss: Entropy vs. Ecology in *The Great Gatsby*." *QQ* 82 (1975): 559–71.

Fitzgerald's novel concretizes the second law of thermodynamics by portraying the corrupting influence of time and wealth. The work may illustrate principles of entropy theory derived from H. Adams's *Degradation of the Democratic Dogma* and W. Thomson's "Universal Tendency in Nature to the Dissipation of Energy" (1852).

Ford Madox Ford (1873–1939)

2310.   Huntley, H. Robert. "*The Good Soldier* and *Die Wahlverwandtschaften*." *CL* 19 (1967): 133–41.

Emphasizes the resemblance of structure and content between Goethe's *Elective Affinities* and Ford's *Good Soldier*. Suggests that Goethe's novel inspired Ford's theme of evolutionary determinism.

Richard Foreman (1937–)

2311.   Falk, Florence A. "Physics and the Theatre: Richard Foreman's *Particle Theory*." *ETJ* 29 (1977): 395–404.

Describes Foreman's attempt to reorient consciousness toward new modes of perception by incorporating metaphors and concepts drawn from physics into the theme and structure of his plays. Stresses Foreman's *Particle Theory*.

John Fowles (1926–)

2312.   Nadeau, Robert L. "Fowles and Physics: A Study of *The Magus, a Revised Version*." *JML* 8 (1980–81): 261–74.

In *The Magus* Fowles gives thematic expression to concepts drawn from quantum theory, relativity, and other aspects of contemporary physics. His knowledge of physics informs his existential outlook.

Max Frisch (1911–)

2313.   Roisch, Ursula. "Max Frischs Auffassung vom Einfluss der Technik auf den Menschen—nachgewiesen am Roman *Homo Faber*." *WB* 13 (1967): 950–67.
Maintains that the novel *Homo Faber* presupposes a break in the original relationship between human beings and nature due to the intervention of technology and scientific accuracy—that artificial domain created by humankind itself. The protagonist, a writer and architect, explores the possibility of finding meaning in a world transformed by technology.

Robert Frost (1874–1963)

2314.   Cook, Raymond A. "Robert Frost: Poetic Astronomer." *EUQ* 16 (1960): 32–39.
Comments on Frost's allusions to astronomical phenomena in poems such as "The Star-Splitter," "Canis Major," "A Loose Mountain," and "It Bids Pretty Fair."

2315.   Harris, Kathryn G. "Robert Frost and Science: The Shaping Metaphor of Motion in the Poems." *DAI* 37 (1976): 967A.
Frost's imagery of motion may stem from his interest in and knowledge of physics, biology, astronomy, and other sciences.

2316.   Hiers, John T. "Robert Frost's Quarrel with Science and Technology." *GaR* 25 (1971): 182–205.
Poems such as "The Star-Splitter," "The Self-Seeker," "The Line-Gang," "Mowing," and "The Pasture" suggest that Frost objected to science and technology because of their elements of crass materialism as well as their tendency to anaesthetize aesthetic sensitivity, though he willingly accorded science due respect for its legitimate accomplishments.

2316a.   Johnson, Andy. "Topical Philosophy of Robert Frost: Science, Politics, Social Philosophy, Education." *DAI* 34 (1973): 2643A.
Deals in part with Frost's view of the limitations of science with respect to humanistic and spiritual concerns.

2317.   Waggoner, Hyatt H. "The Humanistic Idealism of Robert Frost." *AL* 13 (1941–42): 207–23.
Frost's poetry frequently reflects his disillusion with and rejection of the general enthusiasm for science that dominated the intellectual atmosphere of his Harvard years. Waggoner traces the development of Frost's humanistic response to scientism by analyzing passages from poems such as "The Star-Splitter," "Build Soil," "West Running Brook," "Riders," and "Desert Places." He also notes that Frost's humanism is rooted in Emersonian and Jamesian philosophy.

Federico García Lorca (1899–1936)

2318. Beck-Agular, Vera F. de. "Entomological Symbols in the Capeks and García Lorca." *LE&W* 9 (1965): 96–103.

Briefly comments on how García Lorca and J. Capek and K. Capek adapted their knowledge of entomology to the dramatic and symbolic portrayal of human life. Treats Lorca's play *The Spell of the Butterfly* and the Capeks' *World We Live In*.

Gabriel García Márquez (1928–)

2319. Stevens, L. Robert, and Vela G. Roland. "Jungle Gothic: Science, Myth, and Reality in *One Hundred Years of Solitude*." *MFS* 26 (1980–81): 262–66.

Discusses García Márquez's stylistic reconciliation of the apparently disparate scientific-technological and mythopoeic modes of perceiving reality in *One Hundred Years of Solitude*.

André Gide (1869–1951)

2320. Bettinson, C. D. "Gide's Use of Technical Vocabulary—A Note on the Disability of Anthime Armand-Dubois." *ML* 53 (1972): 112–15.

A brief discussion of Gide's satiric use of technical medical terms to describe the character Anthime's disability in *Les caves du Vatican*.

Ellen Glasgow (1873–1945)

2321. Raper, Julius R., Jr. "Ellen Glasgow and Darwinism, 1873–1906." *DA* 27 (1966–67): 2541A–42A.

Traces the impact of C. Darwin's *Origin of Species* on Glasgow's first six novels, two of her early short stories, and her book of poetry.

Dave Godfrey (1938–)

2322. Lecker, Robert. "Quantum Physics and Nouveau Roman. *The New Ancestors*." *American Review of Canadian Studies* 10.2 (1980): 1–15.

The lack of any clear structural pattern and the shifting temporal perspective in Godfrey's *New Ancestors* suggest an indebtedness to the principles of the French *nouveau roman* as well as to postmodern theories of quantum mechanics.

Hermann Hesse (1877–1962)

2323. Derrenberger, John. "Who Is Leo? Astrology in Hermann Hesse's *Die Morgenlandfahrt*." *Monatshefte* 67.2 (1975): 167–72.

Suggests that the characterization of Leo and his relationship to H. H. in Hesse's *Morgenlandfahrt* is based on astrology.

Jakob van Hoddis (1887–1942)

2324.   Arnold, Armin. "Halley's Comet and Jakob van Hoddis' Poem 'Welt-ende.' " *RNL* 9 (1978): 47–58.

Shows that Hoddis wrote the poem "Weltende" in 1910 in the context of the expected arrival of Halley's comet. The poem mocks the hysteria of 1909–10, which the press fueled with pseudoscientific speculations about possible cosmic catastrophes. Later critics, ignorant of the background, have missed the humor and have read the poem as one of the earliest examples of expressionist poetry.

A. E. Housman (1859–1936)

2325.   Haber, Tom Burns. "A. E. Housman: Astronomer-Poet." *ES* 35 (1954): 154–58.

The recurrent circular or elliptical structure of Housman's poems reflects his intense lifelong interest in astronomy. This essay maintains that the astronomer's circle or ellipsis became the norm of Housman's creative, shaping mind.

2326.   ———. "Housman and Lucretius." *CJ* 58 (1962–63): 173–82.

Notes parallels of theme and style between Lucretius's *De rerum natura* and Housman's poetry, emphasizing Housman's indebtedness to Lucretius for cosmological imagery.

2327.   Wysong, J. N. "A. E. Housman's Use of Astronomy." *Anglia* 80 (1962): 295–301.

Housman uses astronomical and astrological imagery in a highly imaginative way in his poetry. Wysong cites examples from poems such as "Reveille," "Revolution," and "Astronomy."

Aldous Huxley (1894–1963)

2328.   Aldridge, Alexandra. "*Brave New World* and the Mechanist/Vitalist Controversy." *CLS* 17 (1980): 116–32.

Maintains that the controversy in the philosophy of science between the scientific reductionism of Cartesian mechanism and the doctrine of vitalism, principally associated with Bergson, significantly informs the theme of Huxley's antiscientistic dystopia. Specifically, Huxley's London society of 632 AF (After Ford) represents the consequences of mechanist philosophy, while the Reservation and John Savage embody vitalist principles.

2329.   Bentley, Joseph G. "Aldous Huxley and the Anatomical Vision." *DA* 22 (1961): 3655–56.

Examines Huxley's satiric use of physiological imagery in *Point Counter Point* and other works.

2330.   ———. "Huxley's Ambivalent Responses to the Ideas of D. H. Lawrence." *TCL* 13 (1967–68): 139–53.

Though in *Point Counter Point* Huxley tried to express D. H. Lawrence's ideas on physical reality sympathetically, the novel's physiological and anatomical satire conflicted with and ultimately negated Lawrence's ideas.

2331. ———. "Semantic Gravitation: An Essay on Satiric Reduction." *MLQ* 30 (1969): 3–19.

"Satiric style makes extensive use of the principle of semantic gravitation; and semantic gravitation is what takes place when an utterance tends to pull the props from under a high-valued, alembicated image." Bentley illustrates the principle by discussing Huxley's use of reductive physiological imagery in works such as *Point Counter Point*, *Eyeless in Gaza*, and *Island*.

2332. Clareson, Thomas D. "The Classic: Aldous Huxley's *Brave New World*." *Extrapolation* 2 (1960–61): 33–40.

Traces the major themes of Huxley's novel, assesses its place in the literary tradition of utopias and dystopias, and comments on his literary extrapolations from fields such as embryology and psychology.

2333. Firchow, Peter. "Science and Conscience in Huxley's *Brave New World*." *ConL* 16 (1975): 301–16.

Examines Huxley's vision of the future in *Brave New World*, discussing influences such as Bertrand Russell, J. B. S. Haldane, and developments in genetics and psychology.

2334. ———. "Wells and Lawrence in Huxley's *Brave New World*." *JML* 5 (1976): 260–78.

Examines how Huxley's antipathy toward Wells's vision of science and scientific utopias affected the composition of *Brave New World*. Also treats Huxley's relation to the social philosophy of D. H. Lawrence.

2335. Marovitz, Sanford E. "Aldous Huxley's Intellectual Zoo." *PQ* 48 (1969): 495–507.

Huxley used animal imagery and zoological allusions to characterize his ideal of the "amphibious" human being—a synthesis of body, mind, and spirit.

2336. Meckier, Jerome. "Quarles among the Monkeys: Huxley's Zoological Novels." *MLR* 68 (1973): 268–82.

In its characters, plot, figures, and ambiance, *Point Counter Point* is a bestiary, the major resident of which is Philip Quarles. Meckier traces Huxley's antievolutionary satire to the anonymous eighteenth-century work *The Hermit*. He also briefly discusses the zoological imagery of *Antic Hay*, *Island*, *Ape and Essence*, and other works.

2337. Quina, James. "The Mathematical-Physical Universe: A Basis for Multiplicity and the Quest for Unity in *Point Counter Point*." *SNNTS* 9 (1977): 428–44.

Huxley uses atomic, cellular, physiological, and evolutionary imagery to suggest the multiplicity of the universe and light imagery to convey the unity. The juxtaposition of mathematical and physical figures with aesthetic and moral symbolism informs the theme and structure of the novel. Quina notes that E. A. Burtt's *Metaphysical Foundations of Modern Science* (1924) influenced Huxley's thought.

2338.   Wheeler, Wayne B. "The Horror of Science in Politics: Prophecy and the Crisis of Human Values in Mary Shelley's *Frankenstein* and Aldous Huxley's *Brave New World.*" *DAI* 40 (1979): 2246A.
See item 1893 for annotation.

2338a.   Whitesel, George E. "Evolution as Metaphor: Patterns of Continuity in the Thought and Aesthetic of Aldous Huxley." *DAI* 31 (1971): 6027A.
Partly concerns the impact of evolutionary principles such as complexity, non-specialization, growth, and wholeness on Huxley's aesthetic.

Robinson Jeffers (1887–1962)

2339.   Schwartz, Delmore. "The Enigma of Robinson Jeffers, Part I: Sources of Violence." *Poetry* 55 (1939–40): 30–38.
This review of *The Selected Poetry of Robinson Jeffers* includes an analysis of Jeffers's poetic critique of science and technology.

2340.   Scott, Robert I. "Robinson Jeffers' Poetic Use of Post-Copernican Science." *DA* 26 (1965): 1049.
Discusses the effectiveness of Jeffers's poetic use of ideas from post-Copernican astronomy, evolution theory, atomism, physics, and nuclear physics.

David Michael Jones (1895–1974)

2341.   Dilworth, Thomas R. "David Jones's Use of a Geology Text for *The Anathemata.*" *ELN* 15 (1977–78): 115–19.
Jones used William Whitehead Watt's *Geology for Beginners* (1929) in composing his poem.

James Joyce (1882–1941)

2342.   DiBernard, Barbara J. "Alchemical Number Symbolism in *Finnegans Wake.*" *JJQ* 16 (1978–79): 433–46.
Explicates the alchemical significance of Joyce's symbolic allusions in *Finnegans Wake* to the numbers 1, 2, 3, 4, and 10. The numbers shape the texture and structure of the work and function on both microcosmic and macrocosmic levels.

2343.   ————. *Alchemy and* Finnegans Wake. Diss. State U of New York, Binghamton, 1976. State U of New York P, 1980. 163 pp. (Abstract in *DAI* 37 (1976): 1540A.)
Rev. Bernard Benstock, *MFS* 27 (1981–82): 310–16; Mary T. Reynolds, *JJQ* 20 (1982–83): 235–40.

Alchemy serves as the principal metaphor for the artistic process in *Finnegans Wake*. This essay examines various aspects of Joyce's use of the pseudoscience and discusses the sources of his alchemical knowledge.

2344. ———. "Alchemy in *Finnegans Wake*." *JJQ* 14 (1976–77): 274–89.
"*Finnegans Wake* is the result of a modern alchemical process. The book contains references to alchemical techniques, processes, chemicals, equipment, and ingredients, as well as to various alchemists and alchemical theories. These form a web of allusions, the explication of which gives us an important underlying metaphor for the artistic process."

2345. Doxey, William S. " 'Ithaca's' Westward-Turning Earth: A New Portal of Discovery in *Ulysses*." *JJQ* 7 (1969–70): 371–74.
Joyce's reference to the westward rotation of the earth at the conclusion of the Ithaca section of *Ulysses* may have been an intentional error intended to satirize Bloom's scientific pretensions.

2346. Fleischman, Avrom. "Science in Ithaca." *WSCL* 8 (1967): 377–91. Rpt. in *Fiction and the Ways of Knowing: Essays on British Novels*. Austin: U of Texas P, 1978. 136–48.
Studies Joyce's creative use of classical mechanics and astronomy and modern science in the Ithaca section of *Ulysses* as background to an approach to some of his central symbolic themes. Considers especially Joyce's relation to Einstein's relativity theory.

2347. Herr, Cheryl T. "The Unity and Limits of Knowledge in James Joyce's *Ulysses*." *DAI* 39 (1979): 7340A.
Chapters 2 and 3 discuss the unity of art and science in *Ulysses*.

2347a. Kumar, Shiv K. "Space-Time Polarity in *Finnegans Wake*." *MP* 54 (1956–57): 230–33.
Maintains that relativity theory is one source of Joyce's concept of space-time polarity, around which the episodes and characters of *Finnegans Wake* revolve.

2348. Langdon, M. "Some Reflections of Physics in *Finnegans Wake*." *JJQ* 17 (1979–80): 359–77.
Relates structural patterns of the *Wake* to basic conceptions of quantum mechanics and to relativistic physics. For example, "enforced matter-antimatter beam collisions" are a dramatic physical analogue to the *Wake*'s structural principle of polarized opposites.

2349. Littmann, Mark E., and Charles A. Schweighauser. "Astronomical Allusions, Their Meaning and Purpose, in *Ulysses*." *JJQ* 2 (1964–65): 238–46.
Astronomical references are integral to the structure of *Ulysses* and to major themes such as parallax, metempsychosis, Shakespeare, science-art relations, cyclic return, and paternity.

2350.   Lyons, John B. *James Joyce and Medicine*. Dublin: Dolmen, 1973. New
        York: Humanities, 1974. 255 pp.
        Rev. Eugene Webb, *MFS* 21 (1975–76): 580–83.
This biography of Joyce emphasizes his experience as a medical student, his
personal medical problems, and the depiction of illness, medicine, chemistry, and
physics in works such as *Ulysses*, *Dubliners*, *A Portrait of the Artist as a Young Man*,
and *Finnegans Wake*. The discussion of *Finnegans Wake* includes a detailed listing of
the medical, chemical, and anatomical terms used.

2351.   Mitchell, Breon. "The Newer Alchemy: Lord Rutherford and *Finnegans
        Wake*." *WN* ns 3 (1966): 96–102.
Analyzes a passage in *Finnegans Wake* (353, lines 22–32) in which Joyce apparently
refers to the physicist Lord Rutherford's successful attempt to "split" an atom in
1919. Mitchell sees Joyce as an "alchemist of the word," paralleling the "alchemy"
of nuclear physics practiced by Rutherford and other modern physicists.

2352.   Overstreet, David. "Oxymoronic Language and Logic in Quantum Me-
        chanics and James Joyce." *Sub-Stance* 28 (1980): 37–59.
The oxymoronic logic informing the modern-physics concepts of wave-particle
complementarity and space-time also informs the structure and language of *Finnegans
Wake*.

2353.   Phillips, Joseph M. "The Uses of Scientific and Philosophical Concepts of
        Space and Time in James Joyce's *Finnegans Wake*." *DA* 32 (1972): 6999A.
Shows that the unity of *Finnegans Wake* is best understood in the light of concepts
of space and time drawn from contemporary physics and philosophy. Focuses on
passages in book 1, chapter 6, and book 3, chapter 1.

2354.   Watson, Edward A. "Stoom-Bloom: Scientific Objectivity versus Romantic
        Subjectivity in the Ithaca Episode of Joyce's *Ulysses*." *UWR* 2.1 (1966):
        11–25.
Analyzes the significance of Joyce's objective, scientific rendering of Bloom's
homecoming in the Ithaca episode of *Ulysses*. Joyce himself maintained that the
section was written in the form of a "mathematical catechism" in which the central
events are "resolved with their cosmic, physical, psychical, etc., equivalents." Watson also treats the relation between the language of science and Joyce's handling of
subjective and emotional reality.

Franz Kafka (1883–1924)

2355.   Norris, Margot. "Darwin, Nietzsche, Kafka, and the Problem of Mimesis."
        MLN 95 (1980): 1232–53.
Describes the impact of C. Darwin's concept of "mimetic adaptation" on Nietzsche's
analysis of consciousness, nationality, and morality. Interprets Kafka's "Report to
an Academy" in the light of his appropriation of the Darwinian and Nietzschean
perspectives on the evolutionary and mimetic nature of consciousness.

Arthur Koestler (1905–83)

2356.   Harris, Harold, ed. *Astride the Two Cultures: Arthur Koestler at 70*. London: Hutchinson, 1975; New York: Random, 1976. 219 pp.
Assesses Koestler's influence in various fields. Essays discuss Koestler as novelist, his psychology of creativity, his philosophy of mind, and his biological writings.

Jerzy Nikodem Kosinski (1933–)

2357.   Cahill, Daniel J. "An Interview with Jerzy Kosinski on *Blind Date*." *ConL* 19 (1978): 133–42.
Briefly relates the philosophy of George Levanter, the hero of Kosinski's *Blind Date*, to the work of the scientist Jacques Monod.

Peter B. Kyne (1880–1957)

2358.   Bode, Carl. "Cappy Ricks and the Monk in the Garden." *PMLA* 64 (1949): 59–69.
Kyne's popular novels (e.g., *Cappy Ricks Comes Back* and *Never the Twain Shall Meet*) reflect the influence of the theory of race Mendel expressed in *Versuche über Pflanzen-Hybriden* (1865).

D. H. Lawrence (1885–1930)

2359.   Glicksberg, Charles I. "D. H. Lawrence and Science." *SciMo* 73 (1951): 99–104.
Outlines Lawrence's repudiation of science in *Apocalypse*, *Fantasia of the Unconscious*, and other works. Also discusses his role amid the general twentieth-century literary revolt against the dominance of scientific mentality.

2360.   Heywood, Christopher. "D. H. Lawrence's 'Blood-Consciousness' and the Work of Xavier Bichat and Marshall Hall." *EA* 32 (1979): 397–413.
Examines the background of the physiological allusions in Lawrence's novels, primarily *Women in Love* and *Lady Chatterly's Lover*, and stresses his belief in the consciousness of the heart and blood and his understanding of involuntary nervous activity. Lawrence relied principally on the physiological systems of Xavier Bichat and Marshall Hall.

2360a.   Jones, Lawrence. "Physiognomy and the Sensual Will in *The Ladybird* and *The Fox*." *DHLR* 13 (1980): 1–29.
To establish how Lawrence uses physical features, especially the eyes and the teeth, as symbols for the development of his characters' inner forces, Jones examines Lawrence's esoteric theories concerning psychology, physiology, and physiognomy.

Ursula Le Guin (1929–)

2361.   Cogell, Elizabeth Cummins. "Setting as Analogue to Characterization in Ursula Le Guin." *Extrapolation* 18 (1976–77): 131–41.

Examines Le Guin's characterization in the Hainish stories, discussing the effect of environment on the geography, physiology, mythology, and psychology of fictional planetary inhabitants. Considers *Rocannon's World*, *Planet of Exile*, *City of Illusions*, *The Left Hand of Darkness*, and "The Word for World is Forest."

2362.   Koper, Peter T. "Science and Rhetoric in the Fiction of Ursula Le Guin." *Ursula K. Le Guin: Voyager to Inner Lands and to Outer Space*. Ed. Joe De Bolt. Port Washington: Kennikat, 1979. 66–86.

The unifying feature of Le Guin's fiction is her examination of the effects of science on the individual. "Le Guin's fiction is a reaction to the rhetoric of science, is itself an argument that science is inherently alienating and an exploration of the process by which alienation is produced and counteracted."

2363.   Tavormina, M. Teresa. "Physics as Metaphor: The General Temporal Theory in *The Dispossessed*." *Mosaic* 13.3–4 (1979–80): 51–62.

The central metaphor of Le Guin's novel *The Dispossessed* is the temporal concept developed by the character Shevek. Tavormina elucidates the principal features of this concept, notes its relation to Einstein's theory of relativity and his quest for a unified field theory, discusses the ethical implications of the concept for the society depicted in the novel, and assesses the literary value of scientific metaphors.

Stanislaw Lem (1921–)

2364.   Fogel, Stanley. "*The Investigation*: Stanislaw Lem's Pynchonesque Novel." *RQ* 6 (1977): 286–89.

"Like Pynchon, Lem is a formalist writer who employs scientific—specifically, in his case, statistical and mathematical—principles and motifs ultimately to undermine the scientific mode of perceiving and structuring the world in any but an artificial way."

2365.   Springer, Michael. "Wissenschaft und Phantastik: Am Beispiel von Albert Einstein und Stanislaw Lem." *Kürbiskern* 1 (1980): 71–88.

Outlines Einstein's contributions to physics and his views on the nature of science and on the social position of the scientist. Shows that Lem, one of the major writers of the scientific-technological revolution, focused on the human confrontation with nature through science and technology. Cites Lem's *Phantastik und Futurologie*, *Astronauten*, and *Solaris*, among other works.

C. S. Lewis (1898–1963)

2366.   Aquino, John. "Shaw and C. S. Lewis's *Space Trilogy*." *ShawR* 18 (1975): 28–32.

Traces the influence of Shaw's concepts of the life-force and creative evolution on C. S. Lewis's *Space Trilogy*.

2367.   Hillegas, Mark R. "*Out of the Silent Planet* as Cosmic Voyage." *Shadows of Imagination: The Fantasies of C. S. Lewis, J. R. R. Tolkien, and Charles*

Williams. Ed. Mark R. Hillegas. Carbondale: Southern Illinois UP, 1969. 41–58.

Maintains that the value of Lewis's novel lies in its contemporary treatment of the cosmic-voyage theme. Outlines some scientific discoveries and theories informing Lewis's handling of the theme.

2368.   Neuleib, Janice. "Technology and Theocracy: The Cosmic Voyages of Wells and Lewis." *Extrapolation* 16 (1974–75): 130–36.
See item 2526 for annotation.

James Franklin Lewis (1903–)

2369.   Waggoner, Hyatt H. "Poet and Scientist." *UR* 13 (1946–47): 148–51.
Notes that science affected the sensibility, beliefs, and conventions of expression in Lewis's poetry and comments on the relation between Lewis's experiences as a chemist and his poetic endeavors.

Sinclair Lewis (1885–1951)

2370.   Rosenberg, Charles E. "Martin Arrowsmith: The Scientist as Hero." *AQ* 15 (1963): 447–58.
Discusses how Lewis depicts the value schema of scientists through the characters of Martin Arrowsmith and Max Gottlieb in *Arrowsmith*. Emphasizes that Paul de Kruif, Jacques Loeb, Frederick G. Novy, and Lewis's own medical and scientific research influenced the creation of these characters.

Wyndham Lewis (1886–1957)

2371.   Edman, John H. "Shamanism and Champagne: A Critical Introduction to the Vorticist Theory of Wyndham Lewis." *DA* 22 (1961): 258.
Surveys Lewis's literary achievement and applies his vorticist theory of art to his novels. Vorticism represents a composite of naturalist, classicist, romanticist, and scientific realist elements of art.

2372.   Materer, Timothy. "Wyndham Lewis: Satirist of the Machine Age." *SNL* 10 (1972–73): 9–18.
Defends Lewis's forgotten novel *Snooty Baronet* (1932), which satirizes both science and mechanism.

Erik Lindegren (1910–68)

2373.   Böhm, Anton. "Lindegren's 'Mannen utan väg' und die Naturwissenschaft." *Scan* 12 (1973): 37–42.
This interpretation of Lindegren's *Mannen utan väg* stresses his negative depiction of the scientific worldview during World War II and compares it with the contem-

porary scientific outlook. Böhm comments on developments in physics, biology, and biochemistry.

Jack London (1876–1916)

2374.   Carlson, Roy W. "Jack London's Heroes: A Study of Evolutionary Thought." *DA* 22 (1961): 2791.
Studies those heroic figures in London's writings who represent the evolutionary ideas of C. Darwin, Spencer, Marx, and Nietzsche.

2375.   Dickason, David H. "A Note on Jack London and David Starr Jordan." *Indiana Magazine of History* 38 (1942): 407–10.
Outlines the role the scientist and educator David Starr Jordan played in London's scientific education, particularly regarding the theories of C. Darwin, Spencer, and T. H. Huxley.

2376.   Gershenowitz, Harry. "Jack London, Quasi-Neo-Lamarckian." *JLN* 11 (1978): 99–101.
In developing his animal and human characters, London was influenced by the "neo-Lamarckianism" of Spencer, C. Darwin, Haeckel, and Burbank.

2377.   Peterson, Clell T. "London and Lorenz: A Brief Note on Men and Dogs." *JLN* 12 (1979): 46–49.
In *King Solomon's Ring* the ethologist Konrad Lorenz charges that London's testimony concerning the behavior of sledge dogs is questionable.

2378.   Schoenecke, Michael K. "The Science Fiction of Jack London: Scientific Theories and Three Fictional Extrapolations, *The Sea Wolf* (1904), *Before Adam* (1906), and *The Iron Heel* (1908)." *DAI* 40 (1980): 6295A.
Explores London's vision of nature and society in the three cited works and concludes that London's "science fiction" was based on evolutionary theory, Marxian socialism, and Nietzschean philosophy.

2379.   Wilcox, Earl J. "Jack London and the Tradition of American Literary Naturalism." *DA* 27 (1966–67): 785A.
Examines the primary sources of literary naturalism, including works by Comte, Spencer, C. Darwin, Marx, Taine, and Zola and studies the extent to which London's writings reflect this tradition. London's *Call of the Wild*, *White Fang*, *Sea-Wolf*, *Martin Eden*, and other works exhibit characteristics of materialistic and naturalistic doctrines.

Benito Lynch (1885–1951)

2380.   Gates, Eunice J. "Charles Darwin and Benito Lynch's 'El inglés de los Güesos.' " *Hispania* 44 (1961): 250–53.
Cites correspondences between Mister James, the protagonist of Lynch's novel, and C. Darwin, noting especially Darwin's style of scientific activity in his *Journal*

of Researches. Apparently, Lynch had Darwin in mind while creating his fictional character.

Archibald MacLeish (1892–1982)

2381.   Waggoner, Hyall [sic] H. "Archibald MacLeish and the Aspect of Eternity." *CE* 4 (1942–43): 402–12.

One effect contemporary science has had on poetry is the stimulation of poetic reflection on humankind's stature in the universe. The metaphysical impulse to attempt to understand life *sub specie aeternitatis* takes a scientific turn in MacLeish's poetry. This essay examines the poet's reliance on the principles and insights of modern physical science for the metaphysical vision of poems such as "Einstein," "Epistle to Be Left in the Earth," and "Conquistador."

Maurice Maeterlinck (1862–1949)

2382.   Chauvin, Remy. "Le point de vue d'un biologiste." *Europe* 40 (1962): 126–32.

Explores the adversarial relation between science and literature by analyzing Maeterlinck's *La vie des abeilles*, a study of how bees communicate, and criticizes its lack of scientific rigor. Also castigates fellow scientists for their obsession with method to the exclusion of humanistic and metaphysical concerns. Concludes that science and literature must work together in order to comprehend the universe.

Norman Mailer (1923–)

2383.   Finholt, Richard D. " 'Otherwise How Explain?' Norman Mailer's New Cosmology." *MFS* 17 (1971–72): 375–86.

In *An American Dream* Mailer transcends post-Darwinian naturalism and develops a cosmology that weds elements of contemporary science with cosmological conceptions analogous to the notion of a great chain of being.

2384.   Held, George. "Men on the Moon: American Novelists Explore Lunar Space." *MQR* 18 (1979): 318–42.

Analyzes Mailer's *Of a Fire on the Moon*, Bellow's *Mr. Sammler's Planet*, and Updike's *Rabbit Redux* to analyze the novelists' attitudes toward the technology of space exploration and their thematic exploitation of the Apollo 11 moon landing of 1969.

Thomas Mann (1875–1955)

2385.   Brown, Calvin S. "The Entomological Source of Mann's Poisonous Butterfly." *GR* 37 (1962): 116–20.

The source for Mann's description of the butterfly *Hetaera esmeralda* in *Doctor Faustus* is Henry Walter Bates's *Naturalist on the River Amazons* (1863).

2386.   Hilscher, Eberhard. "Thomas Manns Beziehungen zur Philosophie und Naturwissenschaft." *NDH* 23 (1976): 40–58.

Maintains that although Mann was prodigiously learned in literary and cultural matters, he had little direct familiarity with contemporary science. For his speculations about time in his novels he relied more on Schopenhauer and Spengler than on Einstein. This essay cites some specific scientific misinformation in his novels.

2387.   Olsen, Henry. "Der Patient Spinell." *OL* 20 (1965): 217–21.
In the novella "Tristan," Mann describes Spinell's disease, Dystrophia adiposo-genitalis, with a physician's understanding.

2388.   Prusok, Rudi. "Science in Mann's *Zauberberg*." *PMLA* 88 (1973): 52–61.
Mann makes extensive use of themes and symbolism drawn from modern physics, biology, medicine, and other sciences. For example, *Der Zauberberg* is structured on the principles of Einstein's theory of relativity.

2389.   ———. "The Use of Science and Technology in the Novels of Thomas Mann." *DA* 28 (1967–68): 2692A.
Examines aspects of contemporary science, such as relativity theory and medicine, that are woven into the symbolic structure of Mann's novels, including *Der Zauberberg* and *Doktor Faustus*.

2390.   Saueressig, H. "Literatur und Medizin: Zu Thomas Manns Roman *Der Zauberberg*." *Deutsche medizinische Wochenschrift* 99 (1974): 1780–86.
Traces the development of Mann's interest in medicine in works such as *Die Buddenbrooks*, "Tristan," and *Der Zauberberg*, identifying the persons on whom Mann based his characters for *Der Zauberberg* and examining his medical expressions in relation to contemporary medicine. Also treats the response of the medical press to *Der Zauberberg* and publishes a letter Mann wrote in answer to this medical discussion.

2391.   Stein, Barbara Molinelli. "Grandezza: Un caso di coscienza, analisi strutturale é riflessioni sul romanzo *Lotte in Weimar* di Thomas Mann." *Aevum* 52 (1978): 515–51.
Pages 532–43 of this study of Mann's *Lotte* treat the influence Goethe's *Farbenlehre* had on the novel, especially on Mann's classification of temperament according to color.

Harry Martinson (1904–78)

2392.   Bergmann, S. A. "Harry Martinson and Science." *Proceedings of the Fifth International Study Conference on Scandinavian Literature, 6–10 July, 1964, University College, London*. London: University Coll., 1964. 99–120.
In the space poem *Aniara*, Martinson grapples with the implications of the second law of thermodynamics and with the theory of relativity.

2393.   Sjöberg, Leif. "Harry Martinson: From Vagabond to Space Explorer." *BA* 48 (1974): 476–85.
Suggests that a major component of Martinson's influence on the English-speaking literary world is the incorporation of scientific and technological themes into his poems and novels.

John Masefield (1878–1967)

2394.   Stevenson, Lionel. "Masefield and the New Universe." *SR* 37 (1929): 336–48.

"The extensive group of reflective poems which rank among the best productions of Masefield's later years constitute a record of the poet's effort to comprehend the new universe which has been revealed by recent science, and to postulate an acceptable relationship between it and the human soul." Masefield's revaluation of humankind's place in the universe resembles the response of leading Victorian poets to the Darwinian hypothesis.

Charles Langbridge Morgan (1894–1958)

2395.   Nourse, Edwin G. "Nature's Power and the Conscience of Man." *VQR* 31 (1955): 337–52.

Analyzes Morgan's play *The Burning Glass*, which treats the relation between social science and natural science in the contemporary quest to harness and control the powers of nature.

Robert Musil (1880–1942)

2396.   Bouveresse, Jacques. "La science sourit dans sa barbe." *Arc* 74 (1978): 8–31.

Establishes Musil's preference for science over philosophy and art. Examines his theories on the superiority of science and on its relation to philosophy as represented by Ulrich in *L'homme sans qualités*.

2397.   Müller, Gerd. *Dichtung und Wissenschaft: Studien zu Robert Musils Romanen* Die Verwirrungen des Zöglings Törless *und* Der Mann ohne Eigenschaften. Acta Universitatis Upsaliensis: Studia Germanistica Upsaliensia 7. Uppsala: U of Uppsala, 1971. 249 pp.

Musil is equally committed to two traditions regarding the relations of literature and science—the German Romantic yearning to fuse literature and science and the naturalist insistence on adapting literature to the latest scientific research. Trained in the sciences, Musil came under the influence of Ernst Mach, one of the foremost representatives of scientific positivism, who espoused precise and analytic descriptions of all states of consciousness. Sensing the limitations of that methodology, Musil sought to transcend scientific rationalism by drawing on the intuitive and spiritual capabilities of human beings. In this he was strengthened by his great predecessors Goethe and Novalis and by his contemporaries Maeterlinck and Bergson. Musil's novels reflect his efforts both to give science its due and to transcend its limitations as a model for human life.

2398.   ———. "Mathematik und Tranzendenz: Die Bedeutung Novalis' für das Werk Robert Musils." *OL* 23 (1968): 265–75.

Maintains that for both Novalis and Musil the laws and methods of mathematics were the means to solve the mysteries concerning the human soul and eternity. Musil finds his own efforts in this regard confirmed and reinforced in the writings of Novalis. However, whereas Novalis bases his concepts of continuity and cognition on the analogy of the infinitesimal calculus, Musil pursues the implications of imaginary numbers into hypothetic and fictive realms, as exemplified in his novels *Die Verwirrungen des Zöglings Törless* and *Der Mann ohne Eigenschaften*.

2399.   White, John J. "Mathematical Imagery in Musil's *Young Törless* and Zamyatin's *We*." *CL* 18 (1966): 71–78.
This brief account of the mathematical principles underlying *Young Törless* and *We* notes especially that the idea of the square roots of minus numbers is important for both novels.

Vladimir Vladimirovich Nabokov (1899–1977)

2400.   Flower, Timothy F. "The Scientific Art of Nabokov's *Pale Fire*." *Criticism* 17 (1975): 223–33.
Nabokov's application of his scientific values to fiction results in a scientific aesthetic, studied here as reflected in *Pale Fire*. "The subject of Nabokov's art . . . can be seen as the interrelation or dialectic between the natural scientist's empirically verifiable reality and art as a created response to this reality."

Anaïs Nin (1903–77)

2401.   Knapp, Bettina L. "Anaïs/Artaud-Alchemy." *Mosaic* 11.2 (1977–78): 65–74.
Nin used alchemical symbolism in the *House of Incest*. Like Artaud's "Alchemical Theater" (1932), Nin's work portrays the creative act as an alchemical process.

Eugene O'Neill (1888–1953)

2402.   Wasserstrom, William. "Notes on Electricity: Henry Adams and Eugene O'Neill." *Psychocultural Review* 1 (1977): 161–78.
Reappraises O'Neill's *Dynamo*, stressing its treatment of the themes of electrical technology and progress in the industrial age and relating the play to "The Virgin and the Dynamo" from *The Education of Henry Adams*.

George Orwell (1903–50)

2403.   Goodman, David. "Countdown to 1984: Big Brother May Be Right on Schedule." *Futurist* 12 (1978): 345–55.
Examines trends in recent science and technology that point to the fulfillment of the vision of Orwell's novel by 1984.

Walker Percy (1916–)

2404.   Lawson, Lewis A. "Walker Percy: The Physician as Novelist." *SAB* 37.2 (1972): 58–63.

Discusses Percy's *Moviegoer* and *Last Gentleman*, stressing how his medical training and subsequent disenchantment with medicine and science may have affected the themes and characterizations of these novels.

André Pieyre de Mandiargues (1909–)

2405. Campanini, Susan. "Alchemy in Pieyre de Mandiargues' 'Le diamant.' " *FR* 50 (1976–77): 602–09.

The thematic and structural details of Mandiargues's "Diamant" symbolize the alchemical process of creating the philosopher's stone—the transformation from *nigredo* to *albedo* and from *albedo* to *rubedo*.

Robert M. Pirsig (1928–)

2406. Benson, Donald. *"Zen and the Art of Motorcycle Maintenance*: Technology Revalued." *Iowa State Journal of Research* 54 (1979): 267–73.

Outlines Pirsig's alternative to the dualistic view of the relation between technology and humanity, which stems from F. Bacon's *Great Instauration* (1620) and proceeds throughout the scientific and industrial revolutions into the contemporary world. In *Zen and the Art of Motorcycle Maintenance*, Pirsig proposes a "right technology" by which human beings, nature, and technology exist in harmony.

Ezra Loomis Pound (1885–1972)

2407. Cavanaugh, Sister M. Stephanie. "Flake of Gold: A Study of Ezra Pound's 'The Alchemist.' " *Washington Square Review* 2.1 (1966): 52–62.

Examines the relation between medieval alchemy and the rhythm, sound, diction, and structure of Pound's "Alchemist." Also studies the association between the poem's dominant theme of metamorphosis and the system of correspondences established by alchemy.

2408. Kayman, M. A. "Ezra Pound and the Phantasy of Science: An Investigation into the Relation between Pound's Poetic Techniques and His Political Ideology, through the Image and Its Scientific Background." *DAI* 39 (1979): 3119C.

"Deals with Pound's quest for acceptability for his art as knowledge, through metaphorical models of science: the synthetic discourse of energetics; the scientific mysticism of the Society for Psychical Research; the subjectivist science of the empirio-critics; and the depth psychology of Bernard Hart." Cites Pound's poem "Mauberley," the *Cantos*, and other works.

2409. Materer, Timothy. "Pound's Vortex." *Paideuma* 6 (1977): 175–76.

Pound's use of the term *vortex*, which first appeared in his poem "Plotinus" (1908), was derived from his study of J. Burnet's *Early Greek Philosophy*, particularly from Burnet's translations of the fragments of Empedocles and Leucippus.

2410.   Nänny, Max. "Ezra Pound's Visual Poetry and the Method of Science."
        ES 43 (1962): 426–30.
Suggests that Pound's adherence to the principles of positivistic science accounts
for the emphasis on the visual in his poetry.

Marcel Proust (1871–1922)

2411.   Béhar, Serge. *L'univers médical de Proust.* Cahiers Marcel Proust. Nouvelle
        série 1. Paris: Gallimard, 1970. 250 pp.
        Rev. Michael R. Finn, *FR* 45 (1971–72): 918–19.
Explores Proust's use of images of physical illness to convey psychological and
emotional states in *A la recherche du temps perdu*. Illness provides a structure and
rhythm for Proust's literary edifice.

2412.   Beyer, Sandra S. "The Sciences in the Works of Marcel Proust." *DAI* 35
        (1974–75): 6128A.
Examines Proust's incorporation of scientific terminology and principles into his
works. Also discusses his scientific background.

2413.   Beznos, Maurice J. "Aspects of Time according to the Theories of Relativity
        in Marcel Proust's *A la recherche du temps perdu*: A Study of the Similitudes
        in Conceptual Limits." *OUR* 10 (1968): 74–102.
Compares the concepts of time in Proust's work and in Einstein's relativity theory.
Discusses their common concern with the epistemological and ontological significance of relativity perspective, the analogy between the velocity of light in Einstein
and the faculty of memory in Proust, and the treatment of the timelessness of events
by both thinkers.

2414.   Bisson, L. A. "Proust and Medicine." *Literature and Science.* Proc. of the
        Sixth Triennial Congress of the International Federation for Modern Lan-
        guages and Literatures. Oxford, 1954. Oxford: Blackwell, 1955. 292–98.
Discusses some parallels between Proust's personal encounters with medical practitioners throughout his incurable illness and his portrayal of doctors and medicine
in his writings.

2415.   Carter, William C. "The Role of the Machine in *A la recherche du temps
        perdu*." *DAI* 32 (1972): 4603A.
Demonstrates Proust's extraordinary knowledge of science and technology by
analyzing the metaphoric and structural role of the machine in this novel.

2416.   Cattaui, Georges. "Proust et les sciences." *Literature and Science.* Proc. of
        the Sixth Triennial Congress of the International Federation for Modern
        Languages and Literatures. Oxford, 1954. Oxford: Blackwell, 1955.
        287–92.
Essentially summarizes previous scholarly work on Proust's attitudes toward science and his personal attempt to develop a science of psychology in *Remembrance of
Things Past*. Cattaui adds his own considerations of Proust and the sciences by
pointing to the frequency and variety of scientific metaphors in Proust's prose.

2417.   Erickson, John D. "The Proust-Einstein Relation: A Study in Relative Point of View." *Marcel Proust: A Critical Panorama*. Ed. Larkin B. Price. Urbana: U of Illinois P, 1973. 247–76.

Examines parallels between Proust's treatment of time in *A la recherche du temps perdu* and Einstein's relativity theory. "The dialectic of time in Proust's work, which gives dimension and reality to phenomena by establishing coordinates by which to define them, operates in a manner strikingly close in nature to the relative coordinate systems through which Einstein's theory views physical phenomena."

2418.   Graham, Victor E. *The Imagery of Proust*. New York: Barnes; Oxford: Blackwell, 1966. 274 pp.
   Rev. Randi Marie Birn, *CL* 19 (1967): 90–91; William S. Bell, *MP* 65 (1967–68): 89–91.

Systematically analyzes and classifies the metaphors, similes, and analogies in *Remembrance of Things Past*. Examines the correlation between theme and imagery in Proust and discusses the sources of his imagery in nature, common objects, literature, the arts, the social and domestic environment, and the sciences of which he displays a technical knowledge, including biology, physics, mathematics, astronomy, and chemistry.

2419.   ———. "Proust's Alchemy." *MLR* 60 (1965): 197–206.

Like an alchemist seeking the philosopher's stone that will transmute base elements into higher forms, Proust discovers in the involuntary memory the means of transforming experience into art, harmonizing the mysteries of creation and life into a single scheme that circumscribes time and death.

2420.   Levy, Sylvia N. "Proust's Realistic Treatment of Illness." *FR* 15 (1941–42): 233–38, 324–29, 421–24.

Proust's portrayal of illness in *A la recherche du temps perdu* is both realistic and remarkably accurate. Levy reviews episodes that illustrate Proust's knowledge of medicine, noting that his sources of information were both personal observation and scientific texts such as Fernand Widal and Adolphe Javal's *La cure de déchloruration dans le mal de Bright et quelques maladies hydrophigènes* (1906).

2421.   Murray, Jack. "Mind and Reality in Robbe-Grillet and Proust." *WSCL* 8 (1967): 407–20.
   See item 2453 for annotation.

2422.   Virtanen, Reino. "Proust's Metaphors from the Natural and the Exact Sciences." *PMLA* 69 (1954): 1038–59.

Examines Proust's use of similes and metaphors drawn from botany, physics, chemistry, biology, astronomy, optics, medicine, and mathematics, with special attention to the artistic value of these scientific allusions.

Thomas Pynchon (1937–)

2423.   Abernethy, Peter L. "Entropy in Pynchon's *The Crying of Lot 49*." *Crit* 14.2 (1972–73): 18–33.

Discusses how Pynchon uses Norbert Wiener's communications theory to treat the entropic tendencies of American society in *The Crying of Lot 49*.

2424.   Cocks, Geoffrey. "War, Man, and Gravity: Thomas Pynchon and Science Fiction." *Extrapolation* 20 (1979): 368–77.
Discusses Pynchon's *Gravity's Rainbow* as a work that extends the limits of the genre of science fiction into metaphysics, metapsychology, and cosmology. Mentions Pynchon's treatment of the mind body dualism, neurosis, and science and technology.

2425.   Cooper, Peter L. " 'An Ominous Logic': Thomas Pynchon and Contemporary American Fiction." *DAI* 39 (1979): 5510A–11A.
Discusses entropic theme and vision in Pynchon, Kesey, Vonnegut, Nabokov, and Barth.

2426.   Cowart, David. "Science and the Arts in Pynchon's 'Entropy.' " *CLAJ* 24 (1980–81): 108–15.
Maintains that in developing the theme of entropy Pynchon alludes more frequently to literature, art, and music than to science.

2427.   Friedman, Alan J., and Manfred Puetz. "Science as Metaphor: Thomas Pynchon and *Gravity's Rainbow*." *ConL* 15 (1974): 345–59.
Relates the compost-garden image to the V-2 rocket. Drawing on his own theory of "entropy management," Pynchon develops metaphors of death, disorder, and decay.

2428.   George, N. F. "The *Chymische Hochzeit* of Thomas Pynchon." *PNotes* 4 (1980): 5–22.
Maintains that significant portions of Pynchon's *Gravity's Rainbow* reflect Jung's alchemical theories as well as ideas of chemical combination based on modern theories of organic synthesis.

2429.   Harris, Charles B. "Death and Absurdity: Thomas Pynchon and the Entropic Vision." *Contemporary American Novelists of the Absurd*. New Haven: College and University, 1971. 76–99.
Discusses how Pynchon applies entropy theory, quantum mechanics, and information theory to his analysis of social disintegration in "Entropy," *V*, and *The Crying of Lot 49*.

2430.   Herzberg, Bruce I. "Illusions of Control: A Reading of *Gravity's Rainbow*." *DAI* 39 (1979): 6756A–57A.
Pynchon uses images from physics, psychology, and technology to convey a sense of the dehumanizing power of formalized knowledge structures.

2431.   Leland, John P. "Pynchon's Linguistic Demon: *The Crying of Lot 49*." *Crit* 16.2 (1974–75): 45–53.
Though entropy serves as the central metaphor of *The Crying of Lot 49*, providing the work's epistemological perspective and informing the action and characterization of the novel, Pynchon goes further and uses language and fiction to create a work that is itself entropic.

2432. Le Vot, André. "The Rocket and the Pig: Thomas Pynchon and Science Fiction." *Caliban* 12 (1975): 111–18.
Examines Pynchon's treatment of the antithesis between nature and science or technology in *Gravity's Rainbow* and discusses the novel's relation to science fiction. "Science fiction has a preeminently cohering function in *Gravity's Rainbow*. It appears as a centripetal force which prevents the book from falling apart, from being fragmented into a multitude of unrelated pieces."

2433. McClintock, James I. "United State Revisited: Pynchon and Zamiatin." *ConL* 18 (1977): 475–90.
This comparative study of Pynchon's *Gravity's Rainbow* and Zamyatin's *We* focuses on the use of entropy theory to express the self-destructive impulses of a scientized society. Both authors "ransack post-Newtonian and post-Darwinian science and technology for metaphors and symbols that indict 'scientized' cultures and seek others that could validate human aspirations."

2434. Mangel, Anne. "Maxwell's Demon, Entropy, Information: *The Crying of Lot 49*." *TriQ* 20 (1971): 194–208.
Pynchon uses concepts drawn from thermodynamics as metaphors for the experiences of Oedipa Maas, a character in *The Crying of Lot 49*. This essay includes brief accounts of entropy, information theory, and James Clerk Maxwell's thought experiment known as Maxwell's demon.

2435. Marquez, Antonio. "Technologique in *Gravity's Rainbow*." *RS* 48 (1980): 1–10.
Focuses on the metaphysical and ontological dimensions of Pynchon's scientific and technological imagery in *Gravity's Rainbow*. "Pynchon makes the provocative assertion that science and technology have been more instrumental than any other factor—social, political, religious, aesthetic—in shaping the consciousness of modern man."

2436. Nadeau, Robert L. "Readings from the New Book of Nature: Physics and Pynchon's *Gravity's Rainbow*." *SNNTS* 11 (1979): 454–71.
Modern physics is not only the source of new ideas in Pynchon's novels but the basis for his radically new conception of human identity.

2437. Ozier, Lance W. "Antipointsman/Antimexico: Some Mathematical Imagery in *Gravity's Rainbow*." *Crit* 16.2 (1974–75): 73–90.
While in earlier novels Pynchon's scientific allusions fail to provide thematic richness, in *Gravity's Rainbow* his references to science and mathematics contribute significantly to the depth of characterization. Ozier studies the mythological, religious, philosophical, and scientific associations raised by Pynchon's use of a mathematical metaphor to characterize Mexico and Pointsman.

2438. ———. "The Calculus of Transformation: More Mathematical Imagery in *Gravity's Rainbow*." *TCL* 21 (1975): 193–210.
Maintains that Pynchon's mathematical references lend coherence to *Gravity's Rainbow*, and discusses his allusions to mathematical analysis, particularly to concepts from calculus, such as continuity, infinitesimals, integration, and differentiation.

2439.   Patteson, Richard F. "Architecture and Junk in Pynchon's Short Fiction."
         Illinois Quarterly 42 (1979): 38–47.
Discusses Pynchon's imagery of junk accumulation as a measure of entropy in
"Entropy," "Mortality and Mercy in Vienna," "The Secret Integration," and "Low-
lands."

2440.   Pearce, Richard. "Thomas Pynchon and the Novel of Motion." *MR* 21
         (1980): 177–95.
Discusses the concept of unchecked, directionless energy and motion in Pynchon's
V, Crying of Lot 49, and *Gravity's Rainbow.*

2441.   Plater, William M. *The Grim Phoenix: Reconstructing Thomas Pynchon.*
         Bloomington: Indiana UP, 1978. 268 pp.
         Rev. Charles Baxter, *Criticism* 21 (1979): 179–82; Roger B. Henkle, *MFS*
         25 (1979): 340–42; Jerome Klinckowitz, *JEGP* 78 (1979): 466–68; Ray-
         mond M. Olderman, *ConL* 20 (1979): 500–07; Khachig Tololyan, *SNNTS*
         11 (1979): 224–34; Steven Weisenburger, *MLQ* 40 (1979): 88–91; James
         H. Justus, *AL* 51 (1979–80): 582–83; David Seed, *JAmS* 14 (1980):
         333–34.
This analysis of Pynchon's fiction is guided by consideration of several recurring
metaphors and themes, chief among them "the thermodynamic situation of entropy
and the disintegration of order into disorder." Pynchon's world is a closed system
that moves, by the law of entropy, toward death. The principles of "uncertainty"
and "complementarity" drawn from modern physics serve as analogues to his main
themes.

2442.   Seed, David. "The Fictional Labyrinths of Thomas Pynchon." *CritQ* 18.4
         (1976): 73–81.
Briefly reviews the themes and complex structures of *V,* "Entropy," *The Crying
of Lot 49,* and *Gravity's Rainbow,* noting especially Pynchon's frequent use of scientific
concepts and terminology.

2443.   Siegel, Mark Richard. *Pynchon: Creative Paranoia in* Gravity's Rainbow.
         Port Washington: Kennikat, 1978. 136 pp.
         Rev. Raymond M. Olderman, *ConL* 20 (1979): 500–07; Khachig Tololyan,
         SNNTS 11 (1979): 224–34; David Seed, *JAmS* 14 (1980): 333–34.
One chapter examines Pynchon's use of metaphors drawn from contemporary
science, technology, mathematics, and other sociocultural phenomena. "Pynchon
uses mythology, the hypothetical constructs of the social sciences, and scientific
analogy and metaphor such as those of rocketry, to explain and order the various
themes of the novel and to present various possibilities for transcendence or failure
within the plot."

2444.   Simberloff, Daniel. "Entropy, Information, and Life: Biophysics in the
         Novels of Thomas Pynchon." *Perspectives in Biology and Medicine* 21
         (1977–78): 617–25.
Discusses the relations among thermodynamics, information theory, and bio-
physics in Pynchon's *V, Crying of Lot 49,* and *Gravity's Rainbow.*

2445.   Slade, Joseph W. *Thomas Pynchon*. New York: Warner Paperback, 1974.
         256 pp.
This work, the first book-length critical study of Pynchon, examines the use of
scientific images and concepts in his short stories and novels. The underlying web
of imagery in *V* derives from *The Education of Henry Adams*, especially the famous
"Virgin and Dynamo" chapter. Images from systems analysis, entropy and communications, and energy flow permeate *The Crying of Lot 49* and *Gravity's Rainbow*.
In addition, *Gravity's Rainbow* draws heavily on chemistry, physics, mathematics,
psychology, and sociology.

2446.   Stark, John O. *Pynchon's Fictions: Thomas Pynchon and the Literature of In-*
         formation. Athens: Ohio UP, 1980. 183 pp.
         Rev. Beverly Lyon Clark, *MFS* 27 (1981–82): 379–80.
Analyzes the techniques of organization in Pynchon's fiction. Includes chapters
on his use of organizing principles drawn from entropy theory, scientific epistemology, mathematics, cybernetics, psychology, history, religion, and film. Concludes with a survey of his allusions to literature and an examination of his literary
theory.

2447.   Tillotson, T. S. "Gravitational Entropy in *Gravity's Rainbow*." *PNotes* 4
         (1980): 23–24.
Notes that gravitational theory provides a better basis for understanding Pynchon's
use of entropy in *Gravity's Rainbow* than does information theory or thermodynamics.

2448.   Tololyan, Khachig. "The Fishy Poisson: Allusions to Statistics in *Gravity's*
         Rainbow." *NMAL* 4 (1979–80): item 5.
Briefly examines Pynchon's unique handling of the Poisson distribution in *Gravity's Rainbow* and his deliberate distortion of statistical practice for literary effect.

Arno Reinfrank (1934–)

2449.   George, Emery. " 'Scientist through the Poet's Garden': The New Lyricism
         of Arno Reinfrank." *PaideiaFS* 6 (1979): 30–42.
This sympathetic appraisal of Reinfrank's lyric technique stresses his skillful
assimilation of scientific facts into his poetry and discusses his lyric cycles *Mutations*
and *Poet of Facts and Other Poems*.

2450.   Stern, Guy. "Science and Literature: Arno Reinfrank as a 'Poet of Facts.' "
         Probleme der Komparatistik und Interpretation: Festschrift für André von Gronicka
         zum 65. Geburtstag am 25.5.1977. Ed. Walter H. Sokel, Albert A. Kipa,
         and Hans Ternes. Bonn: Bouvier, 1978. 316–31.
Outlines Reinfrank's attempts to bridge the worlds of science and poetry through
the development of a poetics based on factual data drawn from science and technology. Among the works discussed are the essay "Zur 'Poesie der Fakten' " and
the poems "Entwurf für ein neues Deutschland," "Sieben Sterne," and "Das weiss-
umrissene Quadrat."

Conrad Richter (1890–1968)

2451.   Edwards, Clifford D. "Conrad Richter's Ohio Trilogy: Its Ideas, Themes, and Relationship to Literary Tradition." *DA* 24 (1963): 1614–15.
Analyzes Richter's philosophy and social criticism in *Human Vibration*, *Principles in Bio-physics*, and *The Mountain on the Desert*. Also includes a close study of the electrophysiological theories that inform his works.

Rainer Maria Rilke (1875–1926)

2452.   De Clery, Adrien R. "Rainer Maria Rilke et la science moderne." *Literature and Science*. Proc. of the Sixth Triennial Congress of the International Federation for Modern Languages and Literatures. Oxford, 1954. Oxford: Blackwell, 1955. 298–302.
Concerns Rilke's essential antipathy toward modern technology, especially aviation, and its scientific background. In discussing Rilke's relationship to Paul Valéry, however, this essay notes that the later poet's study of pure geometry and mathematics inspired Rilke's deep respect and paralleled his own interest in the study of medicine, expressed at various points in his life.

Alain Robbe-Grillet (1922–)

2453.   Murray, Jack. "Mind and Reality in Robbe-Grillet and Proust." *WSCL* 8 (1967): 407–20.
Discusses the view held by both Robbe-Grillet and Proust that a complete gap exists between subjectivity and the external world. Compares their opinions regarding the roles of literature and science in mending the gap. "Proust felt that literature was much better equipped to describe the external world than science, whereas Robbe-Grillet believes that literature would do well to emulate the language and principles involved in the scientific analysis of reality."

2454.   Wylie, H. A. "Alain Robbe-Grillet: Scientific Humanist." *BuR* 15.2 (1967–68): 1–9.
The style and content of Robbe-Grillet's works are informed both by his humanistic concerns and by the theories, methods, and objectivity of science.

Thomas Eugene Robbins (1936–)

2455.   Miller, Patricia E. C. "Reconciling Science and Mysticism: Characterization in the Novels of Tom Robbins." *DAI* 40 (1979): 2666A.
Robbins reconciles the traditionally opposed worldviews of mysticism and scientific rationalism in his novels *Another Roadside Attraction* and *Even Cowgirls Get the Blues*.

2456.   Nadeau, Robert L. "Physics and Cosmology in the Fiction of Tom Robbins." *Crit* 20.1 (1978–79): 63–74.

Robbins's fiction tries to evaluate the impact of ideas from contemporary physics on the moral and intellectual bases of Western values; it links modern physics with Eastern religions' emphasis on the unity and interrelatedness of all things. This essay discusses *Another Roadside Attraction* and *Even Cowgirls Get the Blues*.

Edwin Arlington Robinson (1869–1935)

2457.   Waggoner, Hyatt H. "E. A. Robinson and the Cosmic Chill." *NEQ* 13 (1940): 65–84.

Robinson's first volume of poetry reflects the challenge science poses to theology. Later volumes downplay this obsession but still reflect the chilling effect of science.

Romain Rolland (1868–1944)

2458.   Francis, R. A. "Romain Rolland and Science." *NFS* 10 (1971): 21–32, 74–86.

Outlines the development of Rolland's attitude toward science, noting the effects of historical science on his early perspective and the influence of Einstein, Planck, and Freud on his post–World War I outlook. Francis stresses the relation of science to Rolland's concept of art and creativity in *L'evangile universel de Vivekananda*, *Beethoven*, and *Péquy*.

Arthur Schnitzler (1862–1931)

2459.   Schlein, Rena R. "Arthur Schnitzler: Author-Scientist." *MAL* 1.2 (1968): 28–38.

Reviews Schnitzler's career, briefly commenting on his medical background and on the image of the physician in plays such as *Professor Bernhardi*.

George Bernard Shaw (1856–1950)

2460.   Bernal, J. D. "Shaw the Scientist." *G. B. S. 90: Aspects of Bernard Shaw's Life and Work*. Ed. S. Winsten. London: Hutchinson, 1946. 93–105.

Reviews Shaw's attitudes toward various scientific issues, including his attacks on vivisection and vaccination and his denouncement of Darwinism in favor of a theory of creative evolution derived from Lamarck.

2461.   Bowman, David. "The Eugenicist's Handbook." *ShawR* 18 (1975): 18–21.

The science of eugenics is the major topic of *Man and Superman* and the sole subject of "The Revolutionist's Handbook." Shaw probably derived his knowledge of eugenics from Karl Pearson and Francis Galton.

2462.   Boxill, Roger. *Shaw and the Doctors*. New York: Basic, 1969. 199 pp.

Interprets, with historical background, Shaw's polemical writings on science, vivisection, the germ theory, antisepsis, vaccination, and medical professionalism.

Discusses Shaw's didactic version of the classical and Molièresque comedy of doctors and relates his medical philosophy to the history of ideas and the future of medicine.

2463. Cole, Susan A. "The Utopian Plays of George Bernard Shaw: A Study of the Plays and Their Relationship to the Fictional Utopias of the Period from the Early 1870's to the Early 1920's." *DAI* 32 (1972): 6966A–67A.

This study of the socioeconomic and scientific background of utopian fiction as a literary genre compares Shaw's utopian plays, such as *Major Barbara* and *Back to Methuselah*, to other examples of this genre, such as S. Butler's *Erewhon*, Bellamy's *Looking Backward*, and Wells's *In the Days of the Comet* and *Food of the Gods*.

2464. Glicksberg, Charles I. "Shaw versus Science." *DR* 28 (1948–49): 271–83.

Outlines the deficiencies characteristic of Shaw's bombastic, antagonistic indictment of science, especially Darwinism, the medical profession, and vivisectionist practices. Though impassioned and articulate in his moral and social criticisms of science, Shaw tended to make violently prejudiced and unprofessional remarks. Among the works discussed are *The Doctor's Dilemma*, *The Quintessence of Ibsen*, *Man and Superman*, *Heartbreak House*, and *Back to Methuselah*.

2465. Kagarlitski, Julius. "Bernard Shaw and Science Fiction: Why Raise the Question?" *ShawR* 16 (1973): 59–66.

Explores the relation between Shaw's interest in science fiction and his rejection of modern science, especially Darwinism.

2466. Ketels, Violet B. "Shaw, Snow, and the New Men." *Person* 47 (1966): 520–31.

Outlines the parallels between Shaw's treatment of the ethics of scientism in *Major Barbara* and Snow's portrayal of scientists and scientific ethics in *The New Men*.

2467. Leary, Daniel J. "The Evolutionary Dialectic of Shaw and Teilhard: A Perennial Philosophy." *ShawR* 9 (1966): 15–34.

The philosophic background of Shaw's ideology includes such thinkers as Bergson, Schopenhauer, Hegel, Marx, Lamarck, and Nietzsche. This study emphasizes the parallels between Shaw's concept of evolution and the ideas that Teilhard de Chardin expresses in *The Phenomenon of Man*.

2468. Mills, Carl H. "Shaw's Theory of Creative Evolution." *ShawR* 16 (1973): 123–32.

Shaw's concept of evolution was indebted to Lamarck, Buffon, and E. Darwin but was opposed to the ideas of C. Darwin and is unacceptable by the standards of modern microbiology. This essay elucidates the principal features of his theory as expressed in *Man and Superman*, *Back to Methuselah*, and other works.

2469. Roy, R. N. *Bernard Shaw's Philosophy of Life*. Calcutta: Mukhopadhyay, 1964. Folcroft: Folcroft, 1969. Norwood: Norwood, 1976. Philadelphia: West, 1977. 165 pp.
        Rev. H. A. Smith, *MLR* 61 (1966): 507–08.

Reviews Shaw's political, economic, and social philosophy and studies his doctrine of creative evolution in *Man and Superman* and other works, stressing his indebtedness to Lamarck, C. Darwin, and S. Butler.

2470. Tetzeli v. Rosador, Kurt. "The Natural History of *Major Barbara*." *MD* 17 (1974): 141–53.
Briefly analyzes Shaw's concept of history as a kind of natural history that includes socioeconomic, metabiological, and religious dimensions. The structural and thematic paradoxes of *Major Barbara* can be resolved by reference to this concept.

C. P. Snow (1905–80)

2471. Graves, Nora C. "The Two Culture Theory in C. P. Snow's Novels." *DA* 28 (1967–68): 1434A–35A.
Explains how the "two cultures" theory, implicit in Snow's novels from *Death under Sail* (1932) to *Corridors of Power* (1964), is thematically manifested in the characters and overall structure and continuity of his work.

2472. Ketels, Violet B. "Shaw, Snow, and the New Men." *Person* 47 (1966): 520–31.
See item 2466 for annotation.

2473. Vogel, Albert W. "The Academic World of C. P. Snow." *TCL* 9 (1963–64): 143–52.
Snow's Rede and Godkin lectures, published as "The Two Cultures and the Scientific Revolution" and "Science and Government," provide a theoretical background for understanding his treatment of the theme of education in the eight novels of the *Strangers and Brothers* series and in *The Search*.

2474. Waring, A. G. "Science, Love and the Establishment in the Novels of D. A. Granin and C. P. Snow." *FMLS* 14 (1978): 1–15.
Explores the relation between science and human and social values as reflected in the depiction of scientists in various novels by Snow and Granin.

John Steinbeck (1902–68)

2475. Astro, Richard. *John Steinbeck and Edward F. Ricketts: The Shaping of a Novelist*. Minneapolis: U of Minnesota P, 1973. 259 pp.
Rev. Lester Jay Marks, *AL* 47 (1975–76): 476–78.
The worldview of the marine biologist Edward F. Ricketts was instrumental in shaping the philosophy of life expressed in Steinbeck's novels. Especially influential was Ricketts's holistic and organismal conception of life, his ecological thinking, and his beliefs about human and animal group behavior. Ricketts was also important as a source of Steinbeck's scientific knowledge, and he served as the model for major characters in *The Grapes of Wrath*, *In Dubious Battle*, *Cannery Row*, and several other works.

2476.   ———. "Steinbeck and Ricketts: The Morphology of a Metaphysic." *UWR*
8.2 (1972–73): 24–33.
Steinbeck incorporated aspects of the marine biologist Edward F. Ricketts's worldview into novels such as *In Dubious Battle* and *The Grapes of Wrath*. He fused Ricketts's
holistic philosophy with an organismal scheme of life but rejected Ricketts's nonteleological thinking.

2477.   Benson, Jackson J. "John Steinbeck: Novelist as Scientist." *Steinbeck and
the Sea*. Proc. of a Conference Held at the Marine Science Center Audi-
torium, Newport, Oregon, 4 May 1974. Ed. Richard Astro and Joel W.
Hedgpeth. Corvallis: Oregon State U Sea Grant Coll. Program, 1975.
15–28. Rpt. in *Novel* 10 (1976–77): 248–64.
Surveys Steinbeck's artistic development from his romantic-poetic novels *The Cup
of Gold* and *To a God Unknown* to his naturalistic, nonteleological novels such as *In
Dubious Battle* and *The Grapes of Wrath*. Emphasizes his gradual assimilation of
scientific motifs, resulting from his friendship with the marine biologist Edward F.
Ricketts. Also discusses the influence of science on the theme and structure of
Steinbeck's later novels and assesses his contribution to the evolution of the contemporary novel.

2478.   Benton, Robert M. "The Ecological Nature of *Cannery Row*." *Steinbeck: The
Man and His Work*. Ed. Richard Astro and Tetsumaro Hayashi. Corvallis:
Oregon State UP, 1971. 131–39.
The interrelationship of the characters in *Cannery Row* is based on ecological
principles, revealing Steinbeck's biological interests and concerns.

2479.   ———. "A Scientific Point of View in Steinbeck's Fiction." *StQ* 7 (1974):
67–73.
The importance of science in shaping Steinbeck's literary method is evident in
Cannery Row, which attempts a synecological study emphasizing the ecology of a
community, and in *Sweet Thursday*, an autecological work that examines the interrelations between individuals and their environments.

2480.   Bracher, Frederick. "Steinbeck and the Biological View of Man." *Pacific
Spectator* 2 (1948): 14–29.
Steinbeck's *Sea of Cortez*, a collation of journals written by Steinbeck and the
biologist Edward F. Ricketts, contains many of the novelist's most important biological speculations and serves as an excellent source for the interpretation of the
biological allusions and imagery in his major writings. Among the works discussed
with reference to *Sea of Cortez* are *Of Mice and Men*, *The Wayward Bus*, *Cannery Row*,
and *In Dubious Battle*.

2481.   Brown, Joyce D. C. "Animal Symbolism and Imagery in John Steinbeck's
Fiction from 1929 through 1939." *DAI* 33 (1972–73): 1716A.
Steinbeck displayed his zoological knowledge through animal imagery in works
such as *Tortilla Flat*, *In Dubious Battle*, *Of Mice and Men*, and *The Grapes of Wrath*.

2482. Feied, Frederick. "Steinbeck's Depression Novels: The Ecological Basis." *DAI* 32 (1971): 4227A–28A.

Steinbeck's naturalism in *The Grapes of Wrath*, *Of Mice and Men*, *In Dubious Battle*, and *Sea of Cortez* reflects the biological and ecological ideas acquired from his friendship with the marine biologist Edward F. Ricketts. In fact, Steinbeck wrote *Sea of Cortez* with Ricketts.

2483. Jones, Lawrence William. "Steinbeck and Zola: Theory and Practice of the Experimental Novel." *StQ* 4 (1971): 95–101.

Outlines the principal tenets of Zola's literary naturalism as expressed in "The Experimental Novel" and examines Steinbeck's attempts to implement these principles in his major novels. Neither Zola nor Steinbeck was able to achieve the strict objectivity that true naturalism demands.

2484. Nimitz, Jack. "Ecology in *The Grapes of Wrath*." *HSL* 2 (1970): 165–68.

Maintains that Steinbeck's treatment in *The Grapes of Wrath* of the "ecological web" hypothesis and the principle of group selection indicates his professional understanding of ecological concepts.

2485. Taylor, Horace P., Jr. "The Biological Naturalism of John Steinbeck." *DA* 22 (1961): 3674.

Examines Steinbeck's biological naturalism, stimulated by his friendship with the marine biologist Edward F. Ricketts, and studies its effect on the ideology, characterization, language, and structure of his novels.

2486. ———. "The Biological Naturalism of John Steinbeck." *McNR* 12 (1960–61): 81–97.

Treats the relation between Steinbeck's biological naturalism and his portrayal of human nature and function, values, social conflicts, and history. Examines his major novels in this regard and comments on his concept of nonteleological thinking and racial memory.

Wallace Stevens (1879–1955)

2487. Kessler, Jascha. "Wallace Stevens: Entropical Poet." *WSJour* 1 (1977): 82–86.

Comments on Stevens's poetic attempts to contend with an age demythologized by science. His poetry responds to a world represented by the physics of entropy.

2488. McDaniel, Judith. "Wallace Stevens and the Scientific Imagination." *ConL* 15 (1974): 221–37.

Explores Stevens's assimilation of concepts drawn from contemporary science into poems such as "The Irish Cliffs of Moher," "The Reader," "The Plain Sense of Things," and "Prologues to What Is Possible." These concepts include relativity theory and thermodynamics.

Jules Supervielle (1884–1960)

2489.   Low, Peter. "The Physiological Idiom in the Poetry of Supervielle." *AUMLA*
46 (1976): 266–75.
Discusses Supervielle's poetic use of metaphors based on the physiology of the
human skeletal structure, the circulatory system, and the body's major organs.

Tristan Tzara (1896–1963)

2490.   Caldwell, Ruth L. "From Chemical Explosion to Simple Fruits: Nature in
the Poetry of Tristan Tzara." *PCL* 5 (1979): 18–23.
Examines the development during 1918–61 in Tzara's treatment of earth, sea,
and sky imagery as a means of expressing the totality and unity of nature. Works
discussed include *Vingt-cinq poèmes*, *L'homme approximatif*, *Le signe de vie*, and *Frère
Bois*.

John Updike (1932–)

2491.   Held, George. "Men on the Moon: American Novelists Explore Lunar
Space." *MQR* 18 (1979): 318–42.
See item 2384 for annotation.

2492.   Strandberg, Victor. "John Updike and the Changing of the Gods." *Mosaic*
12.1 (1978–79): 157–75.
Behind Updike's concern with death lies the physical theory of entropy, against
which he sets a personal theology of agape, especially in *The Centaur*.

2493.   Sykes, Robert H. "Paradichlorobenzine in Updike's *Rabbit Run*." *NMAL*
4.3 (1979–80): item 19.
Shows that the chemical molecular structure and bonding of mothballs, which
Updike alludes to at the climax of *Rabbit Run*, parallels the complex relationship
between Harry and Janice.

Paul Valéry (1871–1945)

2494.   Bémol, Maurice. "Paul Valéry et la méthode scientifique en critique littéraire." *Literature and Science*. Proc. of the Sixth Triennial Congress of the
International Federation for Modern Languages and Literatures. Oxford,
1954. Oxford: Blackwell, 1955. 302–08.
Valéry considered scientific process, the adaptation of science to its objects, an
art form in itself. Taking a cue from that observation, Bémol calls for forms of
literary criticism that, while scientifically precise in their approach to texts, would
preserve artistic dimensions.

2495.   Frandon, Ida-Marie. "Le modernisme de Valéry: Expression littéraire et
formulation scientifique." *RSH* 36.144 (1971): 495–510.

Restates Valéry's view that literary composition and scientific analysis share similar problems of formulation, construction, and method. Treats various aspects of communal mental activity through a discussion of Valéry's *Idée Fixe, Introduction à la méthode de Léonard de Vinci, Crise de l'esprit,* and other works.

2496. Gaudin, Albert. "Paul Valéry et les mathématiques." *FR* 19 (1945–46): 271–78.

Demonstrates that Valéry's prose and thought were heavily influenced by mathematical precision and algebraic and geometric concepts and terminology. Valéry's use of these concepts in the construction of images, allusions, and remarks is seen in *La crise de l'esprit, Léonard et les philosophes, L'histoire d'Amphion,* and several other works. Valéry drew from the works of Laguerre, Poincaré, Cauchy, and Maupertuis as well as from Libri's *Histoire des sciences mathématiques* and Maxwell's *Traité d'éléctricité et de magnétisme.*

2497. Gekas-Fachard, Vasiliki. "Scientific Foundations of Time in the *Cahiers* of Paul Valéry: Its Manifestation in 'Conscience' and Art." *DAI* 40 (1980): 6303A.

In defining the concept of time in the *Cahiers,* Valéry attempts to spatialize it and subject it to mathematical and scientific analysis. In the process, he uses fundamental scientific principles such as entropy.

2498. Ince, W. N. "The Sonnet *Le vin perdu* of Paul Valéry." *FS* 10 (1956): 40–54.

Disputes previous interpretations of Valéry's *Vin perdu.* Suggests that the notion of diffusion or discontinuity in the second part of Poincaré's *Valeur de la science* directly inspired Valéry's poetic image of the "vin précieux" and serves as a basis for comprehending this difficult poem.

2499. Jones, Rhys S. "Poincaré and Valéry: A Note on the 'Symbol' in Science and Art." *MLR* 42 (1947): 485–88.

Poincaré's positivistic interest in the importance of relations or "rapports" among empirical objects influenced Valéry's thinking about the objects of poetic creation. In Valéry's view, both science and art are essentially concerned with relational or symbolic reality.

2500. Laurette, Pierre. *Le thème de l'arbre chez Paul Valéry.* Paris: Klincksieck, 1967. 196 pp.

Examines the evolution of the image of the tree in Valéry's poems, including "Jeune parque," "Au platane," "Ebauche d'un serpent," "Palme," and "Dialogue de l'arbre," and argues that Valéry's notebooks reveal the nature and extent of his scientific inspiration. Among those who most influenced Valéry's worldview and his concepts of the structure of observations, analysis, and depiction were Bergson, Cauchy, Edison, Einstein, Kelvin, Maxwell, and Poincaré.

2501. Roditi, Edouard. "Paul Valéry: Poetics as an Exact Science." *KR* 6 (1944): 398–408.

Explains how Valéry's studies of physics and mathematics directly influenced his aesthetics of poetry. Valéry thought that poetry, as a creative act, was analogous in its methods to exact sciences such as physics.

2502.   Sutcliffe, F. E. *La pensée de Paul Valéry*. Paris: Nizet, 1955. 190 pp.
This detailed study of the influence of mathematics on Valéry's thought and poetry includes discussions of *Monsieur Teste*, *Introduction à la méthode de Léonard de Vinci*, *Analecta*, *Note et digression*, *Léonard et les philosophes*, and "Au sujet d'*Eurêka*."

2503.   Virtanen, Reino. "The Irradiations of *Eureka*: Valéry's Reflections on Poe's Cosmology." *TSL* 7 (1962): 17–25.
Though at age 20 Valéry enthusiastically admired Poe's *Eureka*, his attitude changed over the years. His 1921 publication "Au sujet d'*Eurêka*" indicates a critical and skeptical respect.

2504.   ———. "Paul Valéry's Scientific Education." *Symposium* 27 (1973): 362–78.
Contributing to the current work on Valéry's scientific thought that has been prompted by the *Cahiers*, this study traces the development of Valéry's interest in various sciences, especially mathematics, and discusses his view of the analogies between science and art.

2505.   ———. *The Scientific Analogies of Paul Valéry*. University of Nebraska Studies ns 47. Lincoln: U of Nebraska P, 1974. 99 pp. French trans. *L'imagerie scientifique de Paul Valéry*. Essais d'art et de philosophie. Paris: Vrin, 1975. 153 pp.
Surveys the figurative use of images drawn from physics, astronomy, mathematics, biology, and other sciences in Valéry's novels, poems, essays, and notebooks. Comments on his view of the relations between science and the creative imagination.

Elio Vittorini (1908–66)

2506.   Petrucciani, Mario. "Vittorini: 'La cultura è sempre basata sulle scienze.' Le due culture." *Scienza e letteratura nel secondo novecento*. *La ricerca letteraria in Italia tra algebra e metafora*. Turin: Mursia, 1978. 19–37.
Analyzes Vittorini's magazine *Il politecnico* as his effort to promote awareness of the interdependence of science, society, and literature—an effort carried on later by the journal *Il menabo*. Vittorini maintained that literature cannot be independent of science and, thus, should reflect the scientific advancements that characterize contemporary society.

Kurt Vonnegut, Jr. (1922–)

2507.   Nadeau, Robert L. "Physics and Metaphysics in the Novels of Kurt Vonnegut, Jr." *Mosaic* 13.2 (1979–80): 37–47.
Vonnegut often makes inconsistent statements about science, but his fiction reveals a consistent metaphysic based on concepts drawn from contemporary physics. Nadeau

discusses subjectivity, indeterminacy, and simultaneity in works from *Mother Night* to *Breakfast of Champions*.

H. G. Wells (1866–1946)

2508. Bailey, J. O. "Is Science-Fiction Art? A Look at H. G. Wells." *Extrapolation* 2 (1960–61): 17–19.

Appreciation of H. G. Wells's literary art requires the reader to understand the allegorical nature of his imagery, which draws on the contents of Victorian science and related philosophies.

2509. Barber, Otto. *H. G. Wells' Verhältnis zum Darwinismus*. Beiträge zur englischen Philologie 27. Leipzig: Tauchnitz, 1934. New York: Johnson, 1967. 81 pp.

Three years of study at London's Royal College of Science made Wells thoroughly familiar with the sciences of his time, particularly Darwinism. Barber examines Wells's scientific writings on biological Darwinism, social Darwinism, and eugenics as well as fiction based on Darwinism, such as "The Flowering of the Strange Orchid," "The Empire of the Ants," and *The War of the Worlds*.

2510. Beauchamp, Gorman. "*The Island of Dr. Moreau* as Theological Grotesque." *PLL* 15 (1979): 408–17.

Wells's Dr. Moreau is a scientific as well as a theological grotesque. This essay studies the biological, psychological, and theological aspects of Moreau's experiments.

2511. Bergonzi, Bernard. *The Early H. G. Wells: A Study of the Scientific Romances*. Manchester: Manchester UP, 1961. 226 pp.
   Rev. Roger Lancelyn Green, *RES* ns 13 (1962): 423–25.

Studies the literary aspects of Wells's *Time Machine*, *Wonderful Visit*, *Island of Dr. Moreau*, *Invisible Man*, *War of the Worlds*, *When the Sleeper Wakes*, *First Men in the Moon*, and several early short stories. Includes general remarks on Wells's use of imagery drawn from Darwinism, biology, physics, and other sciences.

2512. Bowen, Roger. "Science, Myth, and Fiction in H. G. Wells's *Island of Dr. Moreau*." *SNNTS* 8 (1976): 318–35.

In *Dr. Moreau* Wells casts the myths of Circe and Prometheus in scientific guise, drawing especially on themes from Darwinism and the biological sciences. Images of metamorphosis, creation, and degeneration abound in the work.

2513. Glikin, Gloria. "Through the Novelist's Looking-Glass." *KR* 31 (1969): 297–319.

Remarks on the autobiographical element in Wells's writings, including their reflection of his failed scientific aspirations.

2514. Haynes, Roslynn D. *H. G. Wells, Discoverer of the Future: The Influence of Science on His Thought*. London: Macmillan, 1979. New York: New York UP, 1980. 283 pp.

Rev. Gorman Beauchamp, *Technology and Culture* 22 (1981): 332–35; John
Huntington, *MFS* 27 (1981–82): 327–30.
Provides an overview of Wells's scientific background and thoroughly examines
the extent to which his scientific training influenced the thought, style, and characterization of his scientific romances, utopian writings, and sociological novels.

2515.   Hillegas, Mark R. "Cosmic Pessimism in H. G. Wells's Scientific Ro-
          mances." *PMASAL* 46 (1961): 655–63.
Discusses the extent to which Wells's scientific romances reflect the cosmic pessimism characteristic of T. H. Huxley's views on the evolutionary development of
humankind.

2516.   ———. "The First Invasions from Mars." *MAQR* 66 (1959–60): 107–
          12.
See item 1771 for annotation.

2517.   ———. *The Future as Nightmare: H. G. Wells and the Anti-Utopians.* New
          York: Oxford UP, 1967. Carbondale: Southern Illinois UP, 1974. 200
          pp.
          Rev. Pauline Madow, *ModA* 12 (1967–68): 198–99; Wilbert E. Moore,
          Science 160 (1968): 647–48.
Argues persuasively against the conventional view that twentieth-century dystopian fiction is simply a response to Wells's optimistic, protechnology utopias.
Influenced by T. H. Huxley's *Evolution and Ethics*, Wells's earliest fiction often
portrays a gloomy, oppressive future; such descriptions provided inspiration for anti-
utopias from E. M. Forster's story "The Machine Stops" to Vonnegut's *Player Piano*
and beyond. Hillegas stresses the treatment of science and technology in Wells and
his successors—Forster, Zamyatin, A. Huxley, C. S. Lewis, Orwell, and numerous
science fiction writers.

2518.   Hughes, David Y. "An Edition and a Survey of H. G. Wells' *The War of
          the Worlds.*" *DA* 23 (1963): 2914.
This critical edition of Wells's novel includes a discussion of the scientific and
philosophical determinism underlying the work.

2519.   Jansing, Helmut. *Die Darstellung und Konzeption von Naturwissenschaft und
          Technik in H. G. Wells' "scientific romances."* Europäische Hochschulschriften
          Reihe 14, Angelsächsische Sprache und Literatur 45. Bern, Frankfurt:
          Lang, 1977. 233 pp.
This study of the scientific and Darwinistic content of Wells's early scientific
romances notes the role technology played in these works, which include *The Time
Machine*, *The Island of Dr. Moreau*, *The Invisible Man*, and *The War of the Worlds*.
Also discusses the influence exerted on Wells by such thinkers as T. H. Huxley,
Nietzsche, Tille, and Spencer.

2520.   Kagarlitski, J. "Wells and Jules Verne." *VLit* 6 (1962): 116–33. (Text
          in Russian.)
Compares the accuracy of references to science and the depiction of scientists in

novels by Verne and Wells. Verne's scientists were usually eccentric, while Wells's scientists were generally more realistic.

2521.   Karl, Frederick R. "Conrad, Wells, and the Two Voices." *PMLA* 88 (1973): 1049–65.
See item 2263 for annotation.

2522.   Kirlin, Thomas M. "H. G. Wells and the Geometric Imagination: A Study of Three Science Fiction Novels in the Nineties." *DAI* 35 (1974–75): 2276A–77A.
Studies the impact of C. Darwin, T. H. Huxley, Marx, and Zola on Wells's *Time Machine*, *When the Sleeper Wakes*, and "Story of the Days to Come."

2523.   McConnell, Frank. *The Science Fiction of H. G. Wells*. New York: Oxford UP, 1980. 250 pp.
Rev. John R. Reed, *MFS* 27 (1981–82): 695–98; Murray A. Sperber, *VS* 25 (1981–82): 384–86.
This introduction to the literature of Wells includes a study of his major cultural and scientific influences, noting especially the profound effect exerted on Wells by C. Darwin.

2524.   Morgan, Dean L. "Scientific Method and Vision of Reality: The Short Stories of H. G. Wells." *DA* 28 (1967–68): 4182A–83A.
"Cartesian and/or Baconian methods or techniques of inquiry are at the foundation of Wells' short fiction."

2525.   Morton, Peter R. "Biological Degeneration: A Motif in H. B. [sic] Wells and Other Late Victorian Utopianists." *SoRA* 9 (1976): 93–112.
Examines the post-Darwinian biological idea of natural degeneration, primarily in Wells's *Time Machine* but also in Hudson's *Crystal Age* and Bulwer-Lytton's *Coming Race*.

2526.   Neuleib, Janice. "Technology and Theocracy: The Cosmic Voyages of Wells and Lewis." *Extrapolation* 16 (1974–75): 130–36.
Discusses the similarities and differences between C. S. Lewis's *Out of the Silent Planet* (1938) and Wells's *First Men in the Moon* (1901). Treats the authors' handling of space travel, scientific accuracy, narrative techniques, and thematic orientation.

2527.   Pagetti, Carlo. "*The First Men in the Moon*: H. G. Wells and the Fictional Strategy of His 'Scientific Romances.' " *SFS* 7 (1980): 124–33.
Examines the complex role of the character-narrator Bedford in the expression of Wells's sociological concerns about scientific progress. *The First Men in the Moon* " . . . presents itself as a reflection on the nature of the 'scientific romance,' on the potentialities of the novel as a means of communication, and on the possibility that science itself may become a means of communication."

2528.   Parsons, Coleman O. "Lunar Craters in Science and Fiction: Kepler, Verne, and Wells." *N&Q* 164 (1933): 346–48.
See item 2008 for annotation.

2529.   Philmus, Robert M. "*The Time Machine*: Or, The Fourth Dimension as Prophecy." *PMLA* 84 (1969): 530–35.

Demonstrates how Wells's vision of social disintegration in *The Time Machine* is manifested by the time traveler's journey in the fourth dimension. The futuristic world of 802,701 expresses Wells's concept of evolution as an antihuman, retrogressive force.

2530.   Scheick, William J. "The Fourth Dimension in Wells's Novels of the 1920's." *Criticism* 20 (1978): 167–90.

Suggests that Wells's experiments with fictional form in the 1920s, especially his treatment of space-time relations, were informed by Einstein's relativity theory. Discusses *Men like Gods*, *The Dream*, *Christina Alberta's Father*, *The World of William Clissold: A Novel at a New Angle*, *Meanwhile: The Picture of a Lady*, and *Mr. Blettsworthy on Rampole Island*.

2531.   Suvin, Darko. "*The Time Machine* versus *Utopia* as a Structural Model for Science Fiction." *CLS* 10 (1973): 334–52.

Analyzes Wells's narrative strategy in *The Time Machine* and its relation to evolutionary and devolutionary schemas of social and biological metamorphosis. Includes a brief comparison with T. More's method of extrapolation in *Utopia*.

2532.   ———, and Robert M. Philmus, eds. *H. G. Wells and Modern Science Fiction*. Lewisburg: Bucknell UP; London: Associated University Presses, 1977. 279 pp.
         Rev. William J. Scheick, *SNNTS* 10 (1978): 291–93; George Guffey, *NCF* 34 (1979–80): 112–17.

The essays in this volume treat various aspects of Wells's influence on the science fiction genre. Among the essays are Tatyana Chernysheva's "The Folktale, Wells, and Modern Science Fiction," which surveys Wells's use of ancient folklore images and motifs in his science fiction and discusses their connection with scientific fact and possibility; David Y. Hughes's "The Garden in Wells's Early Science Fiction," which explores how Wells used biological principles and metaphors derived from C. Darwin and T. H. Huxley in his early scientific romances, including *The First Men in the Moon* and *The Time Machine*; and J. P. Vernier's "Evolution as a Literary Theme in H. G. Wells's Science Fiction," which examines the impact of evolution theory on Wells's creative imagination and on his expression of visions of the future in his science fiction. The volume includes a selective bibliography of Wells's scientific journalism and an annotated survey of his books and pamphlets.

Benjamin Lee Whorf (1897–1941)

2533.   Rollins, Peter C. "The Whorf Hypothesis as a Critique of Western Science and Technology." *AQ* 24 (1972): 563–83.

This analysis of Whorf's theory of linguistic relativity includes a discussion of his apocalyptic novel *The Ruler of the Universe* (1924), which portrays the destructive tendencies of modern science.

William Carlos Williams (1883–1963)

2534.   Baker, Beulah P. "Energy and Event as Motive, Motif and Design in the Poetry of William Carlos Williams." *DAI* 37 (1977): 7747A–48A.

The structure of Williams's poems places the reader in contact with a representation of the fluctuating energy forms described by modern physics and A. N. Whitehead's cosmology.

2535.   Donley, Carol C. " 'A Little Touch of / Einstein in the Night—'; Williams' Early Exposure to the Theories of Relativity." *WCWN* 4.1 (1978): 10–13.

Williams's "St. Francis Einstein of the Daffodils," written on the occasion of Einstein's visit to America in 1921, responds to popular-press accounts of the physicist and relativity. Williams's treatment of relativity indicates an interest in the new physics, but his knowledge was too general to issue in any formal poetic analogues.

2536.   ———. "Relativity and Radioactivity in William Carlos Williams' *Paterson*." *WCWN* 5.1 (1979): 6–11.

Williams's knowledge of relativity provided both subject matter and justification for his formal experiments with the "variable foot." Marie Curie's work with radioactive elements gave Williams a rich source of metaphor for *Paterson*.

2537.   Neely, James C. "One Man's Dr. Williams: An Appreciation." *YR* ns 65 (1975–76): 314–20.

Surveying literary debts to medical science, Neely cites Camus's statement that the artist must "simultaneously serve suffering and beauty." Passages from Williams's fiction and poetry (e.g., *Kora in Hell*, *Paterson*, *White Mule*) reflect the assimilation of medical experience into art.

2538.   Perloff, Marjorie. "The Man Who Loved Women: The Medical Fictions of William Carlos Williams." *GaR* 34 (1980): 840–53.

Williams portrayed his true feelings for women through a medical metaphor in *Life along the Passaic River*, a collection of medical stories.

2539.   Schultz, Leon J. "The Doctor-Poet of *Paterson* and the Science of Art." *DAI* 38 (1977): 791A–92A.

Williams's medical and scientific understanding of physical dynamics may be the key to his method of poetic control. This essay studies the dynamics of Williams's *Paterson*, books 1 through 5.

2540.   Slaughter, William R. "William Carlos Williams: Medicine Man." *DAI* 33 (1973): 5201A.

Williams viewed poetry as an extension of his medical practice and, at the same time, practiced medicine in a poetic way. He conceived poetry to be spiritually therapeutic both for himself as creator and for his readers. This essay discusses *In the American Grain*, *Paterson*, "The Descent," "The Desert Music," and "Asphodel" in this regard.

2541.   Trautmann, Joanne. "William Carlos Williams and the Poetry of Medicine." *Ethics in Science and Medicine* 2 (1975): 105–14.
Illustrates the relations between humanistic and medical sensibility through a study of the symbiosis of the two in Williams's dual career as physician and poet. Williams developed an objectivity that served him in both his medical and poetic capacities. Trautmann examines Williams's objectivism in poems such as "The Artist" and "Spring and All" and in his collection of short stories *The Knife of the Times*.

Virginia Woolf (1882–1941)

2542.   Brogan, Howard O. "Science and Narrative Structure in Austen, Hardy, and Woolf." *NCF* 11 (1956–57): 276–87.
See item 1533 for annotation.

2543.   Constein, Carl F. "Relativity in the Novels of Virginia Woolf." *DA* 17 (1957): 851.
Woolf's awareness of contemporary physics, biology, and psychology influenced the portrayal of characters and her treatment of time and reality in her novels.

William Butler Yeats (1865–1939)

2543a.   Adams, Hazard. "Yeatsian Art and Mathematic Form." *CentR* 4 (1960): 70–88.
Though Yeats rejected mathematics "as an expression of materialist science," his use of alchemical and astrological symbolism allowed him to develop an analogy between art and mathematics that informs *A Vision*.

2544.   Glicksberg, Charles I. "William Butler Yeats and the Hatred of Science." *PrS* 27 (1953): 29–36.
Outlines Yeats's extreme antagonism toward science and his concomitant cultivation of imagination, mysticism, and occultism. Yeats considered science "the evil force of abstraction that clipped the poet's wings and destroyed the purity and power of his vision."

2545.   Knapp, Bettina L. "An Alchemical Brew: From *Separatio* to *Coagulatio* in Yeats's *The Only Jealousy of Emer*." *ETJ* 30 (1978): 447–65.
The characters of Yeats's tragedy *The Only Jealousy of Emer* undergo a spiritual transformation that parallels the alchemical transmutation from *prima materia*, or a state of oneness, to states of *separatio* and *coagulatio*.

2546.   Nemerov, Howard. "Poetry and History." *VQR* 51 (1975): 309–28.
The author interprets Yeats's "Tower" and "Nineteen Hundred and Nineteen" to illustrate the relation between poetry, science, and history.

2547.   Schuler, Robert M. "W. B. Yeats: Artist or Alchemist?" *RES* ns 22 (1971): 37–53.

Discusses Yeats's analogy between the alchemical transmutation of matter and spirit and the artistic transmutation of life into art. Analyzes his poetic use of alchemical symbolism.

2548.   Whitaker, Thomas R. "Yeats's Alembic." *SR* 68 (1960): 576–94.

Traces the development of Yeats's passion for spiritual alchemy, analyzing three works that express this interest: "Rosa Alchemica," "The Tables of the Law," and "The Adoration of the Magi."

Author Index

The author index references by item number the authors of all articles and books cited in the bibliography as well as the authors of book reviews. The author of a book review is indicated by an item number followed by a lower case r (e.g., 1741r).

Renner, Stanley, 2266
Reynolds, Barbara, 1666
Reynolds, George F., 1809
Reynolds, Lou A., 602
Reynolds, Mary T., 2343r
Rhodes, S. A., 2072
Ricatte, Robert, 1669
Rice, William N., 1957
Richards, David B., 1296
Richards, I. A., 104a, 150r
Richards, Robert F., 2308
Richter, Karl, 1026–27, 1196, 2177
Rickey, Mary E., 492a
Riddell, James Allen, 715a
Ridge, George Ross, 119r
Ridgely, Beverly S., 716–17, 783, 856–
    57, 942–43, 946
Rienstra, Miller H., 496
Riep, Albert R., 840
Rieser, Max, 105
Riley, Helene M., 1529
Riley, Thomas A., 1197
Ringe, Donald A., 1553
Ringold, Francine, 2305
Rittersbacher, Karl, 1198
Rivers, James C., 2178
Rizzo, Patrick V., 2034a
Robbins, Rossell Hope, 331r
Roberts, Catherine, 106
Roberts, David A., 433
Robertson, D. S., 206r
Robertson, D. W., Jr., 213r
Robertson, J. K., 168
Robertson, William B., 2056
Robin, P. Ansell, 169, 435
Robins, Harry F., 911
Robinson, Erwin Arthur, 1810–11
Robinson, G. S., 2179
Roche, Thomas P., Jr., 414r
Rockwood, Robert J. R., 639
Rodgers, James S., 1316–17
Roditi, Edouard, 2501
Roedel, Reto, 1781
Roger, Jacques, 1029
Roisch, Ursula, 2313
Roland, Vela G., 2319
Rollins, Peter C., 2533
Romey, William D., 107
Roos, David A., 1482a
Root, Robert K., 321
Root, Winthrop H., 1483
Roper, Derek, 1018r

Roppen, Georg, 1484
Rose, Ernst, 1439r
Rose, Phyllis, 1625
Rosen, Edward, 855
Rosenberg, Albert, 753
Rosenberg, Bruce A., 322
Rosenberg, Charles E., 2370
Rosenberg, John D., 1881
Rosenberry, Edward H., 1708
Rosenfeld, Emmy, 1199
Rosenfield, Leonora Cohen, 719
Ross, Frederic R., 1670
Ross, Robert N., 1108
Ross, Ronald, 108
Rossi, Paolo, 741
Rostand, Jean, 2073
Rotermund, H-M., 1200
Roth, Nancy, 1890
Rothenberg, Albert, 109
Rottensteiner, Franz, 2180
Rouillard, C. D., 1372r
Rousseau, George S., 110–13, 128r, 720,
    994r, 1002r, 1248r, 1279, 1281–82,
    1306–08
Routh, H. V., 1447r
Routh, James E., 1738
Rowland, Beryl, 323–25
Roy, R. N., 2469
Royds, Thomas Fletcher, 206
Rudinsky, Norma L., 1822
Rudrum, Alan, 959
Rueckert, William, 2181
Rusche, Harry, 603
Russell, Henry N., 321
Russell, H. K., 436–37
Russo, John Paul, 912
Rutland, William R., 1958
Rutledge, Sheryl P., 325a
Ryan, Steven T., 114, 2306

Sadler, Frank O., 2182, 2273
Sadler, Lynn Veach, 467, 721
Sage, Evan T., 202
Said, Rushdi, 230
Saine, Thomas P., 1031
Sainéan, Lazare, 506
Sait, James E., 1959
Sale, William M., 2158r
Salm, Peter, 1201
Salvatore, Armando, 204
Sampson, Edward C., 1688
Samuelson, David N., 2183, 2259

Subject Index

1522, 1525; Broch, Hermann, 2248;
Fitzgerald, F. Scott, 2309; Mallarmé,
Stéphane, 1780; Martinson, Harry,
239?; Pynchon, Thomas, 2434, 2444,
2447; science fiction, 2187; Stevens,
Wallace, 2488
Thompson, Francis (1859–1907), 1967
Thomson, James (1700–48), 76, 690,
720, 724, 968, 979, 991, 1002,
1007, 1018, 1358; astronomy, 158,
162, 711; evolution, 1359;
geography, 1357; imaginary voyage,
730; influence of Lucretius, 986,
1037, 1351; meteorology, 670;
Newtonianism, 147, 150, 992, 1001,
1019, 1025, 1035, 1045, 1352,
1354; optics, 982, 1356; scientific
rationalism, 1353, 1355
Thomson, James (B.V.) (1834–82), 1428,
1968
Thomson, Sir William (1824–1907), 2309
Thoreau, Henry David (1817–62), 95,
1659, 1705, 1981–82, 1984; as a
scientist, 1970, 1975, 1980, 1990;
astronomy, 1978; attitude toward
science, 56, 1972, 1977, 1979;
Bacon, Francis, 1988; entomology,
1974; geology, 1417–18; limnology,
1976, 1985; magnetism, 1982a;
natural history, 1969, 1973; optics,
1987; phenology, 1989; scientific
method, 1983; travel literature, 1056;
water imagery, 1645
Thornton, Robert John (1768?–1837),
1093
Thucydides (460?–400? BC), 159
Tieck, Ludwig (1773–1853), 973, 1140,
1471, 1487, 1513
Tille, Alexander (1866–1912), 2519
Time, 87, 433, 514, 878a, 1076–77,
2028, 2030, 2108, 2111, 2139,
2162, 2195, 2223, 2227, 2262,
2282, 2285, 2287–88, 2290, 2297,
2305, 2347a, 2353, 2386, 2413,
2417, 2497, 2530
Tirso de Molina (1584?–1648), 951–52
Toland, John (1670–1722), 696
Tolosa Latour, Manuel de (1857–1919),
1823
Tolstoy, Count Leo (1828–1910), 1424,
2193
Tomkis, Thomas (fl. 1614), 437, 953

Topography, 425, 988, 1245
Topology, 2225
Topsell, Edward (1572–1625?), 638
Torre de Rezzonico, Carlo Castone
Gaetano, conte della (1742–96), 965
Tōson, Shimazaki (1872–1943), 1816
Tourneur, Cyril (1575?–1626), 388, 954–
55
Townshend, Chauncey Hare (1798–1868),
1850
Toxicology, 617
Traherne, Thomas (1637?–74), 656, 664,
956, 1018
Travel literature, 836, 1046, 1056–58,
1075, 1245, 1358, 1393, 1431,
1609, 1789, 1799, 2044
Triller, Daniel Wilhelm (1695–1782),
1038
Trilling, Lionel (1905–75), 60, 77, 89
Trotula, 383
Tucker, George (1775–1861), 1830
Turing, Alan Mathison (1912–54), 12
Twain, Mark (1835–1910), 89, 1406,
1992, 1997–99; attitude toward
science, 1993, 2000a; fingerprinting,
2000; geology, 1418; phrenology,
1995; satire of science, 1990a;
scientific determinism, 1991, 1994,
1996
"Two cultures," theory of, 45, 86, 89,
101, 106, 110, 118, 121, 128, 130a,
140, 2099, 2139a, 2218, 2263,
2300; Arnold, Matthew and T. H.
Huxley, 7, 28, 31, 1415, 1482a;
Leavis, F. R. and/or C. P. Snow, 17,
25, 28, 48, 59–60, 64, 70–71, 77,
79, 115, 120, 122–23, 127, 133,
2091, 2471, 2473; Newman, John
Henry, 1410; science fiction, 2190
Tyard, Pontus de (1521–1605), 504
Tyndall, John (1820–93), 1446, 1576,
1943
Tyson, Edward (c. 1650–1708), 1319
Tzara, Tristan (1896–1963), 2490

Uguiccione da Pisa, 341
Unamuno, Miguel de (1864–1936), 2110
Uncertainty principle, 2159, 2227, 2441
Updike, John (1932–), 2155, 2211,
2384, 2492, 2493
Upham, Thomas (1799–1872), 1874
Usinger, Fritz (1895–), 1830a